(510) 882-1400
Smachdoun @ hotmail.com

(510) 912-5000
RICK - NGAY @ HOTMAIL.COM

This text stands out in two key ways:

▶ **SPSS Student Version software** accompanies this textbook. It is not tacked on – it is fully integrated. The *Fourth Edition* uses a single integrated case and dataset throughout the book. Because of this, students will be familiar with the case, the questionnaire, and the scaling assumptions of the questions. This means they can concentrate on understanding how to run SPSS and interpreting the output.

Annotated screen shots in the text help make SPSS an easier tool to use. And an Online SPSS Student Assistant helps students learn how to run SPSS and interpret the output. View it yourself at **www.prenhall.com/burnsbush**.

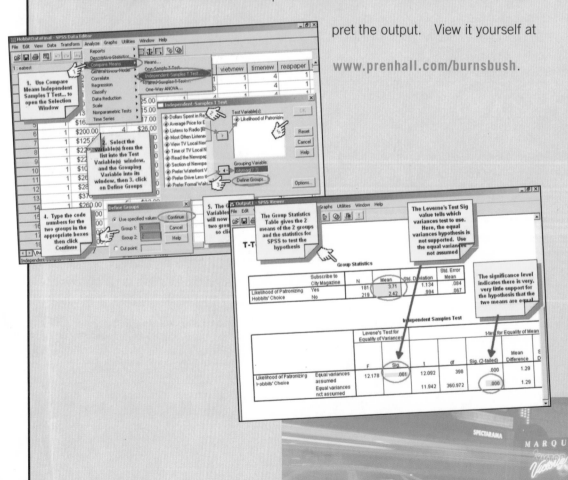

Online marketing research is pervasive in today's marketing research world. Seven marketing research practitioners spearheading this shift have been recruited into the new **Blue Ribbon Panel** feature. In practically every chapter, these practitioners reveal how online research is changing marketing research practice. Students will hear what these practitioners are living. Here are the participants:

BLUE RIBBON PANEL on [Online Research]

▶ Bill MacElroy, President
Socratic Technologies, Inc.

▶ Allen Hogg, President
Burke, Inc.

▶ George Harmon, President
Digital Marketing Services

▶ George Terhanian, Vice President of Internet Research
Harris Interactive

▶ Keith Price, Vice President
Client Development Greenfield Online

▶ Lee Smith, Founder
Insight Express

▶ Doss Struse, Senior Vice President Client Service
Knowledge Networks, Inc.

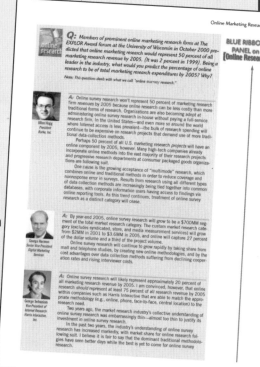

Marketing Research

Online Research Applications

Alvin C. Burns
Louisiana State University

Ronald F. Bush
University of West Florida

Prentice
Hall

PEARSON EDUCATION INTERNATIONAL

Senior Editor: Bruce Kaplan
Editor-in-Chief: Jeff Shelstad
Assistant Editor: Melissa Pellerano
Editorial Assistant: Danielle Rose Serra
Media Project Manager: Anthony Palmiotto
Senior Marketing Manager: Michelle O'Brien
Marketing Assistant: Amanda Fisher
Managing Editor (Production): Judy Leale
Production Editor: Michele Foresta
Production Assistant: Joe DeProspero
Permissions Supervisor: Suzanne Grappi
Associate Director, Manufacturing: Vinnie Scelta
Production Manager: Arnold Vila
Manufacturing Buyer: Michelle Klein
Design Manager: Maria Lange
Art Director: Kevin Kall
Interior Design: Jill Little
Cover Design: Kevin Kall
Cover Illustration/Photo: Image Bank
Illustrator (Interior): UG / GGS Information Services, Inc.
Manager, Print Production: Christy Mahon
Composition: UG / GGS Information Services, Inc.
Full-Service Project Management: UG / GGS Information Services, Inc.
Printer/Binder: Quebecor

Credits and acknowledgments borrowed from other sources and reproduced, with permission, in this textbook appear on pages 627–628.

Microsoft Excel, Solver, and Windows are registered trademarks of Microsoft Corporation in the U.S.A. and other countries. Screen shots and icons reprinted with permission from the Microsoft Corporation. This book is not sponsored or endorsed by or affiliated with Microsoft Corporation.

This edition may be sold only in those countries to which it is consigned by Pearson Education International. It is not to be re-exported and it is not for sale in the U.S.A., Mexico, or Canada.

Pearson Education LTD.
Pearson Education Australia PTY, Limited
Pearson Education Singapore, Pte. Ltd
Pearson Education North Asia Ltd
Pearson Education, Canada, Ltd
Pearson Educación de Mexico, S.A. de C.V.
Pearson Education-Japan
Pearson Education Malaysia, Pte. Ltd
Pearson Education, Upper Saddle River, New Jersey

10 9 8 7 6 5 4 3 2 1
ISBN 0-13-120264-2

Brief Contents

Contents

Chapter **4** DEFINING THE PROBLEM AND DETERMINING
RESEARCH OBJECTIVES 84

Chapter **5** RESEARCH DESIGN 116

Chapter 7 STANDARDIZED INFORMATION SOURCES 180

Chapter 8 OBSERVATION, FOCUS GROUPS, AND OTHER
QUALITATIVE METHODS 202

Chapter **11** DESIGNING DATA COLLECTION FORMS 300

Chapter **13**   DETERMINING THE SIZE OF A SAMPLE 370

Chapter **14**   DATA COLLECTION IN THE FIELD, NONRESPONSE ERROR,
AND QUESTIONNAIRE SCREENING 398

Chapter 18 | **DETERMINING AND INTERPRETING ASSOCIATIONS AMONG VARIABLES 514**

Chapter **19**   **PREDICTIVE ANALYSIS IN MARKETING RESEARCH 548**

Chapter **20**   **PREPARING AND PRESENTING THE RESEARCH
RESULTS 580**

Preface to the Fourth Edition

Marketing Research was created with a particular target in mind: the undergraduate student of marketing research. Accordingly, we have resisted adding techniques that are more appropriate for advanced classes of marketing research. Let's be realistic: typical undergraduate students do not get excited about the theoretical rationale for statistical formulas, so we emphasize a conceptual understanding and a hands-on, practical what-and-how-to-do-it presentation. Our adopters confirm this approach by telling us that their students give the book high marks on course evaluations; they understand the book and find it interesting to read. We believe an understandable book in the hands of a capable professor enhances the chances of student learning, and that is the goal of all of us in academe.

SPSS Integration Our goal has always been to help students use the SPSS software without having techniques and details get in the way of evaluation. Accordingly, we have integrated the software into the text and provided output screens that help students see what to look for in analyzing data. Furthermore, we have developed a Student Assistant tutorial that walks students through the SPSS software.

Our approach has been very well received in the marketplace. In fact, publishing data tell us that _Marketing Research_ is the global leader in the undergraduate marketing research textbook market. We are extremely grateful for the large number of U.S. adopters, and we continue to be delighted as we hear from our foreign adopters. To namedrop a bit, we have been contacted by adopters in Australia, New Zealand, Mexico, Chile, Ecuador, Hong Kong, Taiwan, Peoples Republic of China, Korea, Thailand, India, United Arab Emirates, Egypt, UK, Spain, Holland, and South Africa. Clearly, the approach taken in our book has proven beneficial to many instructors and students.

WHY AND HOW THE FOURTH EDITION IS IMPROVED

In writing the fourth edition, we have continued to "hear the voice of the market" by listening carefully to comments made by students, adopters of the book, and reviewers (both adopters and nonadopters). We have gathered this data in a number of ways including unsolicited e-mail and other comments from our adopters, formal reviews conducted by our publisher, suggestions and recommendations of our students, and our own experiences using the text.

The field of marketing research is truly a moving target, and the velocity of change in the industry has increased dramatically over the life of our third edition. Computer-based and online marketing research practices have proliferated in the last few years, and major parts of the research industry have transitioned rapidly into high-tech status. We have observed this transition, and we have noticed that academic reports, while insightful, lag behind these changes. Consequently, in order to do justice to our treatment of online marketing research in our fourth edition, we have relied on comments from our colleagues in the marketing research industry. In fact, Ron Bush spent an entire sabbatical traveling around the United States visiting key marketing research practitioners, both those from major player companies as well as startup companies doing exciting and innovating things in marketing research.

To keep pace with the online character of marketing research, we have first changed the title of our textbook by adding *"Online Research Applications"* because of the pervasiveness of online research techniques. Second, in the fourth edition, we have sought to integrate a great many examples, comments, and recommendations from practicing marketing researchers about online marketing research. To give students insights into the leaders in the industry and their backgrounds, we've integrated short bios and photos of marketing research practitioners. In short, readers will find a treasury of online marketing research and practitioner-based material carefully integrated in the fourth edition, not simply tacked on at inappropriate places.

Inset excerpt 1:

You can get an idea of the type, number, and services offered by these firms by looking at some online directories of marketing research firms. For example, take a look at the New York chapter of the American Marketing Association's Web site and look through the *Greenbook*, a directory of marketing research firms. Go to www.greenbook.org and click on the picture of the *Greenbook*. Explore this Web site and you will get a better understanding of how to classify external supplier firms. Also visit the different "directory" listings at www.quirks.com.

External Suppliers of Online Survey Research

Inside Research, a confidential newsletter for research industry executives also published by Jack Honomichl, publishes an index to measure the growth of online survey research. The index is based on 30 U.S. marketing research firms and their 27 subsidiaries. These firms reported revenue of $333.5 million in 2001. This represented an increase of 51 percent from 2000. Even though many industries would love to have a 51 percent increase, this was less than expected due to the combination of a weak worldwide economy in 2001 and the economic downturn brought about by the terrorists attacks on New York City in September 2001. Significantly, the participating firms forecast revenues to increase by 46 percent in 2002 in spite of the weak economy.[12] Obviously, online survey research is a fast-growing segment of online research and of the entire research industry.

How Do External Suppliers Organize?

Like internal supplier firms, external supplier firms organize themselves in different ways. These firms may organize by function (data analysis, data collection, etc.), by type of research application (customer satisfaction, advertising effectiveness, new-product development, etc.), by geography (domestic versus international), by type of customer (health care, government, telecommunications, etc.), or some combination of the foregoing functions. Let's look at a few supplier firms to get an appreciation of how they are organized. Burke, Inc. is organized around four main areas of research application and function: Burke Marketing Research is a full-service marketing research division. The Burke Customer Satisfaction Associates offers a standardized service of measuring and managing customer satisfaction. The Burke

See how Burke, Inc. is organized at www.burke.com.

Inset excerpt 2:

sors and spreadsheets that were developed for the PC during this period, applications such as computer-assisted questionnaire programs, touchscreen data collection programs, statistical programs for the PC, and CATI computer telephoning programs were quickly adopted by the marketing research industry.

Globalization–Online Era

We call the time since 1990 the **globalization–online era** since these two major factors have influenced the marketing research industry. First, marketing research companies became much more global during this time period. As business firms grew into multinational operations there was a need for their U.S. research service to be available in other markets of the world as well. The research industry, through acquisition, merger, and expansion, moved into international markets at an unprecedented pace. In the third edition of this book, published in 2000, Jack Honomichl discussed what happened in the research industry during the 1990s. He said some of the world's largest firms, such as Procter & Gamble, Gillette, Coca-Cola, H. J. Heinz, and Johnson & Johnson, obtain more than half their profits from operations outside their home country. Honomichl went on to say that the research firms that cater to the information needs of these multinational giants must serve them all over the world, and this explains the force behind the globalization of the research industry. As an example, Honomichl says that in just 1997 and 1998, the world's largest marketing research firms acquired 55 other firms around the globe.[5] In 2000, the top 50 U.S.-based research firms got 37 percent of their revenues from non-U.S. operations.[6]

Our second influence during the time period from 1990 to the present would have to be online research, the focus of this edition of our text. There have been many forces that have created the growth in online research. The technology, based in the PC technology era of the eighties, continued to evolve and create even more powerful machines and applications software. Globalization meant that not only were firms located far from their customers, but also managers were located far from one another. The need for communications was never greater. Increasing competitive pressures drove the need for operating efficiencies. Consumers' growing concerns for privacy caused researchers to grow wary about the future viability of

Research firms have followed their client firms to new markets all around the world.

A major factor for the success of our earlier editions has been the SPSS Student Version software that accompanies the textbook. In fact, if "imitation is the sincerest form of flattery," we are indeed thrilled that practically all of our competitors have followed our lead and have SPSS Student Version CDs bundled with their texts. However, to stay ahead of the competition, we have redoubled our efforts to integrate SPSS into our fourth edition. One new feature is a single, integrated case and dataset that is used throughout the textbook. This single case is particularly advantageous in the SPSS examples as students do not have to learn about a new situation and new dataset with each technique. Students should be familiar with the case, the questionnaire, and the scaling assumptions of the questions so they can concentrate on understanding how to run SPSS and interpreting the output.

In addition, with this full-color edition, we have created annotated screen shots for SPSS analysis menus as well as SPSS output. We fully expect these to greatly reduce the instructor's burden when teaching SPSS, and we all know that our students require a great deal of tutoring when learning SPSS. Our fourth edition places less emphasis on statistical formulas and more on SPSS output, and our annotated SPSS screen captures will greatly alleviate instructors' workloads when teaching analysis topics. Finally, we have gone online ourselves with an Online SPSS Student Assistant that students can access and study to learn how to run SPSS and interpret the output. In previous editions, the SPSS Student Assistant required installation on a PC's hard drive, but now it is accessible at our Web site: **www.prenhall.com/burnsbush**.

STRENGTHS OF MARKETING RESEARCH, FOURTH EDITION

Marketing Research: Online Research Applications, Fourth Edition, builds on the strengths of earlier editions, and it has some unique features that are new strengths. The key strengths are described below.

Online marketing research examples integrated throughout the textbook. There has been a dramatic shift in the marketing research industry over the past five years to move onto the Internet. While traditional marketing research techniques have remained, online marketing research methods have bloomed and boomed onto the scene. There are many forces behind, benefits to, issues with, and nuances of this exciting format. We have surveyed the emerging literature and talked with a great many marketing research practitioners about online research in an effort to include topics and examples that are integrated throughout the fourth edition.

220   Chapter 8   *Observation, Focus Groups, and Other Qualitative Methods*

MARKETING RESEARCH
INSIGHT
8.3   online research

An Online Application

How an Online Focus Group Helped a U.S. Researcher Understand the Adoption of Western Medicine in Mainland China

Ann Veeck, a marketing professor at Western Michigan University, specializes in the study of Chinese consumers. She has undertaken a number of studies in mainland China over the past decade that trace the changes in Chinese consumers as a result of China's open economy policies and the rapid influx of Western goods and services, such as Kentucky Fried Chicken, McDonald's, and Starbucks, into China's major cities.

When Ann became interested in studying the possible shift away from traditional Chinese medicine, which relies heavily on acupuncture, pressure points, and herbal medications, to Western medicine practices, she realized that a focus group would be a good starting point. However, she was in Kalamazoo, Michigan, and the focus group participants were thousands of miles away in mainland China. She recruited focus groups members via the Internet by working with Dr. Yu Hongyan of Jilin University in Changchun, Jilin Province, People's Republic of China (PRC), as his students had Internet connectivity and online

chat capabilities. Most university students in the PRC do not have personal computers with Internet connections, so they make use of their university's "Web bars" or PC laboratories with PCs that are connected. Also, all students learn a second language, and English, Japanese, and Russian are the most popular languages.

At the appointed time Dr. Yu organized his many students into five teams with English-capable leaders who had good keyboard skills. The time zone differences are such that Changchun is 14 hours ahead of Kalamazoo, so the focus group participants were literally in "tomorrow," while Ann sat at her computer in her office, using a moderator based in a different U.S. city, and with Dr. Yu's students online in Changchun.

Analysis of the online focus group transcript revealed that Western medicine is respected and used mainly by more educated Chinese consumers who can afford this expensive option. Chinese citizens with less education still believe strongly in traditional Eastern medical practices and medicines.

Blue Ribbon Panel of online marketing research practitioners. Because online marketing research is so pervasive in today's marketing research world, we have identified seven marketing research practitioners who are spearheading this shift and recruited them into our "Blue Ribbon Panel." In practically every chapter, they have responded to a question about how online research is changing marketing research practice. Students will hear what these practitioners are living.

SPSS™ Student Version 11.0. SPSS Student Version is state of the art statistical software and SPSS is the most popular statistical software in the marketing research industry. It has been a proven program in colleges and universities for many years. This text is packaged with SPSS Student Version 11.0 CD (0-13-035135-0). This student copy of SPSS will last for one year from the time it is first loaded on a student's computer. For schools having SPSS available in an on-campus computer lab, instructors may order this text without the SPSS Student Version 11.0 CD with a price discount. (0-13-141249-3). There are several improved features of SPSS that adopters and student users will greatly appreciate.

Annotated SPSS menus and output. A significant improvement in our fourth edition is the inclusion of annotated screen captures that show SPSS menu clickstreams as well as SPSS output. As the fourth edition is in full color, these screen captures are faithful to what students will see when they run SPSS, and the annotations are in the form of simulated post-

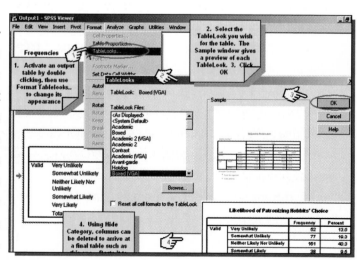

it notes, arrows, circles, colored highlights, and clip art. By looking at the annotated SPSS menu clickstreams, students will learn what menus to use, how to make them appear, and how to use them. With the annotated SPSS output, students' attention will be directed to the precise parts of the output that are relevant, and the annotations show them how to interpret the SPSS output.

A single case integrated throughout the textbook and as chapter cases. Another significant improvement in the fourth edition is a single case study that is integrated throughout the textbook. Students encounter "The Hobbit's Choice Restaurant" case about a proposed upscale restaurant early in the textbook, and the marketing research activities associated with research on consumer reactions/demand for this restaurant are posed as end-of-chapter case questions in most chapters. In addition, the SPSS dataset for this survey is provided on our Web site, and all data analysis topic SPSS examples in the book use this dataset.

More user-friendly descriptions of difficult concepts. Some of our adopters have voiced a desire for less emphasis on statistical formulas and more on interpretation of SPSS output. We have reduced the number of equations, and in some instances, we have moved the equations to boxed items that adopters can opt to include or exclude from student reading assignments. The more complex statistical analyses, such as t-tests, ANOVA, and regression, are more conceptual in description, and more emphasis is placed on how to interpret the SPSS output for these analyses. In our sample size chapter, we have not eliminated formulas, but we have based the idea of sample size around nine tenets so that students will focus on the basic concepts, rather than memorize formulas.

6. How will the data be collected? Should you use the telephone, mail, Internet, or personal interviewing?
7. What about a sample plan? Should this be a national sample or would it be appropriate to sample people in a few cities spread out geographically around the United States, such as New York, Chicago, Dallas and Los Angeles?
8. What is the important information that should be included in the final report?

CASE 2.2   *Your Integrated Case*

This case will appear throughout the book. The case will be used to illustrate concepts covered in the chapter in which the case appears.

The Hobbit's Choice: A Restaurant

Jeff Dean is a restaurant supply sales representative. He works in a large metropolitan area and calls on many of the restaurant owners in the city. His dream is to one day own his own restaurant. He had saved a substantial amount of his earnings during his 15 years in the restaurant supply business and he had recently gone over some financial figures with his banker. He and the banker both agreed that he had enough capital to get serious about investing in his dream. His banker, Walker Stripling, was very optimistic about Dean's potential for

RETURN TO   *Your Integrated Case*

The Hobbit's Choice: A Restaurant to Be or Not to Be*

Although Jeff Dean feels prepared for the business and is encouraged by his banker, Walker Stripling, he has several concerns. He knows that, although he has learned quite a bit about restaurant operation in his area and also quite a bit about upscale restaurants from his friends in other cities, he is not sure if there is an interest in his city for such a restaurant. Even though the metro area is nearly 500,000 in population, he has no assurances that there are enough persons with the income and tastes necessary to

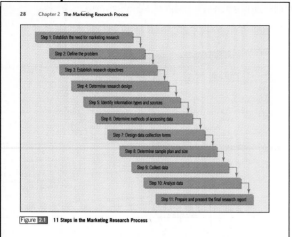

28   Chapter 2 The Marketing Research Process

Step 1: Establish the need for marketing research
Step 2: Define the problem
Step 3: Establish research objectives
Step 4: Determine research design
Step 5: Identify information types and sources
Step 6: Determine methods of accessing data
Step 7: Design data collection forms
Step 8: Determine sample plan and size
Step 9: Collect data
Step 10: Analyze data
Step 11: Prepare and present the final research report

Figure 2.1   11 Steps in the Marketing Research Process

There are caveats to learning a step-by-step process. Although the steps are useful to give you a framework for understanding marketing research, not all projects follow these steps in the exact order shown. Sometimes researchers expand or even skip some of the steps entirely in order to get the job done.

In Michael Lotti's viewpoint about the marketing research process, he actually tells you that this process is not always a step-by-step process. He tells you that researchers sometimes have to expand, or even skip some of the steps. So, instead of being a step-by-step process, marketing research practice is more of an interactive process whereby a researcher, by discovering something in a given step, may move backward in the process and begin again at another step. Finding some new information while collecting data, for example, may cause the researcher to establish different research objectives. Second, as pointed out by Mr. Lotti, any given research project may not involve each and every step shown here. Sometimes you skip steps entirely. The research problem could be resolved, for example, by a review of secondary data, thereby eliminating the need to determine a sample plan or size. What is important for you to know is that, although almost every research project is different, there are enough commonalities among the various procedures and activities to enable us to specify the 11 basic steps of the marketing research process. Thus, learning the research process as a series of steps is necessary to provide you with a framework for understanding marketing research. You just can't view all research projects as moving through a tightly defined series of 11 steps.

An 11-step process approach to marketing research. Because we believe it aids learning marketing research, we kept our process approach by using the 11-step marketing research process that we used in the first three editions. Beginning in Chapter 3, we discuss marketing research as a step-by-step process, and we refer to this process continually as the student makes his or her way through the text. With each new chapter, we highlight the appropriate section of the research process so that the students always know where they are in terms of the overall research process. They are reminded that each section of the research process is linked to some previous section.

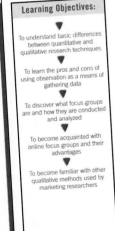

Learning Objectives:

▼

To understand basic differences between quantitative and qualitative research techniques

▼

To learn the pros and cons of using observation as a means of gathering data

▼

To discover what focus groups are and how they are conducted and analyzed

▼

To become acquainted with online focus groups and their advantages

▼

To become familiar with other qualitative methods used by marketing researchers

Streaming Media for Marketing Research

Active >>> group

Practitioner Viewpoint

Flexibility and convenience. Two simple words that are some of the primary reasons that the Internet has become the new medium that is revolutionizing every aspect of business. The flexibility of the Internet allows you to get the goods, services, or information that you want specifically tailored to your needs, and the convenience allows you to receive that information wherever you are and at whatever time you want it.

Flexibility and convenience are also two of the reasons that the marketing research industry is now rushing to embrace the Internet. Although the research industry has sometimes been slow to adopt new technology, the industry embrace of the Internet is encouraging. Now to go along with our first two words is another term: streaming media. This technology has begun to play a more important role not only to the Web in general but also to the research industry in particular.

Streaming media allows clients to watch and participate in qualitative events from their desktops on their own schedules. It will allow consumers to view and rate ads online rather than in a mall facility, and it will eventually allow for true virtual groups in which each respondent and the moderator are all in different places. All of these items are designed to save the client time and money while getting targeted data faster.

David Nelems, President
ActiveGroup

Insights from marketing research practitioners. The fourth edition provides a wealth of current insights and views from practitioners in the marketing research industry. There is a "Practitioner Viewpoint" located at the beginning of every chapter where we have asked our friends in the industry to reflect on certain issues and give us their comments. By involving these individuals—many leaders of large research firms and industry leaders in their own right—the reader has access to up-to-date views of how the marketing research industry operates.

Advice from marketing research practitioners. In our encounters with marketing research companies, we have found practitioners who wish to share their advice with marketing research students. Readers will find this sage advice sprinkled throughout the text.

Meet a marketing researcher. In order to ground our textbook in the marketing research world, we have asked practitioners to provide short biographies and photos. These are scattered throughout the textbook, and students will learn that there are many career paths into marketing research.

New, relevant examples. In an effort to keep students' interest high, we strive to find current examples that are relevant to learning marketing research. *Marketing Research, Fourth Edition,* contains many current, relevant examples. We endeavored to find in-depth examples illustrating each issue being discussed in the text. You will find these examples strategically placed in the text to provide relevant and current illustrations of a concept just introduced to the reader.

Fresh end-of-chapter cases. In addition to the integrated case feature, we replaced many cases in the fourth edition. For example, we have cases focusing on new products such as the Segway™ Human Transporter, online research situations, and a number of cases that relate directly to students' lives and experiences.

right information, typically make the best decisions.

Visit the NewProductWorks at www.newproductworks.com.

MARKETING RESEARCH
INSIGHT
1.1

managers, having the right information, typically make the best decisions. However, in addition to having the right information, success dictates that management must also have the right philosophy, which you have learned as the "marketing concept," and then implement strategies that satisfy customers. Let's discuss these important concepts before we get to marketing research.

Advice from a Marketing Researcher

Not Hearing the "Voice of the Consumer" Can Lead to Failure
Insights from Robert M. McMath

Robert M. McMath probably knows more about product failure than anyone in the world. He developed the New Product Showcase & Learning Center in Ithaca, New York, which in March 2001 became NewProductWorks in Ann Arbor, Michigan. Together, he and the company serve as consultants to firms all over the world that are interested in what makes products succeed and to help them understand why products fail. We appreciate Mr. McMath's special contributions that help provide you, the student of marketing research, with insights on product failure.

One has to understand that in the 1970s, ingredients were "hot buttons" in the introduction of new hair care products. In particular, different shampoos based on unusual and often unique ingredients were being introduced in profuse numbers. In 1974, Clairol's Look of

What Is Marketing Research? **9**

▶ **Meet a Marketing Researcher**

Finding the Right Career Opportunity
Randy Thaman, President/CEO of MRSI

MARKETING RESEARCH
INSIGHT
1.2

Randy Thaman has 25 years of solid research experience. Randy started his career with Burke Marketing Research. A recipient of a Burke Fellowship Award, he next became manager of Marketing Research and Development for Heublien Grocery products and then at Kentucky Fried Chicken. Randy joined MRSI in 1984 and purchased the company in 1989.

In addition to his CEO role, Randy remains very active in the conduct of marketing research studies at MRSI. He serves as an internal consultant for complex studies. He also leads the sales development efforts for MRSI. Randy is an honors graduate of Wright State University (recipient of the Robert Firestone Award for Top Student in Quantitative Business Analysis), with an M.B.A. from the University of Cincinnati.

looks for opportunities for new products. Some of its interests include baby milk sold in disposable bottles, tea and coffee that heat themselves, and a spray that temporarily whitens teeth.[11] MRSI is a marketing research firm that specializes in help-

Will the Segway HT revolutionize personal transportation?

grip to aid in turning. Speed and direction are controlled by the rider shifting weight. It is electric so it is quiet and pollution free. The Segway E series weighs 80 pounds and is designed to carry a 250-pound rider and 75 pounds of cargo. Plans are to allow customization through racks and accessories. Security is enhanced through an intelligent key. Also, in the future, special racks would be available for users to store their Segways, and chains could be

Key Questions the Researcher Should Ask the Manager

Obviously, despite their divergent orientations, marketing managers and marketing researchers must work together to survive. Although understanding the differences presented in Table 4.1 goes a long way toward helping managers and researchers forge a working relationship, much more is required.

There are seven categories of information that the manager and researcher should discuss during their first meeting: (1) symptoms of the problem, (2) the manager's situation, (3) information the manager has about the situation, (4) suspected causes of the problem, (5) possible solutions to the problem, (6) anticipated consequences of these solutions, and (7) the manager's assumptions about any of the prior categories of information. The dialogue between the researcher and the manager is

Despite their differences, managers and researchers must develop a working relationship.

Table 4.1	Eight Fundamental Differences Between Managers and Researchers	
AREA OF DIFFERENCE	MANAGERS	RESEARCHERS
Organizational position	Line	Staff
Responsibility	To make profits	To generate information
Training	General decision making	Technique applications
Disposition toward knowledge	Wants answers to questions	Wants to ask questions
Orientation	Pragmatic	Scholarly
Brand involvement	Highly involved; emotional	Detached; unemotional
Use of the research	Political	Nonpolitical
Research motivation	To make symptoms disappear	To find the truth

INFORMATION GAP	RESEARCH OBJECTIVE(S)
How will prospective residents react to the inclusion of the satellite television programming package with the base apartment?	To what extent do prospective student residents want satellite television?
Will University Estates be more competitive if it adds a satellite television package?	Will University Estates be more attractive than competing apartment complexes if it has the satellite television programming package?

complexes that had cable television? Would they want to live at University Estates more than at an apartment complex that had only basic cable?

As you may have noticed in the University Estates example, whenever an information gap that is relevant to the problem at hand is apparent to the manager, the manager and researcher come to agree that it is a research objective. That is, **research objectives** are specific bits of knowledge that need to be gathered and that serve to close information gaps. These objectives become the basis for the marketing researcher's work. In order to formulate the research objectives, the marketing researcher considers all the current information surrounding the marketing management problem. We have created Table 4.5 to identify the information gaps and appropriate research objectives in the case of University Estates.

The manager and researcher come to agree on research objectives that are based on information gaps.

The problem definition stage is much more difficult when the researcher is working with a global marketing problem because several marketing managers may be involved. Marketing Research Insight 4.2 describes a way to overcome this situation.

▶ A Global Perspective

MARKETING RESEARCH
INSIGHT
4.2

When Undertaking a Global Marketing Research Project, Work with an Angel![1]

Although there are many commonalities between global marketing research and U.S. domestic marketing research, there are fundamental differences between them as well.

According to Joe Plummer, executive vice president, global accounts, McCann-Erickson Worldwide, Inc., the greatest difference is found in the planning stage in which the marketing management problem definition is crystallized and the marketing research methods are decided. Domestic marketing management decision problems tend to have only a single brand manager involved. This situation means that the marketing researcher can have a "sit down" with that manager to define the problem, and that meeting will establish the working relationship between the researcher and the manager that will suffice for the entire research project.

However, the complexity of global marketing typically requires the involvement of several managers, and this fact means that the researcher must determine:

▶ Who is the key manager(s)?
▶ What manager has responsibility and say-so on what issue?
▶ What manager(s) have authority to agree to the researcher's proposal?
▶ Who will be the recipients and ultimate users of the researcher's findings?
▶ Whose budget will be used?

Mr. Plummer advises that during the planning stage, the researcher find an "angel" to work with. An angel is the highest-level executive in the head office of the client organization, preferably the CEO or president, who can compel the underlying managers to work closely together and with the researcher. Of course, the angel will not be involved with the gritty details of the project, but the knowledge that he or she is interested in and watching the project as it unfolds will help immensely when managers disagree or squabble.

Management perspective throughout. Our textbook is written using a manager's perspective. Chapter 4 emphasizes the role of management being involved to define the research problem properly. We present marketing research as a useful source of information, but one that has its own costs. Students are taught that managers must weigh the benefits of more information with the costs of obtaining that information. Throughout the text, a decision-making approach is used. Students are also taught the many trade-offs involved in research that managers constantly make, the use of a probability sample versus a non probability sample, the effects of undersampling, and so on.

Global applications. The marketing world continues to get "smaller." As we note in Chapter 3, revenue from international operations of research firms continues to grow, and online research applications make global research practical and affordable. We highlight our examples of doing marketing research internationally by using the globe icon throughout the book.

Ethical issues confronting the industry. In Chapter 3 we present the major ethical issues confronting the marketing research industry. This discussion includes a presentation of new ethical issues brought about by online survey research and how the industry is beginning to resolve these new issues. In particular, we present CASRO's ideas for properly handling online survey research. We have end-of-chapter cases devoted to ethics. We also provide examples of ethical problems in other chapters, and we use our ethics icon to point out ethical examples to students.

MARKETING RESEARCH
INSIGHT
3.3

An Ethical Issue

Sugging and Frugging
Diane Bowers, President, CASRO

Diane K. Bowers is the president of the Council of American Survey Research Organizations (CASRO), with which she has been associated since 1979. She is also a member of ESOMAR's Professional Standards Committee and sits on the board of advisors of the Masters in Marketing Research programs at the University of Georgia, the University of Texas at Arlington, and the University of Wisconsin at Madison. In addition, Diane is a past president of the Council for Marketing and Opinion Research (CMOR), the Market Research Council (MRC), and the Research Industry Coalition (RIC).

Sugging

"Sugging" or selling under the guise of research is a shorthand term to describe a misuse of the public trust and an abuse of the survey research process that has been promulgated by telemarketers as a means to get a "foot in the door."

This practice had become so commonplace that the public, the research industry, and, ultimately, the federal government decided to put an end to it. In 1994 a federal law was enacted that provided the public and the research industry with a weapon to combat sugging. The Consumer Fraud and Abuse Prevention Act included an amendment requiring telemarketers to promptly state at the beginning of a telephone call that they were selling a good or service.

After the passage of this law the Federal Trade Commission (FTC) promulgated rules for the enforcement of the law, now called the "Telemarketing Sales Rule," affirming the antisugging component. The FTC specifically has emphasized that ". . . the legislative history of the Telemarketing Act noted the problem of deceptive telemarketers contacting potential victims under the guise of conducting a poll, survey, or other type of market research. To address these problems, the Commission believes that in any multiple purpose call where the seller or telemarketer plans, in at least some of those calls, to sell goods or services, the disclosures required . . . must be made 'promptly,' during the first part of the call, before the non-sales portion of the call takes place. Only in this manner will the Rule assure that a sales call is not being made under the guise of a survey research call, or a call for some other purpose."

Recently, the FTC has stepped up its enforcement efforts by recommending that a "National Do Not Call" list be created through which consumers could dictate their desire not to be contacted by telemarketers.

Frugging

"Frugging," or fund raising under the guise of research, is as commonplace and offensive as sugging. In these instances political and social organizations, nonprofit enterprises, charitable, and even educational organizations use the guise of a survey to solicit contributions, support, alumni gifts, membership, and so on for their institution or cause. Examples of frugging include letters from political campaigns or environmental causes that include the words "Survey Enclosed" stamped on the outside of the envelope. The so-called "survey" usually includes only a few leading questions, all with an obvious morally correct answer, such as "Do you favor protecting our children from harm?" At the end of the survey (often in the form of the last question in the survey) is a request for money, support, or membership. The law has not caught up with these abusive practices, probably because the institutions or causes that commit frugging are generally worthwhile and commendable. Industry efforts to educate fruggers have been modestly successful, but the practice continues and public complaints have increased.

Review questions and applications. At the end of each chapter we provide review questions and applications. These materials are provided to aid students' learning of marketing research. Some of the questions require answers that may be taken directly from the text material. Such questions serve the purpose of organizing and reinforcing what the student has just read. Other questions or applications require the students to synthesize the chapter material with other business course material. Finally, there are applications that require extensive work outside of class—for instance—talking with local

REVIEW QUESTIONS/APPLICATIONS

1. List five basic differences between marketing managers and marketing researchers.
2. When a marketing manager and a researcher meet, what are the key questions that the researcher should ask the manager in order to better communicate during their first meeting?
3. When should marketing research be undertaken? When should it not be undertaken?
4. List and describe the elements in a marketing management problem.
5. How does a symptom differ from a cause? How does a cause differ from a potential solution?
6. How do possible causes differ from probable causes?
7. What are are possible solutions, and why is it important to identify all possible ones?
8. How do assumptions lead to research objectives?
9. What leads to an information gap?
10. What is a marketing research proposal and what are its three components?
11. What are constructs, who uses them, and how are they envisioned by the marketing researcher?
12. How does a marketing researcher use relationships and models?

business firms, looking up additional library material, or working with SPSS. Professors can assign different questions/applications to suit their particular course objectives. Adopters who are not using a class project will find adequate supplementary material by focusing on some of the application questions, if desired.

Marginal notes and icons. Students will find comments in the margins. We do this to repeat important points and to serve as effective study guides. Our marginal icons can be seen in this preface. They are readily identifiable visual aids that signal text material that deals with ethical considerations, online research, global applications, our Blue Ribbon panel, or SPSS-related topics.

Bold key terms. We set key terms in bold print. At the point where a key word appears in bold print, we define that term. We list all key terms at the end of the chapter in order to serve as a review and study guide.

New datasets, including the integrated case dataset. Datasets are available to be downloaded from our textbook Web site. In addition to our integrated case, "The Hobbit's Choice Restaurant" dataset, there is a new dataset based on an online survey conducted by an online automobile dealer.   These datasets are provided to aid the students in learning and running various analyses using SPSS.

    In conclusion, we have studied the growth of online marketing research, discussed marketing research issues and practices with individuals who work daily in the marketing research industry, and listened to our students, adopters, reviewers, and the professionals at Prentice Hall and SPSS. We have contemplated the various ways to bring practice and conceptual understanding together and we have created *Marketing Research: Online Research Applications, Fourth Edition.* We are convinced that you will find significant improvements over *Marketing Research, Third Edition.* However, we have also endeavored to retain the winning features of our previous editions, so we emphasize that we have improved the textbook, rather than change it for the sake of change. We hope you'll enjoy learning or teaching from the fourth editon as much as we enjoyed writing it.

INSTRUCTIONAL SUPPORT

We know full well from years of experience that teaching marketing research can be a challenge. The subject matter of marketing research ranges from plain descriptions of research company services to explanations of complicated statistical analysis with many different topics in between. Teaching across all of these topics requires a multifaceted approach. Consequently, we have developed a variety of teaching and learning aids, and adopters of this textbook will receive the following ancillary materials to help them prepare their course and teach it effectively.

Companion Website **(www.prenhall.com/burnsbush).** Consistent with our online applications orientation, we have developed a companion Web site. The Web site was actually developed for the third edition, but it was launched after publication. Our fourth edition Web site is faster and easier to navigate. It has a large number of learning resources for students including popular online sample tests for each chapter, teaching resources for instructors, and other useful information about marketing research. It has a download center for users to access datasets, PowerPoint files, and other items. The authors maintain this Web site.

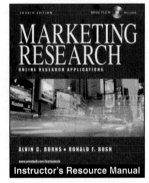

Instructor's Manual. There is a comprehensive instructor's manual prepared by Al Burns. The manual has chapter outlines, key terms, teaching pointers, answers to end-of-chapter questions, and case solutions.

PowerPoint Slides. We have greatly improved our PowerPoint presentation slides with the fourth edition. The presentations are now animated and dynamic, rather than static. The file(s) may be downloaded by students or instructors from the textbook Web site.

Computerized Test Bank. There is a test bank of objective questions, all prepared by the authors and covering all of the material in the fourth edition. This test bank is available from Prentice Hall and can be loaded into Prentice Hall's Test Manager software. Test Manager allows random selection of test questions, modification of individual questions, or insertion of new questions into a test.

SPSS Student Version 11.0. Every textbook is packaged with SPSS Student Version 11.0. The Student Version is identical to the SPSS base version except it is limited to 50 variables and 1,500 cases. Once installed on the hard drive of a PC, SPSS Student Version will remain operational for a full year. For those instructors who want to order the book without the SPSS software CD, use ISBN 0-13-141249-3.

SPSS Student Assistant Online. With previous editions, we created the SPSS Student Assistant, a stand-alone tutorial that teaches students how to use and interpret SPSS. With the fourth edition, the SPSS Student Assistant is located on our textbook Web site, and any user with a high-speed modem may access these explanations and videos without the need to install software. The videos show cursor movements and resulting SPSS operations and output. There is a test for each Student Assistant session so students may assess their learning of the material.

ACKNOWLEDGMENTS

Writing a book takes the cooperation of many people. We are fortunate to have so many friends and colleagues who provide support to us with each edition of *Marketing Research*. First, we want to thank the professional staff at Prentice Hall. Whitney Blake was instrumental in convincing Prentice Hall to make our fourth edition full color, and we are very grateful for her efforts and for her support and assistance in previous editions. Bruce Kaplan took over as our editor in the early stages of the actual writing of the fourth edition. Bruce has been very supportive and responsive during the several months we worked on the fourth edition. The editorial and support staff at Prentice Hall has also been very supportive, and we wish to thank Michele Foresta, Melissa Pellerano, Anthony Palmiotto, Danielle Rose Serra, Kevin Kall, Suzanne Grappi, Judy Leale, and Michelle Klein.

We are thankful for our colleagues at our universities. They provide us with support, comment, and constructive criticism. We thank our deans, Dean Tom Clark of LSU and Dean Ed Ranelli of UWF, for providing us with an environment conducive to pursuing knowledge in our discipline. We thank the members of our support staff who help us with the myriad of detail necessary to write a book. Thank you, Mary McBride, Phyllis Detrick, and Pat Cravat of UWF. Also, we wish to thank Amanda Saveikonis for her computer assistance and Mary Tsao for her research assistance.   Others who worked for us on the research end of our revision are Al's graduate assistants: Anthony Kerr, Gregory "Noah" Mills, Jamye Foster, and Shweta Chaturvedi.

There are always a few people who make special contributions to a book writing project. The entire process of working with outside organizations and acquiring permissions to reprint information is a time-consuming and laborius task. Carolyn Peck was responsible for this task for the fourth edition, and she did an outstanding job. Peggy Toifel is the business reference librarian at the University of West Florida. Peggy does a wonderful job of keeping up with the ever-changing world of IT. We benefit from her knowledge by having up-to-date information in our chapter on secondary information, Chapter 6. Drs. Marcia Howard and Heather Donofrio are experts in the area of communications and report writing. They made major revisions in Chapter 20.

Our friends in the marketing research industry are so important to us in writing an up-to-date book on the marketing research industry. Not only do these people give us information about their firms, but they also share their knowledge on a number of topics. Often, we ask them to read our manuscripts and give us their reactions. Time and again, our friends spend hours reading our manuscript and penning new information based on their special insights. First, we wish to offer special thanks to our Blue Ribbon Panel members, all of whom spent a great deal of time responding to our many questions. Additionally, we wish to especially thank Bill MacElroy of Socratic Technologies and the past president of IMRO as well as Allen Hogg of Burke Interactive. Both of these gentlemen went out of their way to provide us with new and fresh insights. We wish to thank the following individuals for giving us information on new products and services, reviewing our manuscripts, and providing us with many practitioner insights you will find in the book: Janet M. DeVita of ACNielsen; David Nelems of ActiveGroup; Matt Utterback of Affinnova; Allison Groom of the American Heart Association; Yin Chang of Arbitron; Sara Lipson and Randall L. Zeese of AT&T; Don Bruzzone of Bruzzone Research; Burton Ritchie of The Psychodelic Shack; Diane Bowers of CASRO; Ronald Tatham, Carol Brandon, and Nancy Bunn of Burke, Inc.; Stephen F. Moore of Claritas, Inc.; Chet Zalensky of ConsumerMetrics, Inc.; Jerry Thomas and Cristi Allen of Decision Analyst, Inc.; Diane Diaz of Terrabrook; Joe Marinelli of SPSSMR; George Harmon and Shelly Bracken of AOL-Digital Marketing Services; Brent Roderick, David Huffman, Christian Harder, and David Broyles of ESRI Business Information Solutions; Keith Price and Janice Caston of Greenfield Online; Humphrey Taylor, George Terhanian, and Nancy Wong of Harris Interactive; Stephen Pearson of InfoWorld Media Group; Lee Smith, Insight Express; Doss Struse and Melinda Smith de Borrero, Knowledge Networks; Michael Lotti, Kodak; Lawrence D. Gibson, Eric Marder, and Associates; Joan Symmons, Lightspeed; Anne P. Mitchell, MAPS; Randy Thaman, MRSI; Jack Honomichl, Marketing Aid Center; Robert M. McMath, The New Products Showcase and Learning Center; J.J. Klein and Scott McFarlane, OpinionOne; Ed O'Brien, Ping Golf; Dan Quirk, Quirk's Marketing Research Review; B. Venkatesh and Anthony Zahorik, The Burke Institute; Lynda Roguso, Sales & Marketing Management; William D. Neal, SDR Consulting; Michael Zeman and Herb Sorensen, Sorensen Associates; Christopher DeAngelis, Terrence Coen, and Diane Urso, Survey Sampling, Inc.; Dick Thomas, Strategy Research Corp.; Steve Clark, Scientific Telephone Samples; and Howard Gershowitz, Mktg., Inc. All of these dedicated professionals in the research industry gave us their time, opinions, and much valuable information.

We wish to thank the many individuals who served as reviewers for this book. Reviewers for the *Fourth Edition* were:

E. Wayne Chandler, Eastern Illinois University

B. Andrew Cudmore, Florida Institute of Technology

Eric Freeman, Concordia University

Douglas Hausknecht, The University of Akron

Subhash Lonial, University of Louisville

Charles J. Yoos II, Fort Lewis College

We also thank those who reviewed the first, second, and third editions as many of their suggestions and insights are incorporated in these earlier editions:

Linda Anglin, Mankato State University

Silva Balasubramanian, Southern Illinois University

Ron Beall, San Francisco State University

Jacqueline J. Brown, University of Nevada, Las Vegas

Joseph D. Brown, Ball State University

Thomas Cossee, University of Richmond

Corbett Gaulden Jr., University of Texas of the Permian Basin

Ashok Gupta, Ohio University

M. Huneke, University of Iowa

James Leigh, Texas A&M University

Bryan Lilly, University of Wisconsin

Joann Lindrud, Mankato State University

Gary McCain, Boise State University

Sumaria Mohan-Neill, Roosevelt University

V. Padmanabhan, Stanford University

Diane Parente, State University of New York, Fredonia

Don Sciglimpaglia, San Diego State University

Terri Shaffer, Southeastern Louisiana University

Bruce L. Stern, Portland State University

John H. Summey, Southern Illinois University

Nicolaos E. Synodinos, University of Hawaii

Peter K. Tat, The University of Memphis

Dr. William Thomas, University of South Carolina

Jeff W. Totten, Southeastern Louisiana State University

Dr. R. Keith Tudor, Kennesaw State University

Steve Vitucci, University of Central Texas

Once again, only we know how much our wives, Jeanne and Libbo, have sacrificed during the times we have been devoted to this book. We are fortunate in that, for both of us, our wives are our best friends and smiling supporters.

Al Burns,
Louisiana State University

Ron Bush,
University of West Florida

Chapter 1

An Introduction to Marketing Research

Practitioner Viewpoint

You are about to enter the world of marketing research. Welcome! I'm sure you will find this to be a fascinating topic. In this chapter you will learn how marketing research fits into marketing decision making, and you will learn about a relatively new area of marketing research—online marketing research. This chapter introduces you to online marketing research, and you will see applications of it over and over as you move through the chapters of this book. Although a few of you will become marketing researchers, most of you will seek information to aid you in making decisions. By reading this book, you will be taking your first step in understanding the process that generates the information on which you will base those decisions.

Bill MacElroy
Socratic Technologies

IMRO

The Interactive Marketing Research Organization (IMRO) is a new organization in the marketing research industry that was formed as a result of the growing significance of online marketing research. IMRO is a worldwide organization dedicated to providing a forum for the discussion of best practices and ethical approaches to conducting online, or interactive, marketing research. The organization recognizes that online research provides an unprecedented mechanism for the conduct and communication of research worldwide. As such, the tools of online research also have the potential for misuse, particularly regarding the privacy rights of individuals. IMRO, as well as other research organizations such as the AMA, CASRO, MRA, and ESOMAR, will provide guidance to researchers in using the power of online marketing research effectively, efficiently, and ethically.

We are excited to bring you the fourth edition of this book because we are able to offer the significant changes that have occurred in marketing research since the third edition was published. Perhaps the most significant change in the industry has been brought about by technological applications that make use of computer networks, including the Internet. Indeed, some regard the Internet as the cause of a major paradigm shift in both marketing and marketing research.[1] We refer to conducting marketing research using computer networks as "online research." As you are about to see, online research has had a pronounced impact on the marketing research industry. We felt so strongly about this that we named this fourth edition, *Marketing Research: Online Research Applications*. In this book we present to you the latest information on the marketing research industry and, in so doing, we introduce you to online research and its applications. When we discuss online research, you will see the online research icon in the margin.

To introduce you to marketing research and, more specifically, to online marketing research, we invited Mr. Bill MacElroy to provide his special insights at the beginning of this chapter. We chose Mr. MacElroy because he has been a significant industry leader in the area of online research. His firm, Socratic Technologies, specializes in online research, and Mr. MacElroy is the founder and was the first president of the Interactive Marketing Research Organization. IMRO is dedicated to providing a forum for the discussion of the best practices and ethical approaches to research being conducted via the Internet. In this chapter you will learn not only more about IMRO but also how marketing research is related to marketing, the marketing concept, and marketing strategy. You will learn the AMA's definition of marketing research as well as our shorter definition. You will also learn more about online research, examples of online research, and the major companies involved in the area. After reading this chapter, you will know the purpose and uses of marketing research, the types of marketing research studies, and, finally, you will understand how marketing research is related to marketing information systems (MIS).

WHAT IS MARKETING?

We should begin our journey into the field of marketing research by first talking about marketing. Why? Because marketing research is part of marketing. We cannot

The AMA defines marketing as the process of all activities necessary for the conception, pricing, promotion, and distribution of ideas, goods, and services to create exchanges that satisfy individual and organizational objectives.

fully appreciate the role of marketing research unless we know how it fits into the marketing process. So, what is **marketing?**

> *The American Marketing Association has defined marketing as the process of all activities necessary for the conception, pricing, promotion, and distribution of ideas, goods, and services to create exchanges that satisfy individual and organizational objectives.*[2]

Marketers conceive of what the market wants and exchange it for something else, usually money. Nintendo has exchanged many of its video games for sales dollars. Warner Brothers exchanges viewing the movie *Harry Potter and the Sorcerer's Stone* for ticket prices, Harley-Davidson exchanges its motorcycles for sales dollars, and ABC exchanges its entertaining TV production Monday Night Football for high viewer ratings, which it then exchanges for advertising dollars. These companies and many others are successful marketers. Why are these companies so successful? In each case, it is because the marketers have correctly "heard" the consumers' wants and needs and conceived a product (or service), price, promotion, and distribution method that satisfied those wants and needs.

But many companies never "hear the voice of the market." They do not conceive of products or services that meet the needs and wants of the market. They have the wrong price, poor advertising, or poor distribution. Then they become part of the many firms that experience product failure. Our Marketing Research Insight 1.1, written for you by Robert McMath, a leading authority on product failure, illustrates some of the reasons products fail. Fortunately, not all companies and/or their products fail. Peter Drucker wrote that successful companies are those that know and understand the customer so well that the product conceived, priced, promoted, and distributed by the company is ready to be bought as soon as it's available.[3] You will learn in this chapter that one of the reasons leading to success is that managers, having the right information, typically make the best decisions. However, in addition to having the right information, success dictates that management must also have the right philosophy, which you have learned as the "marketing concept," and then implement strategies that satisfy customers. Let's discuss these important concepts before we get to marketing research.

You will learn in this chapter that one of the reasons leading to success is that managers, having the right information, typically make the best decisions.

Visit the NewProductWorks at www.newproductworks.com.

MARKETING RESEARCH
INSIGHT
1.1

Advice from a Marketing Researcher ◄

Not Hearing the "Voice of the Consumer" Can Lead to Failure
Insights from Robert M. McMath

Robert M. McMath probably knows more about product failure than anyone in the world. He developed the New Product Showcase & Learning Center in Ithaca, New York, which in March 2001 became NewProductWorks in Ann Arbor, Michigan. Together, he and the company serve as consultants to firms all over the world that are interested in what makes products succeed and to help them understand why products fail. We appreciate Mr. McMath's special contributions that help provide you, the student of marketing research, with insights on product failure.

One has to understand that in the 1970s, ingredients were "hot buttons" in the introduction of new hair care products. In particular, different shampoos based on unusual and often unique ingredients were being introduced in profuse numbers. In 1974, Clairol's Look of

Buttermilk made its debut in southern test markets, and it was tested for about four years using various approaches. Around 1977, Clairol's Touch of Yogurt entered the market in the same test area. Yogurt, at the time, was enjoying a growing market in the edible category. Apparently scientists thought what consumers were becoming increasingly interested in for healthy eating might translate into "healthy-looking hair." It offered "natural organic protein." Buttermilk, on the other hand, contained protein and a neutral pH factor for an "enriching shampoo and conditioning treatment all in one." In theory, these should have been successful—except that not enough consumers really liked the idea of gooing yogurt or buttermilk in their hair. There is an old saying: "Sell the sizzle, not the steak." Perhaps if these had been branded "A Touch of Elegance with Yogurt," or "The Look of Elegance with Buttermilk," they might have been more acceptable. But apparently the thoughts of putting these slimy ingredients in their hair didn't appeal to enough people to make them successful. Despite these examples that failed, other companies have tried placenta, corn syrup, and even eggs as ingredients—all of which are no longer available.

Clairol also tried a shampoo called "Short & Sassy, the Protein-Enriched Shampoo for Short Hair." Trade sources indicated that this failed because the company was in development with this product for three years. By the time it reached the market for full-scale sales, the hair styles had turned to long hair. Good potential product; wrong time for launching!

Baker Tom's Baked Cat Food, a new product from the bakers of Milk-Bone dog treats, came out as "the only baked cat food" in 1974. But at the time consumers were not concerned about fat in their diets and weren't at all familiar with any type of baked snacks for themselves, much less for their cats. Consumers looked at the line and wondered, "Why should I care?" Another reason it wasn't successful was that the process of baking those little pieces of cat food made them so hard that, "the cats couldn't chew it."

Jell-O for Salads had a reasonably long-running test market in the early 1980s from the General Foods Corporation. Included were flavors such as mandarin orange, pineapple, and Italian salad. Careful examination indicated that when shoppers purchased Jell-O, they might take three of the salad varieties and three regular ones. But when they wanted to make a regular Jell-O dessert for their families and only the salad flavors were on the shelves, they turned to some other type of dessert. The salad varieties were "typecast." Consumers thought of them only for salads and wouldn't use them for anything else, thus not enlarging, over all, the consumption of the brand.

Kimberly-Clark Corporation also introduced a potentially "break-through" product in Avert®, Virucidal Tissues by Kleenex®. Although these tissues would not cure colds, they were designed with special ingredients to "stop major cold-causing viruses before they spread." They were "the first tissue scientifically designed to kill these viruses when

deposited on the tissue by blowing your nose, coughing, or sneezing." But consumers had problems with the designation "virucidal." Words that end in "cidal"—homicidal, suicidal, and partricidal—do not put people in a buying mood. And there was no way to identify the tissues from any other Kleenex product when removed from the box. People didn't necessarily want to use them for removing eye makeup, for example. Perhaps embossing, or putting little blue specks embedded in the tissues, would have differentiated them from other tissues and justified the higher price charged for a box of 60 three-ply tissues, as opposed to the normal 100 sheets of regular types.

Source: NewProductWorks, by permission. Photos by Robert McMath, by permission. McMath e-mail: **rmcmath@cs.com**.

The "Right Philosophy": The Marketing Concept

Okay, so you are thinking: Do I have to read about all this philosophy stuff before these writers tell me what I need to know? Hang on a second. Have you ever thought why your philosophies are so important to you? Give us a chance to explain this and you may be surprised . . . read on! A philosophy may be thought of as a system of values by which you live. Another way of saying this is that a philosophy refers to the set of principles by which you live; therefore, they are important in dictating what you do each and every day. In fact, this is why philosophies are so important; your philosophy affects your day-to-day decisions. For example, you likely have a philosophy similar to this: "I believe that higher education is important because it will provide the knowledge and understanding I will need in the world to enable me to enjoy the standard of living I desire." Are we right? Probably so. So, does this philosophy affect your daily life and the decisions you make every day? I think so. Think about what you are doing right now. You are reading this book, aren't you? Enough said. Well, the same is true for business managers. A manager's philosophy will affect how he or she will make day-to-day decisions in running a firm. There are many different philosophies that managers may use to guide them in their decision making. "We are in the locomotive business; we make and run trains." Or "To be successful we must sell, sell, sell!" The managers who guided their companies by these philosophies guided those companies right out of business. A much better philosophy is called the marketing concept. One of the most prominent marketing professors, Philip Kotler, has defined the marketing concept as follows:

> The **marketing concept** is a business philosophy that holds that the key to achieving organizational goals consists of the company being more effective than competitors in creating, delivering, and communicating customer value to its chosen target markets.[4]

For many years, business leaders have recognized that this is the "right philosophy." And although the marketing concept is often used interchangeably with other terms such as "customer oriented" or "market driven," the key point is that this philosophy puts the customer first. Time has proven that such a philosophy is superior to one in which company management focuses on production, the product itself, or some promotional gimmick. If you satisfy consumers, they will seek to do business with your company. Thus, we've learned that having the "right philosophy" is an important first step in being successful. Still, just appreciating the importance of satisfying consumer wants and needs isn't enough. Firms must put together the "right strategy."

The "Right Marketing Strategy"

A strategy is nothing more than a plan. The term "strategy" was borrowed from military jargon that stressed developing plans of attack that would minimize the enemy's ability to respond. Firms may also have strategies in many different areas such as financial strategy, production strategy, technology strategy, and so on. So, what exactly is marketing strategy?

> A **marketing strategy** consists of selecting a segment of the market as the company's target market and designing the proper "mix" of product/service, price, promotion, and distribution system to meet the wants and needs of the consumers within the target market.

Note how this definition assumes that we have already adopted the marketing concept. A manager not having the marketing concept, for example, wouldn't be concerned that his or her plan addressed any particular market segment and cer-

---

The philosophy called the marketing concept emphasizes that the key to achieving goals consists of the company being more effective than competitors in creating, delivering, and communicating customer value to its chosen target markets.

Marketing strategy consists of selecting a target market and designing the "mix" (product/service, price, promotion, and distribution) necessary to satisfy the wants and needs of that target market.

tainly wouldn't be concerned with consumers' wants and needs. So, to continue, we are thinking like *enlightened* managers; we have adopted the marketing concept. Now, as we shall see, because we have adopted the marketing concept, we can't come up with just any strategy. We have to develop the "right" strategy—the strategy that allows our firm to truly meet the wants and needs of the consumers within the market segment we have chosen. Think of the many questions we now must answer: What is the market? How do we segment the market? What are the wants and needs of each segment? How do we measure the size of each market segment? Who are our competitors, and how are they meeting the wants and needs of each segment? Which segment(s) should we target? Which model of a proposed product will best suit the target market? What is the best price? Which promotional method will be the most efficient? How should we distribute the product/service?

Now we see that many decisions must be made in order to develop the "right" strategy in order to succeed in business. In order to make the right decisions, managers must have objective, accurate, and timely information.

> In order to make the right decisions, managers must have objective, accurate, and timely information.

The need for information is never ending. As environments change, business decisions must be revised again and again to produce the right strategy for the new environment. The bottom line of this entire discussion: To make the right decisions, managers continuously need information. As we shall learn next, marketing research supplies much of this information.

> Environments are forever changing, and this means marketers constantly need updated information about those environments.

WHAT IS MARKETING RESEARCH?

We've established that managers need information. Now you are ready to learn exactly what marketing research is.

> *Marketing research is the process of designing, gathering, analyzing, and reporting information that may be used to solve a specific marketing problem.*

> Marketing research is the process of designing, gathering, analyzing, and reporting information that may be used to solve a specific marketing problem.

This definition tells us that marketing research is a process that results in reporting information, and that information can be used to solve a marketing problem such as determining price, how to advertise, and so on. The focus then is on a process that results in information that will be used to make decisions. That process is what this book is all about. We introduce you to the process in Chapter 2, which serves as a good preview of the rest of the book. Ours is not the only definition of marketing research. The American Marketing Association (AMA) formed a committee several years ago to establish a definition of marketing research. Its definition is:

> *Marketing research is the function that links the consumer, customer, and public to the marketer through information—information used to identify and define marketing opportunities and problems; generate, refine, and evaluate marketing actions; monitor marketing performance; and improve the understanding of marketing as a process.*[5]

> The AMA has defined marketing research as the function that links the consumer, customer, and public to the marketer through information—information used to identify and define marketing opportunities and problems; generate, refine, and evaluate marketing performance; and improve the understanding of marketing as a process.

Which one of these definitions is correct? They are both right. Our definition is shorter. The AMA's definition is longer because it elaborates on the function (we call it the purpose) and uses of marketing research. In the next two sections, we focus on the purpose and uses of marketing research.

What Is the Purpose of Marketing Research?

By now you've probably guessed that the purpose of marketing research has to do with providing information to make decisions. That is essentially correct but the AMA definition includes a reference to the consumer: The **purpose of marketing research** is

> The purpose of marketing research is to link the consumer to the marketer by providing information that can be used in making marketing decisions.

to link the consumer to the marketer by providing information that can be used in making marketing decisions.

The AMA definition expands on our definition by telling us that the information provided by marketing research for decision making should represent the consumer. In fact, by mentioning the consumer, this implies that marketing research is consistent with the marketing concept because it "links the consumer . . . to the marketer." The AMA definition is normative. That is, it tells us how marketing research *should* be used to ensure the firm is consumer oriented. We certainly agree with this but what *should be done* isn't always followed. Kevin J. Clancy and Peter C. Krieg, in their book *Counterintuitive Marketing: Achieve Great Results Using Uncommon Sense*, argue that many failures can be attributed to managers just making "intuitive" decisions. They implore managers to use research.[6] We also want to point out that marketing research information is also collected on entities other than the consumer. Information is routinely gathered on members of distribution channels, employees, and all the environments, including competitors.[7]

Sometimes marketing research studies lead to the wrong decisions. We should point out here that just because a manager uses marketing research doesn't mean that the decisions based on the research are infallible. In fact, marketing research studies are not always accurate. There are plenty of examples when marketing research said a product would fail, yet if the product made it to market in spite of the research prognosis, the product turned out to be a resounding success.

Jerry Seinfeld's popular TV program, *Seinfeld*, is a good example of this. The marketing research that was conducted on the pilot for the Jerry Seinfeld TV show stated the show was so bad that executives gave up on the idea. It was six months before another manager questioned the accuracy of the research and resurrected the show, which became one of the most successful shows in television history.[8] Likewise, marketing research studies also predicted that hair styling mousse and answering machines would fail if brought to market.[9] There are also plenty of failures where marketing research predicted success. Most of these are removed from the shelves with as little fanfare as possible. A classic example of this was Beecham's cold water wash product, Delicare. The new product failed even though marketing research predicted it would unseat the category leader, Woolite. When this happened, there was a great deal of publicity because Beecham sued the research company that predicted success.[10] There are many other examples in which products or services have failed in spite of marketing research studies being conducted that supported them. The products discussed in Marketing Research Insight 1.1 are examples of such failures. But this doesn't mean marketing research is not useful. Remember, most marketing research studies are trying to understand and predict consumer behavior. That's a pretty tough task and we should expect some erroneous predictions. The fact that the marketing research industry has been around for many years and is growing means that it has passed the toughest of all tests to prove its worth—the test of the marketplace. If the industry did not provide value, it would cease to exist.

What Are the Uses of Marketing Research?

Identifying Market Opportunities and Problems Now that you understand the purpose of marketing research, let's take a closer look at the uses of marketing research. In our short definition we simply refer to the use of marketing research as providing information to solve a specific marketing problem. (We will talk more about the word "specific" later in this chapter). The AMA definition, although longer, more clearly elaborates on what some of these problems may be.

For example, the identification of market opportunities and problems is certainly a use of marketing research. Mintel, a British consumer market research firm,

Marketing research *should* be used to ensure the firm is consumer oriented, but some firms do not use marketing research.

▶ **Meet a Marketing Researcher**

Finding the Right Career Opportunity
Randy Thaman, President/CEO of MRSI

Randy Thaman has 25 years of solid research experience. Randy started his career with Burke Marketing Research. A recipient of a Burke Fellowship Award, he next became manager of Marketing Research and Development for Heublien Grocery products and then at Kentucky Fried Chicken. Randy joined MRSI in 1984 and purchased the company in 1989.

In addition to his CEO role, Randy remains very active in the conduct of marketing research studies at MRSI. He serves as an internal consultant for complex studies. He also leads the sales development efforts for MRSI. Randy is an honors graduate of Wright State University (recipient of the Robert Firestone Award for Top Student in Quantitative Business Analysis), with an M.B.A. from the University of Cincinnati.

looks for opportunities for new products. Some of its interests include baby milk sold in disposable bottles, tea and coffee that heat themselves, and a spray that temporarily whitens teeth.[11] MRSI is a marketing research firm that specializes in helping firms find opportunities in the marketplace.

In terms of identifying problems, one of the largest areas of marketing research is that of measuring customer satisfaction. Customer satisfaction studies identify problems early on and allow managers to take corrective action. Burke, Inc., in Cincinnati, Ohio, is known for its high-quality studies in customer satisfaction.

Marketers need information to help them identify market opportunities.

▶ **Advice from a Marketing Researcher**

What It Takes to Be a Marketing Researcher
Insights from Randy Thaman, President and CEO, MRSI

I believe a successful marketing research career is a combination of three elements: creative thinking, the ability to pull many pieces of data together into a cohesive story, and the ability to communicate with everyone from the CEO to the entry-level analyst. Communication is so critical that I encourage you to take a speech class so that you are comfortable presenting in front of people. It is also imperative that you can think logically and that you are very detail oriented.

Make sure your first job is with a company that has a strong training program. If you start with the right fundamen-

tals, you will find that many doors will be open to you. Before choosing that first position, talk to market researchers in corporations and to suppliers. Try to find people in large and small companies, and be prepared with questions. Ask them about their careers, their future plans, and what they feel are keys to success. And ask about what it is like to work in their company. Don't worry about finding the perfect job right out of school—you probably won't find it because you won't know what the perfect job for you is yet! But make sure that any position always gives you the opportunity to learn something new.

MRSI is a marketing research firm that helps companies evaluate opportunities in the marketplace.

Marketers need information to help them determine which strategy will best take advantage of a market opportunity.

Generate, Refine, and Evaluate Potential Marketing Actions Marketing research can also be used to generate, refine, and evaluate a potential marketing action. For example, as AT&T grew from being "the long-distance telephone company" to participating in all forms of the fast-paced telecommunications industry, it wanted a brand image that would connote being a dynamic, unique, creative, and fast-moving company with advanced products and services in many areas. It conducted research that generated the "Boundless" brand advertising campaign. Then it conducted research to evaluate the effectiveness of the campaign.[12] Thus, AT&T is a good example of a firm using marketing research to generate, refine, and evaluate a marketing action. In this case, the "action" was developing a brand that conveyed the image AT&T wanted in the marketplace.

Monitor Marketing Performance The AMA definition also states that marketing research may be used to *monitor marketing performance*. Everyone talks about the Super Bowl commercials in which companies spend millions of dollars for a 30-second spot during the most-watched TV event year in and year out. Bruzzone Research Company monitors the effectiveness of ads on Super Bowl Sunday. Wonder why Tom Cruise and Jack Nicholson earn such big bucks? Their ad for the movie *A Few Good Men* has had the record for getting the highest recognition scores among movie ads shown on Super Bowl Sunday for years.[13] Another example of monitoring research is called tracking research. Tracking research is used to monitor how well products of companies such as Hershey's, Campbell's Soup, Kellogg's, and Heinz are performing in the supermarkets. Research firms such as ACNielsen and Information Resources, Inc. are two of several firms monitoring the performance of products in supermarkets and other retail outlets. They monitor how many units of these products are being sold, through which chains, at what retail price, and so on.

Companies use marketing research to monitor how well their products or services are performing in the marketplace.

Improve Marketing as a Process Finally, our AMA definition says that a use of marketing research is to *improve marketing as a process*. To improve our understanding of the marketing process means that some marketing research is conducted to expand our basic knowledge of marketing. Typical of such research would be attempts to define and classify marketing phenomena, and to develop theories that describe, explain, and predict marketing phenomena. Such knowledge is often published in journals such as the *Journal of Marketing Research* or *Marketing Research*. Much of this research is conducted by marketing professors at colleges and universities and by other organizations, such as the Marketing Science Institute. The latter use could be described as the only part of marketing research that is basic research.

Basic research is conducted to expand our knowledge rather than to solve a specific problem. Research conducted to solve specific problems is called **applied research,** and this represents the vast majority of marketing research studies.

> Basic research is undertaken to extend knowledge by attempting to improve marketing as a process. However, most marketing research is applied research because it is undertaken to solve a specific problem.

CLASSIFYING MARKETING RESEARCH STUDIES

Another way to introduce you to marketing research is to look at a classification of the different types of marketing research studies being conducted in the industry. In Table 1.1 we organize the major types of studies under the usage categories from the AMA definition. Under each of these four categories we provide example studies.

At this point, you should understand how marketing research is used by marketing managers to help them develop the "right" strategies using the marketing concept. You also know how to define marketing research and you know the purpose and uses of marketing research as well as some of the different types of studies conducted. Now we can take a closer look at the hot area of marketing research we talked about in the opening paragraph . . . online marketing research.

ONLINE MARKETING RESEARCH

Computer networks, particularly the Internet, have brought about many changes not only in terms of how people shop, learn, and communicate but also in how businesses operate. Computer networks have impacted how businesses market to one another (B2B) and how businesses market to consumers (B2C). They have affected virtually every type of business worldwide. Marketing research is no exception. In *Online Marketing Research*, Grossnickle and Raskin state: "The advent of the Web has led to a revolution in the research community. Web technology has astronomically reduced the cost of conducting numerous types of research and simultaneously enabled the execution of more complicated and rigorous study designs."[14] The revolution created by online marketing research is likely to be a permanent component of the structure of marketing research in the future. However, as Allen Hogg of

---

Table **1.1** **A Classification of Marketing Research Studies**

A. *Identifying Market Opportunities and Problems*

As the title implies, the key issues among these studies are directed at finding opportunities or problems with an existing strategy. For example, a company conducts a study that determines that one in twenty 12-year-olds is dieting. The company conducts additional research to determine that there is viable demand for diet products for the teen market segment. Therefore, through its research, the company has discovered a new market opportunity.[15]

Market demand determination
Market segments identification
Marketing audits
SWOT analysis
Product/service use studies
Environmental analysis studies
Competitive analysis

Table 1.1   **(continued)**

B. *Generate, Refine, and Evaluate Potential Marketing Actions*

Suppose the foregoing studies determine that there is demand (opportunity) for a new product. The types of research studies in this section are designed to generate, refine, and evaluate marketing mix alternatives that are thought necessary to fulfill that demand. Going back to the "teen diet" example cited earlier, these types of studies would determine alternative ways of appealing to the teen diet market. Would a new diet drink, exercise program, chain of "teen" health clubs, or specially formulated diet pills satisfy this market segment? If research determined that a diet drink had the most appeal, what special formulations of the drink would best serve the market? What price should be used? How should the drink be promoted? Distributed?

> Marketing mix evaluation testing
> In-store new/existing product testing
> Concept tests
> New-product prototype testing
> Reformulating existing product testing
> Pricing tests
> Advertising pretesting
> TV ad recall studies
> Radio listenership studies
> Magazine viewership studies
> In-store promotion effectiveness studies
> Distribution effectiveness studies

C. *Monitor Marketing Performance*

These studies are control studies. They allow a firm that already has a marketing mix placed in the market to evaluate how well that mix is performing. If our example company is marketing its diet drink to teens, it may want to gather market information on the "image" the drink has relative to competitors' offerings among teens, parents, and medical professionals. The company may want to purchase tracking studies that show how many units of the drink are being sold by package type and flavor type and through which retail outlets compared to all the competitive products. It may also want to conduct a customer satisfaction study to determine how its present consumers feel about the drink.

> Image Analysis
> Tracking studies
> Customer satisfaction studies
> Employee satisfaction studies
> Distributor satisfaction studies
> Web site evaluations

D. *Improve Marketing as a Process*[16]

In the following list are a few example studies that could be considered basic research. They are conducted to expand our knowledge of marketing as a process rather than to solve a specific problem facing a company, such as "Should we sell a diet drink targeted to teens?" Note, however, that by having the knowledge generated from these studies, managers may be in a much better position to solve a specific problem within their firm. Basic research on how teens assimilate "traditionally adult products," for example, may be of real value to the company that is thinking of marketing a diet drink to teens. Likewise, basic research conducted to provide cultural explanations for teens' fascination with slender body figures may also prove valuable to any company considering targeting the teen population.

> How managers learn about the market
> Consumer behavior differences in e-business transactions
> Determining the optimum amount that should be spent on
>   e- business and measuring success in e-business
> Predictors of new-product success
> The impact of long-term advertising on consumer choice
> Measuring the advantage to being the first product in the market
> Marketing mix variable differences over the Internet

Burke Interactive pointed out to us, the rate of technological change will continue to impact online research and, therefore, it too will change in the future.[17] In the paragraphs that follow we provide a discussion of online marketing research.

What Is Online Research?

We define **online research** as:

> *The use of computer networks, including the Internet, to assist in any phase of the marketing research process including development of the problem, research design, data gathering, analysis, and report writing and distribution.*

Let's discuss this definition. First, by using the phrase "computer networks," we would include any form of computer connectivity, such as the Internet and intranets. For example, salespersons are asked to fill out a questionnaire describing customers' reactions to a new product they have just presented to the customers. The salespersons are using the company intranet to deliver research concerning potential customers' reactions to a new product. The essential ingredient is that computer networks are being used in the research process.

The second issue in our definition refers to computer networks being used in *any phase* of the research process. This means that online research, to a limited extent, has been around for years, being used in limited applications of the research process since the 1960s. Transfer of data via Bitnet, an early data transfer system predating the Internet, or, more recently, accessing online information services such as Lexis-Nexis, in the 1980s, for example, would constitute online research. So what we have has been more of an evolution than a revolution. Yet it is not incorrect to use the term "revolution" because the last few years have produced a revolutionary number of online research applications throughout the research process. It is the availability and use of these many applications that have created the revolution called online research. Examples of these applications of online research follow.

Examples of Online Research Over the years, the research industry has been designing applications creatively that utilize computer networks to assist in the many activities involved in the marketing research process. Some of these innovative applications include:

Receiving/distributing RFPs (requests for proposals) online and responding online

Designing sample plans, requesting and receiving samples online (Survey Sampling, Inc.'s SSI-SNAP, Greenfield Online's "River")

Designing questionnaires using online questionnaire-design software (WebSurveyor, Market Tool's "Zoomerang," Insight Express)

Distributing questionnaires online and using them to collect data on the Web (AOL/DMS, Harris Interactive, Socratic Technologies, Knowledge Networks, Vividence)

Analyzing data at a central processing location and using the computer networks to distribute data analysis output (SPSS)

Distributing research reports via computer networks in a format allowing users to manipulate output and conduct additional analyses (ConsumerMetrics, Inc., Beyond 20/20, Burke's Digital Dashboard)

Using the Internet for concept testing (Decision Analyst, Inc. and Affinova)

Throughout this text we will illustrate the application of online marketing research tools being used in the industry today at every step of the research process.

Online research may be defined as the use of computer networks, including the Internet, to assist in any phase of the marketing research process including development of the problem, research design, data gathering, analysis, and report writing and distribution.

We will give real-world examples illustrating the actual companies that are partici-pating in this fast-growing segment of marketing research.

Online Research vs. Web-Based Research vs. Online Survey Research

Understanding online research means we should distinguish between two other concepts that are confused with online research. First, by **Web-based research,** we mean research that is conducted *on* Web applications. This type of research, some-times confused with online research, may use traditional methods as well as online research methods in conducting research on Web-based applications. Some Web-based applications would include research on the popularity of the Web pages themselves, such as "site hit counts," effectiveness studies of pop-up ads on Web sites, or research measuring consumers' reactions to various components of Web sites. Any of these Web-based projects could be researched using either online research or traditional research. Because online research refers to using computer networks in conducting the research process, it may be used regardless of the application.

The recent growth in online survey research is sometimes thought to repre-sent online research. **Online survey research** refers to the collection of data using computer networks. Collecting employee satisfaction data using a company's intranet would constitute online survey research. Many research firms, such as Greenfield Online, have been recently created for the purpose of using the Internet to gather survey data. This also would be an example of online survey research. Because online survey research uses computer networks to collect data (part of the research process), we would consider it to be a subset of online research.

Growth of Online Research

There are no estimates of the exact size of online research. However, we would be safe in saying that online research has been experi-encing double-digit growth rates and will likely continue to do so in the next few years. As we have stated, almost daily, new online innovations appear that facilitate the process of marketing research.

Growth of Online Survey Research

Fortunately, we do have some industry figures to estimate the growth of online survey research, a subset of online research. Allen Hogg, director of marketing for Burke Interactive, states that the use of the Internet by marketing researchers is "exploding." Also, Mr. Hogg notes that industry figures likely are very conservative estimates. Why? Industry spending estimates only count research that is reported by the marketing research firms themselves. The reason this underscores the amount spent on research is that the nonmarketing research firms (i.e., Apple, Kodak, Time, AT&T) also do their own "in-house" research. General Mills even created a spinoff firm called InsightTools to do its online research. The amount of online research these firms are conducting is not counted in industry esti-mates, and IMRO (Interactive Marketing Research Organization) estimates that if we added the "in-house" online research we could easily have as much as three or four times more online research going on than is reported by the marketing research firms.[18]

Throughout this text we are going to report to you the opinions of our Blue Ribbon Panel on Online Research (see Preface). We asked these people, all highly recognized in the research industry, a series of questions. Their answers to our ques-tion about their predictions for the future growth of online research are reported in the accompanying box. We also take up this subject again in Chapter 3 when we dis-cuss the industry.

By Web-based research, we mean research that is conducted on Web applications.

Online survey research refers to the collection of data using com-puter networks.

Estimates of the use of online research indicate its use will con-tinue to grow.

BLUE RIBBON PANEL on [Online Research]

Q: *Members of prominent online marketing research firms at The EXPLOR Award forum at the University of Wisconsin in October 2000 predicted that online marketing research would represent 50 percent of all marketing research revenue by 2005. (It was 2 percent in 1999). Being a leader in the industry, what would you predict the percentage of online research to be of total marketing research expenditures by 2005? Why?*

Note: This question deals with what we call "online survey research."

Allen Hogg
President
Burke, Inc.

A: Online survey research won't represent 50 percent of marketing research firm *revenues* by 2005 because online research can be less costly than more traditional forms of research. Organizations are also becoming adept at administering online survey research in-house without paying a full-service research firm. In the United States—and even more so around the world where Internet access is less prevalent—the bulk of research spending will continue to be expensive research projects that demand use of more traditional data-collection methods.

Perhaps 50 percent of all U.S. marketing research *projects* will have an online component by 2005, however. Many high-tech companies already incorporate online methods into the vast majority of their research projects and progressive research departments at consumer packaged goods organizations are following suit.

One cause is the growing acceptance of "multimode" research, which combines online and traditional methods in order to reduce coverage and nonresponse error in surveys. Results from research using all different types of data collection methods are increasingly being tied together into common databases, with corporate information users having access to findings via online reporting tools. As this trend continues, treatment of online survey research as a distinct category will cease.

George Harmon
Senior Vice President
Digital Marketing
Services

A: By year-end 2005, online survey research will grow to be a $700MM segment of the total market research category. The custom market research category (excludes syndicated, store, and media measurement services) will grow from $2MM in 2001 to $3.6MM in 2005, and online will capture 27 percent of the dollar volume and a third of the project volume.

Online survey research will continue to grow rapidly by taking share from mall and telephone studies, by creating new online methodologies, and by the cost advantages over data-collection methods suffering from declining cooperation rates and rising interviewer costs.

George Terhanian
Vice President of
Internet Research
Harris Interactive,
Inc.

A: Online survey research will likely represent approximately 20 percent of all marketing research revenue by 2005. I am convinced, however, that online survey research *should* represent at least 75 percent of all research revenue by 2005 within companies such as Harris Interactive that are able to match the appropriate methodology (e.g., online, phone, face-to-face, central location) to the research need.

Two years ago, the market research industry's collective understanding of online survey research was embarrassingly thin—almost too thin to justify its investment in online survey research.

In the past two years, the industry's understanding of online survey research has increased markedly, with market share for online research following suit. I believe it is fair to say that the dominant traditional methodologies have seen better days while the best is yet to come for online survey research.

Keith Price
Vice President
Greenfield Online

A: Online survey research has gained both credibility and interest over the past few years. Initially, marketing research professionals were hesitant about conducting online survey research, since, unlike telephone and mail research methodologies, online survey research does not have a true "sampling frame" and requires that respondents have access to the Internet. Both factors have been considered by some to be major drawbacks.

Online survey research will never replace traditional research methodologies, but it has gained popularity. The Internet population is forecasted to grow by 65 percent between 2000 and 2003, is predicted to reach 1 billion by the year 2005 (Source: PriceWaterhouse Coopers), and is no longer representative of a small portion of the U.S. population. Although online survey research does not have a true sampling frame, weighting techniques can be applied.

I believe that companies are starting to realize that online survey research can provide an attractive alternative to traditional research methodologies. Now companies are able to quickly and efficiently survey their target audiences and maintain consumer dialogue, which will ultimately lead to customer relationship management (CRM) efforts. Although 50 percent seems to be a large percentage of total marketing research revenue, I believe that our definition of research will change as a result of online survey research and expand beyond traditional research. I predict that 50 percent is altogether feasible, when CRM and custom research panels are taken into account.

Lee Smith
CEO
Insight Express

A: The shifting demographics of the online population are a fundamental force enabling the use of online survey research. As the demographics of the general and online populations converge, the relative quality, projectability, and set of applications for which online research may be used will soar. With these aspects established, marketers and market researchers may leverage the speed, quality, greater access to respondents, and affordability of online survey research with confidence. And once the power of online survey research is experienced, researchers will quickly move mail, telephone, and in-person initiatives to the online methodology to capture all of its benefits—without the need to weigh results.

Doss Struse
Senior Vice President
Client Service
Knowledge Networks,
Inc.

A: The proportion of all survey research accounted for by online survey research will be somewhat lower than the forecasts made in 1999. My estimate would be that it will account for 30 percent to 35 percent in the United States. The reasons for online survey research capturing a smaller share of the total include these factors:

▶ Because of slowed growth in the penetration of the Internet, a significant proportion of the population will not be online.
▶ There will continue to be restrictions on intrusively contacting online consumers. This coupled with the absence of any usable sampling frame will handicap online research in displacing more traditional modes.
▶ Internet firms have disappointed research buyers with their lack of any significant research expertise or experience.
▶ A number of firms entering the online survey research arena with bright prospects in 1999 have stumbled badly in the economic downturn that started at the end of 2000.
▶ There is no infrastructure comparable to that which exists for central location interviewing or telephone interviewing to facilitate all research companies adopting online survey research as a principal mode for connecting with consumers. Although an infrastructure is evolving, it is less developed and less complete for the other dominant modes.
▶ Online research methods that enable research buyers to replace a number of forms of more traditional research have not evolved.

> ▶ Too much emphasis has been placed on implementing traditional research methods faster and more cheaply, and too little emphasis has been placed on using the technology to change the nature of the interaction with consumers.
> ▶ As research shifts from central location and telephone to online, there will be economic pressure to reduce the cost of these traditional modes of research.
> ▶ All of these factors are accentuated outside the United States, making the proportion of survey research that will go online internationally even lower—probably under 20 percent for most developed countries and under 10 percent in less developed areas.

Factors Encouraging the Growth of Online Research The primary reason that online research is growing in popularity is the same reason that computers and Internet technology have been popular: effectiveness and efficiency. Online applications not only get the job done but also accomplish tasks much faster and more cheaply than traditional methods. Consider the old process of acquiring a sample from a professional sampling firm. First, even with a clear understanding of the objectives of the research project at hand, defining the population from which the samples would be drawn took at least a telephone conversation between researcher and sampling firm personnel. Then once agreement was reached and after the sample was generated, the sample forms (hard copy) were mailed (or sent overnight). With online capabilities, however, a researcher can use a Web site to design, order, and receive the sample (in different formats) online in a matter of minutes. Consider another example. A firm wishes to design a survey and obtain a response from 300 persons around the United States. Whereas in the past this may have taken several weeks, the entire process can now be accomplished in a matter of days thanks to online research. The bottom line is that computer/online technology impacts marketing research just as it does many other endeavors. The result is that the job gets done (effectiveness) with a minimum of time and cost (efficiency). In addition, there are other benefits depending on the application. Conducting surveys online, for example, may allow the researcher to view data as they are being entered, interviewer bias is eliminated, and studies are showing that respondents actually prefer online surveys versus telephone, mail, or face-to-face interviews. Gayle Fugitt, vice president of Consumer Insights, General Mills, stated that he believes consumers are more candid and honest when they respond using the Internet. He feels this way because these consumers get to choose when, where, and how they give information, and this leads them to be more helpful. General Mills estimates that by using zTelligence, a firm providing online research, the company saves as much as 50 percent on the cost of research and reduces the time required to gather information by up to 75 percent. Thus, online research is growing because it:

> *The primary reason that online research is growing in popularity is the same reason that computers and Internet technology have been popular: effectiveness and efficiency.*

> ▶ Has applications throughout the marketing research process.
> ▶ Is suitable for both quantitative as well as qualitative research.
> ▶ Is suitable for both attitudinal research (surveys) and behavioral research (observing and tracking what people do online).
> ▶ Allows respondents to view and manipulate stimuli such as video, ads, product prototypes, and so on, in the comfort of their homes.
> ▶ Allows clients/researchers to view data in real time.

> ▶ Is faster than traditional research methods.
> ▶ Is cost-effective.
> ▶ May prove to be the most desirable alternative method of gathering data as telephone, mail, and mall intercept interviewing find growing resistance among potential respondents.

Challenges to Online Research Online research has not evolved without controversy. The controversy primarily centers on online survey research and focuses on three major issues: representativeness of data collected online, spam, and privacy issues. In terms of representativeness, some question whether or not information collected from among only those with online capabilities can represent the total population. Related to this is the question of whether or not those who are willing to take surveys online are even representative of all those consumers who are online.

Online research has not evolved without controversy. The controversy primarily centers on online survey research and focuses on three major issues: representativeness of data collected online, spam, and privacy issues.

Spam refers to unsolicited e-mail. Soon after the Internet provided the electronic "open door" to households, surveyors jumped at the chance to obtain unprecedented numbers of surveys quickly and cheaply by simply sending surveys to e-mail addresses. The reaction was to be expected. Consumer rights groups reacted negatively to the electronic invasion of unwanted surveys (and ads) called spam. Although the research industry has fought vigorously to ban spam surveys, this remains an issue of concern.

Finally, the issue of privacy of information has been controversial. One firm proposed to correlate and sell personal information with online behavior collected without consumer consent. There is an ongoing debate regarding privacy rights of consumers. Online research, because it allows for one-on-one access, is particularly open to privacy concerns. Research conducted on how consumers shop on Web sites, the use of collaborative filtering techniques that allow marketers to guess at what products and services you are most interested in, the use of cookies to identify where consumers have visited within Web sites, and so on, have been challenged by consumer rights groups. Also, standards for blocking spam are being proposed. All of these issues are discussed more fully in Chapter 3 under ethical issues. We will use the ethics icon to point out ethical issues in marketing research to you throughout the book.

THE MARKETING INFORMATION SYSTEM

So far we have presented marketing research as if it were the only source of information. This is not the case, as you will understand by reading this section on marketing information systems.

An MIS is a structure consisting of people, equipment, and procedures to gather, sort, analyze, evaluate, and distribute needed, timely, and accurate information to marketing decision makers.

Decision makers have a number of sources of information available to them. We can understand these different information sources by examining the components of the **marketing information system (MIS)**.

An MIS is a structure consisting of people, equipment, and procedures to gather, sort, analyze, evaluate, and distribute needed, timely, and accurate information to marketing decision makers.[19] The role of the MIS is to determine decision makers' information needs, acquire the needed information, and distribute that information to the decision makers in a form and at a time when they can use it for decision making. However, this sounds very much like marketing research—providing information to aid in decision making. We can understand the distinction by understanding the components of an MIS.

Components of an MIS

As noted previously, the MIS is designed to assess managers' information needs, to gather this information, and to distribute the information to the marketing managers who need to make decisions. Information is gathered and analyzed by the four subsystems of the MIS: internal reports, marketing intelligence, marketing decision support, and marketing research. We discuss each of these subsystems next.

Internal Reports System The **internal reports system** gathers information generated by internal reports, which includes orders, billing, receivables, inventory levels, stockouts, and so on. In many cases, the internal reports system is called the accounting information system. Although this system produces financial statements (balance sheets and income statements, etc.) that generally contain insufficient detail for many marketing decisions, the internal reports system also contains extreme detail on both revenues and costs that can be invaluable in making decisions. For example, a sophisticated internal reports system can yield historical information for a given product, product line, location, or region, including:

- ❱ Revenue
- ❱ Product cost
  - • Purchase price
  - • Shipping or transportation charges
- ❱ Gross margin
- ❱ Direct costs of sale, such as commissions to salespersons
- ❱ Indirect costs, or what is often referred to as "overhead"
  - • Rental or lease cost for retail space
  - • Salaries and wages, including benefits
  - • Operating costs, such as utilities and security[20]

Other information is also collected such as inventory records, sales calls records, and orders. A good internal reports system can tell a manager a great deal of information about what has happened within the firm in the past. When information is needed from sources outside the firm, other MIS components must be called upon.

Marketing Intelligence System A second component of an MIS is the **marketing intelligence system.** The marketing intelligence system is defined as a set of procedures and sources used by managers to obtain everyday information about pertinent developments in the environment. Such systems include both informal and formal information-gathering procedures. Informal information-gathering procedures involve such activities as scanning newspapers, magazines, and trade publications. Formal information-gathering activities may be conducted by staff members who are assigned the specific task of looking for anything that seems pertinent to the company or industry. They then edit and disseminate this information to the appropriate members or company departments. Formerly known as "clipping bureaus" (because they clipped relevant newspaper articles for clients), several online information service companies, such as Lexis-Nexis, provide marketing intelligence. To use its service a firm would enter key terms into search forms provided online by Lexis-Nexis. Information containing the search terms appears on the subscriber's computer screen as often as several times a day. By clicking on an article title, subscribers can view a full-text version of the article. In this way, marketing intelligence goes on continuously and searches a broad

---

The four subsystems of an MIS are the internal reports system, marketing intelligence system, marketing decision support system (DSS), and marketing research system.

The internal reports system gathers information generated by internal reports, which includes orders, billing, receivables, inventory levels, stockouts, and so on.

The marketing intelligence system is defined as a set of procedures and sources used by managers to obtain everyday information about pertinent developments in the environment.

range of information sources in order to bring pertinent information to decision makers.

Marketing Decision Support System (DSS) The third component of an MIS is the decision support system. A **marketing decision support system (DSS)** is defined as collected data that may be accessed and analyzed using tools and techniques that assist managers in decision making. Once companies collect large amounts of information, they store this information in huge databases that, when accessed with decision-making tools and techniques (such as break-even analysis, regression models, and linear programming), allow companies to ask "what-if" questions. Answers to these questions are then immediately available for decision making.

> A marketing decision support system (DSS) is defined as collected data that may be accessed and analyzed using tools and techniques that assist managers in decision making.

Marketing Research System Marketing research, which we have already discussed and defined, is the fourth component of an MIS. Now that you understand the three other components of an MIS, we are ready to discuss the question we raised at the beginning of this section. That is, if marketing research and an MIS both are designed to provide information for decision makers, how are the two different? In answering this question we must see how marketing research differs from the other three MIS components.

First, the **marketing research system** gathers information not gathered by the other MIS component subsystems: Marketing research studies are conducted for a *specific* situation facing the company. It is unlikely that other components of an MIS have generated the particular information needed for the specific situation. When *People* magazine wants to know which of three cover stories it should use, can its managers obtain that information from internal reports? No. From the intelligence system or the DSS? No. This then is how marketing research plays a unique role in the total information system of the firm. By providing information for a *specific problem at hand*, it provides information not provided by other components of the MIS. This is why persons in the industry sometimes refer to marketing research studies as "ad hoc studies." *Ad hoc* is Latin meaning "with respect to a specific purpose." (Recall that earlier in the chapter when we defined marketing research, we told you we would revisit the word *specific*. Now you see why we used that word in our definition.)

> Marketing research studies are for specific problems and are sometimes referred to as "ad hoc studies." They also have a beginning and an end. Hence, they are also referred to as marketing research "projects."

There is another characteristic of marketing research that differentiates it from the other MIS components. Marketing research projects, unlike the previous components, are not continuous—they have a beginning and an end. This is why marketing research studies are sometimes referred to as "projects." The other components are available for use on an ongoing basis. However, marketing research projects are launched only when there is a justifiable need for information that is not available from internal reports, intelligence, or the DSS.

SUMMARY

The marketing concept is a philosophy that states that the key to business success lies in determining and fulfilling consumers' wants and needs. Marketers attempting to practice the marketing concept need information in order to determine wants and needs and to design marketing strategies that will satisfy customers in selected target markets. Environmental changes mean that marketers must constantly collect information to monitor customers, markets, and competition.

We defined marketing research as the designing, gathering, analyzing, and reporting of information that may be used to solve a specific problem. The uses of marketing research are to (1) identify and define marketing opportunities and problems; (2) generate, refine, and evaluate marketing actions; (3) monitor marketing performance; and (4) improve our understanding of marketing. Online marketing research refers to the use of computer networks to assist in any phase of the marketing research process. Web-based research, on the other hand, refers to research (online or traditional) being applied to Web applications such as Web page design. Online survey research is a subset of online research and refers to collecting data using computer networks. Online research is expected to grow because it is proving to be an effective and efficient method of conducting research. Marketing research is one of four subsystems making up a marketing information system (MIS). Other subsystems include internal reports, marketing intelligence, and decision support systems. Marketing research gathers information not available through the other subsystems and is conducted on a project basis as opposed to an ongoing basis.

KEY TERMS

Marketing (p. 4)
Marketing concept (p. 6)
Marketing strategy (p. 6)
Marketing research (p. 7)
Purpose of marketing research (p. 7)
Basic research (p. 11)
Applied research (p. 11)
Online research (p. 13)
Web-based research (p. 14)

Online survey research (p. 14)
Spam (p. 18)
Marketing information system (MIS) (p. 18)
Internal reports system (p. 19)
Marketing intelligence system (p. 19)
Marketing decision support system (DSS) (p. 20)
Marketing research system (p. 20)

REVIEW QUESTIONS/APPLICATIONS

1. Define marketing research.
2. What is marketing? Explain the role of marketing research in the process of marketing management.
3. Distinguish among MIS (marketing information system), marketing research, and DSS (decision support system).
4. Explain why marketing research is not always correct.
5. The chapter includes two definitions of marketing research, and we discussed basic research versus applied research. Is all marketing research applied? Does either definition recognize that marketing research can be both basic and applied?
6. How would you classify marketing research studies? How does this classification relate to the AMA's definition of marketing research?
7. Go to your library and look through several business periodicals such as *Advertising Age*, *Business Week*, *Fortune*, and *Forbes*. Find three examples of companies using marketing research.
8. Select a company in a field in which you have a career interest and look up information on this firm in your library or on the Internet. After gaining some knowledge of this company, its products and services, customers, and competitors, list five different types of decisions that you believe this company's management may have made within the last two years. For each decision, list

the information the company's executives would have needed to make these decisions.

9. What are the differences between online research, Web-based research, and online survey research?
10. Give three examples of online research.
11. Explain why online research has grown as a part of total research.
12. What are some of the challenges facing online research?
13. How would you summarize what our Blue Ribbon Panel has to say about the future growth of online survey research?
14. What is IMRO, and what are its objectives?
15. Kevin Weseman is finishing his M.B.A. degree. He has a B.S. in marketing and has had a few years' work experience with a firm in the health care industry. Kevin took advantage of his school's marketing club and attended the meetings every week. Different speakers from industries including communications, packaged foods, industrial supply, and financial services presented weekly programs. The presentations allowed Kevin to develop insights into career opportunities and expectations within each industry. However, Kevin had an entrepreneurial spirit as well. He was interested in acquiring his own business. Realizing he was lacking in experience, he became interested in franchising. What should Kevin do to satisfy his interest in franchising?

INTERACTIVE LEARNING

Visit the Web site at www.prenhall.com/burnsbush. For this chapter, work through the Self-Study Quizzes, and get instant feedback on whether you need additional studying. On the Web site, you can review the chapter outlines and case information for Chapter 1.

CASE 1.1   Tattoos Aren't Us[21]

When teen actresses Liv Tyler and Alicia Silverstone appeared in the popular video for the Aerosmith song "Crazy," the belly rings they wore created a demand for body piercing in places other than the ear. Also, tattoos, traditionally associated with sailors and tough guys, have become popular. Today body piercing shops and tattoo parlors are often housed in the same establishment.

   The rise in the phenomenon of tattooing and body piercing did not escape the attention of Burton Ritchie, owner of The Psychedelic Shack, a shop that caters to the popular culture market. Burton, a marketing major in college, had developed a successful business by carefully observing trends in the market and sensing which trends would become profitable business lines. His tattooing business was based on solid facts about the market. By the early 2000s, 10 percent of Americans have or have had a tattoo. Research also showed tattooing was a youth phenomenon. Burton knew, based on his experience, that virtually all of his tattooing customers were in the 18- to 24-year-old category. He also knew that the research showed tattooing was equally attractive among males and females, and it was equally appealing to whites, blacks, and Hispanics. It was also inversely related to education. High school graduates or those with less than high school educations were much more likely to be tattooed and have body piercing than college graduates.

   Although Burton Ritchie's shop enjoyed revenue generated by tattooing and body piercing in the late 1990s and early 2000s, Burton wondered what the trend would be in

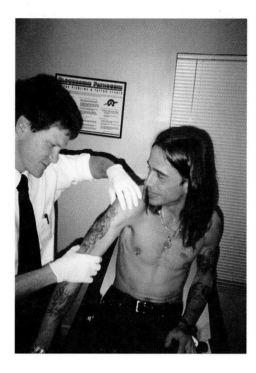

Will there be a huge demand for tattoo removal in the future?

the future. Historically, Burton knew that virtually everything considered "cool" today ends up being "a drag" in the future. A quick look at his high school annual yearbook and the "silly" clothes everyone wore "back then" was all the assurance Burton needed to know that this phenomenon still occurs. But what interested Burton was the fact that tattooing had the major disadvantage of being permanent. He recalled reading research that showed that 91 percent of Americans agree with the statement that "people should be careful about getting tattoos because they are permanent." Sure, there are laser removal devices, but they are very expensive and do not always remove all of the tattoo. What will happen when these teens and twenty-somethings turn 30? What will happen when the next generation of pop artists appear sans tattoos and body jewelry? What will happen when the next pop superstar actually is a nonconformist and speaks out against tattoos? Burton knew all too well what would likely happen, and he was interested in serving the market's needs for tattoo removal just as he had served the market's needs for tattooing.

Burton conducted some research and found the following information in a magazine that reports trends in demographics and values of the population. The magazine had commissioned an online research firm to conduct a national survey about attitudes toward tattoos. The results follow.

What Do People Think About Those Tattoos?

▶ PERCENTAGE OF ADULTS WHO ASSOCIATE THE FOLLOWING TERMS WITH VISIBLE TATTOOS, BY AGE:

	18–24	25–29	30–39	40–49	50–64	65+	Total
Intelligent	42%	38%	33%	10%	1%	10%	28%
Fashionable	60%	52%	10%	6%	2%	18%	25%
Independent	12%	18%	20%	15%	10%	6%	23%
Would Hire	40%	23%	8%	9%	2%	4%	15%

(handwritten margin note: not fav. less 30% based total on all)

Burton reviewed the research findings. He is considering investing in a tattoo removal system that will be effective in totally removing the tattoos. He also knows that developing such a system will be very costly and that the only way to reduce the cost of removal on a per-tattoo basis is to have a large volume of customers. He will not make his decision based on the foregoing research results, but he will decide whether or not to pursue his interests further.

Look at the terms in the table that were shown to the respondents. How should Burton Ritchie interpret the meaning of these terms?

1. Looking only at the total column, what insights do you think the data provide to Burton?
2. Examine the data across the age groups from 18–24 to 65+ for each term. What would you conclude?
3. Should Burton Ritchie continue to pursue his idea of a new, effective, low-cost tattoo removal system?

CASE 1.2   Gym City[22]

Ronny McCall was a director of a state-run rehabilitation program. Running the program had given him great insights on the benefits of staying fit through exercise programs. He also saw that exercise clubs, health clubs, and gyms were not only growing but also seemed to be fully used throughout the day. Although nearing retirement, Ronny was only in his mid-fifties and was interested in starting a gym in his city.

Ronny had observed the existing health clubs and gyms in his city for some time. He knew they had built new, large facilities with ample, modern equipment in the newer suburban areas of the city. In fact, the national chains had completely surrounded the city in the suburbs. He understood why they had moved out to the suburbs. He reasoned that the average age in the suburbs was much younger than in the central city. He figured the chains were trying to capture the youth market. He noticed their ads contained young models and youth-oriented copy. He noticed the radio and TV strategies of the chains targeted the younger generation. There was no question that the gym-chain managers knew what they were doing. At all six gym/health clubs located in the suburbs, the parking lots seemed to be filled from early in the morning until late at night.

Ronny decided to use a geodemographic information system (GIS) program that would allow him to examine demographic profiles in different areas of the city. The GIS program confirmed his premonitions. The suburbs had lower average ages, about 30. But, while using the GIS program, he noticed that there was a fairly large, heavily populated area, of the central city that had a much higher income than any of the suburbs and that there were no health clubs or gyms near this area of the city. However, the residents in the area were older than those in the suburbs. The GIS program showed the average age in the area Ronny defined was about 50. Would the older generation work out?

Lucy Moody, one of Ronny's "fit friends," showed him additional research conducted by Roper Starch Worldwide for the International Health, Racquet & Sportsclub Association (IHRSA). The IHRSA is a Boston-based, nonprofit trade association and its objective in the research was to determine whether consumers have a different perception of fitness than they did 10 or 15 years ago when the emphasis on working out was to produce a hard body look. The IHRSA felt that consumers today are less interested in the pursuit of being "buff" and more interested in the health and emotional benefits derived from exercise. The Roper Starch Worldwide research findings confirmed this change. More people were involved in exercise to reduce emotional stress and to prevent health problems. Also, the findings showed that, of the adults surveyed, 9 percent already were health club members and 18 percent were current members or had been members within the past five years. The research provided the following table which shows membership in health/fitness clubs by age.

Membership in Health/Fitness Clubs by Age

Age	Current Members	Never/Not a Member for Years
18–29	10%	15%
30–39	33%	23%
40–49	22%	23%
50–59	17%	15%
60–69	9%	9%
70+	7%	15%
Median age	41	44

Percentages do not add up to 100 because not all those surveyed responded to the question.
Source: IHRSA

1. Based on the research provided in the case, should Ronny McCall pursue his dream of developing a gym in the central city? Why or why not?
2. What other information should Ronny McCall seek?

Chapter 2

The Marketing Research Process

Learning Objectives:

To gain insights into marketing research by learning the steps in the marketing research process

To understand the caveats associated with "a process"

To be able to know when marketing research may be needed and when it may not be needed

To know which step is the most important in the marketing research process

To have a framework for understanding the topics to be covered in the rest of this book

To understand the research process in a case situation

Kodak

Practitioner Viewpoint

The research process is the map that identifies the researchers' path that leads to a quality understanding of the market. Knowing the steps alone is not enough. Like skilled builders, researchers need to add personal skill to get an outstanding result. Research is a creative process that requires more than the application of mechanical steps. The researcher must assemble a thorough understanding of the business problem and the appropriate research objectives that, when accomplished, provide the information necessary to aid the executive's decision. The researcher needs to balance the need for speed, accuracy, and budget constraints creatively. Depending on requirements, one must know which steps to skip or expand. Each investigation requires a new mix. The Internet as a commercial tool, global competition, and the explosion of information available to customers are all decreasing the time available to do research. New analytical approaches and collection methodologies help researchers to creatively understand the market situation. The Internet is changing the way we reach customers, providing research stimulation, and distributing study results. Creating actionable insights is the payoff of the research process. This is much more than statistical analysis of the data. Powerful insights come from creatively assembling patterns in the responses from the subgroups of the sample.

Michael A. Lotti
Director, Business Research, and Vice President, Corporate Marketing, Eastman Kodak Company

The Marketing Research Process at Kodak

Michael Lotti, who wrote the preceding Practitioner Viewpoint, is responsible for marketing research at Eastman Kodak Company. He not only responds when other Kodak executives present problems to him but also he must be alert to identify problems that others have not identified. Mr. Lotti must also determine if research is justified. If so, he must clearly define the problem and establish the research objectives so that, when reached, they will provide the necessary information to solve the problem. Mr. Lotti will have to decide the proper research design or basic approach the research will take. Will the research objectives require that he conduct a nationwide, representative survey? Will he need to conduct a few focus groups in a couple of cities or will he need tightly controlled experiments? He must determine if the information he needs is already available in secondary data sources or if he needs to collect his own primary data for the project at hand. If he needs primary data, will he access the data through surveys of online panel members, telephone surveys of randomly selected households, or by interviewing customers in shopping malls? He will have to determine what questions he must ask and how to word those questions to get accurate information from the survey respondents. He must determine how he will select the sample of respondents and how many will be selected. Then he must actually collect the data, analyze it, and write up the results to present to the managers who need the information to make a decision. You can see how being the director of research in a major company can keep you pretty busy. But, even though this seems like a myriad of activities, Mr. Lotti knows how to do his job because he understands the process of marketing research.

This chapter introduces you to the steps involved in the marketing research process. When you finish this chapter, you will be able to "see" the marketing research process in the description of Michael Lotti's work at Kodak as we have just described. We are going to briefly take you through the steps in the research process in this chapter. For each step, we are going to give you some examples to help you better understand the process. Finally, you will see that the rest of the book is organized around the steps in the marketing research process.

THE MARKETING RESEARCH PROCESS: 11 STEPS

We identify the 11 **steps in the marketing research process** in Figure 2.1. The steps are (1) establishing the need for marketing research, (2) defining the problem, (3) establishing research objectives, (4) determining research design, (5) identifying information types and sources, (6) determining methods of accessing data, (7) designing data collection forms, (8) determining the sample plan and size, (9) collecting data, (10) analyzing data, and (11) preparing and presenting the final research report.

> There are 11 steps in the marketing research process.

Before we discuss these 11 steps in the marketing research process, we want to point out the caveats of providing you with a step-by-step process. First, although the list does strongly imply an orderly, step-by-step process, it is rare that a research project follows these steps in the exact order that they are presented in Figure 2.1.

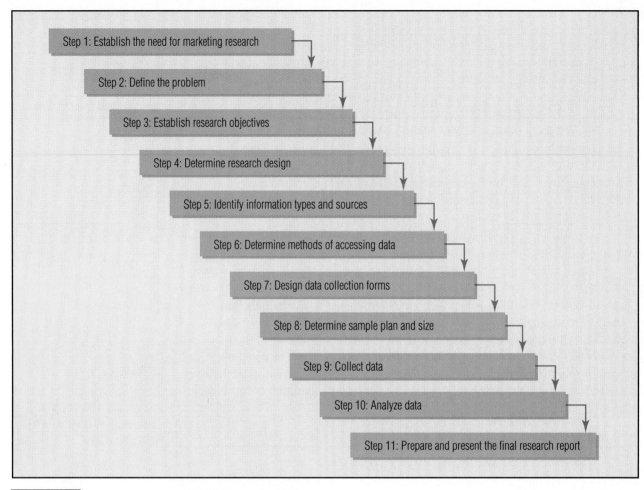

Figure 2.1   11 Steps in the Marketing Research Process

There are caveats to learning a step-by-step process. Although the steps are useful to give you a framework for understanding marketing research, not all projects follow these steps in the exact order shown. Sometimes researchers expand or even skip some of the steps entirely in order to get the job done.

In Michael Lotti's viewpoint about the marketing research process, he actually tells you that this process is not always a step-by-step process. He tells you that researchers sometimes have to expand, or even skip some of the steps. So, instead of being a step-by-step process, marketing research practice is more of an interactive process whereby a researcher, by discovering something in a given step, may move backward in the process and begin again at another step. Finding some new information while collecting data, for example, may cause the researcher to establish different research objectives. Second, as pointed out by Mr. Lotti, any given research project may not involve each and every step shown here. Sometimes you skip steps entirely. The research problem could be resolved, for example, by a review of secondary data, thereby eliminating the need to determine a sample plan or size. What is important for you to know is that, although almost every research project is different, there are enough commonalities among the various procedures and activities to enable us to specify the 11 basic steps of the marketing research process. Thus, learning the research process as a series of steps is necessary to provide you with a framework for understanding marketing research. You just can't view all research projects as moving through a tightly defined series of 11 steps.

Step 1: Establish the Need for Marketing Research

Marketing research is needed when decision makers must make a decision and they do not have the information to help them make the decision. Look back at the AMA's definition of marketing research in Chapter 1 and recall the uses of marketing research that we discussed. For example, the need for marketing research occurs when managers are interested in new opportunities in the marketplace and when they see problems. As we learned in Chapter 1, a firm's MIS should monitor the environments on a continuous basis. Marketing intelligence systems often identify new opportunities in the marketplace, and managers need marketing research to help them make the decision as to whether or not to take advantage of that opportunity. For example, when Internet surveying appeared to be a new, fast, and economical way of gathering data, several companies did the research to determine if Internet surveying represented a viable market opportunity. Greenfield Online, Insight Express, and Socratic Technologies, to name a few, are companies that exist today because they identified online marketing research as a viable opportunity. For products and services that we see today as being very successful and prominent in the marketplace, you should understand that, at one time, they represented a market opportunity. Decision makers did not know if they would be successful. When Bell Labs invented the technology that made cellular telephones possible, many companies conducted marketing research to determine if cell phones represented a viable market opportunity. The early marketing research studies showed cell phones had great promise, and that promise has proven to be true. Will satellite radio be the primary radio medium in the next decade? You better believe that companies are doing research on this opportunity today.

Remember that another use of marketing research is to identify problems. Companies conduct research to identify problems so that they can correct them. Sony is constantly refining its vast line of video cameras, eliminating dislikes, and developing models that have features desired by consumers. Sometimes it's too late when problems are identified. In 2001 alone the following problems arose too late: Digiscents discovered that, although it is technically possible to send scents via the Internet, there was no market for it. Several PC models went under during the year including the NetPliance IOpener, 3COM's Adurey, Dell's Webster, and Gateway's AOL Companion. The Sony computer named the eVilla was dropped during the same week it was introduced.[1] Marketing research is needed to determine what problems exist. We also know that marketing research is needed to generate, refine, and evaluate marketing actions and to monitor marketing performance.

When Marketing Research Is Not Needed   There are several situations in which management should not consider a marketing research project. Here are four situations in which marketing research may be inappropriate.[2]

The Information Is Already Available.   When management knows its markets, competition, and the products and services, it may have the necessary information to make an informed decision without commissioning a market research study.[3] Ping, the very successful golf club manufacturer, knows that it must find real improvements in its clubs in order for customers to pay the $550 price tag for a new driver. Ping knows that cosmetic improvements will not work in the marketplace. Today managers have access to much information about their business because computer technology has provided more firms with good information systems (MISs).[4]

Decisions Must Be Made Now!   Time is often critical in business decision making and sometimes a decision must be made before any research can be conducted. A competitor introduces a new version of a product that experiences an immediate

Visit satellite radio at www.xmradio.com.

Marketing research is needed to determine if there are opportunities in the market.

Marketing research is needed to determine if problems exist, to generate, refine, and evaluate marketing actions, and to evaluate marketing performance.

When information is readily available, there is no need to do marketing research.

and very strong positive reaction from the market. Should executives spend months conducting research on a new version of their own product or should they get something out to compete with the new product as soon as possible? Obviously, they need to do the latter. The market's response to the competitor's product must serve as the "research" in this situation.

We Can't Afford Research. If conducted in-house, marketing research requires a commitment of personnel, facilities, and budget. If conducted by an outside research firm, money as well as personnel time are needed. If there is not enough money to devote to the market research, management must simply make the decision that those resources are better spent elsewhere. Of course, management always runs the risk of discovering that it invested resources in a strategy that marketing research would have identified as being inferior to alternative strategies. This is one of the "catch-22s" for business management: The firms that are strapped for cash and, thus, feel they cannot afford to spend dollars on marketing research are usually the firms that could probably benefit the most by performing the research to help them make the best decisions.[5] Nevertheless, resources may simply not be available for research. Two well-known consultants in business, Kevin J. Clancy and Robert S. Schulman, suggest that one of the myths that kills business is believing that marketing research must always be expensive.[6] Also, there are some guides[7] and examples[8] for conducting marketing research with tight budgets.

Costs Outweigh the Value of the Research. Some decisions have relatively little impact on company sales, profits, consumer loyalty, dealer goodwill, and so on. As a result, they simply do not justify expenditures on research. Other decisions, however, may be very important, thereby justifying research. For example, how a product's packaging is designed for shipment to trade shows may seem relatively unimportant. However, the packaging design used to ship products to dealers could be very important in terms of reducing spillage and spoilage and enhancing dealer loyalty. Also, the package design for the customer is very important. Which package design will gain the most attention on the shelf?

Another aspect to consider when weighing the value to be gained against the cost of the research has to do with the confidence that the manager has in the outcome of a proposed decision. The CEO of the marketing research firm Decision Analyst, Jerry W. Thomas, suggests that research should be done when managers can't afford to be wrong on a decision, when the risks are great, or when the opportunities are big. However, he warns that research should only be conducted when the benefits exceed the costs of the research.[9] The purpose of marketing research is to serve as an aid in decision making, in effect, to reduce the uncertainty in the outcomes of alternative decisions. If the manager feels that he or she knows the possible outcomes, then marketing research should not be used.

Step 2: Define the Problem

Defining the problem is the most important step in the research process. Why? What else matters if we have defined the problem incorrectly? Unfortunately, managers are good at clearly seeing symptoms and are less adept at seeing the real problem. In fact, as we have seen before, research is sometimes used to determine what the problems are. All too often, marketing research studies are commissioned without a clear understanding of the problem the research should address. Take the following situation facing WebMasters, Inc., a Web page design firm. The owner was concerned about declining sales. She hired a consultant who, after one visit to the firm, returned with a proposal to conduct tests of several advertising copy alternatives to be used in the firm's newspaper advertising program. Do you see anything wrong

Marketing researchers at InfoWorld Media Group constantly make decisions as to whether or not to conduct marketing research. By permission, InfoWorld Media Group.

with this situation? How does WebMasters know that sales are declining as a result of problems with ad copy? It does not know, and neither does the consulting firm. The problem has not been defined.

The most important step in the marketing research process is properly defining the marketing manager's problem.

This is a classic situation in which marketing research is proposed that does not address the real problem. A firm may spend literally hundreds of thousands of dollars doing market research but, if it has not correctly identified the problem, those dollars will have been wasted. To avoid this scenario, care must be taken to explore all possible causes of the symptom. This requires time and a great deal of communication between the researcher and the client. Often a form of research, called exploratory research, is needed to clearly define the problem so that the proper research may be conducted. We discuss exploratory research under step 4. The process of defining the problem is discussed in detail in Chapter 4 of this book.

Exploratory research helps to clearly define the problem.

Step 3: Establish Research Objectives

Research objectives, although related to and determined by the problem definition, are set so that, when achieved, they provide the information necessary to solve the problem. Let us consider the following example. Independent insurance agents typically belong to a state association called, for instance, the Independent Insurance Agents of Iowa. The association is responsible for educational programs, lobbying with state insurance boards, and technical advice. If the association were concerned with responding to the needs of its members, reasonable research objectives would include (1) to determine how important each of the association's services are to its members and (2) to assess how satisfied members of the association are with the association's performance of each service.

A good way of setting research objectives is to ask, "What information is needed in order to solve the problem?" Because the association's services are in place, the research objectives would translate as follows:

Determine the average importance level of each service.

Determine the average level of satisfaction for each service.

You should notice that these research objectives are different from the defined problem. Yet, when the information is gathered as a result of carrying out these research objectives, the problem is solved. By collecting the information requested by the first two research objectives, the association is in a position to rank its services based on how important they are to members, and it can identify which highly important services are low in satisfaction. That is, it can identify critical problem areas. Alternatively, it can identify significant strengths indicated by high satisfaction with highly important services, if they exist.

Research objectives identify what specific pieces of information are necessary to solve the problem at hand.

Step 4: Determine Research Design

Almost every research project is different but there are enough similarities among research projects to enable us to categorize them by the research methods and procedures used to collect and analyze data. There are three types of these categories, which are referred to as research designs: (1) exploratory research, (2) descriptive research, and (3) causal research.

Exploratory research is defined as collecting information in an unstructured and informal manner. It is often used when little is known about the problem. Analyzing secondary data in a library or over the Internet is one of the most common ways of conducting exploratory research. An executive reading about demographic trends forecast for the next five years in *American Demographics* would be an example of conducting exploratory research. A manager observing the lines of customers awaiting service at a bank would be an example of exploratory research.

Descriptive research designs refer to a set of methods and procedures that describes marketing variables. Descriptive studies portray these variables by answering who, what, why, and how questions. These types of research studies may describe such things as consumers' attitudes, intentions, and behaviors, or the number of competitors and their strategies. Although most descriptive studies are surveys in which respondents are asked questions, sometimes descriptive studies are observation studies that observe and record consumers' behavior in such a way as to answer the problem. When Bissell Inc. conducted marketing research on the Steam Gun, an elongated cleaning device that used steam to remove stubborn dirt, the company gave the product to families and then observed them using the product in their homes. In addition to learning that they needed to change the name, the company learned several important lessons that led them to successfully market the Steam N' Clean.[10]

The final research design, **causal research,** allows us to isolate causes and effects. We call causal research designs **experiments.** Some researchers conducted an experiment on the effects of Yellow Page ads. The experiment allowed them to conclude that color is better than black and white and that photos are better than line art at causing more favorable customer attitudes and perceptions of quality and credibility. The experiments also showed that these relationships varied across product categories.[11] This is powerful information to companies that spend huge sums of money on Yellow Pages ads each year. We discuss causal designs in Chapter 5.

There are three types of research design: exploratory, descriptive, and causal.

Step 5: Identify Information Types and Sources

Basically, two types of information are available to a marketing researcher: secondary data and primary data. **Secondary data** are information that has been collected for some other purpose. That is, it is being used for a purpose that is secondary to its original function. Sources of secondary data can be external, such as census data, *Sales & Marketing Management's Survey of Buying Power*, and countless other publications. Or sources can be internal, arising from sources inside the firm, such as databases containing customer information. Much may be learned from secondary data. However, when existing information does not suit the problem at hand, researchers must resort to collecting primary data. **Primary data** are information gathered specifically for the research objectives at hand.

Two types of information are available to marketing researchers: secondary data and primary data.

Step 6: Determine Methods of Accessing Data

Once researchers determine which type or types of information are needed, they must determine methods of accessing data. How do they accomplish this? It depends on the type of data needed. Compared to primary data, accessing secondary data is relatively easy. If the data are internal, the manager may gather the information from company records, salespersons, other company executives, marketing information systems, or even scanning systems, which offer a wealth of information.

Methods of accessing external secondary data have greatly improved over the last few years. Not only has the quantity of information available increased but, perhaps more significantly, the Internet has vastly improved our ability to easily and quickly retrieve the information from online information services and from the Web sites of organizations providing such information. Still, much valuable information is available at your local library. Not all information is electronic. Books are still a good resource for information.

The basic methods for collecting primary data include the telephone, mail, and face-to-face methods including door-to-door interviews, mall-intercept studies, and online surveys. Qualitative data are also gathered in observation studies (see Marketing Research Insight 2.1), focus groups, and other methods. The advantages and disadvantages of these methods are discussed in Chapters 8 and 9.

The Internet provides researchers with easy access to secondary data. For example, see www.census.gov.

▶ **Additional Insights**

MARKETING RESEARCH
INSIGHT
2.1

Sorensen Associates, Inc. Accesses Data by Observation

There are many ways that marketing researchers access data. One method is to observe what people do. Sorensen Associates, known as "the in-store research company," conducts observation studies inside supermarkets and other retail stores.

Consumers buy over *$400 billion* of groceries and other consumer packaged goods (CPG) from supermarkets and other retail stores every year. Other than small qualitative studies and a very few larger quantitative studies, very little is known about the actual paths and practices of shoppers in stores. This situation is being remedied by a new research technology called PathTracker™. This system electronically tracks the path of every shopper in the store and correlates their path with the purchases made at the checkout counter. To the right is an example of the "flow" in one supermarket.

What is readily apparent is the general counter-clockwise motion around the perimeter "racetrack." The general drift from the back of the store to the front is also obvious. However, other PathTracker™ studies show a dominance of "excursion" shopping, rather than the commonly expected "zig zag" pattern up and down the aisles. An excursion happens when the shopper leaves her dominant path and then returns to it later. This common behavior is not obvious to an observer because when watching shoppers in aisles, one sees them moving through an aisle, one way or the other. The logical implication is that they are passing through an aisle, and then will pass in the reverse direction through an adjacent aisle. In fact this behavior is not as common as imagined.

Sorensen provides valuable research information to companies marketing products in supermarkets and other retail stores. Understanding how consumers shop in stores is important in determining how firms design product packaging and in determining what type and how much in-store promotion they must use to gain shoppers' attention. We introduce you to the founder of Sorensen Associates, Herb Sorensen in the following Meet a Marketing Researcher.

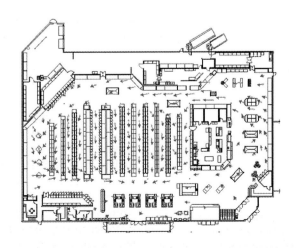

MARKETING RESEARCH
INSIGHT
2.2

Sorensen Associates, Inc.
Herb Sorensen, Ph.D., President

Herb began his career as a chemist with interests in quantum mechanics, electronic structures, and metabolism. From the faculty of Colorado State University in 1971 he moved into the commercial realm as a board certified clinical chemist, where he managed the quality assurance program for a laboratory processing up to 10,000 patients per day. In 1973 Herb established his own consulting and laboratory business providing testing and product development services (including surveys) to the consumer packaged goods industry.

Herb's market research has always focused on shoppers at their point of purchase, hence, the continuing interest of his "in-store research company" in relationships with retailers and the means of fielding an interviewing force over a wide geographic area.

Herb has a Ph.D. in biochemistry from the University of California (1970), a master's degree in biochemistry and nutrition from Nebraska (1965), and undergraduate majors in both chemistry and mathematics (1964). He has been an active member in the American Marketing Association, Institute of Food Technologists, and other associations for many years.

Step 7: Design Data Collection Forms

The design of the data collection form that is used to ask and record information gathered in marketing research projects is critical to the success of the project. Even when the correct problem has been defined and the most appropriate research design planned, asking the wrong questions, or asking the right questions in the wrong order, will destroy the usefulness of the research effort. Whether the research design requires that respondents be asked questions or that their behavior is observed, standardized forms, called questionnaires, record the information. A questionnaire's apparent simplicity (writing a list of questions) is very deceptive. Care must be taken to design a questionnaire that will cooperatively elicit objective information from the respondents. This means avoiding both ambiguous and leading questions. Additional considerations must be made for observation studies. In recent years, software programs have been made available to researchers to assist in creating surveys. Some of the newer software programs allow users to post the surveys on the Web and data are automatically downloaded into a statistical package such as SPSS when respondents complete answers to the survey questions. One such software program is WebSurveyor.

Computer software is now available to aid in the design and use of questionnaires. Visit WebSurveyor at www.websurveyor.com.

Step 8: Determine Sample Plan and Size

Typically, marketing research projects study subsets, called samples, of populations in order to learn about the entire population. General Mills uses a sample of homemakers to learn about the cooking preferences of all homemakers. Pfizer pharmaceuticals studies a sample of physicians in order to learn the preferences of doctors for drug prescriptions. The **sample plan** refers to the process used to select units from the population to be included in the sample. A sample plan, for example, would tell Pfizer how to select physicians for its sample from among all physicians. There are different sample plans and each has advantages and disadvantages. The sample plan determines how representative the sample is of the population. You will learn how to select the appropriate sample plan depending on the objectives of the research objectives in Chapter 12. **Sample size,** as the name implies, refers to determining how many elements of the population should be included in the sample. As a rule, the larger the sample the better, but you can have a sample that is too large, which wastes research dollars. The size of the sample determines the accuracy of the sample results. In Chapter 13 you will learn how to calculate a sample size that is just large enough to give you accurate results. There are research firms, such as Survey Sampling, Inc. and STS Samples, that help researchers with their sample plans and sample size problems.

> The sample plan refers to the *process used to select units from the population* to be included in the sample. Sample size refers to determining *how many units* of the population should be included in the sample.

Step 9: Collect Data

Data collection is very important because, regardless of the data analysis methods used, data analysis cannot "fix" bad data.[12] Data are usually gathered by trained interviewers who are employed by field data collection companies to collect primary data. Many possible errors, called **nonsampling errors** because they are attributable to factors other than sampling errors, may occur during data collection. Such errors include selecting the wrong sample elements to interview, securing subjects who refuse to participate or are simply not at home when the interviewer calls, interviewing subjects who intentionally give out the wrong information, or hiring interviewers who cheat and fill out fictitious survey questionnaires. Even interviewers who honestly complete their interviewers may make inadvertent nonsampling errors by copying down the wrong information on their survey form. Needless to say, good marketing researchers must be aware of the errors that may occur during data collection and should implement plans to reduce these errors. Unlike sampling error, you cannot measure the amount of nonsampling error that may exist in a study. Therefore, it is important to know the possible causes of nonsampling error so that appropriate steps can be taken to limit its occurrence. You will learn the causes of nonsampling errors and how to reduce those errors in Chapter 14.

> Because nonsampling error cannot be measured, researchers must be aware of the sources of this type of error so that appropriate steps can be taken to limit its occurrence.

Step 10: Analyze Data

Once data are collected, data analysis is used to give the raw data meaning. **Data analysis** involves entering data into computer files, inspecting the data for errors, and running tabulations and various statistical tests. The first step in data analysis is **data cleaning,** which is the process by which the raw data are checked to verify that the data have been correctly inputted from the data collection form to the computer software program. Typically, data analysis is conducted with the assistance of a computerized data analysis program such as SPSS. You will learn how to conduct basic descriptive data analysis in Chapter 15, how to make statistical inferences from your data in Chapter 16, how to determine if there are significant differences in Chapter 17, how to determine if there are significant associations in Chapter 18, and how to make predictions in Chapter 19. You will learn all of these types of data analysis using SPSS software.

> Data analysis involves entering data into computer files, inspecting the data for errors, and running tabulations and various statistical tests.

Step 11: Prepare and Present the Final Research Report

The last step in the marketing research process is to prepare and present the final research report—one of the most important phases of marketing research. Its importance cannot be overstated because it is the report, or its presentation, that properly

Preparing the marketing research report involves describing the process used, building meaningful tables, and using presentation graphics for clarity.

communicates the study results to the client. Sometimes researchers not only turn in a written research report but they also make an oral presentation of the research methods used to conduct the study as well as the research findings to their client. In Chapter 20 we show you how to write a marketing research report and we provide you with suggestions on how to give oral presentations.

METRO CIVIC CENTER: A CASE EXAMPLE OF THE MARKETING RESEARCH PROCESS

We are providing a case, Metro Civic Center, to further illustrate the steps in the marketing process. By reading this short case example, you should have a clearer understanding of the research process and how the steps in the research process fit together. Metro Civic Center is an auditorium facility that can seat 20,000 persons. It is a modern building with the ability to host a variety of events including ice shows, basketball games, rock concerts, and so on. The building is owned by the city government and is operated by Civic Center Operators, Inc. (CCO). CCO is in charge of all Metro Civic Center operations and its contract with the city requires that the center earn a profit by the end of the three-year contract period.

Establish the Need for Marketing Research

CCO took over the Metro Civic Center contract in January 2003. The management company had taken over on short notice and had spent most of the first quarter getting organized and running the events previously scheduled by the former manager. CCO management had immediately installed an MIS and its DSS produced pro forma income statements that showed the center was not likely to earn profits during its first half year of operation. Because the Metro Civic Center had not been profitable during its first three years of operation, CCO's contract with the city government required that it earn a profit by the end of the three-year contract period. CCO had two and one-half years to turn the center around. But CCO wanted to perform better than the contract minimum. It wanted to be profitable in each year of operation. CCO management knew, based on their experience in other markets, that a strong profit performance almost always led to contract renewals. But CCO had been bound by contracts left over from the former manager of the center who

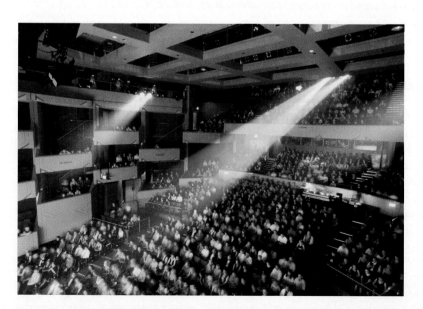

Marketing research provided the information needed to make the Metro Civic Center profitable.

had run the center for the first three years of its operation. The former manager, Tony Smitherman, was the popular mayor's brother and, although a locally popular figure, he had no experience in managing entertainment centers. CCO was accustomed to such situations. Carolyn Peck, CCO's manager, called a meeting of top management. During the meeting Ms. Peck reviewed the income statement projections. Other managers' views confirmed the gloomy outlook. CCO faced a problem: losses in its first year of operation. Management needed to conduct research to determine what do to in order to get the center back in the black.

The identification of a problem often justifies the need for marketing research. In this case, the problem is important—another reason to conduct research.

Define the Problem

Carolyn Peck invited Mary McBride of Bartram and Associates, a marketing research firm, to discuss the situation. Peck told McBride, "We are losing money." McBride and Peck both realized this was a symptom and they began exploring causes for the projected losses. The center had to cover significant fixed costs. It had to make a quarterly payment for the cost of the new, modern building, and other costs such as utilities and personnel costs for the maintenance crews were significant. Peck and McBride agreed that the solution to recouping fixed costs was to ensure that the building did not sit idle. But the former manager had done a good job of scheduling many events. McBride wanted to see an analysis of each event. How many tickets were sold? At what price were the tickets sold? Which events were making money and which were losing money? Three days later, Peck put all the necessary information together and called McBride for a second meeting. The two quickly discovered that, although many events were being scheduled, ticket sales to the events were below par. In fact, only once in the past two years of operation had the center sold out. Other events rarely drew crowds over 3,000 people. As other seats remained empty, revenues were far below the level needed to recoup the fixed and variable costs necessary to earn a profit. Also, revenue from the several dozen concessions that provided food, beverages, and sold merchandise was based on their sales. If there were few people at the event, the concessioners' sales were low as well. The two agreed to meet again the next day.

Problems are sometimes presented as symptoms. Researchers and clients must meet several times and communicate often to properly define the problem.

Early the next morning Peck and McBride conducted some exploratory research. They simply went through the records of the events and categorized them. They were startled to find that a significant percentage of the events were for bluegrass music bands and for tractor-pulls. The latter events featured specially designed trucks and tractors pulling huge weights and engaging in competitions against one another. The records showed that bluegrass bands attracted a small number of ticket buyers. They also found that the tractor-pulls attracted much larger crowds but the ticket prices necessary to attract persons to this event were very low. Peck and McBride asked employees who had been at the center since it was built if they were aware of the large percentage of bluegrass and tractor-pull events. They responded, "Oh certainly! Mr. Smitherman, the mayor's brother, loved bluegrass music and tractor-pulls!" Now Peck and McBride were piecing the puzzle together. They realized that Smitherman was using his own preferences to schedule entertainment groups to the center. They defined the problem as determining which entertainment groups to schedule at the Metro Civic Center so that attendance will be maximized for the given ticket price. McBride asked Peck if she had information from the other centers managed by CCO that would help them schedule popular events. Peck stated that she had some ideas but that she wanted to make some calls around the country to confirm her ideas. The two agreed to meet again the following Monday.

By Monday, Carolyn Peck had conducted additional exploratory research by calling her counterpart at six other civic centers around the country in towns about the size of hers. She reported her findings to McBride. The other managers, Peck stated, confirmed her opinion based on 15 years of experience in the business. There are certain entertainers that will always sell out. Elton John has done this for years and, more recently, other entertainers are part of this elite group such as N'Sync. But, beyond these premiere performers, the popularity of different forms of entertainment varies widely between different markets. In some markets, certain sports events, such as hockey or basketball, never fail to fill the seats. In other markets, rock concerts are the key. And in still other markets, the primary attraction is wrestling. The bottom line was that each market differed markedly. After hearing this, McBride was ready to make a statement. In spite of Smitherman's good intentions, she explained, he had not really been practicing the marketing concept. What did consumers in the two-county service area of the Metro Civic Center really want in terms of entertainment groups? Smitherman had not determined their needs and, because it was obvious from the exploratory research conducted in other markets, they must determine their customers' preferences for entertainment groups.

Establish Research Objectives

Research objectives tell the researcher what must be done in order to solve the manager's problem. The problem stated previously as determining which entertainment groups to schedule at the Metro Civic Center so that attendance will be maximized for the given ticket price can be solved by the following research objective:

> *Determine the rank-order preferences for entertainment groups among residents, 16 years of age and older, in the two-county service area of the Metro Civic Center.*

Now Mary McBride knows that if she carries out the research to achieve the foregoing research objective she will be giving Carolyn Peck the information she needs to solve her problem.

Research objectives tell the researcher what must be done in order to solve the manager's problem.

Determine Research Design

McBride had to decide on the basic blueprint for the research. Exploratory research, as usual, had been used in helping to properly define the problem. The research objective required that a description of consumer preferences be obtained. A descriptive research design was needed. McBride knew that a descriptive research design would involve conducting a survey. These surveys can be taken at one point in time or at multiple times. McBride felt the information could be obtained through one survey of the population.

Both exploratory and descriptive research designs were used.

Identify Information Types and Sources

Secondary data on consumer preferences for entertainment groups among residents in the two-county service area were simply not available. However, McBride decided to do some secondary research on entertainment group popularity. Although this would not tell CCO what its two-county market desired, it might be useful in terms of background information. For this study, primary data were needed.

Both secondary and primary data were needed.

Determine Methods of Accessing Data

McBride considered several methods of collecting the data. The respondents would not have to see or touch anything in order to respond, so she knew that personal, face-to-face interviewing was not necessary. She also knew that CCO would want to have representative information. This meant that McBride would have to ensure that all areas of the two counties would be included in the survey. She discounted sending out a mail survey because it was her experience that few people responded to mail surveys unless a very powerful incentive was included. Simply calling on the telephone seemed a good choice but so did using the Internet. The Internet would be ideal because it was fast and the responses could be collected online and down-loaded into Bartram & Associates SPSS software for data analysis. But McBride was concerned that the two counties had even lower Internet access than the nation as a whole. Although the Internet would give her the results she needed quickly, she was worried about the respondents not being representative of the general population. However, she had heard of Knowledge Networks. Knowledge Networks is an online marketing research company that recruits panel members to respond to surveys by selecting them at random from all over the nation. It then provides its panel members with WebTV and Internet access. So its samples are not based only on persons having Internet access, because they all have Internet access. This seemed the way to go. McBride called Knowledge Networks and, yes, it could offer her access to its sample of panel respondents who live in the two-county area.

Determining the method of accessing data involves consideration of several factors such as response rate, the respondents' need to see, touch, or use an object, and the ability to gain access to a representative sample.

Design Data Collection Forms

Mary McBride had been in the research industry for several years and had kept up with technological developments. She is very much aware of software that is available to help her design survey questionnaires. She uses WebSurveyor, a computer-assisted questionnaire design software that helps her compose questions, and captures the questionnaire in electronic format for her to e-mail to Knowledge Networks. She carefully composes the questions that will provide the data needed to achieve the research objective. She takes the questionnaire to her client, Carolyn Peck, and they review each question to ensure the responses to the questions will be useful.

Researchers often allow a client to give final approval on the design of a questionnaire.

Determine Sample Plan and Size

Because CCO is going to use the data collected in the survey to attempt to schedule entertainment groups at the Metro Civic Center, the data should be representative of the two-county service area. By using Knowledge Networks' panel, McBride is assured of a representative sample because Knowledge Networks used a probability sampling plan to recruit its panel members. By **probability sampling plan,** we mean a plan in which everyone in the county had a chance of being included in the sample. Second, McBride had discussed the accuracy of the findings with Peck. They agreed that they wanted to be 95 percent confident that the survey results would be within 5 percent of the true population's percentage preference for entertainment groups. That is, if the survey showed that 85 percent of the respondents wanted a rock concert with a certain band, Peck could be 95 percent confident that the entire population's percentage of preference fell somewhere between 80 percent and 90 percent. Satisfied with this level of accuracy, McBride calculated that they would need a sample of 400 respondents for the survey.

A probability sampling plan assures a representative sample and the size of the sample determines the accuracy of the sample results.

Collect Data

Knowledge Networks took only three days to collect the data and the data were downloaded to an SPSS file at Bartram & Associates. Knowledge Networks provided McBride with information on how many respondents had been sent the survey and how many responded to the survey. McBride calculated the response rate as 88 percent.

Eighty-eight percent of those sample members eligible to respond did respond. This is called the response rate.

Analyze the Data and Prepare the Final Research Report

While Knowledge Networks was collecting the data, McBride was busy preparing the research report. She prepared the report complete with tables but without data. When the data arrived, McBride used SPSS to determine the average responses to

Data analysis tells you the average response to a question and how far the typical respondent was from this average response. Data analysis also allows you to rearrange or transform categories of responses for purposes of clarity of presentation.

the questions and measures of variability to show how similar to the average response the other responses were. She and Peck had also agreed that other information would be important in the survey. One question determined the likelihood that respondents would attend any type of entertainment event held at the Metro Civic Center. McBride used SPSS to put respondents into categories of "Likelihood of Attending the Metro Civic Center" ranging from "Unlikely to Attend Any Event" to "Very Likely to Attend Events."

When McBride presented the final report, Carolyn Peck asked her to make a formal presentation to the entire management staff. McBride prepared PowerPoint slides and rehearsed her presentation. When she presented the findings, it was very clear to Peck and the rest of the CCO management which entertainment groups to schedule. The top preferences did not include any bluegrass bands or tractor-pulls! The research objective had been met.

Marketing research provides the information necessary to help managers make the right decisions.

Three months later, the first entertainment group chosen based on the marketing research study had performed. Mary McBride called Carolyn Peck the next morning. Carolyn happily reported that the event had drawn 12,500 persons and that the next two events scheduled were sold out! The information provided by the research had led to decisions that resolved the management problem. McBride made a note to follow up in six months to discuss updating the research the following year.

SOME FINAL COMMENTS ON THE MARKETING RESEARCH PROCESS

We don't mean to imply that all marketing research processes are as straightforward as we show in the Metro Civic Center case. Is this case fictitious? No. The case is based on a real-world marketing research project. Only the names and certain details were changed for confidentiality or updating purposes. Although many cases are just as straightforward as we have shown here, the point we want to make is that there is great diversity in marketing research projects. A research project designed to produce a new name for a new type of razor blade is very different from a research project designed to forecast sales in units for a brand-new product. Yet, as we told you at the beginning of this chapter, the steps in the research process still provide you with a good framework for understanding marketing research. In Chapter 3 we continue our introduction to marketing research. You are about to learn about the industry itself as well as the ethical issues facing the industry.

SUMMARY

There is great variability in marketing research projects. Some studies are limited to a review of secondary data; others require complex designs involving large-scale collection of primary data. But even with this diversity of research projects, there are enough commonalities among these projects to enable us to characterize them in terms of "steps of the research process." These steps are (1) establishing the need for marketing research, (2) defining the problem, (3) establishing research objectives, (4) determining research design, (5) identifying information types and sources, (6) determining methods of accessing data, (7) designing data collection forms, (8) determining sample plan and size, (9) collecting data, (10) analyzing data, and (11) preparing and presenting the final research report.

There is value in characterizing research projects in terms of successive steps. First, the steps give researchers and nonresearchers an overview of the entire research process. Second, they provide a procedure in the sense that a researcher, by referring to the steps, knows what tasks to consider and in what order. However, an informed researcher and client should know there are caveats in such a step-by-step procedure. Only by being thoroughly familiar with the research process is a researcher or client in a position to understand some of the problems associated with following a cookbook, step-by-step procedure. Many problems may not require, for example, the collection of primary data, data analysis, and so on. Furthermore, the steps shown in this chapter are interactive. That is, after collecting some data, the researcher may decide that the problem needs to be redefined, and the process may start over. A case, Metro Civic Center, is presented which illustrates the 11-step research process in a marketing research project.

KEY TERMS

Steps in the marketing research
   process (p. 27)
Exploratory research (p. 32)
Descriptive research (p. 32)
Causal research (p. 32)
Experiments (p. 32)
Secondary data (p. 32)

Primary data (p. 32)
Sample plan (p. 35)
Sample size (p. 35)
Nonsampling errors (p. 35)
Data analysis (p. 35)
Data cleaning (p. 35)
Probability sampling plan (p. 39)

REVIEW QUESTIONS/APPLICATIONS

1. What are the steps in the marketing research process?
2. Use an example to illustrate that the steps in the marketing research process are not always taken in sequence.
3. Explain why firms may not have a need for marketing research.
4. Why is defining the problem the most important step in the marketing research process?
5. Explain why research objectives differ from the definition of the problem.
6. What are the three types of research that constitute research design?
7. Which part of the research process ensures that the sample is representative?
8. Which part of the research process ensures the accuracy of the results?
9. Go to the Internet and do a search for marketing research firms. Look through their Web pages. Can you identify examples of what they are presenting to you as relating to steps in the research process?
10. Go to your library or the Internet and look for examples of firms conducting a marketing research study. There are many examples reported in periodicals such as *Advertising Age*, *Marketing News*, *Business Week*, and *Forbes*. Typically, these articles will mention a few details of the research project itself. Identify as many of the steps in the marketing research process as possible that are referred to in the articles you find.
11. Observe any business in your community. Examine what it does, what products or service it provides, its prices, its promotion, or any other aspect of its business. Try to determine whether or not you, if you managed the business, would have conducted research to determine the firm's products, their design, features, prices, promotion, and so on. If you decide that you would not have conducted marketing research on a given area, explain why.

INTERACTIVE LEARNING

Visit the Web site at www.prenhall.com/burnsbush. For this chapter, work through the Self-Study Quizzes, and get instant feedback on whether you need additional studying. On the Web site, you can review the chapter outlines and case information for Chapter 2.

CASE 2.1 Satellite Radio

Technology has been developed that would allow for the broadcast of many radio channels all over the United States and other parts of the world via satellite. Radio signals broadcast from satellite would give consumers the ability to listen to their favorite "local" radio station no matter where they were. Also, a large variety of programmed music may be available on many channels dedicated to a particular type of music, such as classical, r&b, rock, or country. Nonmusic channels featuring talk shows, classic radio, sports, or comedy, for example, may also be available. The signals would be high-quality digital signals and listeners would get a readout on their radio of the names of the program, song title, and artist to which they were tuned. Many channels will be commercial free. Programming partners would include Sesame Workshop, NASCAR, Associated Press, CNBC, CNET, BBC World Service, and BBC Concerts, *USA Today*, AsiaOne, BET, Radio One, The Sporting News, CNN/Sports Illustrated and CNN Financial Network, Bloomberg, Hispanic Broadcast Corporation, C-SPAN Radio, Clear Channel and DIRECTV, *National Lampoon*, Discovery, Firesign Theatre, and MTV. This wide variety would give listeners a large choice of listening preferences.

In order to listen to satellite radio, a listener would have to have a radio equipped with a satellite receiver. Estimates are that radios built with the receivers would retail somewhere around $300. Different models are proposed. One model is for installation in existing car radio housings. Another model is a home, table model, and still a third model is portable and can be used anywhere.

The Federal Communications Commission (FCC) has decided to grant two licenses for satellite radio in the United States. Several companies are considering seeking the satellite radio license from the FCC. After filing for the application, the FCC will award licenses to two applicants.

1. Assume you are considering filing for the FCC license. On what will you base your decision to file or not file?
2. Is it likely that you, as a potential investor in this industry, would already have the information needed to make this decision? If yes, what is the information and what would your decision be? If no, what would now be needed?
3. Assuming you were going to conduct a marketing research study, what do you think the problem and the research objectives would be?
4. Given the research objectives you defined in question 3, do you think the company should conduct exploratory, descriptive, or causal research? Why?
5. Will you need to collect primary or secondary data?
6. How will the data be collected? Should you use the telephone, mail, Internet, or personal interviewing?
7. What about a sample plan? Should this be a national sample or would it be appropriate to sample people in a few cities spread out geographically around the United States, such as New York, Chicago, Dallas and Los Angeles?
8. What is the important information that should be included in the final report?

CASE 2.2 *Your Integrated Case*

This case will appear throughout the book. The case will be used to illustrate concepts covered in the chapter in which the case appears.

The Hobbit's Choice: A Restaurant

Jeff Dean is a restaurant supply sales representative. He works in a large metropolitan area and calls on many of the restaurant owners in the city. His dream is to one day own his own restaurant. He had saved a substantial amount of his earnings during his 15 years in the restaurant supply business and he had recently gone over some financial figures with his banker. He and the banker both agreed that he had enough capital to get serious about investing in his dream. His banker, Walker Stripling, was very optimistic about Dean's potential for

Can marketing research be used to predict the success of a restaurant?

success even though he had seen many failed attempts in the restaurant business. Stripling was confident in Dean because he felt, with his restaurant supply experience, few people knew the restaurant business as well as Dean.

Dean's idea was to not try to compete with everyone else. There were too many restaurants that, except for their décor and a few menu items, offered little new to the market. He had seen many of the "me-too" restaurants falter after a short time of operation. His plan was to offer something not currently available in the market even though the city was fairly large. Dean had traveled extensively during his career. His primary purpose in traveling had been to attend trade shows in the restaurant supply business. There were usually several of these a year and Dean had been diligent about attending these shows as he learned about new products and services his supplier firms were offering for him to sell to his local restaurants. While attending the trade shows, Dean and some of his friends made a habit of visiting restaurants of all types in the various cities. Dean was familiar with restaurants in New Orleans, San Francisco, Dallas, Miami, New York, and many of the other major cities in the United States. These cities all had restaurants like the restaurants he had as clients at home and they had these same types of restaurants by the dozens. But there was one type of restaurant these cities had that was missing from his metro area. His city did not have a fine, upscale restaurant featuring the finest entrées, drinks, and desserts in an elegant atmosphere. He had visited with the owners of these types of restaurants in several of the cities in which he traveled. Many had been very willing to talk with him about what they had learned and how they operated. Dean had planned his restaurant for several years. He took the best ideas from the restaurants he had visited and put them into his plan. His restaurant would be called "The Hobbit's Choice." Dean was a fan of the author J.R.R. Tolkien, and he thought the reference to the Hobbits would be perfect in a name for an upscale restaurant. The Hobbits, characters in Tolkien's writings, were portrayed as good, fun-loving people whose lives primarily centered around eating.

1. What reasons would you give for Jeff Dean to not conduct any marketing research?
2. What reasons would you give for Jeff Dean to conduct marketing research?
3. If you were Jeff Dean, what would you do in terms of not conducting or conducting marketing research? Why?

The Marketing Research Industry

Practitioner Viewpoint

The marketing/advertising/public opinion research industry has benefited enormously from online research made possible by ever-increasing technological advances. Powerful computers handling huge blocks of data and a technology-based infrastructure allow us to capture data at the point of purchase via scanning of UPC codes on products. This has opened new ways to track consumer preference purchases. And with the introduction of preferred customer cards, these data can be linked to specific households, opening the door to more productive analysis of tracking data such as measuring customer reaction to deals. Online research is also impacting the industry's ability to monitor media. Now the Arbitron PPM (personal people meter) is making possible a huge improvement in the measurement of TV, radio, and cable audience size and behavior. Here miniaturization has made possible a small computer weighing about 2 ounces that respondents wear and that is able to record any broadcast signals within their hearing range.

One area of online research, online survey research, is significantly impacting the research industry today. Made possible by the Internet, online survey research has the advantages of speedy turnaround of projects, much larger samples, and the ability to expose respondents to visual stimuli. And that is one reason why interviewing via the Internet is widely used for concept/product tests now. There has been much trial and error as research practitioners strive to utilize the potential of online survey research and overcome some of the disadvantages. But, no doubt, online survey research is a major innovation that's here to stay. Technology continues to change the research industry.

Jack Honomichl
President, Marketing Aid Center

Inside Research with Jack J. Honomichl

As we have with our previous editions of this book, we asked Jack Honomichl to provide us with information and to write the Practitioner Viewpoint for you. We are delighted to have him do this for us because few people know the marketing research industry as well as Mr. Honomichl. Jack Honomichl is the president of Marketing Aid Center, Inc. in Barrington, Illinois. The Marketing Aid Center publishes the industry newsletter *Inside Research*, which targets top management in the research industry. The firm provides consulting, compiles industry statistics such as "The Honomichl Top 50" (see Table 3.1), and conducts research projects.

Having received a B.S. degree from Northwestern University and a master's degree from the University of Chicago, Mr. Honomichl has spent a good part of his life in the research industry. He has held executive positions with the Marketing Information Center, a subsidiary of Dun & Bradstreet; Audits & Surveys, Inc.; MRCA; and the *Chicago Tribune*. He frequently contributes to *Advertising Age* and the AMA's *Marketing News*. His book on the industry entitled *Honomichl on Marketing Research* is published by National Textbook Company, Lincolnwood, Illinois. He has published nearly 400 articles in the trade and the academic press. As you learn about the marketing research industry in this chapter, you will gain many insights from the publications of Mr. Honomichl and others.

Jack J. Honomichl is recognized as a leader in the marketing research industry.

The purpose of this chapter is to provide you with some information about the marketing research industry itself. We begin by giving a brief historical perspective of marketing research. Next, we consider the structure of the industry by examining the types of firms in the industry and we look at firm size by introducing you to "The Honomichl Top 50," which shows the top 50 marketing research firms in terms of revenue. We next look at evaluations of the industry. How has the research industry performed? Finally, we examine the ethical issues facing the industry and, in doing so, we examine closely the additional ethical issues brought on by online research. When you finish this chapter, you will have finished our three-chapter introduction to marketing research. Some of you may have become interested in marketing research as a career. If you want to know more about a career in the industry, we encourage you to read the Appendix on careers that we have provided for you at the end of this chapter.

MARKETING RESEARCH: A BRIEF HISTORY

Pre–Marketing Research Era

Our brief history of marketing research examines the development of marketing research during different time periods or eras. We could refer to the time period from colonization until the industrial revolution as the **pre–marketing research era**. The economy was primarily made up of artisans and craftsmen bartering one good for another. Towns and villages were small and the businesses that served them were also small. Everyone knew what each craftsman or artisan made. Paul Revere was a silversmith. He knew the people with whom he bartered and he didn't need a marketing research study to tell him what they wanted. The significance of this time period is that the craftsmen or small business owners knew their customers personally. When these conditions exist, even today, there is little need for formal marketing research studies. This is true for many small business owners. They know their customers very well, many by name. Not only do their customers tell them about their likes and dislikes, but customers also keep small business owners informed about their likes and dislikes of competitors' offerings as well.[1]

> The significance of the pre–marketing research era is that business owners knew their customers so that there was little need for formal marketing research.

Early Development Era

We refer to the period between the industrial revolution and about 1920 as the **early development era**. The events of this era led to the need for marketing research. First, the industrial revolution made an everlasting impact on humankind. For the first time in the history of the world, we had the ability to mass-produce goods. Second, transportation systems were developed to move large quantities of goods streaming forth from the new factories. The St. Lawrence Seaway was opened, which facilitated water transportation along an east–west route and connected the Great Lakes with the Atlantic. Settlements in the Far West developed and grew, and transportation to these markets was aided by the completion of the transcontinental railroad in 1869. Third, means of communication also improved with the introduction of the telegraph in 1844 and the wireless radio in 1906 and with increased literacy levels. Both of these developments in communications and increases in literacy were important to enable companies with factories located in one part of the country to advertise their products in distant markets. For the first time, companies could mass-produce products and advertise and distribute them to distant markets. This meant that business managers were no longer near or acquainted with their customers. So it was the development of a mass market, separated from the factories of mass production, that led to the development of marketing research. Managers of these new companies, equipped with the tools of production, needed to understand their faraway markets.

> The significance of the early development era is that customers were separated from business managers, and marketing research was needed to understand the distant markets.

Questionnaire Era

We call the third era, the **questionnaire era** (1920–1940). Although the questionnaire survey is said to have first been used in 1824 by some newspapers, and N. W. Ayres and Company is said to have surveyed grain production in each of the states in 1879, questionnaire surveys were in limited use until the 1920s. During World War I, the military used questionnaires for personnel screening. This increased familiarity with this research tool led to its use in opinion polls conducted by magazine publishers.[2] Severe changes in the economy led to increased use of questionnaires. When the "boom" during the 1920s gave way to the Great Depression, beginning in 1929, there was increased interest in the use of the questionnaire as a survey tool.

Questionnaires, still an important tool of marketing research, became prominent in marketing research during the time period from about 1920 to 1940.

Quantitative Era

The time period from 1940 to 1960 we call the **quantitative era.** Census data and, in particular, the taking of the censuses of business led to an interest in statistical analysis. Marketing research was used to set sales quotas and to determine equitable sales territories. It was applied to managerial accounting techniques, such as cost analyses, to determine the costs of distribution. Also, marketing researchers began to borrow methodological techniques from the social sciences. Sampling theory, hypothesis testing, and the application of statistical techniques to hypotheses involving consumers' behaviors, intentions, and attitudes became part of the marketing research industry's tool kit.[3] The study of "why people buy," or motivational research, started during this time period. For the first time, the marketing researcher was aided in his or her task of analysis by a new invention—the computer.[4]

Many quantitative techniques were applied to studying consumers and markets for the first time during the quantitative era—1940 to 1960.

Organizational Acceptance Era

By 1960 marketing research gained acceptance in business organizations. Consequently, we call the period from 1960 to 1980 the **organizational acceptance era.** As the marketing concept was accepted, the marketing research function was established as a formal part of the organization of the firm. The number of firms having their own research departments grew rapidly during this time period. During this era, other changes were also taking place. More firms became involved in international marketing activities requiring management to make decisions about consumers and competition with which they had little, if any, firsthand experience. Worldwide communications and innovations in product and service technologies created a smaller world, but one that was filled with greater diversity and changing environments. To keep up, firms embraced the concept of the marketing information system (MIS), of which marketing research is a key component. Marketing research had not only gained acceptance in the organization but also was recognized as being a key to understanding distant and fast-changing markets. It was needed for survival.

During the organizational acceptance era, management began to realize that, in order to survive, marketing research was needed to implement the marketing concept.

PC Technology Era

We call the period from 1980 to about 1990 the **PC technology era.** Although research firms had access to mainframe computing technology, computer technology was made available to everyone, all the time, through the invention of the personal computer (PC). The PC served as a catalyst for the development of technological applications that would make use of the PC. As these applications evolved, they found a willing market. Because more powerful applications meant new PCs with greater computing power, more storage and faster operating speeds were needed. The marketing research industry, like many industries, has benefited from the significant advances in personal computing during this time period. Although computer

The technological era has brought many new products and services to the research industry that have impacted the way business is conducted.

technology and applications have continued to grow in number and complexity, the foundation was laid during the decade of the eighties. In addition to word processors and spreadsheets that were developed for the PC during this period, applications such as computer-assisted questionnaire programs, touchscreen data collection programs, statistical programs for the PC, and CATI computer telephoning programs were quickly adopted by the marketing research industry.

Globalization–Online Era

We call the time since 1990 the **globalization–online era** since these two major factors have influenced the marketing research industry. First, marketing research companies became much more global during this time period. As business firms grew into multinational operations there was a need for their U.S. research service to be available in other markets of the world as well. The research industry, through acquisition, merger, and expansion, moved into international markets at an unprecedented pace. In the third edition of this book, published in 2000, Jack Honomichl discussed what happened in the research industry during the 1990s. He said some of the world's largest firms, such as Procter & Gamble, Gillette, Coca-Cola, H. J. Heinz, and Johnson & Johnson, obtain more than half their profits from operations outside their home country. Honomichl went on to say that the research firms that cater to the information needs of these multinational giants must serve them all over the world, and this explains the force behind the globalization of the research industry. As an example, Honomichl says that in just 1997 and 1998, the world's largest marketing research firms acquired 55 other firms around the globe.[5] In 2000, the top 50 U.S.-based research firms got 37 percent of their revenues from non-U.S. operations.[6]

Research firms have followed their client firms to new markets all around the world.

Our second influence during the time period from 1990 to the present would have to be online research, the focus of this edition of our text. There have been many forces that have created the growth in online research. The technology, based in the PC technology era of the eighties, continued to evolve and create even more powerful machines and applications software. Globalization meant that not only were firms located far from their customers, but also managers were located far from one another. The need for communications was never greater. Increasing competitive pressures drove the need for operating efficiencies. Consumers' growing concerns for privacy caused researchers to grow wary about the future viability of traditional data collection methods. The opening of the Internet to the public created the pavement needed for the information highway. All of these forces led firms in the marketing research industry to practice online research. We believe online research will continue to evolve, and we believe it will be a significant part of the industry for years to come.

Improved technology and greater need for efficient communications have paved the way for increased online research.

UNDERSTANDING THE INDUSTRY STRUCTURE

In the marketing research industry we refer to providers of marketing research information as **research suppliers.** There are several ways we can classify suppliers. We use a classification developed by Naresh Malholtra,[7] slightly modified for our purposes here. This classification system is shown in Figure 3.1. As shown in this figure, suppliers may be classified as either internal or external.

Internal Suppliers

An internal supplier means an entity within the firm supplies marketing research information.

An **internal supplier** means an entity within the firm supplies marketing research. It has been estimated that these firms spend roughly 1 percent of sales on marketing research, whether it is supplied internally or externally.[8] Kodak, General Mills, General Motors, and DaimlerChrysler have research departments of their own. AT&T has an in-house

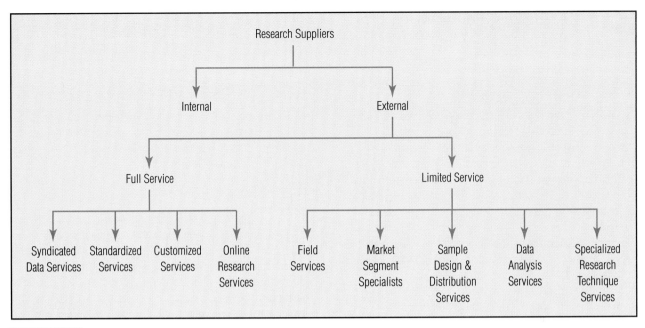

Figure 3.1   **A Classification of Marketing Research Suppliers**

research department that constantly monitors consumer satisfaction and environmental trends. It also provides research support to AT&T's advertising agencies. Internal suppliers exist not only in for-profit firms but also, as we see in Marketing Research Insight 3.1, in not-for-profits, such as the American Heart Association, which has its own marketing research function. It is, thus, an internal supplier.

How Do Internal Suppliers Organize the Research Function?

Internal suppliers of marketing research can elect several organizing methods to provide the research function. They may (1) have their own formal departments, (2) have no formal department but place at least a single individual or a committee responsible for marketing research, or they may (3) assign no one responsibility for conducting marketing research. Most large organizations have the resources to staff their own formal marketing research departments. Firms with higher sales volumes (over $500 million) tend to have their own formal marketing research departments and many large advertising agencies have their own formal research departments.[9] The key to whether a company has its own research department lies in justifying the large fixed costs of supporting the personnel and facilities of the department day in and day out. The major advantage of having your own department is that the staff is fully cognizant of the firm's operations and the changes in the industry. This may give them better insights into identifying opportunities and problems suitable for marketing research action.

Marketing research departments are usually organized according to one or a combination of the following functions: area of application, marketing function, or the research process. By "area of application," we mean these companies organize the research function around the "areas" to which the research is being applied. For example, some firms serve both ultimate consumers as well as industrial consumers. Therefore, the marketing research department may be organized into two divisions: consumer and industrial. Some firms organize their research department around brands or lines of products or services. Marketing research may be organized

Internal suppliers may (1) have their own formal departments, (2) have no formal department but at least a single individual responsible for marketing research, or they may (3) assign no one responsibility for conducting marketing research.

Marketing research departments are usually organized according to one or a combination of the following functions: area of application, marketing function, or the research process.

MARKETING RESEARCH
INSIGHT
3.1

*Internal Suppliers of Marketing Research Include
Not-for-Profit as Well as For-Profit Organizations*
Allison Groom, American Heart Association

Ms. Allison Groom is a marketing research consultant with the American Heart Association's national center in Dallas, Texas. Her responsibilities encompass a wide spectrum of marketing research, including customer satisfaction, public awareness, employee research, market segmentation, and online research. She consults internally with management to apply the data to business decisions affecting strategic planning, product development and marketing, and corporate operations. Before joining the American Heart Association in 1988, Ms. Groom was employed at Bozell & Jacobs advertising agency in Dallas. She holds a master's in advertising from the University of Texas at Austin, and a B.S. in journalism from Texas Christian University at Fort Worth.

When we think of organizations that are internal suppliers with their own, in-house marketing research function, we normally think of for-profit firms such as GE, IBM, and Wal-Mart. But decision makers at the not-for-profits must make important decisions as well. As you can see from the examples of marketing research supplied to us by Allison Groom, the American Heart Association (AHA) conducts marketing research studies itself (internal supplier) as well as obtaining research information from marketing research external supplier firms.

Market Segmentation

The AHA maintains profiles of 26 custom market segments based on health knowledge, attitudes and behavior, donating and volunteering habits, lifestyle and spending habits, demographics, and psychographics. The segments drive product development, marketing, and communications strategies. The segments were created based on data from a national consumer mail panel survey that was overlayed with Claritas segmentation profiles.

Market Tracking Study

The AHA has conducted a biannual tracking study since 1996 among the general public to measure changes in social marketing issues, corporate positioning, and health knowledge, attitudes, and behavior. A mail survey is sent to 5,000 members of a national consumer mail panel and averages a 60 percent response rate. The data allow AHA to adjust strategy based on market changes, as well to update the 26 custom market segments.

Customer Usage and Attitude Study

The AHA recently conducted a usage and attitude study among donors and volunteers that represents a comprehen-

sive investigation into giving and volunteering behavior. A total of 1,300 nationally representative telephone interviews were conducted with adults. Telephone surveys were used to measure top-of-mind awareness.

Online Survey Research

The AHA has recently begun using online survey research when applicable, including surveys among donors, volunteers, fund-raising event participants, Web site visitors, and other customers who are accessible online. Examples of online surveys include: testing fund-raising event prize concepts and T-shirt designs, obtaining usage and satisfaction of emergency cardiovascular care products, testing names for a Web-based program, evaluating an Intranet site, and screening employee participants for an e-training course. The average response rate has been around 30 percent, and turnaround time is typically within two weeks. This methodology has dramatically reduced the AHA's research costs and time lines. Traditional research methodologies, however, are still used heavily by the AHA in order to reach audiences who tend not to be accessible online.

Positioning Research

The AHA conducted a series of qualitative and quantitative research to determine its corporate positioning. The research began with a competitive analysis to identify the positioning strategies used by other major nonprofit health organizations. Focus groups were then held with customers, including donors, volunteers, health care professionals, and general consumers. The focus groups elicited perceptions and expectations that resulted in the creation of five alternative positioning statements. The statements were then tested through a quantitative mail survey. Four key attributes that were important and believable—personal, credible, understandable, and accessible—led to the creation of the AHA's current positioning statement: "The American Heart Association is working for you and your family by getting the best science on heart disease and stroke and making it simple to understand and easy to obtain."

Secondary Research

The AHA subscribes to several standardized information services, as third parties have already explored many health care and fund-raising issues. It also frequently conducts its own online searches over the Internet.

around functional areas such as advertising research, product research, distribution research, and so on. Finally, the research function may be organized around stages in the research process such as data analysis or data collection.

If internal supplier firms elect not to have a formal marketing research department, there are many other organizational possibilities. Assignment for marketing research may be made across company departments or divisions. That is, although there is no formal research department, responsibility for research rests within existing organizational units. One problem with this method is that research activities are not coordinated; a division conducts its own research, and other units of the firm may be unaware of useful information. One way to remedy this is to have a committee whose primary function is to coordinate research activities to ensure that all units of the firm have input into and benefit from any research activity undertaken. In some cases, committees or individuals assigned to marketing research may actually conduct some limited research but typically their primary role is that of helping other managers recognize the need for research and coordinating the purchase of research from external research suppliers. Obviously, the advantage here is limiting fixed costs incurred by maintaining the full-time staff required for an ongoing department. No one may be assigned to marketing research in some organizations. This is rare in large companies but not unusual at all in smaller firms. In very small firms, the owner/manager plays many roles, ranging from strategic planner to salesperson to security staff. He or she must also be responsible for marketing research, making certain to have the right information before making decisions. Fortunately, small business owner/managers can more easily gather certain types of information than can CEOs of large, multinational corporations. This is because small business owners/managers have daily contact with customers and suppliers. In this way, they constantly gather information that helps them in their decision making.

> It is rare to find no one responsible for marketing research in large organizations; small business owners who see their customers daily conduct their own "informal" research constantly.

External Suppliers

External suppliers are outside firms hired to fulfill a firm's marketing research needs. As Allison Groom of the American Heart Association points out in Marketing Research Insight 3.1, the AHA is not only an internal supplier of marketing research but it also purchases research from external suppliers as well. Both large and small firms, for-profits and not-for-profits, and government and educational institutions purchase research information from external suppliers.

> External suppliers are outside firms hired to fulfill a firm's marketing research needs.

Every year Jack Honomichl publishes the "**The Honomichl Top 50.**" Mr. Honomichl's study includes revenues from the top 50 firms (ranked on the basis of revenues earned in the U.S.) and an additional 130 research firms who are members of CASRO (Council of American Survey Research Organizations). The Honomichl Top 50 is published each year in the June issue of the AMA's *Marketing News*. The 2002 study, reporting revenues for the industry for 2001, is shown for you in Table 3.1. Revenues were up from 2000 to 2001 by 4 percent after an adjustment for inflation, real growth was 1.28 percent. This was down from real growth rates of 10 percent in 1998, 7.9 percent in 1999 and 5.6 percent in 2000 but the decline was expected. In fact, many felt the decline in growth would be more than this due to a lackluster economy and the horrendous effects of the tragedy of September 11, 2001. Mr. Honomichl states that the firms offering syndicated services, with long term contracts, were affected less by the 9/11 tragedy and firms depending mainly on ad hoc research project work were affected most. Ad hoc research came to a virtual standstill for several weeks following 9/11. Table 3.1 shows that the amount of research revenues earned in the United States during 2001 by the 130 firms was $5.5 billion. These same firms earned another $3.3 billion in revenues earned outside the United States for a rounded total of $8.9 billion.[10]

> The marketing research industry earns nearly $9 billion in annual revenues.

Table	3.1	The Honomichl Top 50

TOP 50 U.S. MARKET RESEARCH ORGANIZATIONS

U.S. 2001	Rank 2000	Organization	Headquarters	Web Site	U.S. Research Revenues* ($ in millions)	Percent Change From 2000**	WW Research Revenues* ($ in millions)	Non-U.S. Research Revenues* ($ in millions)	Percent Non-U.S. Revenues
1	2	VNU Inc.	New York, NY	vnu.com	1,300.0	8.3	2,400.0	1,100.0	45.8
2	3	IMS Health Inc.	Fairfield, CT	imshealth.com	469.0	11.1	1,171.0	702.0	60.0
3	4	Information Resources Inc.	Chicago, IL	infores.com	420.3	5.6	555.9	135.6	24.4
4	6	The Kantar Group	Fairfield, CT	kantargroup.com	299.1	6.1	962.3	663.2	68.9
5	5	Westat Inc.	Rockville, MD	westat.com	285.8	8.1	285.8		
6	7	Arbitron Inc.	New York, NY	arbitron.com	219.6	9.5	227.5	7.9	3.5
7	—	NOP World US	New York, NY	nopworld.com	206.6	1.7	224.1	17.5	7.8
	12	*NOP World US*	New York, NY	nopworld.com	143.7*	3.2	149.3*	5.6*	3.8
	17	*Roper Starch Worldwide*	Harrison, NY	roperasw.com	62.9*	-2.5	74.8*	11.9*	15.9
8	8	NFO WorldGroup	Greenwich, CT	nfow.com	163.0	-7.9	452.9	289.9	64.0
9	9	Market Facts Inc.	Arlington Heights, IL	marketfacts.com	156.2	-8.6	189.7	33.5	17.7
10	11	Taylor Nelson Sofres USA	London, U.K.	tnsofres.com	150.5	8.4	166.9	16.4	9.8
11	13	Maritz Research	Fenton, MO	maritzresearch.com	127.1	3.5	181.7	54.6	30.0
12	23	Ipsos	New York, NY	ipsos.com	112.9	5.1	204.3	91.4	44.7
13	15	J.D. Power and Associates	Westlake Village, CA	jdpa.com	109.3	24.2	128.0	18.7	14.6
14	14	Opinion Research Corp.	Princeton, NJ	opinionresearch.com	91.4	-3.6	133.6	42.2	31.6
15	10	The NPD Group Inc.	Port Washington, NY	npd.com	88.7	16.1	101.7	13.0	12.8
16	17	Jupiter Media Metrix Inc.	New York, NY	jmm.com	68.6	-27.5	85.8	17.2	20.0
17	18	Harris Interactive Inc.	Rochester, NY	harrisinteractive.com	64.9	-7.0	75.4	10.5	13.9
18	20	Abt Associates Inc.	Cambridge, MA	abtassociates.com	53.4	15.8	62.8	9.4	15.0
19	19	C&R Research Services Inc.	Chicago, IL	crresearch.com	43.6	-5.6	43.6		
20	22	Wirthlin Worldwide	McLean, VA	wirthlin.com	39.6	-5.9	46.8	7.2	15.4
21	24	Lieberman Research Worldwide	Los Angeles, CA	lrwonline.com	38.8	11.8	43.1	4.3	10.0
22	25	Burke Inc.	Cincinnati, OH	burke.com	34.3	-0.3	45.5	11.2	24.6
23	21	MORPACE International Inc.	Farmington Hills, MI	morpace.com	32.4	-23.2	48.3	15.9	32.9
24	26	Market Strategies Inc.	Livonia, MI	marketstrategies.com	30.2	-4.7	31.7	1.5	4.7

Rank	2002 Rank	Company	Headquarters	Web site	U.S. Research Revenue	% Change	Worldwide Research Revenue	Non-U.S. Revenue	% Outside U.S.
25	30	GfK Custom Research Inc.	Minneapolis, MN	customresearch.com	28.9	2.1	29.8	0.9	3.0
26	32	ICR/Int'l Communications Research	Media, PA	icrsurvey.com	28.5	2.5	28.8	0.3	1.0
27	29	M/A/R/C Research	Irving, TX	marcresearch.com	24.0	-18.4	24.5	0.5	2.0
28	31	Elrick & Lavidge Marketing Research	Tucker, GA	elrickandlavidge.com	22.9	-17.9	22.9		
29	36	RDA Group Inc.	Bloomfield Hills, MI	rdagroup.com	22.4	19.8	26.0	3.6	13.8
30	33	Lieberman Research Group	Great Neck, NY	liebermanresearch.com	21.8	4.3	22.3	0.5	2.2
31	—	Knowledge Networks, Inc.	Menlo Park, CA	knowledgenetworks.com	21.4	42.1	21.4		
32	34	Walker Information	Indianapolis, IN	walkerinfo.com	21.3	4.4	26.8	5.5	20.5
33	37	National Research Corp.	Lincoln, NE	nationalresearch.com	17.7	-6.0	17.7		
34	38	Directions Research Inc.	Cincinnati, OH	directionsrsch.com	16.7	-4.6	16.7		
35	48	Marketing and Planning Systems Inc.	Waltham, MA	mapsnet.com	16.5	1.8	19.7	3.2	16.2
36	—	Alliance Research Inc.	Crestview Hill, KY	allianceresearch.com	15.4	5.7	15.4		
37	40	Data Development Corp.	New York, NY	datadc.com	15.3	1.3	15.6	0.3	1.9
38	46	Marketing Analysts Inc.	Charleston, SC	marketinganalysts.com	14.7	2.1	15.1	0.4	2.6
39	—	Marketing Research Services Inc.	Cincinnati, OH	mrsi.com	14.3	20.0	14.3		
40	43	Greenfield Online Inc.	Wilton, CT	greenfield.com	14.2	-4.1	14.2		
41	42	Greenfield Consulting Group Inc.	Westport, CT	greenfieldgroup.com	13.9	-9.2	14.0	0.1	1.0
42	45	Savitz Research Companies	Dallas, TX	savitzresearch.com	13.2	-4.3	13.2		
43	44	The PreTesting Co. Inc.	Tenafly, NJ	pretesting.com	12.4	-7.5	13.1	0.7	5.3
44	39	Schulman, Ronca & Bucuvalas Inc.	New York, NY	srbi.com	11.4	-25.5	12.1	0.7	5.8
45	49	Cheskin	Redwood Shores, CA	cheskin.com	11.2	2.8	14.3	3.1	22.0
46	—	The Marketing Workshop, Inc.	Norcross, GA	mwshop.com	10.6	5.5	10.6		
47	—	Symmetrical Holdings, Inc.	Deerfield Beach, FL	symmetrical.com	10.4	11.8	10.4		
48	—	comScore Networks Inc.	Reston, VA	comscore.com	10.0	525.0	10.0		
49	—	MarketVision Research	Cincinnati, OH	marketvisionresearch.com	10.0	-3.0	10.0		
50	47	The B/R/S Group Inc.	San Raphael, CA	brsgroup.com	8.7	-29.3	10.9	2.2	20.0
		Total			5,033.1	4.3	8,318.2	3,285.1	39.5
		All other (130 CASRO companies not included in the Top 50)***			510.6	1.0	563.1	52.5	9.3
		Total (180 companies)			5,543.7	4.0	8,881.3	3,337.6	37.6

*U.S. and WW (worldwide) and Non-U.S. revenues that include non-research activities for some companies are significantly higher.

**Rate of growth from year to year has been adjusted so as not to include revenue gains or losses from acquisitions or divestitures.

***Total revenues of 130 survey research firms—beyond those in Top 50—that provide financial information, on a confidential basis, to the Council of American Survey Research Organizations (CASRO).

Due to the growth of online research, several online research firms have now joined The Honomichl Top 50.

Another significant finding of "The Honomichl Top 50" is that due to the relatively high growth experienced by online firms for several years now, more of them are appearing in the top 50. The 2002 report shows that Knowledge Networks and comScore Networks have joined other online research firms previously appearing on the list. Those online research firms previously appearing are firms such as Harris Interactive, Greenfield Online, and Jupiter Media Metrix.[11] Mr. Honomichl's report is highly regarded as the best measure of revenue and change in the marketing research industry. You can view "The Honomichl Top 50" table with hyperlinks to the companies at www.marketingpower.org publications (Do a search for Honomichl).

Of course, there are many other research firms in the marketing research industry. These research firms range in size from one-person proprietorships to the large, international corporations shown in the "The Honomichl Top 50." In terms of revenue, VNU Inc., owner of ACNielsen, has been the dominant firm with well over a billion dollars in annual revenue. So, as you can see by looking at Table 3.1, the research industry is made up of a few large firms, several medium-sized firms, and many smaller firms (see that the over 100 CASRO firms had revenues totaling a small percentage of the top 50 firms' revenues).

You can get an idea of the type, number, and services offered by these firms by looking at some online directories of marketing research firms. For example, take a look at the New York chapter of the American Marketing Association's Web site and look through the *Greenbook*, a directory of marketing research firms. Go to www.greenbook.org and click on the picture of the *Greenbook*. Explore this Web site and you will get a better understanding of how to classify external supplier firms. Also visit the different "directory" listings at www.quirks.com.

External Suppliers of Online Survey Research

Inside Research, a confidential newsletter for research industry executives also published by Jack Honomichl, publishes an index to measure the growth of online survey research. The index is based on 30 U.S. marketing research firms and their 27 subsidiaries. These firms reported revenue of $333.5 million in 2001. This represented an increase of 51 percent from 2000. Even though many industries would love to have a 51 percent increase, this was less than expected due to the combination of a weak worldwide economy in 2001 and the economic downturn brought about by the terrorists attacks on New York City in September 2001. Significantly, the participating firms forecast revenues to increase by 46 percent in 2002 in spite of the weak economy.[12] Obviously, online survey research is a fast-growing segment of online research and of the entire research industry.

How Do External Suppliers Organize?

Like internal supplier firms, external supplier firms organize themselves in different ways. These firms may organize by function (data analysis, data collection, etc.), by type of research application (customer satisfaction, advertising effectiveness, new-product development, etc.), by geography (domestic versus international), by type of customer (health care, government, telecommunications, etc.), or some combination of the foregoing functions. Let's look at a few supplier firms to get an appreciation of how they are organized. Burke, Inc. is organized around four main areas of research application and function: Burke Marketing Research is a full-service marketing research division. The Burke Customer Satisfaction Associates offers a standardized service of measuring and managing customer satisfaction. The Burke Training & Development Center provides training in marketing research for supplier firms, whether internal or external suppliers. The Burke Strategic Consulting Group offers intensive consulting to business management. Also, as change occurs,

See how Burke, Inc. is organized at www.burke.com.

we see research companies changing their organizational structure to accommodate the change. For example, as online research has grown, Burke, Inc. added a division to Burke Marketing Research called Burke Interactive.

Opinion Research Corporation (ORC) is organized by geography, type of research application, and function. ORC's three divisions are ORC International, which conducts global marketing research; ORC Macro, which specializes in global social research such as health issues; and ORC ProTel, which is a provider of teleservices.[13]

Strategic Alliances Among External Suppliers Firms in the marketing research industry, as in other industries, form strategic alliances. **Strategic alliances** bring firms together in a way that allows each firm to take advantage of the other firms' expertise and resources. Therefore, each participating firm gains by being in the alliance. The basis of these alliances may be through acquisition, merger, or contractual agreements. For example, several years ago, Burke, Inc. acquired Trendbox, a research firm in Amsterdam, in order to have research capabilities for its Burke clients who were operating in western Europe. Burke gained immediate representation in western Europe for its clients who were operating there and Trendbox gained the advantage of Burke's very large staff with expertise in many areas. Another strategic alliance has been formed between Digital Marketing Services (DMS) and the marketing research division of SPSS, SPSS MR. We present this alliance to you because not only is it a good example of strategic alliance in the research industry but it also represents a significant alliance in online survey research. DMS, an AOL company, created a large base of internet subscribers who were willing to complete online surveys. In 2001 DMS entered into a strategic alliance with SPSS's marketing research division, SPSS MR. So, now this alliance offers a competitive array of services including the talents of these established research firms, a site for online respondents called Opinion Place and data collection and data analytics provided by SPSS MR. This a good example of how reorganizing via a strategic alliance can produce a competitive service.[14] DMS and SPSS MR will work closely to expand online industry survey and sample services through OpinionPlace.com, the online industry's largest portal for reliable survey research respondents.[15]

Classifying External Supplier Firms

As you may recall from Figure 3.1, we can classify all external supplier firms into two categories: full-service or limited-service firms. In the following paragraphs we will define these two types of firms and give you some examples of each.

Full-Service Supplier Firms **Full-service supplier firms** have the ability to conduct the entire marketing research project for the buyer firms. Full-service firms will often define the problem, specify the research design, collect and analyze the data, and prepare the final written report. Typically, these are larger firms that have the expertise as well as the necessary facilities to conduct research studies in their entirety. Firms such as Market Facts, Inc., Burke, Inc., ACNielsen, Roper Starch Worldwide, Information Resources, Inc., and Walker Information are full-service firms. There are certain specializations in the research industry such as syndicated data services, standardized services, or Internet services. ACNielsen, for example, offers syndicated data services. ACNielsen is a very large, full-service firm. These services are not easily offered and, therefore, they are typically provided by the larger, full-service firms. Customized services, meaning research that is custom designed for a particular client problem, may be carried out by a large or small full-service firm.

External suppliers can be classified as either full-service or limited-service supplier firms.

Full-service supplier firms have the ability to conduct the entire marketing research project for the buyer firms. Full-service firms can be further broken down into syndicated data services, standardized services, and customized services.

Syndicated data service firms collect information that is made available to multiple subscribers.

Syndicated data service firms collect information that is made available to multiple subscribers. The information, or data, is provided in standardized form (information may not be tailored to meet the needs of any one company) to a large number of companies, known as a syndicate. Therefore, these companies offer syndicated data to all subscribing members of the syndicate. We will discuss syndicated data service firms in greater detail in Chapter 7.

Standardized service firms provide syndicated services as opposed to syndicated data. Each client gets different data, but the process used to collect the data is standardized so that it may be offered to many clients at a cost less than that of a custom-designed project.

Standardized service firms provide syndicated marketing research services, as opposed to syndicated data, to clients. Each client gets different data, but the *process* used to collect the data is standardized so that it may be offered to many clients at a cost less than that of a custom-designed project. Burke's Customer Satisfaction Associates provides the service of measuring customer satisfaction. RoperAWS offers several segmentation services. Other companies offer the service of test marketing.

Customized service firms offer a variety of research services that are tailored to meet the client's specific needs.

Customized service firms offer a variety of research services that are tailored to meet the client's specific needs. Each client's problem is treated as a unique research project. Customized service firms spend considerable time with a client firm to determine the problem and then design a research project specifically to address the particular client's problem. Such firms include Market Facts, Inc., Elrick & Lavidge, Inc., Burke Marketing Research, and Taylor Nelson Sofres USA. Market Facts, for instance, provides custom marketing research services through a range of research methodologies including test marketing, focus groups, and consumer and industrial surveys.

Online services firms specialize in providing marketing research services online, such as surveys, concept testing of new products, and focus groups.

Online research services firms specialize in providing services online. Recall in Chapter 1 that we defined online research as the use of computer networks, including the Internet, to assist in any phase of the marketing research process including development of the problem, research design, data gathering, analysis, and report distribution. Virtually all research firms today use online research in the sense that they make use of online technology in at least one or more phases of the research process. These firms would be better categorized in one of the other types of firms shown in Figure 3.1. However, there are many firms that specialize in online services. Their "reason for being" is based on the provision of services online. Affinova, for example, exists because it has proprietary, new software that allows consumers to design preferred product attributes into new products online. Knowledge Networks came into being because its founders wanted to provide clients with access to probability samples online. Insight Express was formed by NFO, Inc. to allow clients to develop questionnaires and conduct surveys online. Active Group was formed to conduct focus groups online. Certainly, there are overlapping categories in Figure 3.1. We do not claim that the categories are mutually exclusive. In fact, we could argue that some of these, because they specialize in one step of the research process, could be placed in one of the limited-service supplier categories that follow.

Limited-service supplier firms typically specialize in one or, at most, a few marketing research activities.

Limited-Service Supplier Firms **Limited-service supplier firms** specialize in one or, at most, a few marketing research activities. Firms can specialize in types of marketing research techniques such as eye-testing and mystery shopping, or specific market segments such as senior citizens or certain sports segments such as golf or tennis. The limited-service suppliers can be further classified on the basis of their specialization. These include field services, market segment specialists, sample design and distribution services, data analysis, and specialized research technique service suppliers. Many of these limited-service firms specialize in some form of online research.

Field service firms specialize in collecting data.

Field service firms specialize in collecting data. These firms typically operate in a particular territory conducting telephone surveys, focus group interviews, mall-intercept surveys, or door-to-door surveys.

Because it is expensive and difficult to maintain interviewers all over the country, firms will use the services of field service firms in order to quickly and efficiently gather data. There is specialization even within firms that specialize in field services. Some firms, for example, conduct only in-depth personal interviews; others conduct only mall-intercept surveys. Some firms, such as Irwin Research Associates, are known as "phone banks" and limit their practice to telephone surveying. Its "sister" company, The Irwin Companies, specializes in focus groups.

Opinion One is a good example of a limited-service firm that uses online research. It is a field service firm that specializes in providing the ability to display graphics, including video, in selected malls around the country. Its system allows respondents to view the image and answer questions using touch-screen technology. Respondents' answers are automatically recorded and sent directly to Opinion One's office in Cincinnati, Ohio. Another example of online survey research in a limited-service firm is Insight Express. This company allows a decision maker to design his or her questionnaire online as well as choose sample characteristics (i.e., a particular income group, gender, or type of employment). Then Insight Express gathers respondent data from its online survey respondents and provides data back to the client. All this can be done very quickly and at relatively low expense. The New York–based Meyers Research Center specializes in in-store research using consumer point-of-sale intercept interviews. Quick Test, Inc. offers clients interviewers who have been trained specifically for mall-intercept interviews.

Visit Insight Express at www.insightexpress.com.

Other limited-service firms, called **market segment specialists,** specialize in collecting data for special market segments such as African Americans, Hispanics, children, seniors, gays, industrial customers, or a specific geographic area within the United States or internationally. Strategy Research Corporation is a Market Facts company that specializes in Latin American markets. JRH Marketing Services, Inc. specializes in marketing to ethnic markets, especially to black markets. MedProbe, Inc. specializes in the research of the medical and pharmaceutical markets. Other firms specialize in children, mature citizens, pet owners, airlines, beverages, celebrities, college students, religious groups, and many other market segments. By specializing, these limited-service suppliers capitalize on their in-depth knowledge of the client's industry.

Market segment specialists collect data for special market segments such as, African Americans, Hispanics, children, seniors, gays, industrial customers, or a specific geographic area within the United States or internationally.

Survey Sampling Inc. and Scientific Telephone Samples (STS) are examples of limited-service firms that specialize in **sample design and distribution.** It is not uncommon, for example, for a company with an internal marketing research department to buy its sample from a firm specializing in sampling and then send the samples and a survey questionnaire to a phone bank for completion of the survey. This way, a firm may quickly and efficiently conduct telephone surveys using a probability sample plan in markets all over the country. Survey Sampling, Inc. provides Internet samples, B2B samples, global samples, and samples of persons with characteristics that are hard to find (low-incidence samples).

Sample design and distribution firms specialize in providing samples to firms that are conducting research studies.

Survey Sampling, Inc. (SSI) is one of the oldest and best-known firms specializing in providing samples to marketing research firms. SSI is also an example of a company using online research. Users can design their sample plan online (see SSI-SNAP) and receive their samples online. Go to www.ssi.com.

There are limited-service marketing research firms that offer **data analysis services.** Their contribution to the research process is to provide the technical assistance necessary to analyze and interpret data using the more sophisticated data analysis techniques such as conjoint analysis. SDR Consulting, SPSS MR, and Applied Decision Analysis LLC are examples of such firms.

Specialized research technique firms provide a service to their clients by expertly administering a special technique. Examples of such firms include The Pretesting Company, which specializes in eye movement research. Eye movements are used to

Specialized research technique firms address very specific needs such as eye-tracking, package design, or brand name testing.

determine effectiveness of ads, direct-mail pieces, and other forms of visual promotion. Other firms specialize in mystery shopping, taste tests, fragrance tests, creation of brand names, generating new ideas for products and services, and so on.

We should not leave this section without saying that our categorization of research suppliers does not fit every situation. For example, many full-service firms have the capabilities of offering what we have called a limited service. Taylor Nelson Sofres is a large, full-service firm. It also offers very specialized data analysis services. Also, there are other entities supplying research information that do not fit neatly into one of our categories. For example, universities and institutes supply research information. Universities sponsor a great deal of research that could be classified as marketing research. However, you may recall that we stated in Chapter 1 that this is basic research as opposed to the applied research. Don't forget that a good way for you to learn more about the structure of the industry is to go to www.quirks.com and www.greenbook.com and explore how they categorize marketing research firms in their online directories.

> There are other entities supplying research information that do not fit neatly into one of our categories.

CAN THE MARKETING RESEARCH INDUSTRY IMPROVE ITS PERFORMANCE?

Studies evaluating entire industries are conducted from time to time. Such is the case in the marketing research industry. These reviews indicate that, although the marketing research industry is doing a reasonably good job, there is room for improvement. Here are some striking examples indicating marketing research needs improving. Sony, Chrysler, and Compaq "ignored the customer" when they introduced the Walkman, minivan, and PC network servers to eager markets. Yet, Coca-Cola's first attempt at New Coke and McDonald's McLean Burgers both failed but, in both cases, were supported by extensive marketing research.[16] Mahajan and Wind suggest, however, that marketing research is not fundamentally flawed but that many executives misapply research. They misapply research by not having research professionals involved in high-level, strategic decision making. Instead, too many executives view marketing research as a commodity to be outsourced to "research brokers." To remedy the situation, Mahajan and Wind, highly regarded in academics and business consulting, recommend that researchers (1) focus on diagnosing problems, (2) use information technology to increase speed and efficiency, (3) take an integrative approach, and (4) expand the strategic impact of marketing research.

> In evaluations of the research industry, the basic conclusion is that the industry has performed well, but there is room for improvement.

Marketing Researchers Should Focus on Diagnosing Problems

Mahajan and Wind suggest that marketing researchers should stop using marketing research only to test solutions, such as testing a specific product or service. Instead, researchers should diagnose the market. As an example, consider that customers didn't "ask" for a Sony Walkman or a minivan. Marketing researchers would not have known about these products by asking customers what they wanted. Without having ever seen these products, it is unlikely that customers would have been able to articulate the product characteristics. But had marketing researchers focused on diagnosing the market in terms of unserved markets and unarticulated needs in those markets, they may have produced these products. The Walkman was successful because it met an unserved market's need for portable entertainment. The minivan was successful because it met an unserved market's need for additional space in family vehicles. Marketing research can improve by properly diagnosing the market first, then testing alternative solutions to meet the needs discovered in the market.

Marketing Researchers Should Speed Up Marketing Research by Using IT

It has long been recognized that there is a trade-off between quickly producing marketing research information and doing research in a thorough manner. Marketing researchers want time to conduct projects properly. However, Mahajan and Wind point out that researchers must remember that time is money. There are real dollar losses to being late in introducing products and services to the marketplace. So much so, in fact, that many companies cut many corners in the research they conduct or don't do any marketing research at all. This, of course, often leads to disaster and has recently been labeled "death-wish" marketing.[17] The suggested prescription is for marketing researchers to make use of information technology (IT) for speed and economical efficiency. This is exactly why online research is becoming such a significant part of the research industry. Decision Analysts, Inc. allows companies to test product concepts quickly using online respondents. Affirnova is a new company that allows a company to actually design new products online. Harris Interactive, Knowledge Networks, Greenfield Online, and many others allow surveys to be conducted online. All of these firms use IT to speed up and reduce the cost of research.

Marketing Researchers Should Take an Integrative Approach

Marketing researchers have created silos, which separate themselves from other information. For example, by separating research into qualitative and quantitative research, researchers tend to use one or the other when, in fact, more insights may be gained by integrating the two approaches. The same is true of modeling versus marketing research. Other silos are created when decision support systems are not linked with marketing research. Firms should integrate experiments they conduct instead of conducting one-shot projects that investigate a single issue. Mahajan and Wind also suggest greater integration of marketing research with existing databases and other information sources such as customer complaints, other studies of product/service quality, and external databases. In other words, marketing researchers would improve their results by taking a close look at all existing information instead of embarking on isolated research projects to solve a problem.

Marketing Researchers Should Expand Their Strategic Impact

Marketing research has become too comfortable in providing standard reports using simple measures. This information, although useful, does not allow marketing research to contribute to the important central issues of determining overall strategy. Research becomes relegated to a lower-level function providing information for lower-level decisions. As an example, Mahajan and Wind refer to marketing research periodically providing a report on market shares. Although this information is useful for making tactical decisions for each brand, marketing research should be providing information such defining the market. Should the company look at a broader market than the one defined? Should global market share be considered? How can the company get more from total spending in the market? These are broader, more strategic issues that, if addressed properly by marketing research, would add value to the function of marketing research.

There have been several other investigations of the research industry over the years. Some of these reviews have been made by knowledgeable persons' critiques and others have asked buyers of marketing research studies whether the value of the research performed by the suppliers in the industry is worthwhile. Critical reviews are good for the industry. John Stuart Mill once said that "custom is the enemy of progress."[18] One entire issue of *Marketing Research*, edited by Chuck Chakrapani, was devoted to a number of articles questioning customary practices in marketing research.[19] The debate these articles stirred is good for the industry. In summary, the basic conclusion of these evaluations is that the industry has performed well, but there is room for improvement. Criticism has focused on the following areas of concern: There is a lack of creativity, the industry is too survey oriented, the industry does not understand the real problems that need studying, market researchers show a lack of concern for respondents, the industry has a cavalier attitude regarding nonresponse error, the price of the research is high relative to its value, and that academic marketing research should be more closely related to actual marketing management decisions.[20]

Industry Improvements: Certification, Auditing, and Education

Even though there have been criticisms of the marketing research industry, the industry has performed well by the toughest of all standards, the test of the market-place. As we noted earlier in this chapter, revenues in the research industry have been increasing each year. Clients obviously see value in the marketing research that is being generated. However, the industry is not complacent. Many suggest that the problems are created by a very small minority of firms, most of which simply are not qualified to deliver quality marketing research services. There is obviously a concern among buyers and suppliers with the lack of uniformity in the industry as well. In a study of buyers' and suppliers' perceptions of the research industry, Dawson, Bush, and Stern found that the key issue in the industry is a lack of uniform quality; there are good suppliers and there are poor suppliers.[21]

Certification Some have argued that marketing research attracts practitioners who are not fully qualified to provide adequate service to buyer firms. There are no formal requirements, no education level, no degrees, no certificates, no licenses, and no tests of any kind required to open up a marketing research business. Certainly, the vast majority of research firms have staffs thoroughly trained in research methods and have years of excellent performance. However, some say, it is those few firms with unqualified personnel and management that tarnish the industry's image.

Professor Bruce Stern has argued that all practitioners should be certified by being required to pass a four-part exam on each of the following areas: secondary data, research methods, data analysis, and the fundamentals of marketing. As other professions such as accounting, real estate, and financial analysis have learned, **certification** programs can raise the overall level of competence within an industry.[22] Alvin Achenbaum[23] as well as Patrick Murphy and Gene Laczniak[24] have proposed a professional designation of certified public researchers (CPRs), analogous to CPAs or CFAs. Those arguing against certification point out that it would be difficult, if not impossible, to agree on defining certification standards, particularly for the creative aspect of the research process.[25]

Few would argue that William D. Neal of SDR Consulting has led the battle to create a certification for marketing researchers. We asked Mr. Neal to address this topic for this book. He provides an extract from a presentation he made to the Advertising Research Foundation in Marketing Research Insight 3.2. As you will see, Mr. Neal makes a good argument for certification of marketing researchers. In conclusion, although many believe certification should take place, there is presently no certification program for marketing researchers.

Auditing An alternative to certification is **auditing.** The concept is to have marketing research firms' work be subject to an outside, independent review for the sake of determining the quality of their work. Several years ago, Steve Bernstein, market research manager for Consolidated Freightways, proposed auditing as a means of providing the industry with some professional oversight. Bernstein suggested that the audit include assessments of, for example, research methods and data integrity. An audit would involve procedures such as retabulation from raw data of a random

Many of the problems in the research industry are created by a very small minority of firms, most of which simply are not qualified to deliver quality marketing research services.

The marketing research industry is discussing certification and auditing programs. It has also recently implemented new professional development programs for members of the industry.

The Marketing Research Profession Needs Certification[26]
Insights from William D. Neal, Founder and Senior Executive Officer, SDR Consulting

The certification of marketing researchers has been hotly debated in this country for the last 25 years. Several fact-based articles have been published on the subject along with several notable opinion articles. The two major quantitative studies on the subject (AMA, 1990; McDaniel and Solano-Mendez, Journal of Advertising Research, 1993) show very consistent results—over 60 percent of marketing researchers support certification. Younger and less experienced researchers support certification to a greater degree than their older colleagues.

Certification is a voluntary process whereby individuals receive a document recognizing that they have fulfilled the requirements of and have the knowledge base to practice in the field. Most certification program requirements include passing an objective knowledge test, demonstrating a basic level of experience, abiding to a code of professional practices, and a commitment to engaging in ongoing professional development.

There are numerous reasons our profession needs a certification program. There is too much "bad" research being delivered to clients—by untrained practitioners, by management consultants, and by ill-trained M.B.A.'s and marketing majors. This practice has a major negative impact on user organizations and it greatly depreciates both the profession and the practice of marketing research.

There are no standards or minimum qualifications for entering the field. Anyone can claim he or she is a research professional without knowing a single thing about correct procedure. Unfortunately, too many of these "pseudo-researchers" do some really bad research and the whole profession gets a black eye for the ridiculous results they deliver. On the other hand, many user organizations hire or promote unqualified people into research positions because they have no guidelines on proper credentials—be it training or experience.

Over 50 percent of the M.B.A. programs in the United States do not require a single course in marketing research. Yet, many of our clients are M.B.A.'s. Thus, the outcome is that we often have the uninformed directing the inexperienced to do the impossible, with little or no money. And, as usual, the research profession takes the rap for the usually untenable results. Outside of the handful of dedicated master's programs in marketing research, training of marketing researchers is, for the most part, haphazard and unorganized. Again, there are no standards or generally accepted credentials for the profession.

Much of the business and trade press depreciates the contributions of marketing research. How has this happened? In many cases we have let the "business" of marketing research usurp the "science" of marketing research. We let our clients do focus groups when we know they should be doing quantitative research. We compromise on sampling and sample sizes, and we too often engage in a myriad of other compromises to keep the relationship with the client. Over the years, this has weakened our professional image among the users of our product. In many other cases, we simply have ill-trained researchers overstepping their knowledge base and capabilities due mostly to a lack of adequate training and experience. The result is the same—a weakened professional image.

Certification will provide a platform and process for addressing most of these issues. A comprehensive, well-publicized certification program will finally establish the field of marketing research as a recognized profession. It will improve the practice of marketing research by promoting a core body of knowledge that can be studied and mastered by those wishing to practice in the field. Certification will improve the practice of marketing research by promoting a set of ethical standards to which those in the field would adhere. It would provide a visible signal to employers that the researcher possesses the basic knowledge and experience to practice the craft. Certification will help strengthen the relationship between purchasers and providers of marketing research services by providing a common knowledge base and a common code of professional practice. It will provide a starting point for those wishing to enter the profession. It will greatly assist professionals, especially younger professionals, in planning their careers. It will improve the image of marketing research in the eyes of external constituencies—consumers, the business press, the courts, government, and business managers. Certification will further differentiate marketing researchers from telemarketers and other direct marketers. It will provide a professional identity for both those in the profession and those who use the services of the profession. A comprehensive, well-publicized certification program will provide a signal to the entire business community that not just anyone can do marketing research. Good research takes a trained, experienced professional.

Is certification something new and radical? No. Many other specialized business professions have developed

(*box continues*)

successful certification programs, including the International Association of Business Communicators, the Public Relations Society of America, the International Customer Service Association, the Business Marketing Association, the Center for Direct Marketing, the Association of Incentive Marketing, and the Project Management Institute, to name a few.

All the pieces are in place to develop a comprehensive certification program in marketing research. We have standards of ethical practice published by MRA, AAPOR, CASRO, and others. We have a superb basic training program that is universally available online or through correspondence—the

Marketing Research Institute International's Principles of Marketing Research Program. Included with that program is a comprehensive knowledge test covering all of the basics in the field. We have a wide range of ongoing professional development programs offered annually by the major professional associations, universities, and private firms. All that is needed is for the major associations representing the profession to bring it together, organize it, and administer it.

We are part of a profession that is at least 60 years old. It's time we started acting like a profession and put a certification program in place.

---

sample of descriptive surveys, validation of a sample of questionnaires, and even checking questionnaires for evidence of selling under the guise of marketing research.[27] (We discuss the latter in the following section on ethics.)

Though proposed several years ago for the marketing research industry, the audit concept has lain dormant. However, auditing is increasing in other areas and this may create renewed interest in the concept for marketing research. The American Marketing Association has recently created a certification for **Professional Certified Marketer (PCM).** To achieve the PCM(TM) designation, candidates must fulfill several criteria such as having a bachelor's degree, four years of professional experience, or a master's degree with two years of professional experience. Candidates must also commit to high standards of ethics in the practice of marketing and pass a five-hour test of marketing knowledge. The five areas covered on this exam are legal, ethical, and professional marketing issues; the marketing mix; relationship, information, and resource management; assessment and planning of the strategic marketing process; and marketing evaluation. There are also standards for maintaining the certification such as attending professional seminars and conferences.[28] The Audit Bureau of Circulations (ABC), the auditor of magazine and other periodical circulation for many years, formed ABCi (ABC Interactive) in 2001 for the purpose of auditing traffic on Web sites.[29] Survey Sampling, Inc., a marketing research firm specializing in the provision of samples, has asked ABC to audit its samples. Thus, the use of auditing *may* still be an alternative for the industry.

Education   Although debate continues over the issue of certification and auditing may make a comeback bid, the key issue is that the industry recognizes it has certain problems, and efforts are being made to remedy them. The industry has been involved in very good continuing education programs. The AMA sponsors programs designed to increase skills in the industry. One, the AMA School of Marketing Research, is a program conducted at Notre Dame University designed to benefit the analyst, project supervisor, or manager of marketing research. The other is an annual conference on advanced analytical techniques. Also, the Marketing Research Association started an introductory program on marketing research. Coordinated at the University of Georgia, this program is designed to develop research skills of those being transferred into marketing research or those who want to enter the profession. The Marketing Research Association (MRA), Council for the Association of Survey Research Organizations (CASRO's CASRO University), and the Advertising Research Foundation (ARF) have many excellent training classes and programs frequently scheduled to meet industry needs. Several universities now offer master's-level training in marketing research (see Appendix 3 at the end of this chapter). Certain firms also provide excellent training for the industry. The Burke Institute, a division of Burke, Inc., has provided training programs for many years that are highly regarded in the industry. The institute teaches classes throughout the year on a number of topics including online research, multivariate techniques, questionnaire design, focus group moderating, basic marketing research, and many others. Any review of the industry would agree that the industry is healthy and is being responsive to its many challenges.

ETHICS AND MARKETING RESEARCH

As in most areas of business activity, there exist many opportunities for unethical (and ethical) behavior in the marketing research industry.[30] A recent study by the Ethics Resource Center of Washington, DC, states that the most common ethical problem in the total workplace is "lying to employees, customers, vendors or the public" (26 percent) followed by "withholding needed information" from those parties (25 percent). Only 5 percent of those in the study reported having seen people giving or taking "bribes, kickbacks, or inappropriate gifts." Ninety percent of American workers "expect their organizations to do what is right, not just what is profitable." But one in eight of those polled said they "feel pressure to compromise their organization's ethical standards." And among these respondents, nearly two-thirds said pressure "comes from top management, their supervisors and/or co-workers."[31] Unfortunately, the marketing research industry is not immune to ethical problems.[32] Also, online survey research has brought about several new areas of ethical concern (you will read about these in our Blue Ribbon Panel's answers shown later in this chapter). Our purpose here is to introduce you to the areas in which unethical behavior has existed in the past and hopefully to give you some framework for thinking about how you will conduct yourself in the future when confronted with these situations. We think these ethical issues are so important that we call your attention to them throughout this book using the ethical issue icon that you see at the beginning of this section.

Ethics may be defined as a field of inquiry into determining what behaviors are deemed appropriate under certain circumstances as prescribed by codes of behavior that are set by society. Society determines what is ethical and what is not ethical. In some cases, this is formalized by our institutions. Some behavior, for example, is so wrongful that it is deemed illegal by statute. In many ways, behavior that is illegal is unethical, by definition. However, there are many other behaviors that are considered by some to be unethical but are not illegal. When these types of behaviors are not spelled out by some societal institution (such as the justice system, legislature, Congress, regulatory agencies such as the FTC, etc.), then the determination of whether the behaviors are ethical or unethical is open to debate.

Your Ethical Views Are Shaped by Your Philosophy: Deontology or Teleology

There are many philosophies that may be applied to explain one's determination of appropriate behavior given certain circumstances. In the following discussion we use the two philosophies of deontology and teleology to explain this behavior.[33] **Deontology** is concerned with the rights of the individual. Is the behavior fair and just for each individual? If an individual's rights are violated, then the behavior is not ethical.[34] For example, consider the marketing research firm that has been hired to study how consumers are attracted to and react to a new form of in-store display. Researchers, hidden from view, record the behavior of unsuspecting shoppers as

We think these ethical issues are so important that we call your attention to them throughout this book using the ethical issue icon that you see here.

A number of ethical issues confront the marketing research industry.

Ethics may be defined as a field of inquiry into determining what behaviors are deemed appropriate.

One's philosophy usually determines appropriate, ethical behavior.

One philosophy is called deontology, which focuses on the rights of the individual. If an individual's rights are violated, then the behavior is not ethical.

they walk through the supermarket. A deontologist considers this form of research activity unethical because it violates the individual shopper's right to privacy. The deontologist would likely agree to the research provided the shoppers were informed beforehand that their behavior would be recorded, giving them the option to participate or not to participate.[35]

Teleology is a philosophy that focuses on the trade-off between individual costs and group benefits. If benefits outweigh costs, the behavior is judged to be ethical.

On the other hand, **teleology** analyzes a given behavior in terms of its benefits and costs to society. If there are individual costs but group benefits, then there are net gains and the behavior is judged to be ethical.[36] In our example of the shopper being observed in the supermarket, the teleologist might conclude that, although there is a violation of the right to privacy among those shoppers observed (the cost), there is a benefit if the company learns how to market goods more efficiently, thus reducing long-term marketing costs. Because this benefit ultimately is shared by many more individuals than those whose privacy was invaded during the original study, the teleologist would likely declare this research practice to be ethical.

Thus, how you view a behavior as being ethical or unethical depends on your philosophy. Are you a deontologist or a teleologist? (See Case 3.1 at the end of this chapter). It's difficult to answer that question until you are placed in an ethically sensitive situation. One thing that is for certain is that you will come across ethically sensitive situations during your career. Will you know it's an ethically sensitive situation? How will you respond? We hope you will at least know when you are in an ethically sensitive situation in marketing research. The rest of this section is devoted to teaching you this sensitivity.[37]

The British Market Research Association has a code of ethics. Visit its Web site at www.bmra.org.uk. Also, the Market Research Society of New Zealand has a code of ethics. Visit its Web site at www.mrsnz.org.nz.

Ethical Behavior in Marketing Research

As noted previously, there are many ways a society may prescribe wanted and unwanted behaviors. In business, if there are practices that are not illegal but are nevertheless thought to be wrong, trade associations or professional organizations will often prescribe a **code of ethical behavior.** This has been the case in marketing and, more specifically, in marketing research. The American Marketing Association (www.marketingpower.com), the Council of American Survey Research Organizations (www.casro.org), the Qualitative Research Consultants Association (www.qrca.org), the Marketing Research Association (www.mra-net.org), and the Canadian-based Professional Market Research Society (www.pmrs-aprm.com) all have a code of ethics. The European-based ESOMAR, the European Society for Marketing Research (www.esomar.nl), has a code of ethics that is adopted by many marketing research organizations around the world such as the Market Research Society of Australia, Ltd. All over the world, marketing research organizations are striving to achieve ethical behavior among practitioners of marketing research.

Codes of Ethics   As noted previously, the American Marketing Association has a code of ethics. You can read the code in entirety at its Web site (www.marketingpower.com.). However, the AMA's "full" code contains some specific codes for marketing research as follows. *In the area of marketing research:*[38]

> prohibiting selling (Sugging) or fund raising (Frugging) under the guise of conducting research;
>
> maintaining research integrity by avoiding misrepresentation and omission of pertinent research data;
>
> treating outside clients and suppliers fairly.

Sugging and Frugging   The first provision of the AMA code deals with prohibiting selling or fund raising under the guise of conducting research. **Sugging** refers to "selling under the guise of a survey." Typically, sugging occurs when a "researcher" gains a respondent's cooperation to participate in a research study and then uses the opportunity to attempt to sell the respondent a good or service. Most consumers are quite willing to provide their attitudes and opinions of products and services in response to a legitimate request for this information. Suggers (and Fruggers), however, take advantage of that goodwill by deceiving unsuspecting consumers. Consumers soon learn that their cooperation in answering a few questions has led to their being subjected to a sales presentation. In sugging and frugging there is no good-faith effort to conduct a survey for the purpose of collecting and analyzing data for specific purposes. Rather, the intent of the "fake" survey is to sell or raise money. Of course, these practices have led to the demise of the pool of cooperative respondents. Marketing Research Insight 3.3 fully explains sugging and frugging. The Telemarketing and Consumer Fraud and Abuse Prevention Act of 1994 seeks to put an end to sugging by telemarketers. Under this act, telemarketers will not be allowed to call someone and say they are conducting a survey, and try to sell a product or service. Although telemarketers are not able to legally practice sugging, the act does not prohibit sugging via the mails.[39] **Frugging** is closely related to sugging and stands for "fund raising under the guise of a survey." Because frugging does not involve the sale of a product or service, it is not covered in the Telemarketing and Consumer Fraud and Abuse Prevention Act of 1994, but it is widely considered to be unethical. Actually, sugging and frugging are carried out by telemarketers or other direct marketers. Researchers do not practice sugging and frugging. However, we cover this topic because both sugging and frugging are unethical treatments of potential respondents in marketing research. Also, we give it special attention because both practices have been significant to the industry for several years.

Research Integrity Sometimes research is not totally objective. Information is withheld, falsified, or altered to protect vested interests.

Marketing research information is often used in making significant decisions. The outcome of the decision may impact future company strategy, budgets, jobs, organization, and so forth. With so much at stake, the opportunity exists for a lack of total objectivity in the research process. The loss of **research integrity** may take the form of withholding information, falsifying data, altering research results, or misinterpreting the research findings in a way that makes them more consistent with predetermined points of view. As one researcher stated, "I refused to alter research results and as a result I was fired for failure to think strategically."[40] We now know that this was all too common in the field of auditing. The Enron fiasco of 2002 taught the world that even the highly esteemed field of auditing is subject to a failure of research integrity. A breakdown occurred when Anderson was the auditing firm and also the managerial consulting firm.[41] The impetus for a breach in research integrity may come from either the supplier or buyer. If a research supplier knows that a buyer will want marketing research services in the future, the supplier may alter a study's results or withhold information, so that the study will support the buyer's wishes. The buyer may not be aware of any departure from total objectivity but is very pleased with the study results and, according to the thinking of the supplier firm, is more likely to use the supplier company again in the future.

Breaches of research integrity need not be isolated to those managing the research project. Interviewers have been known to make up interviews and to take shortcuts in completing surveys. In fact, there is some evidence that this is more of a problem than was once thought.[42]

Maintaining research integrity is regarded as one of the most significant ethical issues in the research industry. In a study of 460 marketing researchers, Hunt,

MARKETING RESEARCH
INSIGHT
3.3

Sugging and Frugging
Diane Bowers, President, CASRO

Diane K. Bowers is the president of the Council of American Survey Research Organizations (CASRO), with which she has been associated since 1979. She is also a member of ESOMAR's Professional Standards Committee and sits on the board of advisors of the Masters in Marketing Research programs at the University of Georgia, the University of Texas at Arlington, and the University of Wisconsin at Madison. In addition, Diane is a past president of the Council for Marketing and Opinion Research (CMOR), the Market Research Council (MRC), and the Research Industry Coalition (RIC).

Sugging

"Sugging" or selling under the guise of research is a short-hand term to describe a misuse of the public trust and an abuse of the survey research process that has been promulgated by telemarketers as a means to get a "foot in the door."

This practice had become so commonplace that the public, the research industry, and, ultimately, the federal government decided to put an end to it. In 1994 a federal law was enacted that provided the public and the research industry with a weapon to combat sugging. The Consumer Fraud and Abuse Prevention Act included an amendment requiring telemarketers to promptly state at the beginning of a telephone call that they were selling a good or service.

After the passage of this law the Federal Trade Commission (FTC) promulgated rules for the enforcement of the law, now called the "Telemarketing Sales Rule," affirming the antisugging component. The FTC specifically has emphasized that ". . . the legislative history of the Telemarketing Act noted the problem of deceptive telemarketers contacting potential victims under the guise of conducting a poll, survey, or other type of market research. To address these problems, the Commission believes that in any multiple purpose call where the seller or telemarketer plans, in at least some of those calls, to sell goods or services, the disclosures required. . . must be made 'promptly,' during the first part of the call, before the non-sales portion of the call takes place. Only in this manner will the Rule assure that a sales call is not being made under the guise of a survey research call, or a call for some other purpose."

Recently, the FTC has stepped up its enforcement efforts by recommending that a "National Do Not Call" list be created through which consumers could dictate their desire not to be contacted by telemarketers.

Frugging

"Frugging," or fund raising under the guise of research, is as commonplace and offensive as sugging. In these instances political and social organizations, nonprofit enterprises, charitable, and even educational organizations use the guise of a survey to solicit contributions, support, alumni gifts, membership, and so on for their institution or cause. Examples of frugging include letters from political campaigns or environmental causes that include the words "Survey Enclosed" stamped on the outside of the envelope. The so-called "survey" usually includes only a few leading questions, all with an obvious morally correct answer, such as "Do you favor protecting our children from harm?" At the end of the survey (often in the form of the last question in the survey) is a request for money, support, or membership. The law has not caught up with these abusive practices, probably because the institutions or causes that commit frugging are generally worthwhile and commendable. Industry efforts to educate fruggers have been modestly successful, but the practice continues and public complaints have increased.

Chonko, and Wilcox found that maintenance of research integrity posed the most significant problem for one-third of those sampled.[43]

Treating Others Fairly Several ethical issues may arise in the practice of marketing research that center around how others are treated. Suppliers, buyers, and the public may be treated unethically.

Sometimes firms buying marketing research are treated unethically. For example, they are sold unnecessary research or supplier firms subcontract the work to other firms for less money and, therefore, take profits without doing the research themselves. Buyers also treat supplier firms unethically. Agreements are not honored, payments are delayed, and buyers sometimes ask supplier firms to provide them with research designs without ever intending on contracting with an external supplier.

Buyers. In the Hunt, Chonko, and Wilcox study cited previously, the second most frequently stated ethical problem facing marketing researchers was fair treatment of buyer firms. A little over one-tenth of the respondents claimed this was the most important ethical problem they faced. Unfair treatment of buyers can take many forms. *Passing hidden charges* to buyers, *overlooking study requirements* when subcontracting work out to other supplier firms, and *selling unnecessary research* are examples of unfair treatment of buyer firms. By overlooking study requirements, such as qualifying respondents on specified characteristics or verifying that respondents were interviewed, the supplier firm may lower its cost of using the services of a subcontracting field service firm. A supplier firm may oversell research services to naive buyers by convincing them to use a more expensive research design, such as a causal design in lieu of a descriptive design, or using more subjects than is necessary.

Sharing confidential and proprietary information raises ethical questions. Virtually all work conducted by marketing research firms is confidential and proprietary. Researchers build up a storehouse of this information as they conduct research studies. Most ethical issues involving confidentiality revolve around how this storehouse of information, or "background knowledge," is treated. One researcher stated, "Where does 'background knowledge' stop and conflict exist (as a result of work with a previous client)?"[44] As an example, let us assume that a marketing research firm conducts a number of market surveys for buyer Firm A. Information collected in the survey reveals important customer perceptions of Firm B, one of Firm A's major competitors. After completing the project for Firm A, the research firm recognizes the value of the survey information to Firm B and approaches the management of Firm B to sell it a survey that is "guaranteed" to identify important consumer perceptions about its firm. Is this ethical? Such a situation illustrates how "background knowledge" may be used but violates the confidentiality trust that must be maintained between research suppliers and buyers.

Sharing of "background knowledge" among firms raises ethical questions.

It is common practice among research supplier firms to check their existing list of buyer-clients to ensure there is no conflict of interest before accepting work from a new buyer. Let's say a buyer representing an out-patient medical facility in City A requests research assistance from a supplier firm. Before accepting the work, the supplier firm determines that it already has client firms that would be considered competitors of the new buyer firm. In most cases, the new buyer would be told that it would have to seek services elsewhere since there would be a conflict of interest.

Suppliers. Phony RFPs. Buyers also abuse suppliers of marketing research. A major problem exists, for example, when a firm having internal research capabilities issues a request for proposals (RFPs) from external supplier firms. External firms then spend time and money developing research designs to solve the stated problem, estimating costs of the project, and so on. Now, having collected several detailed proposals outlining research designs and costs, the abusing firm decides to do the job internally. There may be cases in which this is justifiable, but certainly issuing a call for proposals from external firms with no intention of doing the job outside is unethical behavior. Closely related to this practice is that of issuing proposal requests from external firms when another external firm has been awarded the contract. The proposals are used, once again, as a check on costs and procedures.

Failure to honor time and money agreements. Often buyer firms have obligations such as agreeing to meetings or the provision of materials needed for the research project. Supplier firms must have these commitments from buyers in a timely fashion in order to keep to their time schedules. Buyer firms sometimes abuse their agreements to deliver personnel or these other resources in the time to which they have agreed. Also, buyers sometimes do not honor commitments to pay for services. Unethical buyers may claim they may no longer need the research information or that the information provided by the research firm is not of value in an attempt to justify their nonpayment. This is a good reason for the research firm to remain in close communication with the buyer firm throughout the research process. Close communication helps to assure that the information provided is the information of value to the buyer. However, some buyers are simply unethical in terms of not paying their bills. Although this happens in many industries, research suppliers do not have the luxury of repossession although there are, of course, legal recourses.

The Public. *Research on products thought to be dangerous to society.* Ethical issues arise as researchers balance marketing requirements with social issues. This is particularly true in the areas of product development and advertising. For example, marketing researchers have expressed concern over conducting research on advertising to children. Some advertising has had the objective of increasing the total consumption of refined sugar among children via advertising scheduled during Saturday morning TV programs. Other ethical concerns arise when conducting research on products researchers felt were dangerous to the public such as certain chemicals and cigarettes. More recently, television networks are considering changing their policy of not allowing the advertising of alcoholic beverages. Undoubtedly, there will be debate about the appropriateness of this advertising. It is likely that researchers will be asked to conduct research on the effectiveness of televised alcoholic beverage ads. Imagine the ethical dilemma a researcher is faced with if asked to develop an effective advertising message to attract teens to drinking bourbon?

> Ethical concerns arise when marketing researchers are asked to conduct research on advertising to children or on products they feel are dangerous to the public such as certain chemicals, cigarettes, alcohol, or sugar.

Respondents. Respondents are the "lifeblood" of the marketing research industry. Respondent cooperation rates have been going down and the industry is concerned with the ethical treatment of the existing respondent pool.[45]

In 1982, CMOR (Council for Marketing and Opinion Research) began monitoring survey response cooperation. CMOR surveys a large number of consumers from time to time to determine the percentage of the population that has refused to take part in a survey in the past year. The percentages have risen sharply: 1982 (15 percent), 1992 (31 percent), 1999 (40 percent), and in 2002 the percentage was 45 percent.[46]

Marketing researchers must honor promises made to respondents that the respondent's identity will remain confidential or anonymous if they expect respondents to cooperate in requests for information in the future.

The very nature of marketing research requires an invasion, to some degree, of individual privacy. The majority of the U.S. public is concerned about threats to personal privacy.

Deception. Respondents may be deceived during the research process. Kimmel and Smith point out that deception may occur during subject recruitment (they are not told the true identity/sponsor of the research, etc.), during the research procedure itself (they are viewed without their knowledge, etc.), and during postresearch situations (there is a violation of the promise of anonymity). Also, these authors suggest that there are serious consequences to this deception.[47]

Deception can occur in two basic forms. First is by omission (also called **passive deception**) of information to fully inform a respondent. For example, respondents are asked to participate in a study of "choice of a personal bank." They are not told the study is being conducted by the particular bank sponsoring the research. Second, deception by commission (also called **active deception**) refers to intentionally giving the respondent false information. This may be done for many reasons, such as "creating a setting in order to provide a plausible context for an experiment." For example, in a study to determine how consumers behave when they are uncertain of their judgments, to "create" the "uncertainty" researchers may give them false feedback about their judgments on a task.[48] Deception of any sort should be held to minimum use in research. Still, it may be necessary, in some studies, to deceive respondents. In those cases, respondents should be debriefed. Debriefing occurs after a study and should follow the guidelines of the National Research Act of 1974. The respondents should be provided with the complete and truthful description of the study and its sponsors. The researcher should identify and accurately describe any and all deceptions that occurred and present a rationale for their use. The latter is called "dehoaxing." If applicable, an attempt should be made to deal with the negative effect (bad feelings, moods, and emotions) that may have been generated by deception. The attempt to reduce these negative effects is referred to as desensitizing.[49] Case 3.1 deals with a situation involving deception of respondents.

Confidentiality and Anonymity. One way of gaining a potential respondent's trust is by promising confidentiality or anonymity. **Confidentiality** means that the researcher knows who the respondent is but does not identify the respondent with any information gathered from that respondent to a client. So the respondent's identity is confidential information known only by the researcher. A stronger appeal may be made under conditions of **anonymity.** The respondent is, and remains, anonymous or unknown. The researcher is only interested in gathering information from the respondent and does not know who the respondent is. The latter often happens with telephone interviews that have been obtained by randomly dialed telephone numbers.

Ethical issues arise when the respondents are promised confidentiality and anonymity and the researcher fails to honor this promise. There are pressures to identify respondents. Clients are often in the business of identifying leads for sales presentations. Suppose research is conducted to identify consumers' interest in a new service. In order to gain their cooperation, researchers promise potential respondents confidentiality. After the research, the client naïvely asks for the list of names of all those respondents who expressed some interest in the new service. A researcher complying with this request is acting unethically. More egregious is the situation wherein the respondents are told they are anonymous yet the researcher knows their identity and uses that identity in some way such as making a sales contact.

In some cases, however, respondents want to be identified. Suppose a new product or service is being evaluated through research and certain respondents are very interested in the service. They may desire to be contacted as soon as the product or service is available. In such cases, respondents should be asked during the research process if they would like to be contacted. If they would, then identifying the respondent to a client would not be considered unethical.

Invasions of Privacy. Marketing research, by its nature, is invasive. Any information acquired from a respondent has some degree of invasiveness. Ethical issues, some of them legal, abound in the area of invading others' privacy. For many years, marketing researchers have been concerned about issues such as observing others without their permission. Under certain conditions, this should be avoided at all costs. For example, consider a company that decides to conduct research by placing researchers in homes for the purpose of watching consumers' behavior and learning about their attitudes, media habits, purchasing preferences, and so forth. This may be perfectly acceptable as long as the family being studied is aware of the researchers' intention. A few years ago, however, quite a controversy ensued when a researcher from another country was placed in a U.S. family's home posing as an exchange student! The family was totally unaware that they were being observed and studied for commercial purposes. Obviously, this was a terrible violation of privacy rights. But what about a company observing you in a public place and not placing you in a situation that would be considered unsafe? Watching you shop in a supermarket, for example. This is not regarded as unethical by most researchers. As we shall see in the following paragraphs, online research brings with it serious opportunities for violations of privacy rights.

Spam. When online survey research became a possibility by accessing respondents via the Internet, some organizations viewed this as an easy, fast way to gather survey information. They gave little concern to ethical issues when they obtained e-mail lists to use to target survey recipients. They began sending out thousands of surveys to unwary persons. The practice of sending unwanted e-mail is called spamming. An electronic message has been defined as **spam** if (1) the recipient's personal identity and context are irrelevant because the message is equally applicable to many other potential recipients; (2) the recipient has not verifiably granted deliberate, explicit, and still revocable permission for it to be sent; and (3) the transmission and reception of the message appear to the recipient to give a disproportionate benefit to the sender.[50] Although the practice of sending spam ads and surveys continues today, much of it has been stopped thanks to organizations like Mail Abuse Prevention System (MAPS). Visit the MAPS Web site at www.mail.abuse.org.

Marketing Research and Spam Surveys

As we have noted previously, the Internet provides researchers with the ability to access millions of potential respondents. However, how they access these potential respondents is critical in determining whether unethical practices are being used. In the early days of the Internet, before guidelines regarding spam were established, several research firms e-mailed unsuspecting respondents surveys. Still, many may be doing this. Some know that they are spamming and others are simply uninformed. In the section that follows, we present information that clarifies when an e-mailed survey is or is not ethical.

Opt-Out vs. Opt-In Standards[51] There is an ongoing debate regarding what practices actually constitute invasions of privacy. Slowly, legislation is being adopted around the world that helps to define this issue. One common theme in the legislation has been the individual's right of consent. One consent standard is the "**opt-out**" standard. Under this standard, individuals are given the opportunity to not be contacted again and/or to limit the manner in which information they provide may be used. On the other hand, the alternative standard, to "**opt-in**," means that individuals must specifically and affirmatively consent to a specified activity, such as being given an online survey via their e-mail. Opt-in is referred to as "active consent" and has been preferred by many privacy advocates for the reason that it allows the individual full control. That is, respondents never receive the survey unless they have opted-in to take it. Others argue that the ability to opt-out, also known as "passive consent," provides ample control to individuals. To more clearly understand the differences, let's think of the calls you receive from telemarketers. Telemarketing laws exist that allow individuals to be put on lists that telemarketers are not to call. This would be an example of the opt-out standard. Some argue that the problem with this standard is that it puts the burden on the individual to protect his or her privacy rights. They must know how information about themselves is being used and also know the process for the "opt-out." For example, your supermarket may be selling information on what you buy. Under the opt-out standard, you, the consumer must know that this is occurring so that you may pursue an opt-out opportunity. And, once you decide that you do not want this information about you to be used, you must invest in time and effort to learn how you can opt-out. A bill, the Consumer Online Privacy and Disclosure Act, requires Web sites to post privacy policies on their sites as well as provisions for consumers to opt-out of the disclosure of information about them that is collected at the Web site.

Opt-in is a much tougher standard. In terms of telemarketing, for example, the use of an **opt-in** standard would mean you would have to consent to receiving telemarketing calls prior to telemarketers calling you. So, under the opt-in standard, you would have to be told by the supermarket that you could participate in its program to obtain information about your purchases. If you refused to opt-in, your privacy would be protected. Under the opt-in standard you would be protected from others obtaining information about you without your knowledge and it would save you the time and effort of learning how to opt-out. If you don't opt-in, you do not have to opt-out.

Online Research

Legislative bodies will likely continue the debate as to which standard, opt-in versus opt-out, should be used in privacy laws. The marketing research industry has been self-regulating itself through codes of standards using the opt-in standard. CASRO has been an industry leader in helping to shape not only ethical standards for the industry but in also trying to ensure that legislation passed to deal with telemarketers does not include legitimate marketing researchers. Marketing Research Insight 3.4 provides you with information about CASRO.

What Does the CASRO Code of Ethics Say About
Online Survey Research and Spamming?

We asked Diane K. Bowers, director of CASRO, to provide you with some additional information illustrating what online survey researchers can and cannot do when it comes to using the Internet to collect online survey information. We present her guidance to you in the following paragraphs, which first depict a specific statement in the CASRO Code of Ethics followed by further explanation of the application of the code by Ms. Bowers.

The following statements are taken from the CASRO Code of Ethics, Responsibilities to Respondents; Privacy and the Avoidance of Harassment, Section 3. Internet Research:

> *The unique characteristics of Internet research require specific notice that the principle of respondent privacy applies to this new technology and data collection methodology. The general principle of this section of the Code is that survey research organizations will not use unsolicited e-mails to recruit respondents for surveys.*

Ms. Bowers: "Online research is unique in that it is not permissible for online researchers to randomly e-mail individuals requesting participation in online research. For other data collection methods (telephone, for example) a randomly selected sample is not only permitted but is desirable from a statistical standpoint. Current and proposed state laws (1) prohibit the sending of unsolicited e-mails, and/or (2) require adherence to Internet Service Providers'

MARKETING RESEARCH
INSIGHT

3.4

An Ethical Issue ◀

CASRO Fights for Ethical Standards

The Council of American Survey Research Organizations (CASRO) was founded in 1975. As the national trade association of commercial survey research companies, CASRO represents over 170 companies that account for more than 85 percent of the survey revenue in the United States. Members not only join CASRO for its role in the survey research industry, but they also join CASRO because it provides members with additional support and insights in areas such as business operations, staff development, networking, business development, and management.

Purpose

The main objectives of this organization are to educate, to protect, and to represent. CASRO continuously communicates to the industry and the public about the changes taking place in the research arena. Furthermore, CASRO is committed to educate the industry and the public to understand the ongoing changes in the research world. CASRO requires all members to adhere to its Code of Standards and Ethics for Survey Research in order to protect the public's right and privacy. In addition, CASRO set standards for conducting online research because it recognizes the importance of the Internet as a growing data collection medium.

Mission

The following list highlights CASRO's mission

Provides the environment and leadership that will promote the growth and best interests of firms in the survey research industry

Promotes the establishment, maintenance, and improvement of the professional and ethical standards

Communicates the standards, contributions, and achievements of the survey research industry

As the nation's leading survey research trade organization, CASRO plays an important role in shaping the survey research industry. First, it sets research standards and guidelines for the industry and the survey research process. Second, it informs members on the current events affecting the survey research industry. Third, it is involved in the legal and ethical issues that face the survey research industry. In 2001, CASRO adopted the theme "Taking Responsibility for the Future" to communicate its commitment to industry. Therefore, CASRO is prepared to meet the changing environment of the survey research industry.

Contact Information
Council of American Survey Research (CASRO)
3 Upper Devon
Port Jefferson, New York 11777
Phone: (631) 928-6954
Fax: (631) 928-6041
E-mail: **casro@casro.org**
Web site: **www.casro.org**

Source: www.casro.org

policies which prohibit "spamming," and/or (3) prohibit the sending of unsolicited e-mails to people who have requested not to receive further e-mails from a particular company."

Research organizations are required to verify that individuals contacted for research by e-mail have a reasonable expectation that they will receive e-mail contact for research. Such agreement can be assumed when ALL of the following conditions exist.

(1) A substantive pre-existing relationship exists between the individuals contacted and the research organization, the client or the list owners contracting the research (the latter being so identified);

Ms. Bowers: This raises the question of what is a '**substantive pre-existing relationship?**' At CASRO we believe that such a relationship exists when there has been a business transaction or customer/consumer communication or correspondence in which the individual has voluntarily supplied his/her e-mail address for future research, marketing or correspondence contact. The relationship must be evident to the person being e-mailed—in other words, the e-mailed person must have a definable connection with the person contacting him or her. If that connection is with the research company, the research company must be identified. If the relationship is with a client, the client must be identified."

(2) Individuals have a reasonable expectation, based on the pre-existing relationship, that they may be contacted for research;

Ms. Bowers: "We define a reasonable expectation as a sufficient belief on the individual's part that he or she may be contacted via e-mail for research purposes in connection with or as a follow-up to a preexisting relationship with the person doing the contacting."

(3) Individuals are offered the choice to be removed from future e-mail contact in each invitation; and,

Ms. Bowers: "The identified researcher (or client) who has a preexisting relationship with the individual e-mailed for research purposes must give that individual the chance to opt out of the specific online research study and ALL future online research studies in this preexisting relationship."

(4) The invitation list excludes all individuals who have previously taken the appropriate and timely steps to request the list owner to remove them.

Ms. Bowers: "Researchers or clients must maintain a '**do-not-e-mail**' list of those individuals who have opted out of future online research studies."

Research organizations are prohibited from using any subterfuge in obtaining e-mail addresses of potential respondents, such as collecting e-mail addresses from public domains, using technologies or techniques to collect e-mail addresses without individuals' awareness, and collecting e-mail addresses under the guise of some other activity.

Ms. Bowers: "In traditional sampling, it is acceptable to buy lists, use customer databases, buy data in the public domain, and so on. None of this is acceptable in online research unless the sample e-mail addresses are of individuals who have expressly agreed to be contacted for research purposes. Several states require ISPs to obtain the consent of their subscribers prior to selling or releasing subscribers' names or e-mail addresses."

Research organizations are prohibited from using false or misleading return e-mail addresses when recruiting respondents over the Internet.

Ms. Bowers: "Researchers must be straightforward and direct in their relationship with respondents and may not mislead respondents with disguised e-mail addresses. Several states have passed laws against transmission of false e-mails and misrepresentation of point of origin of e-mail."

When receiving e-mail lists from clients or list owners, research organizations are required to have the client or list provider verify that individuals listed have a reasonable expectation that they will receive e-mail contact, as defined, . . . above.

Ms. Bowers: "This restates that clients have the same responsibility as researchers in ensuring that individuals have agreed to be contacted by e-mail for research based on the four assumptions . . . above."

BLUE RIBBON
PANEL on
[Online Research]

Q: *What ethical issues has online marketing research created and how would you evaluate how the industry has handled these issues?*

Bill MacElroy
President
Socratic Technologies

A: Historically, the violations of online etiquette have been committed not out of malice but out of a lack of familiarity with the customs of Web interaction. Many firms are simply doing things the way that things have always been done in the traditional research world. But things like calling people at home without permission, sending people unsolicited business offers, selling magazine subscriber lists, and so on have no acceptable analogous counterparts in the online world. Online these would be considered serious invasions of privacy and spam.

Although the industry is actively examining these types of issues and attempting to create meaningful codes of ethics (like IMRO), new players are continually entering the field (some through acquisition or corporate takeover). We see many instances where the first instinct of financially motivated newcomers is to spam, spam, spam and let the long-run consequences be damned. However, the long run is not that far away. And people who turn respondents off by bad and unacceptable recruitment and survey behavior will only serve to hurt their own business, as well as everyone else's.

George Harmon
Senior Vice President
Digital Marketing
Services

A: Online marketing research has solved more ethical issues than it has created. Online research is unquestionably held to higher standards than off-line research. Online privacy guidelines are far more stringent with regard to contact, collection, and use of information.

Online research's automated interviewing process also has great ethical advantages. Software systems, unlike human interviewers, are less likely to lead respondents to the answers they want to fill daily/weekly quotas, and so on.

George Terhanian
Vice President of
Internet Research
Harris Interactive,
Inc.

A: The market research industry has been quite successful at contending with issues involving the ethical propriety of conducting all forms of research, including online research. Issues that have arisen in recent years, which are not necessarily unique to online research, have involved respondent confidentiality, e-mail etiquette, data transmission, data storage, and data linkage. In general, the major players in the industry exhibited exemplary practices from the start. Industry associations such as CASRO and ESOMAR, as well as online watchdog groups, thereafter have played an important role in contributing to the development and definition of ethical propriety in online research.

Keith Price
Vice President
Greenfield Online

A: Greenfield Online strongly believes that companies using the Internet need to govern the rights of users. From our beginnings, we have taken responsibility for protecting privacy and know that if we abuse the power the Internet and technology brings in reaching out to consumers, we will lose respondent cooperation and encourage government intervention. Greenfield Online is a member of TRUSTe and BBBOnLine. We have helped the research community create guidelines for online research with active participation in CASRO (Council of American Research Survey Organization) and as a founding member of IMRO (Internet Marketing Research Organization). We adhere to the highest consumer privacy standards regarding respondent information.

The online research community as a whole has created a number of organizations that help to govern the usage of online research and, unlike most industries, has truly banded together to develop standards and combat legislation that could negatively impact the online research industry.

A: The issue of import is that of personal privacy. Online research has a potential for facilitating connecting more personally identifying information than traditional measures. This can occur in a variety of ways ranging from how consumers are "invited" to participate to keeping track of these consumers via cookies to installing software on consumers' PCs, which enables recording all of their online activity.

Doss Struse
*Senior Vice President
Client Service
Knowledge Networks,
Inc.*

Associated with this issue is how companies gain informed consent from consumers to gather and use their information. It is easy to create a permission or privacy statement that is so long and detailed that consumers might skip reading it carefully, enabling an unscrupulous firm to hide its intention to use the information obtained very aggressively.

What Do Online Research Industry Leaders Have to Say About Ethical Issues Related to Online Research?

Now that you have an appreciation of ethical issues in marketing research, we wanted you to see what industry leaders have to say about what they see as ethical issues in online research and how they handle these issues.

Ethical issues abound in the practice of marketing research. Treating buyers, suppliers, the public, and respondents fairly is a basic ethical tenet necessary for the health of the research industry. As technology that allows for the tracking of individual behaviors increases, individuals are justifiably more and more concerned with privacy rights. Online research represents yet another possible avenue to invade individuals' cyberspace. However, with organizations such as IMRO, CASRO, and the MRA, marketing researchers are adopting their own standards for the ethical treatment of respondents. Yet, the future is cloudy in terms of how legal actions will affect research. Already, research firms, realizing that respondents are their "lifeblood," are moving in the direction of recruiting their own panels of willing respondents. Recruiting and maintaining a panel requires a considerable investment. **Panel equity,** the value of readily available access to willing respondents, may become more and more important in the future. Marketing research firms, recognizing the value they have in panels, will make even greater effort to ensure fair and ethical treatment of their panel respondents.

SUMMARY

This chapter covered four introductory topics. First, it reviewed the history of the use of marketing research. In the "pre–marketing research era," marketing research was not needed because businesses had many face-to-face contacts with their customers. During the "early development era," the industrial revolution led to marketing to customers in distant markets, which created the need for marketing research to understand those distant markets. Questionnaires began to be used in the "questionnaire era" and statistical concepts and computers were applied to marketing research in the "quantitative era." By 1960 marketing research departments became commonplace in what we call the "organizational acceptance era." During the 1980s marketing research was shaped by the invention of the PC. We call this decade the "PC technology era." Since 1990 two factors have greatly impacted the research industry and we call this time period the "globalization–online research era."

The marketing research industry has a number of unique players, and we described them as internal suppliers and external suppliers of marketing research information. The external suppliers may be further categorized as either full-service or limited-service firms. Syndicated data services, standardized services, customized service firms, and online research service firms are all full-service firms. Limited-service firms include field services, market segment specialists, sample design and distribution services, data analysis services, and specialized research technique firms. Internal suppliers of marketing research have their own formal departments (AT&T, Kodak, GM), have no department but entrust an individual or a committee with the research function, or assign no one with responsibility for marketing research. External supplier firms are outside firms hired to fulfill a firm's marketing research needs. "The Honomichl Top 50" is an annual report that shows the top 50 external supplier firms. The research industry is an $8 billion industry and has experienced growth rates around 8 percent per year. Online research firms' revenues have been growing in double-digit figures for several years. Online research revenues are well over $300 million. External suppliers organize by function, area of research application, geography, by type of customer, or some combination of these. Research firms have recently been forming "strategic alliances," which allow for two or more firms to take advantage of other firms' skills and resources. DMS, for example, develops samples taken from AOL subscribers and SPSS MR supplies expertise in analytics. The combination of these three organizations can provide excellent online survey research studies to client firms.

The marketing research industry's performance is evaluated from time to time. In general, these reviews show that the industry is doing a reasonably good job but there is room for improvement. Suggestions are made for some of these improvements. Some industry leaders have called for a formal certification program for marketing research professionals or even an auditing system to ensure consistency of performance across the industry. The research industry has started several professional development programs for its members in recent years. These educational programs come from industry professional organizations such as CASRO, MRA, and the AMA. Also, there are private educational programs of excellent quality such as the Burke Institute. Finally, colleges and universities are becoming more involved in providing specialized master's-level programs in marketing research. The University of Georgia sponsors an online course in marketing research designed to train those entering the field of marketing research with the fundamentals of marketing research similar to what you will learn in the course you are taking now.

Ethical issues in marketing research are more important today than ever. A number of ethical issues are present in the practice of marketing research. Individuals differ in terms of their sensitivity to the presence of ethical issues. Ethics is defined as a field of inquiry into determining what behaviors are deemed appropriate under certain circumstances as prescribed by codes of behavior that are set by society. How you respond to ethically sensitive situations depends on your philosophy: deontology or teleology. Several organizations in the research industry have codes of ethical behavior for both buyers and suppliers of research. Sugging is illegal. Frugging is very unethical. Ethical issues include research integrity, treating others (buyers, suppliers, the public, and respondents) fairly. Respondent fairness issues include deception, confidentiality, and invasions of privacy. Spam surveys are an invasion of privacy. Special standards are provided to online marketing researchers to protect the privacy of online respondents. In the future, we can probably expect more legislation affecting access to respondents. Research companies, faced with a declining pool of willing respondents in the general public, will rely more heavily on recruiting their own panel members. Your authors believe that by recruiting and maintaining their own panels of respondents, research companies will come to value their "panel equity" and we will see even fairer treatment of respondents in the future.

KEY TERMS

Pre–marketing research era (p. 46)
Early development era (p. 46)
Questionnaire era (p. 47)
Quantitative era (p. 47)
Organizational acceptance era (p. 47)
PC technology era (p. 47)
Globalization–online era (p. 48)
Research supplier (p. 48)
Internal supplier (p. 48)
External suppliers (p. 51)
Strategic alliances (p. 55)
Full-service supplier firms (p. 55)
Syndicated data service firms (p. 56)
Standardized service firms (p. 56)
Customized service firms (p. 56)
Online research services firms (p. 56)
Limited-service supplier firms (p. 56)
Field service firms (p. 56)
Market segment specialists (p. 57)
Sample design and distribution (p. 57)
Data analysis services (p. 57)

Specialized research technique firms
  (p. 57)
Certification (p. 60)
Auditing (p. 60)
Professional Certified Marketer
  (PCM) (p. 62)
Ethics (p. 63)
Deontology (p. 63)
Teleology (p. 64)
Code of ethical behavior (p. 64)
Sugging (p. 64)
Frugging (p. 65)
Research integrity (p. 65)
Passive deception (p. 69)
Active deception (p. 69)
Confidentiality (p. 69)
Anonymity (p. 69)
Spam (p. 70)
Opt-out (p. 70)
Opt-in (p. 71)
Panel equity (p. 75)

REVIEW QUESTIONS/APPLICATIONS

1. Explain why marketing research was not needed during the "pre–marketing research era."
2. Explain why marketing research was needed during the "early development era."
3. Explain what has happened in terms of the history of marketing research since about 1980.
4. We categorized firms as internal and external suppliers of marketing research information. Explain what is meant by each and give an example of each type of firm.
5. Distinguish among full-service, limited-service, syndicated data services, standardized services, and customized service firms.
6. How would you categorize the following firms?
   a. a firm specializing in marketing to kids (6–12)
   b. a firm that specializes in a computerized scent generator for testing reactions to smells
   c. a firm that offers a package for running test markets
   d. a firm that consists of consultants that can offer research on all functional areas (i.e., finance, marketing, production, human resources, etc.)
   e. a firm that collects data on Web site visits and sells this information
7. Provide some examples as to how a not-for-profit organization would use marketing research.
8. What is the advantage in a firm having its own formal marketing research department? Explain three different ways such a department may be internally organized.
9. On evaluating the marketing research industry, what has been the general conclusion on how it is doing? What were given as recommendations for improving marketing research?

10. Explain the pros and cons of how a certification program, an auditing program, or educational programs may work to improve the marketing research industry.

11. What are the two fundamental philosophies that can be used as a basis for making ethical decisions? Give an example of how you would use each in your daily life. Then give an example of the use of each as it could be applied to an ethical issue in the marketing research industry.

12. Discuss the basic issues you would include in a code of ethics for the marketing research industry. What practical value do you believe such codes have for those who are internal suppliers? External suppliers? Respondents? The public?

13. Select any three companies from Table 3.1, "The Honomichl Top 50." Go to your library or the Internet and find out where you can get additional information on these firms. List the sources and the types of information provided.

14. Look up "marketing research" in your Yellow Pages directory. Given the information provided in the Yellow Pages, can you classify the research firms in your area according to the classification system of research firms we used in this chapter?

15. Comment on each practice in the following list. Is it ethical? Indicate your reasoning in each case.

    a. A research company conducts a telephone survey and gathers information that it uses later to send a salesperson to the home of potential buyers for the purpose of selling a product. It makes no attempt to sell the product over the telephone.

    b. Would your answer to (a) change if you found out that the information gathered during the telephone survey was used as part of a "legitimate" marketing research report?

    c. A door-to-door salesperson finds that, by telling people that he is conducting a survey, they are more likely to listen to his sales pitch.

    d. Greenpeace sends out a direct-mail piece described as a survey and asks for donations as the last question.

    e. The cover letter of a mail questionnaire says that it will "only take a few minutes to fill out." But pretests have shown that at least 15 minutes are needed to fill it out.

    f. Telephone interviewers are instructed to assure the respondent of confidentiality only if the respondent asks about it.

    g. A client insists on inspecting completed questionnaires ostensibly to assess their validity, but the researcher suspects that the client is really interested in finding out what specific comments the respondents had about the client.

    h. In the appendix of the final report, the researcher lists the names of all respondents who took part in the survey and places an asterisk beside the names of those who indicated a willingness to be contacted by the client's sales personnel.

    i. A "list" of randomly generated telephone numbers is drawn in order to conduct a telephone survey.

    j. A "list" of randomly generated e-mail addresses is generated using a "Spambot" (an electronic "robot" that searches the Internet looking for and retaining e-mail addresses) in order to conduct a random online research project.

    k. Students conducting a marketing research project randomly select e-mail addresses of other students from the student directory in order to conduct their term project.

l. A department store requests that customers provide them with their e-mail address for "future correspondence" on their monthly bill to the customers. They randomly select e-mail addresses from among those customers supplying the e-mail addresses in order to conduct an online survey.

INTERACTIVE LEARNING

Visit the Web site at www.prenhall.com/burnsbush. For this chapter, work through the Self-Study Quizzes, and get instant feedback on whether you need additional studying. On the Web site, you can review the chapter outlines and case information. You may also want to look at the internship and employment opportunities.

CASE 3.1   Creating Thieves in Name of Research!

Several years ago a company developed a device that was said to use subliminal auditory messages that would affect behavior. The company had received a great deal of publicity in the press by claiming that its "black boxes" would play subliminal messages over a company's sound system and that these messages could, for example, cause real estate agents to get more listings and cause shoppers and employees to reduce shoplifting. When retailers learned there was a way to reduce their high costs due to shoplifting, the company making the "black box" received numerous calls to install the "black box." Executives viewed this wonderful new product as a way of stimulating employees to excel and, for retailers, curbing shoplifting without the use of invasive tactics. But some asked "Does this new method, based on subliminal messages, actually work?"

One of your authors was involved in a marketing research project designed to measure the effects of subliminal messages on shoplifting behavior. The research design consisted of researchers recruiting respondents passing by an office building to take part in a study of the "attitudes and opinions of the public." Respondents were then told that if they agreed to complete the short survey they would be given a very nice gift (a choice of several nice gifts including a watch, pen set, or expensive glassware). Respondents agreeing to the study were then escorted into a private "research office," given a bogus survey measuring attitudes and opinions, and shown a large supply of the free gifts nearby. As the respondents began to take the survey, the researcher interrupted them to tell the respondents that they had to take a break and asked if it would be O.K. with the respondent to "Just select one of the free gifts and lock the door when you leave." Surrounded by many nice products and without any supervision, this situation was designed to create the maximum likelihood that someone would steal. On a random basis, half of the respondents were exposed to a subliminal message consisting of the same message the "black box" company claimed would reduce shoplifting. The other half of the respondents were not exposed to any message. If the subliminal message worked, there would be less stealing when the subliminal message was being played than in the condition when the message was not played.

1. Do you think this study is ethical? Why? Why not?
2. If you think the study is ethical, what is your philosophy? If unethical, what is your philosophy?
3. Do you think deception is used in the study? If so, what type of deception?
4. Should this study have been conducted? Why? Why not?
5. If you felt this study should not have been conducted, under what circumstances would you agree to a study designed to measure the effects of the subliminal "black box" technology?

CAREERS IN MARKETING RESEARCH

Maybe you have been thinking about marketing research as a career choice. There are many career opportunities in the industry and we have prepared this appendix to give you some information about those career choices. More importantly, we give you some sources to pursue additional information about a career in the marketing research industry.

WHAT IS THE OUTLOOK FOR THE INDUSTRY?

Before you seek employment in any industry you should ask about the total outlook for the industry. Buggy whip manufacturing is not exactly a growth industry! What are the growth rates in the industry? What do the experts have to say about the future of the industry?

A good place to find information about the outlook of an industry is the *Occupational Outlook Handbook*. You can access it online at **www.bls.gov/oco/home.htm**. Look under the category "Professional and related" and then under "Economists and market and survey researchers."

The *Occupational Outlook Handbook* forecasts jobs in economics and marketing research to grow faster than average (21 to 35 percent) through 2010. Demand for qualified market research analysts should be healthy because of an increasingly competitive economy. Marketing research provides organizations valuable feedback from purchasers, allowing companies to evaluate consumer satisfaction and more effectively plan for the future. As companies seek to expand their market and consumers become better informed, the need for marketing professionals will increase.

Opportunities for market research analysts with graduate degrees should be good in a wide range of employment settings, particularly in marketing research firms, as companies find it more profitable to contract out for marketing research services rather than support their own marketing department. Other organizations, including financial services organizations, health care institutions, advertising firms, manufacturing firms producing consumer goods, and insurance companies may offer job opportunities for market research analysts.

Opportunities for survey researchers should be strong as the demand for market and opinion research increases. Employment opportunities will be especially favorable in commercial market and opinion research as an increasingly competitive economy requires businesses to more effectively and efficiently allocate advertising funds.[52]

Also, recall that we showed you in this chapter that the research industry has been growing. Industry figures show annual growth rates of 7 to 8 percent in recent years. One of the largest concerns expressed by members in the industry in a 1999 survey conducted by the Advertising Research Foundation was a concern that too few qualified researchers would be available to handle industry needs. The report suggested increasing college graduate recruiting and working with universities to offer meaningful internships and enrichment of existing marketing research courses.[53]

WHAT ARE THE SALARIES?

Another question you should ask is how much the people in this profession earn. Like many professional services, salaries vary widely in the marketing research industry. Nevertheless, we can give you some general guidelines. The *Occupational Outlook Handbook* separates marketing research analysts from survey researchers. The primary difference is that analysts are involved with the total research process and their definition of survey researchers closely matches what we discuss in this chapter as field data collection firms (limited-service firms). Median annual earnings of market research analysts in 2000 were $51,190. The middle 50 percent earned between $37,030 and $71,660. The lowest 10 percent earned less than $27,570, and the highest 10 percent earned more than $96,360. Median annual earnings in the industries employing the largest numbers of market research analysts in 2000 were as follows:

Computer and data processing services	$61,320
Management and public relations	44,580
Research and testing services	43,660

Median annual earnings of survey researchers in 2000 were $26,200. The middle 50 percent earned between $17,330 and $47,820. The lowest 10 percent earned less than $15,050, and the highest 10 percent earned more than $71,790. Median annual earnings of survey researchers in 2000 were $52,470 in computer and data processing services and $18,780 in research and testing services.[54]

Another source stated that entry-level job opportunities are dwindling in the marketing research industry because companies want people who can hit the ground running. The starting salaries for individuals with undergraduate degrees in business or statistics are around $40,000 per year. With more experience, researchers can earn six-figured salaries. On average, in 1999, researchers earned $87,000, a 5.3 percent increase over 1998. Also, 82 percent of marketing researchers earned more than $60,000 in 1999.[55]

Also, to learn about salaries in marketing research (and other fields) try these sites:

Career Center www.govexec.com/careers (federal pay schedules)

Executive Pay Watch www.aflcio.org/paywatch

Job Smart. www.jobsmart.org/tools/salary/index.htm

Salary.com www.salary.com

WHAT KIND OF JOBS ARE THERE?

O.K., so you are still interested! What types of jobs are there in the marketing research industry?

Position titles and the positions themselves vary, depending on whether you work for a full-service firm (account executive/director or project manager), for a limited-service firm (focus group moderator or field supervisor), or within a supplier/buyer firm (director of marketing research or research analyst). Recognizing that position titles vary by company, you could expect entry-level positions to include titles such as marketing research assistant or junior project director. After a year or more, you might advance to assistant marketing research manager or project director. The job titles are not nearly as important as the responsibilities. As you grow in your marketing research career, your assignments will move from problem management to problem definition and project design.

Almost all the large research firms have a job-openings site on their Web sites. For example, try acnielsen.com, ACNielsen's Web page, and go to "Contact" and check out the posted job listings. This will show you the titles and job descriptions of jobs available at ACNielsen. Or take a look at National Family Opinion (NFO) Worldwide's Web site at www.nfow. Go to "Join Us" and then "Career Center." You will see job descriptions and requirements for the positions available at NFOWorldwide. We recommend you do this at several of the Web sites. Check out the companies listed in this chapter in Table 3.1, "The Honomichl Top 50."

WHAT ARE THE REQUIREMENTS?

Do you have what it takes? The traits associated with the most successful and effective marketing researchers include the following: curiosity, high intelligence, creativity, self-discipline, good interpersonal and communication skills, the ability to work under strict time constraints, and feeling comfortable working with numbers. The field is becoming gender neutral. About half of all new researchers are women.[56] Information Resources, Inc. (IRI) states it prefers a degree in marketing or a related area. Although an undergraduate degree is required, there has been a trend toward requiring postgraduate degrees in some firms. Most universities do not offer a degree in marketing research. There are some, reported later, that are quite good. Thus, an M.B.A. with a marketing major is one of the more common combinations for people employed in marketing research. Other possibilities are degrees in quantitative methods, sociology, or economics. Undergraduate training in mathematics or the physical sciences is a very suitable (and employable) background for anyone considering a career in marketing research.

ARE YOU INTERESTED IN A MASTER'S DEGREE IN MARKETING RESEARCH?

Graduate degrees are highly recommended in the marketing research industry. Throughout this book, we have and will continue to introduce you to real people in the industry. In many cases, we show you their biography that includes their formal training. You will notice that almost all of them have graduate degrees. Again, it is not necessary but it is desirable. The following schools were obtained from the MRA Web site:

Santa Clara University
MBA Office
Kenna Hall 323
Santa Clara, CA 95053-0001
408-554-4500
408-554-4571 fax
www.scu.edu
Degree offered: M.B.A. with MR Concentration

University of Georgia
Terry College of Business
Program of Marketing Research
Athens, GA 30602
706-542-3540
www.uga.edu
Degree offered: Master's in MR

Southern Illinois University School of Business
Box 1051
Edwardsville, IL
62026-0001
618-692-3412
618-692-3979 fax
www.siue.edu/MMR/
Degree offered: Master of Science in MR

Rutgers University
92 New Street
Newark, NJ 07102-1895
973-648-5651
973-648-1592 fax
www.rutgers.com
Degree offered: Master's in Marketing with Concentration in MR

City University of New York—Baruch
Office of Graduate Admissions
17 Lexington Ave., Box H-0725
New York, NY 10010-5585
212-802-2330
www.baruch.cuny.edu
Degree offered: Master's in Marketing with Concentration in MR

University of Texas—Arlington
College of Business Administration, Marketing Department
UTA Box 19469

Arlington, TX 76019-0469
(817) 272-2340
817-272-2854 fax
www.uta.edu
Degree offered: Master of Science in MR

University of Wisconsin/Nielsen School
Gradate Program Office
2766 Grainger Hall
975 University Ave.
Madison, WI 53706-1380
608-262-1555
608-265-4192 fax
www.wisc.edu
Degree offered: Master's in Marketing with MR Concentration

LOOKING FOR A JOB

The first thing you should do is go to your university's career center. Make certain you take advantage of the materials it offers and the knowledge of the staff. Remember, your university wants you to find a meaningful career but it can only offer you the resources. You must use those resources. There are some helpful guides available such as:

Career Busters: 22 Things People Do to Mess Up Their Career and How to Avoid Them
Hot Jobs: The No-Holds-Barred, Tell-It-Like-It-Is Guide to Getting the Jobs Everybody Wants
How to Land a Better Job
Successful Job Search Strategies for the Disabled

Look these titles up on your library's search system. Also, visit the Web pages of the American Marketing Association, Marketing Research Association, and CASRO. They all have information to help you in your career search.

Getting a job is hard work. Getting a *good* job requires hard work and a lot of preplanning. Network, take advantage of internships, and get familiar with and read publications about the industry in which you wish to have a career. Join marketing associations, make contacts, and ask them how they got their job and to explain their job to you. Good jobs go to well-trained, enthusiastic, and motivated individuals. Get started now!

Chapter 4

Defining the Problem and Determining Research Objectives

Learning Objectives:

To understand basic differences between marketing managers and researchers

To learn how to dissect a marketing management problem

To know how to itemize the research objectives of a research project

To know what elements go into a marketing research proposal

Practitioner Viewpoint

A problem well defined is a problem half solved says an old but still valid adage. How a problem is defined sets the direction for the entire project. A good definition is necessary if marketing research is to contribute to the solution of the problem. A bad definition dooms the entire project from the start and guarantees that subsequent marketing and marketing research efforts will prove useless.

Nothing we researchers can do has so much leverage on profit as helping marketing define the right problem. Researchers must resist the temptation to "go along" with the first definition suggested. They should take the time to conduct their own investigation and to develop and consider alternative definitions. Researchers have the responsibility to make that special contribution only marketing research can offer.

Lawrence D. Gibson
Independent Consultant and Senior Associate
Eric Marder Associates, Inc.

Where We Are:

1. Establish the need for marketing research
2. Define the problem
3. Establish research objectives
4. Determine research design
5. Identify information types and sources
6. Determine methods of accessing data
7. Design data collection forms
8. Determine sample plan and size
9. Collect data
10. Analyze data
11. Prepare and present the final research report

Theology on Tap: Would God Be Happy with a Brewskie in Gary, Indiana?

The Catholic diocese of Gary, Indiana, serves approximately 200,000 Roman Catholics located in 57 parishes in northeastern Indiana. The diocese noted that although it retained older Catholics, attendance by young adults was very low. In fact, young adult attendance at organized religious ceremonies of almost all religions has been declining for the past several years. This situation has grave implications for the long-term success of the Catholic diocese of Gary as young adults advance into middle-aged and older adults. Without a history of attendance in church activities, these individuals will have little reason to begin attending when they are older. The forecast is for a downward attendance spiral threatening the lifeblood of the diocese.

The diocese turned to Barna Research Group, a Christian marketing research company specializing in periodic surveys and custom research across various religious denominations. With its extensive research on the topic, the Barna Research Group has identified four generations of churchgoers. The four types and their distinguishing characteristics are listed in the table.[1]

Ironically, the Barna research revealed that the young adult "Busters" are in the greatest need of spiritual guidance and comfort as they are the most stressed-out group and struggling the most with doubts about the purposes of their lives. They are also the busiest group as they are faced with job pressures, new and young family needs, and transitions from students to productive young adults.

The diocese came to realize that the problem was to "think out of the box," for it would be fruitless to try to make Busters return to traditional church attendance. The research revealed that Busters are gregarious and social. They have active, busy

The Catholic Church used marketing research to target "Busters" with "Theology on Tap."

lifestyles centered on eating out and social functions. The diocese realized that it must create church-related options that are harmonious with the Busters' lifestyles.

It launched "Theology on Tap," where small groups of Busters can gather at designated restaurants, eat free snacks, drink free beer and wine, and listen and discuss spiritual issues. To date, Busters in Gary, Toledo, and other northeastern Indiana counties are attending this innovative attempt on the part of the Roman Catholic Church to bring them back into the fold.[2]

Name	Age Range	Percentage Who Attend Church Regularly	Percentage Who Are "Stressed Out"	Percentage Who Are Searching For Meaning in Life
Seniors	75 and older	47%	22%	32%
Builders	55 to 74	50%	27%	32%
Boomers	37 to 55	42%	32%	32%
Busters	16 to 36	35%	41%	44%

The Catholic Church uses marketing research to save lost souls.

The previous chapters introduced you to the world of marketing research. This chapter addresses what some marketing researchers claim is the most important step in the marketing research process—defining the nature of the problem confronting the marketing manager, specifying constructs, and determining research objectives. As is evident in the preceding Theology on Tap description, understanding markets is a constant challenge, and marketers need timely and accurate marketing research to sense and take advantage of emerging opportunities. This chapter also discusses the differences between marketing managers and marketing researchers and describes their different orientations to help you understand why a continuous dialogue must take place between these two roles during the problem-formulation and objectives-setting steps. Finally, the components of a research proposal are identified and discussed.

DEFINE THE MARKETING MANAGER'S PROBLEM

Defining the problem is critical to setting the direction for all subsequent steps of the marketing research process. This is particularly true for custom-designed research as opposed to standardized research. Standardized or syndicated research is generic research that is provided in identical fashion to all buyers by the marketing research supplier. Custom-designed research is research that is fashioned to address a unique marketing management problem confronting a client manager. Custom-designed research requires that the marketing researcher fully understand the circumstances of the marketing manager's problem.

Custom marketing research should begin with a thorough problem definition.

Although there are a number of problem-solving techniques that individual managers can use,[3] we will describe a process that works for the marketing manager-researcher situation. It is not unusual for the manager and researcher to conduct many discussions to define the problem as well as the precise nature of the research needed to resolve the problem. For example, the Marriott hotel chain may call in a marketing researcher because it thinks there is a problem with its reservation system. When it contacts the researcher, Marriott may state that it feels that its telephone lines are often tied up and that it loses business travelers who wait on hold too long when they call its toll-free number. If this is the issue to be researched, then a research study could be launched to find out the experience of prospective Marriott hotel patrons when they call the toll-free number. A nationwide telephone study could be undertaken to determine how often business travelers call the number, why they must wait, and what amount of time they do wait before a Marriott reservations representative comes on the line.

However, although this survey would gather much information on this facet of Marriott's reservation system, it might not solve the real problem, which stems from the fact that many business travelers delegate making hotel reservations to their secretaries or company travel agencies, and a competitor has developed an incentive system to reward those employees who make reservations with their hotel chain. Without considering who the "purchasing agents" are, the problem definition is incomplete. Thus, until all dimensions of the issue are explored the problem has not been defined satisfactorily. If the problem is not defined correctly, satisfactory performance at the other steps in the marketing research process will not remedy the situation.

Differences Between Managers and Researchers

Marketing managers and marketing researchers see the world differently because they have different jobs to perform and their backgrounds differ markedly. As illustrated in Table 4.1, managers and researchers actually operate in different worlds. However, during the problem definition phase, their worlds overlap, and they enter into a discussion of the symptoms perceived by the manager. They also discuss the types of research the researcher envisions will be necessary to generate answers to the question of why the symptoms have arisen and what the manager can do to resolve the problem.

Managers' and researchers' backgrounds differ markedly.

Key Questions the Researcher Should Ask the Manager

Obviously, despite their divergent orientations, marketing managers and marketing researchers must work together to survive. Although understanding the differences presented in Table 4.1 goes a long way toward helping managers and researchers forge a working relationship, much more is required.

There are seven categories of information that the manager and researcher should discuss during their first meeting: (1) symptoms of the problem, (2) the manager's situation, (3) information the manager has about the situation, (4) suspected causes of the problem, (5) possible solutions to the problem, (6) anticipated consequences of these solutions, and (7) the manager's assumptions about any of the prior categories of information. The dialogue between the researcher and the manager is

Despite their differences, managers and researchers must develop a working relationship.

Table 4.1	**Eight Fundamental Differences Between Managers and Researchers**	
AREA OF DIFFERENCE	MANAGERS	RESEARCHERS
Organizational position	Line	Staff
Responsibility	To make profits	To generate information
Training	General decision making	Technique applications
Disposition toward knowledge	Wants answers to questions	Wants to ask questions
Orientation	Pragmatic	Scholarly
Brand involvement	Highly involved; emotional	Detached; unemotional
Use of the research	Political	Nonpolitical
Research motivation	To make symptoms disappear	To find the truth

Table 4.2	**Topic Questions the Researcher Should Ask the Marketing Manager to Define the Problem**

PROBLEM DEFINITION AREAS	SAMPLE QUESTION(S)
Symptoms	What has changed that is causing you concern?
Decision maker's situation	How are these changes impacting your objectives? What resources do you have at your disposal? What is the time frame for required action?
Information	What do you know about the circumstances of these changes?
Suspected causes	Why do you think these changes have come about?
Possible solutions	What do you have the power to do about these changes?
Anticipated consequences	If you do the things in your power, what are the most likely results?
Assumptions	Why do you anticipate these responses to your actions to resolve the problem?

The manager and the researcher should discuss at least seven different aspects of the manager's problem.

often a question-and-answer session, and Table 4.2 notes the topic question that the researcher may begin with in each case. We will elaborate on the nature of each of these seven problem definition areas later in this chapter.

The proper way to consider these questions is in the context of what is to be gained or lost. When managers do their homework and thoroughly describe the problem's dimensions, and when they identify reasonable alternatives, noting the resources that can be applied or other pressures operating on the research effort, the communication process is enhanced. At the same time, it is necessary that researchers obtain as complete a preliminary picture as possible by asking pointed questions, reviewing salient materials, or even probing the managers' true motives. Research has demonstrated that the quality of interactions that take place between managers and researchers, plus the level of involvement on the part of researchers, directly affect the managers' utilization of the research.[4] Ultimately, the problem definition stage of enlightened marketing research must be viewed as a partnership, and partnerships can survive only with mutual respect, trust, and open communication.

The manager and researcher should develop a partnership.

DECIDE WHEN MARKETING RESEARCH IS WARRANTED

Marketing managers are responsible for initiating the marketing research process. This means that they must first determine when to embark on a marketing research project. Unfortunately, it is all too easy to commission marketing research without a sober evaluation of whether or not research should be undertaken in the first place.

As explained in Chapter 2, there are at least four instances in which marketing research may not help (pp. 29–30). It is probably wise to forgo the expense of research when any one of these is present. Of course, marketing research is performed every day, so there must be general instances when the manager should go ahead with marketing research.[5] In general, there are four instances in which research should be undertaken:

▶ If it clarifies problems or investigates changes in the marketplace that can directly impact your product responsibility

▶ If it resolves your selection of alternative courses of marketing action to achieve key marketing objectives

▶ If it helps you gain a meaningful competitive advantage

▶ If it allows you to stay abreast of your market(s)

Another way to decide when to do marketing research is to perform a cost–benefit analysis. To do this, the marketing manager estimates how much will be lost if the problem (or opportunity) is not addressed. If the anticipated cost of the research does not exceed this estimate, then the manager should proceed with the research. Some managers fail to compare research cost with its benefits, which is a mistake.[6]

ONLINE ENVIRONMENT FOR MARKETING DECISION MAKING

With the almost universal adoption of the Internet, marketing managers are finding it increasingly necessary to "turn on a dime." In other words, the world is not only becoming smaller, but it is also turning faster because of the avalanche of information pouring through to any managers with marketing information systems. Furthermore, this information can be almost real time if the proper information-gathering and reporting systems are in place. Thus, the good news about the online environment is that marketing decision makers are more informed about all aspects of their marketing responsibilities: Information streams in on a continual basis, and their inquiries are posed more quickly and responded to faster by their assistants and coworkers. The bad news is that there is the danger of information overload, so they must cultivate information management strategies. Another disadvantage of the fast-moving online environment is that both customers and competitors are better armed with information. The old-time fairy tale about the tortoise beating the hare in a race most certainly does not apply, for all of the tortoises are extinct, and the hares are on steroids. Staying on top of the information explosion does not guarantee success, but it is a requirement if one hopes to compete at all.

The online environment requires marketing decision makers to move faster.

Because they are on the firing line, we asked our Blue Ribbon Panel of marketing research practitioners how the online environment is now impacting and will continue to impact the interactions between marketing decision making and marketing research. You will find their views in the "Blue Ribbon Panel on Online Research" section at the end of this chapter.

DEFINE THE MARKETING MANAGEMENT AND RESEARCH OBJECTIVES

There are two types of problems with which a marketing researcher must contend: the marketing management problem and the marketing research objectives. A **marketing management problem** is defined in one of two ways: (1) If the symptoms of failure to achieve a goal are present, the marketing manager must select a course of action to regain the goal, and (2) if the symptoms of the likelihood of achieving a goal are present, the manager must decide on how best to seize the opportunity. Some researchers refer to the second type as **opportunity identification**.

The marketing research problem differs from the marketing management problem.

Once the marketing management problem is fully defined, the marketing researcher must wrestle with the **marketing research objective**, which is defined as providing relevant, accurate, and unbiased information that managers can use to solve their marketing management problems. Obviously, the marketing management problem is critical, for its improper definition will invalidate the researcher's identification of the research objective. Poor problem definition can expose research to a range of undesirable consequences, including incorrect research designs and inappropriate or needlessly expensive data collection, assembly of incorrect or irrelevant data, and poor choice of the sample selection.[7] It is critical, therefore, that the marketing management problem be defined accurately and fully.

As indicated earlier, there are seven assessment areas that help the marketing researcher properly define the marketing management problem. These areas (1) assess the manager's situation, including background of the company, product, and market and the decision maker's circumstances, objectives, and resources; (2) clarify the symptoms of the problem; (3) pinpoint suspected causes of the problem; (4) specify actions that may alleviate the problem; (5) speculate on anticipated consequences of these actions; (6) identify the manager's assumptions about the consequences; and (7) assess the adequacy of information on hand. A discussion of each area follows.

There are seven assessments to a marketing management problem.

Assess the Manager's Situation

It is during the initial meeting between the marketing researcher and the marketing manager that the researcher is informed regarding the **background** of the product or service under investigation, including its performance history and any recent marketing strategy changes. At this meeting, the manager also informs the researcher regarding the company's history, its organizational structure, ownership situation, and overall mission. Additionally, the manager will need to describe the product, including how it works, its composition or production, its various features or benefits, and other aspects of the physical product. The researcher should also be informed about the marketing program, including pricing, distribution, and promotional activities. Some information summarizing key consumer behavior associated with the product will undoubtedly be provided, and the manager will want to describe major competitive players, current trends in the market, and any factors in the environment that are impacting the market. If appropriate, the manager may make a copy of the product's marketing plan along with quarterly or monthly financial documents that track the product's performance. It is also possible that the manager will identify some key news or trade articles that have appeared recently summarizing the industry or otherwise detailing what is going on in the target market. As a result of this initial meeting, the researcher may come away from this meeting with a considerable amount of "homework."

Full sharing of background facts between manager and researcher is necessary during problem definition.

During problem definition, the market researcher learns about the marketing manager's situation.

Managers are employed for the purpose of achieving company or organizational objectives, and they are provided various resources to accomplish these objectives. Moreover, they operate under various pressures and expectations dictated by their superiors or, perhaps, by corporate culture. So it is vital that the researcher gain a feel for the manager's operating circumstances, for they may well dictate the urgency or timing of the research.

It will certainly help to know the reasons the manager has requested research help. This means that the researcher should know the **manager's objectives**, which are tangible statements of a company's expectations. Gaining a feel for the manager's specific objectives will help the researcher understand the gravity of the problem. By comparing recent sales, market share, or profitability level, for instance, with objectives, the researcher can compare how far the brand has strayed from acceptable performance. A pattern may be discerned; that is, was the deviation a slow trend over time, or was it a sudden plunge into an unacceptable condition?

> The manager's objectives are insightful to the nature of the problem he or she is facing.

To achieve objectives, the manager uses a number of resources, including assets, capital, personnel, company time, and so on. Typically, a manager's resources are apparent by inspecting the budget. Some companies do not have detailed budgets, so the researcher may be forced to question the manager about how many salespersons are assigned to the brand, what their sales records look like, how much was spent on advertising and to which media it was allocated, what product improvements have been implemented or committed to, how much division time is spent on this brand, and who has been performing what tasks. Understanding the level of resources and how they have been utilized may shed light on the real problem.

Clarify the Symptoms of the Problem

During the problem definition phase, the manager and researcher must distinguish between **symptoms**, which are changes in the level of some key monitor that measures the achievement of an objective, and their causes. A symptom may also be a perceived change in the behavior of some market factor that suggests adverse consequences or, perhaps, implies an emerging opportunity. Applying market research to analyze marketing opportunities is equally important as applying it to problem definition. At least one marketing research expert has blamed the downfall of the dot-com companies in the late 1990s on their lack of marketing research.[8]

> Symptoms are changes in the level of some key monitor that measures the achievement of an objective.

Marketing managers should continually monitor their situations for changes in market behavior. A sampling of commonly used monitors is provided in Table 4.3. Often these monitors are formal, which means that they are included in the business plan or they are part of the company's monitoring systems. Sometimes they are

Table 4.3 Formal Monitors That Are Helpful in Alerting Managers to Possible Problems

TYPE OF MONITOR	DESCRIPTION
Sales volume	The total units or dollar value of units sold in a given time period
Market share	The percentage of total industry sales accounted for by the company's brand
Profit	The total profit generated by a brand
Dealer orders	The amount of goods ordered by the company's dealers
Complaints	The level of consumer complaints registered
Competitors	Actions of the competition such as price reduction, introduction of new products, style changes, expansion into new territories, and so on

informal and much more subjective. With informal monitors, the problem definition phase is necessarily more protracted because the researcher must construct the activity monitors and track them back in time to gain a feel for when the symptoms moved away from the company's acceptable levels and how much they have wandered into dangerous territory.

Even if formal monitors are in place, they may not present a sufficiently detailed or complete picture of what has happened. This is sometimes referred to as the **iceberg phenomenon**, a situation in which you must look beneath the surface to see the complete picture. The researcher may request a breakdown by sales territory, for example, to see if market share has fallen in all areas. Or he or she may want to look at sales for the industry as a whole to see if the phenomenon is industrywide. An astute researcher will ask questions that sometimes tax the manager's patience, but they are necessary to gain an understanding of all of the facets of the problem.

It is vital to "look beneath the surface" when defining the problem.

Pinpoint Suspected Causes of the Problem

Problems do not arise out of the blue—there always is an underlying **cause**, or the factor that underlies and gives rise to the symptom. For example, sales do not drop without buyers doing something that is different from what they have been doing in the past, customer complaints do not increase unless some dissatisfaction has occurred, and dealers do not report returns unless there is a flaw in the product. In other words, changes in market behavior do not occur randomly.

There is an important reason for looking for causes that underlie the symptoms. Perhaps this funny story will help you realize why.

> *A marketing manager in his mid-fifties and a young pup from his research department took a weekend off to hike in the woods. They were enjoying the crisp air and the quiet of the forest until they walked into a wide clearing where they saw a giant grizzly bear about to charge them.*
>
> *Suddenly, the young man stopped, dropped to the ground, yanked off his hiking boots, and pulled his running shoes out of his backpack.*
>
> *"What are you doing?" screamed the marketing manager. "Those shoes won't help you outrun that bear!"*
>
> *The young man tied his running shoes, jumped up, and sprinted away, leaving his boss huffing and puffing far behind.*
>
> *"I don't have to outrun the bear," the young man shouted back over his shoulder. "I just have to outrun YOU."*[9]

Eliminating a symptom does not solve the problem.

Of course, the researcher was just eliminating a symptom, and the manager was still going to be left with the problem. Actually, seasoned market researchers are quite good at separating symptoms and problems because they deal with problem definition quite often. Read about Lawrence Gibson who contributed the Practitioner Viewpoint at the beginning of this chapter in our Meet a Market Researcher feature. Mr. Gibson, you will discover, actually teaches a "problem-solving" tutorial across the United States.

Often a manager suspects or even has strong opinions concerning the cause of a bothersome symptom. In fact, he or she may even begin the conversation by telling the researcher what to research. However, it is important that the researcher list all **possible causes** in as objective a manner as possible, because if a possible cause is overlooked and that cause turns out to be the real cause, all research will have been wasted.

For every problem, an underlying cause can be found.

To illustrate the importance of pursuing all possible causes of a problem, we present an example involving University Estates, an apartment complex that targets students attending a nearby college. Last year, University Estates experienced a decline in its occupancy rate from 100 percent to 80 percent. The researcher and the

MARKETING R
INSIG

4.1

*Lawrence D. Gibson, Independent Consultant
and Senior Associate of Eric Marder Associates, Inc.*

Larry Gibson has had a long, varied career in marketing and marketing research as marketing research director at General Mills for 20 years, advertising agency researcher, and consultant/supplier for companies such as General Motors, Amoco, and Motorola. He has worked in Western Europe, Latin America, China, and Japan. A frequent speaker at American Marketing Association (AMA) and Advertising Research Foundation (ARF) conferences, chapter meetings, and university classrooms, Larry has also published many articles in professional journals.

For the AMA, Larry is currently an at-large national board member; teaches a tutorial, "Problem Solving with Marketing Research," at Applied Research Methods conferences; leads off the AMA School of Marketing Research at Notre Dame; is a member of the *Marketing Research* editorial review board, and has served on the Marketing Research Council.

Elsewhere, Larry was chair of The Conference Board's Marketing Research Council, a board member of the Marketing Science Institute, and a member of the Business Research Advisory Council of the Bureau of Labor Statistics.

manager of University Estates met and began discussing this symptom, asking themselves why the occupancy rate declined. Over the course of their discussion, they identified four general areas of possible causes: (1) competitors' actions, which had drawn prospective student residents away; (2) changes in the consumers (student target population); (3) something about the apartment complex itself; and (4) general environmental factors. The results of their brainstorming session are presented in Table 4.4. Given this long list, it was necessary to narrow down the possible causes to a small set of **probable causes**, defined as the most likely factors giving rise to the symptoms.

A probable cause differs from a possible cause.

The researcher and the University Estates manager systematically examined every possible cause listed in Table 4.4 and came to the realization that only a few could be probable causes of the decline in occupancy rate. For example, the manager was vigilant to what rents were being charged, and he knew that no competitor had lowered its rents in the past year. Similarly, no new apartment complexes had been built or opened up last year. Through this dialogue, the researcher and the University Estates manager narrowed the list down to two probable causes: (1) competing apartment complexes had added digital cable television in every apartment and (2) some apartment complexes had added on-site workout facilities. With a little more background investigation, it was found that only one competing apartment complex had added a workout facility, and most of the complexes, including University Estates, did not have any workout facility. Thus, the cable television deficiency of University Estates was narrowed down as the the most probable cause for its occupancy decline.

Probable causes are those possible causes that are highly likely to be culprits.

| Table 4.4 | **Possible Causes for University Estates Occupancy Rate Decline** |

1. Competitor's Actions

a. Reduced rents
b. New or additional competitors
c. New services

d. New facilities
e. Better advertising
f. Financial deals such as no deposit

2. Consumers (current and prospective student renters)

a. Loss of base numbers of students
b. Change in financial circumstances
c. Better living opportunities elsewhere
d. Concern for personal safety

e. Gravitating to condominiums
f. Want more value for the money
g. Negative word-of-mouth publicity

3. University Estates Itself

a. Traffic congestion
b. Noisy neighbors
c. Advertising cutback, change

d. Aging facilities and equipment
e. Image as "old" apartments
f. Upkeep issues

4. The Environment

a. Less student financial aid
b. Increased crime rate
c. Housing market oversupply

d. Change in students' preferences
e. Cost of commuting increase
f. Other living alternatives

Specify Actions That May Alleviate the Problem

As you learned earlier, managers have at their disposal certain resources, and these resources constitute the solutions they may attempt to employ to resolve the decision problem at hand. Essentially, possible **solutions** include any marketing action that the marketing manager thinks may resolve the problem, such as price changes, product modification or improvement, promotion of any kind, or even adjustments in channels of distribution. It is during this phase that the researcher's marketing education and knowledge fully come into play; often both the manager and the researcher brainstorm possible solutions. Sometimes this phase is moderated by the marketing researcher. At other times, the manager may independently generate several tactics that might resolve the problem once the probable causes are identified.

Solutions include any marketing action that may resolve the problem.

We cannot emphasize how important it is for the manager to specify all of the actions he or she might consider in attacking the problem. In fact, one marketing research consultant has gone on record with this bold statement, "Unless the entire range of potential solutions is considered, chances of correctly defining the research problem are poor."[10]

With the University Estates problem definition meeting, the manager realized that he needed to look into cable television installations, and this additional service seemed necessary, at minimum, to meet the changes in competitors. However, the manager was not content to just match the competition, so he began considering a satellite television system such as DishTV's Multiple Dwelling Unit Program with its 150 channels, four premium channels of HBO, Starz, Showtime, and Cinemax, plus pay-per-view as one of his likely plans of action. In fact, the manager was quite pleased with his discovery that he could offer satellite television connections in every apartment because the satellite programming seemed far superior to basic cable television.

University Estates can use marketing research to find out why its occupancy rate declined.

Speculate on Anticipated Consequences of the Actions

Research on anticipated **consequences**, or most likely outcomes, of each action under consideration will help determine whether the solution is correct or not. For example, a solution might resolve the problem; on the other hand, it might intensify the problem if the solution is not the correct action. To avoid resolving the problem incorrectly, the manager asks "what if" questions regarding possible consequences of each marketing action being considered. These questions include:

> ▶ What will be the impact not only on the problem at hand but also through-
> out the marketing program if a specific marketing action is implemented?

> ▶ What additional problems will be created if a proposed solution to the cur-
> rent problem is implemented?

To help resolve problems, managers ask "what if" questions.

Typically, the range of consequences of possible marketing actions is readily apparent. For example, if your advertising medium is changed from *People* magazine to *USA Today*, customers will either see less, see more, or see the same amount of advertising. If a nonsudsing chemical is added to your swimming pool treatment, customers will either like it more, less, or have no change in their opinions about it. Most marketing research investigates consumer consequences of marketing solutions, but it is also possible to research dealers' reactions or even suppliers' reactions, depending on the nature of the problem.

With the University Estates problem definition, it seemed reasonable to the manager to speculate that if University Estates added a satellite television system connection in each apartment, University Estates would be seen as more attractive than the other apartment complexes that had surged ahead in occupancy.

Identify the Manager's Assumptions About the Consequences

As they define the problem, the manager and the researcher make certain **assumptions**, which are assertions that certain conditions exist or that certain reactions will take place if the considered actions are implemented. For example, the manager may say, "I am positive that our lost customers will come back if we drop the price to $500," or "Our sales should go up if we gain more awareness by using advertising inserts in the Sunday paper." However, if a researcher questions a manager about his or her beliefs regarding the consequences of certain proposed actions, it may turn out that the manager is not really as certain as he or she sounds. Conversely, the manager may be quite certain and cite several reasons why his or her assumption is valid. It is imperative, therefore, that the manager's assumptions be analyzed for accuracy.

Assumptions deserve researcher attention because they are the glue that holds the decision problem together. Given a symptom, the manager assumes that certain causes are at fault. She or he assumes that, by taking corrective actions, the problem will be resolved and that the symptoms will disappear. If the manager is completely certain of all of these things, there is no need for research. But typically uncertainty prevails, and critical assumptions about which the manager is uncertain will ultimately factor in heavily when the researcher addresses the marketing research problem. Research will help eliminate this uncertainty. At the same time, there may be disagreement on key assumptions within the manager's company, and research may be needed to determine which competing assumption is true.

The key assumptions underlying the University Estates problem definition meeting are that students (1) know about and understand the advantages of satellite television over basic cable TV, and (2) they want satellite television more than they want cable television in their apartments. The manager was also assuming that adding a satellite television connection in each apartment would render University Estates more desirable than the other apartment complexes targeting university students.

Assess the Adequacy of Information on Hand to Specify Research Objectives

As the manager attempts to formulate a decision problem, available information varies in both quantity and quality. As just noted, the manager may have information that greatly reinforces his or her beliefs, or he or she may not have anything more than a "gut feeling." You should recall that it is the researcher's responsibility to provide information to the manager that will help resolve the marketing manager's problem. Obviously, if the manager knows something with a high degree of certainty, it is of little value for the researcher to conduct research to reiterate that knowledge. It is vital, therefore, that the researcher assess the existing **information state**, which is the quantity and quality of evidence a manager possesses for each of his or her assumptions. During this assessment, the researcher should ask questions about the current information state and determine what the desired information state is. Conceptually, the researcher seeks to identify **information gaps**, which are discrepancies between the current information level and the desired level of information at which the manager feels comfortable resolving the problem at hand. Ultimately, information gaps are the basis for marketing research objectives.

With the University Estates situation, the manager felt quite confident about the accuracy of his information that cable television was offered by his competitors because they had advertised this new feature as well as announced this new service with signs outside the apartment complexes. Plus, he was confident that students were into cable television; although, he was not sure about how much they desired the additional programming available on satellite television. Thus, the manager had an information gap because he was unsure of what the reactions of prospective University Estates residents would be if the satellite program package was included in the apartment package. Would they see it as competitive to the other apartment

---

The manager's assumptions deserve researcher attention because they may be incorrect or uncertain.

Research will help to eliminate a manager's uncertainty.

Information gaps serve as the basis for research objectives.

| Table 4.5 | Information Gaps and Research Objectives for University Estates |

INFORMATION GAP	RESEARCH OBJECTIVE(S)
How will prospective residents react to the inclusion of the satellite television programming package with the base apartment?	*To what extent do prospective student residents want satellite television?*
Will University Estates be more competitive if it adds a satellite television package?	*Will University Estates be more attractive than competing apartment complexes if it has the satellite television progamming package?*

complexes that had cable television? Would they want to live at University Estates more than at an apartment complex that had only basic cable?

As you may have noticed in the University Estates example, whenever an information gap that is relevant to the problem at hand is apparent to the manager, the manager and researcher come to agree that it is a research objective. That is, **research objectives** are specific bits of knowledge that need to be gathered and that serve to close information gaps. These objectives become the basis for the marketing researcher's work. In order to formulate the research objectives, the marketing researcher considers all the current information surrounding the marketing management problem. We have created Table 4.5 to identify the information gaps and appropriate research objectives in the case of University Estates.

> The manager and researcher come to agree on research objectives that are based on the information gaps.

The problem definition stage is much more difficult when the researcher is working with a global marketing problem because several marketing managers may be involved. Marketing Research Insight 4.2 describes a way to overcome this situation.

▶ **A Global Perspective**

MARKETING RESEARCH
INSIGHT
4.2

When Undertaking a Global Marketing Research Project, Work with an Angel[11]

Although there are many commonalities between global marketing research and U.S. domestic marketing research, there are fundamental differences between them as well.

According to Joe Plummer, executive vice president, global accounts, McCann-Erickson Worldwide, Inc., the greatest difference is found in the planning stage in which the marketing management problem definition is crystallized and the marketing research methods are decided. Domestic marketing management decision problems tend to have only a single brand manager involved. This situation means that the marketing researcher can have a "sit down" with that manager to define the problem, and that meeting will establish the working relationship between the researcher and the manager that will suffice for the entire research project.

However, the complexity of global marketing typically requires the involvement of several managers, and this fact means that the researcher must determine:

▶ Who is the key manager(s)?
▶ What manager has responsibility and say-so on what issue?
▶ What manager(s) have authority to agree to the researcher's proposal?
▶ Who will be the recipients and ultimate users of the researcher's findings?
▶ Whose budget will be used?

Mr. Plummer advises that during the planning stage, the researcher find an "angel" to work with. An angel is the highest-level executive in the head office of the client organization, preferably the CEO or president, who can compel the underling managers to work closely together and with the researcher. Of course, the angel will not be involved with the gritty details of the project, but the knowledge that he or she is interested in and watching the project as it unfolds will help immensely when managers disagree or squabble.

Now, we must relate to you the most important difference between the marketing manager and the market researcher. The entire time that the dialogue is going on between the manager and the researcher, the manager is fixed on one goal: "How can I solve this problem?" However, the researcher is fixed on a different but highly related goal, "How can I gather information relevant to the problem that will help the manager solve his or her problem?" The researcher must focus on the research proposal which we take up next.

FORMULATE THE MARKETING RESEARCH PROPOSAL

As you have learned, the research objectives are the all important results of the meeting(s) between the manager and researcher in their quest to specify the marketing management problem. That is, the marketing researcher's first task is to talk to the marketing manager and to develop as complete a picture of the marketing management problem as possible. With the marketing management problem statement agreed to, the marketing researcher develops the research objectives and quickly moves to the formulation of a marketing research proposal. A **marketing research proposal** is a formal document prepared by the researcher, and it serves three important functions: (1) It defines the marketing management problem, (2) it specifies the research objectives, and (3) it details the research method proposed by the researcher to accomplish the research objectives.[12]

Define the Marketing Management Problem

The first step in a research proposal is to describe the marketing management problem. This is normally accomplished with a single statement, rarely more than a few sentences long, called the problem statement. The problem statement typically identifies four factors: (1) the company, division, or principals involved; (2) the symptoms; (3) the possible causes of these symptoms; and (4) the anticipated uses of the research information. Of course, if the manager is faced with a marketing opportunity rather than a marketing problem, the "symptoms" would be "signals."

Identifying the company, division, and principals is important for several reasons. First, if the researcher is external to the company requesting the work, it is common courtesy to reference the company. Second, if the proposal will be reviewed internally, identification of the division involved helps the reviewers understand the need for the research because they should be intimately knowledgeable about the division's circumstances. Finally, it is essential to note which manager (or set of managers) has approached the researcher because it is the manager's perceptions that have served to formulate the marketing management problem. Also, because managers sometimes change positions in a company, noting who initiated the work is helpful for the replacement.

The symptoms and causes are noted to verify that the researcher "sees" the decision problem with the manager's eyes. Again, if internal review occurs, there may be some disagreement about these aspects of the problem, and explicitly stating them in an early stage serves to bring these differences of opinion out into a forum for discussion. Finally, noting in general how the information will be used by the decision maker helps clarify the range of alternatives being considered to remedy the situation. In sum, the problem statement section of the formal marketing research proposal is necessary to confirm that the researcher and the manager are "on the same page."

There is one instance when the problem definition work takes place without the manager–researcher dialogue. This situation seemingly saves the researcher a great deal of work, but it places a tremendous burden on the researcher to design an out-

A marketing research proposal does three things: (1) defines the problem, (2) specifies research objectives, and (3) details the research method.

The problem statement identifies (1) the client company and principals, (2) symptoms, (3) possible causes of these symptoms, and (4) anticipated uses of the research.

The research proposal ensures that the researcher and the manager see the problem in the same way.

standing research proposal. Read Marketing Research Insight 4.3 to learn about the good and bad news accompanying RFPs and ITBs.

Translate the Research Objectives to Be Researchable

After describing the marketing management problem in the marketing research proposal, the marketing researcher must reiterate the specific research objectives. As we just described, the research objectives address information gaps that must be closed in order for the manager to go about resolving the marketing management problem. That is, the researcher develops a tentative set of information needs the manager requires to solve the problem.

Generally, the researcher prepares an itemized listing of the information objectives agreed upon by the manager as essential for this purpose. In creating this list, the researcher must keep in mind four important qualities. Each research objective must be precise, detailed, clear, and operational. To be precise means that the terminology is

The proposal itemizes the information objectives agreed to by the manager and researcher.

▶ **Additional Insights**

RFP? ITB? QED?

Occasionally, managers prepare an RFP or *request for proposal*. Another name for an RFP is an ITB or *invitation to bid*. An RFP or an ITB makes the marketing researcher's job a great deal easier as the manager must think through the marketing decision problem a great deal in order to prepare the document. This process takes place without the researcher–manager dialogue that we have described in this chapter.

Although each RFP or ITB is different, there are sections or parts commonly found in all of them. These sections are:

▶ *Introduction.* Identification of the company or organization that originates the RFP, with background information about the company.
▶ *Scope of Proposal.* Description of the basic problem at hand.
▶ *Deliverables.* Specification of the tasks to be undertaken and products to be produced and delivered to the company soliciting the proposal or bid. For example, the deliverable may be "a survey of 1,000 representative recent users of the company's services, described in a report with text, tabulations, figures, and relevant statistical analyses."
▶ *Evaluation Criteria.* The criteria or standards that will be used to judge the proposals, often set up as a point system in which the proposal is awarded a number of points for each area based on the quality of the work that is proposed.

▶ *Deadline.* The date by which the deliverables must be delivered.
▶ *Bidding Specifics.* Necessary items such as the due date for the proposal or bid, specific information required about the bidding company, proposal length and necessary elements (such as sample questions that may appear on the questionnaire), intended subcontract work, payment schedule, contact individual within the origination company, and so on.

As can be seen, a document that specifies these elements of the marketing management problem signals that the managers involved believe they have a firm grasp of the decision. There is no need for the researcher to have a dialogue with the manager(s) about the management problem at hand. As you may have playfully used in your basic trigonometry class, for the designation "QED" that stands for the Latin phrase *quod erat demonstrandum* students often substitute, *"quite easily done"* when they solve an easy trig problem. QED would seem to apply here because the researcher is spared the great deal of time and effort normally invested in the problem definition stage. However, RFPs or ITBs are broadcast to the research industry as a whole, which means that literally any research company can respond with a proposal. Thus, the bad news for the researcher is that there is a great deal more competition for the business in this situation.

understandable to the marketing manager and that it accurately captures the essence of each item to be researched. Detail is provided by elaborating, perhaps with examples, each item. The objective is clear if there is no doubt as to what will be researched and how the information will be presented to the manager. Finally, the objective must be operational. In other words, it implies specific measurement scales and even statistical analyses. These do not need to be in the list of research objectives; however, the manager and researcher may have discussed these in general, and the researcher should have specific operational plans in mind, as we will describe shortly.

Research objectives must be precise, detailed, clear, and operational.

In other words, in preparing the research proposal, the researcher often translates the research objectives into a format that facilitates the research process. Ideally, this translation phase concerns three operations: (1) specify constructs and operational definitions, (2) organize constructs into relationships, and (3) specify a model. We will describe each one in turn.

Specify Constructs and Operational Definitions A marketing researcher generally thinks in terms of constructs when he or she listens to the marketing manager articulate the problem. A **construct** is a marketing term or concept that is somehow involved in the marketing management problem that will be researched. Examples of constructs that are often investigated in marketing research studies are listed in Table 4.6. You should recognize some of them from your previous marketing courses. This is not a complete list; other constructs include lifestyle or psychographics, which are descriptions of how consumers think and behave.

The researcher uses marketing constructs and envisions operational definitions of these constructs.

Although managers and researchers share the language of constructs, the researcher translates the construct into an **operational definition**, which describes

Table 4.6   **A Representative List of Constructs Often Investigated by Marketing Researchers**

Construct	Operational Definition
Brand awareness	Question: Have you heard of Brand A? ____ Yes ____ No
	Measure: Percentage of respondents having heard of the brand
Recall, recognition of advertising	Question: Do you recall seeing an advertisement for Brand A?
	Measure: Percentage who remember seeing a specific ad
Knowledge of product features	Question: Indicate which of Brand A's features you know about.
	Measure: Percentage who know about each feature
Brand familiarity	Question: Are you "unfamiliar," "somewhat familiar," or "very familiar" with Brand A?
	Measure: Percentage for each familiarity category
Comprehension of product benefits	Question: For each product benefit statement, indicate if you agree or disagree.
	Measure: Percentage who agree with each benefit statement
Attitudes, feelings toward brand	Question: Rate Brand A on a 1–5 scale, where 1 = "poor" and 5 = "excellent"
	Measure: Average rating
Intentions to purchase	Question: What is the probability that you will buy Brand A the next time you purchase this product?
	Measure: Average probability
Past purchase or use	Question: Have you used Brand A in the past three months?
	Measure: Percentage who have used it
Brand loyalty	Question: With your last five purchases of the product, how many times did you buy Brand A?
	Measure: Percentage of times
Satisfaction	Question: Rate Brand A on a 1–5 scale, where 1 = "unsatisfied" and 5 = "very satisfied"
	Measure: Average rating

how the marketing researcher intends to measure the construct. That is, an operational definition implies a specific question format that will be used in a survey to gather information about the construct at hand. You can see by examining the operational definitions in Table 4.6 how the researcher measures each construct. In actuality, there are several alternative operational definitions possible for any construct, and there are important considerations that must be determined before the operational definition is finalized. It is premature to delve into these factors at this time; we develop them in detail in Chapter 10. Whereas the marketing manager thinks of constructs as ways to better understand or better respond to this market, the marketing researcher usually envisions them as questions or sets of questions on a questionnaire. Typically, the operational definition of each construct is *not* included in the research proposal. Rather, when the researcher specifies the construct in the research proposal, the operational definition is a mental note he or she makes that will serve as the bridge to the questionnaire design phase of the research project.

An operational definition relates to how the researcher will measure a construct.

Identify Relationships Marketing researchers must consider relationships that connect the various constructs. A **relationship** is a meaningful link believed to exist between two constructs. For instance, one such relationship might be that customers will buy more of a product when the price is lowered and that they will buy less of it when the price is increased. There may be a positive relationship between liking satellite TV and intention to rent an apartment with this feature. You should note that these relationships typically link the marketing manager's decision factors with their anticipated outcomes.

There are two basic sources for the relationships the marketing researcher identifies. The first source is beliefs and assumptions provided by the marketing manager. Granted, there may be some uncertainty involved, but usually the marketing manager is familiar with the basic driving forces in his or her marketing management problem. The second source is the researcher's general marketing knowledge. Where great uncertainty exists or where the marketing manager has not indicated a belief or suspicion, the researcher is likely to fall back on universally accepted relationships.

A relationship is a meaningful link believed to exist between two constructs.

Decide on a Model Once you take a set of constructs and order their relationships with some understandable logic, you have created a **model**. Occasionally, the marketing manager can provide a model that ties together the various constructs and their relationships. Often managers do not have these models in mind so it is up to the researcher to find or create one. Fortunately, a number of models exist that can serve as frameworks for marketing research objectives. One such model, called the "hierarchy of effects," is provided in Table 4.7 in which we have applied it to the satellite television being contemplated by our University Estates manager. The hierarchy of effects traces the steps a consumer goes through in learning about, forming an opinion regarding, trying, and then adopting a product, brand, or service. The steps constitute constructs, and the progression from unawareness to purchase loyalty is the model that ties the constructs together.

A model connects constructs with understandable logic.

The amount of effort that the researcher expends in gaining a feel for the marketing management problem pays off in model specification. By studying the manager's circumstances and resources, pondering the competitive environment, factoring in consumer behavior considerations, and otherwise reflecting on everything he or she has learned during their conversation, the marketing researcher has the opportunity to develop a custom model of possible problem causes, solutions, and consequences. Sometimes these models are elaborate, but often they are simple. For instance, the University Estates manager expects the satellite television to make

Table **How the "Hierarchy of Effects" Model Can Frame Research for University Estates' Satellite Television Decision**

HIERARCHY STAGE	DESCRIPTION	RESEARCH QUESTION
Unawareness	Not aware of your brand	What percentage of prospective student residents are unaware of satellite television?
Awareness	Aware of your brand	What percentage of prospective student residents are aware of satellite television?
Knowledge	Know something about your brand	What percentage of prospective student residents who are aware of it know that satellite television (1) has 150 channels, (2) premium channels, and (3) pay-for-view?
Liking	Have a positive feeling about your brand	What percentage of prospective student residents who know something about satellite televison feel negatively, positively, or neutral about having it in their apartment?
Intention	Intend to buy your brand next	What percentage of prospective student residents who are positive about having satellite television in their apartment intend to rent an apartment with it?
Purchase*	Have purchased your brand in the past	What percentage of the market purchased (tried) your brand in the past?
Repurchase/Loyalty*	Purchase your brand regularly	What percentage of the market has purchased your brand more than other brands in the last five purchases?

*Not applicable to University Estates as the satellite television feature is not currently available.

University Estates more attractive and, thus, to cause more prospective student residents to consider living there.

Detail the Proposed Research Method

Finally, the research proposal will detail the proposed **research method**. That is, it will describe the data collection method, questionnaire design, sampling plan, and all other aspects of the proposed marketing research in as much detail as the researcher thinks is necessary for the manager to grasp the plan. It will also include a tentative timetable and specify the cost of the research undertaking. Proposals vary greatly in format and detail, but most share the basic components we have described: problem statement; research objectives; and proposed research method, including timetable and cost. We realize that you will study in detail all of these topics in chapters that follow so we will not delve into them now.

The proposed research method identifies data collection mode, questionnaire design, sample plan, and other aspects of the anticipated marketing research.

What does a marketing research proposal look like? We have prepared Marketing Research Insight 4.4, which is the proposal written for University Estates based on the way it has been described in this chapter.

PUTTING IT ALL TOGETHER USING THE INTEGRATED CASE FOR THIS TEXTBOOK

In this section, we are going to continue with our integrated case study, "The Hobbit's Choice: A Restaurant." You were introduced to this case in Chapter 2, Case 2.2, pages 42–43. Please go back and read the introduction to this case as it sets the scene for the description we are about to provide for you in this chapter. Again, this integrated case appears in the case section of many chapters, and your instructor may assign these to you either as written assignments or as class discussion items throughout your courses. Here is the continuation of our integrated case.

Here is a marketing research situation that is treated as an integrated case appearing at the end of most chapters of the textbook.

▶ **Additional Insights**

Marketing Research Proposal for University Estates: Proposal to Determine the Attractiveness of Satellite Television to Prospective Student Residents of University Estates

Introduction

This proposal responds to a request on the part of the principals of University Estates, 2525 Bright Drive, New Haven, Connecticut, to provide assistance in its deliberations of adding satellite television to attract prospective university student residents.

Background

University Estates is experiencing an occupancy drop from 100 percent to 80 percent. This decline coincides with the addition of cable television now available in all University Estates competitors but not at University Estates. University Estates principals are contemplating the addition of a satellite television system that will include 150 channels, four premium channels, and pay-for-view. Information is needed to assess prospective student residents' reactions to this possible additional service.

Research Objectives

Discussion with University Estates managers suggests that answers are desired to the following questions:

▶ To what extent do prospective student residents want satellite television?

▶ Will University Estates be more attractive than competing apartment complexes if it has the satellite television programming package?

Research Framework

Based on Research Associates' understanding of the decision facing University Estates principals, and further using the Company's experience in these types of questions, the Company proposes to use the "hierarchy of effects" model

as a framework in which to cast the research questions to be used in the proposed survey.

This framework addresses the decision by breaking it into constructs or factors that delineate a complete picture of the factors that may facilitate or hamper the attractiveness of the satellite programming package.

Using this model, the research questions are:

▶ What percentage of prospective student residents are aware of satellite television?

▶ What percentage of prospective student residents who are aware of it know that satellite television (1) has 150 channels and (2) four premium channels, and (3) pay-for-view?

▶ What percentage of prospective student residents who know something about satellite television have a positive feeling (as opposed to negative or neutral feelings) about having it in their apartment?

▶ What percentage of prospective student residents who are positive about having satellite television in their apartment intend to rent an apartment with it?

▶ Is University Estates with satellite television more attractive than competing apartment complexes with cable television?

Research Method

Research Associates proposes to undertake a telephone survey of 500 full-time university students who live off-campus. Research Associates will prepare and pretest the survey questionnaire, subcontract the telephone survey work, analyze the data, and present the findings to University Estates principals within six weeks of the execution of a contract. The cost of the proposed survey work is $10,000.

RETURN TO *Your Integrated Case*

The Hobbit's Choice: A Restaurant to Be or Not to Be*

Although Jeff Dean feels prepared for the business and is encouraged by his banker, Walker Stripling, he has several concerns. He knows that, although he has learned quite a bit about restaurant operation in his area and also quite a bit about upscale restaurants from his friends in other cities, he is not sure if there is an interest in his city for such a restaurant. Even though the metro area is nearly 500,000 in population, he has no assurances that there are enough persons with the income and tastes necessary to make his business successful. He needs some additional information that would give him some inkling that a market exists. He does not want to lose the money that he has so diligently saved during the last 15 years. There are also other decisions for which he feels he needs additional information. He is not certain how to promote the restaurant in his town. Sure, the owners of the other restaurants have told him what they did but they already had well-established reputations in their city. Where will he promote the restaurant when he first opens? Also, there are many choices to make about the design of the restaurant, the price the market is willing to pay for an upscale entrée, the best location, and so on. Now that his banker is willing to work with him and the financing is in good shape, Jeff Dean is ready to start making the other decisions needed to open The Hobbit's Choice.

Jeff Dean tells Walker Stripling that he is concerned about making the design, location, and promotion decisions. Walker tells him his experience with existing restaurant clients will not be of much help because Jeff's restaurant concept is so new to the market. Walker suggests that Jeff call the local office of CMG Research. CMG is a full-service firm that offers custom-designed research studies. The research firm has been in business for over 30 years and has offices in several cities around the country. Walker gave Jeff a business card from CMG Research, and later in the day, Jeff calls CMG and is referred to Cory Rogers, project director.

Cory Rogers asked Jeff Dean to generally explain what he is looking for from CMG. After Jeff explains that he is interested in gathering some research to help him make some decisions about opening up an upscale restaurant in the area, Cory tells him that he will check to ensure there were no conflicts of interest with other clients and will get back in touch. The next day, Cory calls and asks that Jeff spend one and one-half hours with him.

Later that day, Jeff visits the offices of CMG and is greeted by Cory Rogers. Cory has arranged a comfortable, quiet meeting place and has asked his staff assistant to please not disturb him during the meeting with Jeff. Cory encourages Jeff to talk freely about his concept and assures him that the company has no other clients interested in such a business and that everything Jeff says will be kept in strict confidence. Jeff explains everything to Cory including his desire to open the restaurant after having worked in the industry for 15

Will an upscale restaurant called "The Hobbit's Choice" appeal to the market? Marketing research can answer this question.

years. Cory asks probing questions that center around the steps Jeff will have to take to go into business. Even though Jeff assures Cory that the financing is set and that Walker Stripling at First Bank is enthusiastic about the plans, Cory covers all the details of the financial plans as well. Jeff is surprised when almost two hours have passed so quickly and is surprised again when Cory says, "I would like to investigate some of these issues more thoroughly and then we will need another fairly long meeting right away." Jeff enthusiastically agrees, and another appointment is made.

At the second meeting Jeff is impressed with how informed Cory is about the restaurant business. It is apparent that overnight Cory has learned many facts about the business, such as the importance of tracking food costs, table turnover rates, and financial ratios and operating expense norms for the restaurant business. He has also ordered a marketing research report that was prepared last year about upscale restaurants in general. Jeff feels assured that CMG is a good choice and the two continue their discussion about the decisions that would be necessary to open and operate The Hobbit's Choice.

The second meeting is structured around some issues that Cory says are key to the success or failure of The Hobbit's Choice restaurant.

Is There Demand for an Upscale Restaurant and at What Price Level?

Cory feels that one of the key issues deals with demand. Are there adequate numbers of customers in their metro area to generate profitable revenue? Cory tells Jeff that, based on his research, several successful upscale restaurants operate in metro areas as large as theirs. However, Cory is quick to point out that there are big differences in markets in terms of consumer preferences and income levels. *Population alone is not* a good predictor of success but at least there is evidence that other metro areas of 500,000 support upscale restaurants. The two individuals spend the rest of the appointment discussing operating expenses for the restaurant. Cory tells Jeff he will e-mail him an Excel spreadsheet with a break-even analysis based on their assumptions about operating costs and possible entrée prices. The break-even analysis will tell Jeff how many customers he will need to have weekly in order to break even. Different revenues are included for lunch and dinner meals. The next day, Jeff receives the break-even analysis and calls Cory for another meeting. He tells Cory that he is excited because he feels the break-even figure is easily achievable.

Cory Rogers feels the best way to start off the meeting with Jeff Dean is to make certain that Jeff has not placed too much faith, at this point, in their break-even analysis. Cory points out to Jeff that the purpose of the break-even analysis, at this stage, is to see if they are dealing with a reasonable number of restaurant patrons required to break even. He explains that sometimes CMG has to advise clients, after a rough break-even analysis, that they do not recommend going further with the project even though it means losing their business. "Our philosophy at CMG," Cory states, "is that you will come back to us when you need research in the future. We want to provide research that leads to success." He tells Jeff he views this as only a very rough start that basically has informed them to continue with the planning. Jeff agrees that this exercise is necessary, and he thanks Cory for being "up-front" with him. The last thing Jeff wants is to be led down the path to failure. Cory says what they want to do is to get some other inkling, some measurement from this market, that consumers in their town will support an upscale restaurant. And they want some idea of what this market would be willing to pay for a dinner meal in an upscale restaurant. "We're making a big assumption that the price per meal we've entered in our break-even analysis is valid. I would hypothesize that people in our city would expect an evening dinner entrée to be priced at $18 but I don't have any supporting data."

Cory Rogers then showed Jeff Dean a forecasting model to predict the number of customers expected to patronize a restaurant. One of the most important components in the forecasting model was a measure of the percentage of consumers in the market who stated that they would very likely patronize the restaurant and the average amount these same persons were spending, per capita, in restaurants per month. Also, another important component was the average price consumers would expect to pay for a dinner entrée. Cory explained that they would have to conduct research in their city to determine the amount of these required components to be entered into the forecasting model. Cory told Jeff, "If we can collect valid and reliable information on likelihood to patronize your restaurant, average amount spent in restaurants per month, and the average price to be paid per entrée, we can create a much more accurate break-even analysis and compare that with the number of patrons you can expect. This is the information we need in order to determine if you will have adequate demand for The Hobbits' Choice." In fact, Cory had already made some estimates of demand using the forecasting model. He told Jeff that if only 4 percent of heads of households in the 12 zip code area claimed they were "very likely" to patronize the restaurant and if these same people spent an average of $200 per month in restaurants and were willing to pay an average of $18 for an à la carte entrée, then the model predicted a very successful restaurant operation.

What About Design and Operating Characteristics?

At their next meeting, Cory referred back to questions Jeff raised in their first meeting. Jeff had told Cory there were a number of design and operating characteristics that he had seen in other restaurants but he didn't know what he should use in The Hobbit's Choice. How elegant should the décor be? Should there be live entertainment such as a jazz combo? Should the restaurant have a water view? Should the wait staff be formerly dressed in tuxedos? Should the wait staff be very formal or informal in their behavior? Should the menu include a variety of choices including exotic entrées not found in other restaurants such as elk, bison, or truffles? Would traditional desserts be desirable or should they offer unusual desserts served with fanfare such as flaming Bananas Foster or Baked Alaska? Would patrons view valet parking as a convenience or an extra expense? And what about driving time? Jeff thought if he located in a central section of the city, people from all over the metro area would come if they didn't mind the driving time.

Cory's background research revealed that Jeff was correct in having concerns about all these issues. Successful upscale restaurants in other cities have such a variety of design and operating characteristics that it is impossible to tell what each market values. For example, one very successful, very expensive restaurant has the barest of décor. Its plain brick walls and wooden furniture seem to add to the ambiance for customers in this city. On the other hand, a similar restaurant in terms of menu and prices in another city has very formal décor with curtained walls and large, original antique, upholstered furniture, and expensive chandeliers. Yet another restaurant has no entertainment and another has a jazz combo during dinner hours. It seems that each restaurant owner has discovered what his or her local market desires and this, no doubt, was at least part of the reason for their many years of success in the competitive restaurant business. "Well, we are going to have to rely a great deal on your own personal decisions in terms of how you will specifically design and operate your business," said Cory. "But, we will be able to get some good feedback from our local market when we collect the information we will need to determine demand. I'm just concerned that we don't have a clear handle on the design and operational characteristics that consumers will think important when patronizing a restaurant. We will have to think more about how to clearly determine what these are and how consumers describe them."

Where to Locate The Hobbit's Choice Restaurant?

Jeff is well aware of the old axiom in retail business: The most important three factors for success in retailing are location, location, and location! Even though he knows his restaurant will be unique in the market, the location has to be considered convenient to his patrons. "You are right," said Cory Rogers, "many customers will be willing to drive far out of their way for a unique experience once or maybe even a couple of times. But everything we know about the restaurant business tells us that, if you want repeat business, you must be within a reasonable driving time of your primary target market." This makes perfect sense to Jeff. In almost every case, the owners of the successful upscale restaurants told him, "Sure, we get some business from the out-of-town tourists like yourself, but 80 percent of our revenue comes from our local, repeat customers."

Cory Rogers laid out a map of the city showing the 12 zip code areas of the metro area. Along with the map, Cory had acquired demographic information on each zip code and he categorized them into four groups based on their commonalities. He summarized the information on the zip codes as follows:

Location A: Zip Codes 1, 2. Low-income, older population located in the south-southeastern part of the city. Cory and Jeff both clearly rule this part of the city out.

Location B: Zip Codes 3, 4, and 5. Located in the northwestern part of the city with high-income, older population of retirees and established professionals. Essentially, these are families with inherited wealth, professionals, and entrepreneurs. There is also a growing population of young professionals and managers who are upwardly mobile. Cory explains that these younger families are moving into the area and renovating older homes. Jeff thinks this could possibly be a good area in which to locate. He expresses some concern about an older population and older homes. He recalls how neighborhoods seemed to decline as homes get old. Cory suggests they keep an open mind about this area since the incomes are so high.

Location C: Zip Codes 6, 7, 8, and 9. Almost double the population of areas 3, 4, and 5 who live in the eastern part of the city along the shoreline. These are young, upwardly mobile and older, upper-middle-class households with occupations in management, government, and young entrepreneurs. This is Jeff's part of town and he feels that this area represents an excellent opportunity. Although the incomes are not as high as in zip codes 3, 4, and 5, there are almost twice as many people and they have above-average incomes. Jeff comments that he has told several of his neighbors about his upscale restaurant idea and, without exception, they have each vowed to patronize the business. Also, Jeff is convinced that a waterfront view was important and this was the only section of town where waterfront property could be acquired. Again, Cory suggests they keep an open mind.

Location D: Zip Codes 10, 11, and 12. Middle-class neighborhoods; primarily laborers with occupations in the building and manufacturing trade who are located in the western part of the city. Jeff and Cory quickly eliminate this area as an alternative along with zip code 12, which was primarily an industrialized southwestern part of the city with relatively few permanent residents.

Jeff notes that the demographic information available suggests either a location somewhere within zip codes 3, 4, and 5 or within 6, 7, 8, and 9. Unfortunately, the two sets of zip codes are not close to one another. Cory tells Jeff the decision is going to be one or the other, not a central location. He also explains that they need information from the market to determine which area represents the best location. Once they make the decision as to which area in which to locate, they can start dealing with choosing the specific site because there seem to be good alternatives in both the areas. Cory tells Jeff he is going to start working on a questionnaire that will address the issues they have discussed up to this point. The two set up another meeting a week later.

How to Promote The Hobbit's Choice Restaurant?

At their next meeting Jeff reminds Cory that they have not fully discussed his questions regarding how to best promote the restaurant. He is most concerned about which media and programming to select rather than ad copy. He feels comfortable about what to say in his promotional messages but he is not confident that he knows where to say it. They discuss some ideas for preopening publicity and some direct marketing. Cory recommends a local ad agency to help with these decisions and actually doing some of the work. Jeff eagerly accepts the suggestions knowing that he will be very involved with all the details of getting the restaurant operational. Jeff asks, "But, after the grand opening, where am I going to direct my advertising?" After some discussion, the two agree that Jeff will be using all the media from time to time: radio, television, newspaper, and perhaps the local city magazine. Jeff says he knows which medium to use and where to place the message for virtually every type of restaurant in town. He knows where the fast foods run their ads, where the cafeterias run their ads, where the restaurant/lounges run their ads, and so on. But he does not have a clue as to where to place ads for The Hobbit's Choice.

Cory next shows Jeff the questionnaire he has been working on. It contains the questions needed to measure likelihood of patronizing the restaurant and the other issues the two had agreed needed addressing. Cory then identifies each medium and the two discuss the alternatives. For radio, there are many stations from which to choose and each provides a listenership study that gives some demographics on the audience of each station. But, even with many stations, Cory and Jeff agree they all break down into these station formats: country and western, jazz, easy listening, rock, and talk radio. Each station provides demographic information on its listeners by income. So, once Jeff Dean knows what type of programming to select, he will then need to know which specific stations to select which offer the desired type of programming. By knowing if there are differences in income between customers with different intentions to patronize the restaurant, Dean will be able to select the appropriate radio stations. For television, few local ad opportunities exist except during daytime television, local sporting events, and the news. They both agree that news broadcasts were likely to be the most appealing but which news broadcast will hit their target market? There was a morning, 7:00 A.M. time slot, a noon slot, early evening (6:00 P.M.), and late evening (10:00 P.M.) slot. As for the newspaper, which section did most members of the target market read? Editorial? Business? Local? Sports? Health, Living and Entertainment? Classifieds? Jeff noted that the sports section seems to be a good place to promote restaurants. As far as the local city magazine, Jeff's primary concern is whether or not the target market subscribes to it. It was an attractive, high-quality publication, but it was expensive and he has never heard how many subscriptions the magazine had. He wonders if more than a handful of subscribers will read an expensive ad in the magazine. Jeff recalls that three years ago when the magazine started, the owner gave away many copies in order to develop interest. But for the last two years the magazine has only been mailed to actual subscribers. Cory tells Jeff that he will take the notes from this meeting and add questions to the survey questionnaire he is working on to address the questions Jeff has about promoting The Hobbit's Choice. Cory tells Jeff that if he had answers to the questions they had discussed and advice from an ad agency, Jeff should be in good shape as far as promotion decisions.

Finally, Cory said, "Now I need to put together some standard demographic questions we will ask on the survey. These demographics will help us do a number of things. First, they can tell us about the sample we selected. We will prepare a demographic profile of the sample. We want to know on which group of people we are basing your decisions. Second, we will be able to profile the likely patrons of The Hobbit's Choice. This will help us more clearly understand your target market and will be helpful to you when you make future decisions, such as does the restaurant appeal more to females than males and knowing if media habits vary between males and females?" Jeff thanked Cory and left the meeting feeling more confident than ever that he is on the road to realizing his dream.

*Note: The Hobbit's Choice Restaurant is the integrated case used throughout the textbook and introduced on pages 42–43.

We realize that this case has a great deal of information, but we have included subheadings to show the major concerns of the case. In fact, the subheadings are clues to the primary marketing problems being faced by Jeff Dean in his quest to build and operate The Hobbit's Choice. You will find the six major marketing problems facing Jeff Dean in his Hobbit's Choice Restaurant vision identified in Table 4.8. You will be challenged to use this information to design research objectives in Case 4.2 on page 115, and you will encounter a new marketing research method application challenge at the end of almost every chapter in the textbook.

There are six major marketing problems in our Hobbits' Choice Restaurant integrated case.

| Table **4.8** | **Marketing Problems for The Hobbit's Choice Restaurant** |

PROBLEM ITEM	DESCRIPTION
Will the restaurant be successful?	Will a sufficient number of people patronize the restaurant?
How should the restaurant be designed?	What about décor, atmosphere, specialty entrées and desserts, wait staff uniforms, reservations, special seating, and so on?
What should be the average price of entrées?	How much are potential patrons willing to pay for the entrées as well as for the house specials?
What is the optimum location?	How far from patrons' homes are patrons willing to drive, and are there any special location features (such as waterfront, ample parking, etc.) to take into consideration?
What is the profile of the target market?	What are the demographic and lifestyle profiles of those who are going to patronize The Hobbit's Choice?
What are the best promotional media?	What advertising media should be used to best reach the target market?

Q: Has marketing management decision making, particularly the decision making that is related to marketing research, been affected by the online environments of clients, consumers, and/or competitors, and, if so, how?

BLUE RIBBON PANEL on [Online Research]

Bill MacElroy
President
Socratic Technologies

A: Absolutely, and the biggest impact is, in a word: speed. The traditional process of marketing decision making involves a number of steps including problem identification, research objectives and design, data collection, analysis, recommended actions, management consideration, and, finally, action in the form of broad policy implementation.

With the use of the Internet, however, the management of the marketing mix, which used to take months, is now being conducted in milliseconds through e-commerce technology. Policy formation is being replaced by instantaneous one-to-one modeling capabilities. Pricing "policies," for example, are being replaced by "smart intercepts." In this business model, each consumer who is purchasing a product or service online is offered any one of a number of initial price points. By tracking which prices lead to a consummated sale, an optimal price point (or set of price points) is determined. With each iteration, or consumer, the data on which price is determined grow and the price being offered stabilizes at the price that has proven to increase revenue margins.

These types of technologies will lead to a major upheaval in the way the business of marketing research is conducted.

Allen Hogg
President
Burke, Inc.

A: Proficient marketing managers are taking advantage of the online environment to improve their own decision making, as well as decisions made by information users throughout their organizations. Online applications that provide "real-time" access to research findings are a key way people are being empowered to make data-based decisions.

The quicker turnaround time associated with online data collection is also helping companies move with "Internet speed." With shortening product development cycle times forcing organizations to seek rapid consumer feedback, concept testing has become the number-one online survey application.

Other information now collected is being used to help companies navigate their way through the rapidly changing online world. When designing their organizations' Web presence, expert marketing managers are continually monitoring "the voice of the visitor." Information on Web site behavior is also collected, and systems have been set up to tailor individuals' online experiences according to their prior activity. In addition, marketing managers are seeking to quantify the impact of online advertising when making decisions about its place in their promotional mix. They are also using consumer input to create personalized, direct-marketing e-mail messages.

George Terhanian
Vice President of
Internet Research
Harris Interactive, Inc.

A: Organizations that have benefited substantially from online research include, among others, CPG firms, automotive firms, telecommunications firms, advertising agencies, financial services institutions, pharmaceutical companies, and any company interested in understanding e-business. Online research has improved the salience and amount of evidence available to these companies, thereby allowing them to make better-informed decisions far more quickly. Increasingly, companies that conduct online research are discovering that the ability to move swiftly and to be the first in their industry to recognize and act on an opportunity enables them to achieve competitive advantage.

Online research has also expanded the available supply of design and analysis tools for addressing the concerns of these organizations, thereby creating new opportunities for research. For instance, the Internet has enabled us to employ techniques that were once too costly or unwieldy to employ routinely through traditional data collection modes. When we were evaluating whether to acquire the custom research group of Yankelovich Partners, for example, we explored whether and how we might transfer some of their sophisticated analytic methods to the Internet. To our delight, it turned out that many of these methods were better suited for the Internet than for other modalities. For example, Yankelovich's market structure analyses required respondents to sort "cards" into piles in the presence of a facilitator. This is an unwieldy, time-consuming, expensive activity even among the most able facilitators. The Web technologies that we have developed, however, facilitate card sorting in the absence of a facilitator, thereby reducing significantly the cost and time required for data collection and analysis, as well as the quality of data that we collect.

As my colleague here at Harris Interactive, Humphrey Taylor, chairman of *The Harris Poll*®, likes to say, "Online research is another arrow in our quiver."

Keith Price
Vice President
Greenfield Online

A: As a marketer, what could be more important than knowing what consumers think about your product before making critical decisions? Consumers are the driving force behind brand success, and receiving feedback on an ongoing basis enables marketers to make more informed and effective decisions that ultimately provide immeasurable return on investment by lowering customer acquisition costs and improving retention rates. Consumer loyalty is at an all-time low due, in part, to the fact that the Internet and related technologies have presented innumerable purchase options from vendors all around the world. Communicating on a frequent basis is no longer a "should do"—it is a "must do."

This knowledge has always been valuable, was originally obtained informally, and ultimately evolved into a common practice that paved the way for the principles of marketing research. Marketing research initially was conceived based on marketers' need for more information; advanced technology makes it possible to gather more cost-efficient and timely data, paving the way for ongoing continuous interaction with target audiences.

Internet research affords marketers one of today's most valuable and constrained resources—time. Research now has to fit into abbreviated timetables and provide marketers with more insights than ever before imagined. Decision makers can no longer afford to conduct research and wait weeks for results to be tabulated and analyzed. Consumer opinions now change quickly and feedback that was gathered weeks ago is no longer actionable and/or accurate. Online marketing research makes it possible to gather consumer feedback quickly and efficiently.

Lee Smith
CEO
Insight Express

A: All aspects of business, including marketing management, are being asked to perform more with less. That is, marketers are being required to introduce more products with less staff and generate greater profits with less risk and investment. As markets become more competitive and the pace of business accelerates, research becomes a hidden competitive and essential weapon. Marketers will use real-time feedback as a tool to guide their decisions—big and small. Research, enabled by the online environment, will move from infrequent, strategic, and expensive to daily, tactical, and remarkably affordable. Online research will enable marketers to weave consumer opinion into the fabric of their business—from considering new-product ideas to making decisions regarding mature products. Every decision will involve "checking the market" and will aid in the creation of products that customers want—enabling the marketer to do more with less.

Doss Struse
Senior Vice President
Client Service
Knowledge
Networks, Inc.

A: In general, I think not yet. There are certainly exceptions—firms that conduct much of their business online in fact can establish a dialogue with their consumers, which may be a combination of listening to what consumers request, asking what consumers want or need, and watching how they respond to various offers. However, in most instances online research has been viewed as a way to do traditional forms of research more quickly and more cheaply. The firms that are using online research to innovate new approaches to understanding consumers are still in the early stages of developing these approaches. Although I would expect these to affect marketing decision making, this is still largely in the future.

*To learn about the panel members, see the Preface of this book.

SUMMARY

This chapter began by describing important differences between marketing managers and researchers. Because they have different orientations and work in different worlds, it is essential that an open dialogue be established. Only in this way can the manager's problem be translated into a meaningful marketing research endeavor. The marketing management problem is often complex. It is important that the researcher gain background on the company, product, and market involved. The manager's circumstances, objectives, and resources must be identified as well as any other salient factors in the environment. Symptoms such as slipping market share compel the manager to action, but the researcher and manager must enumerate the possible causes and reasonable courses of action to resolve the problem. During the dialogue, the researcher will become aware of any assumptions or beliefs about the problem or possible solutions held by the manager and will determine where information gaps exist and the needs that must be addressed with a research effort.

The researcher uses the research objectives to formulate a research proposal. In writing the proposal, the marketing researcher thinks in terms of constructs or basic marketing concepts such as brand loyalty or demographic descriptors of buyers. Typically, the researcher thinks ahead and has in mind operational definitions or ways to state the questions and tabulate the results. These constructs are arranged in logical relationships and sometimes there are models of how they fit together. Ultimately, the marketing researcher must create a research proposal that states the problem, specifies the research objectives, identifies relationships, possibly in the form of a model, and suggests a research plan that indicates how the marketing researcher will address the marketing management problem at hand.

KEY TERMS

Marketing management problem (p. 89)
Opportunity identification (p. 89)
Marketing research objective (p. 89)
Background (p. 90)
Manager's objectives (p. 91)
Symptoms (p. 91)
Iceberg phenomenon (p. 92)
Cause (p. 92)
Possible cause (p. 92)
Probable cause (p. 93)
Solutions (p. 94)

Consequences (p. 95)
Assumptions (p. 95)
Information state (p. 96)
Information gaps (p. 96)
Research objectives (p. 97)
Marketing research proposal (p. 98)
Construct (p. 100)
Operational definition (p. 100)
Relationship (p. 101)
Model (p. 101)
Research method (p. 102)

REVIEW QUESTIONS/APPLICATIONS

1. List five basic differences between marketing managers and marketing researchers.
2. When a marketing manager and a researcher meet, what are the key questions that the researcher should ask the manager in order to better communicate during their first meeting?
3. When should marketing research be undertaken? When should it not be undertaken?
4. List and describe the elements in a marketing management problem.
5. How does a symptom differ from a cause? How does a cause differ from a potential solution?
6. How do possible causes differ from probable causes?
7. What are are possible solutions, and why is it important to identify all possible ones?
8. How do assumptions lead to research objectives?
9. What leads to an information gap?
10. What is a marketing research proposal and what are its three components?
11. What are constructs, who uses them, and how are they envisioned by the marketing researcher?
12. How does a marketing researcher use relationships and models?

13. Sony is contemplating expanding its line of three-inch and six-inch portable televisions. It thinks there are three situations in which this line would be purchased: (1) as a gift, (2) as a set to be used by children in their own rooms, and (3) for use at sporting events. How might the research objective be stated if Sony wished to know what consumers' preferences are with respect to these three possible uses?

14. Take the construct of channel (that is, "brand") loyalty in the case of teenagers viewing MTV. Write at least three different definitions that indicate how a researcher might form a question in a survey to assess the degree of MTV loyalty. One example is "Channel loyalty is determined by a stated preference to view a given channel for a certain type of entertainment."

15. You are the staff human resources trainer at General Mills, which markets food products such as Betty Crocker cake mix. A new researcher with a degree in applied statistics but no marketing background whatsoever has just been hired. List and describe five different marketing management concepts that he should understand before interacting with any brand manager at General Mills to discuss undertaking research.

16. The local Lexus dealer thinks that the four-door sedan with a list price in excess of $50,000 should appeal to Cadillac Seville owners who are thinking about buying a new automobile. He is considering a direct-mail campaign with personalized packages to be sent to owners whose Cadillac Sevilles are over two years old. Each package would contain a professional video of all the Lexus sedan's features and end with an invitation to visit the Lexus dealership. This tactic has never been tried in this market. State the marketing management problem and indicate what research objectives would help the Lexus dealer understand the possible reactions of Cadillac Seville owners to this campaign.

INTERACTIVE LEARNING

Visit the Web site at www.prenhall.com/burnsbush. For this chapter, work through the Self-Study Quizzes, and get instant feedback on whether you need additional studying. On the Web site, you can review the chapter outlines and case information for Chapter 4.

CASE 4.1   Segway HT

In late fall of 2001 the Segway Human Transporter (HT) was introduced to widespread fanfare on the ABC show *Good Morning America*. Known by the code names "Ginger" and "IT" for over a year before the invention was introduced on *Good Morning America*, the product received a substantial amount of preintroduction publicity and created a great deal of interest. The Segway HT is the brainchild of the very successful inventor Dean Kamen. Kamen's DKEA Research and Development company operates out of Manchester, New Hampshire. The two-wheeled Segway carries one person, travels around two to three times walking speed and has, as its central innovative feature, a gyroscope stabilizer that makes it difficult to turn over.

(Visit the Segway HT Web site at www.segway.com)

The Segway HT is a scooter-like device but it is very different from conventional scooters and, in fact, it is very different from all vehicles in that it is designed to operate on sidewalks. The gyroscope stabilizer means that the Segway has very good stability. It has a single hand

Will the Segway HT revolutionize personal transportation?

grip to aid in turning. Speed and direction are controlled by the rider shifting weight. It is electric so it is quiet and pollution free. The Segway E series weighs 80 pounds and is designed to carry a 250-pound rider and 75 pounds of cargo. Plans are to allow customization through racks and accessories. Security is enhanced through an intelligent key. Also, in the future, special racks would be available for users to store their Segways, and chains could be used to lock up Segways just like bikes.

The market being sought by the investors of more than $100 million in the project is a personal transportation device to be used on the sidewalks. To ensure that it is safe to be used on crowded sidewalks, the Segway can travel at slow speeds, backs up as soon as it hits anything, has soft tires that roll over things without hurting them, and does not have a rigid frame like vehicles should it bump into something.

The power for the machine is electricity that is so economical it can carry the average rider for a full day for 5 cents worth of electricity. The Segway HT is designed to comfortably move at 6 to 7 mph on the sidewalk, which is about 2 to 3 times walking speed. Decelerating or going downhill generates electricity and extends the range. It takes up to six hours to fully recharge. The Segway HT operates uphill as well as downhill. It operates in rain and ice and snow. For those who have tested the machine, the conclusion is that in bad weather, it works as well as walking.

Plans are to offer an industrial model for use by industry. It is anticipated that the Segway could be used by postal workers, police, and plant workers. For example, companies with large distribution centers with many workers walking all around placing items on conveyor belts for shipping would obviously be very interested in the Segway HT. However, Segway also believes there is a market among consumers. The company has working prototypes and believes the industrial model will have a price tag of about $8,000, and the consumer model is projected to have a lower cost.

1. What are the marketing management problems?
2. What are the research objectives?

| CASE 4.2 | *Your Integrated Case* |

The Hobbit's Choice Restaurant

The background description for this case is found on pages 42–43.

1. For each of the management problem items specified in Table 4.8 (page 109) identify a corresponding research objective.
2. For each of your research objectives, identify relevant constructs and possible ways to measure each construct.

Chapter 5

Research Design

Applications Methodologies

Practitioner Viewpoint

There are several key criteria for successful market research design. The first requirement is to position research at the front end of a business discussion. When the market researcher is able to participate in up-front discussions, he or she can help to frame the business question to be addressed by the research. With full knowledge of the context in which the business question exists, the researcher can better design a research plan that is targeted, relevant, and actionable.

The second key element of successful research design is the ability of the researcher to act like an internal business consultant. In a consultative environment, the researcher is more likely to expand the depth and breadth of the research in order to better address the business issue. An effective research partner will also be less proprietary about research design, freely integrating other data sources, analytic power, and marketing information system resources necessary to get at the heart of the business issue.

A relatively new tool available to the researcher that can contribute to more timely and efficient research for decision making is online research methodology. At AT&T, an increasing number of customer surveys are conducted online, and online focus groups are becoming more common. These online focus groups include online recruitment of participants, a "virtual" moderator, and a back office chat room for clients monitoring the research to communicate with the moderator.

Full use of the entire package of research design tools should be considered. Each case is unique and although most research begins with exploratory research, sometimes it is appropriate to begin with other research such as marketing tracking studies, a type of descriptive research.

Effective research design is dependent upon early involvement, positioning of the researcher as a business partner, and creative use of multiple research tools for optimal research impact.

Sara Lipson, Vice President
AT&T Brand Asset Management

Randy Zeese
AT&T Brand Research Director

Designing Effective Research to Drive Strategic Marketing: AT&T's Boundless Brand Campaign

Shaping the Strategy

In the fall of 2000, AT&T was faced with a strategic business challenge: Although the company continued to enjoy leadership in its traditional core long-distance business and in heritage brand attributes such as trust and high service quality, it lacked momentum in forward-leaning brand attributes such as innovation and dynamism. Customers still primarily associated AT&T with its core consumer long-distance service business, even though it had become a leading player in the wireless, cable TV, and data services industries as well. An opportunity existed for the development of a brand positioning advertising campaign that would redefine AT&T. A strategic research plan was needed to guide the development and execution of this brand repositioning. But only 12 short weeks were available before the launch of this new positioning campaign at the 2000 Summer Olympics!

Designing the Research Plan: Identifying Key Themes

The market research that ultimately resulted in the launch of the successful AT&T Boundless campaign was multifaceted: First, AT&T researchers determined the important heritage attributes that would serve as the foundation for the core strengths of AT&T (quality, reliability, and trust) and then identified the new attributes that would propel it into the future (innovation, differentiation, and dynamism). This was determined through comprehensive reanalysis of continuous survey research from many sources across more than 500 brands.

Developing Campaign Executions

The next phase of research included the development of possible advertising ideas. The most visually striking campaign execution developed by the advertising agency involved the use of the AT&T logo as the key character in the advertising. Research conducted among consumers revealed that there was more than 75 percent unaided awareness of the AT&T globe—more than enough to substantiate the use of the globe in the advertising campaign. Once this was determined, a series of campaign spots was produced.

Advertising Pretesting

The next phase of research involving the pretesting of campaign spots was immediately begun to measure customer reaction (likeability, breakthrough of key messages). The results identified which of the campaign spots were most effective at communicating the message that AT&T was a Boundless brand, providing innovative services and solutions to business and consumer customers alike.

Guiding Media Exposure

Research was conducted to determine the appropriate level of exposure—or advertising weight—that would be required to successfully launch the campaign. Using analyses from previous brand campaigns, it was determined that at least 200 gross

Where We Are:

1. Establish the need for marketing research
2. Define the problem
3. Establish research objectives
4. **Determine research design**
5. Identify information types and sources
6. Determine methods of accessing data
7. Design data collection forms
8. Determine sample plan and size
9. Collect data
10. Analyze data
11. Prepare and present the final research report

rating points (GRPs) of advertising exposure would be required to drive the new message home.

Postlaunch Advertising Effectiveness Measures

Once the AT&T Boundless brand campaign was launched on opening night of the 2000 Summer Olympics, advertising effectiveness measurements were conducted to determine the awareness levels of the campaign itself and association of the campaign message with AT&T. In addition, customer perceptions of AT&T were measured and compared with perceptions of AT&T before the campaign. As a result of this research, AT&T moved forward with the campaign in earnest, and movement of perceptions of the AT&T brand continued throughout 2001 at levels that exceeded expectations.

Ongoing Research for Continued Success

In mid-2001, while the campaign was less than a year old, additional research was conducted to determine possible wearout of the message and to identify additional themes that would further enhance the campaign's effectiveness. As a result of this follow-up research, the campaign was slightly enhanced to reinforce the role of AT&T as a key partner for success among businesses and enabler of communications effectiveness and freedom among consumers. This new messaging was successfully launched during the 2002 Winter Olympics and serves as the cornerstone of the AT&T Boundless campaign today.

Summary: Research Design Is Key!

Effective design of the research plan is critical to making the research insights actionable! Balancing cost and timeliness factors, the market researcher must develop a comprehensive research plan that addresses the key strategic business issues in a compelling and relevant manner. In the AT&T brand management example, a series of research initiatives was used to guide the development, launch, and strategic update of the most successful brand campaign at AT&T to date!

VROOM! AT&T's Boundless ad campaign helps AT&T connote it is a leader "on the move," providing not only long-distance service but many new telecommunications products and services. An excellent research design led to the most successful brand campaign in AT&T history. By permission, AT&T.

Sara Lipson and Randy Zeese of AT&T provide you with an excellent introduction to the concept of research design. Different problems lead to many different research designs. Researchers like those at AT&T must develop new brand images, others must create new-product designs, test proposed brand names, determine what attributes consumers use to evaluate products and services, assess promotion effectiveness, and so on. No one research approach will satisfy all types of research objectives. However, we can design a research plan for each type of research objective that contains the research approaches most suitable to that problem. In this chapter, we introduce you to the concept of research design. An overview is provided of the various types of research design: exploratory, descriptive, and causal. The chapter concludes with a discussion of test marketing. When you finish this chapter, you should be able to determine the different types of research designs used by AT&T in developing its successful new brand image.

RESEARCH DESIGN

Marketing research methods vary from focus groups to simulated test markets to large, nationally representative sample surveys. Some research objectives require only library research, whereas others may require thousands of personal interviews.

▶ **Meet a Marketing Researcher**

Sara Lipson Coordinates Research Design at AT&T

MARKETING RESEARCH
INSIGHT
5.1

Sara Lipson is vice president of brand asset management for AT&T, responsible for managing domestic and global AT&T brand identity, brand licensing, brand experience metrics,

and corporate communication and sponsorships. She also manages market research for public relations, and investor community and human resources groups. Dr. Lipson completed her doctorate in quantitative sociology at Columbia University while on a research fellowship at the Bureau of Applied Social Research and Center for Policy Research. In 1980, Dr. Lipson left academia and joined Young and Rubicam in account market research. She then spent time at Citibank, Lieberman Research, and Shearson Lehman Brothers, specializing in financial services marketing and new-product development. Just prior to joining AT&T, Dr. Lipson spent three years as senior vice president and director of business development at Smith Barney, where she was responsible for creating prospecting and consultative sales tools for retail brokers. Dr. Lipson's marketing role also included new product and service development, advertising, and pricing strategy.

Dr. Lipson's first four years at AT&T were spent building and managing a cross-business unit Customer Sciences organization, which included market research, advertising development, quality tracking, competitive analysis, database modeling, and a new-product development "consumer lab." Dr. Lipson is a member of the board of directors of the Advertising Research Foundation, a frequent speaker at American Marketing Association conferences, and a trustee of the Marketing Sciences Institute.

Each method has certain advantages and disadvantages, and one method may be more appropriate for a given research problem than another. How do marketing researchers decide which method is the most appropriate? After thoroughly considering the problem and research objectives, researchers select a **research design**, which is a set of advance decisions that makes up the master plan specifying the methods and procedures for collecting and analyzing the needed information.

The Significance of Research Design

Every research problem is unique. In fact, one could argue that, given each problem's unique customer set, area of geographical application, and other situational variables, there are so few similarities among research projects that each study should be completely designed as a new and independent project. In a sense this is true; almost every research problem is unique in some way or another, and care must be taken to select the most appropriate set of approaches for the unique problem and research objectives at hand. However, there are reasons to justify the significance placed on research design.

First, although every problem and research objective may seem totally unique, there are usually enough similarities among problems and objectives to allow us to make some decisions in advance about the best plan to use to resolve the problem. Second, there are some basic marketing research designs that can be successfully matched to given problems and research objectives. In this way, they serve the researcher much like the blueprint serves the builder.

As you read the AT&T example at the beginning of this chapter, you were reading about a research design that involved several different types of research studies. This was a complex process that led to a successful conclusion. The proper research design was formulated and applied to the research objective. However, sometimes the wrong research design is formulated and this leads to disaster. Marketing Research Insight 5.2 is provided for you by Lawrence D. Gibson. Mr. Gibson illustrates how a poorly designed research project led to a product "improvement" that lost sales!

THREE TYPES OF RESEARCH DESIGNS

Research designs are classified into three traditional categories: exploratory, descriptive, and causal. The choice of the most appropriate design depends largely on the objectives of the research. It has been said that research has three objectives: to develop hypotheses, to measure the state of a variable of interest (that is, level of brand loyalty), or to test hypotheses that specify the relationships between two or more variables (that is, level of advertising and brand loyalty). Note also that the choice of research design is dependent on how much we already know about the problem and research objective. The less we know, the more likely it is that we should use exploratory research. Causal research, on the other hand, should only be used when we know a fair amount about the problem and we are looking for causal relationships among variables associated with problem and/or research objectives. We shall see how these basic research objectives are best handled by the various research designs. Table 5.1 shows the three types of research designs and the basic research objective that would prescribe a given design.

Research Design: A Caution

We pause here, before discussing the three types of research design, to warn you about thinking of research design solely in a step-by-step fashion. Some may think that it is implied in this discussion that the order in which the designs are presented—that is, exploratory, descriptive, and causal—is the order in which these

---

A research design is a set of advance decisions that makes up the master plan specifying the methods and procedures for collecting and analyzing the needed information.

Although every problem and research objective may seem totally unique, there are usually enough similarities among problems and objectives to allow us to make some decisions in advance about the best plan to use to resolve the problem.

There are some basic marketing research designs that can be successfully matched to given problems and research objectives. In this way, they serve the researcher much like the blueprint serves the builder.

Sometimes the wrong research design is formulated and this leads to disaster.

Research designs are classified into three traditional categories: exploratory, descriptive, and causal.

The choice of the most appropriate design depends largely on the objectives of the research and how much we already know about the problem and the research objectives.

Research design should not be viewed as a step-by-step process. Research may begin with any one of the three types of research designs.

▶ **Advice from a Marketing Researcher**

How Improper Research Design Can Lead to Lost Sales!
Lawrence D. Gibson, Eric Marder Associates, Inc.

Mr. Gibson is an independent consultant and senior associate at Eric Marder Associates, Inc. He is a frequent contributor to the literature on marketing research and is widely respected in the industry for his thought-provoking ideas.

Some years ago, General Mills introduced "new, improved" Trix and promptly lost more than one-third of its Trix volume. The lost sales were recaptured a few months later when original Trix was reintroduced.

The superiority of "new, improved" Trix seemed conclusively demonstrated in test after test. Consumers liked it better than old Trix at the 99 percent confidence level in each of three in-home paired comparison product tests. They preferred the new product in a major central location taste test at the 97 percent confidence level. They rated each of three product variations superior at the 99 percent confidence in a second set of three in-home paired comparison tests. Four

taste tests of final plant-produced product confirmed the superiority of New Trix: three at 95 percent and one at 85 percent confidence levels.

How could consumer testing have been so wrong? Couldn't consumers tell which product they liked better? Was there "taste tiring"? Was it possible that consumers were deliberately misleading us? Were our interviewers cheating?

No. The problem was much simpler. Our research design was wrong. We had simply asked consumers the wrong question. We asked consumers to choose between new Trix and old Trix—a choice they were never going to have in the real world. New Trix was *replacing* old Trix and new Trix would compete with Corn Flakes and Cheerios. Preference for new Trix over old Trix was irrelevant. New Trix should have been tested against its real competitors, Corn Flakes and Cheerios, while old Trix was also tested against Corn Flakes and Cheerios in a matched consumer group.

Years later Coca-Cola repeated the same Trix experiment with the same outcome. Consumer surveys had previously shown that consumers preferred a sweeter cola than regular Coca-Cola. A new sweeter Coca-Cola was developed that was preferred in taste tests among thousands of consumers.

You know what happened. New Coca-Cola was substituted for the old Coca-Cola. Sales plummeted and the "old" Coca-Cola had to be reintroduced. Many Coca-Cola customers were buying it because it was less sweet. Many more consumers did prefer a sweeter "Coke" but they already had one—it was called Pepsi-Cola.

The lesson to be learned is straightforward. If research is to predict real-world choices, the choice in research must be structurally the same as the choice in the real world. Proper research design is essential to valid research recommendations.

Table 5.1   The Basic Research Objective and Research Design

RESEARCH OBJECTIVE	APPROPRIATE DESIGN
To gain background information, to define terms, to clarify problems and hypotheses, to establish research priorities	Exploratory
To describe and measure marketing phenomena	Descriptive
To determine causality, to make "if–then" statements	Causal

designs should be carried out. This is incorrect. Three points should be made relative to the interdependency of research designs. First, in some cases, it may be perfectly legitimate to begin with any one of the three designs and to use only that one design. Second, research is an "iterative" process; by conducting one research project, we learn that we may need additional research, and so on. This may mean that we need to utilize multiple research designs. We could very well find, for example, that after conducting descriptive research, we need to go back and conduct exploratory research. Third, if multiple designs are used in any particular order (if there is an order), it makes sense to first conduct exploratory research, then descriptive research, and finally causal research. The only reason for this order pattern is that each subsequent design requires greater knowledge about the problem and research objectives on the part of the researcher. Therefore, exploratory research may give one the information needed to conduct a descriptive study, which, in turn, may provide the information necessary to design a causal experiment. Now that you have been cautioned about thinking of research design solely in a step-by-step fashion, we begin our discussion of the three types of research design.

Exploratory Research

Exploratory research is most commonly unstructured, informal research that is undertaken to gain background information about the general nature of the research problem. By unstructured, we mean that exploratory research does not have a formalized set of objectives, sample plan, or questionnaire. It is usually conducted when the researcher does not know much about the problem and needs additional information or desires new or more recent information. Often exploratory research is conducted at the outset of research projects. Because exploratory research is aimed at gaining additional information about a topic and generating possible hypotheses to test, it is described as informal. Such research may consist of going to the library and reading published secondary data; of asking customers, salespersons, and acquaintances for their opinions about a company, its products, services, and prices; or of simply observing everyday company practices. Exploratory research is systematic, but it is very flexible in that it allows the researcher to investigate whatever sources he or she desires and to the extent he or she feels is necessary in order to gain a good feel for the problem at hand. In the following sections, we discuss the specific uses of exploratory research as well as the different methods of conducting exploratory research.

Uses of Exploratory Research

Exploratory research is used in a number of situations: to gain background information, to define terms, to clarify problems and hypotheses, and to establish research priorities.

Gain Background Information When very little is known about the problem or when the problem has not been clearly formulated, exploratory research may be used to gain much-needed background information. This is easily accomplished in firms having a marketing information system in which a review of internal information tracked over time can provide useful insights into the background of the firm, brand, sales territories, and so on. Even for very experienced researchers it is rare that some exploratory research is not undertaken to gain current, relevant background information. There is far too much to be gained to ignore exploratory information.

Define Terms Exploratory research helps to define terms and concepts. By conducting exploratory research to define a question such as, "What is bank image?"

Exploratory research is most commonly unstructured, informal research that is undertaken to gain background information about the general nature of the research problem.

Exploratory research is usually conducted when the researcher does not know much about the problem and needs additional information or desires new or more recent information.

Exploratory research is used in a number of situations: to gain background information, to define terms, to clarify problems and hypotheses, and to establish research priorities.

When very little is known about the problem or when the problem has not been clearly formulated, exploratory research may be used to gain much-needed background information.

Exploratory research helps to define terms and concepts.

the researcher quickly learns that "image" is composed of several components—perceived convenience of location, loan availability, friendliness of employees, and so on. Not only would exploratory research identify the components of bank image but it could also demonstrate how these components may be measured.

Clarify Problems and Hypotheses Exploratory research allows the researcher to define the problem more precisely and to generate hypotheses for the upcoming study. For example, exploratory research on measuring bank image reveals the issue of different groups of bank customers. Banks have three types of customers: retail customers, commercial customers, and other banks for which services are performed for fees. This information is useful in clarifying the problem of the measurement of bank image because it raises the issue of which customer group bank image should be measured.

Exploratory research can also be beneficial in the formulation of **hypotheses**, which are statements describing the speculated relationships among two or more variables. Formally stating hypotheses prior to conducting a research study is very important to ensure that the proper variables are measured. Once a study has been completed, it may be too late to state which hypotheses are desirable to test.

> Exploratory research can be beneficial in the formulation of hypotheses, which are statements describing the speculated relationships among two or more variables.

Establish Research Priorities Exploratory research can help a firm prioritize research topics in order of importance, especially when it is faced with conducting several research studies. A quick review of a spreadsheet that calculates sales gains and losses by product, for example, may dictate research priorities. A summary account of complaint letters by retail store may tell management where to devote their attention. One furniture store chain owner decided to conduct research on the feasibility of carrying office furniture after some exploratory interviews with salespeople revealed that their customers often asked for directions to stores carrying office furniture.

> Exploratory research can help a firm prioritize research topics in order of importance.

Methods of Conducting Exploratory Research

A variety of methods are available to conduct exploratory research. These include secondary data analysis, experience surveys, case analysis, focus groups, and projective techniques.

Secondary Data Analysis By **secondary data analysis,** we refer to the process of searching for and interpreting existing information relevant to the research objectives. Secondary data are data that have been collected for some other purpose. Your library and the Internet are full of secondary data, which include information found in books, journals, magazines, special reports, bulletins, newsletters, and so on. An analysis of secondary data is often the "core" of exploratory research.[1] This is because there are many benefits to examining secondary data and the costs are typically minimal. Furthermore, the costs for search time of such data are being reduced every day as more and more computerized databases become available. Knowledge of and ability to use these databases are already mandatory for marketing researchers. You will learn more about secondary data in Chapter 6.

> A common method of conducting exploratory research is to examine existing information.

> For some examples of secondary data often used in marketing research, see www.secondarydata.com, a Web site developed by Decision Analyst, Inc.

Experience Surveys **Experience surveys** refer to gathering information from those thought to be knowledgeable on the issues relevant to the research problem. If the research problem deals with difficulties encountered when buying infant clothing, then surveys of mothers or fathers with infants may be in order. If the research problem deals with forecasting the demand for sulphuric acid over the next two years, researchers may begin by making a few calls to some experts on this issue. Experience surveys differ from surveys conducted as part of descriptive research in

> Experience surveys refer to gathering information from those thought to be knowledgeable on the issues relevant to the research problem.

that there is usually no formal attempt to ensure that the survey results are representative of any defined group of subjects. Nevertheless, useful information can be gathered by this method of exploratory research.

Case Analysis By **case analysis**, we refer to a review of available information about a former situation(s) that has some similarities to the present research problem. Usually, there are few research problems that do not have some similarities to some situation in the past.[2] Even when the research problem deals with a radically new product, there are often some similar past experiences that may be observed. For example, when cellular telephones were invented but not yet on the market, many companies attempted to forecast how many cellular telephones would be sold. Part of the forecasting process was to determine the rate of adoption. These companies looked at adoption rates of consumer electronic products such as televisions and VCRs. A wireless communications company, 21st Century Telesis, used data from a low-power, neighborhood phone system that was very successful in Japan to help it market cellular phones to young people in Japan.[3]

Is this valid? Yes, but researchers must be aware of the caveats in using former case examples for current problems. They should ask themselves questions to determine the relevancy of prior cases. How similar is the phenomenon in the past to the phenomenon in the present? (For example, would adoption rates of Japanese have any relationship with adoption rates of Americans?) What situational factors have changed that may invalidate using the case to predict a future outcome? To the extent that the researcher can adequately answer these questions, the greater should be his or her confidence in using a case analysis as part of exploratory research.

Focus Groups An increasingly popular method of conducting exploratory research is through **focus groups**, which are small groups of people brought together and guided by a moderator through an unstructured, spontaneous discussion for the purpose of gaining information relevant to the research problem.[4] Although focus groups should encourage openness on the part of the participants, the moderator's task is to ensure the discussion is "focused" on some general area of interest. For example, the Piccadilly Cafeteria chain periodically conducts focus groups all around the country. The conversation may seem "freewheeling," but the purpose of the focus group may be to learn what people think about some specific aspect of the cafeteria business, such as the perceived quality of cafeteria versus traditional restaurant food. This is a useful technique for gathering some information from a limited sample of respondents. The information can be used to generate ideas, to learn the respondents' "vocabulary" when relating to a certain type of product, or to gain some insights into basic needs and attitudes.[5] Focus groups are discussed extensively in Chapter 8 and now several companies are offering online focus group services.

Projective Techniques **Projective techniques**, borrowed from the field of clinical psychology, seek to explore hidden consumer motives for buying goods and services by asking participants to project themselves into a situation and then to respond to specific questions regarding the situation. One example of such a technique is the sentence completion test. A respondent is given an incomplete sentence such as, "Andrea Livingston never buys frozen dinners for her family because. . . ." By completing the sentence, ostensibly to represent the feelings of the fictitious Ms. Livingston, the respondent projects himself or herself into the situation. These techniques are explored in greater detail in Chapter 8.

A concluding word about exploratory research is that it should almost always be used at least to some extent. Why? Exploratory research is fast. You can conduct quite a bit of exploratory research online within a matter of minutes. Exploratory

Examining similar situations in the past, called case analysis, is another method of conducting exploratory research.

Researchers should use former similar case situations cautiously when trying to make applications from them to the present research objectives.

Focus groups are small groups of people brought together and guided by a moderator through an unstructured, spontaneous discussion for the purpose of gaining information relevant to the research objectives.

Projective techniques seek to explore hidden consumer motives for buying goods and services by asking participants to project themselves into a situation and then to respond to specific questions regarding the situation.

research is relatively inexpensive. Compared to collecting primary data, exploratory research is cheap. Finally, sometimes exploratory research either provides information to meet the research objective or assists in gathering current information necessary to conduct either a descriptive or causal research design. Therefore, few researchers embark on a research project without doing some exploratory research.

Descriptive Research

Descriptive research is undertaken to describe answers to questions of who, what, where, when, and how. When we wish to know who our customers are, what brands they buy and in what quantities, where they buy the brands, when they shop, and how they found out about our products, we turn to descriptive research. Typically, answers to these questions are found in secondary data or by conducting surveys.

Marketing decision makers often need answers to these basic questions before they can formulate effective marketing strategies. Consider the following examples. *Who* may be defined as the firm's (competitor's) customers. *What* may be defined as the products, brands, sizes, and so on that are being purchased. *Where* may be defined as the places the customers are buying these products. *When* refers to the time or the frequency with which purchases are made. *How* may mean the ways in which customers are using the products. Note that we cannot conclusively answer the question of *why* using descriptive research. Conclusive answers to questions such as why sales increase or decrease if we increase or decrease advertising or why one ad garners greater attention than another are questions that must be answered through causal research designs. Marketing Research Insight 5.3 illustrates how descriptive research studies were used by AT&T to determine the best corporate signature that would allow the company to identify its four independent businesses and yet keep the benefits of the AT&T brand without confusing consumers.

Classification of Descriptive Research Studies

There are two basic descriptive research studies available to the marketing researcher: cross-sectional and longitudinal designs. **Cross-sectional studies** measure units from a sample of the population at only one point in time. A study measuring your attitude toward adding a required internship course in your degree program, for example, would be a cross-sectional study. Your attitude toward the topic is measured at one point in time. Cross-sectional studies are very prevalent in marketing research, outnumbering longitudinal studies and causal studies. Because cross-sectional studies are one-time measurements, they are often described as "snapshots" of the population. As an example, many magazines survey a sample of their subscribers and ask them questions such as their age, occupation, income, educational level, and so on. These sample data, taken at one point in time, are used to describe the readership of the magazine in terms of demographics. Cross-sectional studies normally employ fairly large sample sizes, so many cross-sectional studies are referred to as sample surveys.

Sample surveys are cross-sectional studies whose samples are drawn in such a way as to be representative of a specific population. ABC often conducts surveys on some topic of interest to report on the evening news. The surveys' samples are drawn such that ABC may report that the results are representative of the population of the United States. Nabisco may want to conduct a survey whose results are representative of chain-owned supermarkets in the northeastern United States. Sample surveys require that their samples be drawn according to a prescribed plan and to a predetermined number. Later on, you will learn about these sampling plans (Chapter 12) and sample size techniques (Chapter 13). Ping, the maker of golf clubs

Cross-sectional studies measure units from a sample of the population at only one point in time.

Because cross-sectional studies are one-time measurements, they are often described as "snapshots" of the population.

Sample surveys are cross-sectional studies whose samples are drawn in such a way as to be representative of a specific population.

MARKETING RESEARCH

INSIGHT
5.3

*Using Descriptive Market Research Studies
to Address Brand Architecture Issues*

As mergers and acquisitions, spin-offs, and tracking stocks become more commonplace, issues surrounding strategic brand management arise. At AT&T, where a restructuring of the company has resulted in the establishment of four independent businesses sharing a single brand identity, market research was at the forefront of brand management decision making.

The AT&T Brand Asset Management team faced a unique challenge: defining the essence of the brand and then maximizing the equity of the AT&T brand, while giving individual voice to the branded operating businesses. In other words, it was important that consumers distinguished among the four businesses and, at the same time, perceived all these businesses to be part of AT&T. The brand identity challenge was addressed using descriptive research that provided respondents with a number of corporate signature choices. Following the exposure of these brand identity signatures, respondents were asked to rate AT&T on several dimensions that are important to AT&T, such as trust and quality. The research also measured customer confusion arising from using different business names with the AT&T brand name.

The research results clearly demonstrated that a consistent corporate identity signature was appropriate for use across the independent businesses to ensure that brand equity was maintained. The preferred corporate signature (in the first column in the graphic seen below) allows consumers to differentiate the independent businesses yet understand these are all part of AT&T. This was descriptive research because AT&T wanted to describe how customers rated the different signatures and it wanted to describe the amount of confusion the different signatures may have created.

and other golf equipment, wanted to know how to improve its position as the best-known manufacturer for custom-fitting golf clubs to individuals. It conducted cross-sectional surveys of golfers and gained knowledge that allows it to remain number one in custom-fit golf clubs.

Today serious golfers face a staggering array of choices in clubs featuring different metals, club head designs, shaft flexes, lofts, sweet-spot sizes, grip sizes and compositions, and so on. Ping knows that many golfers prefer having golf clubs custom-fitted to their unique swing, strength, speed, height, and hand size. Ping conducted marketing research to determine what it needed to do to enhance its leadership position in fitting clubs to golfers. Golfers can be fitted either through the Ping Web site or through fitting centers all around the world.

Visit Ping at www.pinggolf.com.

When Ping surveys a sample of golfers at a point in time for the purposes of learning about their attitudes, preferences, and intentions regarding custom-fitting golf clubs, this is a cross-sectional study.

Online survey research is being used to collect data for cross-sectional surveys at faster rates of speed.

Online survey research is being used to collect data for cross-sectional surveys at faster rates of speed. The Turner Entertainment Group worked with Burke Interactive to set up a process for gathering continuous feedback from visitors coming to the Web sites of its TV networks, including TBS, TNT, Turner Classic Movies (TCM), and the Cartoon Network. A mechanism was put in place so that every nth visitor to the site saw a "pop-up window" inviting her or him to participate in a survey. The value of n was determined based on the number of visitors coming to each site, the desired number of completed surveys, and the percentage of visitors receiving the survey invitation who responded. A main goal of the effort was to profile site visitors. Other sections of the survey were designed to understand why visitors came to the site, obtain satisfaction readings, uncover gaps between what site visitors wanted and what they were getting, and examine functional, navigational, and design issues. Individuals who did not have sufficient experience with the site to rate it initially were asked for their e-mail addresses and were recontacted later so they would have another chance to participate in the study. The Turner Entertainment Group then used Burke's Digital Dashboard® online reporting solution to display the results of the studies throughout the organization in real time.[6] (You will read about online reporting systems such as Digital Dashboard in Chapter 20.)

New applications of online research are constantly evolving. One new firm has an innovative method for allowing consumers to design new products online. The company is Affinnova. (See Marketing Research Insight 5.4.) It works with clients to determine the features that make up a product, for example, the cap, neck, and label on soda bottles. It then generates many variations of each of the features and allows consumers to evaluate the different features online. Then, as consumers rate the features, images evolve and change to reflect the best new-product "fit" with consumers' preferences. This type of study illustrates the use of a cross-sectional study to design a new product.

Longitudinal studies repeatedly measure the same sample units of a population over a period of time. Because longitudinal studies involve multiple measurements, they are often described as "movies" of the population. Longitudinal studies are employed by almost 50 percent of businesses using marketing research.[7] To ensure the success of the longitudinal study, researchers must have access to the same members of the sample, called a panel, so as to take repeated measurements. **Panels** represent sample units who have agreed to answer questions at periodic intervals. Maintaining a representative panel of respondents is a major undertaking.

Visit Affinnova at
www.affinnova.com

Longitudinal studies repeatedly measure the same sample units of a population over a period of time. Because longitudinal studies involve multiple measurements, they are often described as "movies" of the population.

Panels represent sample units who have agreed to answer questions at periodic intervals.

MARKETING RESEARCH
INSIGHT
5.4

*Affinnova Uses Cross-Sectional Research
to Design New Products . . . Online!*

Featurize

Starting with a base product concept or brief, Affinnova works with managers to determine the features they wish to test. A product feature can be anything you can see—shape, color, configuration, images, branding, and messaging. Benefit statements and price can also be tested using Affinnova.

Affinnova offers solutions for consumer packaged goods, automotive, consumer electronics, digital and print communications, and toys industries.

Generate Variations

Working with the featurization developed with managers, the next step is to populate the Affinnova solution with all of the variations of each feature to be tested. A handful or thousands of variations can be tested. Images for these variations

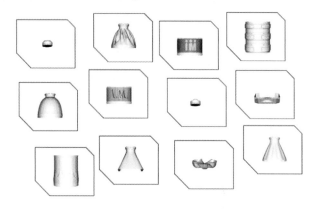

can be taken from sketches, photos, or sophisticated CAD renderings. In addition, Affinnova can embed constraints into a design so that undesirable or infeasible product images will not be shown to consumers.

Evolve with Consumers

To start, consumers are shown an initial set of diverse product images. These images are generated in real time and on the fly using Affinnova's IDEA technology and imaging tools.

Consumers then rate this first set of products. Based on their ratings, the images evolve and change to show consumers products increasingly "fit" for their needs and preferences.

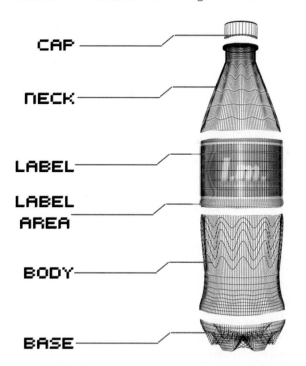

Several commercial marketing research firms develop and maintain consumer panels for use in longitudinal studies.

Several commercial marketing research firms develop and maintain consumer panels for use in longitudinal studies. Typically, these firms attempt to select a sample that is representative of some population. Firms such as NFOWorldwide and ACNielsen have maintained panels consisting of hundreds of thousands of households for many years. In many cases these companies will recruit panel members such that the demographic characteristics of the panel are proportionate to the demographic characteristics found in the total population according to Census Bureau statistics. Sometimes these panels will be balanced demographically not only to the United States in total but also within each of various geographical regions. In this way, a client who wishes to get information from a panel of households in the Northwest can be assured that the panel is demographically matched to the total population in the states making up the northwestern region. Many companies maintain panels to target market segments such as "dog owners," "kids" (ages 6 to 14; see www.Kidzeyes.com). Note that panels are not limited to consumer households. Panels may consist of building contractors, supermarkets, physicians, lawyers, universities, or some other entity.

Online research created the opportunity for several new companies to emerge offering panels recruited to respond to online queries. One such company is Lightspeed Research. Lightspeed's strategy is to employ traditional research over the Internet, thereby giving its clients the advantage of speed. Currently, Lightspeed offers clients panels of consumer households in the United States (us.lightspeedpanel.com), Great Britain (gb.lightspeedpanel.com), and the Netherlands (nl.lightspeedpanel.com).

Certainly, panels play a big role in online survey research. We asked our Blue Ribbon Panel of experts on online research to tell you what they think about the use of panels in online survey research.

Online survey research firms recruit panel members, which allows them access to respondents from whom they gather research information online.

Q: *How have online panels affected marketing research practices, and what do you forecast to be the influence or role of online panels in the next five years?*

Bill MacElroy
President
Socratic Technologies

A: The use of prerecruited panels has been one way that research professionals have gained access to willing online participants. Although panels have sometimes been criticized as being not random and in some cases overused, they are usually better than the alternative. In traditional research, published figures show that less than 15 percent of the U.S. public is willing to take part in randomly dialed phone surveys. By some estimates, less than 5 percent of the American public accounts for 75 percent of all phone survey respondents. Obviously, the noncooperation rate is as critical as nonrandomness. Because willingness to participate is a key screening item for most research, prerecruited panels from which a stratified sample can be scientifically drawn is usually preferable to a very low response rate with the potential for significant nonresponse bias.

Allen Hogg
President
Burke, Inc.

A: The concept of "permission-based" research—sending survey invitations to those who have given their prior consent to receive e-mail messages—has taken a firm hold in the online world. Many research firms have recruited online panels of consumers, and numerous corporations are also creating proprietary online panels of customers and other individuals within their target markets who have expressed interest in participating in research projects.

Organizations should exhibit some caution before relying solely on opinions of online panelists. It is important to consider how well the views of these volunteers represent the entire market. Many companies have learned, however, how to calibrate the input provided by online panelists to accurately predict marketplace outcomes. A key development taking place in the next few years will be the maturation of online panels outside the United States. There will also be more and better online panels providing access to respondents working in specific occupations, so that more and more "business-to-business" research can move online.

Keith Price
Vice President
Greenfield Online

A: Most online research companies would define an online panel as a group of individuals and households that can be contacted to participate in research studies. For Greenfield Online, our panels are far more than that. Our panels are 100 percent comprised of members who not only sign up for the express purpose of participating in surveys but also double-opt-in. This means they must respond to a confirmation message after registration, before they enter the panel, ensuring that a third party does not fraudulently add them. We also collect in-depth information about our members so we can select accurate, quality samples.

Online research panels are best used when it is imperative to have information about a respondent's background, you need to communicate with individual respondents over time, or if a study is to be conducted among low-incidence samples.

Greenfield Online began its business by creating an online panel of respondents in 1994. At this point, the Internet was a new communications vehicle and not much was known about the online population. As such, it was important to conduct panel-based research. As the Internet has evolved, we have realized that additional means of obtaining samples are often viable and, as a result, have partnered with the Microsoft Network to access broader and more varied pools of respondents. It is always important to survey respondents who have opted-in to participate in research studies, but it is not always necessary to conduct panel-based research.

Lee Smith
CEO
Insight Express

A: Traditional research panels provide easy access to low-incidence audiences and enable the tracking of attitudes, opinions, and behaviors over time. Historically, however, panels were created due to the high variable cost of reaching an audience. Although online panels certainly provide value for the tracking of attitudes, opinions, and behaviors over time, this will become the core use of online panels—particularly for customer panels—in the next five years and beyond. Due to easy access through large online communities and a near zero variable cost of recruiting these individuals, the overall importance of traditional research panels will begin to wane within the next five years. This is an example of the online medium having disruptive impact upon the traditional research industry—transforming it forever.

Continuous panels ask panel members the same questions on each panel measurement. Discontinuous panels vary questions from one panel measurement to the next.

There are two types of panels: continuous panels and discontinuous panels. **Continuous panels** ask panel members the same questions on each panel measurement. **Discontinuous panels** vary questions from one panel measurement to the next.[8] Continuous panel examples include many of the syndicated data panels that ask panel members to record their purchases, using diaries or scanners. The essential point is that panel members are asked to record the *same* information (grocery store purchases) over and over. Discontinuous panels, sometimes referred to as omnibus ("including or covering many things or classes") panels may be used for a variety of purposes, and the information collected by a discontinuous panel varies from one panel measurement to the next. How longitudinal data are applied depends on the type of panel used to collect the data. Essentially, the discontinuous panel's primary usefulness is that it represents a large group—people, stores, or some other entity— that is agreeable to providing marketing research information. Discontinuous panels, like continuous panels, are also demographically matched to some larger entity, implying representativeness as well. Therefore, a marketer wanting to know how a large number of consumers, matched demographically to the total U.S. population, feel about two different product concepts may elect to utilize the services of an omnibus panel. In this way, then, discontinuous panels represent existing sources of information that may be quickly accessed for a wide variety of purposes.

The continuous panel is used quite differently. Usually, firms are interested in using data from continuous panels because they can gain insights into *changes* in consumers' purchases, attitudes, and so on. For example, data from continuous panels can show how members of the panel switched brands from one time period to the next. Studies examining how many consumers switched brands are known as **brand-switching studies.**

To illustrate the importance of using continuous panel data to gain insights into how consumers change brands, we compare longitudinal data taken from a continuous panel with data collected from two cross-sectional sample surveys. Figure 5.1 shows data collected from two separate cross-sectional studies, each having a household sample size of 500. (Cross-sectional data are referenced as "Survey 1" or "Survey 2.") Look at how many families used each brand in Survey 1 (red) and then see how many families used each brand in Survey 2 (blue). What would we conclude by examination of these two cross-sectional studies? (1) Pooch Plus has lost market share because only 75 families indicated that they purchased Pooch Plus in the second survey as opposed to 100 Pooch Plus families in the first survey; and (2) apparently, Pooch Plus has lost out to Milk Bone dog treat brand, which increased from 200 to 225 families. Note that Beggar's Bits remained the same. This analysis would lead most brand managers to focus on the strategies that had been used by Milk Bone (since it's "obvious" that Milk Bone took share from Pooch Plus) to increase market share for Pooch Plus.

> Firms are interested in using data from continuous panels because they can gain insights into *changes* in consumers' purchases, attitudes, and so on.

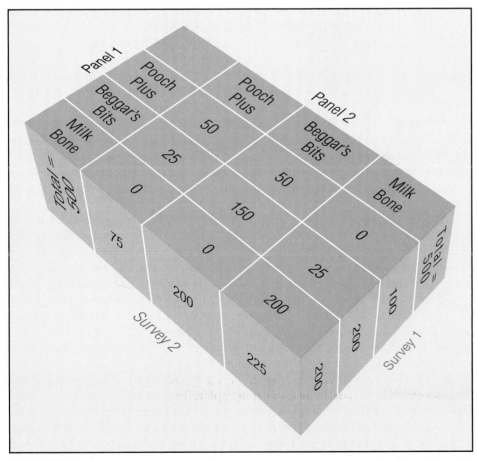

Figure 5.1   **The Advantage of Longitudinal Studies versus Cross-sectional Studies**

Now, having reached a conclusion from the two cross-sectional surveys, let's look at the data assuming we had used longitudinal research. When we examine the longitudinal data, we reach quite a different conclusion from the one we reached by looking at the two cross-sectional studies. Looking at Panel 1 total (red) and Panel 2 total (blue), we see the same data that we saw in the two cross-sectional surveys. Panel 1 totals show us that Pooch Plus had 100 families, Beggar's Bits had 200 families, and Milk Bone had 200 families. (This is exactly the same data found in our first cross-sectional survey.) Now, we later return for a second measurement of the *same families* in Panel 2 and we find the totals are Pooch Plus, 75 families; Beggar's Bits, 200 families; and Milk Bone, 225 families. (Again, we have the same totals as shown by Survey 2 data.) But the real value of the continuous panel longitudinal data is found in the changes that occur between Panel 1 and Panel 2 measurements. With longitudinal data, we can examine how each family changed from Panel 1 to Panel 2 and, as we shall see, the ability to measure change is very important in understanding research data. To see how the families changed, look again at Panel 1 totals (red) and then look at the data *inside the figure* (green) at the Panel 2 results. In Panel 1 (red) we had 100 families using Pooch Plus. How did these families change by the time we asked for Panel 2 information? Looking at the data on the inside of the figure (green) and reading across for Pooch Plus, we see that 50 families stayed with Pooch Plus, 50 switched to Beggar's Bits, and none of the original Panel 1 Pooch Plus families switched to Milk Bone. Now look at the 200 families in Panel 1 (red) who used Beggar's Bits. In Panel 2 data (green) we see that 25 of those 200 families switched to Pooch Plus, 150 stayed with Beggar's Bits, and 25 switched to Milk Bone. Finally, all of the 200 Milk Bone families in Panel 1 stayed loyal to Milk Bone in Panel 2. So, what does this mean? It is clear that Pooch Plus is competing with Beggar's Bits and not with Milk Bone. Milk Bone's total shares increased but at the expense of Beggar's Bits, not Pooch Plus. The brand manager should direct his or her attention to Beggar's Bits, not Milk Bone. This, then, is quite different from the conclusion reached by examining cross-sectional data. The key point being made here is that because longitudinal data allow us to measure the change being made by each sample unit between time periods, we gain much richer information for analysis purposes. It is important to note, at this point, that this type of brand-switching data may be obtained only by using the continuous panel. Because different questions are asked, discontinuous panels do not allow for this type of analysis.

Another use of longitudinal data is that of market tracking. **Market tracking** studies are those that measure some variable(s) of interest, that is, market share or unit sales over time. By having representative data on brand market shares, for example, a marketing manager can "track" how his or her brand is doing relative to a competitive brand's performance. Every three years the American Heart Association (AHA) conducts what it calls the *National Acute Event Tracking Study*. The AHA collects data using a panel to track changes in unaided awareness of heart attack and stroke warning signs. By tracking consumers' awareness of heart attack and stroke warning signs, the AHA can determine the effectiveness of its promotional materials designed to communicate these signs to the public.[9]

Market tracking studies are those that measure some variable(s) of interest, such as market share or unit sales, over time.

Causal Research *cause and effect relationship*

Causality may be thought of as understanding a phenomenon in terms of conditional statements of the form "If *x*, then *y*." These "if–then" statements become our way of manipulating variables of interest. For example, if the thermostat is lowered, then the air will get cooler. If I drive my automobile at lower speeds, then my gasoline mileage will increase. If I spend more on advertising, then sales will rise. As humans, we are constantly trying to understand the world in which we live.

Fortunately for humankind, there is an inborn tendency to determine causal relationships. This tendency is ever present in our thinking and our actions. Likewise, marketing managers are always trying to determine what will cause a change in consumer satisfaction, a gain in market share, or an increase in sales. In one recent experiment, marketing researchers investigated how color versus noncolor and different quality levels of graphics in Yellow Page ads caused changes in consumers' attitudes toward the ad itself, the company doing the advertising, and perceptions of quality. The results showed that color and high-photographic graphics cause more favorable attitudes. But the findings differ depending on the class of product being advertised.[10] This illustrates how complex cause-and-effect relationships are in the real world. Consumers are bombarded on a daily and sometimes even hourly basis by a vast multitude of factors, all of which could cause them to act in one way or another. Thus, understanding what causes consumers to behave as they do is extremely difficult. Nevertheless, there is a high "reward" in the marketplace for even partially understanding causal relationships. Causal relationships are determined by the use of experiments, which are special types of studies. Many companies are now taking advantage of conducting experiments online.[11]

> Causality may be thought of as understanding a phenomenon in terms of conditional statements of the form "If *x*, then *y*." If Yellow Page ads are in color, then consumer attitudes toward the product will be higher than if the ad is in black and white.

> Experiments can be conducted using online research.

EXPERIMENTS (compare two groups: control and other group re: level of change)

An **experiment** is defined as manipulating an independent variable to see how it affects a dependent variable, while also controlling the effects of additional extraneous variables. **Independent variables** are those variables over which the researcher has control *and* wishes to manipulate. Some independent variables include level of advertising expenditure, type of advertising appeal (humor, prestige), display location, method of compensating salespersons, price, and type of product. **Dependent variables,** on the other hand, are those variables that we have little or no direct control over, yet we have a strong interest in. We cannot change these variables in the same way that we can change independent variables. A marketing manager, for example, can easily change the level of advertising expenditure or the location of the display of a product in a supermarket, but he or she cannot easily change sales, market share, or level of customer satisfaction. These variables are typically dependent variables. Certainly, marketers are interested in changing these variables. But because they cannot change them directly, they attempt to change them through the manipulation of independent variables. To the extent that marketers can establish causal relationships between independent and dependent variables, they enjoy some success in influencing the dependent variables.

> An experiment is defined as manipulating an independent variable to see how it affects a dependent variable, while also controlling the effects of additional extraneous variables.

> Independent variables are those variables over which the researcher has control *and* wishes to manipulate. Independent variables could include level of advertising expenditure, type of advertising appeal, display location, method of compensating salespersons, price, and type of product.

> Dependent variables are those variables that we have little or no direct control over, yet we have a strong interest in manipulating, such as net profits, market share, or employee or customer satisfaction.

Extraneous variables are those that may have some effect on a dependent variable but yet are not independent variables. To illustrate, let's say you and your friend wanted to know if brand of gasoline (independent variable) affected gas mileage in automobiles (dependent variable). Your "experiment" consists of each of you filling up your two cars, one with Brand A, the other with Brand B. At the end of the week, you learn that Brand A achieved 18.6 miles per gallon and Brand B achieved 26.8 miles per gallon. Do you have a causal relationship: Brand B gets better gas mileage than Brand A? Or could the difference in the dependent variable (gas mileage) be due to factors other than gasoline brand (independent variable)? Let's take a look at what these other extraneous variables may be: (1) One car is an SUV and the other is a small compact! (2) One car was driven mainly on the highway and the other was driven in the city in heavy traffic. (3) One car has never had a tune-up and the other was just tuned up. We think you get the picture.

> Extraneous variables are those that may have some effect on a dependent variable but yet are not independent variables.

Let's look at another example. Imagine that a supermarket chain conducts an experiment to determine the effect of type of display (independent variable) on sales of apples (dependent variable). Management records sales of the apples in its regular produce bin's position and then changes (manipulates the independent variable) the position of the apples to end-aisle displays and measures sales once again. Assume sales increased. Does this mean that if we change display position of apples from the produce bins to end-aisle displays, then sales will increase? Could there be other extraneous variables that could have affected the sales of the apples? What would happen to apple sales if the weather changed from rainy to fair? If the apple industry began running ads on TV? If the season changed from summer vacation to fall? Yes, weather, industry advertising, and apples packed in school lunch boxes are viewed in this example as extraneous variables, having an effect on the dependent variable, yet themselves not defined as independent variables. As this example illustrates, it would be difficult to isolate the effects of independent variables on dependent variables without controlling for the effects of the extraneous variables. Unfortunately, it is not easy to establish causal relationships but it can be done. In the following section we will see how different experimental designs allow us to conduct experiments.

Experimental Design

An experimental design is a procedure for devising an experimental setting such that a change in a dependent variable may be attributed solely to the change in an independent variable.

An **experimental design** is a procedure for devising an experimental setting such that a change in a dependent variable may be attributed solely to the change in an independent variable. In other words, experimental designs are procedures that allow experimenters to control for the effects on a dependent variable by an extraneous variable. In this way, the experimenter is assured that any change in the dependent variable was due only to the change in the independent variable.

You should carefully study the symbols of experimental design. Without a good grasp of the meaning of these symbols, you will have difficulty with the following sections.

Let us look at how experimental designs work. First, we list the symbols of experimental design:

O = The measurement of a dependent variable

X = The manipulation, or change, of an independent variable

R = Random assignment of subjects (consumers, stores, and so on) to experimental and control groups

E = Experimental effect, that is, the change in the dependent variable due to the independent variable

Time is assumed to be represented horizontally on a continuum.

Subscripts, such as O_1, or O_2, refer to different measurements made of the dependent variable.

Measurements of the dependent variable taken prior to changing the dependent variable are called pretests and those taken after are called posttests.

When a measurement of the dependent variable is taken prior to changing the independent variable, the measurement is sometimes called a **pretest**. When a measurement of the dependent variable is taken after changing the independent variable, the measurement is sometimes called a **posttest**.

There are many research designs available to experimenters. In fact, entire college courses are devoted to this one topic. But our purpose here is to illustrate the logic of experimental design and we can do this by reviewing three designs of which only the last is a true experimental design. A **"true" experimental design** is one that truly isolates the effects of the independent variable on the dependent variable while controlling for effects of any extraneous variables. However, the first two designs we introduce you to are *not* true experimental designs. We introduce you to the first two designs to help you understand the real benefits of using a true experimental design. The three designs we discuss are after-only; one-group, before–after; and before–after with control group.

After-Only Design

The **after-only design** is achieved by changing the independent variable and, after some period of time, measuring the dependent variable. It is diagrammed as follows:

$$X \ O_1$$

where X represents the change in the independent variable (putting all of the apples in end-aisle displays) and the distance between X and O represents the passage of some time period. O_1 represents the measurement, a posttest, of the dependent variable (recording the sales of the apples). Now, what have you learned about causality? Not very much! Have sales gone up or down? We do not know because we neglected to measure sales prior to changing the display location. Regardless of what our sales are, there may have been other extraneous variables that may have had an effect on apple sales. Managers are constantly changing things "just to see what happens" without taking any necessary precautions to properly evaluate the effects of the change. Hence, the after-only design does not really measure up to our requirement for a true experimental design.

Designs that do not properly control for the effects of extraneous variables on our dependent variable are known as **quasi-experimental designs.** Note that in the after-only design diagram there is no measure of E, the "experimental effect" on our dependent variable due solely to our independent variable. This is true in all quasi-experimental designs. Our next design, the one-group, before–after design, is also a quasi-experimental design, although it is an improvement over the after-only design.

One-Group, Before–After Design

The **one-group, before–after design** is achieved by first measuring the dependent variable, then changing the independent variable, and, finally, taking a second measurement of the dependent variable. We diagram this design as follows:

$$O_1 \ X \ O_2$$

The obvious difference between this design and the after-only design is that we have a measurement of the dependent variable prior to and following the change in the independent variable. Also, as the name implies, we have only one group (a group of consumers in one store) on which we are conducting our study.

As an illustration of this design, let us go back to our previous example. In this design, our supermarket manager measured the dependent variable, apple sales, prior to changing the display location. Now, what do we know about causality? We know a little more than we learned from the after-only design. We know the change in our dependent variable from time period 1 to time period 2. We at least know if sales went up, down, or stayed the same. But what if sales did go up? Can we attribute the change in our dependent variable solely to the change in our independent variable? The answer is "no"—numerous extraneous variables, such as weather, advertising, or time of year, could have caused an increase in apple sales. With the one-group, before–after design, we still cannot measure E, the "experimental effect," because this design does not control for the effects of extraneous variables on the dependent variable. Hence, the one-group, before–after design is also not a true experimental design; it is a quasi-experimental design.

Control of extraneous variables is typically achieved by the use of a second group of subjects, known as a control group. By **control group,** we mean a group whose subjects have not been exposed to the change in the independent variable. The **experimental group,** on the other hand, is the group that has been exposed to a change in the independent variable. By having these two groups as part of our experimental design, we can overcome many of the problems associated with the quasi-experimental designs presented thus far. We shall use the following true experimental design to illustrate the importance of the control group.

Before–After with Control Group

The **before–after with control group design** may be achieved by randomly dividing subjects of the experiment (in this case, supermarkets) into two groups: the control group and the experimental group. A pretest measurement of the dependent variable is then taken on both groups. Next, the independent variable is changed only in the experimental group. Finally, after some time period, posttest measurements are taken of the dependent variable in both groups. This design may be diagrammed as follows:

Experimental group (R) $O_1 \, X \, O_2$

Control group (R) $O_3 \quad O_4$

where $E = (O_2 - O_1) - (O_4 - O_3)$.

In this true experimental design, we have two groups. Let us assume we have 20 supermarkets in our supermarket chain. Theoretically, if we randomly divide these stores into two groups—10 in the experimental group and 10 in the control group—then the groups should be equivalent. That is, both groups should be as similar as possible, each group having an equal number of large stores, and small stores, an equal number of new stores and old stores, an equal number of stores in upper-income neighborhoods and lower-income neighborhoods, and so on. Note that this design assumes that the two groups are equivalent in all aspects. An experimenter should take whatever steps are necessary to meet this condition if he or she uses this design. There are other methods for gaining equivalency besides randomization. Matching on criteria thought to be important, for example, would aid in establishing equivalent groups. When randomization or matching on relevant criteria does not achieve equivalent groups, more complex experimental designs should be used.[12]

Looking back at our design, the R indicates that we have randomly divided our supermarkets into two equal groups—one a control group, the other an experimental group. We also see that pretest measurements of our dependent variable, apple sales, were recorded at the same time for both groups of stores as noted by O_1 and O_3. Next, we see by the X symbol that only in the experimental group of stores were the apples moved from the regular produce bins to end-aisle displays. Finally, posttest measurements of the dependent variable were taken at the same time in both groups of stores as noted by O_2 and O_4.

Now, what information can we gather from this experiment? First, we know that $(O_2 - O_1)$ tells us how much change occurred in our dependent variable during the time of the experiment. But was this difference due solely to our independent variable, X? No, $(O_2 - O_1)$ tells us how many dollars in apple sales may be attributed to (1) the change in display location and (2) other extraneous variables, such as the weather, apple industry advertising, and so on. This does not help us very much, but what does $(O_4 - O_3)$ measure? Because it cannot account for changes in apple sales due to a change in display location (the display was not changed), then any differences in sales as measured by $(O_4 - O_3)$ must be due to the influence of other extraneous variables on apple sales. Therefore, the difference between the experimental group and the control group, $(O_2 - O_1) - (O_4 - O_3)$, results in a measure of E, the "experimental effect." We now know that if we change apple display locations, then apple sales will change by an amount equal to E. We have, through experimentation using a proper experimental design, made some progress at arriving at causality.

As we noted earlier, there are many other experimental designs and, of course, there are almost limitless applications of experimental designs to marketing problems. An experimenter, for example, could use the before–after with control group design to measure the effects of different types of music (independent variable) on total purchases made by supermarket customers (dependent variable). Although we have demonstrated how valuable experimentation can be in providing us with knowledge, we should not accept all experiments as being valid. How we assess the validity of experiments is the subject of our next section.

How Valid Are Experiments?   *validity: extent to which research results measure what was intended to be measured.*

How can we assess the validity of an experiment? An experiment is valid if (1) the observed change in the dependent variable is, in fact, due to the independent variable, and (2) if the results of the experiment apply to the "real world" outside the experimental setting.[13] Two forms of validity are used to assess the validity of an experiment: internal and external.

Internal validity is concerned with the extent to which the change in the dependent variable was actually due to the independent variable. This is another way of asking if the proper experimental design was used and if it was implemented correctly. To illustrate an experiment that lacks internal validity, let us return to our apple example. In the experimental design, before–after with control group, we made the point that the design assumes that the experimental group and the control group are, in fact, equivalent. What would happen if the researcher did not check the equivalency of the groups? Let us suppose that, by chance, the two groups of supermarkets had customers who were distinctly different regarding a number of factors such as age and income. This difference in the groups, then, would represent an extraneous variable that had been left uncontrolled. Such an experiment would lack internal validity because it could not be said that the change in the dependent variable was due solely to the change in the independent variable.

Experiments lacking internal validity have little value. Table 5.2 lists some factors that an experimenter should be concerned with in terms of the validity of his or

> An experiment is valid if (1) the observed change in the dependent variable is, in fact, due to the independent variable, and (2) if the results of the experiment apply to the "real world" outside the experimental setting.

> Internal validity is concerned with the extent to which the change in the dependent variable was actually due to the independent variable.

> Experiments lacking internal validity have little value.

Table 5.2   Validity Concerns in Marketing Experimentation

INTERNAL VALIDITY CONCERNS	EXTERNAL VALIDITY CONCERNS
Extraneous Factors Have extraneous events or influences affected the outcome of the experiment?	**Representative Sample** Was the sample used representative of the population to which the results were generalized?
Changes in Subjects Have natural, biological, physiological, or psychological changes occurred in subjects during the course of the experiment?	**Realism** Were the experiment's context and conduct so artificial or unusual as to question how realistically subjects behaved?
Measure Error Was the measuring instrument uniform in its sensitivity and accuracy throughout the experiment?	**Generalizability** Is there any other factor that casts doubt on the generalization of the experiment's results to the actual marketing entity for which it was designed?
Subjects Guessing Were subjects "tipped off" as to the experiment's objectives before or during the experiment?	
Equivalent Groups If groups were compared, were the groups' components identical across all relevant characteristics?	
Dropout Rate If groups were compared, did one group have a different "dropout" rate than the other(s)?	

her experiment. Note that the internal validity concerns are all situations that could cause a change in the dependent variable other than, or in addition to, the independent variable.

External validity refers to the extent that the relationship observed between the independent and dependent variables during the experiment is generalizable to the "real world."[14] In other words, can the results of the experiment be applied to units (consumers, stores, and so on) other than those directly involved in the experiment? There are several threats to external validity. How representative is the sample of test units? Is this sample really representative of the population? Additionally, there exist many examples of the incorrect selection of sample units for testing purposes. For example, executives, headquartered in large cities in cold winter climates, have been known to conduct "experiments" in warmer, tropical climes during the winter. Although the experiments they conduct may be internally valid, it is doubtful that the results will be generalizable to the total population.

Another threat to external validity is the artificiality of the experimental setting itself. In order to control as many variables as possible, some experimental settings are far removed from real-world conditions. Several experiments have been conducted, for example, wherein consumers were invited to a theater and asked to view a "pilot" TV show in which test commercials (containing copy A or B), the real subject of the experiment, were spliced into the "pilot." After viewing the film, consumers were given vouchers and were told they could spend the voucher in the "store" next door to the theater. The "store," of course, was set up for the experiment and contained displays of the products advertised in the test ads. It is arguable that the shopping data results from an experiment like this do not represent the true shopping behaviors of consumers. Consumers may act differently in a real supermarket. Look again at Table 5.2; it presents the various issues that should be of concern to the experimenter in terms of assessing external validity.[15] Note that the external validity concerns all raise questions as to the experimental setting being "real" and, therefore, more generalizable to the real world.

Types of Experiments

Laboratory experiments are those in which the independent variable is manipulated and measures of the dependent variable are taken in a contrived, artificial setting for the purpose of controlling the many possible extraneous variables that may affect the dependent variable.

We can classify experiments into two broad classes: laboratory and field. **Laboratory experiments** are those in which the independent variable is manipulated and measures of the dependent variable are taken in a contrived, artificial setting for the purpose of controlling the many possible extraneous variables that may affect the dependent variable.

To illustrate, let us consider the study we previously mentioned whereby subjects were invited to a theater and shown test ads, copy A or B, spliced into a TV "pilot" program. Why would a marketer want to use such an artificial, laboratory setting? Such a setting is used to control for variables that could affect the purchase of products other than those in the test ads. By bringing consumers into a contrived laboratory setting, the experimenter is able to control many extraneous variables. For example, you have learned why it is important to have equivalent groups (the same kind of people watching copy A as those watching copy B) in an experiment. By inviting preselected consumers to the TV "pilot" showing in a theater, the experimenter can match (on selected demographics) the consumers who view copy A with those who view copy B, thus ensuring that the two groups are equal. By having the consumers walk into an adjoining "store," the experimenter easily controls other factors such as the time between exposure to the ad copy and shopping and the consumers' being exposed to other advertising by competitive brands. As you have already learned, any one of these factors, left uncontrolled, could have an impact on the dependent variable. By controlling for these and other variables, the experimenter can be assured that any changes in the dependent variable were due solely to differences in the independent variable, ad copy A and B. Laboratory experiments, then, are desirable when the intent of the experiment is to achieve high levels of internal validity.

There are advantages to laboratory experiments. First, they allow the researcher to control for the effects of extraneous variables. Second, compared to field experiments, lab experiments may be conducted quickly and with less expense. Obviously, the disadvantage is the lack of a natural setting and, therefore, there is concern for the generalizability of the findings to the real world. For instance, blind taste tests of beer have found that a majority of beer drinkers favor the older beers such as Pabst, Michelob, or Coors, yet new beer brands are introduced regularly and become quite popular,[16] so the generalizability of blind taste tests is questionable.

Field experiments are those in which the independent variables are manipulated and the measurements of the dependent variable are made on test units in their natural setting. Many marketing experiments are conducted in natural settings, such as in supermarkets, malls, retail stores, and consumers' homes. Let us assume that a marketing manager conducts a *laboratory* experiment to test the differences between ad copy A, the company's existing ad copy, and a new ad copy, copy B. The results of the laboratory experiment indicate that copy B is far superior to the company's present ad copy A. But, before spending the money to use the new copy, the manager wants to know if ad copy B will really create increased sales in the real world. She elects to actually run the new ad copy in Erie, Pennsylvania, a city noted as being representative of the average characteristics of the U.S. population. By conducting this study in the field, the marketing manager will have greater confidence that the results of the study will actually hold up in other real-world settings. Note, however, that even if an experiment is conducted in a naturalistic field setting in order to enhance external validity, the experiment is invalid if it does not also have internal validity.

The primary advantage of the field experiment is that of conducting the study in a naturalistic setting, thus increasing the likelihood that the study's findings will also hold true in the real world. Field experiments, however, are expensive and time consuming. Also, the experimenter must always be alert to the impact of extraneous variables, which are very difficult to control in the natural settings of field experimentation.

The example we just cited of using Erie, Pennsylvania, for a field experiment would be called a "test market." Much of the experimentation in marketing, conducted as field experiments, is known as test marketing. For this reason, test marketing is discussed in the following section.

TEST MARKETING

Test marketing is the phrase commonly used to indicate an experiment, study, or test that is conducted in a field setting. Companies may use one or several test market cities, which are geographical areas selected in which to conduct the test. There are two broad classes of uses of test markets: (1) to test the sales potential for a new product or service and (2) to test variations in the marketing mix for a product or service.[17]

Although test markets are very expensive and time consuming, the costs of introducing a new product on a national or regional basis routinely amount to millions of dollars. The costs of the test market are then justified if the results of

The advantages of laboratory experiments are that they allow for the control of extraneous variables and they may be conducted quickly and less expensively than field experiments.

A disadvantage of laboratory experiments is that they are conducted in artificial settings.

Field experiments are those in which the independent variables are manipulated and the measurements of the dependent variable are made on test units in their natural setting.

The advantage of field experiments is that they are conducted in natural settings.

The disadvantages of field experiments are that they are expensive and time consuming.

Test marketing is the phrase commonly used to indicate an experiment, study, or test that is conducted in a field setting.

There are two broad classes of uses of test markets: (1) to test the sales potential for a new product or service and (2) to test variations in the marketing mix for a product or service.

the test market can improve a product's chances of success. Sometimes the test market results will be sufficient to warrant further market introductions. Sometimes the test market identifies a failure early on and saves the company huge losses. The GlobalPC, a scaled-down computer targeted for novices, was tried in test markets. The parent company, MyTurn, concluded that the test market sales results would not lead to a profit and the product was dropped before the company experienced further losses.[18] Test markets are not only conducted to measure sales potential for a new product but also to measure consumer and dealer reactions to other marketing mix variables as well. A firm may use only department stores to distribute the product in one test market and only specialty stores in another test market city to gain some information on the best way to distribute the product. Companies can also test media usage, pricing, sales promotions, and so on through test markets. Marketing Research Insight 5.5 illustrates marketers' use of test marketing.

Types of Test Markets

Test markets have been classified into four types: standard, controlled, electronic, and simulated.[19] The **standard test market** is one in which the firm tests the product and/or marketing mix variables through the company's normal distribution channels. Standard test markets are time consuming, often taking a year or more, and are very expensive, often requiring several hundred thousand dollars. Standard test markets are not confidential; as soon as the test begins, competitors know about the product and can surmise a great deal about the intended marketing strategy for the product. Even with these limitations, however, standard test markets are perhaps the best indicators as to how the product will actually fare in the marketplace. This is because very little is contrived in the standard test market.

Controlled test markets are conducted by outside research firms that guarantee distribution of the product through prespecified types and numbers of distributors. Companies specializing in providing this service, such as RoperASW and ACNielsen, provide dollar incentives for distributors to provide them with guaranteed shelf space. Controlled test markets offer an alternative to the company that wishes to gain fast access to a distribution system set up for test market purposes. The disadvantage is that this distribution network may or may not properly represent the firm's actual distribution system.

Electronic test markets are those in which a panel of consumers has agreed to carry identification cards that each consumer presents when buying goods and services. These tests are conducted only in a small number of cities in which local retailers have agreed to participate. The advantage of the card is that as consumers buy (or do not buy) the test product, demographic information on the consumers is automatically recorded. In some cases, firms offering electronic test markets may also have the ability to link media viewing habits to panel members as well. In this way, firms using the electronic test market also know how different elements of the promotional mix affect purchases of the new product. Firms offering this service include Information Resources, Inc. and ACNielsen. Obviously, the electronic test market offers speed, greater confidentiality, and less cost than standard or controlled test markets. However, the disadvantage is that the test market is not the real market. By virtue of having agreed to serve as members of the electronic panel, consumers in electronic test markets may be atypical. A user firm must evaluate the issue of representativeness. Also, electronic test markets are typically situated in small cities such as Eau Claire, Wisconsin,[20] which is another representativeness consideration.

A standard test market is one in which the firm tests the product and/or marketing mix variables through the company's normal distribution channels.

Controlled test markets are conducted by outside research firms that guarantee distribution of the product through prespecified types and numbers of distributors.

Electronic test markets are those in which a panel of consumers has agreed to carry identification cards that each consumer presents when buying goods and services.

► **Additional Insights**

*Test Marketing Is Conducted to Determine How
the Market Will React to a New Product or Service*

Portable Calzone Anyone?

Pizza Hut, in its second $70 million product launch in less than a year, has debuted the P'Zone, a portable, calzone-like item that officials tout as "the pizza that actually sold out in test market." P'Zone is a medium-sized crust filled with toppings and cheese, folded into a half-moon shape and sealed like a calzone, and then baked.[21]

Dress Up Your Cell Phone?

Carphone Warehouse is test marketing a new stand-alone retail concept called Phone Fashions. The new retail store offers cell phone accessories. The first Phone Fashions-branded store has opened on Wardour Street in London next to a Carphone Warehouse shop. It sells ringtones, all sorts of accessories and games, including exclusive products not available in Carphone Warehouse. The test includes the launch of a Mirror-branded product called Instant Mirror to be sold exclusively in Phone Fashions. It delivers celebrity news, gossip, and football scores direct to customers' phones.[22]

How About Some Really Fast Fast Food?

For those on the go who find drive-through service a tad too slow, McDonald's is test marketing a new idea: McQuick. Offered only at three units (in Bellevue, Kirkland, and Redmond, Washington), the mobile ordering and payment service is about as fast as a restaurant can be. Customers with mobile phones set up a credit card–linked McQuick account online (**www.try.mcquick.com**) or by phone where they create up to five menus of their most frequently ordered meals. When ordering, they simply call the McQuick service and indicate the unit location with a one-button push and the meal desired (no substitutions allowed) with another one-touch command. The service recognizes customers' cell phone numbers and deducts the meal charge from the account. McDonald's says the transaction takes about 10 seconds. McQuick meals can be picked up inside at a designated no-wait mobile order pick-up counter or at the drive-through window.

McDonald's adds a 15-cent convenience charge to each order but waives that fee during the first 60 days after a McQuick account is set up. The Oak Brook, Illinois–based chain is evaluating the service for possible expansion beyond the current test markets.[23]

Want to Invite Samuel Adams?

Big Chair's first TV tests for a new campaign for Boston Beer's Samuel Adams brand uses the tag line, "Mighty tasty" and seeks to position the brew as the ultimate party beer. In one test ad, "Sister," two guys check out a girl in a bar. One says, "She's smart. She's beautiful. Why not?" His pal says, "Because she's my sister, and I'll kill you!" But after he sips some Sam Adams, he introduces his friend to his sister and leaves them to get acquainted. In another test ad, "Tape," a man drinks some Sam Adams and ends up showing his buddies a sexy video he made with his girlfriend. "We wanted to make Sam Adams cool to a young audience," said C. J. Waldman, creative director for the test ads. Previous ads had focused on the beer's quality, featuring beach and bar party footage. The tag line was, "The world's most award-winning beers." The ads, aimed at 21- to 29-year-olds, were run in five test markets: Atlanta; Austin, Texas; Minneapolis; Phoenix; and Richmond, Virginia. Research showed young drinkers don't often order Sam Adams. "It wasn't a party beer," said Waldman. "We wanted to bring it into the vernacular of a younger audience."[24]

Honey, May I Offer You a Dip of Snuff?

Because opinions about smoking are becoming more disputed, the tobacco industry is exploring new venues to expand on its core base of consumers. U.S. Smokeless has a mission to make snuff socially acceptable by providing packets of mint-flavored tobacco that don't break apart in the mouth or trigger the need to spit. They are test-marketing in Topeka, Kansas, and Youngstown, Ohio, under the "Tobacco satisfaction. Anytime. Anywhere" tag. Called "Revel," the product is positioned as a discreet solution for places and situations in which tobacco users are restricted from lighting up or chewing.[25]

Simulated test markets (STMs) are those in which a limited amount of data on consumer response to a new product is fed into a model containing certain assumptions regarding planned marketing programs, which generates likely product sales volume.

Simulated test markets (STMs) are those in which a limited amount of data on consumer response to a new product is fed into a model containing certain assumptions regarding planned marketing programs, which generates likely product sales volume. It is claimed that IBM has suffered business failures such as the ill-fated Aptiva line of PCs because it failed to use STM research.[26]

Typical STMs share the following characteristics:

▶ Respondents are selected to provide a sample of consumers who satisfy predetermined demographic characteristics.

▶ Consumers are shown commercials or print ads for the test product as well as ads for competitive products.

▶ Consumers are then given the opportunity to purchase, or not to purchase, the test product either in a real or simulated store environment.

▶ Consumers are then recontacted after they have had an opportunity to use the product in an effort to determine likelihood of repurchase, as well as other information relative to use of the product.

▶ Information from the preceding process is fed into a computer program that is calibrated by assumptions of the marketing mix and other elements of the environment. The program then generates output such as estimated sales volume, market share, and so on.[27]

There are many advantages to STMs. They are fast relative to standard test markets. STMs typically take only 18 to 24 weeks compared to as many as 12 to 18 months for standard test markets. STMs cost only 5 percent to 10 percent of the cost of a standard test market. STMs are confidential; competitors are less likely to know about the test. Different marketing mixes may be tested and results of STMs have shown that they can be accurate predictors of actual market response. The primary disadvantage is that STMs are not as accurate as full-scale test markets. They are very dependent on the assumptions built into the models. These assumptions must include estimates as to how the distributors will react to the product and the likelihood that consumers will repurchase the product. Standard test markets do not need to assume the impact of these important market factors.[28]

Consumer Versus Industrial Test Markets

When we think of test marketing we normally think of tests of consumer products. Test marketing, however, has been growing in the industrial market, sometimes called the B2B market. Although the techniques are somewhat different between consumer and industrial test markets, the same results are sought—the timely release of profitable products.

Test marketing is used in both consumer markets and industrial or B2B markets as well.

In consumer test markets, multiple versions of a more-or-less finished product are tested by consumers. In industrial test markets, the key technology is presented to selected industrial users who offer feedback on desired features and product performance levels. Given this information, product prototypes are then developed and are placed with a select number of users for actual use. Users again provide feedback to iron out design problems. In this way, the new product is tried and tested under actual conditions before the final product is designed and produced for the total market. The negative side of this process is the time it takes to test the product from the beginning stages to the final, commercialized stages. During this time period, information on the new product is leaked to competitors, and the longer the product is being tested, the more investment costs increase without any revenues being generated. U.S. automakers, for example, take 48 to 60 months to design, refine, and begin production of a new car model. Japanese companies are able to do it in 30 months by having a development team made up of a combination of marketing and production people. DaimlerChrysler and 3M have experimented with this concept. In many firms, future industrial test marketing will be fully integrated with the new-product development process.[29]

So far, our discussion of test marketing has not mentioned the likelihood of having different results between tests conducted in one country versus another. Markets that differ dramatically in terms of demographics and culture should not be expected to respond equally to any single marketing mix. For this reason, some companies are experimenting with "lead country" test marketing.

"Lead Country" Test Markets

A **lead country test market** is test marketing conducted in specific foreign countries that seem to be good predictors for an entire continent. As markets have become more global, firms are no longer interested in limiting marketing of new products and services to their domestic market.

A lead country test market is test marketing conducted in specific foreign countries that seem to be good predictors for an entire continent.

Colgate-Palmolive used lead country test marketing when it launched its Palmolive Optims shampoo and conditioner. The company tested the product in the Philippines, Australia, Mexico, and Hong Kong. A year later, distribution was expanded to other countries in Europe, Asia, Latin America, and Africa.[30] Colgate used two countries as test markets in 1999 to test its battery-powered Actibrush for kids. These two countries brought in $10 million in sales. Colgate moved into 50 countries in 2000 and earned $115 million in sales.[31]

Korea is being used as a lead country test market for digital products and services. Seongnam is a middle-class Seoul suburb with a mix of high-rise apartment blocks, restaurants, and malls. During the next three years, municipal officials plan to transform the town of 930,000 into the world's first digital city. Multiple broadband connections will seek to do away with analog concepts—like cash and credit cards. Seongnam will start equipping citizens with digital cell phones that, in effect, pay for purchases at every store in the city. Cash-free Seongnam is one of many on-the-ground tests being launched in South Korea, a nation preoccupied with all things digital. More than half of South Korea's 15 million households have broadband service and more than 60 percent of Koreans carry cell phones. The country is now so wired that many companies can use entire urban populations as test markets for their latest digital products and services.[32]

Selecting Test Market Cities

There are three criteria that are useful for selecting test market cities: **representativeness, degree of isolation,** and **ability to control distribution and promotion.** Because one of the major reasons for conducting a test market is to achieve external validity, the test market city should be representative of the marketing territory in which the product will ultimately be distributed. Consequently, a great deal of effort is expended to locate the "ideal" city in terms of comparability with characteristics of the total U.S. (or other country) population. The "ideal" city is, of course, the city whose demographic characteristics most closely match the desired total market. For instance, R. J. Reynolds chose Chattanooga, Tennessee, to test market its Eclipse "smokeless" cigarette because Chattanooga has a higher proportion of smokers than most cities, and R. J. Reynolds needed to test Eclipse with smokers.[33]

When a firm test markets a product, distribution of the product and promotion of the product are isolated to a limited geographical area, such as Tulsa, Oklahoma. If the firm advertises in the *Tulsa World* newspaper, the newspaper not only covers Tulsa but also has very little "spillover" into other sizable markets. Therefore, the company, along with its dealers, competitors, and so on, is not likely to get many calls

There are three criteria that are useful for selecting test market cities: representativeness, degree of isolation, and ability to control distribution and promotion

from a nearby city wanting to know why it cannot buy the product. Distribution has been restricted to the test market, Tulsa. Some markets are not so isolated. If you were to run promotions for a product test in the *Los Angeles Times*, you would have very large spillover of newspaper readership outside the Los Angeles geographical area. Note that this would not necessarily be a problem as long as you wanted to run the test in the geographical area covered by the *Los Angeles Times* and you also had arranged for the new product to be distributed in this area.

The ability to control distribution and promotion depends on a number of factors. Are the distributors in the city being considered available and willing to cooperate? If not, is a controlled test market service company available for the city? Will the media in the city have the facilities to accommodate your test market needs? At what costs? All of these factors must be considered before selecting the test city. Fortunately, because it is desirable to have test markets conducted in a city because it brings in additional revenues, city governments as well as the media typically provide a great deal of information about their city to prospective test marketers.

A good example of the application of these three criteria is McDonald's test market of its all-you-can-eat breakfast bar. The test was conducted in Atlanta and Savannah, Georgia, which are representative southeastern cities where McDonald's has control over its outlets and where the promotional media are specific to those markets. The buffet was found to increase weekend family breakfast sales.[34]

Pros and Cons of Test Marketing

The advantages of test marketing are straightforward. Testing product acceptability and marketing mix variables in a field setting provides the best information possible to the decision maker prior to actually going into full-scale marketing of the product. Because of this, Philip Kotler has referred to test markets as the "ultimate" way to test a new product.[35] Test marketing allows for the most accurate method of forecasting future sales, and it allows firms the opportunity to pretest marketing mix variables.

There are, however, several negatives to test marketing. First, test markets do not yield infallible results. There have been many instances in which test market results have led to decisions that proved wrong in the marketplace. No doubt, there have probably been many "would-be successful" products withheld from the marketplace due to poor performances in test markets. Much of this problem, however, is not due to anything inherent in test marketing; rather, it is a reflection of the complexity and changeability of consumer behavior. Accurately forecasting consumer behavior is a formidable task. Also, competitors intentionally try to sabotage test markets. Firms will often flood a test market with sales promotions if they know a competitor is test marketing a product. When PepsiCo tested Mountain Dew Sport drink in Minneapolis in 1990, Quaker Oats Company's Gatorade counterattacked with a deluge of coupons and ads. Mountain Dew Sport was yanked from the market although Pepsi says Gatorade had nothing to do with the decision.[36] These activities make it even more difficult to forecast the normal market's response to a product.

Another problem with test markets is their cost. Estimates are that the costs exceed several hundred thousand dollars even for limited test markets. Test markets involving several test cities and various forms of promotion can easily reach well over six figures. Finally, test markets bring about exposure of the product to the competition. Competitors get the opportunity to examine product prototypes and to see the planned marketing strategy for the new product via the test market. If a company spends too much time testing a product, it runs the risk of allowing enough

Test marketing allows for the most accurate method of forecasting future sales, and it allows firms the opportunity to pretest marketing mix variables.

Test markets do not yield infallible results.

Test markets are expensive, expose the new product or service to competitors, and take time to conduct.

MARKETING RESEARCH
INSIGHT
5.6

▶ **An Ethical Issue**

Ethical Issues in Test Marketing

Yes, ethical issues arise as company executives make test market decisions. Some companies conduct test markets and publicize the results in the trade press. There is nothing unethical about this practice. However, sometimes it is the information that is not reported that causes an ethical problem. Knowing that their test market results will get publicized, some companies have intentionally selected test markets where their distribution and reputation were particularly strong. The test market results, then, are skewed from the outset to make the company's "new product" sound favorable.

Fortunately, the problem of incomplete reporting (whether of a test market or some other marketing practice) has been addressed by the *Wall Street Journal*. In an effort to provide complete information regarding its surveys, the *Wall Street Journal* has begun publishing a boxed insert containing the details of how its sample was drawn and other facts allowing readers to understand its methodology. Some readers will regard this information as superfluous, but it does allow a basis for judging the quality and meaning of the survey results. Also, the Public Affairs Council of the Advertising Research Foundation (ARF) has published "Guidelines for the Public Use of Market and Opinion Research." This document covers the origin, design, execution, and candor of the research being reported.

Source: Murphy, P. E. & Laczniak, G. R. (1992, June). Emerging ethical issues facing marketing researchers. *Marketing Research*, p. 6.

time for a competitor to bring out a similar product and to gain the advantage of being first in the market. In spite of these problems, the value of the information from test marketing makes test marketing a worthwhile endeavor. Finally, as we see in Marketing Research Insight 5.6 , ethical issues arise in terms of how test markets are selected as well as how test market results are reported.

SUMMARY

Research design refers to a set of advance decisions made to develop the master plan to be used in the conduct of the research project. There are three general research designs: exploratory, descriptive, and causal. Each one of these designs has its own inherent approaches. The significance of studying research design is that, by matching the research objective with the appropriate research design, a host of research decisions may be predetermined. Therefore, a research design serves as a "blueprint" for researchers. Selecting the appropriate research design depends, to a large extent, on the research objectives and how much information is already known about the problem. If very little is known, exploratory research is appropriate. Exploratory research is unstructured and informal research that is undertaken to gain background information; it is helpful for more clearly defining the research problem. Exploratory research is used in a number of situations: to gain background information, to define terms, to clarify problems and hypotheses, and to establish research priorities. Reviewing existing literature, surveying individuals knowledgeable in the area to be investigated, and relying on former similar case situations are methods of conducting exploratory research. Exploratory research should almost always be used because it is fast, inexpensive, and sometimes resolves the research objective or is helpful in carrying out descriptive or causal research.

If concepts, terms, and so on are already known and the research objective is to describe and measure phenomena, then descriptive research is appropriate. Descriptive research measures marketing phenomena and answers the questions of who, what, where, when, and how. Descriptive studies may be conducted at one point in time (cross-sectional) or several measurements may be made on the same sample at different points in time (longitudinal). Longitudinal studies are often conducted using panels. Panels represent sample units who have agreed to answer questions at periodic intervals. Continuous panels are longitudinal studies in which sample units are asked the same questions repeatedly. Brand-switching tables may be prepared based on data from continuous panels. Market tracking studies may be conducted using data from continuous panels.

The second type of panel used in longitudinal research is the discontinuous panel. Discontinuous, sometimes called omnibus panels are those in which the sample units are asked different questions. The main advantage of the discontinuous panel is that research firms have a large sample of persons who are willing to answer whatever questions they are asked. The demographics of panel members are often balanced to the demographics of larger geographical areas they are to represent, such as a region or the entire United States. Marketing research firms such as NFOWorldwide and ACNielsen have maintained panels for many years. More recently, online survey research firms use panels to gain access to respondents.

Sometimes the research objective requires the researcher to determine causal relationships between two or more variables. Causal relationships provide relationships such as "If x, then y." Causal relationships may only be discovered through special studies called experiments. Experiments allow us to determine the effects of a variable, known as an independent variable, on another variable, known as a dependent variable. Experimental designs are necessary to ensure that the effect we observe in our dependent variable is due, in fact, to our independent variable and not to other variables known as extraneous variables. The validity of experiments may be assessed by internal validity and external validity.

Laboratory experiments are particularly useful for achieving internal validity whereas field experiments are better suited for achieving external validity. Test marketing is a form of field experimentation. Test market cities are selected on the basis of their representativeness, isolation, and the degree to which market variables such as distribution and promotion may be controlled. Various types of test markets exist (standard, controlled, electronic, simulated, consumer, industrial, and lead country) and, although test markets garner much useful information, they are expensive and not infallible.

KEY TERMS

Research design (p. 120)
Exploratory research (p. 122)
Hypotheses (p. 123)
Secondary data analysis (p. 123)
Experience surveys (p. 123)
Case analysis (p. 124)
Focus groups (p. 124)
Projective techniques (p. 124)
Descriptive research (p. 125)
Cross-sectional studies (p. 125)
Sample surveys (p. 125)
Longitudinal studies (p. 127)
Panels (p. 127)
Continuous panels (p. 130)
Discontinuous panels (p. 130)
Omnibus panels (p. 130)
Brand-switching studies (p. 131)

Market tracking studies (p. 132)
Causality (p. 132)
Experiment (p. 133)
Independent variables (p. 133)
Dependent variables (p. 133)
Extraneous variables (p. 133)
Experimental design (p. 134)
Pretest (p. 134)
Posttest (p. 134)
"True" experimental design (p. 134)
After-only design (p. 135)
Quasi-experimental designs (p. 135)
One-group, before–after design (p. 135)
Control group (p. 135)
Experimental group (p. 135)
Before–after with control group (p. 136)
Internal validity (p. 137)

External validity (p. 138)
Laboratory experiments (p. 138)
Field experiments (p. 139)
Test marketing (p. 139)
Standard test market (p. 140)
Controlled test markets (p. 140)
Electronic test markets (p. 140)

Simulated test markets (p. 142)
Lead country test market (p. 143)
Representativeness (p. 143)
Degree of isolation (p. 143)
Ability to control distribution and
  promotion (p. 143)

REVIEW QUESTIONS/APPLICATIONS

1. How would you match research designs with various research objectives?
2. Give some examples illustrating the uses of exploratory research.
3. What type of research design answers the questions of who, what, where, when, and how?
4. What are the differences between longitudinal studies and cross-sectional studies?
5. In what situation would a continuous panel be more suitable than a discontinuous panel? In what situation would a discontinuous panel be more suitable than a continuous panel?
6. Explain why studies of the "if–then" variety are considered to be causal studies.
7. What is the objective of good experimental design? Explain why certain designs are called quasi-experimental designs.
8. Explain the two types of validity in experimentation and also explain why different types of experiments are better suited for addressing one type of validity versus another.
9. Distinguish among the various types of test marketing.
10. Think of a past job that you have held. List three areas in which you, or some other person in the organization, could have benefited from having information generated by research. What would be the most appropriate research design for each of the three areas of research you have listed?
11. At the beginning of the chapter we introduced you to actual research conducted by AT&T to develop its logo. Can you identifiy the different research designs that were most likely used in this research?
12. Design an experiment. Select an independent variable and a dependent variable. What are some possible extraneous variables that may cause problems? Explain how you would control for the effects these variables may have on your dependent variable. Is your experiment a valid experiment?
13. The Maximum Company has invented an extra-strength, instant coffee brand to be called "Max-Caff" and positioned to be stronger tasting than any competing brands. Design a taste test experiment that compares Max-Caff to the two leading instant coffee brands to determine which brand consumers consider to taste the strongest. Identify and diagram your experiment. Indicate how the experiment is to be conducted, and assess the internal and external validity of your experiment.
14. Coca-Cola markets PowerAde as a sports drink that competes with Gatorade. Competition for sports drinks is fierce where they are sold in the coolers of convenience stores. Coca-Cola is thinking about using a special holder that fits in a standard cooler but moves PowerAde to eye level and makes it more conspicuous than Gatorade. Design an experiment that determines whether the special holder increases the sales of PowerAde in convenience stores. Identify and diagram your experiment. Indicate how the experiment is to be conducted and assess the internal and external validity of your experiment.

15. SplitScreen is a marketing research company that tests television advertisements. SplitScreen has an agreement with a cable television company in a medium-sized city in Iowa. The cable company can send up to four different television ads simultaneously to different households. SplitScreen also has agreements with the three largest grocery store chains, which will provide scanner data to SplitScreen. About 25 percent of the residents have SplitScreen scan cards that are scanned when items are bought at the grocery store and that allow SplitScreen to identify who bought which grocery products. For allowing SplitScreen access to their television hookups and their grocery purchases information, residents receive bonus points that can be used to buy products in a special points catalog. Identify and diagram the true experimental design possible using the SplitScreen system. Assess the internal and external validity of SplitScreen's system.

16. AT&T can afford to hire the best researchers in the world. Read what Lipson and Zeese have to say at the beginning of this chapter. Then go back to our evaluation of the marketing research industry in Chapter 3. See specifically, "Can the Marketing Research Industry Improve Its Performance?" Look at the recommendations made by Mahajan and Wind. Explain why you think AT&T hires good researchers.

INTERACTIVE LEARNING

Visit the Web site at www.prenhall.com/burnsbush. For this chapter, work through the Self-Study Quizzes, and get instant feedback on whether you need additional studying. On the Web site, you can review the chapter outlines and case information for Chapter 5.

CASE 5.1   Swing Jacket[37]

Visit Swing Jacket at www.swingjacket.com.

Swing Jacket is a strap-on training device for golfers. The product's main feature is its patented swing rails that guide a golfer's arms and help produce a better swing. By using the jacket, the golfer's muscles "learn" the correct path to take to ensure a proper swing. Swing Jacket, Inc. faced difficulties with its initial plan to sell the apparatus through golf stores. The product was hard to sell due to its relative technical complexities. Swing Jacket, Inc. decided that the expense was too great to train specialty golf store salespeople across the nation on the proper use of the device. So the company decided to focus its resources on direct sales and hired legendary Script-to-Screen to produce an infomercial.

Within the first two quarters after the infomercial aired, Swing Jacket, Inc. knew it had a problem. Return rates for the product soared at 23 percent. Swing Jacket, Inc. wasn't sure why people were returning the device. The infomercial starred popular PGA tournament player Peter Jacobson and tracked the improvement of three amateur players with varying handicaps. The $150 product was advertised to "significantly lower your score" or consumers could return the product within 90 days. Trials during product development did not show a problem. Golfers who had tried the product before its debut didn't suggest that they were embarrassed to wear the device nor did they find it uncomfortable. Players who had tried the product reported that it helped their golf swing. But yet, the return rate of the Swing Jacket still hovered at nearly 25 percent.

1. Should Swing Jacket, Inc. conduct research? Why or why not?
2. Assuming you believe Swing Jacket, Inc. should conduct research, what type of research design would you recommend?
3. Would you recommend more than one research design?

CASE 5.2   Meridian Research Associates (MRA)

Laura Holladay is a project manager for Meridian Research Associates (MRA). During the week she oversaw a project for General Mills that involved setting up taste tests in locations around the country to compare regional taste differences for three new products. She also made calls on three prospective clients. On Friday afternoon she sat down to review her notes of the three client visits.

Tuesday/A.M. Met with Susan Greer—assumed position as vice president of the Colony Bank last May. Bank only six years in this market. Board meeting suggestion for her to conduct a bank image analysis. Neither Greer nor other officers have any experience with bank image analysis studies. How should they conduct the study? What is bank image analysis? Should they include their competitors in the study? Greer wants MRA to give them guidance; they feel they should do the study. Want to hire us for advice. Next appointment set for 5:30 on 14th.

Wednesday/P.M. Judd Tucker, brand manager for Pooch Plus dog treats. Pooch Plus division of PetcoProducts, Inc. Dog treats business very competitive; constant sales promotions conducted to sway market share from competitors. Tucker very aggressive and wants us to conduct research examining dog treat brand swings in market shares over last five years. What types of promotions lead to greatest share swings? What are the best methods to counter effective promotions of competitors? We will need to track market share and promotion history of dog treats category. (Call Gayla VanZyverden at Information Resources Thursday A.M.) Appointment set up for 8:30 on 19th.

Thursday/P.M. Melissa Duggan of General Mills. Reviewed progress on upcoming taste tests but Duggan interested in a new project. General Mills considering a new hot breakfast cereal. Brand's attributes built around health and nutrition. Concept tests are favorable and now company interested in determining best package design. Which size, color, logo type size combinations will get highest level of customer awareness? Cereal will compete with many brands. Duggan believes new brands "get lost" on store shelves with dozens of other brands competing for customer attention. Wants to make sure GM has the most effective package design so new brand will be seen by customers. Appointment on 22nd at 10:30.

Laura Holladay spent Friday finalizing her taste test project for General Mills. By late afternoon she reviewed the notes of her meetings with the three prospective client/projects. She packed her briefcase and headed for her home in the suburbs. On the way she thought about the three upcoming projects. Within a short period of time she had decided on the research design needed for all three. Finally, she sat back, relaxed, and listened to her favorite radio station, KLAY. When she arrived in her driveway, Holladay called her office message center and recorded notes on the three proposed research designs.

1. What research design do you think Laura Holladay has selected for each of the three situations?
2. For each research design you specify in question 1, describe the reason(s) you selected it.
3. Briefly describe the appropriate research process for each of the three situations. In other words, describe what you think MRA should do for each client.

Chapter 6

Secondary Data and Online Information Databases

Learning Objectives:

To learn how to distinguish between secondary and primary data

To learn a classification of secondary data

To understand databases, both internal and external

To understand the advantages and disadvantages of secondary data

To learn how to evaluate secondary data

To learn how to find secondary data including search strategies needed for searching online information databases

To know the contents of some of the major sources of secondary data provided by the government and private sources

Practitioner Viewpoint

Secondary data can provide information about the size and characteristics of any market—the number of people or households, age, ethnicity and language, education, labor force participation, commuting patterns, household type, marital status, income, housing type, and cost. Demographic profiles are the most common but not the only type of secondary data. Information is also available about crime rates, the location of businesses by industry, shopping centers, bank deposits, school enrollment, facilities such as hospitals or schools, amenities such as parks or museums, even traffic counts and climate conditions.

There is a variety of sources available for secondary data. Public data sources include a number of federal agencies. Compendia of federal data sources can be found at www.fedstats.gov/ or www.whitehouse.gov/fsbr/demography.html. Local agencies can also provide a variety of data for their states or communities. Public data sources are a good starting point for the intrepid market analyst. However, the recency and detail of the data are limited in most public sources. Census 2000 is the most comprehensive demographic database, but the data were already two years old by the time the last tables were released in 2002.

The alternative to public data sources is a private vendor. Private sector sources process the public databases, update the data to current-year and/or five-year forecasts, offer the data for any geographic area, and integrate public databases with a variety of private databases such as consumer surveys and business lists. Data are readily available from private vendors but are not free.

Lynn Wombold
Director, Data Development
ESRI Business Information Solutions

Marketing Research Using Census 2000

Marketers are constantly making decisions about geographical markets. Which markets are growing? Which markets are increasing the most in population? What are the changes in income levels in those markets? What have past sales been in those markets? These are but a few of the many variables marketing managers seek to understand when making business decisions. Fortunately, much of this information does not require primary data collection; it is available in secondary data sources. The *Census of the Population*, taken every decade by the U.S. Census Bureau, provides the backbone of secondary data used by marketing researchers. Information collected by the census is not only used by government policy makers but also is heavily relied on by business organizations collecting secondary data to make business decisions. The Department of Education is very interested in knowing how many 5-year-olds will enter the K–12 schooling system. Toy manufacturers are very interested in this same information. Visit the Census 2000 Web site at **www.census.gov** (see Figure 6.1). The change in population of 33 million people from 1990 to 2000 represented the largest increase between censuses ever recorded. The 1990s was the only decade in the twentieth century in which every state in the United States gained population. The figure below shows that, although all parts of the United States experienced growth, most growth took place in the South and West.[1]

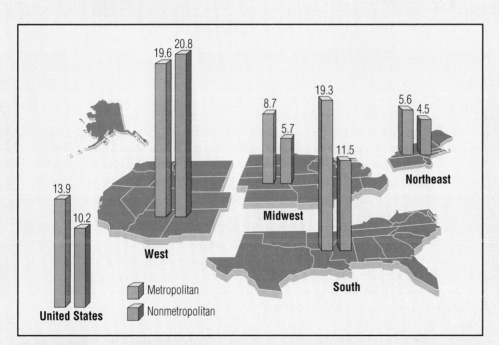

Figure **6.1** **Percentage Change in Metropolitan and Nonmetropolitan Populations by Region: 1990 to 2000**

Source: U.S. Census Bureau, Census 2000 and 1990 census.

Once a marketing researcher determines the apppropriate research design for a research objective, he or she normally turns to secondary data. As our demographer, Lynn Wombold, suggests in her preceding viewpoint and as our introductory example of Census 2000 illustrates, many marketing decisions are based on information supplied by secondary data. By taking a quick tour of the Census Bureau's homepage you can easily see how the type of information provided can be of practical use in making business decisions. The Internet's greatest impact has been making information widely available and easily accessible. Much of this information is available through online databases such as LexisNexis and ABI Inform. Online databases, a part of online research, have had such a significant impact on secondary data search that we included the name in our chapter title. The Internet has greatly increased access to online databases. In just a few years, the Internet has become a very important source of seeking and retrieving secondary data of all types. Imagine how this information would help if you were trying to make marketing decisions. You would be able to quickly and inexpensively make many marketing decisions by accessing such information even though it was gathered by someone else for some other purpose. In this chapter, we introduce you to the sources of secondary data, including online databases. We discuss the advantages and disadvantages of secondary data and how to evaluate secondary data. We have a completely new and updated section that shows you how to search for secondary data, including strategies for searching online information databases. Finally, we take a close-up look at some of the most important secondary data sources for marketing researchers.[2]

SOURCES OF SECONDARY DATA

Primary Versus Secondary Data

As presented in Chapter 2, data needed for marketing management decisions can be grouped into two types: primary and secondary. **Primary data** are information that is developed or gathered by the researcher specifically for the research project at hand. **Secondary data** have previously been gathered by someone other than the researcher and/or for some other purpose than the research project at hand. As government agencies and other organizations gather information in the daily course of business, they gather information that is recorded. U.S. customs officials, for example, record a wealth of information to help us understand the amount and types of goods being imported and exported. Businesses provide information to the government on sales by product or service, number of employees, business locations, and so on. When a consumer completes a warranty card to register a new scuba-diving tank, registers a new puppy, registers an automobile, applies for a driver's license, or subscribes to a magazine, information is recorded. Much of this information is valuable. Government and private organizations provide this information to the public.

The evolution of the Internet has done more to bring fast and easy access of secondary data to end users than anything else since the Gutenberg press. Since the mid-1980s virtually all documents have been electronically produced, edited, stored, and made accessible to users. For several years firms have concentrated on bringing this information to users through specialized services. Today many of these firms offer these services via the Internet. Although some services are available only through a subscription, the Internet provides an incredible stock of free secondary data. Yet, with all the information available to Internet users today, this will likely be viewed as very primitive when Internet2 becomes widely available. Some com-

> **Primary data** are information that is developed or gathered by the researcher specifically for the research project at hand.
>
> **Secondary data** have previously been gathered by someone other than the researcher and/or for some other purpose than the research project at hand.

▶ **Meet a Marketing Researcher**

Demographers Use Secondary Data
Lynn Wombold, ESRI Business Information Solutions

Lynn Wombold manages data development for ESRI Business Information Solutions, including the current processing of Census 2000 data, development of unique databases such as demographic forecasts, consumer spending, and the ACORN market segmentation system, plus the acquisition and integration of third-party data, such as InfoUSA's business database. She is also responsible for custom analysis and modeling projects. Her areas of expertise include population estimates and projections, state and local demography, census data, survey research, and consumer data.

Lynn has been with ESRI BIS since 1988; previously she was senior demographer at the University of New Mexico. Her education includes degrees in sociology, with a specialty in demographic studies from Bowling Green State University in Ohio. Awards include CACI's Eagle Award for Technical Excellence and Encore Achievers.

pare the information highway today to what Internet2 will offer as a cart path compares to an eight-lane superhighway![3] We think secondary data access through the Internet, another form of online research, will contine to grow and become more and more important in the marketing researcher's toolbox.

Secondary data access through the Internet, another form of online research, will contine to grow and become more and more important in the marketing researcher's toolbox.

CLASSIFICATION OF SECONDARY DATA

With so much secondary information available, every marketing researcher must learn to properly manage these data. In fact, secondary data are more important to the marketing researcher today than ever before because so much information is available and it can be very useful. However, the stock of information available can be overwhelming. Marketing researchers must learn to properly handle secondary data. They must know the classifications of secondary data as well as their advantages and disadvantages, and they must know how to evaluate the information available to them.

Internal Secondary Data

Secondary data may be broadly classified as either internal or external. **Internal secondary data** are data that have been collected within the firm. Such data include sales records, purchase requisitions, and invoices. Obviously, a good marketing researcher always determines what internal information is already available. You may recall from Chapter 1 that we referred to internal data analysis as being part of the internal reports system of a firm's marketing information system (MIS). Today a major source of internal data is databases that contain information on customers, sales, suppliers, and any other facet of business a firm may wish to track. *Database marketing* is the term used to refer to uses of these internal databases to

Internal secondary data are data that have been collected within the firm. Such data include sales records, purchase requisitions, and invoices.

target marketing programs directly to consumers. The use of internal databases has grown dramatically for several years.

Internal Databases

Before we discuss internal and external databases, we should understand that a **database** refers to a collection of data and information describing items of interest.[4] Each unit of information in a database is called a **record.** A record could represent a customer, a supplier, a competitive firm, a product, an individual inventory item, and so on. Records are composed of subcomponents of information called **fields.** As an example, a company having a database of customers would have *records* representing each customer. Typical *fields* in a customer database would include name, address, telephone number, e-mail address, products purchased, dates of purchases, locations where purchased, warranty information, and any other information the company thought was important. Although you can have a noncomputerized database, the majority of databases are computerized because they contain large amounts of information and their use is facilitated by computer capability to edit, sort, and analyze the mass of information.

> A database refers to a collection of data and information describing items of interest to the database owner.
>
> Databases are composed of records that represent a unit of information. Subcomponents of information in records are called fields.

   Internal databases are databases consisting of information gathered by a company typically during the normal course of business transactions. Marketing managers normally develop internal databases about customers but databases may be kept on any topic of interest such as members of the sales force, inventory, maintenance, and supplier firms. Companies gather information about customers when they inquire about a product or service, make a purchase, or have a product serviced. Think about the information you may have provided to marketing firms: your name, address, telephone number, fax number, e-mail address, credit card number, your banking institution and account number, and so on. Coupled with a knowledge of what products you have purchased in the past and with other information provided by government and other commercial sources, many companies know quite a bit about you. Companies use their internal databases for purposes of direct marketing and to strengthen relationships with customers called **CRM,** customer relationship management.[5]

   Internal databases can be quite large. Dealing with the vast quantities of data has been a problem with managing information from internal databases. **Data mining** is the name for software that is now available to help managers make sense out of seemingly senseless masses of information contained in databases.[6] However, even simple databases in small businesses can be invaluable. Databases can tell managers which products are selling, report inventories, and profile customers by SKU. Coupled with geodemographic information systems (GIS), databases can provide maps indicating zip codes in which the most profitable and least profitable customers reside. Internal databases, built with information collected during the normal course of business, can provide invaluable insights for managers. We shall discuss GIS more completely in the next chapter.

> Internal databases, built with information collected during the normal course of business, can provide invaluable insights for managers.

   What companies do with information collected for their internal databases can present ethical problems. Should your credit card company share the information on what types of goods and services you bought with anyone who wants to buy that information? Should your Internet Service Provider be able to store information on which Internet sites you visit? As more consumers have grown aware of these privacy issues, more companies have adopted privacy policies.[7]

> What companies do with information collected in their internal databases can present ethical problems.

External Secondary Data

Published Sources   **External secondary data** are data obtained from outside the firm. We classify external data into three sources: (1) *published,* (2) *syndicated services* *data,* and (3) *databases.* **Published sources** are those sources of information that are prepared for public distribution and are normally found in libraries or through a variety of other entities such as trade associations, professional organizations, or companies. Published sources are available in a number of formats including print, CD-ROM, and online via the Internet. Many publications that were formerly available in print only are becoming available in electronic format. Magazines available electronically are called e-zines; journals are called e-journals. Published sources of secondary information come from the government (*Census of the Population*), nonprofit organizations (chambers of commerce, colleges, and universities), trade and professional associations (CASRO, AMA, IMRO, MRA), and for-profits (*Sales & Marketing Management* magazine, Prentice Hall, Inc., McGraw-Hill, and research firms). Many research firms publish secondary information in the form of books, newsletters, white papers, or special reports. Strategy Research Corporation (SRC), for example, specializes in marketing research in Hispanic markets. The company, a Market Facts Company, publishes a Latin America market planning report every two years. In addition, the company publishes the U.S. Hispanic Market Study. For companies marketing products and services to these markets, the secondary data provided by Strategy Research Corporation are valuable information.

> **Published sources are those sources of information that are prepared for public distribution and are normally found in libraries or through a variety of other entities.**

> Visit Strategy Research Corporation at www.strategyresearch.com.

▶ **Meet a Marketing Researcher**

MARKETING RESEARCH
INSIGHT
6.2

Strategy Research Corporation Produces Several Research Publications
Dick Thomas, Senior Vice President, Business Development, Strategy Research Corporation

Dick Thomas has extensive experience in all phases of marketing research. He has designed, proposed, directed, and analyzed concept and product tests, image and strategic studies, major segmentation and market structure studies, and advertising development and tracking studies. He has developed and directed large-scale, multiphased research programs for new-product development, created marketing strategies, and evaluated marketing plans in both the product and service categories. His experience includes projects fielded in the general market, in the U.S. Hispanic market,

and throughout Latin America. His clients have included both domestic and foreign-based companies. He has conducted research for both consumer and business-to-business clients on assignments in consumer package goods, health and beauty aids, retail, IT, financial services, and travel and tourism categories, as well as many others. Dick is a successful presenter and proposer of new studies to both prospective and current clients. He has attained senior-level responsibility on the client, advertising agency, and supplier sides of the industry. Dick is an experienced focus group moderator and has practiced a wide range of qualitative research techniques.

Starting at SRC as a senior project director, Dick moved on to research director before attaining his current account and brand development responsibilities. Prior to his arrival at SRC in 1987, Dick was vice president, associate research director at Foote, Cone and Belding Advertising, Inc. Previous experience also includes employment in marketing research for Pepsi-Cola Company, Seagrams, and MRCA. Dick serves on the board of the International Advertising Association and is a corporate member of the Beacon Council and the Greater Miami Chamber of Commerce. He holds degrees in clinical psychology and business administration from the University of Dayton and has done graduate course work at the New York Law School and the University of Miami.

Understanding the function of different types of publications can help you find the secondary data you need.

A catalog consists of a list of a library's holdings of books.

Indexes are records compiled from periodicals and contain information on the contents of periodicals recorded in fields such as author, title, keywords, date of publication, name of periodical, and so on.

The sheer volume of published sources makes searching this type of secondary data difficult. However, understanding the function of the different types of publications can be of great help to you in successfully searching published secondary information sources. Table 6.1 depicts the different types of publications and gives you their function as well as an example.

Today many libraries enter their holdings of books and other publications in electronic records whose fields are searchable electronically. These electronic libraries allow researchers to search secondary data quickly, conveniently, inexpensively, and thoroughly. Most electronic libraries have information available in two broad categories: catalogs and indexes. A **catalog** consists of a list of a library's holdings of books. (Catalogs sometimes also list the periodicals to which the library subscribes.) Therefore, catalogs are useful for finding *books* by subject, author, title, date of publication, or publisher. **Indexes** are records compiled from periodicals and contain information on the contents of periodicals recorded in fields such as author, title, keywords, date of publication, name of periodical, and so on. Sometimes an index contains the entire contents of the periodical (called full-text indexes). Such indexes are not normally constructed by a library. Rather, they are provided by companies that make them available to libraries or other organizations. We shall talk more about these when we discuss online information databases.

Syndicated Services Data **Syndicated services data** are provided by firms that collect data in a standard format and make them available to subscribing firms. Such data are typically highly specialized and are not available in libraries for the general public. The suppliers syndicate (sell) the information to multiple subscribers, thus making the costs more reasonable to any one subscriber. Examples include Arbitron's radio listenership data, Nielsen Media Research's Television Rating Index, and Information Resources, Inc.'s InfoScan report of products sold in retail stores. In all these cases, these firms supply subscribing firms with external secondary data. We devote more attention to syndicated data services firms in Chapter 7.

External Databases **External databases** are databases supplied by organizations outside the firm. They may be used as sources for secondary data. Some of these databases are available in printed format but, in recent years, many databases are now available online. **Online information databases** are sources of secondary data searchable by search engines online. Some online databases are available free of charge and are supplied as a service by a host organization. However, many online information databases are available from commercial sources that provide subscribers password (or IP address identification) access for a fee. These databases have grown dramatically since the 1980s. During the 1990s and early 2000s many of the companies supplying external databases of secondary data have merged. We have fewer companies but each one is much larger, with the larger firms offering subscribers access to billions of records of information. Different databases are often packaged together by vendors that produce the software that retrieves the information. Sometimes called "aggregators" or "databanks," these services or vendors may offer a wide variety of indexes, directories, and statistical and full-text files all searched by the same search logic. Such services include Gale Group, Proquest, First Search, LexisNexis, and Dialog, among others. Business databases comprise a significant proportion of these databanks. Whereas many of these database services firms offer access through multiple media including print and CD-ROM, the trend has been to offer access through Internet sites.

Table **6.1** **Understanding the Function of Different Types of Publications Can Make You a Better User of Secondary Data**

1. Reference Guides

Function: Refer to *types* of other reference sources and recommend specific titles. Guides tell you where to look to find different types of information.
Example*: Encyclopedia of Business Information Sources.* Detroit: Galegroup, 1970–2001

2. Indexes and Abstracts

Function: List periodical articles by subject, author, title, keyword, etc. Abstracts also provide summaries of the articles. Indexes allow you to search for periodicals by the topic of your research.
Example: *ABI/Inform.* Ann Arbor, MI: Proquest, 1971–present

3. Bibliographies

Function: Lists varied sources such as books, journals, etc. on a particular topic. Tell you what is available, in several sources, on a topic.
Example: *Recreation and Entertainment Industries, an Information Source Book.* Jefferson, NC: Macfarland, 2000

4. Almanacs, Manuals, and Handbooks

Function: These types of sources are "deskbooks" that provide a wide variety of data in a single handy publication.
Example: *Wall Street Journal Almanac.* New York: Ballantine Books, Annual.

5. Dictionaries

Function: Define terms and are sometimes available for special subject areas.
Example*: Concise Dictionary of Business Management.* New York: Routledge 1999.

6. Encyclopedias

Function: Provide essays, usually in alphabetical order, by topic.
Example*: Encyclopedia of Busine$$ and Finance.* New York: Macmillan, 2001

7. Directories

Function: List companies, people, products, organizations, etc. usually providing brief information about each entry.
Example: *Career Guide: Dun's Employment Opportunities Directory.* Parsippany, NJ: Dun's Marketing Services Annual.

8. Statistical Sources

Function: Provide numeric data, often in tables, pie charts, and bar charts.
Example: *Handbook of U.S. Labor Statistics.* Lanham, MD: Bernan Press, Annual

9. Biographical Sources

Function: Provide information about people. Useful for information on CEOs, etc.
Example: *D&B Reference Book of Corporate Management.* Bethlehem, PA: Dun & Bradstreet, 2001

10. Legal Sources

Function: Provide information about legislation, regulations, and case law.
Example: *United States Code.* Washington, DC: Government Printing Office

There are four types of databases categorized according to the nature of data records within the database:

▶ **Bibliographic databases** contain citations to journal articles, newspapers, and government documents. Many bibliographic databases also include full-text articles online. Examples include *ABI Inform*, an index to over 800 business, management, and trade journals, and the *Gale Academic Index ASAP*, an index to over 960 multidisciplinary journals. *Social Science Citation Index*, known as a citation bibliographic database, actually indexes the bibliographies of articles allowing the user to learn which articles "cited" certain sources.

▶ **Numeric or statistical databases** contain statistics or numeric data, such as baseball game attendance records or sales for a given industry over some time period. Examples include the 2000 *Census of Population and Housing*, *County Business Patterns*, and *STAT-USA*.

▶ **Directory or list databases** list information about certain organizations, individuals, government entities, and so on. Examples include *Gale's Associations Unlimited*, which lists more than 80,000 nonprofit membership associations in the United States, and *infoUSA*, which lists addresses and phone numbers for residences and businesses in the United States.

▶ **Comprehensive databases** include many types of information. Examples are *Dow Jones Interactive, Gale Business and Company Resource Center,* and *LexisNexis*.

ADVANTAGES OF SECONDARY DATA

There are four main advantages of using secondary data. First, it can be *obtained quickly*, in contrast to collecting primary data, which may take several months from beginning to end. Second, it is *inexpensive* when compared to collecting primary data. Third, it is *usually available*. Fourth, it *enhances existing primary data*. What do we mean by enhancing primary data? Simply because researchers use secondary data does not mean that they will not collect primary data. In fact, in almost every case, the researcher's task of primary data collection is aided by first collecting secondary data. A secondary data search can familiarize the researcher with the industry, including its sales and profit trends, major competitors, and the significant issues facing the industry.[8] A secondary data search can identify concepts, data, and terminology that may be useful in conducting primary research. A bank's management, for example, hired a marketing research firm and, together, management and the research team decided to conduct a survey measuring the bank's image among its customers. A check of the secondary information available on the measurement of bank image identified the components of bank image for the study. Also, the research team, after reviewing secondary information, determined there were *three* sets of bank customers: retail customers, commercial accounts, and other correspondent banks. When the researchers mentioned this to bank management, the original objectives of the primary research were changed in order to measure the bank's image among all three customer groups.

Secondary data are so important in marketing research that several companies offer Web sites allowing users to link to secondary information sources on the Internet. Decision Analyst, Inc., a marketing research firm, provides the Web site SecondaryData.com for this purpose. The site provides you with access to links that not only allow you to directly access secondary data but it also provides links that teach you how to conduct secondary data research. This type of site illustrates the advantages of secondary data being accessed quickly and inexpensively. Not only is secondary data faster to obtain, more convenient to use, and less expensive to gather than primary research, but it also may solve the research objective!

DISADVANTAGES OF SECONDARY DATA

Although the advantages of secondary data almost always justify a search of this information, there are caveats associated with secondary data. Some of the problems associated with secondary data include *mismatch of the units of measurement, differing definitions used to classify the data, the timeliness of the secondary data,* and *the lack of information needed to assess the credibility* of the data reported. These problems exist because secondary data have not been collected specifically to address the researcher's problem at hand but have been collected for some other purpose. Consequently, the researcher must determine the extent of these problems before using the secondary data. This is done by evaluating the secondary data. We discuss the first three disadvantages in the following paragraphs. Evaluation of secondary data is discussed in the next section.

Sometimes secondary data are reported in *measurement units that do not match the measurement unit* needed by the researcher. In analyzing markets, for example, marketing researchers are typically interested in income levels. Available studies of income may measure income in several ways: total income, income after taxes, household income, and per capita income. Or consider a research project that needs to categorize businesses by size in terms of square footage. Secondary data sources, however, classify businesses in terms of size according to sales volume, number of employees, profit level, and so on. Much information in the United States is recorded in American units of measurement (feet, pounds, etc.), yet most of the rest of the world uses metric units (meter, kilograms, etc.). The United States is slowly becoming metric.[9]

The *class definitions of the reported data may not be usable to a researcher.* Secondary data are often reported by breaking a variable into different classes and reporting the frequency of occurrence in each class. For example, the "Survey of Buying Power" reports the variable, effective buying income (EBI), in three classes. The first class reports the percentage of households having an EBI between $20,000 and $34,999, and the final class reports the percentage of households having an EBI of $50,000 and over. For most studies, these classifications are applicable. However, it is doubtful that Beneteau, Inc., a manufacturer of sailing yachts in South Carolina, could use these income classifications to help it target potential customer markets. Because Beneteau's average customer is thought to have an EBI in excess of $75,000, Beneteau could not use the data reported because of the way the EBI classes were defined. What does the researcher do? Typically, if you keep looking you can find what you need. For example, Beneteau can obtain secondary data that would solve its problem by purchasing *Demographics USA,* published by the same producers of the "Survey of Buying Power." It would find that *Demographics USA* provides information on EBI up through categories of $150,000 or more.[10]

Sometimes a marketing researcher will find information reported with the desired unit of measurement and the proper classifications, however, the *data are "out-of-date."* Some secondary data are published only once. However, even for secondary data that are published at regular intervals, the time that passed since the last publication can be a problem when applying the data to a current problem. Ultimately, the researcher must make the decision as to whether or not to use the data.

The four advantages of secondary data are that secondary data can be obtained quickly and inexpensively, are usually available, and enhance primary data collection.

In almost every case, the researcher's task of primary data collection is aided by first collecting secondary data. Sometimes secondary research will solve the research objective.

Some of the problems associated with secondary data include *mismatch of the units of measurement, differing definitions used to classify the data, the timeliness of the secondary data,* and *the lack of information needed to assess the credibility* of the data reported.

A disadvantage of secondary data is that they are sometimes reported in measurement units that do not match the researcher's needs. For example, a researcher needs to know per capita income and the secondary data source reports income as household income.

A second disadvantage of secondary data is that the data may be categorized into class definitions that are unsuitable for the researcher's needs. A researcher, forecasting demand for a day care center, desires to know how many children ages 3, 4, or 5 reside in each zip code area of a city. Yet, the secondary data source reports age as "children less than 10 years of age."

A third disadvantage of secondary data is that they are out-of-date.

EVALUATING SECONDARY DATA

Hopefully, you have learned that not everything you read is true. In order to properly use secondary data, you must evaluate that information before you use it as a basis for decision making. A reader must be most cautious when using an Internet source because few quality standards are applied to most Internet sites. To determine the reliability of secondary information, marketing researchers must evaluate it. This is done by answering the following five questions:

▶ What was the purpose of the study?
▶ Who collected the information?
▶ What information was collected?
▶ How was the information obtained?
▶ How consistent is the information with other information?[11]

A discussion of each question follows.

What Was the Purpose of the Study?

Studies are conducted for a purpose. Unfortunately, studies are sometimes conducted in order to "prove" some position or advance the special interest of those conducting the study. Many years ago, chambers of commerce were known for publishing data that exaggerated the size and growth rates of their communities. They did this to "prove" that their communities were a good choice for new business locations. However, after a few years, they learned that few people trusted chamber data and today chambers of commerce publish reliable and valid data. But the lesson is that you must be very careful to determine whether the entity publishing the data acted in a fair and unbiased manner. Consider the example of disposable diapers. The disposable diaper industry was created in the 1960s. Environmental concerns became alarming as information became available about the forecasts of huge mountains of disposable diapers that would take 50 years to decompose. Consequently, during the late 1980s, the number of customers buying old-fashioned cloth diapers doubled. Also, more than a dozen state legislatures were considering various bans, taxes, and even warning labels on disposable diapers. Then "research studies" were produced on the environmental effects of disposable versus cloth diapers. It seemed that the "new" research proved that cloth diapers, by adding detergent by-products to the water table, were more harmful to the environment than the ever-lasting plastic disposables! Soon after several of these studies were made available to legislators, the movement against disposables was dead. Who conducted the studies? Procter & Gamble. P&G, owning the lion's share of the market for disposable diapers, commissioned the consulting firm of Arthur D. Little, Inc. to conduct a study of disposable versus cloth diapers. The study found that disposable diapers were no more harmful to the environment than reusable cotton diapers. Another favorable study for the disposables was conducted by Franklin Associates whose research showed disposables were not any more harmful than cloth diapers. But who sponsored this study? The American Paper Institute, an organization with major interests in disposable diapers. But wait, before you become too critical of the disposable diaper folks, let's consider some other "scientific" studies. In 1988, a study was published that showed disposable diapers as being "garbage" and contributing to massive buildups of waste that was all but impervious to deterioration. Who sponsored this study? The cloth diaper industry! Another study published in 1991 found cloth diapers to be environmentally superior to disposable diapers. Guess who

▶ **An Ethical Issue**

MARKETING RESEARCH
INSIGHT
6.3

It Ain't Necessarily So!

Many times research studies are reported in secondary data and sometimes what they report ". . . ain't necessarily so," according to authors Murray, Schwartz, and Licture's book (*It Ain't Necessarily So: How Media Make and Unmake the Scientific Picture of Reality*).[12] These authors illustrate their point by citing a study undertaken by an "activist" group called the Food Research and Action Center whose aim, the authors report, is to highlight the problem of hunger and to increase government spending to fight hunger. The study reported that one out of eight children had gone hungry at some point in the previous year. But the researchers did not measure "hunger" in any direct manner. Instead they used a "proxy" measure of hunger. They measured what people *said* about hunger. (The Census Bureau uses income as a proxy measure of hunger.) Was their measure an accurate measure? Even if it were an accurate measure of actual hunger, CBS Network incorrectly reported the results of the study by stating that the study found one in eight American children under the age of 12 is going hungry (tonight). This is a totally different picture than the number of children who reported being hungry in the last year.[13] Other studies report that coffee is associated with disease, whereas others report that coffee prevents disease.[14]

In another book, Cynthia Crossen, a reporter and editor with the *Wall Street Journal*, writes about the truthfulness of research information. Her conclusions were interesting and led her to title the book *Tainted Truth: The Manipulation of Fact in America*. She warns that, even though Americans

have a fascination with research information, we must understand that much of the "research" we use to help us to buy, elect, advise, acquit, and heal has been created not to expand our knowledge but to sell a product or advance a cause of the sponsor of the research. Furthermore, if the research results contradict a sponsor's agenda, the results are routinely suppressed. Crossen gives some compelling evidence for her thesis including a study that found that 62 percent of Americans want to keep the penny in circulation. The sponsor? The zinc industry (most pennies are made with zinc). Another study found that 70 percent of cellular telephone users reported that the cellular phones made them more successful in business. The sponsor? Motorola. Even studies to test the effectiveness of new drugs are often sponsored by the pharmaceutical company selling the drug! Crossen believes that the explosion of "tainted truth" has come from money. Money is used to "sponsor" (buy) research studies and that even once independent and objective institutions such as universities have given in to the monetary pressures. Few researchers escape the pressures of financial support and they are influenced, whether knowingly or not, by trying to please their financial sponsors. Results can be manipulated by subtle means known to researchers.

Crossen has raised an important ethical issue for the research industry. Are research results totally independent and objective? Crossen's book is one among several that deal with research not being objectively prepared or presented.[15]

---

sponsored this study?[16] Marketing Research Insight 6.3 provides us with more examples that illustrate why it is important for you to know the true purpose behind the study.

Who Collected the Information?

Even when you are convinced that there is no bias in the purpose of the study, you should question the competence of the organization that collected the information. Why? Simply because organizations differ in terms of the resources they command and their quality control. But how do you determine the competency of the organization that collected the data? First, ask others who have more experience in a given industry. Typically, creditable organizations are well known in those industries for which they conduct studies. Second, examine the report itself. Competent firms will almost always provide carefully written and detailed explanations of the procedures and methods used in collecting the information contained in the report. Third, contact previous clients of the firm. Have they been satisfied with the quality of the work performed by the organization?

Research studies are often published and become part of secondary data. However, not all research studies are conducted in a totally objective manner. You must ask who conducted the study.

What Information Was Collected?

There are many studies available on topics such as economic impact, market potential, feasibility, and the like. But what exactly was measured in these studies that constitutes impact, potential, or feasibility? There are many examples of studies that claim to provide information on a specific subject but, in fact, measure something quite different. Consider a study conducted by a transit authority on the number of riders on its bus line. On examination of the methodology used in the study, the number of riders was not counted at all. Rather, the number of fares was counted. A single rider may pay several fares per day. Is this distinction important? It may be or it may not be depending on how the study's user intends to use the information. The important point here is that the user should discover exactly what information was collected!

How Was the Information Obtained?

You should be aware of the methods used to obtain information reported in secondary sources. What was the sample? How large was the sample? What was the response rate? Was the information validated? As you will learn throughout this book, there are many alternative ways of collecting primary data and each may have an impact on the information collected. Remember that, even though you are evaluating secondary data, this information was gathered as primary data by some organization. Therefore, the alternative ways of gathering the data had an impact on the nature and quality of the data. It is not always easy to find out how the secondary data were gathered. However, as noted earlier, most reputable organizations that provide secondary data also provide information on their data collection methods. If this information is not readily available and your use of the secondary data is very important to your research project, you should make the extra effort to find out how the information was obtained.

How Consistent Is the Information with Other Information?

In some cases, the same secondary data are reported by multiple, independent organizations, which provides an excellent way to evaluate secondary data sources. Ideally, if two or more independent organizations report the same data, you can have greater confidence in the validity and reliability of the data. Demographic data, for example, for metropolitan areas (MAs), counties, and most municipalities are widely available from more than one source. If you are evaluating a survey that is supposedly representative of a given geographic area, you may want to compare the characteristics of the sample of the survey with the demographic data available on the population. If you know, based on U.S. census data, that there are 45 percent males and 55 percent females in a city and a survey, which is supposed to be representative of that city, reports a sample of 46 percent males and 54 percent females, then you can be more confident in the survey data. It is indeed rare, however, that two organizations will report exactly the same results. Here you must look at the magnitude of the differences and determine what you should do. If all independent sources report very large differences of the same variable, then you may not have much confidence in any of the data. You should look carefully at what information was collected, how it was collected, and so on for each reporting source. For example, if you were to get the number of businesses in a county from Survey Sampling, Inc., and compare that number to the number of businesses reported by the governmental publication, *County Business Patterns* (*CBP*), you would see a marked difference. Specifically, Survey Sampling's number of businesses would be much larger than the number reported by *CBP*. Why?[17] The answer is found by asking the questions "What information was actually collected?" and "How was this information obtained?" As it turns out, neither organization actually counts the numbers of businesses in a given area. *CBP* counts the number of firms submitting payroll information on their employees. Some firms may not report this information and other small firms with "no paid employees" (whose owners are the employees) are excluded from *CBP* data. Therefore, the *CBP* surrogate indicator used to count the number of business firms is going to have a downward bias because it does not count all firms. On the other hand, Survey Sampling counts the number of business firms by adding up the number of businesses listed in the Yellow Pages.

This brings up the question, "What is a business firm?" One franchise organization may run the McDonald's in a city, yet the Yellow Pages lists nine locations. Is this one business or nine? Survey Sampling would list this as nine separate businesses. Therefore, Survey Sampling's estimates of the number of businesses has an upward bias. Which data source should be used? It would depend on the purpose of your study and how the information would be used. Either source of information may be appropriate for use as long as the user understood exactly what the information represented. The key point is that you must adequately evaluate the various data sources so that you are in a position to select the information that will give you the most valid and reliable results.

A final word about evaluating information sources is that you may be able to get some help in terms of evaluations by others. For example, books are often reviewed and those reviews are published. However, it is far more difficult to evaluate journal articles or Web sites.

LOCATING SECONDARY DATA SOURCES

How does one go about the actual task of locating secondary data sources? We suggest you follow the approach outlined here.[18]

Step 1. Identify what you wish to know and what you already know about your topic. This is the most important step in searching for information. Without having a clear understanding of what you are seeking, you will undoubtedly have difficulties. Clearly define your topic: relevant facts, names of researchers or organizations associated with the topic, key papers and other publications with which you are already familiar, and any other information you may have.

Step 2. Develop a list of key terms and names. These terms and names will provide access to secondary sources. Unless you already have a very specific topic of interest, keep this initial list long and quite general. Use business dictionaries and handbooks to help develop your list. Be flexible. Every time a new source is consulted, you may have to use a new selection of terms.

In printed sources as well as databases, it is important to use correct terminology to locate the most relevant resources. In many cases, the researcher must think of related terms or synonyms for a topic. For example, one database may use the term *pharmaceutical industry* to describe that industry, whereas another may use the term *drug industry*. In addition, the source may require that a broader term be used. *Pharmaceutical industry* may be listed as part of the *chemical industry*. However, there may be a need to use a narrower term. For example, if one is researching a database on the *drug industry*, it would be foolish to put in the term *drugs* because almost everything in that database would include that term. Perhaps a specific drug may be a wiser choice.

Many databases have lists of the terms or subject headings they assign to records of information, such as books or articles. These lists are called thesauri, dictionaries, or subject headings lists. In most library catalogs the Library of Congress (LC) Subject Headings are used. These are standard (sometimes called controlled) terms that are consistently used to describe a particular subject. For example, the term *real property* is standard in the LC Subject Headings instead of the term *real estate*. Using a standard subject heading should result in a more efficient search. Marketing Research Insight 6.4 shows you how to find a standard subject heading using *ABI Inform*.

MARKETING RESEARCH

INSIGHT
6.4

Finding a Standard Subject Heading:
A Way to Improve Your Information Searching Skills

How many times have you used an online information service database only to end up frustrated that you could not find what you really needed? Problems of two types occur. First, you get thousands of "hits," which requires that you read through huge amounts of information still searching for what you wanted to find in the first place. Second, you get information that has your key search terms contained within the article but the articles do not have anything to do with what you really want. Sound familiar? You need to learn an important skill in searching online information databases: finding the standard subject heading.

Imagine that you had several persons who were well trained in evaluating and interpreting the contents of information sources such as books, manuals, special reports, magazine articles, journal articles, and so on. Next, imagine if you had these well-trained persons to look through everything that has been published and to place all the books, articles, reports, and so on that pertained to your topic in one stack. So, you now have all publications on your topic in one category and now imagine that this information is all scanned into an electronic database that you can now search using any one or a combination of search strategies. Wow! Think this would improve your information search skills? The good news is that this has already been done for you. You just need to learn how to take advantage of what we shall call standard subject headings.

Databases have a field called the subject field. When a new piece of information arrives, be it a book, journal article, or

whatever, that information is evaluated to determine its subject matter. For example, let's say that an article is entitled "Miami Blues." The title can be very misleading. In fact, if someone were doing a search about blues music, this article would appear in a results list (along with thousands of other nonrelevant information sources). But why is it misleading? Because the subject of the article is really about *real estate* in Miami. If you were interested in finding information about real estate, chances are you would not find this book using key terms in the title field of your database search engine. But, because those "people who are working for you" have looked over this article and correctly placed it in the category of real estate, we are going to find it. So, **standard subject headings** are specific words or phrases that are used to properly categorize the subject matter of records as they are entered into databases. Let's see how you would do it using *ABI Inform,* an index to business journals.

In *ABI Inform*, there is a list of standard subject headings that one can locate by using the advanced search screen and selecting "browse lists" and then "subjects." In the following example we submit the words "real estate." If that term is listed, then it can be used in a search by subject field.

In the next example, the searcher is using the term "real estate" as a subject term (not as a keyword in any field) to make sure the emphasis of the articles retrieved is on real estate. The searcher combines it with the word "Florida" (as a keyword in any field) to further narrow the search. Please

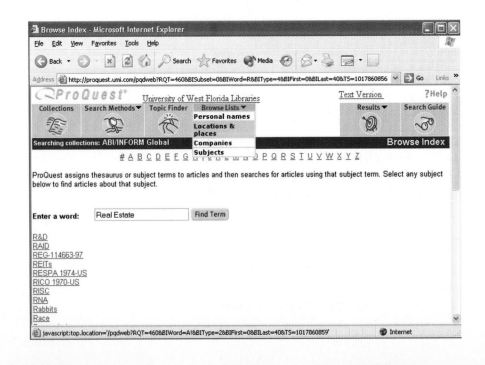

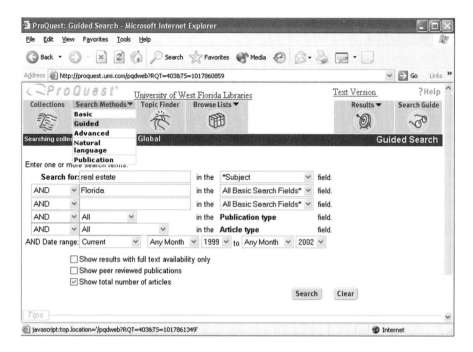

notice that the searcher got to this screen by selecting "search methods" at the top of the screen and then "guided screen."

Finally the search retrieves the results as indicated in the following example. Notice that item 3 entitled "Miami Blues" is a title that would not have been recognizable as an article about real estate. Also notice that the presence of the camera image before the item means that the full-text article is available online.

Although this is just one database from several hundred, a good researcher learns to look for lists of *standard subject headings* whether they are called thesaurus terms, subject headings, terms, and so on. It is also important to check all guide screens and instructions that are made available by each database. Notice that in the preceding example the instructions are listed under the tab marked "Search Guide." Happy searching!

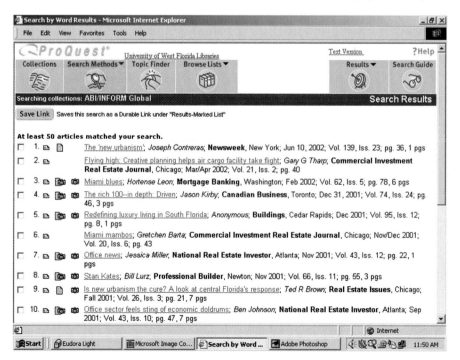

Keyword searching is usually available for searching a database, but using a keyword often retrieves too many false results. A keyword search means that the computer will retrieve a record that has that word anywhere in the record. For example, if someone is searching for the word *banks*, it could be the name of a person, a business, type of bank, a bank of dirt (hill), or any other use of that word. Sometimes to avoid false results the searcher may simply want to search one field in the record as described later in "Field Searching." Keywords may also be used to lead one to better terms to use. If one retrieves a long list of sources, it is wise to select an item that is relevant and examine its record to identify the standard subject heading assigned to that item. Submitting that subject heading should retrieve a much more relevant list of sources (see Marketing Research Insight 6.4).

Step 3. Begin your search using several of the library sources such as those listed in Table 6.2. If you need help in selecting the appropriate sources or databases, refer to Table 6.2 and review the functions of different types of publications.

Search Strategies Used for Searching Online Information Databases

To better understand how to search online databases, the researcher should understand how databases are organized. A common vendor, also known as an aggregator or databank, may provide many databases. For example, the vendor Proquest provides *ABI Inform* and the *Wall Street Journal*. An actual hierarchy exists in the organization of these databases. For example:

Top level – Databank = Proquest

Second level – Databases = *ABI Inform*

Third level – Records = the units describing each item in the database

Fourth level – Fields = parts of the record, such as author, title, SIC number, and so on

Fifth level – Words or numbers = the text of the fields

Usually all databases from the same databank are searched similarly. There may be several methods (basic, advanced, and command) of searching databases. A basic search is often sufficient when searching for books in a catalog or when searching small databases; however, it is often advisable to use the advanced mode when searching for journal articles or complex ideas, so that search refinements can be employed.

Most databanks employ the same search features, but other databanks may use different symbols or interfaces to retrieve results. An interface is the "look and feel" of the database that actually helps the searcher know how to submit a search. Each database has a help screen that is always useful. The following examples of the search techniques are those for a typical library catalog, but each databank, such as First Search, Dow Jones Interactive, and others, may use different searching symbols to accomplish the same results.

Boolean Logic

Boolean logic allows the establishment of relationships between words and terms in most databases. Typical words used as operators in Boolean logic are AND, OR, and NOT. The following examples illustrate the use of Boolean logic:

Operator	Requirements	Examples
AND	Both terms are retrieved	chemical AND industry Exxon AND financial
OR	Either term is retrieved	drug OR pharmaceutical outlook OR forecast
NOT	Eliminates records containing the term	Cherokee NOT jeeps drugs NOT alcohol

Table 6.2 Secondary Information Sources on Marketing

I. Reference Guides

Encyclopedia of Business Information Sources
Detroit: GaleGroup, Annual. For the researcher, this lists marketing associations, advertising agencies, research centers, agencies, and sources relating to various business topics. It is particularly useful for identifying information about specific industries.

II. Indexes

ABI Inform
Ann Arbor, MI: Proquest, 1982. Available online, this database indexes and abstracts major journals relating to a broad range of business topics. Electronic access to some full-text articles is also available.

Business File ASAP
Detroit: Gale Group, 1982. Available online and on CD-ROM. This index covers primarily business and popular journals and includes some full-text articles.

Business Periodicals Index
New York: H. W. Wilson, Co., 1958. Available online and in print. This basic index is useful for indexing the major business journals further back in time than other indexes.

III. Dictionaries and Encyclopedias

Dictionary of Marketing Terms
Hauppauge, NY: Barron's, 2000. Prepared by Jane Imber and Betsy Ann Toffler, this dictionary includes brief definitions of popular terms in marketing.

Encyclopedia of Consumer Brands
Detroit: St. James Press, 1994. For consumable products, personal products, and durable goods, this source provides detailed descriptions of the history and major developments of major brand names.

IV. Directories

Bradford's Directory of Marketing Research Agencies and Management Consultants in the United States and the World
Middleberg, VA: Bradford's, Biennial. Indexed by type of service, this source gives scope of activity for each agency and lists names of officers.

Broadcasting and Cable Yearbook
New Providence, NJ: R. R. Bowker, Annual. A directory of U.S. and Canadian television and radio stations, advertising agencies, and other useful information.

Directories in Print
Detroit: Gale Research, Annual. Provides detailed information on business and industrial directories, professional and scientific rosters, online directory of databases, and other lists. This source is particularly useful for identifying directories associated with specific industries or products.

Gale Directory of Publications and Broadcast Media
Detroit: Gale Research. Annual. A geographic listing of U.S. and Canadian newspapers, magazines, and trade publications, as well as broadcasting stations. Includes address, edition, frequency, circulation, and subscription and advertising rates.

V. Statistical Sources

Datapedia of the United States, 1790–2005
Lanham, MD: Bernan Press, 2001. Based on the *Historical Statistics of the United States from Colonial Times* and other statistical sources, this volume presents hundreds of tables reflecting historical and, in some cases, forecasting data on numerous demographic variables relating to the United States.

Demographics USA—"Survey of Buying Power"
New York: *Sales & Marketing Management* magazine. Annual. A compilation of data published in *Sales & Marketing Management* magazine, which includes statistics on population, income, retail sales, effective buying income, etc., for counties, cities, and metropolitan areas. (This source is discussed at length later in this chapter.)

Editor and Publisher Market Guide
New York: Editor and Publisher, Annual. Provides market data for more than 1,500 U.S. and Canadian newspaper cities covering facts and figures about location, transaction, population, households, banks, autos, etc.

Market Share Reporter
Detroit: Gale Research, Annual. Provides market share data on products and service industries in the United States.

Standard Rate and Data Service
Des Plaines, IL: SRDS, Monthly. In the SRDS monthly publications (those for consumer magazine and agrimedia, newspapers, spot radio, spot television) marketing statistics are included at the beginning of each state section.

Field Searching

Field searching refers to searching records in a database by one or more of its fields. Databases are collections of records, which consist of fields designated to describe certain parts of the record. Searching "by field" may make a search more efficient. For example, if a title is known, a search of the title field should find the desired record. Terms entered as "subjects" may be restricted to specific subject headings (e.g., Library of Congress Subject Headings in most library catalogs), depending on the database. Most databases also allow the use of keyword searching, which searches every word in a record.

Most electronic databases employ the same search strategies for searching databases, but they often vary in the keystrokes designated to perform the search. For example, on the Internet, the keyword "real estate" should be submitted with quotes surrounding the phrase so that the exact sequence of words will be searched; however, to get the same keyword phrase in some library catalogs, one would submit: "real ADJ estate."

Proximity Operators

The preceding *"real estate"* example demonstrates one of the proximity operators, that are available to enhance keyword searching. **Proximity operators** allow the searcher to indicate how close and in which order two or more words are to be positioned within the record. Examples of proximity operators are:

Operator	Requirements	Examples
ADJ	Adjoining words in order specified	Electronic ADJ commerce
NEAR	Adjoining words in any order	Bill NEAR Gates
SAME	Both terms are located in the same field of the record	Microsoft SAME legal

Truncation

Another feature of database searching is **truncation,** which allows the root of the word to be submitted, retrieving all words beginning with that root. The term "forecast?" would retrieve "forecasting, forecasts, forecaster," and so on. The question mark is the truncation symbol for some databases, but other databases may use an asterisk, a plus sign, a dollar sign, or other symbols. In some cases truncation symbols may not be useful. For example, if one wanted "cat" in singular or plural, submitting "cat?" would retrieve "cat, cats, catch, catastrophe," and so on. Using the search "cat OR cats" would be preferred.

Nesting

It is essential that the computer translate the search statement correctly. **Nesting** is a technique that indicates the order in which a search is to be done. For example, if one wishes to search for microcomputers or personal computers in Florida, one would submit "Florida AND (microcomputer? OR personal ADJ computer?)," indicating that "Florida" should be combined with either term. The parenthesis nests the two terms as one. Without the parentheses, "Florida" would be combined with "microcomputer," but every instance of the words "personal computer" would be added to the results. In search engines, there are text boxes that serve much like parentheses to aid in keeping similar terms together.

Limiting

Limiting allows for restricting searches to only those database records that meet specified criteria. For example, searches may be limited to a search of records containing a specific language, location, format, and/or date. These limitations are usually available on the advanced search screen of databases. When searching for current materials, the date limitation is most important to retrieve the correct results.

Step 4. *Compile the literature you have found and evaluate your findings.* Is it relevant to your needs? Perhaps you are overwhelmed by information. Perhaps you have found little that is relevant. Rework your list of keywords and authors. If you have had little success or your topic is highly specialized, consult specialized directories, encyclopedias, and so on, such as the ones listed in this chapter. Again, the librarian may be able to recommend the most appropriate source for your needs.

Step 5. *If you are unhappy with what you have found or are otherwise having trouble and the reference librarian has not been able to identify sources, use an authority.* Identify some individual or organization that might know something about the topic. Such publications as *Who's Who in Finance and Industry, Consultants and Consulting Organizations Directory, Encyclopedia of Associations, Industrial Research Laboratories in the United States*, and *Research Centers Directory* may help you identify people or organizations that specialize in your topic. Do not forget university faculty, government officials, and business executives. Such individuals are often delighted to be of help.

There are several keys to a successful search. First, be well informed about the search process. Reading this chapter is a good place to start. Second, you must be devoted to the search. Don't expect information to fall into your lap; be committed to finding the information. Finally, there is no substitute for a good, professional librarian. Do not be afraid to ask for advice.

Step 6. *Report results.* Locating data may be successful, but if the information is not properly transmitted to the reader, the research is worthless. It is important to outline the paper or report, correctly compose it, and accurately reference the sources that were used. See Chapter 20 for instructions on how to properly write a research report.

KEY SOURCES OF SECONDARY DATA FOR MARKETERS

We hope you understand by now that there are thousands of sources of secondary data that may be relevant to business decisions. However, there are a few sources that are so important that they deserve some attention. In the next few paragraphs we give you additional information about Census 2000 and other government publications, the North American Industrial Classification System (NAICS), which is replacing the Standard Industrial Classification (SIC) system, the "Survey of Buying Power," *Demographics USA*, and the Lifestyle Market Analyst.

Census 2000: *Census of the Population*

The United States Decennial Census, the **Census of the Population,** is considered the "granddaddy" of all market information. Even though the census is conducted only once every 10 years, census data serve as a baseline for much marketing information that is provided in the "in-between" years. Firms providing secondary data commercially, such as ESRI and the "Survey of Buying Power," make adjustments each year to report current information. Besides market data, census data are used to make many governmental decisions such as highway construction, health care services, educational needs, and, of course, redistricting. (You can see why each Census 2000 question was asked at www.census.gov/dmd/www/content.htm.) Because these decisions affect how federal funds are allocated, the method used in taking Census 2000 was highly politicized. Essentially, the Bureau of the Census wanted to use more statistical sampling in order to get more accurate data. Opponents wanted the bureau to continue taking a complete census. Normally, this would not have led

> The United States Decennial Census is considered the "granddaddy" of all market information. Even though the census is conducted only once every 10 years, census data serve as a baseline for much marketing information that is provided in the "in-between" years.

to a political controversy, but it became one as Republicans felt sampling should not be used and Democrats felt sampling would include more population segments (primarily minorities) that were omitted from the 1990 census. Eventually, the Supreme Court had to settle the argument. It ruled that because the Constitution mandates a census, only census (not sampling) data could be used for redistricting.[19] The Census Bureau was allowed to continue using sampling for other components of the census.

The census is composed of a short form, which every household received, and a long form, which was sent to one in six households. You can see both forms at www.census.gov/dmd/www/2000quest.html.

The taking of a census of the U.S. population began in 1790. Prior to 1940, everyone had to answer all the questions that the census used. In 1940, the long form—a form that goes out only to a sample of respondents—was introduced as a way to collect more data, more rapidly, and without increasing respondent burden. In Census 2000, the long form went to one in six housing units. As a result, much of the census data are based on statistical sampling. A great deal of effort went into promoting Census 2000 to the citizenry of the United States due to growing concerns over privacy and declining participation rates in the census since 1970.[20]

Other Government Publications

The U.S. government publishes a huge volume of secondary data. Most of these publications are produced in the U.S. Government Printing Office (GPO). You can visit its Web site at www.po.gov. The *Statistical Abstract of the United States* is a convenient source of statistical secondary data and it is now available to you online. Marketing Research Insight 6.5 identifies the sections of information available in this source.

North American Industry Classification System (NAICS)

NAICS is not a source of secondary information. Rather, it is a coding system that can be used to access information.

The **North American Industry Classification System** (**NAICS**) is pronounced "nakes" and is not actually a source in and of itself. By this, we mean that NAICS is not information per se; rather, it is a coding system that can be used to access information. All marketing research students should be familiar with it because it will be used by so many secondary data sources. Many readers will not be familiar with NAICS, but they will have heard of the **Standard Industrial Classification (SIC) system,** which NAICS is replacing. (We discuss both here because data based on the SIC will be around for several years.) The SIC was created in the mid-1930s when the government required all agencies gathering economic and industrial data to use the same system for classifying businesses. The SIC was a system that classified establishments by the type of activity in which they were engaged. Codes, describing a type of business activity, were used to collect, tabulate, summarize, and publish data. Each industry was assigned a code number and all firms within that particular industry reported all activities (sales, employment, etc.) by this assigned code. The SIC divides all establishments into 11 divisions: Division A, for agriculture, forestry, and fishing; Division B, for mining; Division C, for construction; Division D, for manufacturing; Division E, for transportation, communications, electric, gas, and sanitary services; Division F, for wholesale trade; Division G, for retail trade; Division H, for finance, insurance, and real estate; Division I, for services; Division J, for public administration; and Division K, for nonclassifiable establishments. Divisions are then subdivided into a second level of classification dividing the industry into "major groups." Major groups are numbered consecutively 01 through 99. Division A, for example, contains major groups 01 through 09. A major group within Division A is agricultural production—crops; this is major group 01. Division B contains major groups 10 through 14: 10 is metal mining, 11 is coal mining, and so on. Each major group is further divided into two other categories, which provide greater specificity of classification.[21]

Visit the NAICS site, which allows you to convert SIC codes to NAICS codes at www.census.gov/epcd/www/naics.html.

The SIC is being replaced by NAICS as a result of the North American Free Trade Agreement (NAFTA).

The SIC is being replaced by NAICS as a result of the North American Free Trade Agreement (NAFTA). The system will allow reports conducted by the

▶ **Additional Insights**

MARKETING RESEARCH
INSIGHT
6.5

Statistics Online: Statistical Abstract of the United States

The *Statistical Abstract of the United States* was first published in 1878 and is still a much-used reference for summary statistics on social, political, and economic sectors of the United States. It serves not only as a convenient, one-volume source for statistical data on a wide variety of topics, but it also is a reference guide to aid users in finding more detailed statistical information on their subject areas. The printed copy of the book is available for purchase at bookstore.gpo.gov or you can access the electronic copy of the book at www.census.gov/statab/www/.

Contents include by section:

1. Population—by age, sex, race/ethnic origin
2. Vital Statistics—births, deaths, life expectancy
3. Health and Nutrition—health expenditures, facilities, food consumption
4. Education—projections, degrees conferred, Internet access
5. Law Enforcement, Courts, and Prisons—arrests, child abuse, inmates
6. Geography and Environment—land and water, air quality, hazardous waste
7. Elections—vote results, campaign finances
8. State and Local Government Finances and Employment
9. Federal Government Finances and Employment
10. National Defense and Veterans Affairs
11. Social Insurance and Human Services—social security, aid
12. Labor Force, Employment and Earnings—projections, minimum wage
13. Income, Expenditures and Wealth—GDP, family income, poverty
14. Prices—purchasing power of the dollar, cost-of-living index
15. Business Enterprise—economic census data
16. Science and Technology

17. Agriculture—farms, farmland, farm income, crops, livestock
18. Natural Resources—timber, fishery, mineral, petroleum, gas
19. Energy and Utilities—consumption
20. Construction and Housing—spending, home sales, remodeling
21. Manufacturing—summary statistics
22. Domestic Trade—retail, wholesale, e-commerce
23. Transportation—air, highways, motor vehicles
24. Information and Communications—newspapers, Internet access and use, telecommunications, book purchasing
25. Banking and Finance—financial institutions, interest rates, stocks and bonds
26. Arts, Entertainment and Recreation—performing arts, NCAA, leisure activities, and travel
27. Accommodation, Food Services and Other Services—professional scientific and technical, advertising, administrative support and waste management, tax-exempt organizations
28. Foreign Commerce and Aid
29. Outlying Areas—Puerto Rico, Virgin Islands, Guam, American Samoa, and Northern Mariana Islands
30. Comparative International Statistics—world population, vital statistics, economic measures, finance

It's important to remember that the information contained in the *Statistical Abstract of the United States* did not originate with the abstract. Always reference the original source of secondary information. The original source for information reported in the *Statistical Abstract* is provided in the publication. Also, agencies preparing the data are listed along with telephone numbers, addresses, and Internet sites.

Source: U.S. Census Bureau (2001). *Statistical Abstract of the United States:* 2001, 121st ed. Washington, DC: U.S. Government Printing Office.

Mexican, Canadian, and U.S. governments to share a common language for easier comparisons of international trade, industrial production, labor costs, and other statistics. NAICS will have improvements over the SIC and yet will allow for comparative analyses with past SIC-based data. In fact, Dun & Bradstreet is marketing software that provides a crossover from SIC codes to NAICS codes.[22] NAICS will classify businesses based on similar production processes; special attention is being given to classifying emerging industries such as services and high technology, and more classifications will be assigned to certain industry groups such as eating and drinking places. Under the SIC, all restaurants—beaneries, caterers, hamburger stands, and five-star restaurants—fall under the same category: Eating and Drinking Places. NAICS will break this down into several categories, which will be more useful to researchers.[23]

NAICS groups the economy into 20 broad sectors as opposed to the 11 SIC divisions. Many of these new sectors reflect recognizable parts of the SIC, such as the Utilities and Transportation section broken out from the SIC Transportation, Communications and Utilities division. Because the service sector of the economy has grown so much in recent years, the SIC division for Services Industries has been broken into several new sectors including Professional, Scientific, and Technical Services; Management, Support, Waste Management and Remediation Services; Education Services; Health and Social Assistance; Arts, Entertainment and Recreation; and Other Services except Public Administration. Other new NAICS sectors are composed of combinations of pieces from more than one SIC division. For example, the new information sector is composed of components from Transportation, Communications and Utilities (broadcasting and telecommunications); Manufacturing (publishing); and Services Industries (software publishing, data processing, information services, and motion pictures and sound recording).

The NAICS uses a six-digit classification code instead of the old SIC four-digit code. The additional two digits allow for far greater specificity in identifying special types of firms. However, the six-digit code is not being used by all three NAFTA countries. The three countries agreed on a standard system using the first five digits and the sixth digit is being used by each country in a manner allowing for special user needs in each country. Note that the NAICS code doesn't tell you anything per se. However, knowing a NAICS number that represents a type of business will allow you to find all kinds of secondary information about the firms in that business.

"Survey of Buying Power"

The **"Survey of Buying Power"** is an annual survey that is published every August in *Sales & Marketing Management* magazine. The survey contains data for the United States on population, income, and retail sales for food, eating and drinking places, appliances, and automotives. These data are broken up into metropolitan (MSA), county, and city levels, and media market levels. Five-year projections are also provided. Because the data for the survey are extrapolated from census data, the data are current with each year's publication. In addition to the general data, the survey also reports the **effective buying income (EBI)** and the **buying power index (BPI)**. Table 6.3 illustrates secondary data taken from the "Survey of Buying Power."

EBI is defined as disposable personal income. It is equal to gross income less taxes and, therefore, reflects the effective amount of income available for expenditure on goods and services. This is important because taxes differ widely depending on geographic location. BPI is an indicator of the relative market potential of a geographic area. It is based on the factors that make up a market: People, ability to buy, and willingness to buy. The BPI is an index number that represents a market's percentage of the total buying power in the United States.

How to Calculate the Buying Power Index (BPI) The BPI is one of the main reasons that managers and researchers find the "Survey of Buying Power" so useful. With all the demographic information available to marketers, the BPI is useful because it takes the three factors making up a market (people, ability to buy, and willingness to buy) and calculates those factors into a quantitative index that repre-

NAICS groups the economy into 20 broad sectors as opposed to the 11 SIC divisions.

The NAICS uses a six-digit classification code instead of the old SIC four-digit code.

The "Survey of Buying Power" is an annual survey that is published every August in *Sales & Marketing Management* magazine. Visit *Sales & Marketing Management* magazine's Web site at www.salesandmarketing.com.

BPI is an indicator of the relative market potential of a geographic area. The BPI is an index number that represents a market's percentage of the total buying power in the United States.

Table 6.3   Secondary Data from the "Survey of Buying Power"

The 10 Metros with the Highest Median Household EBI

MARKET	EBI	2001	2000
1. Bridgeport–Stamford–Norwalk–Danbury, CT	$75,312	1	1
2. San Jose, CA	$72,124	2	2
3. Middlesex–Somerset–Hunterdon, NJ	$64,333	3	3
4. Nassau–Suffolk, NY	$60,941	4	4
5. San Francisco, CA	$58,670	5	11
6. Seattle–Bellevue–Everett, WA	$57,183	6	7
7. Trenton, NJ	$57,246	7	6
8. Washington, DC	$57,056	8	5
9. Ventura	$56,574	9	12
10. Santa Cruz–Watsonville	$55,490	10	15

The 10 Metros with the Highest Total Retail Sales

METRO	($000)
1. Los Angeles–Long Beach	$111,276,587
2. Chicago	107,339,981
3. New York	87,695,524
4. Detroit	66,249,125
5. Philadelphia	65,740,609
6. Atlanta	64,611,440
7. Washington	63,408,444
8. Boston–Lawrence–Lowell–Brockton	59,744,476
9. Houston	57,622,352
10. Minneapolis–St.Paul	54,213,658

The 10 Metros with the Highest Hispanic Origin Population

MARKET	(000s)
1. Los Angeles–Long Beach	4,310.9
2. New York	2,373.4
3. Chicago	1,462.1
4. Miami	1,318.9
5. Houston	1,293.9
6. Riverside–San Bernardino	1,274.0
7. Orange County, CA	900.1
8. Phoenix–Mesa	855.9
9. Dallas	847.6
10. San Antonio	830.8

Source: 2001 Survey of Buying Power, SMM Magazine. These data were taken from **www.mysbp.com**, by permission.

sents the buying power of a market. We provide you the formula and illustrate how to calculate the BPI as follows:

BPI = (Population of Market Area A/Total U.S. Population) × 2
+ (EBI of Market Area A/Total U.S. EBI) × 5
+ (Retail Sales of Market Area A/Total U.S. Retail Sales) × 3

The market areas that can be selected are regions, states, counties, MSAs, cities, or DMAs (Designated Market Areas represent television markets). Population is used to represent the market factor: *people.* EBI is used to represent the market factor: *ability to buy.* However, since *willingness to buy,* the third market factor, is a mental construct representing something consumers are going to do in the future, the "Survey of Buying Power" (SBP) uses a surrogate indicator of what consumers will buy. The surrogate is past retail sales, which is used because what people bought yesterday is a good indicator of what they will buy today. The foregoing formula gives you the BPI that, as we've said, is an index number. For example, the BPI for a large market, such as Chicago or Los Angeles, may be around 3.3333. This means that 3.3333 percent of the nation's total buying power is within that market. Casper, Wyoming, may have a BPI around 0.026. This means that Casper has 0.026 percent of the nation's buying power.

Advantages of the "Survey of Buying Power." First, a major advantage of the SBP is that it provides demographic data updated each year. Second, it also provides five-year projections each year. Third, by calculation of the index numbers making up the BPI, the SBP quantifies markets. Like all index numbers, the BPI is useful when used to evaluate a market over a time period. This could be achieved by plotting the BPI for a market over a five-year period. In this way, a manager or researcher would have an indication as to the trend in buying power for that market area. A second useful way to use the BPI is to compare one market with other markets. The BPI represents a quantifiable measure of markets' buying power and, therefore, is an objective measure that is useful for comparing markets. Specific uses of the BPI include selection of new markets, dividing markets into sales territories having equal buying power, and allocating media expenditure based on the potential buying power in a market. A fourth advantage of the SBP is that it is inexpensive and easy to access.

Disadvantages of the SBP. There are two weaknesses of using data reported in the "Survey of Buying Power." As we mentioned earlier, one disadvantage of using secondary data is that the data are not classified in categories useful to the user. The example we gave was that data for EBI is reported in the SBP in only three categories, the last being $50,000 and over. Limited categories of data reported in the SBP can be overcome by using another publication called *Demographics USA.* A second disadvantage of the SBP lies in the logic of the calculation of the BPI. The BPI is a general index in that it uses the entire population, all levels of EBI, and total retail sales in a market area. However, for some products, a general BPI may not be an accurate predictor of buying power. Again, by knowing which secondary data source to consult, researchers can sometimes remedy shortcomings of one source of secondary data with another. We explain how *Demographics USA* overcomes the problem of the SBP's "general BPI" next.

Demographics USA

Another useful source of secondary data is found in the publication *Demographics USA.*[24] Published by Bill Communications, the same company that publishes the "Survey of Buying Power," *Demographics USA* is much more expensive than the SBP. It not only provides much more detailed information but it also overcomes some of the disadvantages of the SBP. First, as we noted earlier, the SBP has a limited number of categories by which it reports data. *Demographics USA* expands these categories. For example, it reports EBI in seven categories with the highest category being "$150,000 and above." Instead of providing only the general BPI, *Demographics USA* offers other market indexes, such as **Total Business BPI, High-Tech BPI, Manufacturing BPI, BPI for economy-priced products, BPI for moderately priced products, BPI for premium-priced products, BPI for business-to-business markets, and BPI for high-tech markets.** These market indexes are calculated as follows:

A major advantage of the SBP is that it provides demographic data updated each year, provides five-year projections and the BPI, and it quantifies markets.

There are two weaknesses of using data reported in the "Survey of Buying Power."

One disadvantage of using secondary data is that the data are not classified in categories useful to the user.

A second disadvantage of the SBP lies in the logic of the calculation of the BPI.

Demographics USA is much more expensive than the SBP. It not only provides much more detailed information but it also overcomes some of the disadvantages of the SBP.

Instead of providing only the general BPI, *Demographics USA* offers other market indexes.

Special Indexes in *Demographics USA*

Total Business Buying Power Index (B2B)

Total establishments with:

1–19 employees, weight = .1

20–99 employees, weight = .2

100–499 employees, weight = .4

with 500+ employees, weight = .3

Hi-Tech Buying Power Index

Total employment: electronic and related equipment (SIC 36), weight = .2

Engineers, weight = .4

Computer specialists, weight = .4

Manufacturing BPI

Total employment: food and kindred products (SIC 20), weight = .2

Apparel and other textiles (SIC 23), weight = .4

Instruments and related products (SIC 38), weight = .4

Economy-Priced Products

Households with incomes less than $15,000, weight = .6

Food store sales, weight = .3

Total number of households, weight = .1

Moderately Priced Products

Households with incomes $15,000 to $24,999, weight = .6

Total retail sales, weight = .3

Number of three- and four-person households, weight = .1

Premium-Priced Products

Households with incomes greater than $25,000, weight = .6

Combined apparel/furniture/appliance sales, weight = .3

Households with householder 35–64 years old, weight = .1

Even with these additional choices, some firms may want to calculate their own customized BPI. A **customized BPI** is an index that uses market factors selected for their relevancy to a particular product or service in terms of how they best represent the buying power for that particular product or service. As an example, let's suppose you were making a decision to locate new dealerships for a new luxury automobile. Which markets represent the highest buying power for a luxury automobile? You might be predisposed to using the premium-priced products index from *Demographics USA,* but let's say you want an even better indicator of buying power for your very expensive new luxury car. A customized BPI may consist of (1) households with incomes of $75,000 or more, (2) automobile sales, and (3) households with householder 35–64 years old. Of course, you would now have the problem of actually calculating your customized BPI for each market you want to consider. Another advantage of *Demographics USA* is the specificity of the geographic detail of the reporting units. In addition to providing the standard reporting units (MSAs, DMAs, etc.), *Demographics USA* also provides data by zip code and information about the business market, such as the number of establishments within nine business categories (e.g., agriculture, manufacturing, retailing, and services).

> A customized BPI is an index that uses market factors selected for their relevancy to a particular product or service in terms of how they best represent the buying power for that particular product or service.

The *Lifestyle Market Analyst* is a printed source of information that analyzes several dozen lifestyle categories such as Avid Book Readers; Own a Cat; Take Cruise Ship Vacations; and Golf.

Lifestyle Market Analyst

A unique source of secondary data is the **Lifestyle Market Analyst.** This printed source of information analyzes several dozen lifestyle categories such as Avid Book Readers; Own a Cat; Take Cruise Ship Vacations; Golf; Own a Camcorder; Have Grandchildren; Shop by Catalog/Mail; Stock/Bond Investments; Improving Health; and Donate to Charitable Causes. Information is organized into sections that have different objectives. First, you can examine markets (defined as DMAs). Not only will you get some standard demographic data for the DMA but you will also be able to determine the dominant (and least dominant) lifestyles in that market. This information helps "paint a personality portrait" of a market for users who otherwise see only a sea of numbers describing markets. Another section of the book focuses on each lifestyle. There you will find the demographic profile of the participants in that lifestyle category as well as other information. For example, to understand the lifestyle of a bicycling enthusiast, one may answer the following questions:

▶ What are the demographics of bicyclists?
▶ In what other activities are bikers involved?
▶ Which markets have the heaviest concentration of bikers?
▶ Which magazines do bikers read?

As another example, a *Lifestyle Market Analyst* profile of boating/sailing enthusiasts reveals that they also enjoy scuba diving, snow skiing, recreation vehicles, vacation property, and fishing, but they have little interest in devotional reading or needlework. Obviously this type of consumer is an appropriate target for outdoor equipment sales.

Your SPSS Student Assistant Online
SPSS Quick Tour: Part I

SUMMARY

We can group data into two categories: primary and secondary. Primary data are gathered specifically for the research project at hand. Secondary data are data that have been previously gathered for some other purpose. Secondary data may be internal. Internal secondary data are data already gathered within the firm for some other purpose. For example, in normal business transactions, much information is obtained and recorded. Sales receipts record customer names, types, quantities and prices of goods or services purchased, delivery addresses, shipping dates, salesperson making the sale, and so on. Storing internal data in electronic databases has become increasingly popular. External secondary data are data obtained from sources outside the firm. These data may be classified as (1) published, (2) syndicated services data, and (3) databases. There are different types of published secondary data such as reference guides, indexes and abstracts, bibliographies, almanacs, manuals and handbooks, and so on. Different types of secondary data have different functions and understanding the different functions is useful in researching secondary data. Online information databases are sources of secondary data searchable by search engines online. When several databases are offered under one search engine, the service is called either an aggregator or a databank. Examples include LexisNexis and Proquest. The four types of databases include bibliographic, numeric or statistical, directories or lists, and comprehensive databases.

Secondary data have the advantages of being quickly gathered, being readily available, being relatively inexpensive, and often adding helpful insights should primary data be needed. Disadvantages are that the data are often reported in measurement units or class definitions that are incompatible with the researchers' needs, and secondary data may be outdated. Evaluation of secondary data is important; researchers must ask certain questions in order to ensure the integrity of the information they use.

Finding secondary data involves understanding what you need to know and understanding key terms and names associated with the subject. Indexes and bibliographies may first be consulted; they list sources of secondary information by subject. Consult the sources and evaluate the information. Make use of computerized data searches from databases, if available. A good way to increase searching skills of online information databases is to learn how to find standard subject headings. Seek the services of a reference librarian to help you improve your searching skills.

Using online information databases requires understanding how these databases are organized and the fundamental search strategies used including Boolean logic, field searching, proximity operators, truncation, nesting, and limiting.

Examples of important secondary data for business decisions are the *Census of the Population* from the U.S. Bureau of the Census and the *Statistical Abstract of the United States*, both of which are available online. The North American Industry Classification System (NAICS) is replacing the Standard Industrial Classification (SIC) system as the government's classification system for business. Because NAICS groups businesses into 20 sectors (instead of the 11 used by the SIC) and uses codes of up to six digits to classify businesses (instead of the four-digit code used by the SIC), NAICS offers a classification system that is much better at specifying types of industries. A privately produced secondary data source that is useful to marketers is the "Survey of Buying Power" (SBP). The SBP is useful because it provides a quantitative index, called the buying power index (BPI), to measure the buying power of various geographical markets in the United States. Demographics in the SBP are updated annually. A second privately produced source of secondary information is *Demographics USA*, which provides useful demographic information that is updated annually. In addition to calculating the BPI (as is provided in the SBP), *Demographics USA* provides several other indexes to quantify the buying power of both industrial and retail markets. Firms may also calculate customized BPIs that are specifically formulated to measure the buying power for their specific product or service. The *Lifestyle Market Analyst* is a unique publication in that it provides information on lifestyles. It contains information on several dozen lifestyles such as bicycling enthusisasts, dog owners, snow skiing enthusiasts, and so on. Demographic profiles of each lifestyle are reported along with what other lifestyle interests (and noninterests) apply.

KEY TERMS

Primary data (p. 152)
Secondary data (p. 152)
Internal secondary data (p. 153)
Database (p. 154)
Internal databases (p. 154)
Data mining (p. 154)
External secondary data (p. 154)
Published sources (p. 155)
Catalog (p. 156)
Indexes (p. 156)
Syndicated services data (p. 156)
External databases (p. 156)
Online information databases (p. 156)
Bibliographic databases (p. 158)
Numeric or statistical databases (p. 158)
Directory or list databases (p. 158)
Comprehensive databases (p. 158)
Standard subject headings (p. 164)

Boolean logic (p. 166)
Field searching (p. 168)
Proximity operators (p. 168)
Truncation (p. 168)
Nesting (p. 168)
Limiting (p. 168)
Census of the Population (p. 169)
North American Industry Classification System (NAICS) (p. 170)
Standard Industrial Classification (SIC) system (p. 170)
"Survey of Buying Power" (p. 172)
Effective buying income (EBI) (p. 172)
Buying power index (BPI) (p. 172)
Demographics USA (p. 174)
Total business BPI (p. 174)
Hi-tech BPI (p. 174)
Manufacturing BPI (p. 174)

Economy-priced products (BPI) (p. 174)   High-tech markets (BPI) (p. 174)
Moderately priced products (BPI) (p. 174)   Customized BPI (p. 175)
Premium-priced products (BPI) (p. 174)   *Lifestyle Market Analyst* (p. 176)
Business-to-business markets (BPI) (p. 174)

REVIEW QUESTIONS/APPLICATIONS

1. How would you find information about the 2000 census?
2. What are some of the disadvantages of data provided by public data sources, such as the government?
3. What are secondary data and how do they differ from primary data?
4. How would you classify secondary data?
5. Name four types of publications and describe their function.
6. What is the difference between a library catalog and an index?
7. Explain what a database is and describe how databases are organized.
8. What is data mining and why is it used?
9. What are online information databases and what are the four types of these databases?
10. Discuss three advantages of secondary data. Discuss three disadvantages of secondary data.
11. How would you go about evaluating secondary data? Why is evaluation important?
12. Discuss how you would go about finding secondary data in your own library.
13. Explain why it is important to know the purpose of a study reported in secondary data.
14. What is a standard subject heading and explain why knowing how to find a standard subject heading would help increase your information searching skills when using online information databases.
15. Explain what is meant by Boolean logic.
16. Why would searching by field help you efficiently search online information databases?
17. Describe the purposes of the U.S. *Census of the Population*.
18. Briefly identify information collected on the short form and the long form of the 2000 census.
19. Name five publications listed as being published by the GPO.
20. Access the *Statistical Abstract of the United States* online and find information relevant to any topic you are presently studying in your coursework.
21. Why is the NAIC system important? How would you use a NAICS code once you have identified the appropriate code? List three industries in which you have a career interest. What are the appropriate NAICS codes for these industries?
22. What is the BPI and what is its significance?
23. Explain why a marketer would use each of the indexes published in *Demographics USA*.
24. Explain how a marketer of boats could use the *Lifestyle Market Analyst*.
25. The CEO of a national retail jewelry chain is considering expanding its stores into several retail malls in the Southeast. The chain already owns several stores in this region of the country. Imagine that you are the director of marketing research for this chain and the CEO has asked you to provide information at next Monday's Executive Committee meeting that will help in making the decision about the selection of the cities in which to open new stores. What kind of internal information would you seek? What kind of external secondary data would you seek? In what way would you use these two sources of information in order to place them in a format that would enable you to contribute to the decisions to make?[25]

INTERACTIVE LEARNING

Visit the Web site at www.prenhall.com/burnsbush. For this chapter, work through the Self-Study Quizzes, and get instant feedback on whether you need additional studying. On the Web site, you can review the chapter outlines and case information for Chapter 6.

CASE 6.1   U.S. Sporting Goods Market: Using the Internet to Find Information[26]

John Bonner, vice president for marketing research at Wilson Sporting Goods, has been reviewing last year's marketing plan and product revenues for the U.S. market. He reflects that sales revenues for the product lines are up and that the company exceeded its marketing goals. However, he notes that the trends for the next year are not as promising as the last. The economy has been in recession and it is apparent that a discretionary item such as sports equipment may be tough to sell in the upcoming year. He decides that a specialized task force of product researchers should be put together to analyze how the sporting goods industry will perform during the next year.

The research team's first task is to understand the industry for sporting goods products. Certain team members attack the problem by surveying the relevant online secondary research services that provide sporting goods product data. Other members of the team observe the industry trade association Web sites that provide data on the sporting goods industry. Given the importance of understanding the nature of the intense competition in this market, a few team members analyze Wilson's competitive environment by accessing research on the Internet.

Search the following Internet Web sites to find the required information:

1. The current size of the U.S. sporting goods industry in dollars
   (http://nsga.org/public/pages/index.cfm?pageid=55).
2. Top industry competitors and their relative market shares
   (http://www.hoovers.com/industry/snapshot/0,2204,55,00.html).
3. Year over year industry sales growth (same link as #1).
4. Sporting goods product categories (same link as #1).
5. Consumer demographics and related identifiers
   (http://sportsillustrated.cnn.com/adinfo/si/mriframe.html).

CASE 6.2   *Your Integrated Case*

The Hobbit's Choice: A Restaurant

After the first meeting between Jeff Dean and Cory Rogers of CMG Research, Cory decided to conduct some secondary data analysis on the restaurant business. He knew he could benefit from doing this because he could conduct the research quickly and inexpensively, and he also knew he was very likely to find information in these secondary data sources that would be helpful to his client, Jeff Dean. First, Cory walked into CMG's library. The library had a reference guide, the *Encyclopedia of Business Information Sources*, almanacs, handbooks, and special business dictionaries. In addition, Cory had Internet access in his office.

1. Based on the published sources available in CMG's library, which book would you recommend as the first book Rogers should consult? The second book? Why?
2. Conduct a search of the Internet that you think Cory would have conducted. Describe the kind of information you retrieved about the restaurant industry and provide the Web sites from which you gathered the information.
3. Based on the information you retrieved from your Internet search, did you find any examples illustrating the weaknesses of secondary data? What are the weaknesses?
4. Assuming that Cory earns $55,000 a year, estimate what CMG's costs are for Cory doing the search that you conducted over the Internet. You can exclude other fixed costs such as the costs of Internet access, building, utilities, and so on. Just estimate the amount of Cory's salary allocated to the search.

Chapter 7

Standardized Information Sources

Learning Objectives:

To learn how to distinguish standardized information from other types of information

To know the differences between syndicated data and standardized services

To understand the advantages and disadvantages of standardized information

To see some of the various areas in which standardized information may be applied

To understand some specific examples of standardized information sources in each of four areas of application

To know the meaning of single-source data

Practitioner Viewpoint

Answering the four most important marketing questions of who *your customers are,* where *they are located,* how *to reach them, and* how *to find more like them is the primary marketing challenge both for traditional and e-commerce marketing. In today's faster business environment, it's even more critical to find the right audience. Marketing automation tools such as demographics, segmentation, targeting, and customer profiling coupled with information technology is a powerful component of business success. These tools can be used to build successful marketing campaigns. Precision is key to marketing success in your neighborhood and the world. Remember, the more you know about your customers, no matter where they are . . . the better you can serve their needs!*

David Huffman
Managing Director
ESRI Business Information Solutions

Imagine Trying to Understand over 100 Million U.S. Households. Impossible? Not with ACORN!

In 1971 ACORN (A Classification of Residential Neighborhoods) was developed. Census block groups, each with an average of about 400 households, are used to represent neighborhoods. ACORN then assigns each of the 220,000 neighborhoods in the United States into one of 43 different market segments by using current statistics such as income, home value, occupation, education, and so on. These 43 different segments are grouped into nine summary segments which are shown here. Also shown is a map of the Chicago area in which dominant ACORN segments have been identified. A critical component of the system is linking spending patterns and lifestyle choices to the various 43 market segments. For example, the segment called "Wealthy Seaboard Suburbs" likes casino gambling whereas another segment, "Top 1 Percent," prefers playing the stock market. Another segment, "Successful Suburbanites," is the best segment for PCs in terms of spending and time spent. The segment "College Campuses" makes the heaviest use of online time. ESRI Business Information Solutions works with clients to determine which of the 43 segments make up the majority of their customers. Using ACORN, ESRI Business Information Solutions can then help clients determine the market potential of various geographic markets, select the most effective media and most appropriate message to use, locate new sites, identify sales territories, and help optimize the marketing mix.

Where We Are:

1. Establish the need for marketing research
2. Define the problem
3. Establish research objectives
4. Determine research design
5. **Identify information types and sources**
6. Determine methods of accessing data
7. Design data collection forms
8. Determine sample plan and size
9. Collect data
10. Analyze data
11. Prepare and present the final research report

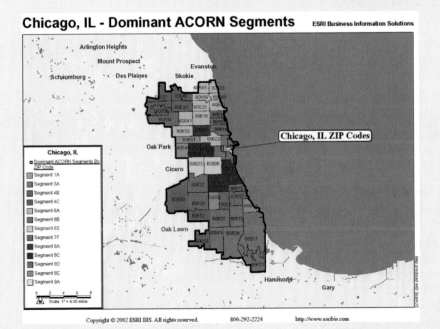

ACORN's 43 market segments are grouped under nine summary segments and ESRI Business Information Solutions knows the neighborhoods in which each segment dominates the residences. By permission, ESRI Business Information Solutions.

Our example of the ACORN system illustrates the topic of this chapter, standardized information. In this case, ESRI Business Information Solutions provides a standard process, the ACORN system, to clients who seek to better understand their customers. Imagine how your job as a marketing manager would be enhanced if you could answer the questions raised by David Huffman in his Practitioner's Viewpoint. ACORN has been a successful standardized service because it has answered these questions for many clients since it was established in 1971. In this chapter we are going to introduce you to the different types of standardized information: syndicated data and standardized services. We begin by defining what we mean by these types of standardized information.

WHAT IS STANDARDIZED INFORMATION?

Standardized information is a type of secondary data in which the data collected and/or the process of collecting the data are standardized for all users. Two broad classes of standardized information are syndicated data and standardized services.

Syndicated data are data that are collected in a standard format and made available to all subscribers.

Standardized services refers to a standardized marketing research *process* that is used to generate information for a particular user.

Standardized information is a type of secondary data in which the data collected and/or the process of collecting the data are standardized for all users. There are two broad classes of standardized information: syndicated data and standardized services. **Syndicated data** are data that are collected in a standard format and made available to all subscribers. The Nielsen TV ratings, for example, consist of data on TV viewing collected using a standardized method. The resulting data are made available to anyone wishing to purchase the information. **Standardized services** refers to a standardized marketing research *process* that is used to generate information for a particular user. ESRI's **ACORN** is a standardized process that is used to profile residential neighborhoods. This information is purchased by clients desiring to better understand who their customers are, where they are located, how to find them, and how to reach them. We discuss both of these types of information next.

Syndicated data are a form of external, secondary data that are supplied from a common database to subscribers for a service fee. Recall from our discussion of the types of firms in the marketing research industry in Chapter 3 that we call firms providing such data syndicated data service firms. Such information is typically detailed information that is valuable to firms in a given industry and is not available in libraries. Firms supplying syndicated data follow standard research formats that enable them to collect the same standardized data over time. These firms provide specialized, routine information needed by a given industry in the form of ready-to-use, standardized marketing data to subscribing firms. We mentioned the Nielsen TV ratings earlier. As another example, Arbitron supplies syndicated data on the number and types of listeners to the various radio stations in each radio market. This standardized information helps advertising firms reach their target markets; it also helps radio stations define audience characteristics by providing an objective, independent measure of the size and characteristics of their audiences. With syndicated data both the process of collecting and analyzing the data and the data themselves are standardized. That is, neither is varied for the client.[1] On the other hand, standardized services rarely provide clients with standardized data. Rather, it's the *process* they are marketing. The application of that standardized process will result in different data for each client. For example, a standardized service may be measurement of customer satisfaction. Instead of a user firm trying to "reinvent the wheel" by developing its own process for measuring customer satisfaction, it may elect to use a standardized service for measuring customer satisfaction. This is also true for several other marketing research services such as test marketing, naming new brands, pricing a new product, or using mystery shoppers.

With syndicated data, the data and the process used to generate the data are standardized across all users. With standardized services, the process of collecting data is standardized across all users.

▶ **Meet a Marketing Researcher**

*David Huffman Uses Standardized Services
for Many Marketing Applications*
David Huffman, Managing Director, ESRI Business Information Solutions

David Huffman is the managing director for ESRI Business Information Solutions, a leading provider of geodemographic and target marketing information. Mr. Huffman has over 14 years of experience in the marketing information industry working for CACI International Inc., National Decision Systems, Urban Decision Systems, and National Research Bureau.

Mr. Huffman has held positions in each of these organizations including senior systems analyst, product manager, production manager, director of PC products, and various sales positions. Through his technical expertise and application knowledge, Mr. Huffman has provided database marketing solutions for companies that include AT&T, Ben & Jerry's, Hair Cuttery, Gerber, Ernst & Young, Kroger, *TV Guide* and the Association of Handicapped Artists. Application areas of expertise include site selection, site success modeling, direct mail, response modeling, sales forecasting, market penetration and optimization, encroachment, category management, and customer profiling and segmentation.

ADVANTAGES AND DISADVANTAGES OF STANDARDIZED INFORMATION

Syndicated Data

One of the key advantages of syndicated data is *shared costs*. Many client firms may subscribe to the information; thus, the cost of the service is greatly reduced to any one subscriber firm. When costs are spread across several subscribers, other advantages result. Because syndicated data firms specialize in the collection of standard data and because their viability, in the long run, depends on the validity of the data, the *quality of the data collected is typically very high*. With several companies paying for the service, the syndicating company can go to great lengths to gather a great amount of data as well. Another advantage of syndicated data comes from the routinized systems used to collect and process the data. This means that the *data are normally disseminated very quickly* to subscribers because these syndicated data firms set up standard procedures and methods for collecting the data over and over again on a periodic basis. The more current the data, the greater their usefulness.

Although there are several advantages to syndicated data, there are some disadvantages. First, *buyers have little control over what information is collected*. Since the research is not custom research for the buyer firm, the buyer firm must be satisfied that the information received is the information needed. Are the units of

Advantages of syndicated data are shared costs, high quality of the data, and speed with which data are collected and made available for decision making.

Disadvantages of syndicated data are that there is little control over what data are collected, buyers must commit to long-term contracts, and competitors have access to the same information.

measurement correct? Are the geographical reporting units appropriate? A second disadvantage is that *buyer firms often must commit to long-term contracts* when buying standardized data. Finally, there is *no strategic information advantage in purchasing syndicated data* because all competitors have access to the same information. However, in many industries firms would suffer a serious strategic disadvantage by not purchasing the information.

Standardized Services

The key advantage of using a standardized service is taking advantage of the *experience of the research firm offering the service.* Often a buyer firm may have a research department with many experienced persons but no experience in a particular process that is now needed. Imagine a firm setting out to conduct a test market for the very first time. It would take the firm several months to gain the confidence needed to conduct the test market properly. Still, lessons would be learned by trial and error. Taking advantage of others' experiences with the process is a good way to minimize potential mistakes in carrying out the research process. A second advantage is the *reduced cost* of the research. Because the supplier firm conducts the service for many clients on a regular basis, the procedure is efficient and far less costly than if the buyer firm tried to conduct the service itself. A third advantage is *speed* of the research service. The efficiency gained by conducting the service over and over translates into reduced turnaround time from start to finish of a research project. The speed in which the service is conducted by standardized services firms is usually much faster than if the buyer firm were to conduct the service on its own.

There are disadvantages of using standardized services as well. Standardized means not customized. The *ability to customize some projects is lost* when using a standardized service. Although some services offer some customization, the ability to design a project for the project at hand is lost when using a standardized service. Second, the company providing the *standardized service may not know the idiosyncrasies of a particular industry* and, therefore, there is a greater burden on the client to ensure that the standardized service fits the intended situation. Client firms need to be very familiar with the service provided including what data are collected on which population, how the data are collected, and how the data are reported before they purchase the service.

APPLICATION AREAS OF STANDARDIZED INFORMATION

Although there are many forms of standardized information that may have many applications, we will illustrate four major application areas in the remainder of the chapter. We will explore the use of standardized information applied to measuring consumer attitudes and opinion polls, defining market segments, conducting market tracking, and monitoring media usage and promotion effectiveness.

Measuring Consumer Attitudes and Opinion Polls

Several firms offer measurements of consumer attitudes and opinions on various issues. The **Yankelovich Monitor,** started in 1971, measures changing social values and how these changes affect consumers. It has specialized in generational marketing and studied matures, baby boomers, and Generation Xrs.[2] The data are syndicated meaning they are available to anyone who wishes to purchase the data, and the information can be used for a variety of marketing management decisions. Data are collected annually through 90-minute in-home interviews and a one-hour questionnaire among 2,500 men and women aged 16 and over using a nationally representative sample.[3] For global marketing, the company offers a standardized service called the Global Monitor. Yankelovich's clients choose the country or countries in which they have an interest as well as the topics of interest. Then the Global Monitor reports information on those topics for the countries selected by the client firm.[4]

The **Harris poll** measures consumer attitudes and opinions on a wide variety of topics. Owned by Harris Interactive, the Harris poll started in 1963 and is one of the longest running, most respected surveys of consumer opinion. Harris polls are conducted on topics such as the economy, environment, politics, world affairs, legal issues, and so on. You can see some examples of recent Harris polls by going to HarrisInteractive.com and following the menu for the Harris Poll Library. The Harris poll uses a sample of 1,000 representative adults aged 18 and older. Polls are taken weekly and, because many of the same questions are asked over and over, the Harris poll is a good source to identify trend lines. Since these data are standardized information, we use it as another example of syndicated data. However, client firms may have Harris Interactive conduct customized surveys.[5]

The **Gallup poll** surveys public opinion, asking questions on domestic issues, private issues, and world affairs, such as "Do you consider the income tax you have to pay this year to be fair?" (Although 85 percent said "yes" in 1943, only 58 percent said "yes" in 2002.) Business executives can track attitudes toward buying private brands or attitudes toward credit by following questions asked in the Gallup poll. The Gallup poll is available each year, and back issues covering each year begin with 1935.[6] Like the Harris poll, the Gallup Organization can conduct customized surveys for clients. However, we treat the Gallup poll here as syndicated data since it collects attitude and opinion information and makes that information available to all who wish to purchase it. Visit its Web site and view some poll results. This will give you an idea of the service provided by the Gallup Organization.

Defining Market Segments

Defining market segments requires placing customers sharing certain attributes (age, income, stage in the family life cycle, etc.) into homogenous groups or market segments. Once in these groups, marketers gather information about the members of the market, compiling profiles of the attributes describing the consumers that make up each segment. Marketers can then decide which segments are presently being served or not served by the competition. They can also determine the size, growth trends, and profit potential of each segment. Using these data, a segment, or group of segments, can be targeted for marketing.

Several standardized information sources provide marketers with information about customers in the market. Some of these sources provide information on members of the industrial market, and others provide information on members of the consumer market.

Providing Information on Members of the Industrial Market

A great deal about the industrial market can be learned through the use of the Standard Industrial Classification (SIC) system and the North American Industry Classification System (NAICS), the government's method of classifying business firms (discussed in Chapter 6). Although achieving the basic objectives of allowing you to identify, classify, and monitor standard statistics about certain member firms, the SIC falls short of allowing you to target customers in a highly specific industry. NAICS partially remedies this problem by going from the SIC's four-digit code to a six-digit code. NAICS allows users to select more specific types of firms instead of the broad categories available through SIC codes.

One standardized information service firm supplies additional information that allows the user to make even better use of the government's classification systems.

The Harris poll measures consumer attitudes and opinions on a wide variety of topics. Visit the Harris poll at HarrisInteractive.com.

The Gallup poll provides syndicated data by making available polls of consumer attitudes and opinions to all who subscribe to its service. Visit the Gallup poll at www.gallup.com.

NAICS allows marketers to define industry types more specifically than the SIC classification system.

Dun's Market Identifiers (DMI), published by Dun & Bradsteet, provides information on over 4 million firms that it updates monthly. The real benefit of DMI is its service that provides eight-digit codes to classify businesses. By having more digits, the service can provide many more categories of firms than other classification systems. This is important if a firm is trying to target specific business firms, however narrow their classification.

> By classifying firms using an eight-digit code, Dun & Bradstreet offers a standardized information service that allows firms to locate all firms in a narrowly defined industry group.

For example, one marketing researcher worked with a manufacturing firm, BasKet Kases, a manufacturer of wooden gift baskets, to secure a listing of all firms that wholesale gift baskets for the purposes of targeting these firms with a marketing campaign. Using the SIC Classification Manual, it was determined that SIC numbers with a 51 prefix were wholesalers of nondurable goods. By examining all of the 51 prefix descriptions, the SIC code of 5199 was found to represent wholesalers of "miscellaneous, nondurable goods," which included baskets. Without additional information, a list of firms with an SIC code of 5199 would have included wholesalers of all types of baskets, including wooden baskets for shipping fruit, freight, and so on. However, with the use of the additional codes supplied by DMI, it was found that the eight-digit code 51990603 represented "wholesalers of gift baskets." This was exactly what the researcher was seeking. By finding the firms sharing this eight-digit code, the researcher was able to identify 45 wholesale firms of gift baskets in the United States for BasKet Kases.

Providing Information on Members of the Consumer Market Many standardized information services are available to help marketers understand the consumer market. Information on segmenting consumers by lifestyle[7] is available through the **VALS-2** study, which is Stanford Research Institute's (SRI) survey that places consumers in segments based on their psychological and demographic characteristics. Some examples of these different groups of consumers include "Actualizers" who are sophisticated, successful, take-charge people with abundant resources and high self-esteem. Their possessions reflect the finer things in life. "Experiencers" are young, enthusiastic, compulsive, and rebellious. They are not committed to many beliefs and are involved in outdoor activities, sports, and social activities. They spend much of their income on fast food, clothing, videos, and movies. SRI Consulting Business Intelligence uses the VALS system to help firms identify characteristics of their customers. The VALS system is standardized in that SRI has the process for identifying consumer VALS segments. The usefulness of the concept lies in knowing in which VALS segments most of a firm's customers are categorized. For example, knowing that 80 percent of a firm's customers fall into one VALS segment allows firms to know much more about the values and lifestyles of their customers. You can determine your VALS segment by completing the VALS survey online at www.sric-bi.com/VALS/. You can also learn more about the other VALS categories at this Web site.[8]

> VALS is a standardized service that offers a system for segmenting consumers by lifestyle.

Geodemographics is the term used to describe the classification of arbitrary, usually small, geographic areas in terms of the characteristics of their inhabitants. Aided with computer programs called **GIS** (geodemographic information systems), geodemographers can access huge databases and construct profiles of consumers residing in geographic areas determined by the geodemographer. Instead of being confined to consumer information recorded by city, county, or state, geodemographers can produce this information for geographic areas thought to be relevant for a given marketing application (such as a proposed site for a fast-food restaurant).

> *Geodemographics* is the term used to describe the classification of arbitrary, usually small, geographic areas in terms of the characteristics of their inhabitants.

Firms specializing in geodemographics combine census data with their own survey data or data that they gather from other sources. Claritas Inc. is the firm that pioneered geodemography. By accessing zip codes and census data regarding census tracks, census block groups, or blocks, which make up a firm's trading area(s), Claritas can compile much information about the characteristics and lifestyles of the people within these trading areas. Or a firm may give Claritas a descriptive profile of its target market and Claritas can supply the firm with geographic areas that most closely match the prespecified characteristics. This service is referred to as **PRIZM** (potential ratings index for Zip+4 markets). The PRIZM system defines every neighborhood in the United States in terms of 62 demographically and behaviorally distinct clusters. By knowing which clusters make up a firm's potential customers, Claritas can help target promotional messages to consumers making up those clusters. Marketing Research Insight 7.2 gives you some background information on Claritas and describes some of its standardized services that can be used for market segmentation.

> **Firms specializing in geodemographics combine census data with their own survey data or data that they gather from other sources. PRIZM is a standardized information service that categorizes neighborhoods in one of 62 different clusters.**

▶ **Additional Insights**

MARKETING RESEARCH

INSIGHT

7.2

Claritas Standardized Services for Market Segmentation

Founded in 1971, Claritas Inc. is widely regarded as the leading provider of precision marketing solutions, developed, in part, through intricate customer segmentation systems and other data delivery and analysis software/Internet systems. The company serves clients within the automotive, financial services, media, retail, real estate, restaurant, telecommunications, and energy/utilities industries, many of which are major *Fortune* 500 companies. Claritas is a division of the VNU Marketing Information Group (VNU/MIG), an established leader in providing a wide variety of industries with innovative, precision-marketing solutions including geodemographic information and qualitative audience research. VNU/MIG is a subsidiary of VNU Inc., which also includes AC Nielsen, Nielsen Media Research, Spectra Marketing Services, Scarborough Research, VNU Business Publications, VNU eMedia, and VNU Expositions.

With information generated through its segmentation systems and databases, Claritas enables businesses to address key marketing issues, such as:

▶ Who are my best customers and prospects?
▶ How many are there and where do they live?
▶ What is the most effective way to reach them?
▶ Which markets, locations, or industries offer the most potential?
▶ How should I allocate marketing resources to maximize my return on investment?

Some Claritas Products Used for Market Segmentation

PRIZM—Defines every neighborhood in the United States in terms of 62 demographically and behaviorally distinct clusters. A precision tool for lifestyle segmentation and analysis, PRIZM offers an easy way to identify, understand, and target consumers down to the block level.

MicroVision—A segmentation and consumer targeting system classifying every U.S. household into one of 50 unique market segments. Classifications are based on the demographic, lifestyle, socioeconomic, buying, media, and behavior characteristics of households within every ZIP+4 geography.

MicroVision Banking—Classifies every U.S. household into 31 segments based on financial service usage, aggregated consumer demand information, and census demographics.

MicroVision Insurance—Classifies every U.S. household into one of nine strategic groups, comprised of segments having statistically similar insurance usage characteristics.

MicroVision Daytime—This segmentation system classifies employees working in a geographic area by MicroVision segment. Helps locate where target segments work and determines an area's potential demand for products and services during the daytime.

P$YCLE—A market segmentation system that differentiates households in terms of financial behavior. The 42-segment system predicts which households will use which types of financial products and services.

LifeP$YCLE—A household-level segmentation system designed for insurance marketers. Analyzes sales potential for specific insurance products as well as profile and target consumers based on insurance buying habits.

ConneXions—A household-level segmentation system for targeting video, voice, and data services.

By permission, Claritas Inc.

ESRI Business Information Solutions, formerly CACI Marketing Systems, is another geodemography firm that we introduced at the beginning of this chapter. We illustrate a GIS application provided for you by ESRI Business Information Solutions in Marketing Research Insight 7.3. Study this example carefully and you will understand the basics of using a GIS program and the benefits of geodemography. You can find out more about GIS systems at esri.com.

MARKETING RESEARCH
INSIGHT
7.3

Additional Insights ◄

ESRI Business Information Solutions Using GIS and ACORN to Solve Business Problems

ArcView® Business Analyst is a GIS software product with many users throughout the world. The program is a set of tools and data designed specifically for business applications, allowing users to analyze markets and customers, see trends and patterns on maps, and generate comprehensive demographic reports. The software has an easy-to-use wizard interface that guides the user through complex tasks, and the data and analysis procedures are built in. Typical users include those working in retail, banking, insurance, manufacturing, real estate, local government, health care, telecommunications, oil and gas, and utilities.

Retail market analysis is a primary function for which ArcView Business Analyst is perfectly suited, and retail and commercial operations of all kinds use the software to identify the best places to target their marketing efforts. To illustrate how this GIS program works, we examine a fictitious

firm, Z.Z. Sporting, a sporting goods chain in Tennessee that wanted to analyze how its stores in the greater Nashville area were doing. The firm also wanted to learn some things about the marketplace generally and figure out where to focus some specific marketing efforts for a particular store.

A key concern was whether, and to what degree, the three Z.Z. Sporting stores in the area might be "cannibalizing" one another, that is, each store "competing" with itself by taking customers away from one another. That can create problems for retailers; in some cases where tough decisions have to be made, retailers might not know whether to close a store or stores or whether they should dramatically change their approach to marketing and advertising.

In the first map, three stores are identified by location, and customers for each are identified by small colored dots (blue, red, and green, respectively). By having a data file

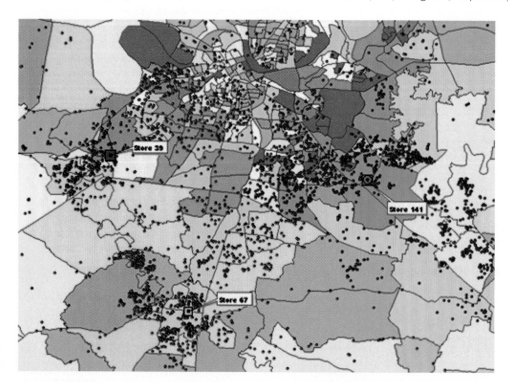

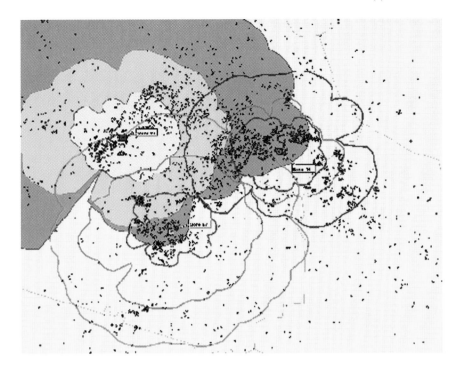

with customers' addresses, a firm can use GIS to visually display customer locations. Assigning the addresses to a location on a map is a process referred to as geocoding. Seeing the locations of customers geocoded on a map is one benefit of ArcView Business Analyst; store managers are able to see to what extent the customer bases of each store overlap.

The second map, which also shows to what extent the customer bases of each store overlap, allows the user to determine the extent to which the stores compete with one another. This is determined by closely examining the overlap of the rings. The rings around each store also show where 80, 60, and 40 percent of the stores' revenues come from (respectively, from the innermost rings outward). The rings analysis is particularly important because it shows managers the precise geographical areas where customers live and where varying levels of sales are derived.

Another major benefit of ArcView Business Analyst is its integration of ACORN® marketing data. ACORN (A Classification of Residential Neighborhoods) is a lifestyle segmentation system that divides neighborhood segments into 43 clusters and nine summary groups (see beginning of this chapter). The lifestyle classification system is used for market research and site selection by thousands of businesses and organizations in the retail and commercial business fields. (ACORN, developed by the former CACI Marketing Systems Group, is now provided by ESRI

Business Information Solutions, a new company that was formed after the acquisition of CACI Marketing Systems Group by ESRI in 2002.)

Using the mapping function of ArcView Business Analyst coupled with the ACORN data, store managers are able to determine the types of customers living near each store, an important factor in figuring out how to market to these groups. For example, in the first map, pink-colored areas are neighborhoods where the predominant ACORN classification is "Middle America," gray areas are predominantly "Prosperous Baby Boomers," tan areas are where "Successful Suburbanites" live, light brown areas are home to "Semirural Lifestyle" people, and darker greenish areas are where "Enterprising Young Singles" are dominant. Each of these groups is defined differently in terms of age, marital status, household income, net worth, purchasing habits, and other factors that are determinants of consumer behavior. Once store managers in our example understood where specific kinds of people—and potential purchasers of sporting goods equipment—lived, they could begin to formulate smarter and better marketing plans.

The third map generated by ArcView Business Analyst was helpful in showing market penetration for one of the stores. In varying shades of green, the number of customers as a percentage of the total number of people in a census block (or neighborhood) group is represented; darker shades tell managers the geographic areas where the highest degrees of revenue are generated.

(box continues)

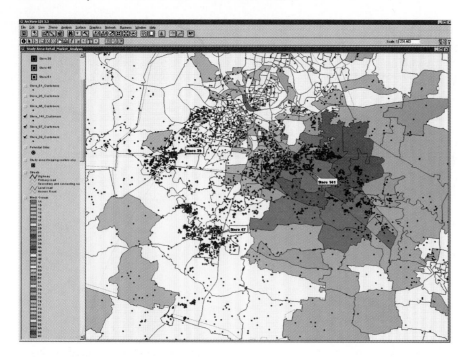

The fourth map developed with ArcView Business Analyst's data-crunching abilities displays a yellow area (comprised of four zip codes) showing where 67 percent of a particular store's sales originate. The yellow area became the key geographic zone where managers specifically targeted advertising for that store, and past "shotgun" mass mailings to a wider geographic area were abandoned, resulting in a significant savings of money.

By permission, ESRI Business Information Solutions. The authors wish to thank ESRI's Industry Solutions department and ESRI Press for providing maps and text for this hypothetical case study. ArcView® Business Analyst is a registered trademark of ESRI of Redlands, California, a world leader in GIS software. ACORN® is a registered trademark of ESRI Business Information Solutions.

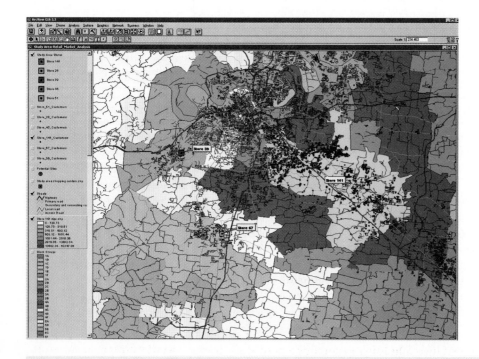

Conducting Market Tracking

By **tracking studies** we mean studies that monitor, or track, a variable over time. For example, companies conduct market tracking to track sales of their brands as well as sales of competitors' brands over time. The "tracks" moving up and down or stable serve as important monitors as to how the market is reacting to a firm's marketing mix. Many variables may be monitored in a tracking study including market share, customer satisfaction levels, measures of promotional spending, prices, stockouts, inventory levels, and so on. You may ask why a company needs to know what its own sales are. Wouldn't a company know, through sales receipts, how much it has sold of a particular product? Although a company may monitor its own sales, sales measured by a firm's own sales receipts provide an incomplete picture. By monitoring only its own sales, a firm does not know what is going on in the channel of distribution. Products are not distributed instantaneously. Rather, inventories are built up and depleted at various rates among the different distributors. Just because household sales of a product increase does not mean that a producer will experience a sales increase of that product. To really know what is happening in the industry, marketers need to monitor the movement of goods at the retail level. Recognizing this need, market tracking is conducted at both the retail store level and at the household level. And tracking studies, as noted, also provide data on competitors' brands that otherwise would not be available to management. So, for these reasons, tracking studies are an important service provided by research firms.[9] Data are collected by scanners and by retail store audits. We provide examples of each in the following paragraphs.

Market Tracking at the Retail Level *ACNielsen Scantrack Services.* ACNielsen's **Scantrack Services** is based on syndicated retail **scanning data** and is recognized as an industry standard in terms of providing tracking data gathered from the stores' scanners. Data are collected weekly from approximately 4,800 food, drug, and mass merchandise stores representing about 800 different retailers in 50 markets in the United States. ACNielsen Scantrack tracks thousands of products as they move through retail stores allowing brand managers to monitor sales and market share and to evaluate marketing strategies. Scantrack reports can be provided at many different levels of information. For example, a report may be ordered for just one category of products across the 50 U.S. markets.[10] Or a report can be generated for one brand in a single market. ACNielsen also provides services for tracking products sold in convenience stores through its Convenience Track Service.[11]

InfoScan Syndicated Data Service. Information Resources, Inc. (IRI) syndicated data service, **InfoScan,** gathers data by scanners in supermarkets, drugstores, and mass merchandisers. InfoScan collects data in over 32,000 stores and provides subscribers access to information across 266 InfoScan categories. The eight major categories for which data are collected include Health & Beauty Care, Frozen, Bakery, Nonedible Grocery, General Merchandise, Dairy, Deli, and Edible Grocery. IRI offers many other standardized information services. The primary advantage of scanning data is that the data are available very quickly to decision makers. There is a minimum delay from the time the data are collected and the time the information is available to decision makers. The disadvantage is that a company may have products distributed through smaller stores that do not have scanners.

Retail Store Audits. Some tracking services do not rely solely on data collected in retail stores by scanners. **Retail store audits** also are used. In retail store audits, auditors are sent to stores and they record merchandising information needed for tracking studies. Store audits are particularly useful for smaller stores that do not have

Tracking studies are those that monitor, or track, a variable such as sales or market share over time.

Tracking studies can tell a firm how well its own products are selling in retail outlets around the world and also provide sales data for competitors' products.

ACNielsen's Scantrack provides firms with tracking data based on scanner-collected data. Visit ACNielsen at www.acnielsen.com.

IRI's InfoScan provides firms with tracking data based on scanner-collected data. Visit IRI at www.infores.com.

In retail store audits, auditors record merchandising information needed for tracking studies.

scanner equipment such as convenience stores. Sales are estimated by calculating the following:

$$\text{Beginning Inventory} + \text{Purchases Received} - \text{Ending Inventory} = \text{Sales}$$

Auditors not only record this information for many products but also note other merchandising factors such as the level and type of in-store promotions, newspaper advertising, out-of-stock products, and shelf facings of products. ACNielsen and RoperASW are two companies that provide tracking data collected by store audits. Like data collected by scanning services, data collected by audit are stored in a common database and made available to all who subscribe. The standardized information produced by these services would be examples of syndicated data.

Market Tracking at the Household Level Information is gathered in homes using scanning devices, diaries, and audits. In-home scanner devices are provided to panel members who agree to scan the UPC codes on products they have purchased. Other services ask panel members to record purchases in diaries that are subsequently mailed back to the research firm. Finally, a few research firms collect data by actually sending auditors into homes to count and record information. Almost all of these methods rely on consumer household panels whose members are recruited for the purpose of recording and reporting their household purchases to one of the standardized data services firms. We shall give you some examples of each.

InfoScan's Combined Outlet Consumer Panel. Information Resources, Inc. also maintains a panel of consumer households that record purchases at outlets by scanning UPC codes on the products purchased. Using IRI's handheld ScanKey scanning wand, panel members record their purchases and this information is transmitted via telephone link back to IRI. In the summer of 2002, IRI had 70,000 shoppers as part of its consumer panel. Like many panels, an advantage of this panel is that it provides not only information on products purchased but also purchase data that are linked to the demographics of the purchasers.[12]

ACNielsen Homescan Panel. This panel, started in 1989, recruits panel members who use handheld scanners to scan all bar-coded products purchased and brought home from all outlets including warehouse clubs and convenience stores. Panel members also record the outlet at which all the merchandise was purchased and which family member made the purchase, as well as price and causal information such as coupon usage. This panel allows ACNielsen to track data on products whether they are bought in a store with or without scanners and from any store. It also allows the company to provide data on products with and without UPC codes. The Homescan Panel consists of households that are demographically and geographically balanced and projectable to the total United States. In addition, local markets can be tracked. ACNielsen's Worldwide Panel Service also provides home tracking services for eighteen countries around the world.

Diary. Several companies offer tracking data collected by household diaries. Panel members are asked to complete diaries containing information such as the type of product, name brand, manufacturer or producer, model number, description, purchase price, store from which the item was purchased, and information about the person making the purchase. This information can then be used to estimate important factors such as market share, brand loyalty, brand switching, and demographic profile of purchasers. The panel members are typically balanced geographically to the United States and regions of the United States. Also, many companies have special-purpose panels. NFO, for example, has a Chronic Ailment Panel (CAP), which consists of more than 250,000 persons suffering from 60 chronic ailments.

Information for tracking studies is gathered in homes using scanning devices, diaries, and audits.

IRI's InfoScan's Combined Outlet Consumer Panel has members who scan products they purchase and send the data back to IRI to be used in tracking studies.

ACNielsen's Homescan Panel has panel members who scan products they purchase using a handheld scanner. The products are purchased from many types of outlets such as warehouse clubs and convenience stores. You can read more about Homescan at www.acnielsen.com/products/reports/homescan.

Some services gather tracking data by having panel members record their purchases in a household diary.

This panel offers firms involved in the health care industry valuable insights on how consumers select medical treatment. NFO also has special panels for babies, adults 50+, and families that are moving.[13]

Audit. Some companies collect data from households by sending auditors into homes. NPD's Complete Kitchen Audit records ingredients, kitchen utensils, and appliances in homes. The information is provided to manufacturers of kitchen products and food producers.[14]

Some firms collect tracking data by sending auditors into households to count and record data of interest.

Turning Market Tracking Information into Intelligence One of the disadvantages of today's information technology is that a user of information can easily be swamped with information producing "information overload." You can imagine the quantity of information that could flow to a manufacturer who subscribes to tracking data. The information flows in frequently and in large quantities. Various companies have created a host of products to help decision makers use vast quantities of information for intelligent decisions. Variously labeled decision support systems, data mining systems, expert systems, and the like, these systems use analytical tools to attach meaning to data, allowing managers to make decisions in response to quickly changing market conditions. Some examples include **IRI's Builder** services and **ACNielsen's Category Business Planner.** To give you an example of how these services work, we shall discuss ACNielsen's Category Business Planner. Category Business Planner is a web-based category planning tool that aids managers in making better decisions based on sales information of products in the consumer packaged goods industry. What is unique about Category Business Planner is that it allows a manufacturer to move from retailer to retailer to view how its product is performing within each retailer's proprietary view of the category containing the product. This allows a manufacturer to evaluate product performance the same way a retail customer would evaluate the manufacturer's product, allowing them to better collaborate when developing their business plans for each product category.

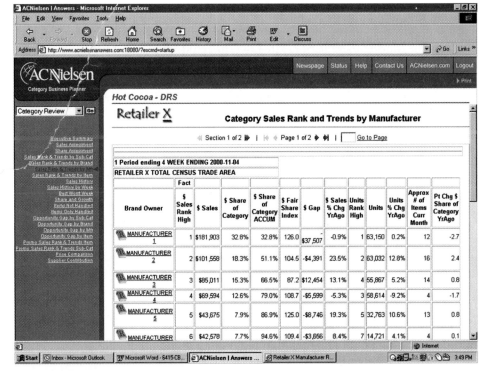

ACNielsen Category Business Planner makes huge volumes of information manageable to aid in decision making.

By permission, ACNielsen.

Manufacturers now will be able to determine how their particular product is performing within each retail customer's category even though retailers may define their categories differently. Users of the service also receive alerts in the form of headlines that relate to key category management metrics. Category Business Planner was also built to be more time-efficient, providing users with instant access to information. It employs a "headlines to details" design, which allows retailers and manufacturers to quickly view relevant insights about a category, and then drill to additional levels of detail if and when required.

Monitoring Media Usage and Promotion Effectiveness

Business firms typically conduct studies to measure their effectiveness, readership, listenership, and so on. This information is useful to firms contemplating advertising expenditures. Because there is a need for some objective measure of promotional effectiveness, several syndicated data service companies have evolved over the years to supply such information to subscribing firms. Some of these services specialize in a particular medium; a few others conduct studies on several forms of media. A discussion of both types of these organizations follows.

Monitoring the number of persons watching TV programs is a syndicated data service provided by the Nielsen Television Index.

Television For many years the **Nielsen Television Index (NTI)** has been the major provider of TV ratings. Since 1999 Nielsen TV Index has been owned by VNU, a Netherlands-based publishing and research firm. VNU also owns the marketing research firm ACNielsen. Few TV watchers have been unaffected by the Nielsen Television Index; their favorite show has been canceled or, because the index showed a large audience, the show has run for many years. Obviously, firms in the TV industry are constantly trying to achieve higher viewership than their competition. High viewership allows them to charge higher prices to advertise on the "more popular" programs.

Until the last few years, the size and characteristics of TV audiences by program were determined by panels made up of approximately 2,000 families that recorded their TV viewing habits in a diary or through an electronic device, the audiometer, that was attached to their TV set. Data were gathered twice a year. The data collection period became known as "sweeps" month, and this affected network and cable programming during these periods. In 1987, in an effort to gain greater objectivity, Nielsen changed the method of measuring the size and characteristics of the audiences to the **people meter,** an electronic instrument that automatically measures when a TV set is on and who is watching which channel. Family members are asked to enter their names (by codes) into the people meter each time they watch TV. Data from the people meter are transmitted directly back to Nielsen, allowing the firm to develop estimates of the size of the audience for each program by reporting the percentage of TV households viewing a given show.[15] NTI reports a rating and a share for each program telecast. A rating is the percentage of households that have at least one set tuned to a given program for a minimum of 6 minutes for each 15 minutes the program is telecast. A share is the percentage of households with at least one set tuned to a specific program at a specific time.

The people meter records what TV program a household member is watching.

The Nielsen Television Index also provides subscribers with other audience characteristic information that allows potential advertisers to select audiences that most closely match their target markets' characteristics. Ratings are reported by the number of households, by whether the women are employed outside the home, by age group for women (18+, 12–24, 18–34, 18–49, 25–54, 35–64, 55+), by age group for men (18+, 18–34, 18–49, 25–54, 35–65, 55+), and by age group of children (children ages 2 and older, ages 6 to 11, and teenagers).

Arbitron provides syndicated data on radio station listening using panels who record the stations to which they are listening in diaries. Arbitron is testing a Personal Portable Meter that automatically records audio and video signals to which a person carrying the meter is exposed.

Radio **Arbitron** provides syndicated data on radio station listening. Since 1964, radio listenership has been measured by Arbitron's national and regional panels whose members complete diaries reporting radio listening for one week. Panel members record information in a weekly paper-and-pencil diary. They indicate the time of day; how long the station was tuned in; which station was on; where the listening was done (at home, in a car, at work, or other place); and the panel member's age, gender, and home address. Although paper-and-pencil diaries are still being used, Arbitron has been testing a **personal portable meter (PPM)**, the size of a pager, which would automatically record stations listened to. (We have more to say about the PPM in the upcoming section on multimedia services). Data from the diaries are used to measure and report a number of variables indicative of radio listenership. Listenership is measured in 15-minute intervals and data are also reported by age and gender to aid in profiling audience characteristics. Subscribers to Arbitron Radio Market Reports can view the data on the computer and select the output formats in which they wish to view the data. How can radio stations and businesses use this information to formulate marketing strategy? For instance, knowing where a person is listening may affect the type of message an advertiser wishes to employ. A station with a high concentration of in-car listening may appeal to car dealers, auto-part stores, transmission repair shops, and tire stores. Understanding where the listening occurs is also helpful in determining programming elements such as traffic reports, contests, newscasts, and other information and entertainment segments. Arbitron also conducts other customized marketing research studies to suit individual clients' problems.[16]

Print **RoperASW's Starch Readership Service** is known as the most widely used source for measuring the extent to which magazine ads are seen and read. Starch conducts personal interviews with a minimum sample of 100 readers of a given issue of a magazine, trade publication, or newspaper. Interviews are carried out in 20 to 30 urban localities for each magazine issue analyzed. Interviews are conducted only with respondents who have read the issue prior to the interview. Therefore, Starch readership studies are not designed to determine the number of readers who read a particular issue of a magazine. Rather, Starch determines what readers saw and read in a study issue when they first looked through it. Starch studies over 25,000 ads in 400 individual print publications a year and interviews more than 40,000 people annually. Starch then uses the following readership levels in its reports:

> Noted—the percentage of issue readers who remember having previously seen any part of the advertisement in the study issue.
>
> Associated—the percentage of issue readers who not only noted the ad but also saw or read some part of it that clearly indicated the brand or advertiser.
>
> Read Some—the percentage of issue readers who read any part of the ad's copy.
>
> Read Most—the percentage of issue readers who read one-half or more of the written material in the advertisement.

In addition to these readership levels, Starch reports a number of other analytical measures such as an ad's rank, which shows the relative standing of an ad in terms of its Noted and Associated percentages to all other ads in the magazine issue. In addition to evaluating individual ads, Starch also analyzes the impact of many other variables on readership such as ad size, number of pages, black and white, color, special position (cover, center spread, etc.), and product category, among several others.[17] To further help marketers make decisions about what comprises a good ad, Starch also provides another syndicated data service called Adnorms. **Adnorms** provides readership scores by type of ads. For example, Adnorms could calculate the average readership scores for one-page, four-color computer ads appearing in *Business Week*. This allows an advertiser to compare his or her ad

RoperASW's Starch Readership service provides syndicated data on magazine readership. Visit Starch Readership Service at www.roperasw.com.

scores with the norm. In this way, advertising effectiveness may be assessed. Users learn the effect of ad size, color, and even copy on readership.[18] There are other standardized information services that evaluate print media. One such firm is Millward Brown's IntelliQuest's Computer Industry Media Study. Marketing Research Insight 7.4 discusses how one firm, InfoWorld Media Group, uses these syndicated data.

Some firms provide syndicated data on several media, such as Simmons Study of Media and Markets.

Multimedia Some standardized information sources firms provide information on a number of media. **Simmons Study of Media and Markets** provides information on magazines, Sunday magazines, newspapers, television, radio, cable, outdoor, Yellow Pages, and syndicated television. It reports media audiences, product/brand usage in over 800 product and brand categories, demographic data, and psychographic data. Simmons uses an index system to report data. An index of 100 equals "average." For example, let's take the product heavy rock music CDs. The 18–24 age group may have a very high index, let's say about 300, whereas the age group of 65 and older has a low index around 10. This indicates that the 18–24 age group is the

To learn more about InfoWorld, go to www.infoworld.com.

MARKETING RESEARCH
INSIGHT
7.4

In the TV business, Nielsen ratings are used to a great extent to gauge viewership of different TV programs. Similarly in radio, Arbitron ratings are used to assess the number of radio listeners who tune in to radio stations and specific programs. For print publications, data from Millward Brown's IntelliQuest's Computer Industry Media Study (CIMS) helps media planners determine which magazines reach people involved in the purchase of computer and Internet-related products and services.

InfoWorld subscribes to CIMS and members of the research department at InfoWorld use specialized computer programs to carry out "runs." ("Runs" is industry jargon for extrapolating results from a syndicated research study like CIMS to identify characteristics of a certain target group.) As an example, a researcher at InfoWorld conducted runs per a request passed along from an ad agency, in which the agency wanted to see coverage and composition numbers for all publications covered in the IntelliQuest CIMS study against the target, which was defined as "chief information officers or IT director or IT manager in companies with 500+ employees." There are specific codes assigned to each of these items, and by entering the proper coding in a specialized computer application, users can find the results for this target group matched against all magazines included in the study. The syndicated data allow users to find out information about a target group for each one of the magazines, including those published by InfoWorld Media Group. InfoWorld then supplies the requesters with an electronic spreadsheet containing the information so that they may

then use the results and enter other information, such as editorial content and circulation data, to determine if they will purchase ad space in InfoWorld and other publications.

InfoWorld Media Group provides cutting-edge coverage and evaluations of IT products, technology, and services for technology experts in senior IT management. InfoWorld reaches the most influential senior technology experts—who drive their enterprises' technology purchases—through integrated online, print, research, and events channels. InfoWorld also provides specialized IT coverage for the chief technology officers, the senior-most company executives who possess deep technology expertise and experience.

InfoWorld Media Group's coverage of key IT products and technologies is supported by original research done in InfoWorld's $23 million, dedicated multiplatform, enterprise test center. Since 1978, InfoWorld has performed the industry's most trusted testing of technology and products. InfoWorld Media Group is a division of IDG, the world's leading technology media, research, and event company. Founded in 1964, IDG had 2000 revenues of $3.1 billion and has more than 12,000 employees worldwide. IDG offers the widest range of media options, which reach more than 100 million technology buyers in 85 countries representing 95 percent of worldwide IT spending. IDG's diverse product and services portfolio spans six key areas including print publishing, online publishing, events and conferences, market research, education and training, and global marketing services.

Because Arbitron's PPM records signals from several media sources, data from the PPM will provide multimedia monitoring information.

prominent market for heavy rock music. What about magazine readership? *Hot Rod* magazine readership for buyers of heavy rock music has a very high index, about 230, and *Barron's* magazine has a low index of around 20. In terms of TV viewership, the programs with the highest index numbers are shows like *Saturday Night Live*, *Comedy Central*, and MTV programs. So you can see how this information could be very useful to marketers in a particular business. Not only does the service give them demographics of users and nonusers but it also gives them a method to determine where to spend their promotional dollars.

We discussed Arbitron with regard to radio earlier. However, Arbitron's Personal Portable Meter (PPM) is a measure of multimedia including TV, radio, and the Web. The company's development of the Personal Portable Meter (PPM) could prove to be a significant innovation in today's world where consumers are exposed to a variety of media types in a variety of locations other than in their own living rooms. The PPM has been under development since 1992 and Arbitron has been testing the device extensively.[19] The PPM works by embedding a code into the audio portion of the signals of TV networks including cable channels, radio broadcasts, and Web pages. When a survey respondent is exposed to a medium's broadcast, the PPM captures the code identifying the medium. In the evening, respondents are asked to place their PPM in a base unit that recharges the unit and records the data collected so that it may be transmitted via modem to Arbitron. Arbitron panel members are encouraged to wear the PPM a minimum of 8 hours a day. The PPM may allow Arbitron to measure audiences for radio, television, cable, satellite, video games, CDs, VCR tapes, and even audio on the Internet. With recent technological advances making more media alternatives available (more channels on TV, satellite radio, wireless Internet, and so on), there is a growing demand for multimedia measurement services.[20]

Arbitron's Personal Portable Meter (PPM) could prove to be a significant innovation in today's world where consumers are exposed to a variety of media types in a variety of locations other than in their own living rooms.

SINGLE-SOURCE DATA

Single-source data are recorded continuously from a panel of respondents to measure their exposure to promotional materials (usually TV as well as in-store promotions) and subsequent buying behavior. Armed with this information, marketers know whether consumers who saw one of their ads actually bought their product.

Several technological developments have led to the development of single-source data, including the universal product code (UPC) and scanning equipment that electronically records and stores data gathered at the point of purchase. As we shall explain in the following paragraphs, when coupled with computer and MIS technological developments, powerful "single-source" databases are built that are capable of providing a wealth of information on consumer purchases down to the UPC level.

Single source data are data that contain information on several variables such as promotional message exposure, demographics, and buyer behavior. Single-source data can help managers determine causal relationships between types of promotions and sales.

Although scanner-based databases can provide up-to-the-minute reports on the sale of virtually any consumer product by store, date, time of day, price, and so on, these same powerful databases cannot provide any information at all as to *who* bought the product. However, several marketing research services, such as Information Resource's **BehaviorScan,** can supply demographic data on the consumers' purchasing of various products. BehaviorScan is a standardized service that consists of panels of consumers in several cities around the United States who are provided with an electronic card that is scanned as they check out of participating retailers. BehaviorScan can control TV ads sent to its panel members. Having the ability to know which ads panelists have been exposed to and also knowing which products these same panelists have purchased gives BehaviorScan subscribers access to powerful causal data. Thus, from a single data source, a marketer may obtain information about media exposure as well as purchases. Consequently, with single-source data, marketers have not only the ability to determine who is purchasing what, when, and where, but they also know the media and in-store promotions to which the buyers were exposed. Therefore, from this one database (single source) marketers should have the ability to answer cause-and-effect questions concerning how marketing mix variables actually affect sales.

When the concept of single-source data was introduced a few years ago, some thought it would revolutionize the marketing research industry. Others believed that it would not be so revolutionary and that there would always be a place for traditional marketing research studies. Today, single-source studies are a small part of total research studies but their use is growing. ITV's tvSPAN, for example, recently expanded its single-source service from 750 households to 3,000 households.[21] As technology improves and as these systems earn confidence among users, we are likely to see single-source services grow even more.[22]

IRI's BehaviorScan is an example of a standardized service source for single-source data.

While single-source data have not replaced traditional marketing research studies during the last decade, use of the service is increasing.

SUMMARY

Your SPSS Student Assistant Online
SPSS Quick Tour: Part II

Standardized information is a type of secondary data in which the data collected and/or the process of collecting the data are standardized for all users. There are two classes of standardized information. Syndicated data are data being collected in a standard format and being made available to all subscribing users. An example would be the Nielsen TV ratings. Standardized services offer a standardized marketing research process that is used to generate information for a particular user. ACORN is a system of classifying neighborhoods into 43 different segments. That process is standardized; it is the same for all users of ACORN. The information from the process is then applied to generate different data for each user. With syndicated data, the data are the same for each user and with standardized services the process of generating data for each user is the same.

Syndicated data have the advantages of shared costs of obtaining the data among all those subscribing to the service, high data quality, and the speed with which data are collected and distributed to subscribers. Disadvantages are that buyers cannot control what data are collected, buyers must commit to long-term contracts, and there is no strategic information advantage to buying syndicated data because the information is available to all competitors.

Standardized services have the advantage of use of the supplier firm's expertise in the area, reduced costs, and speed with which supplier firms can conduct the service. The disadvantages of standardized services are that the process cannot easily be customized, and the supplier firm may not know the idiosyncrasies of the industry in which the client firm operates.

Four major areas in which standardized information sources may be applied are measuring consumers attitudes and opinions, defining market segments in both the industrial/B2B markets as well as the consumer market, conducting market tracking studies, and monitoring media usage and promotion effectiveness. The Harris poll is an example of a syndicated data source providing information on consumers' attitudes and opinions. ACORN is an example of a standardized service that defines consumer market segments. Scantrack is an example of a syndicated data source for tracking the sales of consumer product goods sold in retail stores. Arbitron radio listenership studies are an example of a syndicated data source for monitoring radio listenership.

Single-source information sources use sales data recorded by scanners that record sales at the UPC level by brand, store, date, price, and so on. Those data are then coupled with information on the buyer's demographics and media exposure. Having information on who bought what, where, and when after being exposed to promotional materials in one single database may give marketers the ability to answer important cause-and-effect questions on, for example, which marketing mix variable X caused the sale of product Y. IRI's BehaviorScan is an example of a standardized service providing single-source information.

KEY TERMS

Standardized information (p. 182)
Syndicated data (p. 182)
Standardized services (p. 182)
ACORN (p. 182)
Yankelovich Monitor (p. 184)
Harris poll (p. 185)
Gallup poll (p. 185)
Dun's Market Identifiers (DMI) (p. 186)
VALS-2 (p. 186)
Geodemographics (p. 186)
GIS (p. 186)
PRIZM (p. 187)
MicroVision (p. 187)
MicroVision Banking (p. 187)
MicroVision Insurance (p. 187)
MicroVision Daytime (p. 187)
P$YCLE (p. 187)
LifeP$YCLE (p. 187)
ConneXions (p. 187)
ArcView® Business Analyst (p. 188)
Tracking studies (p. 191)
Scantrack Services (p. 191)

Scanning data (p. 191)
InfoScan (p. 191)
Retail store audits (p. 191)
InfoScan's Combined Outlet Consumer Panel (p. 192)
ACNielsen Homescan Panel (p. 192)
Diary (p. 192)
Audit (p. 193)
IRI's Builder (p. 193)
ACNielsen's Category Business Planner (p. 193)
Nielsen Television Index (NTI) (p. 194)
People meter (p. 194)
Arbitron (p. 194)
Personal portable meter (PPM) (p. 195)
RoperASW's Starch Readership Service (p. 195)
Adnorms (p. 195)
Simmons Study of Media and Markets (p. 196)
Single-source data (p. 198)
BehaviorScan (p. 198)

REVIEW QUESTIONS/APPLICATIONS

1. What is meant by standardized information?
2. Distinguish between syndicated data and standardized services.
3. What are the advantages and disadvantages of syndicated data?
4. What are the advantages and disadvantages of standardized services?
5. Name four broad types of applications of standardized information and give an example of each.
6. What is geodemography and how can it be used in marketing decisions? Give an example.
7. What is the firm that is best known for conducting studies of radio listenership? Briefly describe the service it provides.
8. What is single-source data? Describe how a marketing manager could make use of single-source data to make (a) pricing decisions and (b) in-store promotions decisions.
9. Contact a radio or TV station or perhaps a newspaper in your town. Ask managers how they measure listenership, viewership, or readership and for what purposes they use this information. In most cases, these firms will be happy to supply you with a standard package of materials answering the preceding questions.
10. Given what you know about syndicated services, which firm would you call on if you had the following information needs?
    a. You want to know which magazines have the heaviest readership among tennis players.
    b. You have decided to conduct a test market but you have no research department within your firm and no experience in test marketing.
    c. You need to know how a representative sample of U.S. households would answer seven questions about dental hygiene.
    d. You are thinking about a radically new advertising theme but you are very concerned about consumer reaction to the new theme. You want some idea as to how the new theme will impact sales of your frozen dinners.
11. Go to ACNielsen's home page at www.acnielsen.com. Explore the products and services offered. Read about these products and services. Name four of these services and discuss why you believe these services are either syndicated data or standardized services.

INTERACTIVE LEARNING

Visit the Web site at www.prenhall.com/burnsbush. For this chapter, work through the Self-Study Quizzes, and get instant feedback on whether you need additional studying. On the Web site, you can review the chapter outlines and case information for Chapter 7.

CASE 7.1   Jazzy Teen Fashions[23]

Jazzy Teen Fashions is a chain of nine specialty stores located in enclosed malls in the Boston, Massachusetts, area. In business for five years, Jazzy Teen stores sell upscale clothing, shoes, and accessories to girls ages 10 to 15. With revenues increasing every year, Jazzy Teen was ready to expand and open three new stores in greater New England. The obvious choice was to look at other enclosed malls, but Jazzy Teen wanted to be sure that its new locations were in the correct market areas. The challenge was to identify and find the best three areas for the new stores. Jazzy Teen turned to ESRI Business Information Solutions to assist with the analyses.

The first step was to learn about the types of people who were Jazzy Teen customers. This was done by profiling the existing Jazzy Teen customers using data collected from several sources, including customer receipts, loyalty programs, coupons, phone numbers, and zip codes. After the customer data were collected and collated, ESRI Business Information Solutions appended ACORN segmentation data to each customer record and grouped them into segments according to their demographic similarities.

ACORN (**A C**lassification **o**f **R**esidential **N**eighborhoods) is the industry's original and most trusted segmentation system in existence today. It operates on the premise that people with similar interests and lifestyles tend to live in similar neighborhoods. ACORN can tell you how they live, where they live, what products and services they buy, and how you can reach them.

The ESRI Business Information Solutions (formerly CACI Marketing Systems) data demography staff grouped all of the U.S. neighborhoods into 40 residential and three nonresidential neighborhood segments using lifestyle characteristics such as age, income, household type, occupation, education, and other key behavioral variables. Several analytic techniques were used to produce statistically reliable solutions and to handle an immense amount of information.

ACORN may be used for a wide range of marketing applications including:

- *Consumer Profiling*—ACORN can find who the best consumers and prospects are by their demographic characteristics. By knowing who a client's consumers are, ACORN can help its client find more like them.
- *Data Appending*—ACORN is overlaid on many consumer lists. By adding ACORN segmentation data to a customer file, users may more precisely target current and potential customers.
- *Direct Marketing*—ACORN may be used to tailor direct-marketing messages to reach the consumers who might buy a client's product or service. ACORN segments the consumer types for direct-marketing campaigns.
- *Media Planning*—ACORN can help determine the types of media that will most effectively reach preferred consumers and prospects. Ad dollars may be saved by placing ads only in the media vehicles preferred by top consumers.
- *Merchandise Mix*—ACORN may be used to determine which products would appeal to the consumers in existing or potential locations.
- *Site Selection and Evaluation*—ACORN can profile the types of people who live and work near your sites. You can evaluate the performance of each site using lifestyle characteristics to determine merchandise mix.
- *Target Marketing*—Marketing campaigns can be planned to reach only those who would be interested in your product or service. ACORN can accurately segment targeted trade areas using demographic variables that fit your consumer profiles.

From the ACORN segmentation analysis, a typical customer profile emerged that Jazzy Teen could use as its prototype customer profile. Jazzy Teen learned that the obvious segments were families with girls in the 10–15 age bracket, but surprisingly strong targets were also found in segments of affluent seniors.

After the customer profile was created, ESRI Business Information Solutions added more precision to the Jazzy Teen profile with supplemental data such as purchase and spending potential indices and traffic data studies. Purchase potential data provide information about the possibility of a targeted segment to purchase certain products and services. Spending potential data provide information about the spending habits of a certain population segment. Because most of its customer base did not drive, ESRI Business Information Solutions added traffic studies to determine how far parents or friends might drive to reach a Jazzy Teen store.

Other factors considered in its evaluation were the cost of advertising and marketing promotions for each new store and the available real estate in the targeted areas. Based on these analyses, Jazzy Teen selected three sites and opened the new stores. In six months, each store had generated more than $1 million! Jazzy Teen plans further expansion and will use these analyses in its next series of evaluations.

1. Without using a standardized information service, what other alternatives could Jazzy Teen have used to make its new location decisions?
2. What advantages and disadvantages does the ACORN system have over other methods that Jazzy Teen could have used?

Chapter 8

Observation, Focus Groups, and Other Qualitative Methods

Learning Objectives:

To understand basic differences between quantitative and qualitative research techniques

To learn the pros and cons of using observation as a means of gathering data

To discover what focus groups are and how they are conducted and analyzed

To become acquainted with online focus groups and their advantages

To become familiar with other qualitative methods used by marketing researchers

Practitioner Viewpoint

Flexibility *and* convenience. *Two simple words that are some of the primary reasons that the Internet has become the new medium that is revolutionizing every aspect of business. The flexibility of the Internet allows you to get the goods, services, or information that you want specifically tailored to your needs, and the convenience allows you to receive that information wherever you are and at whatever time you want it.*

Flexibility and convenience are also two of the reasons that the marketing research industry is now rushing to embrace the Internet. Although the research industry has sometimes been slow to adopt new technology, the industry embrace of the Internet is encouraging. Now to go along with our first two words is another term: streaming media. *This technology has begun to play a more important role not only to the Web in general but also to the research industry in particular.*

Streaming media allows clients to watch and participate in qualitative events from their desktops on their own schedules. It will allow consumers to view and rate ads online rather than in a mall facility, and it will eventually allow for true virtual groups in which each respondent and the moderator are all in different places. All of these items are designed to save the client time and money while getting targeted data faster.

David Nelems, President
ActiveGroup

Focus Group Research Helps Kool Aid Target Its Heavy Users

The wide grin on the Kool Aid pitcher dropped quite a bit in the late 1990s. Despite selling about 500 million gallons per year and enjoying virtually universal awareness among mothers of small children and about one-third penetration in all U.S. households, sales declined steadily through the end of the last decade of the twentieth century. Why the decline? Kool Aid managers scratched their heads and some hypothesized that sugary drinks were becoming unpopular, whereas others commented on the growing trend toward ready-to-drink-or-go beverages, such as Fruitopia and Crystal Lite, that are a better fit to families' hectic lifestyles than is mix-it-up Kool Aid.

Kool Aid turned to market research and commissioned a focus group company to conduct 11 focus groups, ordered by Kool Aid usage with its heavy users as well as with light or former Kool Aid buyers. The findings for the heavy users were amazingly insightful. Heavy Kool Aid users were typically African Americans who fell into a lifestyle segment called "home-centered entertainers," meaning that they were families that stayed at home more than other segments. In addition, the focus groups with the heavy users revealed that they added a lot more than just water to their Kool Aid. These individuals buy Kool Aid at least once per month on the average, and they often add fruits such as grapes, oranges, or pineapples to their Kool Aid. At other times, they add club soda or fruit juice to fortify the taste. They make Kool Aid concoctions like Banana Yogurt Smoothie, Tropical Tornado Punch, and Orange-Pineapple Shake. Because they are home centered, they have no problem with the mix-it-up-at-home aspect of Kool Aid, and they do not worry about carrying their Kool Aid places as it is consumed at home. Furthermore, the adults in the heavy users segment are just as likely to drink Kool Aid as are their kids.

Marketing research helped Kool Aid understand its market.

Where We Are:

1. Establish the need for marketing research
2. Define the problem
3. Establish research objectives
4. Determine research design
5. Identify information types and sources
6. **Determine methods of accessing data**
7. Design data collection forms
8. Determine sample plan and size
9. Collect data
10. Analyze data
11. Prepare and present the final research report

Qualitative research helped Kool Aid find its really heavy users.

Fortified with this information, Kool Aid's advertising agency brainstormed ad themes and used focus groups to get reactions from the heavy Kool Aid users. It was found that multigenerational family-and-friends themes centered in the house or the backyard were very appealing to these consumers. Furthermore, the revelation that they "customize" their Kool Aid led to an ad feature in which Kool Aid users are shown describing what they add to their Kool Aid to jazz it up.[1]

This chapter deals with qualitative methods, referred to by some people as the "soft side" of marketing research. But as the Kool Aid example reveals, these methods can be very illuminating. At the same time, they are increasingly combined with high-tech systems to maximize their effectiveness. Qualitative methods are techniques that typically do not generate the huge amounts of data associated with surveys. You will find that each qualitative method has its place in the marketing research process, and that each has its unique advantages and disadvantages as well. Because focus groups are a popular qualitative marketing research technique, an in-depth discussion of them is included. We begin with a discussion of quantitative, qualitative, and pluralistic research.

QUANTITATIVE, QUALITATIVE, AND PLURALISTIC RESEARCH

The means of data collection during the research process can be classified into three broad categories: quantitative, qualitative, and pluralistic. There are vast differences between the first two methods, and it is necessary to understand their special characteristics in order to make the right selection. To start, we briefly define these two approaches and then we describe pluralistic research.

Quantitative research is the traditional mainstay of the research industry, and it is sometimes referred to as "survey research." For our purposes in this chapter, **quantitative research** is defined as research involving the use of structured questions in which the response options have been predetermined and a large number of respondents is involved. When you think of quantitative research, you might envision a nationwide survey conducted with telephone interviews. That is, quantitative research often involves a sizable representative sample of the population and a formalized procedure for gathering data. The purpose of quantitative research is very specific, and this research is used when the manager and researcher have agreed that precise information is needed. Data format and sources are clear and well defined, and the compilation and formatting of the data gathered follows an orderly procedure that is largely numerical in nature.

> Quantitative research involves a structured questionnaire and a large sample.

Qualitative research, in contrast, involves collecting, analyzing, and interpreting data by observing what people do and say. Observations and statements are in a qualitative or nonstandardized form. Because of this, qualitative data can be quantified but only after a translation process has taken place. For example, if you asked five people to express their opinions on a topic such as gun control or promoting alcoholic beverages to college students, you would probably get five different statements. But after studying each response, you could characterize each one as "positive," "negative," or "neutral." This translation step would not be necessary if you instructed them to choose predetermined responses such as "yes" or "no." Any study that is conducted using an observational technique or unstructured questioning can be classified as qualitative research, which is becoming increasingly popular in a number of research situations.[2]

> Qualitative research involves observing and/or asking open-ended questions, usually with a small number of informants.

Qualitative research reveals how shoppers react to store displays.

Why would you want to use such a "soft" approach? Occasionally, marketing researchers find that a large-scale survey is inappropriate. For instance, Procter & Gamble may be interested in improving its Tide laundry detergent, so it invites a group of homemakers to sit down with some of Tide's marketing personnel and brainstorm how Tide could perform better, how its packaging could be improved, or discuss other features of the detergent. Listening to the market in this way can generate excellent packaging, product design, or even product positioning ideas. As another example, if the Procter & Gamble marketing group were developing a special end-of-aisle display for Tide, it might want to test one version in an actual supermarket environment. It could place one in a Safeway grocery store located in a San Francisco suburb and videotape shoppers as they encountered the display. The marketing group would then review the videotape and see if the display generated the types of responses they hoped it would. For instance, did shoppers stop there? Did they read the copy on the display? Did they pick up the displayed product and look at it? Qualitative research techniques afford rich insight into consumer behavior.[3]

With the rush to online quantitative research that produces huge amounts of data, qualitative research is sometimes overlooked.[4] However, it is our goal in this chapter to show you the value of qualitative research techniques and, as you will see very soon, to convince you of the need for qualitative research and quantitative research to work hand in hand.

Although there are proponents of both types of research, many marketing researchers have adopted **pluralistic research,** which is defined as the combination of qualitative and quantitative research methods in order to gain the advantages of both. With pluralistic research, it is common to begin with exploratory qualitative techniques as, for example, in-depth interviews of selected dealers or a series of group discussions with customers in order to understand how they perceive your product and service as compared to those of competitors. Even an observational study could be used if it is helpful in understanding the problem and bringing to the surface issues in the research project. These activities often help crystallize the problem or otherwise open the researcher's eyes to factors and considerations that might be overlooked if he or she rushed into a full-scale survey. The qualitative phase serves as a foundation for the quantitative phase of the research project because it

Pluralistic research combines the advantages of both qualitative research and quantitative research.

With pluralistic research, the qualitative phase is the foundation for the quantitative phase.

Pluralistic research enables marketers to completely understand their target markets.

provides the researcher with firsthand knowledge of the research problem. Armed with this knowledge, the researcher's design and execution of the quantitative phase are invariably superior to what they might have been without the qualitative phase. With pluralistic research, the qualitative phase serves to frame the subsequent quantitative phase, and in some cases, a qualitative phase is applied after a quantitative study to help the researcher understand the findings in the quantitative phase.

The pluralistic approach is becoming increasingly popular, especially with emerging and complex marketing phenomena. We have provided Marketing Research Insight 8.1 that shows how a pluralistic program combined qualitative and quantitative research techniques to yield an understanding of the differences between men and women online as well as identifying different online segments with each gender. Speaking of online, the flexibility of Web-based research facilitates pluralistic research. For example, *The Arizona Republic* has a research system in which online focus groups are used for brainstorming, and the outcomes of these sessions are then expanded into online surveys. Through this pluralistic approach, *The Arizona Republic* has identified local news and happenings and transportation issues/information to be the most important topics to its readers, whereas politics and sports are the least important topics. It has responded with its content accordingly.[5]

It is best to consider qualitative and quantitative methods as partners and not as competitors.

OBSERVATION TECHNIQUES

Observation methods typically rely on recording devices as the researcher's memory alone can be faulty.

Qualitative techniques include the class of **observation methods**—techniques in which the researcher relies on his or her powers of observation rather than communicating with a person in order to obtain information. Observation requires something to observe, and because our memories are faulty, researchers depend on recording devices such as videotapes, audiotapes, handwritten notes, or some other tangible record of what is observed. As we describe each observation technique, you will see that each is unique in how it obtains observations.

Types of Observation

At first glance, it may seem that observation studies can occur without any structure; however, it is important to adhere to a plan so that the observations are consistent and comparisons or generalizations can be made without worrying about any

▶ **An Online Application**

MARKETING RESEARCH
INSIGHT
8.1

Pluralistic Research Identifies Online Buyer Segments and Distinct Purchasing Behaviors

Because online purchase behavior is an emerging phenomenon, a pluralistic approach that utilizes both qualitative research techniques and quantitative methods is the most appropriate way to investigate it. Accordingly, market researchers combined the following research techniques as a strategy to reveal online buyer market segments.

Focus groups, which are moderated discussions conducted with groups of 8 to 12 online buyers, were used to gain a basic understanding of online buying such as why, where, when, and how often. The focus groups uncovered basic differences between women and men online buyers.

Depth interviews, which are personal interviews lasting from 30 to 45 minutes, were then utilized in order to probe motivations for online purchasing, including functional as

well as emotional reasons for buying online. These depth interviews also sought to tap into personal styles for online information search and processing.

An online survey was conducted via e-mail invitations to about 40,000 Internet users. The online questionnaire contained questions about demographics, lifestyle, Internet usage, preferences for Internet delivery formats, and importance of various Internet content types (such as news, entertainment, travel, family, etc.).

The online survey data were subjected to various analyses, and they resulted in the discovery of five distinct female online user segments as well as five separate male online user segments. The segments and their key differences are noted in the following table.

Online Segments and Key Differences Revealed by Pluralistic Research

SEGMENT	PERCENT	DEMOGRAPHICS	KEY ONLINE USAGE	ONLINE FAVORITES
Female Segments				
Social Sally	14%	30–40, college educated	Making friends	Chat and personal Web space
New Age Crusader	21%	40–50, highest income level	Fight for causes	Books and government information
Cautious Mom	24%	30–45, with children	Nurture children	Cooking and medical facts
Playful Pretender	20%	Youngest, many are students	Role play	Chat and games
Master Producer	20%	Tends to be single	Job productivity	White pages and government information
Male Segments				
Bits and Bytes	11%	Young and single	Computers and hobbies	Investments, discovery, software
Practical Pete	21%	40ish, some college, above-average income	Personal productivity	Investments, company listings
Viking Gamer	19%	Young or old, least college education	Competing and winning	Games, chat, software
Sensitive Sam	21%	Highest education and income of males	Help family and friends	Investments, government information
World Citizen	28%	50 and older, most with college education	Connecting with world	Discovery, software, investments

These are only thumbnail descriptions of these 10 different online market segments. Much more detail is provided in the original descriptions,[6] and it is important to note that

such complete understanding of these emerging online types is possible only through the use of pluralistic research.

conditions of the observation method that might confound the findings. There are four general ways of organizing observations: (1) direct versus indirect, (2) disguised versus undisguised, (3) structured versus unstructured, and (4) human versus mechanical.

Direct Versus Indirect

Observing behavior as it occurs is called **direct observation.**[7] For example, if we are interested in finding out how much shoppers squeeze tomatoes to assess their freshness, we can observe people actually picking up the tomatoes. Direct observation has been used by Kellogg to understand breakfast rituals, by a Swiss chocolate maker to study the behavior of "chocoholics," and by the U.S. Post Office's advertising agency to come up with the advertising slogan "We Deliver."[8] It has also been used by General Mills to understand how children eat breakfast, leading to the launch of "Go-Gurt," a midmorning snack for school children.[9]

In order to observe types of hidden behavior, such as past behavior, we must rely on indirect observation. With **indirect observation,** the researcher observes the effects or results of the behavior rather than the behavior itself. Types of indirect observations include archives and physical traces.

Archives are secondary sources such as historical records that can be applied to the present problem. These sources contain a wealth of information and should not be overlooked or underestimated. Many types of archives exist. For example, records of sales calls may be inspected to determine how often salespersons make cold calls. Warehouse inventory movements can be used to study market shifts. Scanner data may afford insight on the effects of price changes, promotion campaigns, or package size changes.

Physical traces are tangible evidence of some event. For example, we might turn to "garbology" (observing the trash of subjects being studied) as a way of finding out how much recycling of plastic milk bottles occurs. A soft-drink company might do a litter audit in order to assess how much impact its aluminum cans have on the countryside. A fast-food company such as Wendy's might measure the amount of graffiti on buildings located adjacent to prospective location sites as a means of estimating the crime potential for each site.[10]

Observation may be direct or indirect.

Archives and physical traces are forms of indirect observation.

Physical traces of graffiti can help Wendy's find desirable new locations.

Disguised Versus Undisguised

With **disguised observation**, the subject is unaware that he or she is being observed. An example of this method might be a "secret shopper" who is used by a retail store chain to record and report on sales clerks' assistance and courtesy. One-way mirrors and hidden cameras are a few of the other ways that are used to prevent subjects from becoming aware that they are being observed. This disguise is important because if the subjects were aware of the observation, it is possible that they would change their behavior, resulting in observations of atypical behavior. If you were a store clerk, how would you act if the department manager told you that he would be watching you for the next hour? You would probably be on your best behavior for the next 60 minutes. Disguised observation has proved illuminating in studies of parents and children shopping together in supermarkets.[11] With direct questions, parents might feel compelled to say that their children are always on their best behavior while shopping.

Sometimes it is impossible for the respondent to be unaware of the observation, and this is a case of **undisguised observation.** Laboratory settings, observing a sales representative's behavior on sales calls, and people meters (a device that is attached to a television set to record when and to what station a set is tuned) must all be used with the subject's knowledge. Because people might be influenced by knowing they are being observed, it is wise to always minimize the presence of the observer to the maximum extent possible.

The use of observation raises ethical questions. Should people being observed be informed of the observation, and, if so, what changes might they make in their behavior in order to appear "normal" or conform to what they think is expected? The researcher wants to observe behavior as it actually occurs even if it is unusual or out of the ordinary. However, people being observed might feel uncomfortable about their habits or actions and try to act in more conventional ways. For instance, if a family agrees to have its television set wired so a researcher can track what programs the family watches, will the parents make sure that the children watch mainly wholesome shows such as those on the Disney Channel? Sometimes researchers resort to deceit in order to observe people without their knowledge, but this is an unethical practice. The ethical practice is to inform people ahead of time and give them an "adjustment period" or, if such a period is not feasible, to fully debrief them of the observation afterward.

> With disguised observation, subjects are unaware they are being studied, whereas with undisguised observation, they are aware they are being studied.

Structured Versus Unstructured

When using **structured observation** techniques, the researcher identifies beforehand which behaviors are to be observed and recorded. All other behaviors are "ignored." Often a checklist or a standardized observation form is used to isolate the observer's attention to specific factors. These highly structured observations typically require a minimum of effort on the part of the observer.

Unstructured observation places no restriction on what the observer would note: All behavior in the episode under study is monitored. The observer just watches the situation and records what he or she deems interesting or relevant. Of course, the observer is thoroughly briefed on the area of general concern. This type of observation is often used in exploratory research. For example, Black and Decker might send someone to observe carpenters working at various job sites as a means of better understanding how the tools are used and to help generate ideas as to how to design the tools for increased safety.

> Observation may be structured or unstructured.

Human Versus Mechanical

With **human observation,** the observer is a person hired by the researcher, or, perhaps, the observer is the researcher. However, it is often possible, desirable, and economical[12] to replace the human observer with some form of static observing device,

Scanners and audiometers are forms of mechanical observation.

as in **mechanical observation.** This substitution may be made because of accuracy, cost, or functional reasons. Auto traffic counts may be more accurate and less costly when recorded by machines that are activated by car tires rolling over them. Besides, during rush hour, a human observer could not count the number of cars on most major metropolitan commuter roads. Nor would it be possible to count the number of fans entering a gate at a professional football title game, so turnstile counts are used instead. Scanning devices are used to count the number and types of products sold (see Chapter 7). Mechanical devices may also be used when it is too expensive to use human observers. For example, a people meter is used instead of a human observer to record families' television viewing habits. As these examples illustrate, mechanical observation has moved into the high-technology area recently, and the combination of telecommunications, computer hardware, and software programs has created a very useful research tool.

Appropriate Conditions for the Use of Observation

Certain conditions must be met before a researcher can successfully use observation as a marketing research tool. These conditions are the event must occur in a short time interval, the observed behavior must occur in a public setting, and when the possibility of faulty recall rules out collecting information by asking the person.

Successful observations are of short duration, are public, and when conditions leading to faulty recall are present.

Short time interval means that the event must begin and end within a reasonably short time span. Examples include a shopping trip in a supermarket, waiting in a teller line at a bank, purchasing a clothing item, or observing children as they watch a television program. Some decision-making processes can take a long time (for example, buying a home), and it would be unrealistic in terms of the time and money required to observe the entire process. Because of this factor, observational research is usually limited to scrutinizing activities that can be completed in a relatively short time span or to observing certain phases of those activities with a long time span.

Public behavior refers to behavior that occurs in a setting the researcher can readily observe. Actions such as cooking, playing with one's children, or private worshipping are not public activities and are, therefore, not suitable for observational studies such as those described here.

Faulty recall occurs when actions or activities are so repetitive or automatic that the respondent cannot recall specifics about the behavior under question. For example, people cannot recall accurately how many times they looked at their wristwatch while waiting in a long line to buy a ticket to a best-selling movie, or which FM radio station they listened to last Thursday at 2:00 P.M. Observation is necessary under circumstances of faulty recall to fully understand the behavior at hand. For instance, an observation technique called "actual radio measurement" using a high-gain antenna, digital frequency scanner, and computer can be used to determine which radio stations were listened to by commuters in their cars.[13]

Advantages of Observational Data

Sometimes observation is the only way to gain an accurate picture of the behavior of interest.

Ideally, the subjects of observational research are unaware they are being studied. Because of this they react in a natural manner, giving the researcher insight into actual, not reported, behaviors. As previously noted, observational research methods also mean that there is no chance for recall error. The subjects are not asked what they remember about a certain action. Instead, they are observed while engaged in the act. In some cases, observation may be the only way to obtain accurate information. For instance, children who cannot yet verbally express their opinion of a new toy will do so by simply playing or not playing with the toy. Retail marketers commonly gather marketing intelligence about competitors and about their own employees' behaviors by hiring the services of "mystery shoppers" who pose as customers but who are actually trained observers.[14] In some situations, data can be obtained with better accuracy and less cost by using observational methods as opposed to other means. For example, counts of in-store traffic can often be made by means of observational techniques more accurately and less expensively than by using survey techniques.

Such advantages of observational research methods should not be interpreted as meaning that this technique is always in competition with other approaches. A resourceful researcher will use observation techniques to supplement and complement other techniques.[15] When used in combination with other techniques, each approach can serve as a check on the results obtained by the other. Actually, observation of humans in their natural context is the approach that has been used by anthropologists for over 100 years and has recently become accepted as a method of marketing research.[16]

Observation can be used to supplement and complement other research techniques.

Limitations of Observational Data

The limitations of observation are the limitations inherent in qualitative research in general. With direct observation, typically only small numbers of subjects are studied and usually under special circumstances, so their representativeness is a concern.[17] This factor, plus the subjective interpretation required to explain the observed behavior, usually forces the researcher to consider his or her conclusions to be tentative. Certainly, the greatest drawback of all observational methods is the researcher's inability to pry beneath the behavior observed and to interrogate the person on motives, attitudes, and all of the other unseen aspects of why what was observed took place.

Due to small samples and the need for interpretation, conclusions based on observation are usually considered to be tentative.

To recap, a limitation of observation is that motivations, attitudes, and other internal conditions cannot be observed. Only when these feelings are relatively unimportant or readily inferred from the behavior is it appropriate to use observational research methods. For example, facial expression might be used as an indicator of a child's attitudes or preferences for various types of fruit drink flavors because children often react with conspicuous physical expressions. But adults and even children usually conceal their reasons and true reactions in public, and this fact necessitates a direct questioning approach because observation alone cannot give a complete picture of why and how people act the way they do.

With observation, you cannot tell what is going on beneath the surface behavior.

FOCUS GROUPS

As we indicated, there are several types of qualitative research, but the technique most often associated with this category is the focus group. A **focus group** is a small group of people brought together and guided by a moderator through an unstructured, spontaneous discussion about some topic. The goal of a focus group is to draw out ideas, feelings, and experiences about a certain issue that would be obscured or stifled by more structured methods of data collection. The use of a small group allows the operation of group dynamics and aids in making the participants feel comfortable in a strange environment. It is called a "focus" group because the moderator serves to focus the discussion on the topic and does not let the group move off onto tangents or irrelevant points. Focus groups have become so popular in marketing research that every large city has a number of companies that specialize in performing focus group research. You can be assured that you will encounter focus group research if you become a practicing marketing manager. "Almost nothing gets done without them,"[18] says Bill Hillsman, a successful advertising executive

Focus groups are small group discussions led by a trained moderator.

whose campaigns have worked for the Minnesota Twins, the Dales shopping centers, and Arctic Cat snowmobiles. Focus groups are an invaluable means of regaining contact with customers when marketers have lost touch, and they are very helpful in learning about new customer groups.

Some Objectives of Focus Groups

Focus groups have four main objectives.

There are four main objectives of focus groups: to generate ideas; to understand consumer vocabulary; to reveal consumer needs, motives, perceptions, and attitudes on products or services; and to understand findings from quantitative studies.

To generate ideas means to use the focus group as a starting point for new product or service ideas, uses, or improvements. Read Marketing Research Insight 8.2 as it depicts how this brainstorming can occur in a focus group. Notice the improvements that are suggested for Fujifilm's digital cameras.

To understand consumer vocabulary means to use the focus group to stay abreast of the words and phrases consumers use when describing products so as to improve product or service communication with them. Such information may help

---

MARKETING RESEARCH
INSIGHT
8.2

Additional Insights ◀

What a Brainstorming Focus Group "Sounds" Like

Background: Fujifilm is considering redesigning its digital cameras and film to make them more user friendly, and it is using focus group research to understand what problems consumers encounter when using digital cameras. Here is part of the transcript. Notice how the moderator directs or focuses the discussion, and notice also how the focus group participants stimulate each others' comments.

Moderator: What other problems have you encountered with your digital camera?

Mary: Well, we have a digital camera that has a lot of automatic features such as focusing and sensing when the flash should be used. Oh, and it has a red eye feature that eliminates those red demon eyes that people have when you use a regular flash.

Moderator: What about problems with the camera? Let's talk about difficulties or frustrations with your digital camera.

Mary: Oh, it is a bit of a problem to hook up my USB cable to it. The "plug-in" thingy only goes one way, and it take me a couple of tries to get it right.

Sally: Yes, and sometimes you use up all of your storage capacity without warning. I have lost one or two good photo opportunities because my digital camera was full.

Gene: Yes, I agree. It's a pain having to review your shots and decide which ones to delete so you can free up more storage space.

Mary: I bet there is some way that they could make a storage cartridge that would snap into the camera when you run out of storage space.

Gail: Yes, but first I would want them to give me some warning that I was about to run out. With conventional cameras, you can see how many shots you have taken and easily figure out how many you have left before you need to change the film.

Gene: Yes, I agree that it would be great to have a counter that would tell me how many shots I have left. When I use my digital camera, I take two or three snaps of the same shot to make sure I will have one good one, so I often find that I am out of storage space. And the pop-in extra cartridge would be great, too.

Gail: Yes, that's what we need—a countdown feature and maybe a warning tone or beep when I am close to using up all of the storage space in the cartridge I have in the camera.

Moderator: Can you think of any other ways that the companies that market digital cameras might be able to change their products so they are more helpful to you?

Sally: I have a problem seeing details in my pictures when I use the viewer in bright sunlight. I have to put my hand over the viewer screen like a visor to shade it so I can see the detail. I practically have to run inside in order to see if I took a good picture.

Moderator: What else about the photo reviewing system? Does anyone have any ideas on a better system?

in advertising copy design or in the preparation of an instruction pamphlet. This knowledge refines research problem definitions and also helps structure questions for use in later quantitative research.

To reveal consumer needs, motives, perceptions, and attitudes on products or services means to use the focus group to refresh the marketing team as to what customers really feel or think about a product or service. Alternatively, managers may need early customer reactions to changes being considered in products or services.[19] Focus groups are commonly used during the exploratory phase of research.[20] This application is useful in generating objectives to be addressed by subsequent research.

To understand findings from quantitative studies means to use focus groups to better comprehend data gathered from other surveys. Sometimes a focus group can reveal why the findings came out a particular way.

Warner-Lambert is a company that has successfully used focus groups to accomplish all four of these objectives. Its consumer health products group, which markets over-the-counter health and beauty products as well as nonprescription drugs, uses focus groups extensively.[21] In fact, Warner-Lambert uses a combination of qualitative research techniques to gain background information, to reveal needs and attitudes related to health and beauty products, to interpret the results of qualitative studies, and to stimulate brainstorming new ideas. Focus groups have been useful in understanding basic shifts in consumer lifestyles, values, and purchase patterns.

> A focus group will help a marketer "get in touch" with target customers.

Operational Questions About Focus Groups

Before a focus group is conducted, certain operational questions should be addressed. It is important to decide how many people should take part in a focus group, who they should be, how they will be selected and recruited, and where they should meet. General guidelines exist for answering these questions. A discussion of each follows.

What Should Be the Size of a Focus Group? According to industry wisdom, the optimal size of a focus group is 6 to 12 people. A small group (fewer than six participants) is not likely to generate the energy and group dynamics necessary for a truly beneficial focus group session. With fewer participants, it is common that one or two of the participants do most of the talking in spite of the moderator's efforts. At the same time, a small group will often result in awkward silences and force the moderator to take too active a role in the discussion just to keep the discussion alive. Similarly, a group with over a dozen participants will ordinarily prove too large to be conducive to a natural discussion. As a focus group becomes larger in size it tends to become fragmented. Those participating may become frustrated by the inherent digressions and side comments. Conversations may break out among two or three participants while another is talking. This situation places the moderator in the role of disciplinarian in which he or she is constantly calling for quiet or order rather than focusing the discussion on the issues at hand.

> The accepted size of a focus group is 6 to 12 participants.

Unfortunately, it is often difficult to predict the exact number of people who will attend the focus group interview. Ten may agree to participate and only 4 may show up. Fourteen may be invited in hopes that 8 will show up, and all 14 may arrive. Of course, if this occurs, the researcher faces a judgment call as to whether or not to send some home. In the worst case, a researcher may run into a situation in which no one attends, despite promises to the contrary. There is no guaranteed method that will ensure a successful participation ratio. Incentives (which will be discussed later) are helpful but definitely not a certain way of gaining acceptance. So although 6 to 12 is the ideal focus group size range, it is not uncommon to have some groups with fewer than 6 and some with more than 12.

> With a focus group of fewer than 6 participants, group dynamics may not work well, and with more than 12, control of the group is difficult.

Who Should Be in the Focus Group? It is generally believed that the best focus groups are ones in which the participants share homogenous characteristics. This requirement is sometimes automatically satisfied by the researcher's need to have particular types of people in the focus group. For instance, the focus group may be comprised of executives who use satellite phones, it may involve building contractors who specialize in building customer residences over $500,000 in value, or it might involve a group of salespeople who are experiencing some common customer service difficulty.

> Focus groups work best with participants who share similar characteristics.

The need for similar demographic or other relevant characteristics in the focus group members is accentuated by the fact that the focus group participants are typically strangers. In most cases, they are not friends or even casual acquaintances, and many people feel intimidated or at least hesitant to voice their opinions and suggestions to a group of strangers. But participants typically feel more comfortable once they realize they have similarities such as their age (they may all be in their early thirties), job situations (they may all be junior executives), family composition (they may all have preschool children), purchase experiences (they may all have bought a new car in the past year), or even leisure pursuits (they may all play tennis). Furthermore, by conducting a group that is as homogenous as possible with respect to demographics and other characteristics, the researcher is assured that differences in these variables will be less likely to confuse the issue being discussed.

How Should Focus Group Participants Be Recruited and Selected? As you can guess, the selection of focus group participants is determined largely by the purpose of the focus group. For instance, if the purpose is to generate new ideas on digital camera improvements, the participants must be consumers who have used a digital camera. If the focus group is intended to elicit building contractors' reactions to a new type of central air-conditioning unit, it will be necessary to recruit building contractors. It is not unusual for companies to provide customer lists or for focus group recruiters to work from secured lists of potential participants. For instance, with building contractors, the list might come from the local Yellow Pages or a building contractor trade association membership roster. In any case, it is necessary to initially contact prospective participants by telephone to qualify them and then to solicit their cooperation in the focus group. Occasionally, a focus group company may recruit by requesting shoppers in a mall to participate, but this approach is rare.

> Focus group participants are often recruited by telephone and are provided an incentive for participating.

As we noted earlier, "no shows" are a problem with focus groups, and researchers have at least two strategies to entice prospective participants. First, incentives of various types are used. These range from monetary compensation for the participant's time to free products or gift certificates. Second, many focus group companies use call-backs during the day immediately prior to the focus group to remind prospective participants that they have agreed to take part. If one prospective participant indicates that some conflict has arisen and he or she cannot be there, it is then possible to recruit a replacement. Neither approach works perfectly, as we indicated earlier, and anticipating how many participants will show up is always a concern. Some focus group companies have a policy of overrecruiting, and others have lists of people they can rely on to participate, given that they fit the qualifications.

> "No shows" are a worry with focus groups, and overrecruiting is one way to deal with this problem.

The difficulties encountered by focus group companies in recruiting focus group participants have led to some questionable practices. Some people like to participate in focus groups, and a focus group company may keep a list of willing participants. Other participants may want to take part simply for the monetary compensation, and their names may be on the focus group company's list as well. In either case, inclusion of those people who have previously participated in numerous focus groups can lead to serious validity problems. Some researchers will explicitly disallow a focus group company to use these participants because of this concern. As a matter of policy, some focus group companies will always report the last time, if ever, that each focus group member participated in a focus group. Other companies will do so only if the client firm makes an explicit request for this information.

Where Should a Focus Group Meet? Obviously, if a group discussion is to take place for a period of 90 minutes or more, it is important that the physical arrangement of the group be comfortable and conducive to group discussion. So focus groups ideally are conducted in large rooms set up in a roundtable format. An advertising company conference room, a moderator's home, a respondent's home, the client's office, hotels, and meeting rooms at churches are all locations in which focus groups can be held. Aside from a seating arrangement where participants can all see one another, the second critical requirement in selecting a meeting place is to find one quiet enough to permit an intelligible audiotaping of the sessions.

The ideal setting for a focus group is a **focus group facility**, which is a set of rooms especially designed for focus groups at a marketing research company specializing in conducting focus groups. The focus group room itself contains a large table and comfortable chairs, a relaxing atmosphere, and a one-way mirror so that clients can view the interviewing process. Ample space for video and audio equipment should also be provided. An example of a typical floor plan for a focus group facility is provided in Figure 8.1. Because focus group research is qualitative, it generates many diverse pieces of information. Rather than relying on memory, which can be faulty, or relying on the moderator's taking notes, which can slow down and distract the process, most focus groups are audiotaped and many are videotaped. You can see from the floor plan in Figure 8.1 that a focus group company's facilities have recording capabilities designed into them. Microphones are built into the walls or ceiling or otherwise set in the center of the table, and videotape equipment often operates from an inconspicuous location. One-way mirrors also allow clients to observe the focus group as it takes place.

In the past, companies have tried to hide or disguise the equipment they used to record respondents' reactions. This was done in an attempt to remove any feelings of self-consciousness or awkwardness that might result in the respondents' interviews by being taped. However, such a practice is unethical, and few participants are tricked anyway. Now it is common practice to let participants know about the recording aspect when they are recruited. If they have any objections, they can decline at that time.

The Focus Group Moderator's Role and Responsibilities By now, you realize that the most crucial factor influencing the effectiveness and usefulness of a focus group is the moderator.[22] A **focus group moderator** is a person who conducts the entire session and guides the flow of group discussion across specific topics desired by the client. The moderator must strive for a very delicate balance between stimulating, natural discussions among all of the group members while ensuring that the focus of the discussion does not stray too far from the topic. A good moderator must have excellent observation, interpersonal, and communication skills to recognize and overcome threats to a productive group discussion. He or she must be prepared, experienced, and armed with a detailed list of topics to be discussed.[23] It is also helpful if the focus group moderator can eliminate any preconceptions on the topic from his or her mind. The best moderators are experienced, enthusiastic, prepared, involved, energetic, and open-minded.[24]

The focus group's success depends on the participants' involvement in the discussion and in their understanding of what is being asked of them. Productive involvement is largely a result of the moderator's effectiveness, which in turn is

Focus group facilities operated by focus group companies have the best locations for focus groups because of their layouts and equipment.

Focus groups are recorded on audiotape and sometimes videotape.

A successful group requires an effective moderator.

A good moderator is experienced, enthusiastic, prepared, involved, energetic, and open-minded.

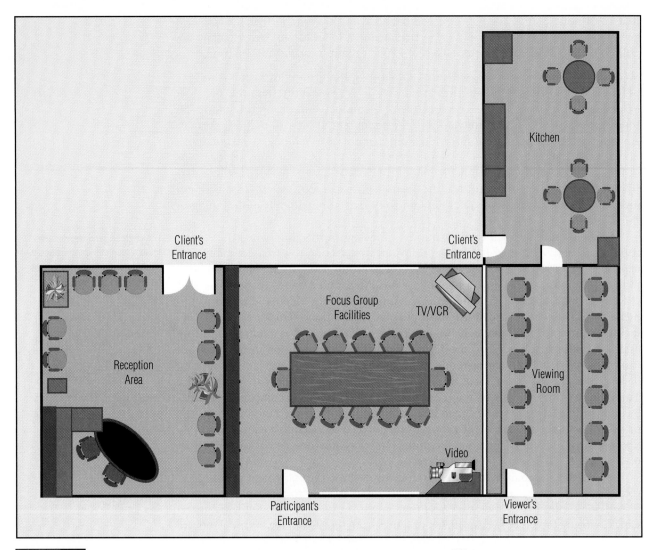

Figure 8.1   **The Floor Plan of a Focus Group Facility Reveals How One Operates[25]**

dependent on his or her understanding of the purpose and objectives of the inter-view. Unless the moderator understands what information the researcher is after and why, he or she will not be able to phrase questions effectively. It is good policy to have the moderator contribute to the development of the project's goals so as to guide the discussion topics. By aiding in the formation of the topics (questions), he or she will be familiar with them and will be better prepared to conduct the group. It is important when formulating questions that they be organized into a logical sequence and that the moderator follow this sequence to the furthest extent possible. With an incompetent moderator, the focus group can become a disaster. Unfortunately, there are no industry standards or certification systems for focus group moderators, but we have found some trade secrets of successful moderators. You will find them in Table 8.1.

The moderator's introductory remarks are influential; they set the tone of the entire session. All subsequent questions should be prefaced with a clear explana-tion of how the participants should respond, for example, how they really feel per-

The focus group topic guide should be prepared with the moderator's involvement.

| Table **8.1** | **Focus Group Moderators' "Tricks of the Trade"** |

The following trade secrets were divulged by experienced focus group moderators at a recent panel at the annual conference of the Qualitative Research Consultants Association.[26]

QUESTION	TRICKS OF THE TRADE
How do you make your groups great every time?	• Be prepared. • Be energized. • Be nice but firm. • Make sure *everything* about the experience is comfortable.
How do you build rapport quickly?	• Make meaningful eye contact during each person's introduction. • Learn and remember names. • Let them create their own name cards. • Welcome folks as they come into the room and use small talk.
How do you bring a drifting group back into focus?	• Tell them the topic is "for another group" and that they need to focus on the topic for this group. • Make a note and tell them that they will come back to this topic if there is time. • Tell them the topic is "interesting" but not the subject at hand and refer to the next question. • Suggest that they can talk about it on their own after the focus group is over.
How do you get them to talk about deeper things than top-of-the-mind answers?	• Play naïve or dumb and ask them to help you understand by explaining. • Use probes such as "Tell us more about that," or "Can you go deeper on that?" • Ask for specifics such as "Tell me about the last time that you . . ." • Pair them up and give them 10 minutes for each pair to come up with a solution or suggestion.
What about management of the "back room" where your clients are observing?	• Orient clients with a 10-minute overview of focus groups, research objectives, and what to expect. • Check with the client(s) during breaks, written exercises, and so on to make sure things are going well. • Have an associate or colleague there to work with the client(s). • If you don't have an associate for the back room, ask the client to select one person to be the point person to communicate with you.

sonally, not how they think they should feel. This allows the moderator to establish a rapport with participants and to lay the groundwork for the interview's structure.

Reporting and Use of Focus Group Results As we noted earlier, focus groups report some of the subtle and obscure features of the relationships among consumers and products, advertising, and sales efforts. They furnish qualitative data on such things as consumer language; emotional and behavioral reactions to advertising; lifestyle; relationships; the product category and specific brand; and unconscious consumer motivations relative to product design, packaging, promotion, or any other facet of the marketing program under study. But focus group results are qualitative and not perfectly representative of the general population.

Focus group transcripts must be translated before they are reported.

Two important factors must be remembered when analyzing the data. First, some sense must be made by translating the qualitative statements of participants into categories and then reporting the degree of consensus apparent in the focus groups.[27] Second, the demographic and buyer behavior characteristics of focus group participants should be judged against the target market profile to assess to what degree the groups represent the target market.

Focus group information is evaluated by an analyst who carefully observes the recorded tapes several times, transcribing any relevant statements that seem evident. These statements are then subjected to closer evaluation. This evaluation is based on the analyst's knowledge of the history and statement of the problem plus his or her own interpretation of the responses. A detailed report is prepared for the client's review.

A focus group analysis should identify the major themes as well as salient areas of disagreement among the participants.

The focus group report reflects the qualitative aspect of this research method. It lists all themes that have become apparent, and it notes any diversity of opinions or thoughts expressed by the participants. It will also have numerous verbatim excerpts provided as evidence.[28] In fact, some reports include complete transcripts of the focus group discussion. This information is then used as the basis for further research studies or even for more focus groups. If the information is used for subsequent focus groups, the client uses the first group as a learning experience, making any adjustments to the discussion topics as needed to improve the research objectives. Although focus groups may be the only type of research to tackle a marketing problem or question, they are also used as a beginning point for quantitative research efforts. That is, a focus group phase may be used to gain a feel for a specific survey that will ultimately generate standardized information from a representative sample.

Online Focus Groups

An **online focus group** is one in which the respondents and/or the clients communicate and/or observe by use of the Internet. Typically, the participants are seated at their own computers, while the moderator operates out of his or her online focus group company. The online focus group is "virtual" in that it communicates electronically, and it does not have face-to-face contact in the traditional focus group sense. Although some experts hold that online focus groups are not equivalent to traditional focus groups, online focus groups offer many advantages with few disadvantages. Recently, the Qualitative Research Consultants Association's Online Qualitative Research Task Force published its investigations into online focus groups[29] and its major conclusions are listed in Table 8.2.

Online focus groups have the following advantages over traditional focus groups: (1) No physical set up is necessary, (2) transcripts are captured on file in real time, (3) participants can be in widely separated geographic locations, (4) participants are comfortable in their home or office environments, and (5) the moderator can exchange private messages with individual participants. Innovative approaches are possible as some researchers combine online with telephone communications for maximum effectiveness.[30] Marketing Research Insight 8.3 illustrates how an online focus group can take place with the participants in one country while the moderator and client(s) can be in another part of the globe.

On the flip side, there are some disadvantages to online focus groups, such as (1) observation of participants' "body language" is not possible, (2) participants cannot physically inspect products or taste food items, and (3) participants can lose interest or become distracted.[31] Of course, as Table 8.2 indicates, both traditional and online focus groups require recruitment and compensation of participants, scheduling and notification, and a prepared and skilled moderator.

| Table 8.2 | Online Focus Groups FAQs[32] | |

QUESTION	ANSWER
Can online focus groups substitute for face-to-face ones?	Yes, as long as the online environment is consistent with the study's objectives.

For what situations are online focus groups best suited?	Some are:
	    Low-incidence respondents
	    Geographically dispersed respondents
	    B2B professionals

What is "lost" with online focus groups?	You cannot:
	    See body language
	    Show prototypes or models of products
	    Conduct taste tests

Can I recruit online focus group participants via e-mail invitation?	Yes, if they have valid e-mail accounts that they use regularly.
What incentives should I use to recruit my focus group participants?	The going rate is about $40 in cash or the equivalent, but B2B participants may require twice this amount.
How many participants should I plan for in my online focus group?	A common number is 15 to 20.
How long should it last?	Up to 90 minutes is typical.
How secure is the online focus group environment?	If you use a commercial chat program, there are password systems that can be used to maintain security.
Can my clients observe the online focus group?	Yes, there are systems in which the client(s) can observe the focus group while online at their own computers. The clients can communicate privately with the moderator online as well.
Are the moderator's skills different with an online focus group?	In addition to basic focus group moderator skills, there needs to be more care in preparation of the discussion topic guide wording to avoid misinterpretation, probes phrased to include all participants, good typing ability, and familiarity with chat room slang.
Are participants more or less candid with online focus groups?	They tend to be more candid as they have anonymity. Also, they tend to compose answers to topic questions without reading others' responses, so the comments are more unique to each participant.

A variation of the online focus group is one that is conducted in a traditional setting, but the client watches online. With the use of streaming media and high-speed Internet connections, ActiveGroup has pioneered this research technique. Marketing Research Insight 8.4 describes ActiveGroup's capabilities.

What is in store for the future of online focus groups? Here is an opinion shared by many, "We're poised for growth. Online focus groups are a viable research methodology."[33]

Advantages of Focus Groups

Now that you understand the basics of focus groups, we can turn to a brief description of their advantages, disadvantages, and other issues researchers are confronted with when they rely on focus groups. There are four major advantages to using focus groups as a form of qualitative research: They generate fresh ideas, they allow clients to observe the group in action, they are generally versatile, and they work well with special respondents. We describe each in turn.

Key advantages of focus groups include the generation of ideas, client interaction, versatility, and the ability to tap special respondents.

MARKETING RESEARCH
INSIGHT
8.3

online research

How an Online Focus Group Helped a U.S. Researcher Understand the Adoption of Western Medicine in Mainland China

Ann Veeck, a marketing professor at Western Michigan University, specializes in the study of Chinese consumers. She has undertaken a number of studies in mainland China over the past decade that trace the changes in Chinese consumers as a result of China's open economy policies and the rapid influx of Western goods and services, such as Kentucky Fried Chicken, McDonald's, and Starbucks, into China's major cities.

When Ann became interested in studying the possible shift away from traditional Chinese medicine, which relies heavily on acupuncture, pressure points, and herbal medications, to Western medicine practices, she realized that a focus group would be a good starting point. However, she was in Kalamazoo, Michigan, and the focus group participants were thousands of miles away in mainland China.

She recruited focus groups members via the Internet by working with Dr. Yu Hongyan of Jilin University in Changchun, Jilin Province, People's Republic of China (PRC), as his students had Internet connectivity and online

chat capabilities. Most university students in the PRC do not have personal computers with Internet connections, so they make use of their university's "Web bars" or PC laboratories with PCs that are connected. Also, all students learn a second language, and English, Japanese, and Russian are the most popular languages.

At the appointed time Dr. Yu organized his many students into five teams with English-capable leaders who had good keyboard skills. The time zone differences are such that Changchun is 14 hours ahead of Kalamazoo, so the focus group participants were literally in "tomorrow," while Ann sat at her computer in her office, using a moderator based in a different U.S. city, and with Dr. Yu's students online in Changchun.

Analysis of the online focus group transcript revealed that Western medicine is respected and used mainly by more educated Chinese consumers who can afford this expensive option. Chinese citizens with less education still believe strongly in traditional Eastern medical practices and medicines.

Generate Fresh Ideas Creative and honest insights are often the result of focus groups. Because the respondents are not alone with the interviewer, they feel more at ease and free to express honest opinions rather than the ones they think will please the interviewer. The effect of "snowballing," or of one comment triggering another, is also common in a focus group situation. A "group creativity" factor is often observed in brainstorming sessions in which one person's idea stimulates others to generate their own ideas. Focus groups are excellent arenas for this sort of effect.

Allow Clients to Observe the Group A frequent complaint of marketing research clients is that they have difficulty understanding the complex quantitative techniques used and the statistical results produced. This lack of understanding invariably leads to an underutilization of the information provided. However, because managers can be involved throughout the focus group process by helping with the design of objectives and by observing the focus group, the results make more of an impression on them and are more likely to result in action. In fact, managers sometimes formulate and begin executing action plans based on their focus group observations even before the focus group data are analyzed and submitted as a formal report.

> The ability to observe focus groups greatly facilitates client understanding.

Generally Versatile A virtually unlimited number of topics and issues can be discussed in a focus group interview situation. It is even possible to incorporate the use of other qualitative techniques such as role playing into the session, thus increasing the productivity of the discussion. Prototypes of products can be demonstrated, concepts can be described, and product performance test results can be disclosed. Even advertising copy can be evaluated with a focus group.[34] The modera-

▶ An Online Application

MARKETING RESEARCH INSIGHT 8.4

ActiveGroup Pioneers Streaming Media Focus Groups

Here is a description of ActiveGroup's capabilities supplied by David Nelems, president. David's biography is in the "Meet a Marketing Researcher" insight found at the end of this feature.

ActiveGroup, the pioneer and leader in Internet broadcasting for marketing research, allows you to view Web casts of your qualitative research. Your interviews still take place in the physical facility, but you or your colleagues no longer have to be there. This state-of-the-art technology allows you the option of having your event broadcast over the Internet to be viewed via your computer from any remote location. Clients can view the event as it occurs live or come back to a Web page devoted exclusively to their research over the period of a month and watch the video on demand whenever they wish.

ActiveGroup always includes the Client Lounge feature, which embeds the video in a secure chat room Web page so that all of the clients who are viewing the groups around the globe can interact with each other while viewing. In other words, the Client Lounge allows viewers to communicate back and forth with each other just as if they were physically at your facility watching the groups from behind the mirror. To participate in the Client Lounge, viewers simply type in their name and message in the appropriate space. The message appears instantaneously as can be seen in the accompanying screen capture.

Clients can also have links made to the profile sheets, moderator outline, screener, moderator biography, or just about any other document they can think of. When viewers go to the Web pages devoted exclusively to their research, the documents are simply a click away. And with the ability to view the event on demand, the viewers have complete fast-forward and rewind capabilities. If viewers wish to skip past the introduction and jump right into the heart of the group, they can click on the fast-forward button and do just that.

The standard package also includes a CD-ROM of all of the groups that the client can distribute.

The key to all of this is the flexibility it gives a client. No longer do all the clients have to attend a facility to view the event. Instead, they can monitor the groups from anywhere

they have Internet access—whether it be an office, a hotel room, or their very own home. ActiveGroup expands the audience of clients for the research allowing many more people to collaborate and have input into the research without all of the scheduling, budgeting, and travel constraints that traditional qualitative events impose

Another useful component is ActiveNotes. ActiveNotes is a new kind of software that will allow you to use your notes as a personal bookmark and index of your research event. ActiveNotes will fundamentally change the way you recall, communicate, and share experiences by enabling you to use your personal notes to pinpoint, share, and publish audio/video highlights of your research event—for yourself or for your colleagues. With ActiveNotes, you can be anywhere in the world monitoring your event while you type your notes on your computer. Then ActiveNotes will link up those notes with the audio/video of the event—live or on demand. Every time you see or hear something you like just type a comment. Our patent-pending software will automatically keep track of the audio/video so you can instantly refer to it later. You can then easily make video clips out of your notes and send these clips to your colleagues and clients.

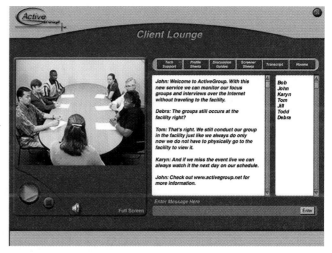

---

tor is also allowed to probe more deeply into the opinions of the participants, something not allowed in highly structured quantitative methods. A different aspect of this advantage is the flexibility of focus groups afforded by technology. Some companies regularly conduct focus groups with participants at diverse geographical locations through the use of videoconferences.[35] Even business supply companies such as Kinko's Copies have videoconference centers available for rent, and focus groups can be conducted with executives, for instance, with the use of

Focus groups using videoconferencing and Internet chat rooms demonstrate the versatility of this technique.

MARKETING RESEARCH
INSIGHT
8.5

Meet a Marketing Researcher ◀
David M. Nelems
President, ActiveGroup

David is president and founder of ActiveGroup, the pioneer and leader in delivering qualitative research live and on demand over the Internet. Prior to founding ActiveGroup, David was chief technical officer for the Marketing Workshop, Inc. (MWI), a nationally recognized, full-service research firm. He is also the son of Jim Nelems, president of that 30-year-old full-service firm.

At MWI, David's primary function was in determining where MWI should go on a technology basis one to two years down the road and developing computer solutions to get there. He was responsible for the Internet web sites of the Marketing Workshop, Inc. and Compass Marketing Research. He also managed a staff that created all of the electronic presentations for MWI's clients. David has developed over a dozen proprietary software programs for marketing research. These programs range from scheduling systems for managing 300 interviews in a CATI center, to a

database management system that handles every step of a project—from proposal to final invoice, to multimedia CDs that have replaced MWI's traditional paper brochures and reports.

His primary focus with ActiveGroup is to manage the explosive growth of the company as it begins its global expansion, forge partnerships with key industry players in both the marketing research and Internet industries, and determine where the technology is going to take the company with qualitative research and streaming media next. With a 15-year background in traditional marketing research, he has been in the back rooms with clients and has seen focus groups and in-depth interviews from every point of view firsthand.

David has a B.S. degree in aerospace technology from Georgia State University. He is married to a focus group moderator and has two small children.

---

these facilities or the videoconference facilities now in place in many focus group company office areas. Some services are now providing focus groups on the Internet where net users will enter chat rooms where certain topics are identified and all chat room members can submit their comments and reactions in a public forum. Some Internet focus groups take place over extended time periods using newsgroup postings.

Work Well with Special Respondents Another major advantage of focus groups is that they permit the researcher to study respondents who might not respond well under more structured situations. In some situations, such as those involving hard-to-interview groups such as lawyers or doctors, the format gives them an opportunity to associate with their peers and to compare notes. Otherwise, they might refuse to take part in a survey. Creative variations of focus groups are successful in studies on children. Both Kid2Kid and Doyle Research Associates have innovative approaches in which children interact with other children in structured team activities, storytelling, and other interactions that the children treat as games.[36] Of course, accommodations must be planned for special respondents. For instance, focus groups can be successful with disabled respondents, but provisions must be in place for each type of disability.[37]

Focus groups are successful with hard-to-interview groups.

Disadvantages of Focus Groups

No research technique is flawless, and focus groups are no exception.[38] Some weaknesses are readily apparent, whereas others are less obvious. There are three major weaknesses: They may not represent the general population, their interpretation is subjective, and their cost-per-participant is high. A discussion of these weaknesses follows.

May Not Represent the Population Focus group results should not be viewed as conclusive research because the participants are not likely to be representative of the general population the researcher is studying. Generally, those who agree to participate in focus groups are more outgoing than the average person. They are more accessible and probably more compliant. Coupled with the small sample size and homogenous group design, these unique characteristics render many focus groups unrepresentative of the marketer's target population. Furthermore, because it is not possible to ensure that all of the participants who agree to take part will show up, semiprofessional respondents are sometimes "on call" for last-minute emergencies. Consequently, tight controls and a sober evaluation of the representativeness of focus groups' participants are mandatory.

> It is important to remember that a focus group may not be representative of the total group under study.

Interpretation Is Subjective Selective use of the data collected by focus groups is a typical problem. Individuals with preconceived notions can almost always find something to support their views, ignoring anything that does not support their opinions. So focus group analysts are constantly on guard against bias entering into qualitative research.[39] The subjectivity problem is compounded by involvement of management personnel during the design and conduct of the focus groups. It is not uncommon for a manager to enter the process with a preconceived notion of what the research will find (or what it should support). Because focus group research typically allows the manager and his or her team to suggest topics and to add specific questions as well as to observe the groups in progress, a danger exists that certain preconceptions will enter into their impressions of the research findings. In fact, as we mentioned earlier, they may even take these impressions and convert them to action before the focus groups are analyzed and the summary report delivered to the client. If a researcher senses that premature actions are a danger, he or she will advise the client to wait until a trained focus group analyst has interpreted the complete set of focus group transcripts, and experienced researchers know that this process takes time.[40]

> Managers may engage in subjective interpretation of a focus group, so it is advisable to use a trained analyst.

Cost-per-Participant Is High A variety of expensive items contribute to the high cost-per-participant. One is participant recruitment. Numerous telephone calls are usually needed to recruit the desired number of required participants. The average charge for this service is around $25 and more for hard-to-reach or rare respondents. Next is the incentive cost. Some sort of compensation is offered to those who show up (usually around $30). This should be given to all respondents who arrive, even if they are not required to participate. These costs are minor compared to the moderator and facilities rental fees. A qualified moderator's salary can range from $1,500 to $2,000 per session. This amount includes his or her participation in developing the objectives, conducting the focus groups, transcribing the videotapes, and writing and presenting a full report to management. Last, rental of the focus group facility plus its videotaping equipment are additional costs to be considered. The rental cost varies greatly, depending on where the focus group takes place, but a fully equipped focus group facility usually charges hundreds of dollars per hour of use. A final cost factor involves hidden costs. Such costs include time spent by the marketing manager and his or her team working and traveling that are absorbed by the manager's budget but not necessarily assigned as a cost of the focus groups by the company's accounting system. Sometimes managers may even review all of the videotapes pertaining to a set of focus groups, resulting in many hours of time, which also draws them away from their other responsibilities. Not counting hidden costs that are difficult to estimate, a typical focus group may cost from $150 to $200 per participant, whereas a "ballpark" telephone survey cost is between $10 and $15 per respondent.

> Although focus group information is valuable, it bears a high cost-per-participant.

Final Comments on Focus Groups

Focus groups are an appealing qualitative research method.

The focus group approach is firmly entrenched in the marketing research world as a mainstay technique. Because they are easy to interpret, of reasonable total cost when compared to large-scale quantitative surveys involving a thousand or more respondents, adaptable to managers' concerns, and capable of yielding immediate results, focus groups are an appealing qualitative research method. Moreover, face-to-face focus groups are becoming common worldwide, and online focus groups are boosting the popularity of focus groups with new capabilities. They are a unique research method because they permit marketing managers to see and hear the market. Managers become so engrossed in their everyday problems and crises that they find it very refreshing to see their customers in the flesh. It is common for marketing managers to come away from a focus group session observation stimulated and energized to respond to the market's desires.

OTHER QUALITATIVE RESEARCH TECHNIQUES

Although focus group interviews and many of the observation methods we have described thus far are clearly the most frequently used qualitative research techniques, they are not the only type of nonstructured research available to marketing researchers. Other popular methods include depth interviews, protocol analysis, various projective techniques, and physiological measurement.

Depth Interviews

Depth interviews with consumers may reveal what they are thinking or why they have acted in a certain way.

A **depth interview** is defined as a set of probing questions posed one-on-one to a subject by a trained interviewer so as to gain an idea of what the subject thinks about something or why he or she behaves in a certain way. It is conducted in the respondent's home or possibly at a central interviewing location such as a mall-intercept facility where several respondents can be interviewed in depth in a relatively short time period. The objective is to obtain unrestricted comments or opinions and to ask questions that will help the marketing researcher better understand the various dimensions of these opinions as well as the reasons for them. Of primary importance is the compilation of the data into a summary report so as to identify common themes. New concepts, designs, advertising, and promotional messages can arise from this method.[41] If used properly, depth interviews can offer great insight into consumer behavior.[42,43]

Depth interviews are especially useful when the researcher wants to understand decision making on the individual level, how products are used, or the emotional and sometimes private aspects of consumers' lives.[44,45]

A depth interview uncovers conscious reasons that interviewees may not disclose without probing questions.

The depth interview is typically conducted by a trained field-worker who is equipped with a list of topics or, perhaps, open-ended questions. In other words, the respondent is not provided a list of set responses and then instructed to select one from the list. Rather, the respondent is encouraged to respond in his or her own words, and the interviewer is trained in asking probing questions such as "Why is that so?" "Can you elaborate on your point?" or "Would you give me some specific reasons?" These questions are not intended to tap subconscious motivations; rather, they simply ask about conscious reasons to help the researcher form a better picture of what is going on in the respondent's head. The interviewer may tape-record responses or may take detailed notes. Although it is typical to do face-to-face depth interviews, they can be done over the telephone when interviewees are widely dispersed.[46]

Depth interviews are versatile, but they require careful planning, training, and preparation.[47]

The summary report will look very similar to one written for a focus group study. That is, the analyst looks for common themes across several depth interview transcripts, and these are noted in the report. Verbatim responses are included in the report to support the analyst's conclusions, and any significant differences of opinion that are found in the respondents' comments are noted as well. Again, it is vital to use an analyst who is trained and experienced in interpreting the qualitative data gathered with depth interviews.

Protocol Analysis

Protocol analysis involves placing a person in a decision-making situation and asking him or her to verbalize everything he or she considers when making a decision. It is a special-purpose qualitative research technique that has been developed to peek into the consumer's decision-making processes. Often a tape recorder is used to maintain a permanent record of the person's thinking. After several people have provided protocols, the researcher reviews them and looks for commonalities such as evaluative criteria used, number of brands considered, types and sources of information utilized, and so forth.

Protocol studies are useful in two different purchase situations. First, they are helpful for purchases involving a long time frame in which several decision factors must be considered, such as when buying a house. By having people verbalize the steps they went through, a researcher can piece together the whole process. Second, when the decision process is very short, recall may be faulty and protocol analysis can be used to slow down the process. For example, most people do not give much thought to buying chewing gum, but if Dentine wanted to find out why people buy spearmint gum, protocol analysis might provide some important insights regarding this purchasing behavior. A variation of the protocol technique is "customer case research," and we have provided a description and examples of its revelations in Marketing Research Insight 8.6.

Protocol studies require subjects to "think aloud."

Projective Techniques

Projective techniques involve situations in which participants are placed in (projected into) simulated activities in the hopes that they will divulge things about themselves that they might not reveal under direct questioning. Projective techniques are appropriate in situations in which the researcher is convinced that respondents will be hesitant to relate their true opinions. Such situations may include behaviors such as tipping waitresses, socially undesirable behaviors such as smoking or alcohol consumption, questionable actions such as littering, or even illegal practices such as betting on football games.

With a projective technique, people often divulge something about themselves they would not divulge in a direct questioning situation.

There are five common projective techniques used by marketers: the word association test, the sentence completion test, the picture test, the cartoon or balloon test, and role-playing activity. A discussion of each follows.

Word Association Test
A **word association test** involves reading words to a respondent who then answers with the first word that comes to his or her mind. These tests may contain over 100 words and usually combine neutral words with words being tested in ads or words involving product names or services. The researcher then looks for hidden meanings or associations between responses and the words being tested on the original list. This approach is used to uncover people's real feelings about these products or services, brand names, or ad copy. The time taken to respond, called "response latency," and/or the respondents' physical reactions may be measured and used to make inferences. For example, if the response latency to the word "duo" is long, it may mean that people do not have an immediate association with the word.

Word association tests can help marketers to analyze potential brand names.

MARKETING RESEARCH

INSIGHT
8.6

How Customer Case Research Leads to Eureka!

When a company is experiencing a customer problem that it finds very difficult to research via conventional methods, an option to try is customer case research, referred to as CCR. CCR is defined as an "exploratory, qualitative market research method that conducts in-depth, chronological case studies of actual purchases," and this Marketing Research Insight is based on a recent exposition of the CCR method.[48,49]

CCR poses seven questions to draw out consumers' stories about their experiences. More often than not, interpretation of the stories of a handful of consumers triggers a *Eureka!*-type revelation for the marketing managers involved. Here are the seven questions with the interpretations of a representative case and the *Eureka!*

CCR QUESTION	REPRESENTATIVE INTERPRETATION	EUREKA!
1. *What started you on the road to making this purchase?*	When asked about taking scuba lessons, many customers said they did so to prepare for a honeymoon in the Caribbean.	The scuba shop realized that brides' magazines can be an effective advertising vehicle.
2. *Why did you make this purchase now?*	Downtown Chicago workers said that they walk by the Chicago River tour boat docks daily but only thought about the trip when visitors were coming to stay with them.	The tour boat owners realized that they could target passersby with a "best thing to do when your relatives visit" theme.
3. *What was the hardest part of this process? Was there any point where you got stuck?*	It was revealed that for men, giving jewelry to a significant other was much more difficult than selecting it.	Jewelry store clerks were supplied with clever, romantic, and novel ways to use to "pop" the jewelry gift on that special person.
4. *When and how did you decide the price was acceptable?*	It was found that for a summer music festival those in the pavilion seats compared the price to winter indoor concerts.	The festival organizers were able to raise the pavilion seat prices with no objections.
5. *Is there someone else with whom I should talk to get more of the story behind this purchase?*	With B2B research, often the presumedly informed manager will say, "I am not the best one to ask. You should talk to ____."	The research should lead to the actual decision maker in the company for the product or service.
6. *If you've purchased this product before, how does the story of your last purchase differ from this one?*	It was determined that seeing a local television channel's news vans and news personnel around town entices curious news viewers to watch that channel's news that evening.	The local station repainted its vans with vivid colors and logo and required its visible news folks to wear easily identifiable clothing.
7. *At what point did you decide you trusted this organization and this person to work in your best interests?*	Prospective honeymooners are clueless about scuba equipment, but they indicated that when the salesperson asked about their specific needs, they began to trust him or her.	Sales clerks were trained to ask about and to be sensitive to the expected uses of the scuba equipment so as to build rapport with first-time customers who are potentially going to buy an expensive set of scuba equipment.

Table 8.3	**Results of an Online NameWave™ Session to Find a Brand Name for a Fortified Health Drink**	

CATEGORIES USED WERE "GOOD TASTING" AND "POWERFUL"

ArcticBowl
CrossThrust
DynaAcceleration
DynaPump
DynamicForce
FruitBonanza
GoodFest
HydroPump
NuclearYield
OmniWatts
SolarCore
VelocityGrid

The NameStormers™ of Largo Vista, Texas, has been very successful with its variation of word association brand-name brainstorming, and its clients include GTE, Blue Cross, Hewlett-Packard, and Frito-Lay. It brainstorms unique combinations of words and coined words that are associated with the benefits and features of the product or service being named, plus the brand names can be very distinct and memorable. This company has an online service called NameWave™ that generates such brand-name candidate words. Table 8.3 shows the results of the candidate brand names that were generated for a new, good-tasting, and powerful sports drink. Which one of these do you think works best in immediately communicating this drink's benefits?

Sentence Completion Test With a **sentence completion test,** respondents are given incomplete sentences and asked to complete them in their own words. The researcher then inspects these sentences to identify themes or concepts that exist. The notion here is that respondents will reveal something about themselves in their responses. For example, suppose that Lipton Tea was interested in expanding its market to teenagers. A researcher might recruit high school students and instruct them to complete the following sentences:

> Write in words to complete these sentences. What does it tell you about your attitude toward drinking hot tea?

Someone who drinks hot tea is _____.

Tea is good to drink when _____.

Making hot tea is _____.

My friends think tea is _____.

The researcher would look at the written responses and attempt to identify central themes. For instance, the theme identified for the first sentence might be "healthy," which would signify that tea is perceived as a drink for those who are health conscious. The theme for the second sentence might be "hot," indicating that tea is perceived as a cold weather drink, whereas the theme for the third sentence may turn out to be "messy," denoting the students' reaction to using a tea bag. Finally, the last sentence theme might be found as "okay," suggesting there are no peer pressures working to cause high school students to avoid drinking tea. Given this information, Lipton might deduce that there is room to capitalize on the hot tea market with teens.

Picture Test With a **picture test,** a picture is provided to participants who are instructed to describe their reactions by writing a short story about the picture. The researcher analyzes the content of these stories to ascertain feelings, reactions, or

> Picture tests are useful ways to test potential advertisements for impact and reactions.

concerns generated by the picture. Such tests are useful when testing pictures being considered for use in brochures, advertisements, and on product packaging. For example, a test advertisement might depict a man holding a baby, and the ad headline might say, "Ford includes driver and passenger airbags as standard equipment because you love your family." A picture test may well divulge something about the picture that is especially negative or distasteful. Perhaps unmarried male respondents cannot relate to the ad because they do not have children and have not experienced strong feelings for children. On the other hand, it may turn out that the picture has a much more neutral tone than Ford's advertising agency intended. It may be that the picture does not generate feelings of concern and safety for the family in married respondents with young children. In any case, without the use of a picture test, it would be very difficult to determine the audience's reactions.

Take the balloon test on this page.

Cartoon or Balloon Test With a **balloon test**, a line drawing with an empty "balloon" above the head of one of the actors is provided to subjects who are instructed to write in the balloon what the actor is saying or thinking. The researcher then inspects these thoughts to find out how subjects feel about the situation described in the cartoon. For example, when shown a line drawing of a situation in which one of the characters is making the statement, "Here is a pair of patent leather dress shoes on sale for $39.99," the participant is asked how the other character in the drawing would respond. Feelings and reactions of the subject are judged based on their answers. An example of a cartoon test is provided in Figure 8.2. Feel free to fill in the balloon. It may interest you to know that some undergraduate students have written quotes indicating that this sunbather is not worried about skin damage from the sun, whereas others have written quotes about how this woman would not dare recline like this in the sun unless she had a very powerful sunblock on.

Role-play this: What would your best friend say if you bought a pair of $200 "Astronaut" Ray-Bans?

Role-Playing Activity With **role playing**, participants are asked to pretend they are a "third person," such as a friend or neighbor, and to describe how they would act in a certain situation or to a specific statement. By reviewing their comments, the researcher can spot latent reactions, positive or negative, conjured up by the situa-

Figure 8.2   **A balloon test: What is she saying about her protection from the sun's ultraviolet rays?**

tion. It is believed that some of the respondents' true feelings and beliefs will be revealed by this method because they can pretend to be another individual. For example, if Ray-Ban is thinking about introducing a new "Astronaut" sunglasses model with superior ultraviolet light filtration, space-age styling, and a cost of about $200, role playing might be used to fathom consumers' initial reactions. In this use of role playing, subjects could be asked to assume the role of a friend or close work-mate and to indicate what they would say to a third person when they learned that their friend had purchased a pair of Astronaut sunglasses. If consumers felt the Astronaut model was overpriced, this feeling would quickly surface. On the other hand, if the space-age construction and styling were consistent with these consumers' lifestyles and product desires, this fact would be divulged in the role-playing comments.

As with depth interviews, all of these projective techniques require highly qualified professionals to interpret the results. This increases the cost per respondent compared to other survey methods. Because of this aspect, projective techniques are not used extensively in commercial marketing research, but each one has value in its special realm of application.[50]

Other and Emerging Qualitative Research Techniques

The various techniques described thus far are in no way a complete list, for a number of other techniques are used by enthnographers, anthrophologists, psychologists, and sociologists to study human behavior. Plus, there are promising analytical techniques for interpreting the marketing strategy implications of qualitative data.[51] However, each new-to-marketing-research qualitative research technique brings with it a need to understand the theoretical and practical aspects of that technique in order to apply it properly, so it is best to hire a specialist with expertise in the particular qualitative research technique. Indeed, companies that specialize in these new techniques report that clients are cautious about them at first.[52] At the same time, qualitative techniques are fast and relatively inexpensive, and companies such as Bissell, which changed the name of its cleaner unit from the Steam Gun to Steam N' Clean after qualitative research found that children would want to use a Steam Gun to threaten their siblings, have found qualitative research to be very satisfactory when funds are low and time is short.[53]

Physiological Measurement

Physiological measurement involves monitoring a respondent's involuntary responses to marketing stimuli via the use of electrodes and other equipment. Most people who are monitored find the situation strange and may experience uneasiness during the monitoring. Because of this factor and the necessary hardware, this technique is rarely used in marketing research.

Physiological measures are sometimes used in marketing research, but they are unnatural and difficult to interpret.

We briefly describe two physiological measures to round out this chapter on qualitative research: the pupilometer and the galvanometer. The **pupilometer** is a device that attaches to a person's head and determines interest and attention by measuring the amount of dilation in the pupil of the eye. It actually photographs the movement of a person's iris when he or she views different pictures. Theoretically, a person's iris enlarges more with an interesting image than when an uninteresting one is viewed. Eye-tracking has a new application in the Internet marketing arena. For example, AT&T has begun to use eye-tracking coupled with depth interviewing to understand how AT&T customers interact with its customer service Web site.[54]

The **galvanometer** is a device that determines excitement levels by measuring the electrical activity in the respondent's skin. It requires electrodes or sensing pads to be taped to a person's body in order to monitor this activity. When a person encounters an interesting stimulus, the electrical impulses in the body become excited. Physiological measures are useful under special circumstances, such as testing sexually oriented stimuli where many people are embarrassed or may not tell the truth, and they require special skills to be administered correctly. There are two disadvantages to using physiological measurement techniques. First, the techniques are unnatural and subjects may become nervous and emit false readings. Second, even though we know that the respondent reacted to the stimulus, we do not know if the response was positive or negative.[55]

Here is how our Blue Ribbon Panel members answered our question about qualitative marketing research techniques.

BLUE RIBBON PANEL on [Online Research]

online research

Q: *What changes or trends are occurring with respect to the use of qualitative marketing research techniques as a result of advances in computer technology and online communication?*

Note: To learn about the panel members, see the Preface of this book.

Bill MacElroy
President
Socratic Technologies

A: Qualitative techniques have remained one of the last, most technology-resistant areas of research. Although many technologies are available for conducting "qualitative-like" studies online, few of them possess the capture of personal and emotional responses that are hallmarks of traditional qualitative methods. For example, "online focus groups" mimic some of the aspects of group dynamics but have not to date been able to replicate the intrinsic characteristics of interpersonal debate, spontaneous concept generation, group dialog, or emotional essence. Online techniques have been good when it comes to removing human interference (e.g., interviewer bias) from the process but have not successfully supplanted those areas where human interaction is key to the procedure.

Allen Hogg
President
Burke, Inc.

A: Many organizations first delved into the online research arena by trying "online focus groups," timed "chat" sessions in which geographically disperse participants interact with each other while also typing responses to questions posed by a moderator. Development of online focus group software has made it easier to present multimedia stimuli in these groups and integrate these qualitative discussions with quantitative surveying. The use of "online bulletin boards" to collect qualitative information seems to be on the rise as well. Bulletin board participants are asked to come to a Web site and provide input several times over the course of a set time period.

Online technology is also transforming the in-person focus group experience. Secure online "broadcasts" of these sessions can eliminate the need for organizational stakeholders to travel to focus group sites. Internet access is also being brought into focus group sessions, and qualitative input regarding Web sites, for example, is now being linked with participants' online behavior.

In the future, we can expect that audio and video transmissions will be integrated with online communications, so that organizations will be able to obtain vocal and visual input, as well as typed comments, from participants in online qualitative research.

George Harmon
Senior Vice President
Digital Marketing
Services

A: Bulletin boards and other posting technology enable guided or unbridled ideation. In general, online focus groups are becoming less qualitative and more quantitative. The ability of respondents to expresses themselves verbally and for moderators to "read" emotions and body language will continue to limit online qualitative research—at least until the moderators and clients can hear and see participants.

George Terhanian
Vice President of Internet Research Harris Interactive, Inc.

A: Several market research firms have demonstrated remarkable proficiency and creativity with online qualitative techniques, notably chat rooms and bulletin boards. At Harris Interactive, for example, we have used bulletin boards to collect qualitative information longitudinally from groups of carefully chosen panelists to facilitate and expedite the ideation process required for new-product development. We have also been able to allay client concerns over the absence of facial expressions, body language, and the like among participants in online chat sessions. Our clients who have witnessed online qualitative research have observed, for example, that online qualitative research participants are adept at expressing emotion through the creative use of text. For these reasons alone, the future of online qualitative research looks promising. I suspect, moreover, that online qualitative methods will continue to improve as new technologies become available, or at least become less expensive. The increasing ubiquity and decreasing cost of Web-cams, for instance, will soon allow us to visually link respondents to the moderator (and the client) and perhaps to other participants as well, thereby reducing further any lingering concerns about the limitations of the methodology.

Keith Price
Vice President Greenfield Online

A: Online qualitative research is going beyond traditional focus groups. New tools have been developed, including online brainstorming, which can be achieved by the use of a threaded bulletin board. The technique can be used to dialogue with consumers over extended periods of time, which is something that is typically impossible off-line. Online brainstorming can be a valuable tool when conducting product testing, attitude and usage, and long-term acquisition studies.

Although online qualitative studies will not replace off-line, traditional face-to-face focus groups, enhancements are being made to online qualitative tools, which will help to simulate off-line focus group sessions. Now images and audio and video clips can be inserted into online qualitative tools to present concepts and enhance the user experience.

Lee Smith
CEO Insight Express

A: With powerful and cost-effective online surveys, the demand for traditional qualitative market research is beginning to subside. However, new technology such as Web-attached video cameras hold enormous promise to drive interest in rapid turnaround qualitative research—overcoming many of the limitations commonly associated with online, chat-based focus groups.

Doss Struse
Senior Vice President Client Service Knowledge Networks, Inc.

A: There are several directions depending on how far out one wants to peer into the possible.

▶ With the spread of broadband and video camera/digital camera technology, online focus groups and real-time "face-to-face" interaction will be possible, without the limitations of bringing people together at a focus group room. The current implementation of online focus groups or video focus groups is a far cry from the live version.

▶ It may be possible to use an "avatar" to engage in an online dialogue with consumers. This avatar would combine the skill of an interviewer/moderator with the knowledge and experience of a brand manager. This might allow research that would dynamically switch between qualitative exploration and quantitative confirmation. This would enable these qual-quant to be done on any scale.

The technology required to implement an avatar would also support connecting brand managers into a true dialogue with consumers. In this scenario research would be completely integrated within the marketing function and not exist as a specialty except to develop and maintain the technology.

SUMMARY

This chapter described the various qualitative research techniques employed by marketing researchers. Qualitative research is much less structured than quantitative approaches. We described the various types of observation alternatives possible such as disguised versus undisguised, structured versus unstructured, and human versus mechanical. We noted that the circumstances most suitable to observational studies are instances of (1) short time interval, (2) public behavior, and (3) lack of recall.

The chapter next described the use of focus groups, or moderated small group discussions, which is a very popular form of research. We noted that a focus group should include from 6 to 12 participants sharing similar characteristics. Recruiting and selection may be problems due to "no shows." Focus group facilities exist in most major cities, but any large room with a central table can be used. The moderator's role is key to a successful focus group. There are, however, a few drawbacks to focus groups, and assessing the representativeness of the group is one of them. Also, interpretation is subjective and the cost-per-participant is high. Nevertheless, focus groups are a mainstay marketing research technique, and online focus groups are boosting the popularity of focus groups.

We wrapped up the chapter with descriptions of some of the other qualitative techniques used in marketing research. Depth interviews, for instance, have been adapted to probe into consumer motivations and hidden concerns. Protocol analysis induces participants to "think aloud" so the researcher can map the decision-making process being used while a consumer goes about making a purchase decision. Projective techniques, such as word association, sentence completion, or role playing, are also useful in unearthing motivations, beliefs, and attitudes that subjects may not be able to express well verbally. Finally, there are some physiological measurements such as pupil movement or electrical activity in the skin that can be used in special circumstances to better understand consumer reactions.

KEY TERMS

Quantitative research (p. 204)
Qualitative research (p. 204)
Pluralistic research (p. 205)
Observation methods (p. 206)
Direct observation (p. 208)
Indirect observation (p. 208)
Archives (p. 208)
Physical traces (p. 208)
Disguised observation (p. 209)
Undisguised observation (p. 209)
Structured observation (p. 209)
Unstructured observation (p. 209)
Human observation (p. 209)
Mechanical observation (p. 210)
Focus group (p. 211)

Focus group facility (p. 215)
Focus group moderator (p. 215)
Online focus group (p. 218)
Depth interview (p. 224)
Protocol analysis (p. 225)
Projective techniques (p. 225)
Word association test (p. 225)
Sentence completion test (p. 227)
Picture test (p. 227)
Balloon test (p. 228)
Role playing (p. 228)
Physiological measurement (p. 229)
Pupilometer (p. 229)
Galvanometer (p. 229)

REVIEW QUESTIONS/APPLICATIONS

1. Define quantitative research. Define qualitative research. List the differences between these two research methods. What is pluralistic research?
2. What is meant by an "observation technique"? What is observed, and why is it recorded?

3. Indicate why disguised observation would be appropriate for a study on how parents discipline their children when dining out.

4. Describe at least three different uses of focus groups.

5. How are focus group participants recruited, and what is a common problem associated with this recruitment?

6. Should the members of a focus group be similar or dissimilar? Why?

7. Describe what a focus group company facility looks like and how a focus group would take place in one.

8. Should the marketing manager client be a focus group moderator? Why or why not?

9. Indicate how a focus group moderator should handle each of the following cases: (a) A participant is loud and dominates the conversation; (b) a participant is obviously suffering from a cold and goes into coughing fits every few minutes; (c) two participants who, it turns out, are acquaintances, persist in a private conversation about their children; and (d) the only minority representative participant in the focus group looks very uncomfortable with the group and fails to make any comments.

10. What should be included in a report that summarizes the findings of a focus group?

11. Indicate the advantages and disadvantages of client interaction in the design and execution of a focus group study.

12. How does an online focus group differ from a traditional focus group? What is gained and what is lost with an online focus group versus a traditional one?

13. What is meant by the term "projective" as in projective techniques?

14. Describe (a) sentence completion, (b) word association, and (c) balloon test. Create one of each of these that might be used to test the reactions of mothers whose children are bedwetters to an absorbent underpant that their child would wear under his or her nightclothes.

15. Johnny Walker Red Label Scotch is concerned about the shifting attitudes of the public regarding the consumption of alcohol. However, managers think that scotch whiskey may be seen differently because it is normally consumed in small quantities as opposed to beer, wine, or even other hard liquors such as vodka. Select two projective techniques. First, defend your use of a projective technique. Second, describe in detail how your two chosen techniques would be applied to this research problem.

16. Your university is considering letting an apartment management company build an apartment complex on campus. To save money, the company proposes to build a common cooking area for every four apartments. This area would be equipped with an oven, burners, microwave oven, sink, food preparation area, garbage disposal, and individual mini-refrigerators with locks on them for each apartment. Two students would live in each apartment, so eight students would use the common cooking area. You volunteer to conduct focus groups with students to determine their reactions to this concept and to brainstorm suggestions for improvements. Prepare the topics list you would have as a guide in your role as moderator.

INTERACTIVE LEARNING

Visit the Web site at www.prenhall.com/burnsbush. For this chapter, work through the Self-Study Quizzes, and get instant feedback on whether you need additional studying. On the Web site, you can review the chapter outlines and case information for Chapter 8.

CASE 8.1   Backroads Adventure Experience

Backroads is a unique travel service that specializes in guided biking, walking, and multi-sport trips in the most beautiful and exotic places on the globe. Backroads is unique in that it combines very high quality lodging and gourmet cuisine with athletic activities. Most Backroads tours are six days, five nights such as the following European tours: Province Walking, Loire Valley Biking, and Ireland Multisport. There are Asia-Pacific tours such as Bali Multisport, Latin American tours such as Costa Rica Walking, African tours like Morocco Multisport, and North American tours such as Vermont Walking or Yellowstone/Tetons Multisport. Each Backroads trip is set up with 5 to 10 start-and-end dates that are scheduled for peak season when the weather is most favorable and the sights are most spectacular.

Backroads is dedicated to excellence, and even though its trips are popular and many are sold out, it believes in constantly monitoring its customers. Backroads has commissioned a company to conduct focus groups with its "first-timers," or individuals who have gone on a Backroads tour for the first time in the past six months. Here is an excerpt from the transcript of the first focus group. This group was comprised of single males and females between the ages of 25 and 40 and took place in San Francisco, California.

Moderator: Does anyone else have a reaction to his or her Backroads trip?

John: Yes, I really enjoyed my trip because everything was planned out from dawn to bedtime, and all of the equipment—bikes, kayaks, and snorkeling gear—was provided.

Curtis: I absolutely agree. It was so nice not to worry about lining up the equipment rentals at the local places or worrying that the equipment will be really bad. Backroads equipment is first class, and its guides are outstanding. They know everything there is to know about the area.

Jill: I did have difficulty lining up my transportation to and from the departure point. I did the Dordogne Biking trip, and I had to get to Brive, France, on my own. Getting flights to Paris at high tourist season is not fun at all, and I almost lost it at DeGaulle Airport because everything was so confusing.

Peter: Same with me. I did the New Zealand Multisport in January, so the season was not a problem, but the cost was a lot more than I expected. Those Backroads tour prices are not cheap to begin with, and they do not include the transportation to and from the departure point. So, I spent probably $2,500 more than I expected to.

John: Wow, that's a lot. I did multisport on the Monterey Peninsula, so I just jumped into my Lexus and I was there in less than two hours.

Amber: My strongest reaction is that I think the singles group trips are perfect. I have done sport trips with mixed groups, and you are always being held back by the slow ones. The complainers are the worst. Two years ago in Thailand with a different sport tour company, all we heard was constant whining from a spoiled 12-year-old all the way from Bangkok to Chang Mai.

Jill: The Backroads singles group tours are the best. I met someone special, and we have plans to do the San Juan Biking tour together this coming October.

Peter: Oh, I did that one last year, but I gained 5 pounds. The gourmet food on the Backroads trips was so good, and I enjoyed it so much.

Using these excerpts as representative of the entire focus group transcript, answer the following questions.

1. How is Backroads perceived? That is, what are its apparent strengths?
2. What are some areas of possible service improvement for Backroads?
3. Are the findings of this focus group generalizable to all of Backroads' "first-timers?" Why or why not?

CASE 8.2   *Your Integrated Case*

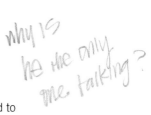

Hobbit's Choice Restaurant

This is your integrated case described on pages 42–43.

Cory Rogers, project director at CMG Research, was excited because he had just talked to Jeff Dean on the phone, and Jeff had given him the go-ahead to conduct some focus groups on The Hobbit's Choice Restaurant project. To refresh his memory on the project, Cory checked his notes, searching for a summary table that he and Jeff had devised in the problem definition phase. Here is the table (the same one you saw in Chapter 4, page 109).

Marketing Problems for The Hobbit's Choice Restaurant

PROBLEM ITEM	DESCRIPTION
Will the restaurant be successful?	Will a sufficient number of people patronize the restaurant?
How should the restaurant be designed?	What about decor, atmosphere, specialty entrées and desserts, wait staff uniforms, reservations, special seating, and so on?
What should be the average price of entrées?	How much are patrons willing to pay for the standard entrées as well as for the house specials?
What is the optimum location?	How far from their homes are patrons willing to drive, and are there any special location features (such as waterfront, ample parking, etc.) to take into consideration?
What is the profile of the target market?	What are the demographic and lifestyle profiles of those who are going to patronize The Hobbit's Choice?
What are the best promotional media?	What advertising media should be used to best reach the target market?

1. Which one of these marketing problem areas should be addressed with focus group research, and why?
2. What types of informants should be recruited for these focus groups?
3. Draft a focus group topic list that a moderator could use as a guide when conducting these focus groups.

Chapter 9

Survey Data Collection Methods

Learning Objectives:

To learn about the advantages and disadvantages of surveys

To become knowledgeable about the details of different types of survey data collection methods such as personal interviews, telephone interviews, and computer-assisted interviews, including online surveys

To appreciate the impact of online surveys on traditional survey methods

To comprehend the factors researchers consider when choosing a particular survey method

Practitioner Viewpoint

Marketing research, with its many resources, continues to design and develop measurements that provide and support a more complex and sophisticated marketplace that is quickly evolving into a global market. As a visionary and pioneer, Opinion One stands with a handful of other pioneers, continuing to create interviewing solutions and data collection methodologies that improve the ability of researchers, scientists, statisticians, marketers, advertisers, media, and others to make accurate decisions and forecasts. Improved and advanced data collection and sampling techniques and methods are required to form an infrastructure for the industry's thirst for and responsibility to communicate with consumers and understand consumer needs and trends in different geographic areas.

Internet-based data collection technologies have provided promises for the market research industry. However, the greatest promise and threat to researchers and data collectors is the industry's ability to improve its capability to communicate with respondents throughout the world regardless if the respondent lives in a penthouse on Park Avenue in New York City or in a hut outside of New Delhi. Interviewing and collecting information from a specified population group can be enhanced with new and existing data collection methodologies and technologies. Opinion One is assisting the global market research community with these efforts through its pioneering work in creating the first new interviewing methodology in 30 years, Computer-Assisted Visual Interviewing (CAVI™). Our vision is to provide the industry with communication methodologies that enable researchers throughout the world to secure and improve respondent cooperation and get closer to the truth. I strongly believe that my vision, goal, and pioneering efforts will help to guide the industry into the future.

"JJ" Klein
Chief Executive, Opinion One, LP

Jstreetdata.com Streamlines Physician Surveys with Its Online Panel and Three Wizards

online research

It is estimated that over $1 billion is spent annually in the United States on researching the medical market. In the past, a typical medical market research project was priced in the $35,000–$45,000 range and required up to two months of activities such as study design; recruiting respondents; data collection via fax, mail, or telephone interview; and data analysis.

Jstreetdata.com, a medical market research specialist, realized that an online panel greatly accelerates the entire research process with a 20 percent to 30 percent savings. This company has recruited 6,000 physicians of all specialties, including some who are very difficult to access such as cardiologists, who have agreed to respond to e-mail invitations to fill out a questionnaire posted on the jstreetdata.com Web site.

Jstreetdata.com uses three online wizards for its services. The Survey Wizard™ walks a researcher through the steps of constructing an online questionnaire. The Survey Wizard™ has a number of question formats that permit yes–no questions, numerical and graphical scales, multiple-choice questions, or open text. When the researcher is satisfied with his or her questionnaire, it is posted on the Web site. The Recruitment Wizard™ is then used to identify specific medical personnel types, such as cardiovascular surgeons, who are on the panel. With this wizard, the researcher sends out a mass e-mail invitation to all eligible panelists. Of course, the 24/7 feature of jstreetdata.com's online surveys is very advantageous as physicians work long hours, and they need this time flexibility to fill out and submit the online questionnaire quickly. During the survey, the researcher can view graphical presentations of survey results, and at the end of the survey, the full data set can be downloaded by the researcher for extensive analysis. The Focus Wizard™ is the third wizard, which is an online chat feature where researchers can conduct online focus groups with targeted panelists.[1]

There are three general ways of obtaining primary data in marketing research—survey, observation, and experiment. Although exact figures are not available, it is well known that surveys are the most widely used method of data collection in commercial marketing research. They are also used extensively in monitoring public opinion, noting social trends, and even being used as evidence in court cases.[2] The bulk of marketing research surveys is sometimes called cross-sectional studies or surveys of large cross sections of populations. Alternatively, the survey may be very targeted such as the online medical research service of jstreetdata.com described earlier. Consequently, we devote much attention to collecting data via surveys in this chapter. First, we note the advantages of surveys. Next, we describe the pros and cons of the three basic survey modes: (1) person-administered surveys, (2) computer-assisted surveys, and (3) self-administered surveys. After these, we give descriptions of several commonly used data collection methods such as mall intercepts, telephone interviews, and mail surveys. Finally, we discuss factors a market researcher should consider when deciding which data collection method to use.

ADVANTAGES OF SURVEYS

Key advantages of surveys include standardization, ease of administration, ability to tap the "unseen," suitability to tabulation and statistical analysis, and sensitivity to subgroup differences.

Compared to observation or other qualitative methods, survey methods allow the collection of significant amounts of data in an economical and efficient manner, and they typically allow for much larger sample sizes. There are five advantages of using survey methods: (1) standardization, (2) ease of administration, (3) ability to tap the "unseen," (4) suitability to tabulation and statistical analysis, and (5) sensitivity to subgroup differences (see Table 9.1).

Standardization

Because questions are preset and organized in a particular arrangement on a questionnaire, survey methods ensure that all respondents are asked the same questions and are exposed to the same response options for each question. Moreover, the researcher is assured that every respondent will be confronted with questions that address the complete range of information objectives driving the research project.

Ease of Administration

Mail surveys are self-administered, the simplest form of administration for researchers.

Sometimes an interviewer is used, and survey modes are easily geared to such administration. On the other hand, the respondent may fill out the questionnaire unattended. In either case, the administration aspects are much simpler than, for instance, conducting a focus group or utilizing depth interviews. Perhaps the simplest case is a mail survey in which questionnaires are sent to prospective respondents. There is no need for tape recording, taking notes, or analyzing projective or physiological data; there is not even a need to read the questions to the respondent. All the researcher needs to do is mail the questions to prospective respondents.

Ability to Tap the "Unseen"

The four questions of what, why, how, and who help uncover "unseen" data. For instance, we can ask a working parent to tell us how important the location of a preschool was in his or her selection of the child's preschool. We can inquire as to how many different preschools he or she seriously considered before deciding on one, and we can easily gain an understanding of the person's financial or work circumstances with a few questions on income, occupation, and family size. Much information is unobservable and requires direct questions.

Table **9.1** **Five Advantages of Survey Research**

ADVANTAGE	DESCRIPTION
Standardization	All respondents react to questions worded identically and presented in the same order. Response options (scales) are the same, too.
Administration ease	Interviewers read questions to respondents and record their answers quickly and easily. In some cases, the respondents fill out the questionnaires themselves.
Tap the "unseen"	It is possible to ask questions about motives, circumstances, sequences of events and mental deliberations.
Tabulation/analysis	Large sample sizes and computer processing allow quick tallies, cross-tabulations, and other statistical analyses.
Subgroup differences	Respondents can be divided into segments or subgroups for comparisons in the search for meaningful differences.

Surveys allow researchers to compare market segments.

Suitability to Tabulation and Statistical Analysis

The marketing researcher ultimately must interpret the patterns or common themes sometimes hidden in the raw data he or she collects. Statistical analysis, both simple and complex, is the preferred means of achieving this goal, and large cross-sectional surveys perfectly complement these procedures. Qualitative methods, in contrast, prove much more frustrating in this respect because of their necessarily small samples, need for interpretation, and general approach to answering marketing managers' questions. Increasingly, questionnaire design software includes the ability to perform simple statistical analyses, such as tabulations of the answers to each question, as well as the ability to create color graphs summarizing these tabulations.

Questionnaire design programs include statistical analysis packages as a natural extension of survey research.

Sensitivity to Subgroup Differences

Because surveys involve large numbers of respondents, it is relatively easy to "slice" up the sample into demographic groups or other subgroups and then to compare them for market segmentation implications. In fact, the survey sample design may be drawn up to specifically include important subgroups as a means of looking at market segment differences. In any case, the large sample sizes that characterize surveys facilitate subgroup analyses and comparisons of various groups existing in the sample.

THREE ALTERNATIVE DATA COLLECTION MODES

There are three major ways to collect information from respondents: (1) Have a person ask the questions, either face-to-face or voice-to-voice without any assistance from a computer. (2) Have a computer assist or direct the questioning in a face-to-face or voice-to-voice survey. (3) Allow respondents to fill out the questionnaire themselves, without computer assistance. We will refer to these three alternatives as

Three data collection modes are person-administered, computer-administered, and self-administered surveys.

person-administered, computer-administered, and self-administered surveys, respectively. Each one has special advantages and disadvantages that we describe in general before discussing the various types of surveys found within each category. Specific advantages and disadvantages on these various types are discussed later.

Person-Administered Surveys (Without Computer Assistance)

A **person-administered survey** is one in which an interviewer reads questions, either face-to-face or over the telephone, to the respondent and records his or her answers. It was the primary administration method for many years. However, its popularity has fallen off as communications systems have developed and computer technology has advanced. Nevertheless, person-administered surveys are still used, and we describe the advantages and disadvantages associated with these surveys next.

Advantages of Person-Administered Surveys Person-administered surveys have four unique advantages: They offer feedback, rapport, quality control, and adaptability.

> Person-administered surveys have the four unique advantages of feedback, rapport, quality control, and adaptability.

1. *Feedback.* Interviewers often must respond to direct questions from respondents during an interview. Sometimes respondents do not understand the instructions, or they may not hear the question clearly, or they might become distracted by some outside factor during the interview. A human interviewer may be allowed to adjust his or her questions according to verbal or nonverbal cues. When a respondent begins to fidget or look bored, the interviewer can say, "I have only a few more questions." Or if a respondent makes a comment, the interviewer may jot it down as a side note to the researcher.

> Personal interviewers can build rapport with respondents who are initially distrustful or suspicious.

2. *Rapport.* Some people distrust surveys in general, or they may have some suspicions about the survey at hand. It is often helpful to have another human being present to develop some rapport with the respondent early on in the questioning process. Once a bridge of trust and understanding has been established, most respondents will become visibly more relaxed with the interview and will open up more to the various questions being posed.

3. *Quality control.* An interviewer sometimes must select certain types of respondents based on gender, age, or some other distinguishing characteristic. Personal interviewers may be used to ensure respondents are selected

Without a personal interviewer present, respondents may fail to understand survey questions.

correctly. Alternatively, some researchers feel that respondents are more likely to be truthful when they respond face-to-face.

4. *Adaptability*. Personal interviewers can adapt to respondent differences. It is not unusual, for instance, to find an elderly person who must be initially helped step by step through the answering process in order to understand how to respond to questions asking if the respondent "strongly agrees," "somewhat agrees," "somewhat disagrees," or "strongly disagrees." By the same token, an engineer quickly grasps very complicated numerical rating scales. An interviewer may be allowed to adjust the directions accordingly or have the respondent do tasks such as sorting cards with brand names into piles or examining a mockup of an ad.

Personal interviewers can easily adapt to the needs and styles of different respondents.

Disadvantages of Person-Administered Surveys The drawbacks to using human interviewers pertain to exactly that, humans. That is, personal interviewers are slower; they are prone to errors; and although pictures, videos, and graphics can be handled by personal interviewers, they cannot accommodate them as easily. Often personal interviewers simply record respondents' answers using pencil and paper, which necessitates a separate data-input step to build a computer data file. But increasing numbers of data collection companies have shifted to the use of laptop computers that immediately add the responses to a data file. Naturally, the use of a face-to-face interviewer is more expensive than mailing the questionnaire to respondents. Ideally, personal interviewers are highly trained and skilled and their use overcomes the expense factor. A less expensive person-administered survey is a telephone interview.

Person-administered surveys are relatively slow and/or expensive.

Computer-Administered Surveys

As our introductory example illustrates, computer technology represents a viable option with respect to survey mode, and new developments occur almost every day. Although person-administered surveys are still the industry mainstay, computer-administered survey methods are growing very rapidly and will rival person-administered surveys in the foreseeable future. Computer-assisted surveys are in an evolutionary state, and they are spreading to other survey types. For instance, a computer may house questions asked by a telephone interviewer, or a questionnaire may be posted on the Internet for administration. Basically, a **computer-administered survey** is one in which computer technology plays an essential role in the interview work. Here either the computer assists an interview or it interacts directly with the respondent. In the case of Internet-based questionnaires, the computer acts as the medium by which potential respondents are approached, and it is the means by which respondents submit their completed questionnaire. As with person-administered surveys, computer-administered surveys have their advantages and disadvantages.

Advantages of Computer-Administered Surveys There are variations of computer-administered surveys. At one extreme, the respondent answers the questions on his or her PC, often online, and the questions are tailored to his or her responses to previous questions, so there are no human interviewers. At the other end, there are computer programs in which a telephone or personal interviewer is prompted by the computer as to what questions to ask and in what sequence. Regardless of which variation is considered, at least five advantages of computer-administered surveys are evident: speed; error-free interviews; use of pictures, videos, and graphics; real-time capture of data; and reduction of "interview evaluation" concern in respondents.

Computer-administered surveys are fast, error free, capable of using pictures or graphics, able to capture data in real time, and are less threatening for some respondents.

1. *Speed*. The computer-administered approach is much faster than the human interview approach. Computers can quickly jump to questions

Person-administered surveys have the advantage of feedback, rapport, quality control, and adaptability.

based on specific responses, they can rapidly dial random telephone numbers, and they can easily check on answers to previous questions to modify or otherwise custom-tailor the interview to each respondent's circumstances. The speed factor translates into cost savings, and there is a claim that Internet surveys are about one-half the cost of mail or phone surveys.[3]

2. *Error-free interviews.* Properly programmed, the computer-administered approach guarantees zero interviewer errors such as inadvertently skipping questions, asking inappropriate questions based on previous responses, misunderstanding how to pose questions, recording the wrong answer, and so forth. Also, the computer neither becomes fatigued nor cheats.

3. *Use of pictures, videos, and graphics.* Computer graphics can be integrated into questions as they are viewed on a computer screen. So rather than having an interviewer pull out a picture of a new type of window unit air conditioner, for instance, computer graphics can show it from various perspectives. CD-ROM disk capabilities allow high-quality video windows to appear so the respondent can see the product in use or can be shown a wide range of visual displays.

The real-time capture of data by computer-administered surveys is an important advantage of this data collection method.

4. *Real-time capture of data.* Because respondents are interacting with the computer and not a human who is recording their answers on a questionnaire, the information is directly entered into a computer's data storage system and can be accessed for tabulation or other analyses at any time. Once the interviews are finished, final tabulations can be completed in a matter of minutes. This feature is so beneficial that some interview companies have telephone interviewers directly linked to computer input when they conduct their interviews.

5. *Reduction of "interview evaluation" concern in respondents.* When involved in responding to questions in a survey, some people become anx-

ious about the possible reaction of the interviewer to their answers. Questions about personal hygiene, political opinions, financial matters, and even age are considered to be "personal" by many people, and the presence of a human interviewer may deter them from answering, or they may give false answers that they believe the interviewer will accept. On the other hand, some respondents try to please the interviewer by saying what they think the interviewer wants to hear. In any case, some researchers believe that respondents will provide more truthful answers to potentially sensitive topics when interacting with a machine.

Disadvantages of Computer-Administered Surveys Obviously, computer-assisted surveys must have some disadvantages; otherwise, more surveys would make use of computer technology. Although computers are relatively inexpensive at present, there are costs involved in computer design, programming, debugging, and setup, which must be incurred with each survey. Depending on what type of computer-administered survey is under consideration, these costs, including the time factor associated with them, can render computer-administered delivery systems for surveys less attractive relative to other data collection options. At the same time, there are a number of moderate to low-cost computer-administered options such as e-mail surveys or Web-based questionnaires with user-friendly development interfaces that are fueling the rush toward online research around the world.

> Some types of computer-administered surveys incur relatively high setup costs, but others are very reasonable and easy to use.

Self-Administered Surveys

A **self-administered** survey is one in which the respondent completes the survey on his or her own. It is different from other survey methods in that there is no agent—human or computer—administering the interview. So, we are referring to the prototypical "pencil-and-paper" survey here. Instead, the respondent reads the questions and responds directly on the questionnaire. Normally, the respondent goes at his or her own pace, and in most instances he or she selects the place and time to complete the interview. He or she also may decide when the questionnaire will be returned. As with other survey methods, those that are self-administered have their advantages and disadvantages.

Advantages of Self-Administered Surveys Self-administered surveys have three important advantages: reduced cost, respondent control, and no interviewer-evaluation apprehension.

> Self-administered surveys are attractive because they are low in cost, they give respondents control, and they avoid interviewer-evaluation apprehension.

1. *Reduced cost.* By eliminating the need for an interviewer or an interviewing device such as a computer program, there can be significant savings in cost.
2. *Respondent control.* Respondents can control the pace at which they respond, so they may not feel rushed. Ideally, a respondent should be relaxed while responding, and a self-administered survey may affect this state.
3. *No interviewer-evaluation apprehension.* As we just noted, some respondents feel apprehensive when answering questions, or the topic may be sensitive, such as gambling,[4] smoking, or dental work.

The self-administered approach takes the administrator, whether human or computer, out of the picture, and respondents may feel more at ease. Self-administered questionnaires have been found to elicit more insightful information than face-to-face interviews.[5]

> There is potential for respondent error with self-administered surveys.

Disadvantages of Self-Administered Surveys As you can see, self-administration places control of the survey in the hands of the prospective respondent. Hence, this type of survey is subject to the possibilities that respondents will not complete the

> If respondents misunderstand or do not follow directions, they may become frustrated and quit.

survey, will answer questions erroneously, will not respond in a timely manner, or will refuse to return the survey at all.

The major reason for these drawbacks is that no opportunity exists to monitor or interact with the respondent during the course of the interview. For example, in conducting a survey for a mass-transit system, one question might be, "Have you used this city's subway system to commute to and from work in the past three months?" The questionnaire may then instruct respondents who indicate "no" to skip the next set of questions, whereas those responding "yes" would continue on and answer questions about the subway's cleanliness, the degree of crowding, its adherence to published schedules, and so on. If a respondent who indicated "no" somehow failed to realize that he or she should skip these questions, there is the possibility that he or she would become frustrated at the questions about the subway's features and throw the questionnaire away. Alternatively, in conducting a survey of aspirin use, one question might ask the respondent to rank five different brands of aspirin from "most preferred" to "least preferred" by writing the rank number beside each brand. However, the respondent might misunderstand and just check off his or her most-preferred brand. In either case, if an interviewer were present, the error would be quickly spotted and resolved; but, because the interviewer is not present, the respondent may well commit numerous similar errors while fully believing that he or she has responded properly.

Due to the absence of the interviewer or an internal computer check system, the burden of respondent understanding falls on the questionnaire itself. It must have very clear instructions, examples, and reminders throughout. Although questionnaire design is a complete topic that we take up in Chapter 11, the point to remember here is that the respondent, not the interviewer, has control with self-administered surveys. Thus, the potential for error is very high, and market researchers must take great care to reduce this error factor.

DESCRIPTIONS OF REPRESENTATIVE DATA COLLECTION MODES

Now that you have an understanding of the pros and cons of person-, computer-, and self-administered surveys, we can describe the various interviewing techniques used in each method. There are 11 different data collection methods used by marketing researchers (Table 9.2):

1. In-home interview
2. Mall-intercept interview
3. In-office interview
4. "Traditional" telephone interview
5. Central location telephone interview
6. Computer-assisted telephone interview (CATI)
7. Fully computerized interview
8. Online and other Internet-based surveys
9. Group self-administered survey
10. Drop-off survey
11. Mail survey

Person-Administered Interviews

There are at least four variations of person-administered interviews, and their differences are largely based on the location of the interview. These variations include the in-home interview, the mall-intercept interview, the in-office interview, and the telephone interview (which includes the "traditional" and central location telephone interviews).

Table 9.2	**Ways to Gather Data**
DATA COLLECTION METHOD	**DESCRIPTION**
In-home interview	The interviewer conducts the interview in the respondent's home. Appointments may be made ahead by telephone.
Mall-intercept interview	Shoppers in a mall are approached and asked to take part in the survey. Questions may be asked in the mall or in the mall-intercept company's facilities located in the mall.
In-office interview	The interviewer makes an appointment with business executives or managers to conduct the interview at the respondent's place of work.
"Traditional" telephone interview	Interviewers work out of their homes to conduct telephone interviews with households or business representatives.
Central location telephone interview	Interviewers work in a data collection company's office using cubicles or work areas for each interviewer. Often the supervisor has the ability to "listen in" to interviews and to check that they are being conducted correctly.
Computer-assisted telephone interview	With a computer-assisted telephone interview, the questions are programmed for a computer screen and the interviewer then reads them off. Responses are entered directly into the computer program by the interviewer.
Fully computerized interview	A computer is programmed to administer the questions. Respondents interact with the computer and enter in their own answers by using a keyboard, by touching the screen, or by using some other means.
Online or other Internet-based survey	Respondents fill out a questionnaire that resides on the Internet, or otherwise accesses it via the Internet such as receiving an e-mail attachment or downloading the file online.
Group self-administered survey	Respondents take the survey in a group context. Each respondent works individually, but they meet as a group and this allows the researcher to economize.
Drop-off survey	Questionnaires are left with the respondent to fill out. The administrator may return at a later time to pick up the completed questionnaire, or it may be mailed in.
Mail survey	Questionnaires are mailed to prospective respondents who are asked to fill them out and return them by mail.

In-Home Interviews Just as the name implies, an **in-home interview** is conducted in the home of the respondent. Two important factors justify the use of in-home interviews. First, the marketing researcher must believe that personal contact is essential to the success of the interview. Second, he or she must be convinced that the in-home environment is conducive to the questioning process.

Let us analyze these factors more completely. With respect to the first factor, the survey may incorporate a set of advertisements the researcher wants viewed, it might require the respondent to see and touch a product, the respondent may have to perform a complicated task such as sorting cards with brand names on them into piles, or it might be vital that the interviewer make visual confirmation of the respondent's qualifying characteristics or nonverbal cues. On the second factor, it is often believed that conducting an interview in the home greatly improves the quality of responses and facilitates the rapport between interviewer and interviewee. When a respondent is in a secure, comfortable environment, the likelihood of distraction is

In-home interviews are conducted in the security and comfort of respondents' homes.

In-home interviews facilitate interviewer–interviewee rapport.

reduced, and it is believed that respondents take more care in responding to various questions. Also, most in-home interviews take considerable time, and by allowing the interview to take place in his or her home, the respondent is implicitly expecting it to take some time, certainly longer than would be expected for a telephone survey, for instance.

Mall-Intercept Interviews   Although the in-home interview has important advantages, it has the significant disadvantage of cost. The expense of in-home interviewer travel is high, even for local surveys. Patterned after "man-on-the-street" interviews pioneered by opinion-polling companies and other "high-traffic" surveys conducted in settings where crowds of pedestrians pass by, the **mall-intercept interview** is one in which the respondent is encountered and questioned while he or she is visiting a shopping mall. A mall-intercept company generally has its offices located within a large shopping mall, usually one that draws from a regional rather than a local market area. Typically, the interview company negotiates exclusive rights to do interviews in the mall and, thus, forces all marketing research companies that wish to do mall intercepts in that area to use that interview company's services. In any case, the travel costs are eliminated because the respondents incur the costs themselves by traveling to the mall.

Mall-intercept interviewing has acquired a major role as a survey method due to its ease of implementation.[6] Shoppers are intercepted in the pedestrian traffic areas of shopping malls and either interviewed on the spot or asked to move to a permanent interviewing facility located in the mall office. Although some malls do not allow marketing research interviewing because they view it as a nuisance to shoppers, many do permit mall-intercept interviews and may rely on these data themselves to fine-tune their own marketing programs.

In addition to low cost, mall interviews have most of the advantages associated with in-home interviewing. Perhaps the most important advantage is the presence of an interviewer who can interact with the respondent.[7] However, a few disadvantages are specifically associated with mall interviewing, and it is necessary to point them out here. First, sample representativeness is an issue, for most malls draw from a relatively small area in close proximity to their location. Some people shop at malls more frequently than others and, therefore, have a greater chance of being interviewed.[8] Recent growth of nonmall retailing concepts such as catalogs and stand-alone discounters such as Wal-Mart mean that more mall visitors are recreational shoppers rather than convenience-oriented shoppers, resulting in the need to scrutinize mall-intercept samples as to what consumer groups they actually represent.[9] Also, many shoppers refuse to take part in mall interviews for various reasons. Nevertheless, special selection procedures called quotas, which are described in Chapter 12, may be used to counter the problem of nonrepresentativeness.

A second shortcoming of mall-intercept interviewing is that a shopping mall does not have a comfortable home environment that is conducive to rapport and close attention to details. The respondents may feel uncomfortable because passersby stare at them; they may be pressed for time or otherwise preoccupied by various distractions outside the researcher's control. These factors may adversely affect the quality of the interview. As we indicated earlier, some interview companies attempt to counter this problem by taking respondents to special interview rooms located in the interview company's mall offices. This procedure minimizes distractions and encourages respondents to be more relaxed. One company, Opinion One, has innovated an oversized monitor with touchscreen technology that immerses respondents in the survey, thereby minimizing distractions and capturing the responses as they are given. In Marketing Research Insight 9.1 you can meet "JJ" Klein, the chief executive of Opinion One.

Mall-intercept interviews are conducted in large shopping malls, and they are less expensive per interview than are in-home interviews.

Mall-intercept interview companies make this method easy and popular.

The representativeness of mall interview samples is always an issue.

Mall interview companies use rooms in their small headquarters areas to conduct private interviews in a relaxed setting.

▶ **Meet a Marketing Researcher**

"JJ" Klein, Chief Executive, Opinion One, LP

"JJ" Klein, chief executive of Opinion One, is a marketing and research professional with more than 25 years of experience in designing, developing, and implementing research methodologies and programs. Mr. Klein is Opinion One's primary visionary.

Mr. Klein began his marketing and research career as a project director for Simmons Market Research Bureau, where he rose through a number of management positions to become associate executive vice president. He was involved in the design and development of the annual

Simmons "Study of Selective Markets" and was director of the "Simmons Local Index." In addition, he was instrumental in designing and developing the first online interactive data analysis and delivery system made available to a variety of markets, including advertisers and their agencies.

Mr. Klein left Simmons Research to form Three Sigma Research Center. As partner and chief operating officer, Mr. Klein created Three Sigma's "Syndicated Study of Major Markets." This was the first major syndicated-local market newspaper audience measurement system implemented in the United States. This syndicated program eventually became the Scarborough Report, based on more than 100,000 interviews, which continues to be an industry standard. Following the sale of Three Sigma, Mr. Klein joined Audits & Surveys Worldwide as a director, principal, and member of the senior management group. He was involved in developing a number of the company's domestic and international businesses, including consumer marketing and retail audit and distribution tracking services.

Mr. Klein brings a unique blend of experience in developing local, national, and international marketing, sales, advertising, and retail information businesses. In addition, he is a member of the American Marketing Association (cofounder of the Gold Coast Chapter) and European Society for Opinion and Marketing Research. Mr. Klein is a frequent guest speaker at domestic and international conferences.

In-Office Interviews Although the in-home and mall-intercept interview methods are appropriate for a wide variety of consumer goods, marketing research conducted in the business-to-business or organizational market typically requires interviews with business executives, purchasing agents, engineers, or other managers. Normally, **in-office interviews** take place in person while the respondent is in his or her office, or perhaps in a company lounge area. Interviewing businesspersons face-to-face has essentially the same advantages and drawbacks as in-home consumer interviewing. For example, if Texas Instruments wanted information regarding user preferences for different features that might be offered in a new ultra-high-speed laser printer designed for business accounting firms, it would make sense to interview prospective users or purchasers of these printers. It would also be logical that these people would be interviewed at their places of business.

As you might imagine, in-office personal interviews incur relatively high costs. Those executives qualified to give opinions on a specific topic or individuals who would be involved in product purchase decisions must first be located. Sometimes names can be obtained from sources such as industry directories or trade association membership lists. More frequently, screening must be conducted over the telephone by calling a particular company that is believed to have executives of the type needed. However, locating those people within a large organization may be time

In-office interviews are conducted at executives' or managers' places of work because they are the most suitable locations.

Centralized telephone interviews are fast, high quality, and relatively inexpensive.

consuming. Once a qualified person is located, the next step is to persuade that person to agree to an interview and then set up a time for the interview. Finally, an interviewer must go to the particular place at the appointed time. Even with appointments, long waits are sometimes encountered and cancellations are not uncommon because businesspeople's schedules sometimes shift unexpectedly. Added to these cost factors is the fact that interviewers who specialize in businessperson interviews are more costly in general because of their specialized knowledge and abilities. They have to navigate around gatekeepers such as secretaries, learn technical jargon, and be conversant on product features when the respondent asks pointed questions or even criticizes questions as they are posed to him or her.

In-office personal interviews incur costs due to difficulties in accessing qualified respondents.

Telephone Interview   As we have mentioned previously, the need for a face-to-face interview is often predicated on the necessity of the respondent's actually seeing a product, advertisement, or packaging sample. On the other hand, it may be vital that the interviewer watch the respondent to ensure correct procedures are followed or otherwise to verify something about the respondent or his or her reactions. If, however, physical contact is not necessary, telephone interviewing is an attractive option. There are a number of advantages as well as disadvantages associated with telephone interviewing.

Advantages of telephone interviews are cost, quality, and speed.

The advantages of telephone interviewing are many, and they explain the popularity of phone surveys. First, the telephone is a relatively inexpensive way to collect survey data. Long-distance telephone charges are much lower than the cost of a face-to-face interview. A second advantage of the telephone interview is that it has the potential to yield a very high-quality sample. If the researcher employs random dialing procedures and proper callback measures, the telephone approach may produce a better sample than any other survey procedure. A third and very important advantage is that telephone surveys have very quick turnaround times. Most telephone interviews are of short duration anyway, but a good interviewer may complete several interviews per hour. Conceivably, a study could have the data collection phase executed in a few days with telephone interviews. In fact, in the political polling industry in which real-time information on voter opinions is essential, it is not unusual to have national telephone polls completed in a single night.

Unfortunately, the telephone survey approach has several inherent shortcomings. First, the respondent cannot be shown anything. This shortcoming ordinarily eliminates the telephone survey as an alternative in situations requiring that the respondent view product prototypes, advertisements, packages, or anything else. A second disadvantage is that the telephone interview does not permit the interviewer to make the various judgments and evaluations that can be made by the face-to-face interviewer. For example, judgments regarding respondent income based on the home they live in and other outward signs of economic status cannot be made. Similarly, the telephone does not allow for the observation of body language and facial expressions, nor does it permit eye contact. On the other hand, some may argue that the lack of face-to-face contact is helpful. Self-disclosure studies have indicated that respondents provide more information in personal interviews, except when the topics are threatening or potentially embarrassing. Questions on alcohol consumption, contraceptive methods, racial issues, or income tax reporting will probably generate more valid responses when asked in the relative anonymity of the telephone than when administered face-to-face.[10]

A third disadvantage of the telephone interview is that the marketing researcher is more limited in the quantity and types of information that he or she can obtain. Very long interviews are inappropriate for the telephone, as are questions with lengthy lists of response options that respondents will have difficulty remembering when they are read over the telephone. Respondents short on patience may hang up during interviews, or they may utter short and convenient responses just to speed up the interview. Obviously, the telephone is a poor choice for conducting an interview with many open-ended questions.

The telephone is a poor choice for conducting a survey with many open-ended questions.

A last problem with telephone interviews is the growing threat to its existence by the increased use of answering machines, caller recognition, and call-blocking devices being adopted by consumers.[11] The research industry is concerned about these gatekeeping methods, and it is just beginning to study ways around them.[12] Another difficulty is that legitimate telephone interviewers must contend with the negative impression people have of telemarketers.[13]

Telephone interviewers must contend with the negative impression people have of telemarketers.

There are two types of telephone interviews: traditional and central location. As you can guess, telephone interviewing has been and continues to be greatly impacted by advances in telephone systems and communications technology. As you will see, the traditional telephone approach has largely faded away, whereas the central location approach has embraced technological advances in telephone systems.

Traditional Telephone Interviewing. Technology has radically changed telephone surveys; however, it is worthwhile to describe this form of telephone interviewing as a starting point. Prior to central location and computer-assisted telephone interviewing, these **traditional telephone interviews** were those that were conducted either from the homes of the telephone interviewing staff or, perhaps, from telephone stalls located in the data collection company's offices. Everything was done mechanically. That is, interviewers dialed the telephone number manually, they read questions off a printed questionnaire, they were responsible for following special instructions on how to administer the questions, and they checked off the respondent's answers on each questionnaire. Quality control was limited to training sessions, sometimes in the form of a dress rehearsal by administering the questionnaire to the supervisor or another interviewer, and to callback checks by the supervisor to verify that the respondent had taken part in the interview.

Obviously, the traditional telephone interview method offers great potential for errors. In addition to the possibilities of misdialing and making mistakes in administering the questions, there are potential problems of insufficient call-backs for not-at-homes, and a host of other problems. Also, because the actual hours worked

Traditional telephone interviewing has great potential for errors.

while performing telephone interviews are difficult to track, most interview companies opt for a "per completion" compensation system. That is, the interviewer is compensated for each questionnaire delivered to the office that is completely filled out. As you can imagine, there have been instances of dishonest interviewers turning in falsified results.

 A concern with traditional telephone interviewing is interviewer cheating. Although most traditional telephone interviewers are honest, only minimal control and supervision can be used with this method. Consequently, there are temptations for cheating such as turning in bogus completed questionnaires or conducting interviews with respondents who do not qualify for the survey at hand. When traditional telephone interviewing is used, checks should be more extensive and may include the following:

1. Have an independent party call back a sample of each interviewer's respondents to verify that they took part in the survey.
2. Have interviewers submit copies of their telephone logs to validate that the work was performed on the dates and in the time periods required.
3. If long-distance calls were made, have interviewers submit copies of their telephone bill with long-distance charges itemized to check that the calls were made properly.
4. If there is a concern about a particular interviewer's diligence, request that the interviewer be taken off the project.

A researcher should always check the accuracy and validity of interviews, regardless of the data collection method used.

Central Location Telephone Interviewing. This form of telephone interviewing is in many ways the research industry's standard. With **central location telephone interviewing,** a field data collection company installs several telephone lines at one location, and the interviewers make calls from the central location. Usually, interviewers have separate enclosed work spaces and lightweight headsets that free both hands so they can record responses. Everything is done from this central location. Obviously, there are many advantages to operating from a central location. For example, resources are pooled, and interviewers can handle multiple surveys, such as calling plant managers in the afternoon and households during the evening shift.

The reasons for the prominence of the central location phone interview are savings and control. Apart from cost savings, perhaps the most important reason is quality control. To begin, recruitment and training are performed uniformly at this location. Interviewers can be oriented to the equipment, they can study the questionnaire and its instructions, and they can simulate the interview among themselves over their phone lines. Also, the actual interviewing process can be monitored. Most telephone interviewing facilities have monitoring equipment that permits a supervisor to listen in on interviewing as it is being conducted. Interviewers who are not doing the interview properly can be spotted and the necessary corrective action taken. Ordinarily, each interviewer will be monitored at least once per shift, but the supervisor may focus attention on newly hired interviewers to ensure they are doing their work correctly. The fact that each interviewer never knows when the supervisor will listen in guarantees more overall diligence than would be seen otherwise. Also, completed questionnaires are checked on the spot as a further quality control check. Interviewers can be immediately informed of any deficiencies in filling out the questionnaire. Finally, there is control over interviewers' schedules. That is, interviewers report in and out and work regular hours, even if they are evening hours, and make calls during the time periods stipulated by the researcher as appropriate interviewing times.

Computer-Administered Interviews

Computer technology has impacted the telephone data collection industry significantly. There are two variations of computer-administered telephone interview systems. In one, a human interviewer is used, but in the other, a computer, sometimes with a synthesized or tape-recorded voice, is used. At the same time, there are important computer-assisted interview methods that have recently emerged, which we describe in this section as well.

Computer-Assisted Telephone Interview (CATI) The most advanced companies have computerized the central location telephone interviewing process; such systems are called **computer-assisted telephone interviews (CATI)**. Although each system is unique, and new developments occur almost daily, we can describe a typical situation. Here each interviewer is equipped with a hands-free headset and is seated in front of a computer screen that is driven by the company's computer system. Often the computer dials the prospective respondent's telephone automatically, and the computer screen provides the interviewer with the introductory comments. As the interview progresses, the interviewer moves through the questions by pressing a key or a series of keys on the keyboard. Some systems use light pens or pressure-sensitive screens. The questions and possible responses appear on the screen one at a time. The interviewer reads the question to the respondent, enters the response code, and the computer moves on to the next appropriate question. For example, an interviewer might ask if the respondent owns a dog. If the answer is "yes," there could appear a series of questions regarding what type of dog food the dog owner buys. If the answer is "no," these questions would be inappropriate. Instead, the computer program skips to the next appropriate question, which might be "Do you own a cat?" In other words, the computer eliminates the human error potential that would exist if this survey were done in the traditional paper-and-pencil telephone interview mode. The human interviewer is just the "voice" of the computer.

> With CATI, the interviewer reads the questions off a computer screen and enters respondents' answers directly into the computer program.

> With CATI, the interviewer is the "voice" of the computer.

The computer can even be used to customize questions. For example, in the early part of a long interview you might ask a respondent the years, makes, and models of all cars he or she owns. Later in the interview you might ask questions about each specific car owned. The question might come up on the interviewer's screen as follows: "You said you own a Lexus. Who in your family drives this car most often?" Other questions about this car and others owned would appear in similar fashion. Questions like this can, of course, be dealt with in a traditional or central location manual interview, but they are handled much more efficiently in the computerized version because the interviewer does not need to physically flip questionnaire pages back and forth or remember previous responses.

The CATI approach also eliminates the need for editing completed questionnaires and creating computer data files by later manually entering every response with a keyboard. There is no checking for errors in completed questionnaires because there is no physical questionnaire. More to the point, in most computerized interview systems it is not permitted to enter an "impossible" answer. For example, if a question has three possible answers with codes "A," "B," and "C," and the interviewer enters a "D" by mistake, the computer will ask for the answer to be reentered until an acceptable code is entered. If a combination or pattern of answers is impossible, the computer will not accept an answer, or it may alert the interviewer to the inconsistency and move to a series of questions that will resolve the discrepancy. Data entry for completed questionnaires is eliminated because data are entered directly into a computer file as the interviewing is completed.

> Most CATI systems are programmed to make wrong answers impossible.

This second operation brings to light another advantage of computer-assisted interviewing. Tabulations may be run at any point in the study. Such real-time

> CATI systems permit tabulation in midsurvey.

reporting is impossible with pencil-and-paper questionnaires in which there can be a wait of several days following interviewing completion before detailed tabulations of the results are available. Instantaneous results available with computerized telephone interviewing provide some real advantages. Based on preliminary tabulations, certain questions may be dropped, saving time and money in subsequent interviewing. If, for example, over 90 percent of those interviewed answered a particular question in the same manner, there may be no need to continue asking the question.

Tabulations may also suggest the addition of questions to the survey. If an unexpected pattern of product use is uncovered in the early interviewing stages, questions can be added to further delve into this behavior. So the computer-administered telephone survey affords an element of flexibility unavailable in the traditional paper-and-pencil survey methods. Finally, managers may find the early reporting of survey results useful in preliminary planning and strategy development. Sometimes survey project deadlines run very close to managers' presentation deadlines, and advance indications of the survey's findings permit managers to organize their presentations in advance rather than all in a rush the night before. The many advantages and quick turnaround of CATI and CAPI (computer-assisted personal interviewing) make them mainstay data collection methods for many syndicated omnibus survey services.[14,15]

In sum, computer-administered telephone interviewing options are very attractive to marketing researchers because of the advantages of cost savings, quality control, and time savings over the paper-and-pencil method.[16] Looming on the horizon, however, is a serious challenge to CATI, especially for global marketing research. For example, Opinion One has developed a proprietary system called CAVI™, which stands for Computer-Assisted Visual Interviewing, that "... includes the integration of many components including but not limited to understanding eye movement and direction, color, text, sound and motion, etc. Opinion One's CAVI™ screen designs are attractive, engaging and provide respondents with an enjoyable experience. This leads to better respondent cooperation."[17] This innovative approach was referred to in our Practitioner Viewpoint by "JJ" Klein, chief executive at Opinion One, in the introduction to this chapter. Read Marketing Research Insight 9.2 to learn about why CATI's importance to the marketing research world may diminish very rapidly.

CATI's popularity may fall as online surveys and panels rise in use.

Fully Computerized Interview (Not Online) Some companies have developed **fully computerized interviews,** in which the survey is administered completely by a computer, but *not online*. With one such system, a computer dials a phone number and a recording is used to introduce the survey. The respondent then uses the push buttons on his or her telephone to make responses, thereby interacting directly with the computer. In the research industry, this approach is known as **completely automated telephone survey (CATS).** CATS has been successfully employed for customer satisfaction studies, service quality monitoring, election day polls, product/warranty registration, and even in-home product tests with consumers who have been given a prototype of a new product.[18]

CATS eliminates the need for a human interviewer.

In another system, the respondent sits or stands in front of the computer unit and reads the instructions off the screen. Each question and its various response options appear on the screen, and the respondent answers by pressing a key or touching the screen. For example, the question may ask the respondent to rate how satisfied, on a scale of 1 to 10 (where 1 is very unsatisfied and 10 is very satisfied), he or she was the last time he or she used a travel agency to plan a family vacation. The instructions would instruct the respondent to press the key with the number appropriate to his or her degree of satisfaction. So, the respondent might press a "2" or a "7," depending on his or her experience and expectations. If, however, a "0" or

With fully computerized interviewing, respondents interact directly with the computer and enter their responses manually.

Several varieties of computer-assisted interview formats are available.

▶ **A Global Perspective**

CATI's Achilles' Heel Makes Certain Its Demise for Global Research[19]

MARKETING RESEARCH
INSIGHT
9.2

Despite the efficiencies and other advantages of its computerized system, computer-assisted telephone interviewing still has an Achilles' heel, namely, telephone interviewers. Although the computer can take care of virtually every other aspect of a telephone interview, there remains the need to have a human interviewer to conduct the interview over the telephone. The human interviewer factor becomes complicated in global studies when there is a need for translation of the questionnaire, and call centers are located in various countries. The necessary communication between call centers, training, interviewing, and client service invariably takes many hours of work.

Recently, Raymond Pettit, president of ERP Associates, and Robert Monster, CEO of Global Market Insite, compared CATI to two online data collection methods for a 10-minute survey of 1,000 respondents in 10 different countries. One online method used lists of respondent prospects who were bulk e-mailed invitations to take the survey, whereas the other online method used target e-mail invitations to a panel of individuals who had agreed to fill out online surveys. Here are the startling findings.

Item	Global CATI	Online with List	Online with Panel
Number of individuals contacted	138,889	1,111,111	17,544
Incidence rate	30%	30%	95%
Cooperation rate	24%	3%	50%
Person-hours elapsed	11,574	60	10
Data processing hours	170	10	5
Time to completion	10–12 weeks	5–7 days	4–5 days
Approximate data collection cost	$175,000	$35,000	$15,000
Approximate total survey cost	$225,000	$85,000	$100,000

Pettit and Monster comment that with worldwide cooperation rates falling, online survey with panels are becoming more and more attractive for global research. The only factor preventing the immediate demise of global CATI research is the small number of online panels around the globe.

some other ineligible key were pressed, the computer could be programmed to beep, indicating that the response was inappropriate, and instruct the respondent to make another entry.

All of the advantages of computer-driven interviewing are found in this approach, plus the interviewer expense or extra cost of human voice communication capability for the computer is eliminated. Because respondents' answers are saved in a file during the interview itself, tabulation can take place on a daily basis. Even if the interviews are conducted in remote locations across the United States, it is a simple matter to download the files via telephone lines and high-speed modems to the central facility for daily tabulations. Some researchers believe that the research industry should move to replace pen-and-paper questionnaires with computer-based ones.[20]

Online and Other Internet-Based Interviews Online research may take on any of a number of faces, but the **Internet-based questionnaire** in which the respondent answers questions online is becoming the industry standard for online surveys. For example, Procter & Gamble, which spends $150 million to conduct thousands of surveys each year, conducted 15 percent of its surveys online in 1999, and increased that number to 50 percent in 2001. Plans are to continue this trend.[21] Internet-based questionnaires are fast, easy, and inexpensive.[22] These questionnaires accommodate all of the standard question formats, and they are very flexible, including the ability to present pictures, diagrams, or displays to respondents. In fact, this ability is a major reason why researchers tracking advertising effects prefer online surveys to

Online surveys are fast, easy, and inexpensive.

telephone surveys, which have been a standard data collection for advertising tracking for a great many years.[23] The researcher can check the Web site for current tabulations whenever he or she desires, and respondents can access the online survey at any time of the day or night. Online data collection is and will continue to profoundly change the marketing research landscape.[24] For instance, in the case of customer satisfaction instead of "episodic" research in which a company does a large study one time per year, it allows for "continuous market intelligence" in which the survey is posted permanently on the Web and modified as the company's strategies are implemented. Company managers can click up tabulated customer reactions on a daily basis.[25] Some researchers refer to this advantage of online surveys as "real-time research."[26]

Are online surveys better than other survey types? This question can be answered by inspecting Figure 9.1, which is a comparison created by Dr. William H. MacElroy, president of Socratic Technologies, and his associates, presenting the various aspects of a survey on a grid.[27] One axis of the grid is how important the feature is to the researcher, identified as moderately or highly important, whereas the other axis is how online surveys compare to traditional surveys such as telephone interviews, face-to-face interviews, or mail surveys. The second axis is separated into gradations of the better or worse performance of online surveys relative to the traditional types.

Figure 9.1 clearly shows that online surveys have important advantages of speed and low cost, plus real-time access of data; however, there are drawbacks of sample

Online surveys have significant advantages over traditional surveys, and their use will increase in the future.

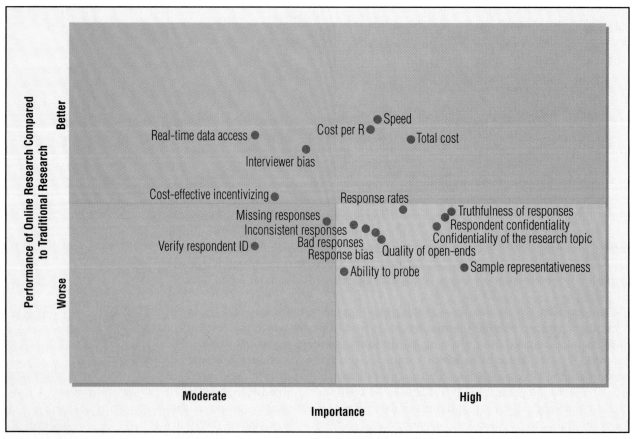

Figure **9.1** **Online Data Collection Methods Have Significant Advantages, But They Have Some Drawbacks, Too**[28]

representativeness, respondent validation, and difficulty in asking probing types of questions. Sample representativeness is most troublesome when global market research is involved, and firms are finding that considerable investments are required to achieve this goal.[29] Read Marketing Research Insight 9.3 to see why. Nevertheless, as Internet connectivity becomes more widespread and integrated into daily life, and as software advances to provide more flexibility and features on Web-based questionnaires, online surveys will undoubtedly become the most prevalent data collection mode. In fact, companies such as Knowledge Networks, Inc. are overcoming the sample representativeness problem by recruiting online panels whose demographic and purchasing profiles are consistent with target markets. These online panels provide accurate research data very quickly.[30]

▶ **A Global Perspective**

MARKETING RESEARCH
INSIGHT
9.3

Global Internet Penetration Differences: An Opportunity or a Challenge for Online Surveys?[31]

Nielsen//NetRatings, the premier Internet penetration authority, periodically releases statistics on its measurement of the Internet audience worldwide. As you would expect, the penetration varies considerably in total numbers and in percentages of each country's population. With regard to total number of individuals with home PC Internet connection, Nielsen//NetRatings has provided the following graph.

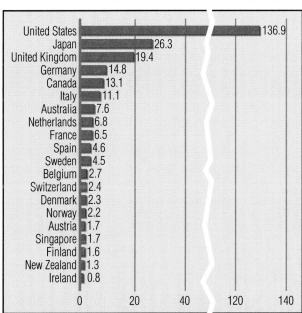

The graph above reveals that global market researchers have ready access to many millions of consumers. In other words, online surveys represent an unparalleled opportunity to accomplish global research quickly and inexpensively.

The percentages show a very different situation, however, as can be seen in the following table.

COUNTRY	% ACCESS AT HOME	% ACCESS AT WORK
Australia	43	28
Austria	29	24
Belgium/Luxembourg	32	20
Denmark	47	35
Finland	43	37
France	13	5
Germany	23	18
Ireland	33	22
Italy	23	13
Netherlands	48	26
New Zealand	44	28
Norway	53	40
Singapore	50	22
Spain	14	12
Sweden	49	36
Switzerland	39	41
United Kingdom	42	24

These figures reveal that even in some heavily industrialized countries, such as Germany, online surveys will eliminate, at minimum, 50 percent and in some countries close to 90 percent of a country's residents because they do not have ready Internet access. In other words, these penetration percentages suggest that online surveys fail to represent large segments of practically every country's consumers.

Self-Administered Surveys

You may be having a bit of difficulty with the "self-administered" designation as online surveys are taken by respondents alone, but the following survey modes are, for the most part, all paper-and-pencil situations in which the respondent fills out a static copy of the questionnaire. Probably the most popular type of self-administered survey is the mail survey; however, there are other variations—the group self-administered surveys and drop-off surveys—that are discussed first.

Group Self-Administered Survey Basically, a **group self-administered survey** entails administering a questionnaire to respondents in groups, rather than individually, for convenience or to gain certain economies. One way to be more economical is to have respondents self-administer the questions. For example, 20 or 30 people might be recruited to view a TV program sprinkled with test commercials. All respondents would be seated in a viewing room facility, and a videotape would run on a large television projection screen. Then they would be given a questionnaire to fill out regarding their recall of test ads, their reactions to the ads, and so on. As you would suspect, it is handled in a group context primarily to reduce costs and to provide the ability to interview a large number of people in a short time.

Variations for group self-administered surveys are limitless. Students can be administered surveys in their classes; church groups can be administered surveys during meetings; social clubs and organizations, company employees, movie theater patrons, and any other group can be administered surveys during meetings, work, or leisure time. Often the researcher will compensate the group with a monetary payment as a means of recruiting the support of the group's leaders. In all of these cases, each respondent works through the questionnaire at his or her own pace. Granted, a survey administrator may be present, so there is some opportunity for interaction concerning instructions or how to respond, but the group context often discourages the respondents from asking all but the most pressing questions.

Drop-Off Survey Another variation of the self-administered survey is the **drop-off survey,** in which the survey representative approaches a prospective respondent, introduces the general purpose of the survey to the prospect, and leaves it with the respondent to fill out on his or her own. Essentially, the objective is to gain the prospective respondent's cooperation. The respondent is told the questionnaire is self-explanatory, and it will be left with him or her to fill out at leisure. Perhaps the representative will return to pick up the questionnaire at a certain time, or the respondent may be instructed to complete and return it by prepaid mail. Normally, the representative will return on the same day or the next day to pick up the completed questionnaire. In this way, a representative can cover a number of residential areas or business locations in a single day with an initial drop-off pass and a later pick-up pass. Drop-off surveys are especially appropriate for local market research undertakings in which travel is necessary but limited. They have been reported to have quick turnaround, high response rates, minimal interviewer influence on answers, and good control over how respondents are selected; plus, they are inexpensive.[32]

Variations of the drop-off method include handing out the surveys to people at their places of work, asking them to fill them out at home, and then to return them the next day. Some hotel chains have questionnaires in their rooms with an invitation to fill them out and turn them in at the desk on checkout. Stores sometimes have short surveys on customer demographics, media habits, purchase intentions, or other information that customers are asked to fill out at home and return on their next shopping trip. A gift certificate drawing may even be used as an incentive to participate. As you can see, the term "drop-off" can be stretched to cover any situa-

---

Group self-administered surveys economize in time and money because a group of respondents participates at the same time.

With a self-administered survey, each respondent works at his or her own pace.

Drop-off surveys must be self-explanatory.

Several variations of drop-off surveys exist.

tion in which the prospective respondent encounters the survey as though it were "dropped off" by a research representative.

Mail Survey A **mail survey** is one in which the questions are mailed to prospective respondents who are asked to fill them out and return them to the researcher by mail. Part of its attractiveness stems from its self-administered aspect: There are no interviewers to recruit, train, monitor, and compensate. Similarly, mailing lists are readily available from companies that specialize in this business, and it is possible to access very specific groups of target respondents. For example, it is possible to obtain a list of physicians specializing in family practice who operate clinics in cities larger than 500,000 people. Also, one may opt to purchase computer files, printed labels, or even labeled envelopes from these companies. In fact, some list companies will even provide insertion and mailing services. There are a number of companies that sell mailing lists, and most, if not all, have online purchase options. If you want to see an example, look at the guided tour on the USAData Web site (www.usadata.com/). On a per-mailed respondent basis, mail surveys are very inexpensive. In fact, they are almost always the least expensive survey method in this regard. But mail surveys incur all of the problems associated with not having an interviewer present, which we discussed earlier in this chapter.

> An example of a mailing list firm with online purchase capability is USAData (www.usadata.com/).

Despite the fact that the mail survey is described as "powerful, effective, and efficient"[33] by the American Statistical Association, the mail survey is plagued by two major problems. The first is **nonresponse,** which refers to questionnaires that are not returned.[34] The second is **self-selection bias,** which means that those who do respond are probably different from those who do not fill out the questionnaire and return it and, therefore, the sample gained through this method is nonrepresentative of the general population. To be sure, the mail survey is not the only survey method that suffers from nonresponse and self-selection bias. Failures to respond are found in all types of surveys, and marketing researchers must be constantly alert to the possibilities that their final samples are somehow different from the original list of potential respondents because of some systematic tendency or latent pattern of response. Whatever the survey mode used, those who respond may be more involved with the product, they may have more education, they might be more or less dissatisfied, or they may even be more opinionated in general than the target population of concern.[35]

> Mail surveys suffer from low response rates and self-selection bias.
>
> Self-selection bias means respondents who return surveys by mail may differ from the original sample.

When informing clients of data collection alternatives, market researchers should inform them of the nonresponse problems and biases inherent in each one being considered. For example, mail surveys are notorious for low response, and those respondents who do fill out and return a mail questionnaire are likely to be different from those who do not. At the same time, there are people who refuse to answer questions over the telephone, and consumers who like to shop are more likely to be encountered in mall-intercept interviews than are those who do not like to shop. Each data collection method has its own nonresponse and bias considerations, and a conscientious researcher will help his or her client understand the dangers represented in the methods under consideration.

Thus, nonresponse and the subsequent danger of self-selection bias is greatest with mail surveys, for typically mail surveys of households achieve response rates of less than 20 percent. Researchers have tried various tactics to increase the response rate. There are eight of these tactics listed in Table 9.3. Take the true-false test in the table to see if you can guess the mail survey experience of Toyota Motor Sales, USA.

Although Toyota's experience is probably typical, despite a great deal of academic research,[36,37] we still do not have a clear understanding of the effectiveness and efficiency of these various techniques.[38] Despite this situation, mail surveys are

| Table 9.3 | **A Researcher's True-or-False Test on Ways to Increase Mail Survey Response[39]** |

Mr. David Fish, strategic research manager at Toyota Motor Sales USA, Inc., has created this test. Answers are found at the end of this chapter.

STATEMENT	CIRCLE YOUR ANSWER	
1. The use of color will increase mail survey response rates.	True	False
2. Stamps on the return envelope will have a greater response rate than preprinted postage-paid envelopes.	True	False
3. A mail survey questionnaire's length greatly affects the response rate.	True	False
4. A recognizable brand name will increase the response rate.	True	False
5. Monetary and other incentives used to increase mail survey response rates are cost-effective.	True	False
6. Money works better than nonmonetary incentives.	True	False
7. The response rate will increase if you prenotify respondents with a postcard.	True	False
8. "Reminder" postcards will increase the response rate.	True	False

To cope with low response to mail surveys, some companies have turned to mail panels.

viable in countries with high literacy rates and dependable postal systems.[40] Remember, however, that consumers and business respondents are constantly changing, and the inducement that works today may not necessarily work the same way in the future. One way research companies have sought to cope with the low response for mail surveys is to create a mail panel in which respondents agree to respond to several questionnaires mailed to them over time, and some see this approach as a preferred option.[41] Others are shifting to Internet communication systems that are faster and cheaper. Of course, the panel members are carefully prescreened to ensure that the mail panel represents the company's target market or consumers of interest.

CHOICE OF A PARTICULAR SURVEY METHOD

At the outset of the discussion of the various types of interviewing used in marketing research, we made the comment that the marketing researcher is faced with the problem of selecting the one survey mode that is optimal in a given situation. Each data collection method has unique advantages, disadvantages, and special features, and we have summarized them for you in Table 9.4. How do you decide which is the best survey mode for a particular research project? When answering this question, the researcher should always have quality as a foremost objective. He or she should strive to choose a survey mode that achieves the highest quality of data allowable with the cost, time, and other special considerations involved with the research project at hand. We will discuss the time horizon, researcher's budget, and special considerations in turn.

In selecting a data collection mode, the researcher balances quality against cost and time.

The Survey Data Collection Time Horizon

Regardless of its nature, every marketing management decision has a deadline when it must be resolved, and this deadline directly impacts the amount of time allowed, or the time horizon, for a particular marketing research survey. In some instances, the deadline is distant, and the marketing researcher is allowed the luxury of choosing his or her data collection methods. Frequently, however, the time period is compressed, and the researcher is forced into choosing a data collection method that may not be his or her first choice but is one that does a reasonable job within the permissible time horizon.

A short deadline may dictate which data collection method to use.

Choice of a Particular Survey Method

Table 9.4	**Key Advantages and Disadvantages of Alternative Data Collection Methods**		
METHOD	**KEY ADVANTAGES**	**KEY DISADVANTAGES**	**COMMENT**
In-home interview	Conducted in privacy of the home, which facilitates interviewer–respondent rapport	Cost per interview can be high; interviewers must travel to respondent's home	Often much information per interview is gathered
Mall-intercept interview	Fast and convenient data collection method	Only mall patrons are interviewed; respondents may feel uncomfortable answering questions in the mall	Mall-intercept company often has exclusive interview rights for that mall
In-office interview	Useful for interviewing busy executives	Relatively high cost per interview; gaining access is sometimes difficult	Useful when respondents must examine prototypes or samples of products
Central location telephone interview	Fast turnaround; good quality control; reasonable cost	Restricted to telephone communication	Long-distance calling is not a problem
CATI	Computer eliminates human interviewer error; simultaneous data input to computer file; good quality control	Setup costs can be high	Losing ground to online surveys and panels
Fully computerized interview	Respondent responds at his or her own pace; computer data file results	Respondent must have access to a computer or be computer literate	Many variations and an emerging data collection method with exciting prospects
Online questionnaire	Ease of creating and posting; fast turnaround; computer data file results	Respondent must have access to the Internet	Fastest-growing data collection method; very flexible; online analysis available
Group self-administered survey	Cost of interviewer eliminated; economical for assembled groups of respondents	Must find groups and secure permission to conduct the survey	Prone to errors of self-administered surveys; good for pretests or pilot tests
Drop-off survey	Cost of interviewer eliminated; appropriate for local market surveys	Generally not appropriate for large-scale national surveys	Many variations exist with respect to logistics and applications
Mail survey	Economical method; good listing companies exist	Low response rates; self-selection bias; slow	Many strategies to increase response rate exist

As we described the various interviewing methods, you probably realized intuitively that some approaches, such as mail surveys, door-to-door interviews, and personal interviews, require long time periods; whereas others, principally telephone studies and mall-intercept surveys, typically take much less time. An example will help you understand the impact of time deadlines on the choice of survey method.

The marketing director of a large bank was informed on Tuesday by the bank president that a number of complaints had been telephoned in by anonymous callers. The complaints focused on a new advertising campaign that used an old Tom Petty tune called "Runin' Down a Dream," and the callers felt that it promoted irresponsible drinking and driving. The advertising schedule allowed for a two-week radio ad before the television spots appeared, meaning that the television spots would begin in 10 days. The marketing director, under pressure from the president, thought of inviting people to view the prospective television ads along with other ads and to ask their opinions, but there was insufficient time to recruit respondents and run them through the viewings. The local mall-intercept firms were booked up for the next week, so this method was eliminated. About the only method left was

By their very nature, some survey data collection methods take longer than others.

A telephone survey helped this bank test its radio ads in a few days.

telephone surveys, which disallowed visual exposures. Because the complaints had all been leveled at the radio spots, it was decided to use the telephone and to have respondents listen to the ad over the telephone. Then their reactions could be solicited even if they had not heard the ad on the radio. They quickly generated a list of respondents from bank customer files, and the interviewing was completed in two evenings. It turned out that no one objected strongly to the theme, and the marketing director concluded that the complaints were competitors trying to unsettle the president. The television ads were shown on schedule without incident. In this example, the short survey time horizon disqualified certain survey data collection modes. In other instances, the time horizon may be longer, which would permit consideration of modes that require more time to implement and complete.

The Survey Data Collection Budget

The commercial marketing researcher frequently encounters situations in which the budget available for a study greatly influences the survey method used. In truth, the budget alone does not dictate the choice of a survey interviewing method; rather, the budget constraints in combination with other considerations influence the survey mode choice. For example, if a researcher wanted to have a final sample of 500 respondents, and the data collection portion of the budget was $5,000, it would not be feasible to hire personal interviewers if the going rate was in excess of $20 per completed interview because the interviewing bill alone would be $10,000. On the other hand, mall-intercept, telephone, and self-administered methods are more within the expense limit for this example. Budgets are sometimes set more arbitrarily than we would prefer, and a budget constraint such as the one described here must be dealt with by selecting a workable data collection mode if the survey is to be done. As you would suspect, a reason for the popularity of online research is its low cost. The questionnaire can be designed easily, and there are no interviewers to train and compensate.

Special Considerations

Time and budget are important factors in the choice of a survey mode, but sometimes one or more special considerations affect the survey, and the researcher must take these into account in this decision. For instance, there may be tasks such as card sorting or examining an ad portfolio that require extensive instructions that can only be delivered by a personal interviewer. Or there may be a great many questions, and this consideration may preclude a mode such as the telephone that is normally of short duration. There may be respondent considerations to factor in. For instance, children have short attention spans, elderly consumers have difficulty with written instructions, recent immigrants may have language barriers, and heavy Internet shoppers may rarely visit a shopping mall.

The selection of a particular survey mode is accomplished by simultaneously considering all of the previously mentioned factors. Of course, certain considerations will take priority over others. Sometimes the deadline for completing the research is close, and this disallows consideration of personal interviews or a mail survey, for instance, which take more time than a telephone interview. On the other hand, there may be a great number of complicated questions and tasks that are involved in a survey, and telephone administration is eliminated from consideration for this reason. At the same time, a researcher may have a favored survey mode with which he or she feels especially comfortable, and this factor may largely determine the selection. It is important that the manager allow the marketing researcher to decide on the survey mode because he or she has a unique understanding of how question characteristics, respondent characteristics, and survey resources and objectives come into play. Choice of survey method can be made by answering the ques-

---

Budget constraints may disallow consideration of the more expensive data collection methods.

Quality, time, and budget are usually combined in the objective, "What data collection method will generate the most complete and generalizable information within the time horizon and without exceeding the allowable expenditure for data collection?"

tion "What data collection method will generate the most complete and generalizable information within the time horizon and without exceeding the allowable expenditure for data collection?"

Here is how our Blue Ribbon Panel members answered our question about online versus traditional data collection methods.

Q: *When designing a research project, what are the key factors that would indicate the use of online survey research? What are the key indicators that would indicate the use of traditional data collection methods (mail, telephone, mall, etc.)?*

Note: To learn about the panel members, see the Preface of this book.

Bill MacElroy
President
Socratic Technologies

A: First and foremost in the decision as to whether to use an online method or not is the population being studied. At Socratic Technologies we have a rule of thumb that unless 60 percent of the population can be reasonably expected to be found "online," the study should be done either by traditional methods or a hybrid mix of both online and off-line techniques. We resist "data transformation" schemes in which data collected online are "manipulated" to weight opinions of some sample attributes in order to simulate off-line responses. Our experience is that these methods are not stable (e.g., can't be reliably reproduced) and produce systematic errors. One key distinguishing factor between online survey takers and off-line participants is that the online group tends to be more technology friendly and tend to be early adopters. For some studies, these psychographic characteristics can't be weighted out of an online sample in order to come up with a total U.S. population opinion projection.

Allen Hogg
President
Burke, Inc.

A: For an increasing number of companies, choosing to conduct research online is a forgone conclusion. They have e-mail addresses of customers (or other members of the target population) and the cost and timing advantages of online research are too compelling to use other methods. People with Internet access also tend to prefer the convenience of taking surveys online, so using online methods alone or in conjunction with more traditional methods can reduce potential nonresponse bias and result in stronger relationships with respondents.

Online research should not be used as the sole survey method when the individuals who will respond via the Internet will not represent the whole population to be studied. In some cases, there will not be available online sample sources that will represent the populations of interest, but the project requires showing visual or multimedia stimuli that cannot be adequately presented via mail or telephone research. In these cases, an online survey might be programmed but traditional recruitments methods will be used. People can be called or sent a letter inviting them to go to a survey Web site, for example, or computers for research can be set up at mall facilities.

George Harmon
Senior Vice President
Digital Marketing Services

A: Most research projects under 15 to 18 minutes in length, without requirements to immediately taste or touch things are well suited for online research projects. Studies with visual or audio stimuli are ideal, too.

The online population continues to be more reflective of the general population but quota controls may be required, especially if the characteristics may influence or interact with the survey subject. For example, a study about potential online services may require quotas based on online usage to assure light users are adequately represented.

George Terhanian
Vice President of Internet Research Harris Interactive, Inc.

A: We would rely on empirical data coupled with cost–benefit analysis to decide whether to recommend moving forward with the online approach. We would also exercise good judgment. For instance, if the aim of the research were to understand why people do not participate in online surveys, we would not mount online research. And if the aim of the research were to estimate the incidence of homelessness in Chicago, we would quite likely dispatch a core of live interviewers into targeted areas within Chicago, after developing a suitable definition of homelessness, which is by no means a simple or straightforward task.

Keith Price
Vice President Greenfield Online

A: Often many research professionals view online research as a way to execute projects quickly and inexpensively. Although it is true that certain online projects do provide cost and timing advantages when compared to off-line research, it is best to think that online research now makes the impossible possible. Projects that were once too costly or time consuming to conduct are now feasible when conducted online.

The Internet does afford a degree of anonymity, which is an important point to consider when conducting a study that involves sensitive subject matters. Respondents are more likely to answer these types of questions online.

Lee Smith
CEO Insight Express

A: Previously, online research was limited to situations when fast answers were needed and the target audience was well represented online. With the growing penetration of the Internet and the convergence of the online population to the general U.S. population, there are few, if any, situations that would require the use of mail, telephone, or other traditional research methods.

Doss Struse
Senior Vice President Client Service Knowledge Networks, Inc.

A: The three principal considerations should be (1) what is the nature of the interaction with the consumer; (2) are there any considerations concerning the selection of consumers to participate dictating one method of contact over another; and (3) is there anything in the task consumers are to perform that dictates one method over another. For example, the need to show pictures or offer a multimedia experience would usually make telephone or mail less appropriate and favor online or in-person interviewing. An example with regard to the second consideration might be if consumers were to drive a new car and then report on their reactions to certain features of the car. Online and telephone surveys would offer little advantage since the research company would have to either bring the consumer to the cars or the cars to the consumer. With regard to the third factor, there are studies in which it is essential that the researcher make visual, objective assessment of the respondent and the circumstances of the interview. This could dictate a personal interview.

SPSS Student Assistant Online
Milk Bone Biscuits: Modifying
Variables and Values

SUMMARY

This chapter described the various methods available to marketing researchers to survey respondents. Surveys provide the important advantages of standardization, easy administration, getting at motives for behaviors, simple tabulation, and ability to investigate subgroupings of respondents. We noted that personal interviews are advantageous because they allow feedback, permit rapport building, facilitate certain quality controls, and capitalize on the adaptability of a human interviewer. However, they are slow and prone to human errors. Computer-administered interviews, on the other hand, are faster, error free, may have pictures or graphics capabilities, allow for real-time capture of data, and may make respondents feel more at ease because another person is not listening to their answers.

We described 11 different survey data collection methods: (1) in-home interviews, which are conducted in respondents' homes; (2) mall-intercept interviews, conducted by approaching shoppers in a mall; (3) in-office interviews, conducted with executives or managers in their places of work; telephone interviews, either conducted (4) by an interviewer working in his or her home, or (5) from a central location telephone interviews, conducted by workers in a telephone interview company's facilities; (6) computer-assisted telephone interviews, in which the interviewer reads questions off a computer screen and enters responses directly into the program; (7) fully computerized interviews, in which the respondent interacts directly with a computer; (8) online and other Internet-based surveys; (9) group self-administered surveys, in which the questionnaire is handed out to a group for individual responses; (10) drop-off surveys, in which the questionnaire is left with the respondent to be completed and picked up or returned at a later time; and (11) mail surveys, in which questionnaires are mailed to prospective respondents who are requested to fill them out and mail them back. The specific advantages and disadvantages of each data collection mode were discussed.

Researchers must take into account several considerations when deciding on a survey data collection mode. The major concerns are (1) the survey time horizon, (2) the researcher's budget, and (3) special considerations. The research project deadline, money available for data collection, and desired quality of data are taken into consideration. Ultimately, the researcher will select a data collection mode with which he or she feels comfortable and one that will result in the desired quality and quantity of information without exceeding time or budget constraints.

KEY TERMS

Person-administered survey (p. 240)
Computer-administered survey (p. 241)
Self-administered survey (p. 243)
In-home interview (p. 245)
Mall-intercept interview (p. 246)
In-office interviews (p. 247)
Traditional telephone interviews (p. 249)
Central location telephone interviewing (p. 250)
Computer-assisted telephone interviews (CATI) (p. 251)

Fully computerized interviews (p. 252)
Completely automated telephone survey (CATS) (p. 252)
Internet-based questionnaire (p. 253)
Group self-administered survey (p. 256)
Drop-off survey (p. 256)
Mail survey (p. 257)
Nonresponse (p. 257)
Self-selection bias (p. 257)

REVIEW QUESTIONS/APPLICATIONS

1. List the major advantages of survey research methods over qualitative methods. Identify the major drawbacks.
2. What aspects of computer-administered surveys make them attractive to marketing researchers?
3. What are the advantages of person-administered surveys over computer-administered ones?
4. Indicate the differences between (a) in-home interviews, (b) mall-intercept interviews, and (c) in-office interviews. What do they share in common?
5. Why are telephone surveys popular?
6. Indicate the pros and cons of self-administered surveys.
7. What advantages do online surveys have over other types of self-administered surveys?

8. How does a drop-off survey differ from a mail survey?

9. What are aspects of the researcher's resources and objectives that have considerable influence in the determination of which survey mode will be used? How does each one affect the decision?

10. Is a telephone interview inappropriate for a survey that has as one of its objectives a complete listing of all possible advertising media a person was exposed to in the last week? Why or why not?

11. NAPA Car Parts is a retail chain specializing in stocking and selling both domestic and foreign automobile parts. It is interested in learning about its customers, so the marketing director sends instructions to all 2,000 store managers telling them that whenever a customer makes a purchase of $150 or more, they are to write down a description of the customer who made that purchase. They are to do this just for the second week in October, writing each description on a separate sheet of paper. At the end of the week, they are to send all sheets to the marketing director. Comment on this data collection method.

12. Discuss the feasibility of each of the types of survey modes for each of the following cases:
    a. Fabergé, Inc. wants to test a new fragrance called "Lime Brut."
    b. Kelly Services needs to determine how many businesses expect to hire temporary secretaries for those who go on vacation during the summer months.
    c. The *Encyclopedia Britannica* requires information on the degree to which mothers of elementary school-aged children see encyclopedias as worthwhile purchases for their children.
    d. AT&T is considering a television screen phone system and wants to know people's reaction to it.

13. With a telephone survey, when a potential respondent refuses to take part or is found to have changed his or her telephone number or moved away, it is customary to simply try another prospect until a completion is secured. It is not standard practice to report the number of refusals or noncontacts. What are the implications of this policy for the reporting of nonresponse?

14. Compu-Ask Corporation has developed a stand-alone computerized interview system that can be adapted to almost any type of survey. It can fit on a palm-sized computer, and the respondent directly answers questions using a stylus once the interviewer has turned on the computer and started up the program. Indicate the appropriateness of this interviewing system in each of the following cases:
    a. A survey of plant managers concerning a new type of hazardous waste disposal system.
    b. A survey of high school teachers to see if they are interested in a company's videotapes of educational public broadcast television programs.
    c. A survey of consumers to determine their reactions to a nonrefrigerated variety of yogurt.

15. A researcher is pondering what survey mode to use for a client who markets a home security system for apartment dwellers. The system comprises sensors that are pressed onto all of the windows and magnetic strips that are glued to each door. Once plugged into an electric socket and activated with a switch box, the system emits a loud alarm and simulates a barking guard dog when an intruder trips one of the sensors. The client wants to know how many apartment dwellers in the United States are aware of the system, what they think of it, and how likely they are to buy it in the coming year. Which consid-

eration factors are positive and which ones are negative for each of the following survey modes: (a) in-home interviews, (b) mall intercepts, (c) online survey, (d) drop-off survey, and (e) CATI survey?

INTERACTIVE LEARNING

Visit the Web site at www.prenhall.com/burnsbush. For this chapter, work through the Self-Study Quizzes, and get instant feedback on whether you need additional studying. On the Web site, you can review the chapter outlines and case information for Chapter 9.

CASE 9.1   FAW-VW of the PRC

With the dawn of the twenty-first century, the People's Republic of China (PRC) represents what is perhaps the greatest phenomenon in marketing history as it transitions from a communist/agrarian economy into a free enterprise/industrial country. The shift has given rise to classes of hardworking upper-management personnel and entrepreneurs who are acquiring wealth at a rapid pace. These consumers are rushing to adopt Western, European, and other world goods and services, and many companies from these counties are joint-venturing with Chinese companies or the Chinese government to deliver them to these eager consumers. Despite the relatively high incomes of these Chinese consumers, only a small percentage of them can afford to own a car.

FAW-VW (First Auto Works-Volkswagen) is one such joint venture with its manufacturing facility located in northeastern China. The Chinese automobile market growth potential is immense. With only about 2.3 million cars registered, there are estimates that this number will increase by 1 or 2 million per year through 2010. To meet this demand, FAW-VW manufactures and markets the following models: Audi, Bora (introduced in 2001), and Jetta and sells these models through its dealer network with locations in 20 major Chinese cities such as Beijing, Shanghai, Nanjing, and Guangzhou. For the past several years, FAW-VW has been one of the market share leaders, and it intends to hold or improve its position through 2010. In order to keep tabs on the fast-growing sedan market, FAW-VW intends to conduct an annual automobile image and intentions survey. This survey will consist of 5,000 respondents. It will assess the image of each FAW-VW model as well as the images of each competing sedan model, and it will gather information on Chinese consumer automobile buying intentions useful for planning and market segmentation.

Major Chinese cities have transitioned or are in the process of transitioning themselves into modern urban centers with greatly improved road systems, modern apartment buildings, good communications, including cellular phones, and shopping malls. Internet penetration is low but growing rapidly. In contrast to Western consumers, PRC consumers have not been assailed by telemarketers, nor have they been deluged with junk mail.

1. What data collection modes do you think are viable candidates, and why? Why are the others not viable?
2. FAW-VW is considering the use of a central telephone interviewing company that has facilities in most of the major Chinese cities. The telephone interviewers will call phone numbers at random. Is this a good choice? Why or why not?
3. If the FAW-VW PRC consumer car image and buying intentions survey is to be conducted annually for the next 10 years, should the same data collection method be used every year, or should the data collection method change from year to year?

CASE 9.2   METREC

METREC is an acronym for Metropolitan Recreation Services, which operates all public park and recreation facilities and programs in the greater metropolitan area. The facilities it maintains and the programs it runs annually include 20 playgrounds, each with organized playgroups for children 3 to 5 years old, six 18-hole golf courses, two 18-hole disc golf courses, a BMX race-way, air gun and archery ranges, a cycling velodrome, a horse activity area for equestrian and other riding activities, five family fitness centers, two mountain bike trails, six tennis court areas, seven outdoor swimming pools, 15 senior citizen activity centers, six nature areas, including MetroZoo, and two art galleries. In addition, METREC operates junior, adult, and masters sports leagues for softball, basketball, soccer, volleyball, and bowling.

Although METREC has a large budget for maintenance of its many facilities, it does not have a sufficient budget for personnel, so it relies very heavily on volunteers, and particularly involved with its organized team sports where coaches, officials, and support personnel are vital. Obviously, constant and good communication from METREC to these volunteers is critical to the smooth operation of the multitude of organized sports leagues throughout the year. Recently METREC has been thinking about expanding its organized team sports services, and the METREC director has decided to conduct two surveys, one with the players in the various sports leagues, and the other with the volunteers. The purposes of the research are to find (1) additional organized team sports activities that the participants enjoy and (2) volunteers' opinions of the quality and quantity of information being supplied to them by METREC. METREC has budgeted $3,000 to accomplish both surveys.

There are approximately 300 organized sports teams across the five different sports leagues with six age groups (7–10; 11–14; 15–18; 20–29, 30–39, masters). During the sport's season, each team meets anywhere from three to five times each week to get organized, practice, and play its games.

Approximately 7,500 volunteers have been involved with METREC over the past 10 years. There is a list with all 7,500 names in the department's headquarters. METREC estimates that about one-quarter of the volunteers are currently actively working with some organized sports league. The remaining three-fourths either have permanently stopped volunteering either because their children no longer compete in METREC sports, or they are temporarily involved with other work and may become active volunteers in the future.

Answer the following questions by reviewing the selection factors discussed in the textbook, and be sure to note important strengths or weaknesses of the method you have chosen in each case.

1. What data collection method do you think is appropriate for the volunteers assuming that only active volunteers' opinions are desired?
2. What data collection method do you think is appropriate for the METREC sports leagues participants?

CASE 9.3   *Your Integrated Case*

The Hobbit's Choice Restaurant

This is your integrated case described on pages 42–43.

Cory Rogers presented his interpretations of the focus groups he had subcontracted for Jeff Dean's The Hobbit's Choice Restaurant to get a feel for what patrons wanted in the décor, atmosphere, entrées, specialty items, and other aspects of the restaurant's operation. Jeff was impressed with the amount of information that had been collected from just three focus groups. "Of course," noted Cory, "we have to take all of this information as tentative because we talked with so few folks, and there is a good chance that they are just a part of your target market. But we do have some good exploratory research that will guide us in the survey."

Jeff agreed with Cory's assessment and asked, "What's next?" Cory said, "I need to think about how we will gather the survey data. There are several options that I must consider in order to make the best choice to survey the entire metropolitan area."

1. Is a mail survey a good choice? Why or why not?
2. Should Cory recommend a telephone survey? What are the pros and cons of telephone data collection for The Hobbit's Choice Restaurant survey?
3. What about an online survey? Compare the use of an online survey to a telephone survey, and indicate which one you recommend that Cory use.

ANSWERS TO THE TRUE-FALSE TEST IN TABLE 9.3, PAGE 258.

False
False
True
True
False
True
False*
True*

*However you need to balance the added cost with the expected increase in response.

Chapter 10

Measurement in Marketing Research

Reducing the risks in decision making.

Practitioner Viewpoint

In most cases, we must actually measure concepts that we are studying as we conduct marketing research. How we measure "sales potential," "demand," "attitudes," "intentions," and so on is very important when it comes time to interpret our study. The way the researcher decides how to measure a concept greatly impacts what he or she can or cannot say about these concepts. For instance, brand loyalty can be defined as the last brand acquired, or it can be defined as the person's most preferred brand. If a competitor is giving away free samples, the first definition will give a false reading on brand loyalty, whereas the second one will yield a truer measurement. A good understanding of measurement is basic knowledge among marketing researchers.

William D. Neal, Senior Executive Officer,
SDR Consulting (www.sdrnet.com)

Branding in the Third Millennium

This opening case is supplied by William D. Neal, senior executive officer at SDR Consulting. You will "meet" Mr. Neal later in this chapter.

"Marko's Wheels—The Best Iron Rimmed Wheels West of the Tiberius." One can imagine a sign similar to this hanging outside Marko's wheel shop—circa 243 BC. Branding, initially in the form of trademarks, has been with us since humans formed villages and learned to specialize in making things. And as we enter the third millennium, many marketing managers are still trying to figure out how to manage their brands and improve brand equity.

Despite the many prognoses that branding will become obsolete in the age of the Internet, I believe the opposite is true. Indeed, I believe the Internet will drive out regional pricing differences, information access inequalities, and inequalities due to variations in availability—putting the end user back in direct contact with the producer and making brand equity the main arbitrator among products and services that are only marginally differentiated. That's been the norm since the beginning of time. Intermediaries and channels that do survive in the Internet age will have to add true value beyond that provided by the manufacturer—not just access convenience.

In the third millennium there will be new and expanded opportunities to create brand value. Just think of the great brands that have been created in the last 10 to 20 years—Microsoft, Intel, America Online, Gateway, Cisco, and so many others. I think this is just the beginning. The opposite is also true; many of our old familiar brands will die, as many already have in the last 20 years through overextension, poor management, or lack of investment in building brand value.

Brand value can be created through real product differentiation, including rebundling and debundling. The key to creating value through product differentiation

Research can determine the impact of the Internet on brand equity.

is value pricing—showing buyers how to trade off specific performance levels against product or service price. The ability to customize production and service delivery to meet the needs of individual customers is reemerging as one of the major business trends of the twenty-first century under the labels of mass customization and one-on-one marketing. Isn't it strange how we are reversing the mass-marketing thinking of the late twentieth century, reverting to the norm of the previous 2,000 years?

Brand value can also be created by channels. But, for traditional channels to meet the challenge of the Internet, a channel's value-added services must be made obvious to the end user, not just the producer. The Internet will overwhelm location and availability convenience for many product and service categories, supplanting them with electronic channels and innovative delivery systems.

I believe brand equity will be the key to building brand value in the new millennium—it is the glue that makes any value proposition believable and relevant. Brand equity currently offers the best opportunity to improve overall brand value in many product and service categories. In industrial and B2B categories, in which branding is often weakest, branding initiatives represent a huge opportunity for sustainable competitive advantage. There are still many unfulfilled opportunities to successfully brand components and ingredients. But ultimately let us not forget that positive brand equity must be backed up with strong and consistent product and service performance.

Brand equity can be viewed as the set of intangible attributes surrounding a brand name that has value. If products are not greatly differentiated and channels are not unique, only price and brand equity remain to differentiate products or services in a category. In the absence of strong brands, the only marketing lever remaining is price. Strong brand equity can prevent or reverse product and service commoditization.

Finally, I believe that building brand value will become, and should become, the yardstick for measuring marketing success and evaluating marketing management. Brand value and its components—price (dis)utility, product attribute utility, channel attribute utility, and brand equity—can be measured and tracked and, therefore, can be used to quantitatively evaluate marketing success or failure. Return on marketing investment (ROMI) then becomes a real number. We only need to get the financial community to buy into it.

Although there is no methodological consensus at this time, brand value and brand equity are being measured and quantified, primarily using marketing research methods. Some methods rely on attitudinal questions; others rely on more sophisticated research procedures such as conjoint and discrete choice experiments. At SDR Consulting we use a combination of conjoint and discrete choice experiments to measure both total brand value and brand equity.

——————

This chapter is the first of two devoted to the questionnaire design phase of the marketing research process. Its primary goal is to develop the foundation for understanding measurement in marketing research. This is done by first describing the six question–response formats available, then defining basic concepts in measurement, and, finally, explaining the various scale formats commonly used in marketing research.

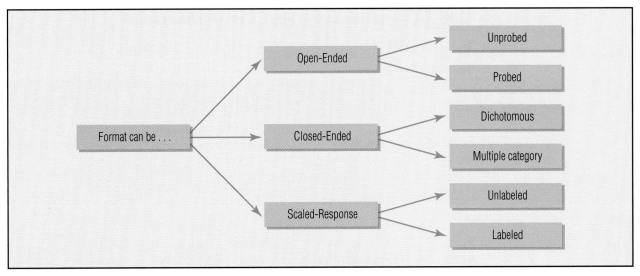

Figure 10.1 **A Diagram of Six Alternative Question–Response Formats**

BASIC QUESTION–RESPONSE FORMATS

Designing a questionnaire from the ground up is akin to Eric Clapton composing a song, Stephen King writing a short story, or an artist painting a landscape. That is, it requires creativity. Still, there are some basic aspects to questionnaire design that can be described. This chapter is concerned with the response side of the question, and it will introduce you to measurement issues. To begin, you should be aware of the three basic question–response formats from which a researcher has to choose: open-ended, closed-ended, and scaled-response questions. Figure 10.1 illustrates the three types and indicates two variations for each one. Pros and cons of each format are provided in Table 10.1 on page 272. A description of each format follows.

> Six basic response format options are available to the researcher.

Open-Ended Response Format Questions

An **open-ended question** presents no response options to the respondent. Rather, the respondent is instructed to respond in his or her own words. The response depends, of course, on the topic. An **unprobed format** seeks no additional information from the respondent. Sometimes the researcher wants a comment or statement from the respondent, or perhaps the researcher simply wants the respondent to indicate the name of a brand or a store.[1] In this case, the researcher uses a **probed format,** which includes a **response probe** instructing the interviewer to ask for additional information, saying, for instance, "Can you think of anything more?" The intent here is to encourage the respondent to provide information beyond the initial and possibly superficial first comments.

> Question–response formats can be open-ended, close-ended, or scaled-response formats.

Closed-Ended Response Format Questions

The **closed-ended question** provides response options on the questionnaire that can be answered quickly and easily.[2] A **dichotomous closed-ended question** has only two response options, such as "yes" or "no." If there are more than two options for the response, then the researcher is using a **multiple-category closed-ended question.**

Table **10.1** **Pros and Cons of Alternative Response Formats**

RESPONSE FORMAT	EXAMPLES: PROS (+) AND CONS (−)
Unprobed open-ended question	*"What was your reaction to the Sony DVD player advertisement you last saw on television?"* + Allows respondent to use his or her own words. − Difficult to code and interpret. − Respondents may not give complete answers.
Probed open-ended question	*"Did you have any other thoughts or reactions to the advertisement?"* + Elicits complete answers. − Difficult to code and interpret.
Dichotomous closed-ended question	*"Do you agree or disagree with the statement 'Sony DVD players are better than Panasonic DVD players'?"* + Simple to administer and code. − May oversimplify response options.
Multiple-category closed-ended question	*"If you were to buy a DVD player tomorrow, which brand would you be most likely to purchase? Would it be, (a) Panasonic, (b) General Electric, (c) Sony, (d) JVC, or (e) some other brand?"* + Allows for broad range of possible responses. + Simple to administer and code. − May alert respondents to response options of which they were unaware. − Must distinguish "pick one" from "pick all that apply."
Unlabeled scaled-response question	*"On a scale of 1 to 7, how would you rate the Sony DVD player on ease of operation?"* + Allows for degree of intensity/feelings to be expressed. + Simple to administer and code. − Respondents may not relate well to the scale.
Labeled scaled-response question	*"Do you disagree strongly, disagree, agree, or agree strongly with the statement 'Sony DVD players are a better value than General Electric DVD players'?"* + Allows for degree of intensity/feelings to be expressed. + Simple to administer and code. + Respondents can relate to the scale. − Scale may be "forced" or overly detailed.

Both the dichotomous and multiple-category closed-ended question formats are very common on questionnaires because they facilitate the questioning process as well as data entry. They also standardize these questions on the questionnaire.

Scaled-Response Questions

The **scaled-response question** utilizes a scale developed by the researcher to measure the attributes of some construct under study. The response options are identified on the questionnaire. With an **unlabeled scaled-response format,** the scale may be purely numerical or only the endpoints of the scale are identified. The **labeled scaled-response format** uses a scale in which all of the scale positions are identified with some descriptor. We describe both of these formats in detail later in this chapter. Researchers deal with question formats all the time. You will now meet Bill Neal who is an expert in this area.

▶ **Meet a Marketing Researcher**

Bill Neal Is a Measurement Expert
William D. Neal, SDR Consulting

William D. Neal is founder and senior executive officer of SDR Consulting. He has personally authored over 60 articles, tutorials, and seminars on marketing research meth-

ods and procedures. Most recently, he has been highly involved in the development and utilization of models for measuring brand value, brand equity, and customer loyalty.

Bill has previously served as chairman of the board of directors for the American Marketing Association (AMA). He also served the AMA as vice president of the Marketing Research Division, chairman of the Strategic Planning Committee, regional vice president and president of the Atlanta Chapter.

Bill is a past chairman of the board of directors of the Marketing Research Institute International. He is on the editorial review boards of *Marketing Management* and *Marketing Research* magazines and is an ad hoc reviewer for several other marketing management and marketing research publications. In 1995 Bill was the fourth person to receive AMA's Lifetime Achievement Award for service to the profession of marketing research. Recognizing his long-term contributions to the profession of marketing research, the Marketing Research Association awarded Bill with an honorary lifetime membership in 1997. In 2001 Bill was elected to receive the Parlin Award—the oldest and most prestigious award in marketing research. At SDR Bill serves as a senior consultant and practice leader.

CONSIDERATIONS IN CHOOSING A QUESTION–RESPONSE FORMAT

All of the six different question formats we have just described are eligible formats for any question on a questionnaire. So how does the researcher decide on which option to use? At least five considerations serve to narrow the choice down: (1) the nature of the property being measured, (2) previous research studies, (3) the data collection mode, (4) the ability of the respondent, and (5) the scale level desired.

Nature of the Property Being Measured

As will become clear later in the chapter when we describe basic concepts in measurement, the inherent nature of the property of a construct often determines the question–response format. For example, if Alka Seltzer wants to know if respondents have bought its brand of flu relief medicine in the last month, the only answers are "yes," "no," or perhaps "do not recall." If we ask marital status, a woman is married, separated, divorced, widowed, single, or she may be cohabiting. But when we ask how much a person likes Hershey's chocolate, we can use a scaled-response approach, because "liking" is a subjective property with varying degrees.

The properties of the construct being measured often determine the appropriate response format.

A dichotomous, closed-ended question could be used to determine if a consumer purchased Alka Seltzer flu relief in the past month.

Previous Research Studies

On some occasions, a survey follows an earlier one, and there may be a desire to explicitly compare the new findings with the previous survey. In this case, it is customary to simply adopt the question format used in the initial study. On the other hand, a particular scale or question format may have been developed by others who have measured the construct. Some scales are published or available for use by marketing researchers at no cost, whereas others may reside within the researcher's own company as a result of its work with several clients over time. For instance, some research companies specialize in customer satisfaction studies, and they have refined their own scales tapping this construct.[3] In any case, if a researcher believes a question format to be reliable and valid, and it suits the purpose of the study at hand, it is good practice to adapt it rather than inventing a new one.

Researchers try to use question formats that are tried and true.

Data Collection Mode

As you know, certain data collection modes are better suited for certain question formats. For instance, a telephone interview is hampered by the respondent's inability to see the response categories, so the interviewer must read them off. It is very difficult to administer certain types of response formats over the telephone as some require detailed explanation before the respondent can envision the response-scale items.[4] On the other hand, a mail or other self-administered questionnaire accommodates scaled-response questions well because the respondent can see the response categories on the questionnaire itself.

The method of data collection determines the appropriate response format.

Ability of the Respondent

It is advantageous to match the question format with the abilities of the respondents. For instance, if a researcher feels that the respondents in a particular study are not articulate or that they will be reluctant to verbalize their opinions, the open-ended option is not a good choice. Similarly, if the respondent is unaccustomed to rating objects on numerical scales, it is appropriate to use a label format, or perhaps to move back to a dichotomous closed-ended question format in which the respondent simply indicates "agree" or "disagree."[5]

Some respondents may relate better to one type of response format than another.

Scale Level Desired

As you will learn in subsequent chapters, certain statistical analyses incorporate assumptions about the nature of the measures being analyzed, so the researcher must bear these requirements in mind when selecting a question format. For example, if the response options are simply "yes" or "no," the researcher can report the percentage of respondents who answered in each way, but if the question asks how many times respondents used an ATM machine in the past month, the researcher could calculate an average number of times. An average is different from a percentage, one reason being that a dichotomous yes–no response option is less informative than a scaled-response option such as "0," "1," "2," and so on. If a researcher desires to use higher-level statistical analyses, the question's response format must embody the correct scale assumptions. This point brings us to the concepts involved with measurement.

BASIC CONCEPTS IN MEASUREMENT

Questionnaires are designed to collect information. How is this information collected? It is gathered via **measurement,** which is defined as determining the amount or intensity of some characteristic of interest to the researcher. For instance, a marketing manager may wish to know how a person feels about a certain product, or how much of the product he or she uses in a certain time period. This information, once compiled, can help solve specific questions such as brand usage.

Measurement is determining how much of a property is possessed by an object.

But what are we really measuring? We are measuring properties—sometimes called attributes or qualities—of objects. Objects include consumers, brands, stores, advertisements, or whatever construct is of interest to the researcher working with a particular manager. **Properties** are the specific features or characteristics of an object that can be used to distinguish it from another object. For example, assume the object we want to research is a consumer. As depicted in Table 10.2, the properties of interest to a manager who is trying to define who buys a specific product are a combination of demographics such as age; income level; gender; and buyer behavior, which includes such things as the buyer's impressions or perceptions of various brands. Note that each property has the potential to further differentiate consumers. For example, Table 10.2 also compares three consumers' ages, income levels, perceptions, and gender. Once the object's designation on a property has been deter-

In this chapter you will learn how to measure the image of a company like Red Lobster.

Table **10.2** **Measuring the Properties of an Object and Differentiating Among Three Consumers' Properties**

THE OBJECT	PROPERTIES	MEASUREMENT DESIGNATIONS
A consumer (Mr. Able)	Age	35 years
	Income level	$55,000
	Gender	Male
	Brand last bought	Gillette
	Evaluation of "our" brand	"Fair"

PROPERTIES	MEASUREMENT DESIGNATIONS		
	Mr. Able	*Ms. Black*	*Mr. Colby*
Age	35	42	21
Income	$55,000	$65,000	$45,000
Gender	Male	Female	Male
Brand last bought	Gillette	Schick	Gillette
Evaluation of "our" brand	"Fair"	"Good"	"Excellent"

mined, we say that the object has been measured on that property. Measurement underlies marketing research to a very great extent because researchers are keenly interested in describing marketing phenomena. Furthermore, researchers are often given the task of finding relevant differences in the profiles of various customer types. Marketing Research Insight 10.2 indicates how Wrigley's Chewing Gum targets demographic market segments based on a measurement of gum chewing.

MARKETING RESEARCH

INSIGHT
10.2

Additional Insights ◀

Wrigley's Wants to Know "Who Puts Their Chewing Gum on the Bedpost Overnight?"[6]

Measurement is a way to determine what people do, think, feel, or believe. In the first case, Wrigley's Chewing Gum wants to know how often people chew gum. Moreover, it is vital for target marketing purposes to find demographic groups that are heavy gum chewers versus those who are light gum chewers. When Wrigley's discovers which consumers buy and chew gum on a regular basis, it can focus its marketing efforts on that group in order to maximize its market share.

Here are the findings of a recent study that measured the frequency of gum chewing.

Wrigley's Target Market

	TOTAL	Age Range					
		16–24	**25–34**	**35–44**	**45–54**	**55–65**	**65+**
Everyday	17%	**33%**	**28%**	14%	16%	6%	3%
Once or twice a week	11%	**24%**	**17%**	10%	7%	6%	1%
Very occasionally	25%	**28%**	**33%**	33%	27%	19%	11%
Never	46%	**16%**	**22%**	43%	50%	69%	85%
Average	2.0	**2.8**	**2.5**	1.9	1.9	1.5	1.2

This survey measuring frequency of gum chewing shows plainly that Wrigley's prime markets are 16–24 and 25–34 age groups.

On the surface, measurement may appear to be a very simple process. It is simple as long as we are measuring **objective properties,** which are physically verifiable characteristics such as age, income, number of bottles purchased, store last visited, and so on. However, marketing researchers often desire to measure **subjective properties,** which cannot be directly observed because they are mental constructs such as a person's attitude or intentions. In this case, the marketing researcher must ask a respondent to translate his or her mental constructs onto a continuum of intensity—no easy task. To do this, the marketing researcher must develop question formats that are very clear and that are used identically by the respondents. This process is known as scale development.

> Objective properties are observable and tangible. Subjective properties are unobservable and intangible, and they must be translated onto a rating scale through the process of scale development.

SCALE CHARACTERISTICS

Scale development is designing questions to measure the subjective properties of an object. There are various types of scales, each of which possesses different characteristics. The characteristics of a scale determine the scale's level of measurement. The level of measurement, as you shall see, is very important. There are four characteristics of scales: description, order, distance, and origin.

> Scale characteristics are de[...] tion, order, distance, and ori[...]

Description

Description refers to the use of a unique descriptor, or label, to stand for each designation in the scale. For instance, "yes" and "no," "agree" and "disagree," and the number of years of a respondent's age are descriptors of a simple scale. All scales include description in the form of characteristic labels that identify what is being measured.

Order

Order refers to the relative sizes of the descriptors. Here, the key word is "relative" and includes such descriptors as "greater than," "less than," and "equal to." A respondent's least-preferred brand is "less than" his or her most-preferred brand, and respondents who check the same income category are the same ("equal to"). Not all scales possess order characteristics. For instance, is a "buyer" greater than or less than a "nonbuyer"? We have no way of making a relative size distinction.

> An ordered scale has descriptors that are "greater than," "less than," and "equal to" one another.

Distance

A scale has the characteristic of **distance** when absolute differences between the descriptors are known and may be expressed in units. The respondent who purchases three bottles of diet cola buys two more than the one who purchases only one bottle; a three-car family owns one more automobile than a two-car family. Note that when the characteristic of distance exists, we are also given order. We know not only that the three-car family has "more than" the number of cars of the two-car family, but we also know the distance between the two (one car).

Origin

A scale is said to have the characteristic of **origin** if there is a unique beginning or true zero point for the scale. Thus, 0 is the origin for an age scale just as it is for the number of miles traveled to the store or for the number of bottles of soda consumed. Not all scales have a true zero point for the property they are measuring. In fact, many scales used by marketing researchers have arbitrary neutral points, but they do not possess origins. For instance, when a respondent says, "No opinion," to the question "Do you agree or disagree with the statement, The Lexus is the best car on the road today?" we cannot say that the person has a true zero level of agreement.

> A neutral category is not a true zero value for a scale.

Perhaps you noticed that each scaling characteristic builds on the previous one. That is, description is the most basic and is present in every scale. If a scale has order, it also possesses description. If a scale has distance, it also possesses order and description, and if a scale has origin, it also has distance, order, and description. In other words, if a scale has a higher-level characteristic, it also has all lower-level characteristics. But the opposite is not true, as is explained in the next section.

LEVELS OF MEASUREMENT OF SCALES

You may ask, "Why is it important to know the characteristics of scales?" The answer is that the characteristics possessed by a scale determine that scale's level of measurement. Throughout this chapter, we try to convince you that it is very important for a marketing researcher to understand the level of measurement of the scale he or she selects to use. Let us now examine the four levels of measurement. They are nominal, ordinal, interval, and ratio. Table 10.3 shows how each scale type differs with respect to the scaling characteristics we have just discussed.

Table 10.3 also introduces two new concepts: categorical versus metric scales. A categorical scale is one that is typically composed of a small number of distinct values or categories such as "male" versus "female," or "married" versus "single" versus "widowed." As you can see in the table, there are two categorical scale types: nominal and ordinal. These will be described in detail in this section. The other concept is a metric scale, which is composed of numbers or labels that have an underlying measurement continuum. There are two metric scales that are also described in this section, and they are interval and ratio scales.

> There is a hierarchy of scales; ratio scales are the "highest" and nominal scales are the "lowest."

Nominal Scales

> Nominal scales simply label objects.

Nominal scales are defined as those that use only labels; that is, they possess only the characteristic of description. Examples include designations as to race, religion, type of dwelling, gender, brand last purchased, buyer/nonbuyer; answers that involve yes–no, agree–disagree; or any other instance in which the descriptors cannot be differentiated except qualitatively. If you describe respondents in a survey according to their occupation—banker, doctor, computer programmer—you have used a nominal scale. Note that these examples of a nominal scale label only the consumers. They do not provide other information such as "greater than," "twice as large," and so forth. Examples of nominal-scaled questions are found in Table 10.4A on page 279.

Ordinal Scales

> Ordinal scales indicate only relative size differences between objects.

Ordinal scales permit the researcher to rank-order the respondents or their responses. For instance, if the respondent was asked to indicate his or her first, second, third, and fourth choices of brands, the results would be ordinally scaled.

Table **10.3** **Measurement Scale Levels Differ by What Scale Characteristics They Possess**

	Scale Characteristics Possessed			
LEVEL OF MEASUREMENT	DESCRIPTION	ORDER	DISTANCE	ORIGIN
Categorical Scales				
Nominal scale	+	−	−	−
Ordinal scale	+	+	−	−
Metric Scales				
Interval scale	+	+	+	−
Ratio scale	+	+	+	+

Table 10.4 Examples of the Use of Different Scaling Assumptions in Questions

A. Nominal-Scaled Questions

1. Please indicate your gender. ____ Male ____ Female
2. Check all the brands you would consider purchasing.
   ____ Sony
   ____ Zenith
   ____ RCA
   ____ Curtis Mathes
3. Do you recall seeing a Delta Airlines advertisement for "carefree vacations" in the past week?
   ____ Yes ____ No

B. Ordinal-Scaled Questions

1. Please rank each brand in terms of your preference. Place a "1" by your first choice, a "2" by your second choice, and so on.
   ____ Arrid
   ____ Right Guard
   ____ Mennen
2. For each pair of grocery stores, circle the one you would be more likely to patronize.
   Kroger versus First National
   First National versus A&P
   A&P versus Kroger
3. In your opinion, would you say the prices at Wal-Mart are
   ____ Higher than Sears
   ____ About the same as Sears
   ____ Lower than Sears

C. Interval-Scaled Questions

1. Please rate each brand in terms of its overall performance.

BRAND	RATING (CIRCLE ONE)									
	Very Poor								Very Good	
Mont Blanc	1	2	3	4	5	6	7	8	9	10
Parker	1	2	3	4	5	6	7	8	9	10
Cross	1	2	3	4	5	6	7	8	9	10

2. Indicate your degree of agreement with the following statements by circling the appropriate number.

STATEMENT	STRONGLY DISAGREE				STRONGLY AGREE
a. I always look for bargains.	1	2	3	4	5
b. I enjoy being outdoors.	1	2	3	4	5
c. I love to cook.	1	2	3	4	5

3. Please rate Pontiac Firebird by checking the line that best corresponds to your evaluation of each item listed.
   Slow pickup ____ ____ ____ ____ Fast pickup
   Good design ____ ____ ____ ____ Bad design
   Low price ____ ____ ____ ____ High price

D. Ratio-Scaled Questions

1. Please indicate your age.
   ____ Years
2. Approximately how many times in the last month have you purchased anything over $5 in value at a convenience store?
   0 1 2 3 4 5 More (specify: ____)
3. How much do you think a typical purchaser of a $100,000 term life insurance policy pays per year for that policy?
   $____
4. What is the probability that you will use a lawyer's services when you are ready to make a will?
   ____ percent

Similarly, if one respondent checked the category "Buy every week or more often" on a purchase-frequency scale and another checked the category "Buy once per month or less," the result would be an ordinal measurement. Ordinal scales indicate only relative size differences among objects. They possess description and order, but we do not know how far apart the descriptors are on the scale because ordinal scales do not possess distance or origin. Examples of ordinal-scaled questions are found in Table 10.4B on page 279.

Interval Scales

Interval scales use descriptors that are equal distances apart.

Interval scales are those in which the distance between each descriptor is known. The distance is normally defined as one scale unit. For example, a coffee brand rated "3" in taste is one unit away from one rated "4." Sometimes the researcher must impose a belief that equal intervals exist between the descriptors. That is, if you were asked to evaluate a store's salespeople by selecting a single designation from a list of "extremely friendly," "very friendly," "somewhat friendly," "somewhat unfriendly," "very unfriendly," or "extremely unfriendly," the researcher would probably assume that each designation was one unit away from the preceding one. In these cases, we say that the scale is "assumed interval." As shown in Table 10.4C, these descriptors are evenly spaced on a questionnaire; as such, the labels connote a continuum and the check lines are equal distances apart.[7] By wording or spacing the response options on a scale so they appear to have equal intervals between them, the researcher achieves a higher level of measurement than ordinal or nominal. With higher-order scales, the researcher is permitted to apply more powerful statistical techniques such as correlation analysis.

Ratio Scales

Ratio scales have a true zero point.

Ratio scales are ones in which a true zero origin exists—such as an actual number of purchases in a certain time period, dollars spent, miles traveled, number of children, or years of college education. This characteristic allows us to construct ratios when comparing results of the measurement. One person may spend twice as much as another or travel one-third as far. Such ratios are inappropriate for interval scales, so we are not allowed to say that one store was one-half as friendly as another. Examples of ratio-scaled questions are presented in Table 10.4D.

WHY THE MEASUREMENT LEVEL OF A SCALE IS IMPORTANT

Why all the fuss over scale characteristics and the level of measurement? There are two important reasons. First, the level of measurement determines what information you will have about the object of study; it determines what you can say and what you cannot say about the object. For example, nominal scales measure the lowest information level and, therefore, they are sometimes considered the crudest scales. Nominal scales allow us to do nothing more than identify our object of study on some property. Ratio scales, however, contain the greatest amount of information; they allow us to say many things about our object. Yet, it is not always possible to have a true zero point. A second important reason for understanding the level of measurement your scale possesses is that the level of measurement dictates what type of statistical analyses you may or may not perform. Low-level scales necessitate low-level analyses whereas high-level scales permit much more sophisticated analyses. In other words, the amount of information contained in the scale dictates the limits of statistical analysis. You will read more about this in Chapters 15 through 19.

Measurement level is important because it determines (1) what you can or cannot say about your object and (2) which statistical analysis you may use.

As a general recommendation it is desirable to construct a scale at the highest appropriate level of measurement possible. Of course, appropriateness is determined by the properties of the object being scaled and to some extent by the mental abilities of your respondents. You can, for example, always "collapse" a scale down to a lower level, but it is practically impossible to climb to a higher level once the data are collected. For instance, the intensity of disagreement or negativism represented by responses such as "strongly disagree" or "somewhat disagree" on an interval scale can be collapsed into the "disagree" category found on a nominal scale, but the reverse is not true.

WORKHORSE SCALES USED IN MARKETING RESEARCH

We noted in our opening comments that marketing researchers often wish to measure subjective properties of consumers. There are many variations of these properties, but usually they are concerned with the psychological aspects of consumers. There are many different terms and labels given to these constructs, including attitudes, opinions, evaluations, beliefs, impressions, perceptions, feelings, and intentions. All of these constructs share the measurement difficulty we discussed earlier. That is, because these constructs are unobservable, the marketing researcher must develop some means of allowing respondents to express the direction and the intensity of their impressions in both a convenient and understandable manner. To do this, the marketing researcher uses scaled-response questions, which are designed to measure unobservable constructs. In this section, we will describe the basic scale formats that are most common in marketing research practice. You will find these scale formats time and again on questionnaires; hence, we call them **workhorse scales** because they do the bulk of the measurement work.

Scaled-response questions are used to measure unobservable constructs.

Because most of these psychological properties exist on a continuum ranging from one extreme to another in the mind of the respondent, it is common practice to design scaled-response questions in an assumed interval-scale format. Sometimes numbers are used to indicate a single unit of distance between each position on the scale. Usually, but not always, the scale ranges from an extreme negative through a neutral to an extreme positive designation (Table 10.5). The neutral point is not considered zero or an origin; instead, it is considered a point along a continuum.

As we noted earlier, it is not good practice to invent a novel scale format with every questionnaire. Instead, marketing researchers often fall back on standard

Table 10.5   The Intensity Continuum Underlying Scaled-Response Question Forms

EXTREMELY NEGATIVE		NEUTRAL				EXTREMELY POSITIVE
	Strongly Disagree 1	Somewhat Disagree 2	Neither Agree nor Disagree 3	Somewhat Agree 4	Strongly Agree 5	
Extremely Dissatisfied 1	Very Dissatisfied 2	Somewhat Dissatisfied 3	No Opinion 4	Somewhat Satisfied 5	Very Satisfied 6	Extremely Satisfied 7
Extremely Unfavorable 1	Very Unfavorable 2	Somewhat Unfavorable 3	No Opinion 4	Somewhat Favorable 5	Very Favorable 6	Extremely Favorable 7

types used by the industry. These workhorse scales include the modified Likert scale, the life-style inventory, and the semantic differential, all three of which we describe next. Of course, sometimes no previous scale exists; or if one exists, it may have been developed in a context different from the one the researcher has in mind.

The Modified Likert Scale

A scaled-response form commonly used by marketing researchers[8] is the **modified Likert scale,** in which respondents are asked to indicate their degree of agreement or disagreement on a symmetric agree–disagree scale for each of a series of statements. The value of the modified Likert scale should be apparent because respondents are asked how much they agree or disagree with the statement. That is, the scale captures the intensity of their feelings. Table 10.6 presents an example of its use in a telephone interview. You should notice the directions given by the interviewer to properly administer this scale.

The Likert-type response format, borrowed from a formal scale development approach developed by Rensis Likert, has been extensively modified and adapted by marketing researchers, so much, in fact, that its definition varies from researcher to researcher. Some assume that any intensity scale using descriptors such as "strongly," "somewhat," "slightly," or the like is a Likert variation. Others use the term only for questions with agree–disagree response options. We tend to agree with the second opinion and prefer to refer to any scaled measurement other than an agree–disagree dimension as a "sensitivity" or "intensity" scale. But this convention is only our preference, and you should be aware that different researchers embrace other designations.

The Lifestyle Inventory

There is a special application of the modified Likert question form called the **lifestyle inventory** (or psychographics inventory), which takes into account the values and personality traits of people as reflected in their unique activities, interests, and opinions (AIOs) toward their work, leisure time, and purchases. The technique was originated by advertising strategists who wanted to obtain descriptions of groups of consumers as a means of establishing more effective advertising. The underlying belief is that knowledge of consumers' lifestyles, as opposed to just demographics,

Table **10.6** **The Likert Question Format Can Be Used in Telephone Surveys, but Respondents Must Be Briefed on Its Format or Otherwise Prompted**

(INTERVIEWER: READ) I have a list of statements that I will read to you. As I read each one, please indicate whether you agree or disagree with it.
Are the instructions clear? (IF NOT, REPEAT)
(INTERVIEWER: READ EACH STATEMENT. WITH EACH RESPONSE, ASK) Would you say that you (dis)agree STRONGLY or (dis)agree SOMEWHAT?

STATEMENT	STRONGLY DISAGREE	DISAGREE	NEUTRAL	AGREE	STRONGLY AGREE
Levi's Engineered jeans are good looking.	1	2	3	4	5
Levi's Engineered jeans are reasonably priced.	1	2	3	4	5
Your next pair of jeans will be Levi's Engineered jeans.	1	2	3	4	5
Levi's Engineered jeans are easy to identify on someone.	1	2	3	4	5
Levi's Engineered jeans make you feel good.	1	2	3	4	5

offers direction for marketing decisions. Many companies use psychographics as a market targeting tool.[9]

Lifestyle questions measure consumers' unique ways of living. These questions can be used to distinguish among types of purchasers such as heavy versus light users of a product, store patrons versus nonpatrons, or media vehicle users versus nonusers. They can assess the degree to which a person is price-conscious, fashion-conscious, an opinion giver, a sports enthusiast, child oriented, home centered, or financially optimistic. These attributes are measured by a series of AIO statements, usually in the form presented in Table 10.7.[10] Each respondent indicates his or her degree of agreement or disagreement by responding to the Likert-like categories. In some applications, the questionnaire may contain a large number of different lifestyle statements ranging from very general descriptions of the person's AIOs to very specific statements concerning particular products, brands, services, or other items of interest to the marketing researcher. Ideally, more than one statement for each lifestyle dimension should be used. Each respondent's indications on the related items are then usually added or averaged together. Then a single score is given for each person on each lifestyle dimension.

Lifestyle inventories are valuable to marketers in a number of ways, not the least of which is as a market segmentation basis and tool. To perform market segmentation, a researcher must use a very large number of lifestyle statements, and a great many respondents must be involved in the survey. Herein lies a dilemma, for potential respondents, even panel members who are compensated for their partici-

> Lifestyle questions measure a person's activities, interests, and opinions with a Likert scale.

Table 10.7 Examples of Lifestyle Statements on a Questionnaire

Please respond by circling the number that best corresponds to how much you agree or disagree with each statement.

STATEMENT	STRONGLY DISAGREE	DISAGREE	NEITHER AGREE NOR DISAGREE	AGREE	STRONGLY AGREE
I shop a lot for "specials."	1	2	3	4	5
I usually have one or more outfits that are of the very latest style.	1	2	3	4	5
My children are the most important thing in my life.	1	2	3	4	5
I usually keep my house very neat and clean.	1	2	3	4	5
I would rather spend a quiet evening at home than go out to a party.	1	2	3	4	5
It is good to have a charge account.	1	2	3	4	5
I like to watch or listen to baseball or football games.	1	2	3	4	5
I think I have more self-confidence than most people.	1	2	3	4	5
I sometimes influence what my friends buy.	1	2	3	4	5
I will probably have more money to spend next year than I have now.	1	2	3	4	5

MARKETING RESEARCH
INSIGHT
online research
10.3

What If You Have a REAAALLY Long Online Questionnaire?[11]

With the use of a sensitivity scale such as a 5-point agree–disagree Likert scale to measure lifestyle or psychographics, it is not unusual for the number of lifestyle statements to expand very rapidly. For example, a complete lifestyle inventory may quickly balloon to over 200 statements. When these are combined with product and services purchasing and usage behavior questions, the result is a very long questionnaire.

Refusals-to-participate and break-offs during the survey are major problems no matter what the data collection method; however, online surveys seem particularly vulnerable because potential respondents can scroll the questionnaire to see how long it is and decide immediately not to participate after scanning many, many questions. Plus, online respondents are notoriously flighty, and they can become bored with a long questionnaire.

One strategy to use is a split-questionnaire design, which breaks the questionnaire into a core component and a number of subcomponents. For example, if there are 100 questions on the questionnaire, these might be split into 25 core questions and three subcomponents with 25 questions each. No respondent need answer more than 50 questions as he or she would answer the 25 core questions and one randomly assigned set of 25 subcomponent questions.

The accompanying illustration shows that Respondent A answered the core and subcomponent set 1, B answered the core and set 3, C did the core and set 1, while D answered the core and subcomponent set 2.

RESPONDENT	CORE SET	SUBCOMPONENT QUESTION SETS		
		1	2	3
A	▓	▓		
B	▓			▓
C	▓	▓		
D	▓		▓	

With online surveys, it is not unusual to have thousands of respondents, so although some subcomponent question sets are not answered in this simple example, all of them would be answered by a large number of respondents in an actual online survey.

The result will be a very large data set with "missing values," but it is acceptable in this case to substitute the average response of those respondents who did answer a question as the response for those who did not answer it. More sophisticated procedures, which are beyond the scope of this book, are available if the researcher wishes to have more accurate estimates.

A consumer's lifestyle may be measured in terms of his or her activities, interests, and opinions.

pation in surveys, dislike long questionnaires. We have included Marketing Research Insight 10.3 that describes a way to greatly reduce the size of the questionnaire but still achieve the goal of a lifestyle market segmentation survey.

The Semantic Differential Scale

The semantic differential is a good way to measure a brand, company, or store image.

A specialized scaled-response question format that has sprung directly from the problem of translating a person's qualitative judgments into quantitative estimates is the **semantic differential scale.** Like the modified Likert scale, this one has been borrowed from another area of research, namely semantics. The semantic differential scale contains a series of bipolar adjectives for the various properties of the object under study, and respondents indicate their impressions of each property by indicating locations along its continuum. The focus of the semantic differential is on the measurement of the meaning of an object, concept, or person. Because many marketing stimuli have meaning, mental associations, or connotations, this type of scale works very well when the marketing researcher is attempting to determine brand, store, or other images.

The construction of a semantic differential scale begins with the determination of a concept or object to be rated. The researcher then selects bipolar pairs of words or phrases that could be used to describe the object's salient properties. Depending on the object, some examples might be "friendly–unfriendly," "hot–cold," "convenient–inconvenient," "high quality–low quality," and "dependable–undependable." The opposites are positioned at the endpoints of a continuum of intensity, and it is customary, although not mandatory, to use seven separators between each point. The respondent then indicates his or her evaluation of the performance of the object, say a brand, by checking the appropriate line. The closer the respondent checks to an endpoint on a line, the more intense is his or her evaluation of the object being measured.

Table 10.8 shows how this was done for a survey for Red Lobster. The respondents also rated Jake's Seafood Restaurant on the same survey. You can see that each respondent has been instructed to indicate his or her impression of various restaurants such as Red Lobster by checking the appropriate line between the several bipolar adjective phrases. As you look at the phrases, you should note that they have been randomly flipped to avoid having all of the "good" ones on one side. This flipping procedure is used to avoid the **halo effect**,[12] which is a general feeling about a store or brand that can bias a respondent's impressions on its specific properties.[13] For instance, suppose you have a very positive image of Red Lobster. If all of the positive items were on the right-hand side and all the negative ones were on the left-hand side, you might be tempted to just check all of the answers on the right-hand side. But it is entirely possible that some specific aspect of the Red Lobster might not be as good as the others. Perhaps the restaurant is not located in a very convenient place, or the menu is not as broad as you would like. Randomly flipping favorable and negative ends of the descriptors in a semantic differential scale minimizes the halo effect. There is some evidence that when respondents are ambivalent on the

When using the semantic differential scale, you should control for the halo effect.

Table 10.8	**The Semantic Differential Scale Is Useful When Measuring Store, Company, or Brand Images**

Indicate your impression of Red Lobster restaurant by checking the line corresponding to your opinion for each pair of descriptors.

High prices	___ ___ ___ ___ ___ ___ ___	Low prices
Inconvenient location	___ ___ ___ ___ ___ ___ ___	Convenient location
For me	___ ___ ___ ___ ___ ___ ___	Not for me
Warm atmosphere	___ ___ ___ ___ ___ ___ ___	Cold atmosphere
Limited menu	___ ___ ___ ___ ___ ___ ___	Wide menu
Fast service	___ ___ ___ ___ ___ ___ ___	Slow service
Low-quality food	___ ___ ___ ___ ___ ___ ___	High-quality food
A special place	___ ___ ___ ___ ___ ___ ___	An everyday place

PRESENTATION OF THE RESULTS SHOWS RED LOBSTER'S COMPETITIVE STRENGTHS

High prices	___ ___ ___ ___ ___ ___ ___	Low prices
Inconvenient location	___ ___ ___ ___ ___ ___ ___	Convenient location
For me	___ ___ ___ ___ ___ ___ ___	Not for me
Warm atmosphere	___ ___ ___ ___ ___ ___ ___	Cold atmosphere
Limited menu	___ ___ ___ ___ ___ ___ ___	Wide menu
Fast service	___ ___ ___ ___ ___ ___ ___	Slow service
Low-quality food	___ ___ ___ ___ ___ ___ ___	High-quality food
A special place	___ ___ ___ ___ ___ ___ ___	An everyday place

_____ Red Lobster
- - - - Jake's Seafood Restaurant

survey topic, it is best to use a balanced set of negatively and positively worded questions.[14]

One of the most appealing aspects of the semantic differential scale is the ability of the researcher to compute averages and then to plot a "profile" of the brand or company image. Each check line is assigned a number for coding. Usually, the numbers 1, 2, 3, and so on, beginning from the left side, are customary. Then an average is computed for each bipolar pair. The averages are plotted as you see them, and the marketing researcher has a very nice graphical communication vehicle with which to report the findings to his or her client, as can be seen in the bottom half of Table 10.8.

> With a semantic differential scale, a researcher can plot the average evaluation on each set of bipolar descriptors.

Other Scaled-Response Question Formats

There are a great many variations of scaled-response question formats used in marketing research. If you choose a career in the marketing research business, you will realize that each marketing research company or marketing research department tends to rely on tried-and-true formats that they apply from study to study. Several examples are provided in Table 10.9.

> Researchers tend to rely on tried-and-true scale formats.

There are some very good reasons for this practice of adopting a preferred question format. First, it expedites the questionnaire design process. That is, by selecting a standardized scaled-response form that has been used in several studies, there is no need to be creative and to invent a new form. This saves both time and costs.[15] Second, by testing a scaled-response format across several studies, there is the

---

Table 10.9 **Scaled-Response Question Formats Can Have Various Forms**

SCALE NAME	DESCRIPTION AND EXAMPLES
Graphic rating scale	Use of a line or pictorial representation to indicate intensity of response: Unimportant ◀- - - - - - - - - - - - - - - - - - -▶ Extremely Important ☺ ☺ ☺ ☺ ☺
Itemized rating scale	Use of a numbered or labeled continuous scale to indicate intensity of response: ☐ 1　　☐ 2　　☐ 3　　☐ 4　　☐ 5 　　　　　　　　　　　　Very Poor　　Fair　　Good　　Good　　Excellent ____　____　____　____　____
Stapel scale	Use of numbers, usually −5 to +5 to indicate the intensity of response: Fast checkout service　−5　−4　−3　−2　−1　+1　+2　+3　+4　+5
Percentage scale	Use of percentages to indicate the intensity of response: Unlikely to purchase　　　　　　　　　　　　　　　　　　Likely 　　　　　　　　　　　　　　　　　　　　　to purchase 0%　10%　20%　30%　40%　50%　60%　70%　80%　90%　100% Very　　　　　　　　　　　　　　　　　　　Very dissatisfied　　　　　　　　　　　　　　　　satisfied 0%　　　　　25%　　　　50%　　　　75%　　　100%

opportunity to assess its reliability as well as its validity. Both of these topics are discussed in detail in a later section of this chapter, which introduces the basic concepts involved with reliability and validity of measurements.

Issues in the Use of Sensitivity Scales

Using scaled-response formats requires the researcher to confront two issues. First is the question of whether or not to include the middle, neutral-response option. Our modified Likert scale, lifestyle, and semantic differential examples all have a neutral point, but some researchers prefer to leave out the neutral option on their scales. Valid arguments exist for both options.[16] Those arguing for the inclusion of a neutral option believe that some respondents do not have opinions formed on that item, and they must be given the opportunity to indicate their ambivalence. Proponents of not including a neutral position, however, believe that respondents may use the neutral option as a dodge or a method of hiding their opinions.[17] Eliminating the neutral position forces these respondents to indicate their opinions or feelings.

Use a neutral response option when you think respondents have a valid "no opinion" response.

The second issue concerns the need to have a completely symmetric scale. Sometimes common sense causes the researcher to conclude that only the positive side is appropriate. For example, when you think of how important something is to you, you do not usually think in terms of degrees of "unimportance." In fact, for many constructs symmetric scales are awkward or nonintuitive and should not be used.[18]

Consequently, some scales contain only the positive side, because very few respondents would make use of the degrees of intensity on the negative side. When in doubt, a researcher can pretest both the complete and the one-sided versions to see whether the negative side will be used by respondents. As a general rule, it is best to pretest a sensitivity scale to make sure it is being used in its entirety. Some individuals, such as Hispanics, have tendencies to use only one end of a scale,[19] and pretests should be used to find a scale that will be used appropriately.

Use common sense in deciding whether to have a completely symmetric scale.

Although scales are vital to market researchers' work, and researchers use them on a daily basis, there are formidable issues when a scale is used across countries.[20] Not only are there language differences to contend with, but also there are critical questions about construct, scalar, measurement, and sample equivalence. Marketing Research Insight 10.4 describes these issues and offers a remedy.

WHAT SCALE TO USE WHEN

It has been our experience that when you study each workhorse scale and the other scaled-response question formats described in this chapter, each one makes sense. However, when faced with the actual decision as to which scale to recommend in a given situation, it is difficult for neophyte marketing researchers to sort these scales out.

As we indicated in Chapter 4, the market researcher's mind-set is geared toward the actual survey steps, and questionnaire design is a vital step that he or she must think about when formulating the marketing research proposal. We indicated in Chapter 4 that market researchers use constructs or standard marketing concepts, and, more important, we indicated that the researcher typically has a mental vision of how each construct will be measured. This mental vision, we indicated, is called an **operational definition,** and Table 4.6 on page 100 previewed this topic.

Since you now understand the basic concepts of measurement and have become acquainted with the workhorse scales and other scales used by market researchers,

MARKETING RESEARCH
INSIGHT
10.4

Construct Measurement Issues with Global Market Segmentation Situations[21]

Market segmentation can be based on marketing constructs such as:

▶ individualism versus collectivism
▶ masculinity versus femininity
▶ future-oriented versus tradition oriented
▶ adoption propensity

The goal of global market segmentation is to identify the relevant constructs, develop or adapt scales to measure these constructs, administer these scales to representative samples of different countries, and to discover the differences that are found between the various countries. For example, a global market segmentation result might look like the following.

Construct	Country A	Country B	Country C
Individualism	Individualistic	Collective	Collective
Masculinity	Masculine	Masculine	Feminine
Future Orientation	Future oriented	Tradition oriented	Tradition oriented
Adoption	Fast adopter	Moderate adopter	Slow adopter

Unfortunately, global market segmentation is riddled with four measurement equivalence issues: (1) construct, (2) scalar, (3) measurement, and (4) sample. Construct equivalence means that a construct may differ in its interpretation based on the culture. For instance, Americans value the future, but many Eastern cultures value the past, so a construct such as "progressive" is different between cultures. Scalar equivalence refers to the number of scale points in the scale. In the United States a 5-point scale is common, but in other cultures, individuals are very comfortable with many more scale points, perhaps as many as 20. Measurement equivalence refers to what the standard measures are for the construct in a culture. For instance, "well educated" may mean possessing a college degree in the United States, but it may mean a high school diploma or even less in African or Central American countries. Last, sample equivalence means that the individuals who respond to the global market segmentation survey, regardless of the country, are very similar. However, accessibility differences, literacy levels, and the willingness of citizens to take surveys differ dramatically.

When performing global marketing research, researchers are advised to "think globally, act locally." In other words, market researchers can use global marketing research to identify market segments within countries or regions, but they must apply in-depth local marketing research to understand every culture's nuances and special circumstances.

we have provided Table 10.10 as a quick reference to appropriate scales pertaining to the constructs most often measured by market researchers. Of course, this is not a complete list of marketing constructs, but the constructs in Table 10.10 are often involved in marketing research undertakings.

We have included some nominally scaled constructs in Table 10.10, namely, the awareness, possession, recall, and recognition constructs are measured with yes–no scales. If there is a list, and the respondent checks all that apply, the researcher can use a **summated scale**, meaning that the number of checks will be counted for each respondent, and that number will stand as the measure of the construct. For example, if there is a list of 10 kitchen appliances that a person could have in his or her kitchen, those respondents with many appliances will have high summated scale numbers, whereas those with few will have low summated scale numbers.

If you are still confused about what scale to use at different times, do not feel badly as scales are not an easy concept to understand at first reading. Although we did not include it as one of our workhorse scales, a very commonly used scale is the simple 5-point anchored scale. An **anchored scale** is one in which the endpoints are identified by the opposite ends of the measurement continuum and are associated with the beginning and ending numbers of the scale. For example, a telephone interviewer might say,

Table 10.10 **Commonly Used Scales for Selected Constructs**

CONSTRUCT	RESPONSE SCALE
Awareness or possession	Yes–No OR check mark from a list of items Example: *Which of the following kitchen appliances do you own?* *(Check all that apply.)*
Brand/store image	Semantic differential (with 4 to 7 scale points) using a set of bipolar adjectives Example: *Refer to example on page 285.*
Demographics	Standard demographic questions (gender, age range, income range, etc.) Examples: *Indicate your gender* ____Male ____Female *What is your age range?* ____ 20 or younger ____ 21–30 ____ 31–40 ____ 41–50 ____ 51 or older
Frequency of use	Labeled (Do Not Use, Infrequently, Occasionally, Often, Quite Often, Very Often) OR number of times per relevant time period (e.g., last month). Example: *How often do you buy takeout Chinese dinners?*
Importance	Labeled (Unimportant, Slightly Important, Important, Quite Important, Very Important) OR numbered rating using 5 scale points Example: *How important is it to you that your dry cleaning service has same-day service?*
Intention to purchase	Labeled (Unlikely, Somewhat Likely, Likely, Quite Likely, Very Likely) OR 100% probability Example: *The next time you buy cookies, how likely are you to buy a fat-free brand?*
Lifestyle/opinion	Likert (Strongly Disagree–Strongly Agree with 5 scale points) using a series of lifestyle statements Example: *Indicate how much you agree or disagree with each of the following statements.* 　1. *I have a busy schedule.* 　2. *I work a great deal.*
Performance or attitude	Labeled (Poor, Fair, Good, Very Good, Excellent) OR numbered rating using 5 scale points OR Stapel using 5 scale points Example: *Indicate how well you think Arby's performs on each of the following features.* 　1. *Variety of items on the menu* 　2. *Reasonable price* 　3. *Location convenient to your home*
Recall or recognition	Yes–No OR check mark from a list of items Example: *Where have you seen or heard an ad for Pets-R-Us in the past month? (Check all that apply.)*
Satisfaction	Labeled (Not Satisfied, Somewhat Satisfied, Satisfied, Quite Satisfied, Very Satisfied) OR 100% satisfaction scale Example: *Based on your experience with Federal Express, how satisfied have you been with its overnight delivery service?*

MARKETING RESEARCH
INSIGHT
10.5

Reader's Digest Trusted Brands Survey Illustrates the Global Usefulness of a 5–Point Scale[22]

The *Reader's Digest*, believed to be the most widely read magazine in the world, conducts an annual consumer trust survey each year in 18 different European countries to identify the most trusted consumer brands in at least 30 different product categories. To accomplish this end, the survey instrument asks each respondent to indicate his or her most trusted brand in each product category. Respondents are then asked to rate each brand on an unanchored 5-point scale. The ratings are gathered for each of four aspects of trust: (1) quality, (2) value, (3) strong image, and (4) understanding customer needs. Below are some of the product evaluation categories that appear in the English version of the *Reader's Digest* Trusted Brands Survey.

Because of the diversity of languages in Europe and because *Reader's Digest* is published in many languages, the questionnaire is printed in 20 languages. The ability of a 5-point unanchored scaled to span so many languages is, indeed, its strong point and places it high on the choice list of marketing researchers doing multinational or single-country surveys. *Reader's Digest's* use of the simple 5-point interval scale of intensity demonstrates that it is applicable across Western cultures.

Here is a sample of the findings of the most trusted consumer brands—across countries—in Europe in 2002.

Almost 32,000 people completed and returned the mail survey.

The Top Eight Brands in Europe

Product Category	Brand Name	Number of European Countries Where Brand Is Most Trusted
Mobile phone handset	Nokia	18
Credit card	Visa	16
Skin care	Nivea	16
Hi-fi/audio equipment	Sony	14
Cameras	Canon	14
Toothpaste	Colgate	12
Personal computers	IBM	10
Soap powder	Ariel	7

The Trusted Brands Survey is conducted annually, and it has been expanded to cover other topics. Refer to **www.rdtrustedbrands.com** for up-to-date information on this global survey. We highly recommend that you visit this site as it has a number of insights into European consumers, their trusted brands, Internet usage, and other valuable pieces of information about this part of the globe.

"Please tell me how satisfied you were with your CD-burner software where a 1 means 'unsatisfied,' and a 5 means 'very satisfied.'" Another example is this, "Please rate the music quality of your PC's audio system where 1 means 'poor,' and 5 means 'excellent.'" An **unanchored scale** is one in which the endpoints are not identified as, for example, "Please indicate on a scale of 1 to 5 how satisfied you were with your CD-burner software." It is implicit with an unanchored scale that, as the scale numbers rise, the evaluation is more positive. So, 1 would be the least positive response, whereas 5 would be the most positive response. Nevertheless, it is important to indicate how the numbers relate to the respondent's evaluation in the instructions for that rating scale.

Marketing Research Insight 10.5 describes an application of the 5-point unanchored scale[23] by *Reader's Digest* in its annual "most trusted brands" survey conducted in various countries in Europe. As you read this item, notice the global flexibility of a simple 5-point scale.

RELIABILITY AND VALIDITY OF MEASUREMENTS

Ideally, a measurement used by a market researcher should be reliable and valid. A **reliable measure** is one in which a respondent responds in the same or in a very similar manner to an identical or nearly identical question. Obviously if a question elicits wildly different answers from the same person and you know that the person is

Reliable measures obtain identical or very similar responses from the same respondent.

unchanged from administration to administration of the question, there is something very wrong with the question.

Validity, on the other hand, operates on a completely different plane than reliability; it is possible to have perfectly reliable measurements that are invalid. Validity is defined as the accuracy of the measurement: It is an assessment of the exactness of the measurement relative to what actually exists. So, a **valid measure** is one that is truthful. To illustrate this concept and how it differs from reliability, think of a respondent who is embarrassed by a question about his income. This person makes under $40,000 per year, but he does not want to tell it to the interviewer. Consequently, he responds with the highest category, "Over $100,000." In a retest of the questions, the respondent persists in his lie by stipulating the highest income level again. Here the respondent has been perfectly consistent (that is, reliable), but he has also been completely untruthful (that is, invalid). Of course, lying is not the only reason for invalidity. The respondent may have a faulty memory, may have a misconception, or may even be a bad guesser, which causes his responses to be inexact from reality.[24]

When a researcher develops questions for his or her questionnaire, he or she uses an intuitive form of judgment called **face validity** to evaluate the validity of each question. Face validity is concerned with the degree to which a measurement "looks like" it measures that which it is designed to measure.[25] Thus, as each question is developed, there is an implicit assessment of its face validity. Often a researcher will ask a colleague to look at the questions to see if he or she agrees with the researcher's face validity judgments. Revisions strengthen the face validity of the question until it passes the researcher's subjective evaluation. Unfortunately, face validity is considered by academic marketing researchers to be a very weak test, so marketing research practitioners are faced with an ethical dilemma when they work with scales. We describe this ethical dilemma next.

> Validity is the accuracy of responses to a measure.

> Face validity: Does the question "look like" it measures what it is supposed to measure?

▶ **An Ethical Issue**

Researchers Face an Ethical Dilemma in Scale Development

MARKETING RESEARCH
INSIGHT
10.6

The proper way to develop a scale is very lengthy and expensive because there are several different criteria that should be used to assess the quality of a scale. To meet these criteria, it is expected that a scale will be developed over a series of administrations. Statistical tests are used after each one to refine the scale, and each subsequent administration tests the new version, which leads to further refinement. It is not unusual for scales that are published in academic journals to go through three or four administrations involving hundreds of respondents.

Although a few research firms have pursued scale development, and they have developed proprietary instruments that are protected by copyright, most marketing research practitioners do not have the time and their clients are unwilling to supply the monetary resources necessary to thoroughly develop scales.

The ethical dilemma is especially evident when a marketing researcher is attempting to maximize his or her profit.

Proper scale development does not take place due to the fact that clients do not appreciate the time and cost factors. In fact, they may not even believe these procedures are warranted and will refuse to pay for them, meaning that if such tests are performed, they will reduce the marketing researcher's profits. Consequently, the vast majority of marketing researchers are forced to design their measures by relying on face validity alone.

The unfortunate truth is that some researchers do not concern themselves at all with reliability or validity measurements. On the other hand, it is unethical for a researcher to find reliability and/or validity problems and not strive to resolve them. Some researchers hold that not assessing reliability and validity is an unethical practice in itself. However, a conscientious market researcher will devote as much time and energy as possible to ensure the reliability and validity of the research throughout the entire process.

The formal development of reliable and valid measures is a long and complicated process that is largely entrusted to academic marketing researchers. In other words, marketing professors who work on the cutting edge of research often labor for long periods of time to develop reliable and valid measures of the marketing constructs with which they are working. Fortunately, these labors are ultimately published in academic journals that place these measures in the public domain, meaning that marketing research practitioners can use them freely.

In fact, a series of *Marketing Scales Handbooks* by Gordon C. Bruner II, Karen E. James, and Paul J. Hensel, editors, containing hundreds of these scales is published by the American Marketing Association. These handbooks save the time and effort that would need to be expended in searching for scales in journal articles or other similar academic sources. (See: www.marketingpower.com.)

Here is how our Blue Ribbon Panel members answered our question about how online research is affecting the measurement of marketing constructs.

BLUE RIBBON PANEL on [Online Research]

Q: *Has online survey research changed the way researchers are measuring fundamental marketing constructs? That is, are our measures of brand image, attitudes, intentions, and so on better, worse, or the same. If not the same, what changes are apparent?*

Note: To learn about the panel members, see the Preface of this book.

Bill MacElroy
President
Socratic Technologies

A: I don't think the basic rules of good survey design change much in the online environment. Technical aspects of research design such as balanced scales, nonleading questions, single construct questions, exhaustive choice sets, and so on are all just as valid online as off-line. Some aspects of question layout and visual presentation can be more dynamic in the online environment, but these should be considered embellishments to good design, not substitutes.

Allen Hogg
President
Burke, Inc.

A: There is evidence that, on some items, people responding to Web surveys will respond differently from people responding to more traditional surveys, especially those that are administered by interviewers, such as telephone research. For example, on traditional purchase-intent questions using semantic scales, phone respondents are more likely than Web respondents to use the scale endpoints. Results gathered through telephone or other off-line research may, therefore, need to be recalibrated to be compared appropriately with online research findings. Companies that specialize in predicting market shares of new consumer package goods and tracking retail sales in such categories as clothing and restaurant meals are among those that have been faced with the daunting task of keeping historical information relevant while transitioning to online data collection methods.

It should be noted that responses to Web surveys can also differ based on how questions appear on a computer screen. Asking people to type in a number, for example, can lead to responses that are different from those that will be obtained using "radio button" or "drop-down box" scales. When interpreting findings, researchers need to be aware of how an online survey was put together and the implications of that approach.

George Harmon
*Senior Vice President
Digital Marketing
Services*

A: In general no, but the quality of the information is better. Respondents can be more discriminating with their responses when they see graphic scales and the scaling intervals that cannot be shown in phone interviews.

With self-administered questionnaires respondents tend to be more truthful when an interviewer is absent. We have seen this especially with purchase-intent scores, where respondents give lower top box ratings than when an interviewer is present. We've also seen it in comparability studies with sensitive subjects where we see online responses that are more consistent with actual sales.

George Terhanian
*Vice President of
Internet Research
Harris Interactive,
Inc.*

A: Online research has indeed changed the way researchers are measuring fundamental marketing constructs. Time, for example, has become a major factor in many marketing programs. Prior to the emergence of the Internet as a channel for marketing and research, most marketing plans coordinated tactics to achieve a desired strategic outcome within a broad time frame (months or quarters). Companies that conduct online research understand that they must move more quickly to achieve competitive advantage.

Programs are created, measured, and managed to achieve weekly goals. This is not simply a research phenomenon, but also it results from a feedback loop where Internet measurement provides the metrics for success and direction for continued marketing actions. The first marketing organizations to take advantage of this have been those that conduct a significant portion of business on the Internet, such as financial services firms or cataloguers. Increasingly, however, we're seeing the advent of market response models using Internet metrics employed in more traditional consumer packaged goods marketing.

Lee Smith
*CEO
Insight Express*

A: Online research is both challenging and changing the way researchers measure marketing fundamentals. With declining cooperation rates via telephone and mail, these historical "gold standard" methodologies are increasingly being viewed as "bronze standards." As efforts to reconcile measurement differences acquired from online and other methodologies continue, new opportunities to drive research quality are becoming apparent. Leveraging the ability to blend text, audio, video, and other forms of stimuli into a research instrument forces us to think about new measurement techniques. For example, no longer will text or verbal descriptions of television commercials be sufficient to test ad awareness levels. Ad awareness will be measured by respondents being exposed to video clips of the actual ads. Similarly, brand awareness will be measured through the display of logos, not a text or verbal description. Through these improved techniques, we will shift our perceptions of research excellence to entirely new standards.

Doss Struse
*Senior Vice President
Client Service
Knowledge Networks,
Inc.*

A: I would judge that there has been limited progress to date. However, I think there are two directions that are promising. The first is to enable more nonverbal responses. Much of the survey research in the United States, especially that done by telephone, is verbally based. Respondents are asked questions verbally and must encode their answers into words— even when the researcher is trying to understand phenomena that may be intrinsically nonverbal. The second is to enable a different mental model for consumers to interact with research. Verbally based research also imposes a "recall" mental model. Respondents are asked what they remember in connection to verbal cues or constructs. The online world because it allows multimedia interaction can enable a recognition mental model. One need only look to one's own ability to recall names versus recognizing faces to see the difference.

SPSS Student Assistant Online
Coca-Cola: Sorting, Searching, and
Inserting Variables and Cases

SUMMARY

This chapter discussed the concepts involved in measurement of the subjective properties of marketing phenomena. We began by reviewing the three basic question–response option formats of open-ended, closed-ended, and scaled-response questions and then we introduced you to the four types of scales used in marketing research: (1) nominal or simple classifications; (2) ordinal or rank order; (3) interval scales, which include number scales and other equal-appearing spaced scales; and (4) ratio scales, which have a true zero point. As you move from the lowest (nominal) to the highest (ratio) type of scale, you gain more information in measurement.

Marketing researchers have a set of commonly used scale types, and the chapter included descriptions of three of these. First, there is the modified Likert scale, which appears as an agree–disagree continuum with five to seven positions. Next, we described lifestyle questions, which use a modified Likert approach to measure people's attitudes, interests, and opinions. Third, we illustrated how the semantic differential scale uses bipolar adjectives to measure the image of a brand or a store.

Finally, reliability and validity of measurement were discussed. Reliability is the degree to which a respondent is consistent in his or her answers. Validity, on the other hand, is the accuracy of responses. It is possible to have reliable measures that are inaccurate. Researchers use face validity, or intuitive judgment, when developing questions that "look like" they are eliciting valid answers. The American Marketing Association publishes handbooks on marketing scales that have been developed and published in journals by academic market researchers.

KEY TERMS

Open-ended question (p. 271)
Unprobed format (p. 271)
Probed format (p. 271)
Response probe (p. 271)
Closed-ended question (p. 271)
Dichotomous closed-ended question (p. 271)
Multiple-category closed-ended question (p. 271)
Scaled-response question (p. 272)
Unlabeled scaled-response format (p. 272)
Labeled scaled-response format (p. 272)
Measurement (p. 275)
Properties (p. 275)
Objective properties (p. 277)
Subjective properties (p. 277)
Scale development (p. 277)
Description (p. 277)

Order (p. 277)
Distance (p. 277)
Origin (p. 277)
Nominal scales (p. 278)
Ordinal scales (p. 278)
Interval scales (p. 280)
Ratio scales (p. 280)
Workhorse scales (p. 281)
Modified Likert scale (p. 282)
Lifestyle inventory (p. 282)
Semantic differential scale (p. 284)
Halo effect (p. 285)
Operational definition (p. 287)
Summated scale (p. 288)
Anchored scale (p. 288)
Unanchored scale (p. 290)
Reliable measure (p. 290)
Valid measure (p. 291)
Face validity (p. 291)

REVIEW QUESTIONS/APPLICATIONS

1. List each of the three basic question–response formats. Indicate the two variations for each one, and provide an example for each.
2. Identify at least four considerations that determine a question's format and indicate how each one would determine the format.
3. What is measurement? In your answer, differentiate an object from its properties, both objective and subjective.
4. Distinguish the four scale characteristics that determine the level of measurement with a scale.
5. Define the four types of scales and indicate the types of information contained in each.
6. Explain what is meant by a continuum along which a subjective property of an object can be measured.
7. What are the arguments for and against the inclusion of a neutral response position in a symmetric scale?
8. Distinguish among a modified Likert scale, a lifestyle scale, and a semantic differential scale.
9. What is the halo effect, and how does a researcher control for it?
10. What is an operational definition? Provide operational definitions for the following constructs:
    a. brand loyalty
    b. intentions to purchase
    c. importance of "value for the price"
    d. attitude toward a brand
    e. recall of an advertisement
    f. past purchases
11. How does reliability differ from validity? In your answer, define each term.
12. Mike, the owner of Mike's Market, which is a convenience store, is concerned about low sales. He reads in a marketing textbook that the image of a store often has an impact on its ability to attract its target market. He contacts the All-Right Research Company and commissions it to conduct a study that will shape his store's image. You are charged with the responsibility of developing the store image part of the questionnaire.

    Design a semantic differential scale that will measure the relevant aspects of Mike's Market's image. In your work on this scale, you must do the following: (a) brainstorm the properties to be measured, (b) determine the appropriate bipolar adjectives, (c) decide on the number of scale points, and (d) indicate how the scale controls for the halo effect.
13. Each of the following examples involves a market researcher's need to measure some construct. Devise an appropriate scale for each one. Defend the scale in terms of its level of measurement, number of response categories, use or nonuse of a "no opinion" or neutral response category, and face validity.
    a. Mattel wants to know how preschool children react to a sing-along video game in which the child must sing along with an animated character and guess the next word in the song at various points in the video.
    b. TCBY is testing five new flavors of yogurt and wants to know how its customers rate each one on sweetness, flavor strength, and richness of taste.

    c. A pharmaceutical company wants to find out how much a new federal law eliminating dispensing of free sample prescription drugs by doctors will affect their intentions to prescribe generic versus brand-name drugs for their patients.

14. Harley-Davidson is the largest American motorcycle manufacturer, and it has been in business for several decades. Harley-Davidson has expanded into "signature" products such as shirts that prominently display the Harley-Davidson logo. Some people have a negative image of Harley-Davidson because it was the motorcycle favored by the Hell's Angels and other motorcycle gangs. There are two research questions here. First, do consumers have a negative feeling toward Harley-Davidson, and, second, are they disinclined toward the purchase of Harley-Davidson signature products such as shirts, belts, boots, jackets, sweatshirts, lighters, and key chains? Design a Likert measurement scale that can be used in a nationwide telephone study to address these two issues.

15. In conducting a survey for the Equitable Insurance Company, Burke Marketing Research assesses reliability by selecting a small group of respondents, calling them back, and readministering five questions to them. One question asks, "If you were going to buy life insurance sometime this year, how likely would you be to consider the Equitable Company?" Respondents indicate the likelihood on a probability scale (0 percent to 100 percent likely). Typically, this test–retest approach finds that respondents are within 10 percent of their initial response. That is, if a respondent indicated that he or she were 50 percent likely in the initial survey, he or she responded in the 45 percent to 55 percent range on the retest.

    The survey has been going on for four weeks, and it has two more weeks before the data collection will be completed. Respondents who are retested are called back exactly one week after the initial survey. In the last week, reliability results have been very different. Now Burke is finding that the retest averages are 20 percent higher than the initial test. Has the scale become unreliable? If so, why has its previous good reliability changed? If not, what has happened, and how can Burke still claim that it has a reliable measure?

16. General Foods Corporation includes Post, which is the maker of Fruit and Fibre Cereal. The brand manager is interested in determining how much Fruit and Fibre consumers think it is helping them toward a healthier diet. But the manager is very concerned that respondents in a survey may not be entirely truthful about health matters. They may exaggerate what they really believe so they "sound" more health conscious than they really are, and they may say they have healthy diets when they really do not.

    The General Foods Corporation marketing research director suggests a unique way to overcome the problem. He suggests that they conduct a survey of Fruit and Fibre customers in Pittsburgh, Atlanta, Dallas, and Denver. Fifty respondents who say that Fruit and Fibre is helping them toward a healthier diet and who also say they are more health conscious than the average American will be selected, and General Foods will offer to "buy" their groceries for the next month. To participate, the chosen respondents must submit their itemized weekly grocery trip receipts. By reviewing the items bought each week, General Foods can determine what they are eating and make judgments on how healthy their diets really are. What is your reaction to this approach? Will General Foods be able to assess the validity of its survey this way? Why or why not?

INTERACTIVE LEARNING

Visit the Web site at www.prenhall.com/burnsbush. For this chapter, work through the Self-Study Quizzes, and get instant feedback on whether you need additional studying. On the Web site, you can review the chapter outlines and case information for Chapter 10.

CASE 10.1   Amos Brown Chevrolet of Reno

The Amos Brown Chevrolet dealership, located in Reno, Nevada, wanted to know how people who intended to buy a new American-made automobile in the next 12 months view their purchase. The owner, Amos Brown, called the marketing department at the University of Nevada–Reno and arranged for a class project to be taken on by Professor Thomas Clary's undergraduate marketing research students. Professor Clary had a large class that semester, so he decided to divide the project into two groups and to have each group compete against the other to see which one designed and executed the better survey.

Both groups worked diligently on the survey over the semester. They met with Mr. Brown, discussed the dealership with his managers, conducted focus groups, and consulted the literature on brand, store, and company image research. Both teams conducted telephone surveys, whose findings are presented in their final reports.

Professor Clary offered to grant extra credit to each team if it gave a formal presentation of its research design, findings, and recommendations.

1. Contrast the different ways these findings can be presented in graphical form to the Amos Brown Chevrolet management group. Which student team has the ability to present its findings more effectively? How and why?
2. What are the managerial implications apparent in each team's findings? Identify the implications and recommendations for Amos Brown Chevrolet as they are evident in each team's findings.

Findings of Professor Clary's Marketing Research Teams

▶ TEAM ONE'S FINDINGS FOR AMOS BROWN CHEVROLET

Importance of Features of Dealership in Deciding to Buy There

Feature	Percent
Competitive prices	86
No high pressure	75
Good service facilities	73
Low-cost financing	68
Many models in stock	43
Convenient location	35
Friendly salespersons	32

Image of Amos Brown Chevrolet Dealership Percent Responding "Yes"

Feature	Percent
Competitive prices	45
No high pressure	32
Good service facilities	80
Low-cost financing	78
Many models in stock	50
Convenient location	81
Friendly salespersons	20

▶ TEAM TWO'S FINDINGS FOR AMOS BROWN CHEVROLET

Importance and Image of Amos Brown Chevrolet Dealership

Feature	Importance[a]	Rating[b]
Competitive prices	6.5	1.3
No high pressure	6.2	3.6
Good service facilities	5.0	4.3
Low-cost financing	4.7	3.9
Many models in stock	3.1	3.0
Convenient location	2.2	4.1
Friendly salespersons	2.0	1.2

[a]Based on a 7-point scale where 1 = "unimportant" and 7 = "extremely important."
[b]Based on a 5-point scale where 1 = "poor" and 5 = "excellent performance."

CASE 10.2 Extreme Exposure Rock Climbing Center Faces the Krag

For the past five years, Extreme Exposure Rock Climbing Center has enjoyed a monopoly. Located in Sacramento, California, Extreme Exposure was the dream of Kyle Anderson who has been into freestyle extreme sports of various types including outdoor rock climbing, hang gliding, skydiving, mountain biking, snowboarding, and a number of other adrenalin-pumping sports. Now in his mid thirties, Kyle came to realize in the year of his thirtieth birthday that after three leg fractures, two broken arms, and numerous dislocations, he could not participate on the extreme edge like he used to. So, he found an abandoned warehouse, recruited two investors and a friendly banker, and opened up Extreme Exposure.

Kyle's rock climbing center has over 6,500 square feet of simulated rock walls to climb, with about 100 different routes up to a maximum of 50 vertical feet. Extreme Exposure's design permits the four major climbing types: top-roping where the climber climbs up with a rope anchored at the top, lead-climbing where the climber tows the rope that he or she fixes to clips in the wall while ascending, bouldering where the climber has no rope but stays near the ground, and rappelling where the person descends quickly by sliding down a rope. Climbers can buy day passes or monthly or yearly memberships. Shoes and harnesses can be rented cheaply, and helmets are available free of charge as all climbers must wear protective helmets. In addition to individual and group climbing classes, Extreme Exposure has several group programs including birthday parties, a kids' summer camp, and corporate team-building classes.

Another rock climbing center called the Krag will be built in Sacramento within the next six months. Kyle notes the following items about the Krag that are different from Extreme Exposure: (1) The Krag will have climbs up to a maximum of 60 vertical feet, (2) it will have a climber certification program, (3) there will be day trips to outdoor rock climbing areas, (4) there will be group overnight and extended-stay rock climbing trips to the Canadian Rockies, and (5) the Krag's annual membership fee will be about 20 percent lower than the one for Extreme Exposure.

Kyle chats with Dianne, one of his Extreme Exposure members who is in marketing, during a break in one of her climbing visits, and Dianne summarizes what she believes Kyle needs to find out about his current members. Dianne's list follows.

1. What is the demographic and rock climbing profile of Extreme Exposure's members?
2. How satisfied are the members with Extreme Exposure's climbing facilities?
3. How interested are its members in (a) day trips to outdoor rock climbing areas, (b) group overnight and/or extended-stay rock climbing trips to the Canadian Rockies, and (c) a rock climber certification program?

4. What are members' opinions of the annual membership fee charged by Extreme Exposure?

5. Will members consider leaving Extreme Exposure to join a new rock climbing center with climbs that are 10 feet higher than the maximum climb at Extreme Exposure?

6. Will members consider leaving Extreme Exposure to join a new rock climbing center with climbs that are 10 feet higher than the maximum climb at Extreme Exposure and whose annual membership fee is 20 percent lower than Extreme Exposure's?

For each of Dianne's questions, identify the relevant construct and indicate how it should be measured.

Chapter 11

Designing Data Collection Forms

Practitioner Viewpoint

Consider art. Consider good fine art. You are drawn into it. It engages. Initially, you are not aware of how it was painted or presented; you are simply drawn into it. Similarly, a good survey engages the recipients and draws them in with a compelling invitation, followed by a natural and logical sequence of questions. *For online surveys, this means the invitation and initial presentation must captivate the audience; the survey itself must be highly interactive, dynamic, and engaging. As with any survey, the first question or two must capture the attention of survey respondents so they become committed and, thus, are more likely to complete the survey. In this chapter you will learn the basics of designing questionnaires and you will learn how to use WebSurveyor to help you with this task.*

Bruce Mancinelli
President/CEO
WebSurveyor

WebSurveyor: A Useful Tool for Online Survey Research

We started this book by telling you that online research is becoming a significant component of marketing research. Conducting surveys online, called online survey research, is a part of online research. Online survey research has many advantages. Respondents are easy to access, questionnaires are sent to them quickly and inexpensively via the Internet, and respondents may easily answer questions at their own computer and return their attitudes, opinions, intentions, and so on at the click of a mouse. However, just as with other forms of data collection (e.g., mail, telephone, and personal interview), the questionnaire plays an important role in the process. The "magic" of online electronic delivery, although adding significant benefits, does nothing to lessen the importance of a well-designed, properly worded, logically organized questionnaire. The burden is still on the questionnaire to compel the respondents to cooperate and engage them in meaningful communication. As Mr. Mancinelli's well-chosen words state, a well-designed questionnaire is like fine art. WebSurveyor is one of several electronic questionnaire design and delivery software programs that are available today to help marketing researchers take part in online survey research. As you can see by the accompanying WebSurveyor screen in Figure 11.1, you can write and edit surveys, manage the survey project, and analyze survey results using WebSurveyor. (We are certain you would answer the question about studying with no less than 12 hours, right?)

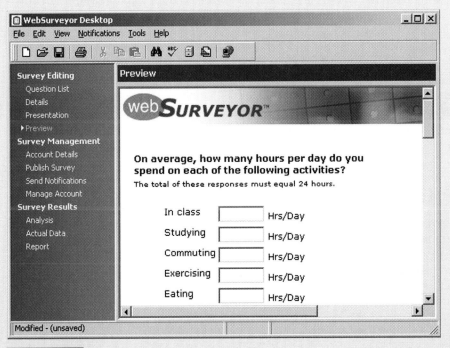

Figure 11.1

We are now ready to discuss how to design the forms on which responses will be recorded. This includes both questionnaires, which are used to ask respondents questions, as well as observation forms, which are designed to record the respondents' actions. In this chapter you will learn the functions of a questionnaire, the process of developing questionnaires, how to word questions, and how to avoid biased questions. You will also learn how to organize the components of a questionnaire and how to precode. We introduce you to computer-assisted questionnaire design programs and, specifically, illustrate how you can use WebSurveyor. Finally, we discuss the importance of pretesting your questionnaire and we discuss the basics of designing observation forms.

THE FUNCTIONS OF A QUESTIONNAIRE

Questionnaires translate research objectives into specific questions, standardize questions and response categories, foster respondent cooperation, serve as permanent records, can speed the process of data analysis, and can serve as the basis for reliability and validation measures.

A questionnaire serves six key functions. (1) It translates the research objectives into specific questions that are asked of the respondents. (2) It standardizes those questions and the response categories so every participant responds to identical stimuli. (3) By its wording, question flow, and appearance, it fosters cooperation and keeps respondents motivated throughout the interview. (4) Questionnaires serve as permanent records of the research. (5) Depending on the type of questionnaire used, a questionnaire can speed up the process of data analysis. Online questionnaires, for example, can be transmitted to thousands of potential respondents in seconds. In the case of WebSurveyor, questionnaires can be delivered and returned online. Some printed questionnaires may be designed to allow respondents' responses to be scanned into a statistical package. (6) Finally, questionnaires contain the information on which reliability assessments may be made, and they are used in follow-up validation of respondents' participation in the survey.

Questionnaire design is very important. It is difficult to overcome defects in questionnaires.

Given that it serves all of these functions, the questionnaire is a very important element in the research process. In fact, studies have shown that questionnaire design directly affects the quality of the data collected. Even experienced interviewers cannot compensate for questionnaire defects.[1] The time and effort invested in developing a good questionnaire are well spent. As you will soon learn, questionnaire development is a systematic process in which the researcher contemplates various question formats, considers a number of factors characterizing the survey at hand, and ultimately words the various questions very carefully. Questionnaire design is a process that requires the researcher to go through a series of interrelated steps.

THE QUESTIONNAIRE DEVELOPMENT PROCESS

We now turn to a discussion of the steps a researcher goes through and how the questionnaire fits into this process. Figure 11.2 offers a flowchart of the various phases in a typical marketing research survey. The first two steps have already been covered in this book. During the problem definition phase, the researcher and manager will have determined the survey objectives for the study, and the researcher knows the resources to be applied to the project plus any special circumstances or constraints involved. The primary data collection method will be agreed on in the early stages of this process (see Chapter 9). Also, we considered basic question response formats and measurement issues discussed in Chapter 10. Questionnaire design begins, as shown by the interior outlined box in Figure 11.2, after these issues are resolved.

It is normal to go through several versions of a questionnaire, revising it with each version.

A questionnaire will ordinarily go through a series of drafts before it is in acceptable final form. In fact, even before the first question is constructed, the researcher mentally reviews alternative question formats to decide which ones are

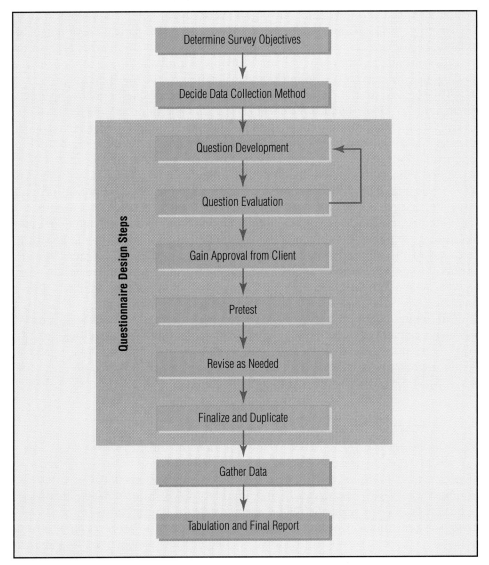

Figure **11.2** **Steps in the Questionnaire Development Process**

best suited to the survey's respondents and circumstances. As the questionnaire begins to take shape, the researcher continually evaluates each question and its response options for face validity. Changes are made, and the question's wording is reevaluated to make sure that it is asking what the researcher intends. Also, the researcher strives to minimize **question bias,** defined as the ability of a question's wording or format to influence respondents' answers.[2]

There is little doubt that how we word questions affects how others answer. Consider this example: A young monk once asked his superior if he could smoke while he prayed. After being chastised by the superior, a friend of the monk suggested: "Why don't you ask him if you could pray while you smoke?"[3] The wording of a question can greatly affect the response. Researchers are interested in objective information and they must avoid biasing questions.

We will describe aspects of this iterative process in more detail in succeeding sections of this chapter. For now, it is important only that you realize that with a

Question bias refers to the ability of a question's wording or format to influence respondents' answers.

A researcher should strive to minimize question bias.

Questionnaires are systematically checked and revised throughout the questionnaire design process. Clients should review the questionnaire to ensure that it covers the issues appropriate to the research objectives.

custom-designed research study, the questions on the questionnaire, along with its instructions, introduction, and general layout, are systematically evaluated for potential error and revised accordingly. Generally, this evaluation takes place at the researcher's end, and the client will not be involved until after the questionnaire has undergone considerable development and evaluation by the researcher.

The client is given the opportunity to comment on the questionnaire during the client approval step, in which the client reviews the questionnaire and agrees that it covers all of the appropriate issues. This step is essential, and some research companies require the client to sign or initial a copy of the questionnaire as verification of approval. There are several good reasons for client approval of a proposed questionnaire. First, it serves as a check that the researcher is still in tune with the survey's objectives. The client may not appreciate all of the technical aspects of questionnaire design, but he or she is vitally concerned with the survey's objectives and can comment on the degree to which the questions on the questionnaire appear to address these objectives. Second, client approval ensures that the client will be apprised of the survey's progress. Third, approval and the initialed questionnaire ensure that the researcher is protected against the remote possibility that the manager will claim that the questions were incomplete or done incorrectly after the findings are revealed.

Client involvement and approval of the questionnaire are necessary to assure that the research will be on target in meeting the client's information needs. It is wise for clients to give signature approval of questionnaires.

Questionnaires should be pretested using sample members taken from the population.

Following client approval, the questionnaire normally undergoes a pretest, which is an actual field test using a very limited sample to reveal any difficulties that might still lurk in wording, instructions, administration, and so on. We describe pretesting more fully later in this chapter.[4] Revisions are made based on the pretest results, and the questionnaire is finalized.

DEVELOPING QUESTIONS

Knowledge is acquired by either asking questions or through observation. There are several types of questions including nonverbal questions (a shrug of the shoulders or a hand gesture), verbal questions, rhetorical questions (more of an expression where no answer is expected), and nonrhetorical questions that explicitly seek information. Peterson has defined a specific type of nonrhetorical question as a research question. According to Peterson, a **research question** is employed in research projects to obtain overt, verbal communication from individual study participants. Its intended function is to elicit meaningful verbal responses from study participants, whether in writing or orally, and regardless of where it is asked—in the laboratory, home, or on the street.[5] Marketing researchers are concerned with developing research questions because they measure (1) attitudes, (2) beliefs, (3) behaviors, and (4) demographics.[6]

A research question is employed in research projects to obtain overt, verbal communication from individual study participants. Its intended function is to elicit meaningful verbal responses from study participants, whether in writing or orally, and regardless of where it is asked—in the laboratory, home, or on the street.

Developing a question's precise wording is not easy. Even one word can make a difference in how study participants respond to a question. There is considerable research to illustrate this. In one study researchers changed only one word. They asked, "Did you see the broken headlight?" to one group of participants and asked, "Did you see a broken headlight?" to another group. Only the "a" and the "the" were different, yet the question containing the "the" produced more "don't know" and "Yes" answers than did the "a" question.[7] We have claimed that developing questions for a questionnaire is an art. But just as there is good art and bad art, there are good questions and bad questions. In developing any question, the ultimate goal is to devise a way to tap the person's true response without influencing him or her either overtly or subtly. Compounding this problem is the fact that the researcher will have only one chance to accomplish this goal, so the wording of each question is critical.

Even one word may make a difference in how respondents answer questions.

Unfortunately, there is far greater potential to generate unreliable or inaccurate responses than we care to admit.[8] Table 11.1 illustrates how certain words cause problems in questionnaires.[9]

As we noted earlier, question bias occurs when the phrasing of a question influences a respondent to answer unreliably or with other than perfect accuracy. Ideally, every question should be examined and tested according to a number of crucial factors known to be related to question bias. For convenience, we discuss these factors as "shoulds" and "should nots."[10]

The Five "Shoulds" of Question Wording

There are five "shoulds" of question wording: (1) The question should be focused on a single issue or topic; (2) the question should be brief; (3) the question should be interpreted the same way by all respondents; (4) the question should use the respondent's core vocabulary; and (5) the question should be a grammatically simple sentence if possible. A discussion of these "shoulds" follows.

The Question Should Be Focused on a Single Issue or Topic
The researcher must stay focused on the specific issue or topic. For example, take the question "What type of hotel do you usually stay in when on a trip?" The focus of this question is hazy because it does not narrow down the type of trip or when the hotel is being used. For example, is it a business or a pleasure trip? Is the hotel at a place en route or at the final destination? A more focused version is "When you are on a family vacation and stay in a hotel at your destination, what type of hotel do you typically use?" As a second example, consider how "unfocused" the following question is: "When do you typically go to work?" Does this mean when do you leave home for work or when do you actually begin work once at your workplace? A better question would be "At what time do you ordinarily leave home for work?"

The Question Should Be Brief
Unnecessary and redundant words should always be eliminated, regardless of the data collection mode. This requirement is especially important when designing questions that will be administered verbally, such as over the telephone. Brevity will help the respondent to comprehend the central question and reduce the distraction of wordiness. Here is a question that suffers from a lack of brevity: "What are the considerations that would come to your mind while you are confronted with the decision to have some type of repair done on the automatic icemaker in your refrigerator assuming that you noticed it was not making ice cubes as well as it did when you first bought it?" A better, brief form would be "If your icemaker was not working right, how would you correct the problem?"

The Question Should Be Interpreted the Same Way by All Respondents
All respondents should "see" the question identically. For example, the question "How many children do you have?" might be interpreted in various ways. One respondent might think of only those children living at home, whereas another might include children from a previous marriage. A better question is "How many children under the age of 18 live with you in your home?"

The Question Should Use the Respondent's Core Vocabulary
The core vocabulary is the everyday language respondents use to converse with others like themselves, but it does not include slang or jargon. Obviously, if a question includes words with which some but not all respondents are familiar, these words are a potential source of error for those who do not interpret them properly. Sometimes the technical aspects of a product or marketing activity will slip into a question and violate the rule of using core vocabulary. For instance, "Did the premiums offered by the store attract you to it?" assumes that respondents know what premiums are

Table 11.1 Problem Words in Questionnaire Design

Problem Word	Reason for Difficulty
All	A "dead-giveaway" word. Some people have a negative reaction to opinion questions that hinge on all-inclusive or all-exclusive words. They may be generally in agreement with a proposition but, nevertheless, hesitate to accept the extreme idea of *all, always, each, every, never, nobody, only, none,* or *sure.* *Would you say that all cats have four legs?* *Is the mayor doing all he can for the city?* It is correct, of course, to use an all-inclusive word if it correctly states the alternative. But you will usually find that such a word produces an overstatement.
Always	Another dead-giveaway word. *Do you always observe traffic signs?* *Is your boss always friendly?*
America, American	Be careful of two things with words like these. First, they may be heavily loaded, emotional concepts. Answers may be given in terms of patriotism instead of the issue at hand. Second, these are very indefinite words referring to whole continents or parts of continents, to Native Americans, or even to that sometimes misused phrase—100% Americans.
Any	The trouble with "any" is that it may mean "every," "some," or "one only" in the same sentence or question, depending on the way you look at it. Another difficulty with "any" is that when used in either the "every" or the "not any" context it becomes as much a dead-giveaway word as are "every" and "none."
Anybody	Words with the "any" root are subject to the same trouble as "any" itself.
Bad	Experience indicates that people are generally less willing to criticize than they are to praise. Because it is difficult to get them to state their negative views, sometimes the critical side needs to be softened. For example, after asking *What things are good about your job?*, we may be wise not to apply the "bad" stigma but to ask *What things are not so good about it?*
Best	This is a dead-giveaway word. Few people do the *best* they can, for example.
Could	It should not be confused with "should" or "might." "Could" means that something *can* be done.
Country	What is meant by this word—the nation as a whole or rural areas?
Daily	Which is intended—five days a week or all seven?
Ever	Tends to be a dead giveaway. "Ever" is such a long time and so inclusive that it makes it seem likely that something may have happened during the time period of "ever." *Have you ever seen Seinfeld?* "Yes—I suppose I must have at some time or other."
Every	Another dead giveaway. Putting forth *every* effort is pretty extreme, for example.
Fair	When used in the sense of "just" or "reasonable," it can be taken to mean "average."
Few	We cannot assume that this word has definite limits. One person's few is another's several.
Government	It is sometimes used as a definite word meaning the U.S. federal government; sometimes as an inclusive term for federal, state, and local government; sometimes as an abstract idea; and sometimes as the party in power as distinct from the opposition party. The trouble is that the respondent does not always know which "government" is meant.
It, Its	These words necessarily refer to some antecedent, and it is best to repeat the full antecedent except where it is unmistakably clear.
Just	A word with conflicting meanings. "Just as much," for example, may mean "only" as much or "fully" as much.
Know	Knowing varies greatly in degree, from mere recognition to full information. Some respondents may hesitate to say they know something when they don't know it for sure or completely. A person may know a song without knowing the words.
Less	This word is usually used as an alternative to "more," where it may cause a minor problem. The phrase "more or less" has a special meaning all its own in which some respondents do not see an alternative. Thus, they may simply answer "yes, more or less" to a question such as *Compared with a year ago, are you more or less happy in your job?* The solution to this problem is to break up the "more or less" expression by introducing an extra word or so or to reverse the two: *Compared with a year ago, are you more happy or less happy in your job?* *Compared with a year ago, are you less or more happy in your job?*
Like	This word is a problem only because it is sometimes used to introduce an example. The problem with bringing an example into a question is that the respondent's attention may be directed toward the particular example and away from the general issue it is meant to illustrate. The choice of an example can affect the answers to the question—in fact, it may materially change the question, as in these two examples: *Do you think that leafy vegetables like spinach should be in the daily diet?* *Do you think that leafy vegetables like lettuce should be in the daily diet?* Because many people do not like spinach, they would answer "no" to the first question.

PROBLEM WORD	REASON FOR DIFFICULTY
Might	Do not think of this as synonymous with "could" or "should." Whereas "could" refers to whether something can be done, "might" refers to a probability that something will be done.
More	This word has more or less been discussed under the word "less." It is a problem for another reason also: When "more" is used in the comparative sense, it is usually advisable to indicate the basis for comparison—more than what? *Are you finding question wording more complicated?*
Most	This word can introduce tricky double thoughts as shown by this question: *Where would you be doing the most useful work?* Which is meant—the most work that is useful or work that is the most useful?
Much	"Much" is an indefinite word. The "how much" type of question leads to unnecessarily wide variations in response—questions should be worded such that it is clear that the responses are expressed in specific terms of dollars, doughnuts, percents, fractions, and other measures.
Never	A dead-giveaway word.
Nobody	This is yet another dead-giveaway word. Nobody can use "nobody" with impunity.
None	This also can be a dead-giveaway word.
Now	For a word that appears reasonably clear, "now" can be almost too definite in the sense of "right this minute," leading to situations like this: *What kind of work are you doing now?* "I'm answering foolish questions."
Own	This definite-sounding word is not always so definite. Some homeowners think that they will not own their homes until they pay off the mortgage. Some stockholders have no feeling of owning part of their company.
Possible	An alternative that uses "possible" in the ultimate sense ("as much as possible") is a dead giveaway.
Quite	This word is quite frequently misused. "Quite a little," for example, has no sensible meaning. If in a question the word "entirely" can be substituted for "quite" without changing the meaning, then "quite" is being properly used. However, in such proper use, "quite" may become a dead-giveaway word.
Saw, See, Seen	These words are sometimes used in the sense of visiting someone, but they may be interpreted literally. *When did you see your dentist last?* "Yesterday, on the golf course."
Service	Here is another indefinite word. Try, for example, to put down exactly what you mean when you speak of the "service" of the electric utility company.
Should	This is one of the three words that should not, could not, might not be used as though synonymous.
Such	Beware of this word because it is often used to introduce examples. When we discussed "like" we pointed out that the particular example may supplant the general issue in the minds of respondents. "Would you use such a product to clean your carpet?" may deflect the respondent's attention from *this* product to another one.
That, These, This, Those	These are antecedent words. Do not use them except when you are reasonably sure that their antecedents are clear.
Today	This may be interpreted too literally, just as "now" may be. *Are farmers getting a fair price for milk today?* "Do you mean right today? You know the price dropped this morning."
Trip	This word needs to be qualified—"one-way trip" or "round-trip," for example.
Where	The frames of reference in answers to a "where" question may vary greatly. *Where did you read that?* "In the *New York Times*." "At home in front of the fire." "In an advertisement."
You	In most questions, "you" gives no trouble whatever. However, the word may sometimes have a collective meaning as in a question asked of computer repairpersons: *How many computers did you repair last month?* This question seemed to work all right until one repairperson in a large shop countered with, "Whom do you mean, me or the whole shop?" Sometimes "you" needs the emphasis of "you yourself," and sometimes it just isn't the right word to use, as in the aforementioned situation.

Source: Adapted from Payne, S. L. (1951). *The art of asking questions*, First printing, 1951, Princeton University Press. These examples were taken from the 1980 edition, Chapter 10. By permission of Princeton University Press.

and can relate them to being attracted to the store. So a better question would be "Was the offer of a free gift a reason for your last visit to The Village clothing store?" Core vocabularies differ from subculture to subculture and from one profession to another. The difficulty of dealing with this issue is the subject of Marketing Research Insight 11.1.

The Question Should Be a Grammatically Simple Sentence if Possible A simple sentence is preferred because it has only a single subject and predicate, whereas compound and complex sentences are busy with multiple subjects, predicates, objects, and complements. The more complex the sentence, the greater the potential for respondent error. There are more conditions to remember, and more information to consider simultaneously, so the respondent's attention may wane or he or she may concentrate on only one part of the question. To avoid these problems, the researcher should strive to use only simple sentence structure—even if two separate sentences are necessary to communicate the essence of the question. Take the question, "If you were looking for an automobile that would be used by the head of your household who is primarily responsible for driving your children to and from school, music lessons, and friends' houses, how much would you and your spouse discuss the safety features of one of the cars you took for a test drive?" A simple approach is, "Would you and your spouse discuss the safety features of a family car?" followed by (if yes), "Would you discuss safety 'very little,' 'some,' 'a good deal,' or 'to a great extent'?"

The 11 "Should Nots" of Question Wording

There are more "should nots" than "shoulds" in question construction. In fact, there are 11. A discussion of these "should nots" follows.

The Question Should Not Assume Criteria That Are Not Obvious Questions frequently require respondents to make judgments, and judgment assumes that certain criteria are being applied. But sometimes the criteria on which the judgments are to be made are not obvious, and a danger exists in respondents using criteria different from those assumed by the question designer. A frequently omitted criterion is the respondent's frame of reference. The question "How important do you think it is for a Circle K convenience store to have a well-lighted parking lot?" has the potential for respondents to think in terms of the needs of others rather than their own. Perhaps a respondent never goes to a Circle K after dark, but he or she thinks that those who do should have good lighting. The better approach is to phrase the question as, "How important is it for you that a Circle K store has a lighted parking lot?"

The Question Should Not Be Beyond the Respondent's Ability or Experience Questions should not transcend the respondent's experience. For example, it makes little sense to ask teenagers what type of family automobile they will purchase when they are married, just as it makes little sense to ask their parents about whether their teenagers would drink nonalcoholic beer at a party. Teenagers cannot predict this purchase decision accurately because they are not (usually) married and are unlikely to have bought a new automobile, and the conditions for a family automobile purchase are unknown. Similarly, most parents do not know what goes on at teenagers' parties, so their answers would be guesses at best.

The Question Should Not Use a Specific Example to Represent a General Case The danger in using a specific example to measure a broader situation lies in the possibility that the respondent will concentrate only on that example. The question "Do you recall any advertising for Sears in the last week such as the inserts that are sometimes placed in your newspaper?" will cause some respondents to concentrate only on the newspaper inserts, but the intent of the question is to ask about all advertising.

Margin notes:

When questions require respondents to make judgments, those judgments assume criteria. A well-designed questionnaire specifies the criteria upon which judgments should be based.

It would make little sense to ask a respondent what factors are important to him or her in buying a car when the respondent has never bought a car. Questions should not be beyond a respondent's ability or experience.

The problem with using a specific example to represent a general case is that respondents will concentrate on the specific example.

▶ **Meet a Marketing Researcher**

*Using the Respondent's Core Vocabulary Requires
Understanding Subcultural Differences*
David Morse, CEO, Access Worldwide Cultural Access Group, Los Altos, California

Understanding subcultural differences is a unique advantage offered to clients by Access Worldwide. "Our strength lies not only in our knowledge of multicultural groups, but how we translate our understanding of cultural nuances into concrete, measurable marketing results for our clients."

Before coming to Access Worldwide, David Morse managed marketing research for Levi Strauss & Company. He worked as a brand manager for Gillette de Mexico where he managed marketing and advertising for the Paper Mate brand. Mr. Morse also held senior marketing and marketing research positions with Southern Pacific Transportation Company and American Honda Motor Company. He founded an import-export company in Mexico, worked as a management consultant for *Fortune* 500 companies, and taught English in Japan. He has a B.A. in psychology and Japanese studies and a master's degree in international management from Thunderbird, the American Graduate School of International Management. Mr. Morse is fluent in Japanese and Spanish.

Although we hear that the world is getting smaller due to telecommunications, researchers must remember that the

world is still made up of thousands of different subcultures, and core vocabularies differ between each of these subcultures. Designing a questionnaire to elicit responses from any group of people must take these subcultural differences into consideration. Even within subcultures, there are affinity groups, and these differences create headaches for market researchers. For instance, there are over 16 million Hispanic consumers in the continental United States representing over $100 billion in purchasing power. However, Hispanics comprise subgroups such as people of Cuban, Tex-Mex, Cal-Mex, and Puerto Rican descent.[11] Although members of these groups speak Spanish, differences exist across the subgroups' language forms and idioms. Researchers must prepare questionnaires so that proper translation is made by all the Hispanic subgroups.[12]

Care in preparing questionnaires is especially important when dealing with international markets. Winston Churchill once noted of the United States and England that "we are two nations divided by a common language." The late Joel Axelrod of BRX/Global, Inc., a marketing research firm, sent a fax to his colleagues in France who were conducting a survey for a cosmetic manufacturer. Dr. Axelrod asked his French counterparts to interview 150 Caucasian women. The next day BRX/Global received a panicky phone call: How could they conceivably be expected to locate 150 women in Paris who were born and raised in the Caucasus?! Caucasians to the French are people from the Caucasus mountain system. This term for *white* is so commonly accepted that even when Dr. Axelrod described the situation to an American researcher, there was a blank look on the part of the listener as though to say that it was impossible for anybody to misunderstand his request. Conducting another study in Germany for this same manufacturer, it took BRX/Global three days to identify the precise translation in German for "pancake makeup." In an industrial study done in Italy, BRX/Global designed a questionnaire asking, in the English version, for comments about a certain brand of industrial seals. When it received the Italian translation and translated it back to English, "seals" had been converted to bee's wax.[13]

Striving to use core vocabularies among all respondents is a desirable goal in designing a questionnaire. The many cultures and languages of the world, however, make this a difficult task for marketing researchers.

A better version is "Did you notice any newspaper, television, radio, or mailed advertising for Sears in the last week?" See the word "like" in Table 11.1 on page 307.

The Question Should Not Ask the Respondent to Recall Specifics When Only Generalities Will Be Remembered Sometimes a question designer forgets that people do not have perfect memory, and the detail requested in the question is beyond the respondent's abilities to reconstruct what actually happened. For instance, "How much was the price per gallon of gasoline when you last bought some at a convenience store?" certainly will require some respondents to think back several months, and it is very unlikely that they will recall the exact price per gallon. A more appropriate way to ask this question is to tap the generalities that the respondent will remember. For example, "The last time you bought gasoline at a convenience store, do you recall it costing more, less, or about the same per gallon as at a gasoline station?"[14]

Keep in mind that respondents do not have a perfect memory. Do not ask questions that require respondents to recall specifics that they are not likely to remember.

The Question Should Not Require the Respondent to Guess a Generalization When asked to respond to a question involving a generality, respondents may be inclined to respond with what they think "must" have happened or what "should" happen. This encourages guessing. Although guesses may be accurate, they are more likely to be inaccurate. Consider these two examples: "When you buy fresh fish at the supermarket, do you worry about its freshness?" and "If you bought a new 35-millimeter automatic focus camera at a catalog showroom store, would you ask the store clerk about its warranty?" Both of these encourage the respondent to answer in the affirmative by tapping into generalizations. One generalization is that freshness is virtually always assessed when buying seafood, and the other is that a common concern of buyers of expensive cameras should be the warranty. A strategy for avoiding the generalization factor is to require specificity from the respondent. For instance, with the fresh fish example, the question might be posed as, "In the last five times you bought fresh fish at the supermarket, how many times did you worry about its freshness?" For the camera question, it would be advantageous to use a likelihood scale: "Would you be 'unlikely,' 'somewhat likely,' 'likely,' or 'extremely likely' to ask the clerk about the camera's warranty?"

Instead of requiring the respondent to guess a generalization, ask a question with greater specificity.

The Question Should Not Ask for Details That Cannot Be Related Marketers sometimes ask for information that is impossible to remember. For example, a question that asks respondents if they use e-mail to specify how many total minutes they have used e-mail and to how many persons have they sent e-mail is asking for information that is too detailed to be recalled. It would be better to ask the total number of minutes spent on e-mail, on average, during a day.[15]

Avoid questions that ask for information that is too detailed to remember.

The Question Should Not Use Words That Overstate the Condition Avoid using words that overstate conditions. It is better to present the question in a neutral tone rather than in a positive or a negative tone. Here is an example that might be found in a survey conducted for Ray-Ban sunglasses. An overstated question might ask, "How much do you think you would pay for a pair of sunglasses that will protect your eyes from the sun's harmful ultraviolet rays, which are known to cause blindness?" As you can see, the overstatement concerns the effects of ultraviolet rays, and because of this overstatement, respondents will be compelled to think about how much they would pay for something that can prevent their blindness and not about how much they would really pay for the sunglasses. A more toned-down and acceptable question wording would be, "How much would you pay for sunglasses that will protect your eyes from the sun's rays?"

Overstatements, either positive or negative, should be replaced with neutral statements.

The Question Should Not Have Ambiguous Wording Ambiguity in wording allows respondents to apply their own situations, experiences, or interpretations to them.

Two forms of ambiguous wording can occur: First, the question designer might use a word that has several legitimate connotations for any one respondent. For example, a Society for the Prevention of Cruelty to Animals survey may ask, "When your puppy has an accident, do you discipline it?" There are two ambiguous words in this question. An "accident" could mean urinating on the floor, or spilling water out of the feeding dish, or any number of different mishaps. The definition of "discipline" is vague, and as you can imagine, the nature and severity of canine discipline can vary greatly. A series of questions would be needed to reduce the ambiguity by specifying the types of accidents and nature of the discipline applied. Second, the question designer might inadvertently select a word that has different interpretations for different subgroups of respondents. For example, ambiguous questions are evident in regional differences in the use of words. Let's say Oscar Mayer wants to perform a survey on the use of meats in sandwiches. A type of sandwich that is called a "grinder" in New England is referred to as a "submarine," "hero," "hoagie," or a "poor boy" in other parts of the United States. New Englanders cannot relate to a "poor boy" any more than someone living in New Orleans can relate to a "grinder." Obviously, Oscar Mayer would need to be concerned about the regional ambiguity of these words.

The Question Should Not Be "Double-Barreled" A **double-barreled question** is really two different questions posed in one question. With two questions posed together, it is difficult for a respondent to answer either one directly. Consider a question asked of patrons at a restaurant "Were you satisfied with the food and service?" How does the respondent answer? If they say "yes" does that mean they were satisfied with the food? The service? A combination? The question would be much improved by asking about a single item: one question for food and another question for service. Sometimes double-barreled questions are not as obvious. Look at the following question designed to ask for occupational status:

____Full-time employment

____Full-time student

____Part-time student

____Unemployed

____Retired

How does one who is retired and a full-time student answer the question? An improvement could be made by asking one question about occupational status and another about student status.[16]

> Make certain you ask one question at a time.

The Question Should Not Lead the Respondent to a Particular Answer A **leading question** is worded in such a way as to give the respondent a clue as to how to answer. Therefore, it biases responses. Consider the question used by Alreck and Settle to illustrate a leading question: "Don't you see some danger in the new policy?"[17] Obviously, the respondent is being led because the question wording stresses one side (in this case, the negative side) of the issue. Therefore, the respondents would expect that there are dangers in the new policy and, therefore, will likely respond with some of these dangers. Rephrasing the question as "Do you see any danger in the new policy?" is a much more objective request of the respondent. Here the respondent is free—that is, not led—to respond "yes" or "no." Examine the following questions for other forms of leading questions:

▶ Cadillac owners will be satisfied car owners, won't they? This is a leading question because the wording presupposes a state of mind. By saying ". . . won't they?" presupposes that the respondent should agree.

▶ Have you heard Celine Dion's new CD everyone is talking about? This is a leading question due to its possessing the ability to condition the respondent in terms of answering in a socially desirable manner. In other words, few people would want to admit they are clueless about something "everybody is talking about."[18]

Closed-ended questions can be leading as well. When an answer alternative that should not be included is provided or when a legitimate answer is not provided, the closed-ended question is leading. Peterson gives an example of a closed-ended leading question similar to the following:

▶ How well do you like the Holiday Host Online Reservation Service?

____ Extremely well

____ Very well

____ Pretty well

____ Not too well

This is a leading question because only positive responses are given.[19]

The Question Should Not Have "Loaded" Wording or Phrasing Leading questions are biased in that they direct the respondent to answer in a predetermined way. By contrast, a loaded question is more subtle, yet, they also are biased questions. Identifying this type of bias in a question requires more judgment, because a **loaded question** has buried in its wording elements that allude to universal beliefs or rules of behavior. It may even apply emotionalism or touch on a person's inner fears. For example, a company marketing mace for personal use may use the question, "Should people be allowed to protect themselves from harm by using mace as self-defense?" Obviously, most respondents will agree with the need to protect oneself from harm, and self-defense is an acceptable and well-known legal defense. Eliminating the loaded aspect of this question would result in the question "Do you think carrying a mace product is acceptable for people who are worried about being attacked?"

As you can see, the phrasing of each question should be examined thoroughly to guard against the various sources of question bias error. Seasoned researchers develop a sixth sense about the pitfalls we have just described; however, because the researcher can become caught up in the research process, slips do occur. This danger explains why many researchers use "experts" to review drafts of their questionnaires. For example, it is common for the questionnaire to be designed by one employee of the research company and then given to another employee who understands questionnaire design for a thorough inspection for question bias as well as face validity (if the questions "look right").

A leading question is worded in such a way as to give the respondent a clue as to how to answer and, therefore, it biases responses.

A loaded question has buried in its wording elements that allude to universal beliefs or rules of behavior and, therefore, is biased and should be avoided.

Researchers often get other researchers' opinions on questionnaire design in an attempt to ensure that the questionnaire will be answered by respondents in an objective manner and that the answers will properly address the research objectives.

QUESTIONNAIRES DEVELOPED FOR ONLINE RESEARCH

Now that we have discussed "shoulds" and "should nots" for *all* surveys we want to give you another perspective on questionnaire design from some people that design online surveys for a living. First, we asked Allen Hogg of Burke Interactive to give you his perspective on the do's and dont's of online survey questionnaires. Mr. Hogg's insightful response is contained in Marketing Research Insight 11.2. Second, we asked our Blue Ribbon Online Research Panel to address the question of what is unique about designing questionnaires for online survey research. As you will see by reading the responses of these professionals, they believe that online questionnaires are different in that they must be easily understood and easy to answer. The slightest bit of difficulty or "unattractiveness" will cause potential respondents to "click off."

► **Additional Insights**

Do's and Dont's of Questionnaires Designed for Online Survey Research
By Allen Hogg, Director of Marketing, Burke Interactive[20]

Do start with an "interesting" question. In online surveys, the highest percentage of "drop outs" comes before the first question gets answered. It is usually a good idea to start with a question that hints at the overall theme of the questionnaire.

Don't start a survey with sensitive demographic questions. Even if researchers only want their surveys to be taken by people in certain income categories, with certain racial-ethnic profiles, or belonging to certain religions, putting such questions at the very start of the questionnaire will likely drive potential respondents away. Ask less sensitive questions first—and be careful about the message delivered when people are "screened out" of surveys. People will get offended if they are led to believe that they are not "good enough" to take a survey because of such demographic characteristics.

Do include instructions for any complex tasks. Some, in fact, would recommend including instructions for *all* tasks, just in case respondents include some people who are new to filling out online forms. It is a good idea to include the instructions as close to the task as possible and not expect people to remember them from previous screens.

Don't include unnecessary "clutter" in surveys. Audio clips, animation effects, and other "cool" features might seem quite reasonable to include with a survey when using a network directly connected to the Internet backbone. The same survey, however, could be incredibly sluggish when accessed by respondents using relatively slow connections.

Do indicate to respondents where they are in a survey. It can also be useful to let respondents know before beginning how long, on average, a survey will take. Putting in accurate indicators can be challenging due to "skip patterns" that might make the survey longer or shorter for certain respondents. Letting respondents know that they are close to finishing, however, can encourage them not to drop out just before the survey's end.

Don't include unnecessary questions. This is good to keep in mind for off-line as well as online research, but because the cost of obtaining "live" telephone respondents tends to be relatively high, researchers are often tempted to "squeeze" as much information out of them as possible. This will backfire in online surveys, as the drop-out rate will skyrocket and the population that completes the survey will likely be less representative of the target population.

Do group together similar questions on the same screen. The number of survey screens, as well as the overall study length, has been found to relate to drop-out rates. Showing just one question per screen can be tiring for the respondent. On the other hand, having just one long screen that respondents must scroll through can be daunting as well. Try to find the right balance between these extremes.

Don't overload a Web survey with "open-ended" questions. Although many respondents will type in lengthy responses to open-ended questions, asking them to do so frequently can make the survey extremely lengthy and increase drop-out rates.

Do let respondents help "code" their own open-ended responses. Sorting through typed responses can be a time-consuming chore for researchers. Allowing respondents to categorize their own response after typing it can cut down on this time considerably.

Don't make it too easy to "rush through" a survey. Researchers should not unduly burden respondents' time, but they can also unintentionally encourage respondents not to pay much attention to survey questions by including repetitive tasks that can be "clicked through" mindlessly. Using drop-down boxes instead of simpler radio buttons, for example, may lead respondents to use a wider range of scale points on a series of rating questions.

Do be cautious about asking respondents to "check all that apply." Respondents are likely to check two or three items, think they have done enough, and move on without considering all the possibilities on the list. Consider designing the question instead as a series of "yes" or "no" items. If a survey does list a large number of items using a "check all that apply" format, it is a good idea to randomize or rotate response options to avoid any order bias.

Don't put a "default" answer in a drop-down box. Instead, put in a default message with a statement such as "click here to respond." Providing a default answer has great potential to lead to measurement error.

Do carefully consider whether to include a "don't know" or "no response" option. When such options are included, more people will use them on Web surveys than in telephone research, where they are typically accepted but not volunteered by the interviewer as a possible response. Omitting such options has *not* been shown to increase Web survey drop-out rates. On the other hand, when asking people to respond to items when they might have no legitimate basis for an opinion, it makes sense to include such an option.

Don't overestimate the security of confidential material. Steps can be taken to protect graphic images of new concepts and other proprietary information. No method is foolproof, however. This is also true for off-line research, but the speed with which confidential material can be transmitted on the Internet has made some researchers more sensitive to the issue when surveys are being conducted online.

Do include information with surveys about whom to contact in case problems are encountered. Such assistance can encourage people to complete the survey. It can also help make researchers aware of troubles, so that they might better understand why surveys did not turn out as expected.

BLUE RIBBON PANEL on [Online Research]

online research

Q: *What is unique about designing questionnaires for online survey research?*

Bill MacElroy
President
Socratic Technologies

A: One thing that distinguishes good online surveys from poor ones is the concept of "usability." Usually reserved for software or Web site design, usability is also very important for surveys. In general, people are very visual in the online mode of communication. They like surveys with a high degree of what I call "visual intuity," which means that they can figure out the task just by looking at it without a long, complex written set of instructions. Respondents are very resistant to the concept of needing to "learn" how to use the technology being employed in an online survey environment or how to answer questions.

At Socratic Technologies we have spent many years experimenting with the use of differentiating color, layout, animation, the amount of information on a page, and so on, in order to produce very fast and efficient surveys. For many online participants, *speed and efficiency* are the two most influential drivers in determining satisfaction with the online survey process. The longer that people have been online, the less interested they are in graphics and unrelated content, and the more focused they become on "rapid task completion."

Allen Hogg
President
Burke, Inc.

A: Online survey research is not so different from more traditional data-collection methods that researchers can ignore good questionnaire design techniques that apply to, for example, mail and phone surveys. In some sense, online research can be thought of as a hybrid between mail surveys, which are also self-administered, and computer-aided telephone interviews, which are programmed to make possible such things as "skip patterns," order rotations, and logic checks.

Some argue that aesthetics is a more important issue with Web questionnaire design and that an attractive interface will make taking the survey more engaging. It is wise, however, to avoid unnecessary "clutter" that will increase survey download speeds—especially if the sample population includes people who have relatively slow online access.

One fundamental thing to keep in mind is that the Internet attention span tends to be short. Lengthy online surveys can have very high drop-out rates. This can impact survey findings: Respondents who drop out will tend to be those less interested in the survey topic. Therefore, results from individuals who complete a long survey will likely overstate, for example, the interest in purchasing products that would otherwise be found in the overall population of interest. Don't forget to read my previous Do's and Don'ts of designing online survey questionnaires on page 313!

George Harmon
Senior Vice President
Digital Marketing
Services

A: Writing engaging, naturally flowing questionnaires has always been an art but it is especially important for online surveys. Questions written for telephone or mall studies are too wordy for a self-administered format, creating fatigue among online respondents acclimated to a visual medium. Appropriate uses of color, bolding, underlining, and italics in questions are employed for emphasis and rapid comprehension. Graphics can also be used in questions to make the survey more interesting, especially if the questionnaire is long or with young respondents.

George Terhanian
Vice President of
Internet Research
Harris Interactive,
Inc.

A: The Internet, as a mode, is quite different from other data collection modes. In some ways, it combines the best features of CATI, CAPI, face-to-face, and any mode that does not require the involvement of a live interviewer. It is perhaps the only mode, for example, through which <u>all</u> forms of advertising (print, radio, television, and online) can be tested efficiently and effectively. The industry's understanding of how to ask questions in this mode was, however, quite primitive just a few years ago, despite the fact that measurement error can lead to disastrous decisions. For this reason, among others, we have expended considerable resources on reducing measurement error in online surveys through experimental research—we have mounted hundreds of experiments on a host of issues. We then use the resulting information to train our researchers to understand how inherent differences between online research and research conducted via other modes may impact the designs of their online surveys. In contrast to other modes of research, for example, online surveys should take advantage of sophisticated visual techniques and technical enhancements of the Internet, for example, by expanding the number of response choices offered for graded scales. The additional response choices allow for greater precision and differentiation among respondents, resulting in increased validity of results. Above and beyond scale precision, visual enhancements are useful for presenting graphics, using complex programming logic to skip respondents in and out of portions of a questionnaire, providing links to useful information, and allowing for Web site visits.

Due to the absence of interviewers, we encourage our researchers to anticipate respondents' questions in advance, being sure to provide extra clarification and direction when necessary. We also encourage them to recognize that for off-line surveys, responses such as "decline to answer" may not be read as choices by interviewers but may be recorded as responses if the respondent speaks them aloud. As a result, the percentage of respondents endorsing these choices on the Internet (when they have been explicitly presented) is often significantly higher. We encourage our researchers to take specific steps to eliminate this discrepancy in results.

Our quality assurance group also reviews every survey before it is programmed to ensure that it conforms with best practices. Finally, every survey includes eight standard evaluation questions for respondents. We then combine their responses with the survey suspend rate to issue a survey report card. This allows us to diagnose and correct problems very rapidly.

Keith Price
Vice President
Greenfield Online

A: Online survey capabilities have evolved over the past few years, and it is now possible to execute "complex" questionnaires online. Skipping, question rotation, and piping were initially difficult to program into online surveys and questions were structured accordingly. These obstacles are no longer apparent, as survey technologies have progressed and questions are typically modified only somewhat when adapted from telephone or mail surveys.

Lee Smith
CEO
Insight Express

A: Surveys for the online environment are fundamentally different from other forms of surveys. Due to their self-administered nature and the ability for respondents to terminate their participation at the "click of a mouse," online surveys must be:
- Warm, in terms of an invitation
- Thoughtfully and well constructed
- Sensitive to the workload and time commitment being requested from the respondent (10–15 minutes, maximum)
- Relevant (be of interest) to the respondent

Although these elements are not specifically unique regarding the online environment, deviation from these rules will result in poor completion rates and impact the quality of the collected data due to the inability to hold the attention of online respondents.

Doss Struse
Senior Vice President
Client Service
Knowledge Networks,
Inc.

A: We are dealing with an interactive media that incorporates audio and visual/video. The look and feel of questionnaires affect the completeness of the information gathered, the perceived workload by the consumer, the reliability of the information, and the validity of the information.

QUESTIONNAIRE ORGANIZATION

The Introduction

The introduction may be a cover letter or a verbal statement depending on the method of data collection.

The introduction is very important in questionnaire design. If the introduction is written to accompany a mail survey or online survey, it is normally referred to as a **cover letter.** If the introduction is to be verbally presented to a potential respondent, as in the case of a personal interview, it may be referred to as the opening comments. Of course, each survey and its target respondent group are unique, so a researcher cannot use a standardized introduction. In this section, we discuss the five functions to be provided by the introduction. The introduction serves five functions:

1. Identification of the surveyor/sponsor
2. Purpose of the survey
3. Explanation of respondent selection
4. Request for participation/provide incentive
5. Screening of respondent

The first function of the introduction is to introduce the research firm and/or sponsoring client to the respondent.

First, it is not only common courtesy but it is also expected that you will introduce yourself at the beginning of a conversation. Some research companies opt for the direct approach with a statement such as, "Hello, my name is ____, and I am a telephone interviewer working with Nationwide Opinion Research Company here in Milwaukee. I am not selling anything." Here the researcher has identified himself or herself and the prospective respondent has been made aware that this is a bona fide survey and not a sales pitch. Additionally, the sponsor of the survey should be identified. There are two options with respect to sponsor identity. The sponsor may be undisguised or disguised. With an **undisguised survey,** the sponsoring company is identified, but with a **disguised survey,** the sponsor's name is not divulged to respondents. The choice of which approach to take rests with the survey's objectives or with the researcher and client who agree whether disclosure of the sponsor's name or true intent can in some way influence respondents' answers. Another reason for disguise is to prevent alerting competitors to the survey. However, as you read in Chapter 3, there is growing concern that all respondents should be debriefed as to the true sponsor of the research.

The second purpose of the introduction is to tell the prospective respondent the purpose of the research.

Second, the purpose of the survey should be described clearly and simply. In a cover letter, the purpose may be expressed in one or two sentences: "We are conducting a survey on personal computer presentation graphics packages used by successful executives such as yourself." Note that respondents aren't interested in the specific purposes of the survey. Rather, they are interested in knowing the subject you will address as you ask them questions. Consider a bank having a survey conducted by a marketing research firm. The actual purpose of the survey is to determine the bank's image relative to that of its competitors. However, the research firm need only say, "We are conducting a survey on customers' perceptions of financial institutions in this area." This satisfies the respondent and does not divulge the name of the bank. Also, it doesn't bore the prospective respondent with details of the actual purpose of the survey.

The third purpose of the introduction is to tell the respondents how and why they were selected for the study.

Third, prospective respondents must be made aware of how and why they were selected. Just a short sentence to answer the respondent's question of "Why me?" will suffice. Telling respondents that they were "selected at random" usually is sufficient. Of course, you should be ethical and tell them the actual method that was used. If their selection wasn't random, you should inform them as to which method was used.

Fourth, you must ask for their participation. "Will you please take five minutes to complete the attached questionnaire and mail it back to us in the postage-paid, preaddressed envelope provided?" If you are conducting a personal interview or a telephone interview, you might say something like "I would now like to ask you a few questions about your experiences with automotive repair shops. OK?" You should be as brief as possible yet let the respondent know that you are getting ready for him or her to participate by answering questions. This is also the appropriate time to offer an incentive to participate. **Incentives** are offers to do something for the respondent in order to increase the probability that the respondent will participate in the survey. There are various incentives that may be used by the researcher to encourage participation. As consumers have become more resistant to telemarketers and marketing researchers' pleas for information, researchers are reporting they must offer increased incentives.[21] Offering a monetary incentive, a sample of a product, or a copy of study results are examples. A more complete list is found in Chapter 14, which deals with nonresponse error and how it can be minimized. Other incentives encourage respondent participation by letting them know the importance of their participation: "You are one of a select few, randomly chosen, to express your views on a new type of automobile tire." Or the topic itself can be highlighted for importance: "It is important that consumers let companies know whether or not they are satisfied."

Other forms of incentives address respondent anxieties concerning privacy. Here again, there are methods that tend to reduce these anxieties and, therefore, increase participation. The first is **anonymity,** in which the respondent is assured that neither the respondent's name nor any identifying designation will be associated with his or her responses. The second method is **confidentiality,** which means that the respondent's name is known by the researcher, but it is not divulged to a third party, namely, the client. Anonymous surveys are most appropriate in data collection modes where the respondent responds directly on the questionnaire. Any self-administered survey qualifies for anonymity as long as the respondent does not indicate his or her identity and provided the questionnaire does not have any covert identification tracing mechanism. However, when an interviewer is present, appointments and/or callbacks are usually necessary, so there typically is an explicit designation of the respondent's name, address, telephone number, and so forth on the questionnaire. In this case, confidentiality may be required. Often questionnaires have a callback notation area for the interviewer to make notes indicating, for instance, whether the phone is busy, the respondent is not at home, or a time at which to call back when the respondent will be available. Here the respondent will ordinarily be assured of confidentiality, and it is vital that the researcher guard against the loss of that confidentiality.

A fifth function of the introduction is to screen respondents. Respondents are screened for their appropriateness to take part in the survey. **Screening questions** are used to screen out respondents who do not meet qualifications necessary to take part in the research study. Whether you screen respondents depends on the research objectives. If the survey's objective is to determine the factors used by consumers to select an automobile dealer for the purpose of purchasing a new car, you may want to screen out those who have never purchased a new car or those who have not purchased a new car within the last, say, two years. "Have you purchased a new car within the last two years?" For all those who answer "no," the survey is terminated with a polite "Thank you for your time." Some would argue that you should put the screening question early on so as to not waste the time of the researcher or the respondent. This should be considered with each survey. We place screening questions as last in the introduction because we have found it awkward to begin a con-

The fourth function of the introduction is to ask for the potential respondent's cooperation.

Incentives are used to increase the likelihood a potential respondent will take part in the research.

Anonymity means the respondent is never identified with the data collected.

Confidentiality means that the respondent is known by the researcher but his or her name is not divulged to a client or any other third party.

Screening questions are used to screen out respondents who do not meet qualifications necessary to take part in the research study.

versation with a prospective respondent without first taking care of the first four items we just discussed. We place screening questions in the introduction because it is common practice to place them near the beginning of the questionnaire.[22]

The creation of the introduction should entail just as much care and effort as the development of the questions on the questionnaire. The first words heard or read by the prospective respondent will largely determine whether he or she will take part in the survey. It makes sense, therefore, for the researcher to labor over a cover letter or opening until it has a maximum chance of eliciting the respondent's cooperation to take part in the survey. If the researcher is unsuccessful in persuading prospective respondents to take part in the survey, all of his or her work on the questionnaire itself will have been in vain.

Typical Question Sequence

Attention should be given to placing the questions developed into a logical sequence to ease respondent participation. Screening questions are among the first to be asked.

Each research objective gives rise to a question or a set of questions. As a result, questions are usually developed on an objective-by-objective basis. However, to facilitate respondents' ease in answering questions, the organization of these sets of questions should follow some understandable logic. A commonly seen sequence of questions found in questionnaires is presented in Table 11.2. As we discussed in the

Table **11.2**   **The Location of Questions on a Questionnaire Is Logical**

QUESTIONNAIRE ORGANIZATION

Question Type	Question Location	Examples	Rationale
Screens	First questions asked	"Have you shopped at Gap in the past month?" "Is this your first visit to this store?"	Used to select the respondent types desired by the researcher to be in the survey
Warm-ups	Immediately after any screens	"How often do you go shopping?" "On what days of the week do you usually shop?"	Easy to answer; shows respondent that survey is easy to complete; generates interest
Transitions (statements and questions)	Prior to major sections of questions or changes in question format	"Now, for the next few questions, I want to ask about your family's TV viewing habits." "Next, I am going to read several statements and, after each, I want you to tell me if you agree or disagree with this statement."	Notifies respondent that the subject or format of the following questions will change
Complicated and difficult-to-answer questions	Middle of the questionnaire; close to the end	"Rate each of the following 10 stores on the friendliness of their sales-people on a scale of 1 to 7." "How likely are you to purchase each of the following items in the next three months?"	Respondent has committed himself or herself to completing the questionnaire; can see (or is told) that there are not many questions left
Classification and demographic questions	Last section	"What is the highest level of education you have attained?"	Questions that are "personal" and possibly offensive are placed at the end of the questionnaire

previous section, the first few questions are normally screening questions, which will determine whether the potential respondent qualifies to participate in the survey based on certain selection criteria that the researcher has deemed essential.[23] Of course, not all surveys have screening questions. A survey of all charge account customers for a department store, for example, may not require screening questions. This is true because, in a sense, all potential respondents have already been qualified by virtue of having charge accounts with the store.

Once the individual is qualified by the screening questions, the next questions may serve a "warm-up" function. **Warm-up questions** are simple and easy-to-answer questions that are used to get the respondents' interest and to demonstrate the ease of responding to the research request. Warm-up questions may or may not pertain to the research objectives. In the latter case, if the first question dealing with a research objective is difficult, a warm-up question may be used to heighten the respondent's interest so that he or she will be more inclined to deal with the harder questions that follow. Some of our Blue Ribbon Panel members strongly recommend questions that get the respondents' interest near the beginning of online survey questionnaires.

Transitions are statements made to let the respondent know that changes in question topic or format are forthcoming. A statement such as "Now, I would like to ask you a few questions about your family's TV viewing habits" is an example of a transition statement. Such statements aid in making certain that the respondent understands the line of questioning. Transitions include "skip" questions. A **skip question** is one whose answer affects which question will be answered next. For example, a transition question may be "When you bake a cake, do you usually do it from scratch or do you use a box mix?" If the person responds that he or she uses a box mix, questions asking more details about baking from scratch are not appropriate, and the questionnaire will instruct the respondent (or the interviewer, if one is being used) to skip over or to bypass those questions. "Skip" questions are tricky. It's a wise idea to check them over several times before finalizing a questionnaire. Some experienced researchers believe it's a wise idea to keep skip questions to a minimum because they are so prone to producing errors.

Deeper in the questionnaire you will find the most complicated and difficult-to-answer questions. Scaled-response questions such as semantic differential scales, Likert-type response scales, or other questions that require some degree of mental activity such as evaluation, voicing opinions, recalling past experiences, indicating intentions, or responding to "what if" questions are found here. There are at least two reasons for this placement. First, by the time the respondent has arrived at these questions, he or she has answered several relatively easy questions and is now caught up in a responding mode in which he or she feels some sort of commitment. Even though the questions in this section require more mental effort, the person will feel more compelled to complete the questionnaire than to break it off. Second, if the questionnaire is self-administered, the respondent will see that only a few sections of questions remain to be answered. That is, once he or she is through the present difficult section, the respondent will be finished. If the survey is being administered by an interviewer, the questionnaire will typically have prompts included for the interviewer to notify the respondent that the interview is in its last stages. Also, experienced interviewers can sense when respondents' interest levels sag, and they may voice their own prompts, if permitted, to keep the respondent on task.

The last section of a questionnaire is reserved for classification questions. **Classification questions,** sometimes called demographic questions, are used to classify respondents into various groups for purposes of analysis. For instance, the researcher may want to classify respondents into categories based on age, gender,

---

Warm-up questions are used near the beginning of the survey to get the respondent's interest and demonstrate the ease of responding to the research request.

Transitions are statements made to let the respondent know that changes in question topic or format are forthcoming.

A skip question is one whose answer affects which question will be answered next.

The more complicated and difficult-to-answer questions are placed later in the questionnaire.

Classification questions, sometimes called demographic questions, are used to classify respondents into various groups for purposes of analysis.

Classification, or demographic, questions should be placed at or near the end of the questionnaire because they are more personal questions. Some respondents will consider them to be an invasion of privacy and may terminate the survey.

income level, and so on. Therefore, demographic items are normally placed here. This placement is industry tradition, and it embodies the strategy of placing questions that may cause respondents to break off the survey at the end of the interview. Some respondents will consider certain demographic questions "personal," and they may refuse to give answers to questions about the highest level of education they attained or about their income level. In these cases, if the respondent refuses to answer, the refusal comes at the very end of the questioning process. If it occurred at the very beginning, the interview would begin with a negative vein, perhaps causing the person to think that the survey will be asking any number of personal questions. As a result, the respondent may very well refuse to take part in the survey at that point.

There are different approaches that can be taken to organizing the flow of questions in a questionnaire.

The funnel approach uses a general-to-specific flow.

Approaches to Question Flow The flow of questions we have just described is generally used by questionnaire designers, but there are at least three specific approaches to questionnaire organization that we can describe: the funnel approach, the work approach, and the sections approach. The **funnel approach** uses a wide-to-narrow or general-to-specific flow of questions that places inquiries at the beginning of a topic on the questionnaire that are general in nature and those requiring more specific and detailed responses later on.[24]

The work approach is employed when the researcher realizes that respondents will need to apply different mental effort to groups of questions.

As a rule, closed-ended questions require the least work on the part of the respondent, followed by scaled-response questions. Open-ended questions are the most taxing for respondents.

The **work approach** is employed when the researcher realizes that respondents will need to apply different mental effort to groups of questions. When questions tap responses that are deeper than simple recall, respondents must apply a higher degree of concentration in answering them. Difficult questions are customarily placed deep in the questionnaire. As a rule, closed-ended questions are easier to answer than either scaled-response or open-ended questions. Open-ended questions are thought to be the most taxing questions for respondents. In fact, some researchers recommend rarely using open-ended questions or using a minimum of open-ended questions.[25]

As we just noted, when the respondent encounters the work questions, he or she should be caught up in the responding mode or otherwise committed to completing the questionnaire. If this is the case, the respondent will be more inclined to expend the extra effort necessary to answer them.

A sections approach organizes questions into sets based on a common objective of the questions in the set.

Perhaps the simplest format is to arrange the questions in logical sets on the questionnaire, referred to as the sections approach. A **sections approach** organizes questions into sets based on a common objective of the questions in the set. For example, several questions may be measuring media habits, others may be measuring frequency of purchasing different products, other sets of questions may all be measuring preferences for restaurant services and features. Sometimes the research objectives define the sections. Sections could also be based on question format. All Likert questions are placed in one section, for example. In our earlier baking example, we could have separate sections of questions for baking cakes, baking pies, baking cookies, baking from scratch, baking with box mixes, and so forth. Elsewhere on the questionnaire, the researcher may want to know respondents' opinions of baking by conventional oven, baking by microwave, and how well a certain brand of baking soda performs—all of these items can be placed in a single section in which the respondent is instructed to indicate his or her agreement with each statement along a seven-point, agree–disagree scale.

No one single approach to the flow of questions is best. The best flow of questions is the one which encourages repondents to answer with valid and complete responses.

Which approach is best? There is no single questionnaire format that fits all cases. In fact, the three approaches we have just described are not mutually exclusive, and there is no reason a researcher cannot use a combination of approaches in a single questionnaire. In fact, a researcher may find that the survey topics influence the placement or approach used in question flow.[26] However, while any one or a combination of these approaches may be used, the guiding issue should be which approach best facilitates respondents in answering the questions. Researchers can analyze questions in any sequence they wish; it's the respondents that are important here.

As we indicated earlier, designing a questionnaire is a blend of creativity and adherence to simple, commonsense guidelines. The most important principle to keep in mind, though, is to design the questionnaire's flow of questions so as to make it respondent friendly[27] by minimizing the amount of effort necessary to respond to it while maximizing the probability that each respondent will fill it out reliably, accurately, and completely.[28] To achieve these results, the researcher selects logical response formats, provides clear directions, makes the questionnaire appearance visually appealing, and numbers all sections plus all items in each section.[29]

PRECODING THE QUESTIONNAIRE

A final task in questionnaire design is **precoding** questions, which is the placement of numbers on the questionnaire to facilitate data entry after the survey has been conducted. Precodes are included as long as they are not confusing to respondents or interviewers.

The logic of precoding is simple once you know the ground rules. The primary objective of precoding is to associate each possible response with a unique number or letter. Ordinarily, a number is preferred for two reasons. First, numbers are easier and faster to keystroke into a computer file. Second, computer tabulation programs are more efficient when they process numbers. Table 11.3 illustrates code designa-

---

Table **11.3** **Examples of Precodes on the Final Questionnaire**

1. Have you purchased a Godfather's pizza in the last month?
   ____ Yes (1) ____ No (2) ____ Unsure (3)
2. The last time you bought a Godfather's pizza, did you (check only one):
   ____ Have it delivered to your house?   (1)
   ____ Have it delivered to your place of work? (2)
   ____ Pick it up yourself?   (3)
   ____ Eat it at the pizza parlor?   (4)
   ____ Purchase it some other way?   (5)
3. In your opinion, the taste of a Godfather's pizza is (check only one):
   ____ Poor   (1)
   ____ Fair   (2)
   ____ Good   (3)
   ____ Excellent (4)
4. Which of the following toppings do you typically have on your pizza? (Check all that apply.)
   ____ Green pepper (0;1)
   ____ Onion   (0;1) (Note: the 0;1 indicates the
   ____ Mushroom   (0;1) coding system that will be used.
   ____ Sausage   (0;1) Typically, no precode such as this
   ____ Pepperoni   (0;1) is placed on the questionnaire. Each
   ____ Hot peppers (0;1) response category must be defined
   ____ Black olives (0;1) as a separate question.)
   ____ Anchovies   (0;1)
5. How do you rate the speediness of Godfather's in-restaurant service once you have ordered?
   (Circle the appropriate number if a 1 means very slow and a 7 means very fast.)
   Very   Very
   Slow   1   2   3   4   5   6   7   Fast
6. Please indicate your age: ____ Years (Note: No precode is used as the respondent will write in a two-digit number.)

tions for selected questions. When words such as "yes" and "no" are used as literal response categories, precodes are normally placed alongside each response and in parentheses. With scaled-response questions in which numbers are used as the response categories, the numbers are already on the questionnaire, so there is no need to use precodes for these questions.

There is one instance in which precoding becomes slightly complicated; but, again, once you learn the basic rules, the precoding is fairly easy to understand. Occasionally, a researcher uses a question that asks the respondent to indicate "all that apply" from a list of possible responses. For example, if Fruit of the Loom were interested in the type and color of underpants men own, there might be a question in a mail survey such as "What type or types of underpants do you own? (Please check all that apply.)" The response categories could be (1) plain white boxer style, (2) colored boxer style, (3) colored brief style, (4) plain white brief style, and (5) colored bikini style. You should note that if the respondent were instructed to select only one style, the precodes would be 1, 2, 3, 4, and 5; but because more than one response category can be checked, there are numerous different possible combinations (1 and 2; 1 and 3; 1, 2, and 3; and so on). Rather than list all possible combinations with a unique code number for each, the standard approach is to have each response category option coded with a 0 or a 1. The designation "0" will be used if the category is not checked, whereas a "1" is used if it is checked by a respondent. In other words, there would be five separate precodes of 0 or 1, each associated with one of the response options. Question number 4 in Table 11.3 is an example of multiple-answer precoding. Note that each response category must be defined as a separate question for data analysis purposes.

It is becoming less common, however, for precodes to actually appear on the final questionnaire as the marketing research industry moves further into the high-technology side of questionnaire design and administration. There is no need for precodes to appear on the questionnaire using computer-assisted questionnaire design programs such as WebSurveyor because the codes are embedded in the software instructions. Still the researcher must know how to code the responses.

COMPUTER-ASSISTED QUESTIONNAIRE DESIGN

Questionnaire design has been impacted by technology. **Computer-assisted questionnaire design** software programs allow users to use computer technology to develop and disseminate questionnaires and, in some cases, to retrieve and analyze data gathered by the questionnaire. Several companies have developed computer software that bridges the gap between composing questions on a word processor and generating the final, polished version complete with boxes, circles, and coded questions. In fact, most of these special-purpose personal computer programs have the ability to interface with statistical analysis packages such as SPSS. Also, some of these software programs allow users to display their questionnaires on the Internet and allow respondents to enter data on the Internet. The data are then downloaded and made available for analysis. One such computer-assisted questionnaire design program is WebSurveyor. In the following paragraphs we use WebSurveyor to illustrate how these computer-assisted questionnaire design programs work. The question shown at the beginning of this chapter was designed using WebSurveyor.

Features of Computer-Assisted Questionnaire Design Systems

There are several significant advantages of computer-assisted questionnaire design software packages: They are easier, faster, friendlier, and provide significant functionality beyond that available with a traditional word processor. One such program is WebSurveyor. We will introduce you to its features in the following paragraphs. In addition to simplifying the process of questionnaire layout, many of these programs also have the ability to publish surveys to the Internet where survey participants can easily respond to the researcher's questions. These software packages can often retrieve responses automatically into their own data analysis programs and export raw data to other software packages such as SPSS, for detailed statistical analysis. Just to give you a feel for the power of computer-assisted questionnaire design, we describe three major advantages of these programs: survey creation, creation of data files, and data analysis and reporting.

Survey Creation Feature The typical questionnaire design program will query the designer on, for example, type of question, number of response categories, whether multiple responses are permitted, if skips are to be used, and how response options will appear on the questionnaire. The survey creation feature sometimes takes the form of a menu of choices, or it might appear as a sequence of format inquiries for each section of the questionnaire. Let's take a look at the survey creation feature in WebSurveyor.

▶ *Question List*. Allows users to create survey questions. Question formats may be closed-ended, open-ended, numeric, or scaled-response (matrix) questions. WebSurveyor allows you to select the format of your questions from a menu of question types. You select "Add . . . ," then choose the question type from those listed. Formats include Select only one (show all), Select only one (horizontal layout), Select only one (pull-down menu), Select all that apply, Open ended text (limited), Open ended text (unlimited), Numeric value, Date value, Select only one matrix, Select all that apply matrix, Data block, HTML snippet, Hidden field, and Rank order. The question editor allows you to enter the question text and response options, assign coding for analysis and export, and identify skip groups based on respondent answers. Additionally, you can implement data validation or data entry rules, which help to prevent data entry mistakes, and specify questions that must be answered by respondents. (See Figure 11.3.)

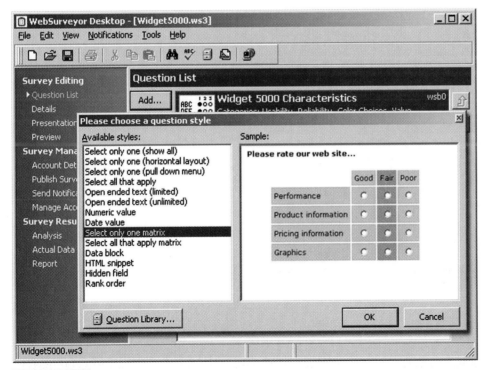

Figure **11.3**

▶ *Question Libraries.* WebSurveyor includes a number of question libraries from which you may select predefined questions or to which you can save questions you use regularly in the question library.

▶ *Details.* You can define the survey title, introductory paragraph (which may include instructions), closing paragraph, and URL where the respondents are directed after completing the survey.

▶ *Survey Appearance.* You choose the background color and graphics of the survey from a range of Display Templates, or you can create your own using WebSurveyor's Template Manager. This is especially useful for creating a survey template that matches the design criteria of an existing Web site.

▶ *Preview.* WebSurveyor lets users preview the questionnaire throughout the development process, testing interactivity, reviewing or updating question content and background design to suit their needs. (See Figure 11.4.)

▶ *Publish.* Once the survey is written, you select "Publish Survey" from the "Account Management" screen. This creates the HTML form, posts it to a unique Web page, creates a database to collect results on the WebSurveyor hosting server, and provides you with a unique URL to which you direct your respondents.

▶ *Send Notifications.* WebSurveyor includes WebEmailer, a tool to create, personalize, and track e-mail–based survey invitations.

Creation of Data Files and Data Collection Many computer-assisted questionnaire design packages create data files as the surveys are being written. For some solutions, this means that a CATI survey data file is ready to collect results as the telephone surveyors call respondents. In other cases, it simplifies traditional data entry from mailed surveys, or allows the researcher to scan forms.

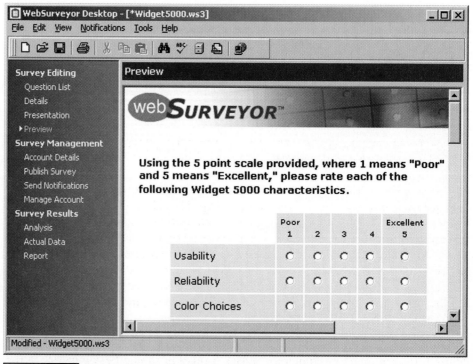

Figure 11.4

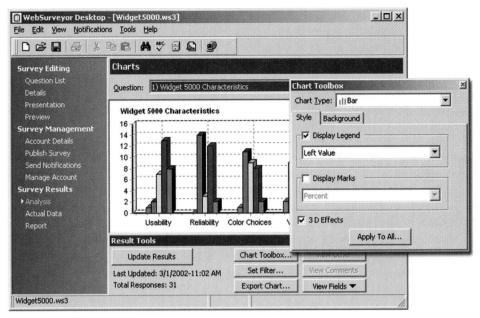

Figure **11.5**

Since WebSurveyor is specifically designed for creating and managing online surveys, the data file is built to collect responses online as they are submitted by survey respondents. The data file is created automatically on WebSurveyor's hosting server when the survey is published to the Internet. If you change or update the survey, the data file is also updated. If respondent data have already been collected, you can choose whether or not to keep results previously collected. It is especially useful to be able to change and republish surveys if you have identified new response options or other features that you need to add to the questionnaire while the survey is active.

WebSurveyor data collection is extremely simple. After each respondent completes the survey and presses "Submit," the encoded data are transferred over the Web to the data file. You can download the data securely at any time, allowing you to analyze real-time results while the survey is running. To download data to WebSurveyor, you select "Analysis" and press "Update Results." Only new responses are collected to speed up data retrieval.

Data Analysis and Reports Many of the software programs for questionnaire design also have provisions for data analysis, graphic presentation, and report formats of results. Some packages offer only simplified graphing capabilities, where others offer different statistical analysis options.

WebSurveyor provides an executive overview of results, by graphing responses to each question automatically, as illustrated in Figure 11.5. Users may export each graph or chart directly into Microsoft Word, PowerPoint, or other software package used to create a presentation or report on results. WebSurveyor also includes tools that allow you to filter results based on specific responses given (select cases in SPSS), cross-tabulate results from different questions, or view and edit raw data in WebSurveyor's "Actual Data" window. Of course, all raw data or selected response sets can be exported to other software packages, such as SPSS, for more detailed statistical analysis.

PERFORMING THE PRETEST OF THE QUESTIONNAIRE

Before finalizing the questionnaire, one last evaluation should be conducted on the entire questionnaire. Such an evaluation uses a pretest to ensure that the questions will accomplish what is expected of them. A **pretest** involves conducting a dry run of the survey on a small, representative set of respondents in order to reveal questionnaire errors before the survey is launched. It is very important that pretest participants are in fact representative, that is, selected from the target population under study. Before the questions are administered, participants are informed of the pretest, and their cooperation is requested in spotting words, phrases, instructions, question flow, or other aspects of the questionnaire that appear confusing, difficult to understand, or otherwise a problem.

Normally, from 5 to 10 respondents are involved in a pretest, and the researcher looks for common problem themes across this group.[30] For example, if only one pretest respondent indicates some concern about a question, the researcher probably would not attempt modification of its wording, but if three mention the same concern, the researcher would be alerted to the need to undertake a revision. Ideally, when making revisions, researchers should place themselves in the respondent's shoes and ask the following questions: "Is the meaning of the question clear?" "Are the instructions understandable?" "Are the terms precise?" and "Are there any loaded or charged words?" However, because researchers can never completely replicate the respondent's perspective, a pretest is extremely valuable.[31]

DESIGNING OBSERVATION FORMS

You should recall that a survey is only one of the ways primary information can be gathered.[32] Another means is through observation. As we indicated in our discussion on qualitative research techniques in Chapter 8, there is one class of qualitative research in which a human observer watches some episode of behavior and takes notes on what he or she sees. **Observation forms** are prepared for researchers to record the behaviors observed by researchers in observations studies. The remainder of this chapter describes some considerations and guidelines pertaining to recording observations. First, we discuss why it is important to develop a useful structure or categorization scheme for the observations, and then we contrast the build-up and break-down approaches to developing observation categorization systems.

Structuring Observational Studies

Let us do some role playing to help you understand the importance of structuring observational studies. Let us assume that you are working part-time for a marketing research company that is being used by Minute Maid orange juice to do an observational study on how consumers buy juice in the grocery store. When you come to work, your supervisor tells you to go to the nearby Kroger grocery store. She has arranged with the Kroger store manager for you to dress as a clerk so you will not be conspicuous to shoppers.

You begin your observations by selecting a shopper as she enters the store. This shopper happens to be a woman in her early thirties. She has two children with her, both of whom are girls, aged about 7 and 3. The 7-year-old girl walks alongside her mother, and the 3-year-old girl sits in the child seat of the grocery cart being pushed by the mother. Your shopper starts shopping with the normal flow of shoppers and stops at the vegetable bins. She picks up an orange. Now, you are thinking that the observation might be relevant, so you make a note. As you do, she puts it back down and picks up another, apparently squeezing it to determine its freshness. She does this several more times before selecting a total of six oranges that she places in her cart.

She moves on, selecting various other items, and finally arrives at the aisle with juices. She immediately picks out a large Welch's grape juice bottle and puts it in her cart. She picks up a can of V-8 Light and seems to read the label with interest.

Meanwhile, the 7-year-old girl picks up a can of Donald Duck orange juice and asks the mother to buy it. The mother says no, puts the V-8 Light and Donald Duck cans back and moves on. You make a note of this episode.

Now, you notice that she has arrived at the dairy products. After selecting low-fat milk, she reaches for a carton of Tropicana orange juice. When she does, the 3-year-old girl begins crying because the 7-year-old girl has grabbed her doll. The mother turns and sternly tells the 7-year-old girl to stop. The older child gives the doll back to the little one who stops crying. Your shopper then continues on, apparently forgetting about the Tropicana she was about to pick up. You make a note of this incident.

Last, when she passes the frozen foods, your shopper stops and buys a container of Sealtest brand rocky road flavor ice cream. As she puts it in her cart, you notice her spot the frozen fruit juices. She looks back at the dairy counter and seems to think for a minute. Then she picks up the largest frozen Minute Maid orange juice container in that section of the frozen foods and puts it in her cart. You make a note of this event. By the end of your day observing shoppers in that Kroger grocery store, you have followed 20 shoppers on their trips, and you have about a dozen pages of scribbled notes from your observations.

How do you structure your observational study so you can summarize your observations into a coherent report? Certainly, the first task would be to group them into logical categories. One scheme you might begin with is to group them by the type of juice bought: (1) fresh oranges, (2) bottled, (3) canned, (4) refrigerated fresh, and (5) frozen. Then, for each one of these, you might identify alternative approaches to selection of a brand such as (1) picked brand immediately, (2) picked brand after inspecting others, (3) inspected but did not buy, or (4) did not stop at this area. A separate categorical scheme would be the shopping party. Was it one shopper, two adults, one adult and child(ren), or some other grouping, and what were the sexes and apparent ages of the shoppers? Did they use a shopping cart, a carry basket, or neither?

Build-Up and Break-Down Approaches

Your work in creating this categorization system might be referred to as the **build-up approach** in which you must perform the observations first, and then the categories for reporting them are built on these observations. An opposite method might be called the **break-down approach** in which the categories are created before the observer goes into the field, and they are provided on an observation record form. This approach requires the researcher to think through and map out all of the relevant behaviors before the actual observation phase is undertaken.

In general, a break-down approach is better than a build-up method for at least three reasons. First, it offers consistency. That is, because the form has specific observation categories, some comment should be on each category for every shopper observed. Without the form, observations are vulnerable to observer distraction or fatigue. Second, it offers structure. In other words, the observer does not make random or arbitrary comments. Instead, the observations are structured, and even though the researcher is working with qualitative data, there is some inherent logic to the categories that will help make sense out of the multitude of observations when they are analyzed. Third, it offers completeness. If the observation form designer has done all of the necessary planning, the form will have a thorough inventory of all of the relevant behaviors. In this way, the researcher will not be concerned about the differences among observers when they are left on their own to decide what to itemize in their notes or what to leave out of their records. Differences among observers will be minimized.

SUMMARY

This chapter described questionnaire design and the creation of observation forms. Questionnaires serve several functions. A step-by-step questionnaire development process should be followed. Clients should approve questionnaires before data are collected. Next, developing questions became the focus, and we listed five different "shoulds" and 11 separate "should nots" regarding question wording. The introduction section of the questionnaire serves several functions including identification, purpose, and request for participation, and it screens potential respondents to ensure that they are qualified to take part in the survey. There are alternative question flow approaches, so we described the typical sequence along with the funnel approach, the work approach, and the sections approach. We also showed you that a pretest is helpful in fine-tuning the questionnaire into final form.

The chapter also introduced you to the notion of precoding or placing the codes to be put in the computer data file on the questionnaire itself. In addition, some companies have developed computer software that performs questionnaire design, and the chapter briefly described the features of these programs. We illustrated such a computer-assisted questionnaire design program by showing you how WebSurveyor works. We discussed observational studies and illustrated how important it is to design a structured observation form that is easy for observers to record the various behaviors that are of interest to the researcher.

KEY TERMS

Question bias (p. 303)
Research question (p. 304)
Double-barreled question (p. 311)
Leading question (p. 311)
Loaded question (p. 312)
Cover letter (p. 316)
Undisguised survey (p. 316)
Disguised survey (p. 316)
Incentives (p. 317)
Anonymity (p. 317)
Confidentiality (p. 317)
Screening questions (p. 317)
Warm-ups (p. 319)

Transitions (p. 319)
"Skip" questions (p. 319)
Classification questions (p. 319)
Funnel approach (p. 320)
Work approach (p. 320)
Sections approach (p. 320)
Precoding (p. 321)
Computer-assisted questionnaire design
  (p. 322)
Pretest (p. 326)
Observation forms (p. 326)
Build-up approach (p. 327)
Break-down approach (p. 327)

REVIEW QUESTIONS/APPLICATIONS

1. What are the functions of a questionnaire?
2. What is meant by the statement that questionnaire design is an iterative process?
3. What is meant by question bias? Write two biased questions.
4. Explain the client's role during questionnaire development.
5. What is a research question?
6. What are five "problem words" that should be avoided in a questionnaire? Write a question using each of the five you have chosen. Rewrite the question without using the problem word.
7. Indicate the functions of (a) screening questions, (b) warm-ups, (c) transitions, (d) "skip" questions, and (e) classification questions.

8. Differentiate the funnel approach from the work approach to questionnaire design.

9. Using a campus escort service as the topic of a survey, define and give examples of questions that (a) are loaded, (b) are leading, (c) are double-barreled, and (d) use assumed criteria.

10. A researcher writes the following question to assess occupational status of survey participants:

   ____ Full-time employment
   ____ Full-time student
   ____ Part-time student
   ____ Unemployed
   ____ Retired

   What is the problem with the question? Write out an improved way to ask the question.

11. What is meant when questions (a) overstate the condition, (b) require the respondent to guess a generalization, (c) lack focus, (d) use a specific example to represent a general class, and (e) use a complex sentence?

12. Describe precoding and give examples of precoding for a (a) closed-ended question, (b) scaled-response question, and (c) "check-all-that-apply" question.

13. Why should the researcher expend so much effort on the cover letter or opening comments of a questionnaire?

14. Distinguish anonymity from confidentiality.

15. Differentiate the "build-up" from the "break-down" approach to observational studies.

16. Listed here are five different aspects of a questionnaire to be designed for the crafts guild of Maui, Hawaii. It is to be administered by personal interviewers who will intercept tourists as they are waiting at the Maui Airport in the seating areas of their departing flight gates. Indicate how the arrangement of these items could differ on a questionnaire if the researcher used the funnel approach, the work approach, the sections approach, or some combination of these approaches.

   a. Determine how they selected Maui as a destination.
   b. Discover what places they visited in Maui and how much they liked each one.
   c. Describe what crafts they purchased, where they purchased them, when they bought them, how much they paid, who made the selection, and why they bought those particular items.
   d. Specify how long they stayed and where they stayed while on Maui.
   e. Provide a demographic profile of each tourist interviewed.

17. The Marketing Club at your university is thinking about undertaking a moneymaking project. Coeds will be invited to compete and 12 will be selected to be in the "Girls of (insert your school) University" calendar. All photographs will be taken by a professional photographer and tastefully done. Some club members are concerned about the reactions of other students who might think that the calendar will degrade women. Taking each "should not," phrase questions that violate the "should not" such that the response would tend to support the view that such a calendar would be degrading. Indicate how the question is in error, and provide a version that is in better form.

18. Go to a local movie theater and observe the food-buying behavior exhibited by the patrons. Be sure to note the following:

   a. When the food was bought.
   b. What food was bought.
   c. Who bought what food.

    d. How buying differed for adults versus children.

    e. How food buying differed for mixed-sex versus same-sex groups of teenagers.

    f. How moviegoers reacted to the theater's popcorn and soft drink prices.

       Write up your observations and present your summary in class. (Note: It is a good idea to ask the manager's permission to observe the moviegoers for a class exercise ahead of time.)

INTERACTIVE LEARNING

Visit the Web site at www.prenhall.com/burnsbush. For this chapter, work through the Self-Study Quizzes, and get instant feedback on whether you need additional studying.

CASE 11.1   Park Place Psychiatric Hospital

Park Place Hospital opened last year in Tucson, Arizona. It specializes in psychiatric care and mental health services. Both inpatient and outpatient services are provided, although the hospital is quite small and can only accommodate up to 20 inpatients at any one time. Because the hospital is new and its location is in the desert on the outskirts of Tucson, it has invested in an extensive advertising campaign using billboards, newspaper, and radio spots. By the end of its first year of operation, Park Place has experienced only 45 percent occupancy, but it is optimistic about the future.

    The management of Park Place has decided that in order to grow, it must reach out to its patient population in Tucson by being more aggressive in its program offerings. Among the services being considered is a series of seminars on selected mental health care problems and a set of companion programs that will cover the various topics more extensively. The marketing manager contacts a local research company and works with some of its personnel to formulate a list of research objectives. These objectives address his concerns about the effectiveness of the marketing program, the hospital's location situation, the decision-making process for a family member who detects another family member having a problem, and an interest in various programs and seminars. These objectives include the following:

> ▶ To determine the level of interest in each of the following two-hour evening seminars that cost $25 each: stop smoking, weight control, stress management, substance abuse, Alzheimer's disease, understanding anxiety, and coping with teenagers.
> ▶ To assess the degree of interest in enrolling in any of the two-month-long programs previously listed that cost $250 each.
> ▶ To evaluate where a person or family would seek help if a mental health problem requiring professional counseling were evident.
> ▶ To determine if prospective clients recall Park Place Hospital advertising, and if so, in which advertising medium.
> ▶ To evaluate the importance of location in the selection of a mental health care facility for a family member, either as an inpatient or an outpatient.
> ▶ To obtain target market information.

Random digit dialing will be used to select prospective respondent households.

    1. Design a questionnaire suited for a telephone survey of 500 Tucson households to be conducted with the "adult head of the household who is responsible for the family's health care."

    2. Justify your choice of the type of question response format for each question. If you have used the same format for a group of related questions, you should indicate your rationale for the group rather than for each question in the group.

    3. Identify the organization aspects of your questionnaire. Identify the question flow approach you have used and indicate why. Also, identify all screening questions, warm-ups, transition questions, and skip questions that you have used.

CASE 11.2   Kendalures

About 10 years ago, Larry Kendall, a retired postal worker living in Maine, began experimenting with the design of a new fishing lure in the hopes that he would invent one that would become as successful as the Johnson Silver Spoon or the Jitterbug. Because of his familiarity with coldwater fish such as trout, Larry's lure took the shape of a wavy spoon with a treble hook on the end. Its action in the water when retrieved or trolled at slow speed simulates a wounded minnow. He paid a machine shop to make a die and stamp out 500, and a paint shop to paint them either gold, silver, metallic red, or metallic green.

Although Larry has used the lure with success, and he has given many away to his friends who report that they have caught fish with it, he has had great difficulty convincing retailers to stock the lure. Despite much effort on Larry's part, only about 10 small bait shops in New Hampshire and Maine stock the item, and most of these have only bought one display card that holds 24 lures for sale. The lure sells for $2.50 retail for the 1/4-ounce size and $3.00 for the 1/2-ounce size. Larry has made inquiries with Kmart, Wal-Mart, Sears, and L.L. Bean, but all have declined to buy his lures.

One of Larry's nephews is a marketing manager with New England Bell, and the nephew suggests that if Larry had some convincing marketing research results about the desirability of the lure, he might have a stronger case to present to the large retail chains. The nephew recommends a "product placement" approach where fishermen would be given the lure if they promised to try it. Reactions Larry would like to know about his lure include its action; its colors; how well it casts; its appearance; what and how many fish, if any, the fishermen caught with it; how much they used the lure; and the weather conditions. There is also a number of other factors that might be helpful in marketing the Kendalure. These items include its appropriate price, what causes fishermen to try a new lure, where they buy lures, sizes of lures purchased, and how much fishing they do.

The plan is to intercept fishermen at boat launches, secure their cooperation to use the lure sometime during their fishing trip that day, meet them when they return, and verbally administer questions to them. As an incentive, each respondent will receive three lures to try that day, and five more will be given to each fisherman who answers the questions at the end of the fishing trip.

1. Design the questionnaire for fishermen who will use the lures.
2. What opening comments should be verbalized when approaching fishermen who are launching their boats? Draft a script to be used when asking these fishermen to take part in the survey.

CASE 11.3   *Your Integrated Case*

The Hobbit's Choice

(Note: This case requires that you have read Case 2.2, The Hobbit's Choice.)

Cory Rogers now felt he had a good grasp of the research objectives needed in order to conduct the research study for Jeff Dean. He sat down and started working on the questionnaire that he would need. He knew he would need to write a cover letter and he knew he needed a screening question. Would everyone's opinion be useful? "Certainly not," he thought. Why would we want the opinion of persons who rarely eat out in restaurants? Cory then turned to the other issues he knew he needed to address. He knew he needed input for the forecasting model so several questions would need to be designed dealing with demand assessment. Also, he needed several questions dealing with the design and operating characteristics questions as well as the advertising placement decisions. Finally, Cory knew he would have to address the location issue.

1. Carefully go over Case 2.2 and design a questionnaire for The Hobbit's Choice.

Chapter 12

Determining the Sample Plan

Learning Objectives:

To become familiar with sample design terminology

To learn about practical and "sufficiency of information" reasons for selecting a sample

To understand the differences between "probability" and "nonprobability" sampling methods

To acquire the skills to administer different types of samples, including online samples

To be able to develop a sample plan

Practitioner Viewpoint

If a sample is not correctly drawn, the research may produce misleading conclusions. As you will learn, careful attention to the sample plan helps researchers reach their objectives.

Linda Piekarski
Vice President, Research & Database
Survey Sampling, Inc.

Survey Sampling Helps Researchers Sample Their World!

In the short span of about 25 years, Survey Sampling, Inc. has grown from a tiny start-up operation to one of the largest specialty marketing research firms in the United States. As its name suggests, Survey Sampling, Inc. deals in samples, and it specializes in household as well as business samples. Currently, Survey Sampling, Inc. operates in 18 countries and it has more than 60 professionals who staff its operations, including Linda Piekarski who provided the preceding Practitioner Viewpoint. The ad lists Survey Sampling, Inc.'s major sample products. Here is a brief description of each one.

- Internet samples (e-samples)—e-mail addresses of individuals suitable for e-mail–delivered surveys. Buyers can select from any of approximately 300 different categories such as type of pet ownership, food products purchases, or sports participation.
- SSI-SNAP—downloadable software that permits users to identify population types by geography, demographic characteristics, lifestyle market segment type, sample selection method, and other parameters. The sample is delivered via e-mail attachment to the user.
- Business-to-business samples—business samples that can be identified by Standard Industrial Classification (SIC) code number. A user can use up to eight SIC code digits, meaning that the industry category can be quite precise, such as 791104 (hula instruction companies). The sample can be targeted or limited to companies with a certain number of employees or sales revenues.
- Global samples—household and business samples are available from selected countries.
- Targeted LITE samples—households that are "low incidence" or only have a small presence in the population. The database of 48 million numbers is compiled and updated based on warranty cards, online surveys, and other ways that individuals can identify their characteristics, hobbies, product usage, and so on.

Survey Sampling, Inc.'s products are used by marketing researchers to obtain samples that represent the target markets, business competitors, potential customers, or other groups that they wish to survey. Survey Sampling, Inc. does not provide custom or syndicated market research services. It has found a unique niche in the marketing research industry, and it is highly regarded by marketing research professionals as a company with high-quality samples that are delivered very quickly at a reasonable price.

International markets are measured in hundreds of millions of people, national markets comprise millions of individuals, and even local markets may constitute hundreds of thousands of households. To obtain information from every single person in a market is usually impossible and obviously impractical. For these reasons, marketing researchers make use of a sample. This chapter describes how researchers go about taking samples. We begin with definitions of basic concepts such as population, sample, and census. Then we discuss the reasons for taking samples. From here, we distinguish the four types of probability sampling methods from the four types of nonprobability sampling methods. Because online surveys are becoming popular, we discuss sampling aspects of these surveys. Last, we present a step-by-step procedure for taking a sample, regardless of the sampling method used.

BASIC CONCEPTS IN SAMPLES AND SAMPLING

To begin, we acquaint you with some basic terminology used in sampling. The terms we discuss here are *population, sample, sample unit, census, sampling error, sample frame,* and *sample frame error.*

Population

The population is the entire group under study as defined by research objectives.

A **population** is defined as the entire group under study as specified by the objectives of the research project. Managers tend to have a less specific definition of the population than do researchers. This is because the researcher must use the description of the population very precisely, whereas the manager uses it in a more general way.

For instance, let us examine this difference for a research project performed for Terminix Pest Control. If Terminix were interested in determining how prospective customers were combating roaches, ants, spiders, and other insects in their homes, the Terminix manager would probably define the population as "everybody who might use our services." However, the researcher in charge of sample design would use a definition such as "heads of households in those metropolitan areas served by Terminix who are responsible for insect pest control." Notice that the researcher has converted "everybody" to "households" and has indicated more precisely who the respondents will be in the form of "heads of households." The definition is also made more specific by the requirement that the household be in a metropolitan Terminix service area. Just as problem definition error can be devastating to a survey so can population definition error because a survey's findings are applicable only to the population from which the survey sample is drawn. For example, if the Terminix population is "everybody who might use our services," it would include industrial, institutional, and business users as well as households. If a large national chain such as Hilton Hotels or Olive Garden Restaurants were included in the survey, then the findings could not be representative of households alone.

Sample and Sample Unit

The sample is a subset of the population, and the sample unit pertains to the basic level of investigation.

A **sample** is a subset of the population that should represent that entire group.[1] Once again, there is a difference in how the manager uses this term versus how it is used by the researcher. The manager will often overlook the "should" aspect of this definition and assume that any sample is a representative sample. However, the

The population is defined precisely by the researcher.

researcher is trained in detecting sample errors and is very careful in assessing the degree of representativeness of the subgroup selected to be the sample.

As you would expect, a **sample unit** is the basic level of investigation. That is, in the Terminix example, the unit is a household. For a Weight Watchers survey, the unit would be one person, but for a survey of hospital purchases of laser surgery equipment, the sample unit would be the hospital purchasing agents because hospital purchases are being researched.

Census

Although a sample is a subset of a group, a **census** is defined as an accounting of the complete population. Perhaps the best example of a census is the U.S. census taken every 10 years by the U.S. Census Bureau (www.census.gov). The target population in the case of the U.S. census is all households in the United States. In truth, this definition of the population constitutes an "ideal" census, for it is virtually impossible to obtain information from every single household in the United States. At best, the Census Bureau can reach only a certain percentage of households, obtaining a census that provides information within the time period of the census-taking activity. Even with a public-awareness promotional campaign budget of several hundred thousand dollars that covered all of the major advertising media forms such as television, newspaper, and radio, and an elaborate follow-up procedure method, the Census Bureau admits that its numbers are inaccurate.[2]

A census requires information from everyone in the population.

The difficulties encountered by U.S. census takers are identical to those encountered in marketing research. For example, there are instances of individuals who are in transition between residences, without places of residence, illiterate, incapacitated, illegally residing in the United States, or unwilling to participate. Marketing researchers undertaking survey research face all of these problems and a host of others. In fact, researchers long ago realized the impracticality and outright impossibility of taking a census of a population. Consequently, they turned to the use of subsets, or samples, which were chosen to represent the target population.

Sampling Error

Sampling error is any error in a survey that occurs because a sample is used. Sampling error is caused by two factors: (1) the method of sample selection and (2) the size of the sample. You will learn in this chapter that some sampling methods minimize this error, whereas others do not control it well at all. Also, in the next chapter, we show you the relationship between sample size and sampling error.

Whenever a sample is taken, the survey will reflect sampling error.

Sample Frame and Sample Frame Error

To select a sample, you will need a **sample frame**, which is some master list of all the sample units in the population. For instance, if a researcher had defined a population to be all shoe repair stores in the state of Montana, he or she would need a master listing of these stores as a frame from which to sample. Similarly, if the population being researched were certified public accountants (CPAs), a sample frame for this group would be needed. In the case of shoe repair stores, a list service such as American Business Lists of Omaha, Nebraska, which has compiled its list of shoe repair stores from Yellow Pages listings, might be used. For CPAs, the researcher could use the list of members of the American Institute of Certified Public Accountants, located in New York City, which contains a listing of all accountants who have passed the CPA exam. Sometimes the researcher is hampered by the lack of a physical list, and the sample frame becomes a matter of whatever access to the population the researcher can conceive of, such as "all shoppers who purchase at least $25 worth of merchandise at a Radio Shack store during the second week of

A sample frame is a master list of the entire population.

March." Here, because some shoppers pay by credit card, some by check, and some with cash, there is no physical master list of qualified shoppers, but there is a stream of shoppers that can be sampled.

A sample frame invariably contains **sample frame error**, which is the degree to which it fails to account for all of the population. A way to envision sample frame error is by matching the list with the population and seeing to what degree the list adequately matches the targeted population. What do you think is the sample frame in our shoe repair store sample? The primary error involved lies in using only Yellow Pages listings. Not all shops are listed in the Yellow Pages, as some have gone out of business, some have come into being since the publication of the Yellow Pages, and some may not be listed at all. The same type of error exists for CPAs, and the researcher would have to determine how current the list is that he or she is using.[3]

Whenever a sample is drawn, the amount of potential sample frame error should be judged by the researcher.[4] Sometimes the only available sample frame contains much potential sample frame error, but it is used due to the lack of any other sample frame. It is a researcher's responsibility to seek out a sample frame with the least amount of error at a reasonable cost. The researcher should also apprise the client of the degree of sample frame error involved.

A listing of the population may be inaccurate and, thus, contain sample frame error.

REASONS FOR TAKING A SAMPLE

Taking a sample is less expensive than taking a census.

There are two general reasons a sample is almost always more desirable than a census. First, there are practical considerations such as cost and population size that make a sample more desirable than a census. Taking a census is expensive as consumer populations may number in the millions. If the population is restricted to a medium-sized metropolitan area, hundreds of thousands of individuals can be involved. Even when using a mail survey, accessing the members of a large population is cost prohibitive.

Second, typical research firms or the typical researcher cannot analyze the huge amounts of data generated by a census. Although computer statistical programs can handle thousands of observations with ease, they slow down appreciably with tens of thousands, and most are unable to accommodate hundreds of thousands of observations. In fact, even before a researcher considers the size of the computer or tabulation equipment to be used, he or she must consider the various data preparation procedures involved in just handling the questionnaires or responses and transferring these responses into computer files. The sheer physical volume places limitations on the researcher's staff and equipment.

Approaching sufficiency of information from a different tack, we can turn to an informal cost–benefit analysis to defend the use of samples. If the project director of our Terminix household survey had chosen a sample of 500 households at a cost of $10,000 and had determined that 20 percent of those surveyed "would consider" switching to Terminix from their current pest control provider, what would be the result if a completely different sample of the same size were selected in identical fashion to determine the same characteristic? For example, suppose the second sample resulted in an estimate of 22 percent. The project would cost $10,000 more, but what has been gained with the second sample? Common sense suggests that very little in the form of additional information has been gained, for if the project director combined the two samples he or she would come up with an estimate of 21 percent. In effect, $10,000 more has been spent to gain 1 percent more of information. It is extremely doubtful that this additional precision offsets the additional cost.

You may be wondering why we are dwelling on populations, samples, and sample selection when you know that there are companies with Internet-based panels that guarantee findings representative of specific population segments. These panel companies offer custom-made or omnibus surveys that obviate the need for a client to worry about sample selection. In truth, panel companies are prevalent, growing, and popular, but there is a "dark side" to the sample representativeness of Internet panels that has recently become known through the investigations of J. Michael Dennis, vice president and managing director at Knowledge Networks, Inc. We have provided Marketing Research Insight 12.1 so you can learn of the two dangers of using Internet-based panels as samples.

▶ **An Online Application**

Is There a "Dark Side" to the Sample Representativeness of Internet Panels?[5]

MARKETING RESEARCH
INSIGHT
12.1

As a result of rising fears and suspicions about telemarketers, a good deal of market research has gravitated to the use of consumer panels comprised of individuals who agree to participate in surveys on an ongoing basis. Internet-based panels afford significant benefits to researchers, including (1) fast data collection, (2) minimal nonresponse, (3) stored database records on respondents, and, perhaps most important, (4) good representativeness of target populations.

Presently, Internet-based samples are evolving, and although the experience base of marketing researchers with Internet-based samples is growing, knowledge about certain dangers that may be inherent in the use of panel samples is low.

There are two conceivable sample representativeness distortions or biases that may lurk in the findings of Internet-based panels. Each one is described next.

1. *"Professional" respondents.* Individuals who are approached and agree to participate on Internet-based panels may feel the need to be more prepared to take surveys than is the typical respondent. For example, if a panel participant thinks a future survey may involve DVD players, the panelist may be more vigilant to advertising, pay more attention to friends' casual comments, or even do background research on this topic. On a more subtle level, panelists may actually become aware and learn about products, services, and brands through exposure to these concepts in early surveys. They are then more attuned and knowledgeable than the typical consumer when asked about these topics in future surveys.

2. *Sample selection bias.* It is impossible to select an Internet-based sample that perfectly mirrors the general population because some individuals do not own computers, and there is uneven access to the Internet among owners. Even those panels whose participants can use WebTV harbor some degree of selection bias as not everyone has a television, nor does everyone own a hardwired telephone (required to connect WebTV to the Internet), and some individuals use cellular phones exclusively.

To investigate these two dangers, Knowledge Networks, Inc., a consumer panel research company that does utilize WebTV, investigated the presence of professional respondents and sample selection bias.

Professional respondents, or panel conditioning, were examined in a number of ways with Knowledge Networks 5,700 panel participants across several topics including non-alcoholic beverages, distilled beverages, attitudes toward new products, personal finances, sensitive questions, and political opinions. Systematically comparing new panelists to those who had been on the panel for various numbers of weeks up to 12 months, the findings uncovered only slight evidence of a "dark side" of respondent bias based on length of participation on the panel.

Sample selection bias was analyzed by inspecting several key sample demographics such as gender and age to see if the patterns shift over the duration of the panel's existence. That is, with attrition of panel members, is there a systematic decrease or increase in any demographic group's representation in the sample? In this investigation, the Knowledge Networks panel did not exhibit any worrisome evidence of sample selection bias.

Can these findings be generalized to all Internet-based panels? Knowledge Networks' panel is designed as follows:

> We developed the only Web-enabled panel founded on the science of probability sampling. While most Web-based surveys are limited to interviewing users who already have Internet access and happen to participate, Knowledge Networks uses a random sample of all Americans, including non-Internet households. We provide all Panelist households with a custom-designed Web device and Internet access so that anyone with a telephone can be represented in our Panel. No training or Web experience is necessary to take part in our surveys.[6]

Because the Knowledge Networks panel is a sample that represents this unique system of panel recruitment, replacement, incentives, and questionnaire administration, the findings of this study pertain only to its Internet-based panel.

TWO BASIC SAMPLING METHODS: PROBABILITY VERSUS NONPROBABILITY

In the final analysis, all sample designs fall into one of two categories: probability or nonprobability. **Probability samples** are ones in which members of the population have a known chance (probability) of being selected into the sample. **Nonprobability samples**, on the other hand, are instances in which the chances (probability) of selecting members from the population into the sample are unknown. Unfortunately, the terms "known" and "unknown" are misleading for, in order to calculate a precise probability, one would need to know the exact size of the population, and it is impossible to know the exact size of the population in most marketing research studies. If we were targeting, for example, readers of the magazine *People*, the exact size of the population changes from week to week as a result of new subscriptions, old ones running out, and fluctuations in counter sales as a function of whose picture is on the cover. You would be hard-pressed, in fact, to think of cases in which the population size is known and stable enough to be associated with an exact number.

The essence of a "known" probability rests in the sampling method rather than in knowing the exact size of the population. Probability sampling methods are those that ensure that, if the exact size of the population were known for the moment in time that sampling took place, the exact probability of any member of the population being selected into the sample could be calculated. In other words, this probability value is really never calculated in actuality, but we are assured by the sample method that the chances of any one population member being selected into the sample could be computed.

With nonprobability methods there is no way to determine the probability even if the population size is known because the selection technique is subjective. As one author has described the difference, nonprobability sampling uses human intervention whereas probability sampling does not.[7] So it is the sampling method rather than the knowledge of the size of the sample or the size of the population that determines probability or nonprobability sampling.

With probability sampling, the chances of selection are "known," but with nonprobability sampling, they are "unknown."

With probability sampling, the method determines the chances of a sample unit being selected into the sample.

Probability Sampling Methods

There are four probability sampling methods: simple random sampling, systematic sampling, cluster sampling, and stratified sampling (Table 12.1. A discussion of each method follows.

With simple random sampling, the probability of selection into the sample is "known" and equal for all members of the population.

Simple Random Sampling With **simple random sampling**, the probability of being selected into the sample is "known" and equal for all members of the population. This sampling technique is expressed by the following formula:

Formula for sample selection probability   Probability of selection = sample size/population size

So, with simple random sampling, if the researcher was surveying a population of 100,000 recent DVD player buyers with a sample size of 1,000 respondents, the probability of selection on any single population member into this sample would be 1,000 divided by 100,000, or 1 out of 100, calculated to be 1 percent. There are a number of examples of simple random sampling, including the "blind draw" method and the table of random numbers method.

The "blind draw" is a form of simple random sampling.

The Blind Draw Method. The **blind draw method** involves blindly choosing participants by their names or some other unique designation. For example, suppose that you wanted to determine the attitudes of students in your marketing research class

Table 12.1 Four Different Probability Sampling Methods

Simple Random Sampling

The researcher uses a table of random numbers, random digit dialing, or some other random selection procedure that guarantees each member of the population has an identical chance of being selected into the sample.

Systematic Sampling

Using a list of the members of the population, the researcher selects a random starting point for the first sample member. A constant "skip interval" is then used to select every other sample member. A skip interval must be used such that the entire list is covered, regardless of the starting point. This procedure accomplishes the same end as simple random sampling, and it is more efficient.

Cluster Sampling

The population is divided into groups called clusters, each of which must be considered to be very similar to the others. The researcher can then randomly select a few clusters and perform a census of each one. Alternatively, the researcher can randomly select more clusters and take samples from each one. This method is desirable when highly similar clusters can be easily identified.

Stratified Sampling

If the population is believed to have a skewed distribution for one or more of its distinguishing factors (e.g., income or product ownership), the researcher identifies subpopulations called strata. A simple random sample is then taken of each stratum. Weighting procedures may be applied to estimate population values such as the mean. This approach is better suited than other probability sampling methods for populations that are not distributed in a bell-shaped pattern.

toward a career in marketing research. Assume that the particular class that you have chosen as your population has 30 students enrolled. To do a blind draw, you first write the name of every student on a 3-by-5 index card, then take all of these cards and put them inside a container of some sort. Next, you place a top on the container and shake it very vigorously. This procedure ensures that the names are thoroughly mixed. You then ask some person to draw the sample. This individual is blindfolded so that he or she cannot see inside the container. You would instruct him or her to take out 10 cards as the sample. (For now, let us just concentrate on sample selection methods. We cover sample size determination in the next chapter.) In this sample, every student in the class has a known and equal probability of being selected with a probability of 10/30 or 33 percent. In other words, each student has a 1 out of 3 chance of being selected into that sample. Of course, you could use ID numbers or some other designation for each population member as long as there were no duplicates.

Random Numbers Method. A more sophisticated application of simple random sampling is to use a computer-generated number based on the concept of a **table of random numbers,** which is a listing of numbers whose random order is assured. Before computer-generated random numbers were widespread, researchers used physical tables that had numbers with no discernible relationship to each other. If you looked at a table of random numbers, you would not be able to see any systematic sequence of the numbers regardless of where on the table you begin and whether you went up, down, left, right, or diagonally across the entries.

To use the random number method to draw the sample in your careers in marketing research study, assign each student in the class a number, say 1 through 30. Granted, we will select only 10 students, but every member of our population must be uniquely identified before we begin the selection process. Or you might use social

A random number table embodies simple random sampling assumptions.

security numbers because these are unique to each person. If each student is given a number from 1 to 30, it is a simple matter to use a table of random numbers to draw the sample. Of course, using a computer is much more convenient.

Marketing Research Insight 12.2 shows the steps involved in using random numbers generated by a spreadsheet program to select students from this 30-member population. Beginning with the first generated random number, you would progress through the set of random numbers to select members of the population into the sample. If you encounter the same number twice within the same sample draw, the number is skipped over, because it is improper to collect information twice from the same person. Such an occurrence would constitute overrepresentation of that person in the sample and violate our "and equal" requirement.

Advantages and Disadvantages of Simple Random Sampling. Simple random sampling is an appealing sampling method simply because it embodies the requirements necessary to obtain a probability sample and, therefore, to derive unbiased estimates of the population's characteristics. This sampling method guarantees that every member of the population has a known and equal chance of being selected into the sample; therefore, the resulting sample, no matter what the size, will be a valid representation of the population.

However, there are some disadvantages associated with simple random sampling. To use either the blind draw or the random numbers approach, it is necessary to predesignate each population member. In the blind draw example, each student's

Using random numbers to draw a simple random sample requires a complete accounting of the population.

MARKETING RESEARCH
INSIGHT
12.2

How to Use Random Numbers to Select a Simple Random Sample

STEP 1: Assign all members of the population a unique number.

NAME	NUMBER
Adams, Bob	1
Baker, Carol	2
Brown, Fred	3
Chester, Harold	4
Downs, Jane	5
. . .	↓
Zimwitz, Roland	30

STEP 2: Generate random numbers in the range of 1 to N (30 in this case) by using the random number function in a spreadsheet program such as Microsoft Excel. Typically, such random number functions generate numbers from 0.0 to 1.0, so if you multiply the random number by N and format the result as an integer,[8] you will have random numbers in the range of 1 to N. The following set of random numbers was generated this way.

23	12	8	4	22	17	6	23	14	2	13

Select the first random number and find the corresponding population member. In the following example, number 23 has been chosen as the starting point.

STEP 3: Select the person corresponding to that number into the sample.

#23—Stepford, Ann

STEP 4: Continue to the next random number and select that person into the sample.

#12—Fitzwilliam, Roland

STEP 5: Continue on in the same manner until the full sample is selected. If you encounter a number selected earlier such as the 23 that occurs at the eighth random number, simply skip over it because you have already selected that population member into the sample. (This explains why eleven numbers were drawn.)

name was written on an index card, whereas in the random numbers example, each student was assigned a specific number. In essence, simple random sampling necessarily begins with a complete listing of the population, and current and complete listings are sometimes difficult to obtain. It is also very cumbersome to manually provide unique designations for each population member. Numbering from 1 through an unknown total population size (N) is tedious and invites administrative errors.

Simple Random Sampling Used in Practice. There are three practical applications in which simple random sample designs are employed quite successfully: small populations, random digit dialing, and computerized databases.

Obviously, one of the most troublesome aspects of simple random sampling is a listing of the population. Consequently, in those marketing research studies in which "small" and stable populations are involved, it is wise to use simple random sampling. For instance, the regional distributor for Anheuser-Busch desired that a customer satisfaction survey be administered to its many accounts. The distributor wanted to know how its delivery system compared to that of its key competitors: Coors Beer and Miller Beer. The Anheuser-Busch accounts were divided into "on-premises" locations where the beer products were consumed at the location. These locations included restaurants, bars, taverns, and sports arenas. The "off-premises" locations were where buyers purchase beer and carry it away. These locations included supermarkets, convenience stores, and package stores. The beer distributor had detailed computer lists of approximately 200 on-premises clients and about 600 off-premises clients. It was a simple matter to generate two separate lists, number each account, and to use the random selection feature of Microsoft Excel to draw a sample of each type of buyer.

Other situations in which simple random sampling is commonly used rely on a computer to generate the numbers and select the sample. One instance in which simple random sampling is employed quite successfully is through the use of random digit dialing. **Random digit dialing (RDD)** is used in telephone surveys to overcome the problems of unlisted and new telephone numbers. Unlisted numbers are a growing concern not only for researchers in the United States but in all industrialized countries such as those in Europe as well.[9]

In random digit dialing, telephone numbers are generated randomly with the aid of a computer. Telephone interviewers call these numbers and administer the survey to the respondent once the person has been qualified.[10] However, random digit dialing may result in a large number of calls to nonexisting telephone numbers. A popular variation of random digit dialing that reduces this problem is the **plus-one dialing procedure** in which numbers are selected from a telephone directory and a digit, such as a "1," is added to each number to determine which telephone number is then dialed.[11]

Finally, there is the possibility of selecting respondents from computer lists, company files, or commercial listing services, which have been converted into databases. Practically every database software program has a random number selection feature, so simple random sampling is very easy to achieve if the researcher has a computerized database of the population. The database programs can work with random numbers of as many digits as are necessary, so even social security numbers with nine digits are no problem. Companies with credit files, subscription lists, or marketing information systems have the greatest opportunity to use this approach, or a research company may turn to a specialized sampling company such as Survey Sampling to have it draw a random sample of households or businesses in a certain geographic area using its extensive databases.

Three practical applications of simple random sampling are small populations, random digit dialing, and computerized lists.

Random digit dialing overcomes problems of unlisted and new telephone numbers.

Plus-one dialing is a convenient variation of random digit dialing.

SPSS allows you to randomly select subsets of cases in a file.

Simple random sampling was used by a beer distributor to select a sample of its accounts in a service satisfaction survey.

These three cases—small populations, random digit dialing, and sampling from databases—constitute the bulk of the use of simple random sampling in marketing research. In the special situation of a large population list that is not in the form of a computer database, such as a telephone book, the time and expense required to use simple random sampling are daunting. Fortunately, there is an economical probability sampling method called systematic sampling that can be used effectively.

Without computer assistance, simple random sampling has practical implementation problems.

Systematic Sampling At one time, **systematic sampling**, which is a way to select a random sample from a directory or list that is much more efficient (uses less effort) than with simple random sampling, was the most prevalent type of sampling technique used. However, its popularity has fallen as computerized databases and generated random number features have become widely available. However, in the special case of a physical listing of the population, such as a membership directory or a telephone book, systematic sampling is often chosen over simple random sampling based primarily on the economic efficiency that it represents. In this instance, systematic sampling can be applied with less difficulty and accomplished in a shorter time period than can simple random sampling. Furthermore, in many instances, systematic sampling has the potential to create a sample that is almost identical in quality to samples created from simple random sampling.

Systematic sampling is more efficient than simple random sampling.

To use systematic sampling, it is necessary to obtain a hard-copy listing of the population, just as in the case of simple random sampling. As noted earlier, the most common listing is a directory of some sort. The researcher decides on a **skip interval**, which is calculated by dividing the number of names on the list by the sample size. Names are selected based on this skip interval, which is computed very simply through the use of the following formula:

One must calculate a skip interval to use systematic sampling.

Formula for skip interval   Skip interval = population list size/sample size

Researchers would not actually count every listing in a telephone directory. Rather, they estimate the population list size by determining the average listings per page.

For example, if one were using the local telephone directory and calculated a skip interval of 250, every 250th name would be selected into the sample. The use of this skip interval formula ensures that the entire list will be covered. Marketing Research Insight 12.3 shows how to take a systematic sample.

▶ **Additional Insights**

How to Take a Systematic Sample

STEP 1: Identify a listing of the population that contains an acceptable level of sample frame error.

Example: the telephone book for your city

STEP 2: Compute the skip interval by dividing the number of names on the list by the sample size.

Example: 25,000 names in the phone book, sample size of 500, so skip interval = every 50th name

STEP 3: Using random number(s), determine a starting position for sampling the list.

Example: *Select:* random number for page number
Select: random number for the column on that page

Select: random number for name position in that column (say, Jones, William P.)

STEP 4: Apply the skip interval to determine which names on the list will be in the sample.

Example: Jones, William P. (skip 50 names) Lathum, Ferdinand B.

STEP 5: Treat the list as "circular." That is, the first name on the list is now the initial name you selected, and the last name is now the name just prior to the initially selected one.

Example: when you come to the end of the phone book names (Zs), just continue on through the beginning (As)

Why Systematic Sampling Is Efficient. Systematic sampling is probability sampling because it employs a random starting point, which ensures there is sufficient randomness in the systematic sample to approximate a known and equal probability of any member of the population being selected into the sample. In essence, systematic sampling envisions the list as a set comprising mutually exclusive samples, each one of which is equally representative of the listed population.

How does the random starting point take place? One option would be to count or estimate the number of population members on the list, and to generate a random number between 1 and *N* (the population size). Then you would have to count the list until you came to that member's location. But a more efficient approach would be to first generate a random number between 1 and the number of pages to determine the page on which you will start. Suppose page 53 is drawn. Another random number would be drawn between 1 and the number of columns on a page to decide the column on that page. Assume the 3rd column is drawn. A final random number between 1 and the number of names in a column would be used to determine the actual starting position in that column. Let us say the 17th name is selected. From that beginning point, the skip interval would be employed. The skip interval would ensure that the entire list would be covered, and the final name selected would be approximately one skip interval before the starting point. It is convenient to think of the listing as a circular file, like an old-fashioned Rolodex file, such that A actually follows Z if the list were alphabetized, and the random starting point determines where the list "begins."

The essential difference between systematic sampling and simple random sampling is apparent in the use of the words "systematic" and "random." The system used in systematic sampling is the skip interval, whereas the randomness in simple random sampling is determined through the use of successive random draws. Systematic sampling works its way through the entire population from beginning to end, whereas random sampling guarantees that the complete population will be covered but without a systematic pattern. The efficiency in systematic sampling is gained by two features: (1) the skip interval aspect and (2) the need to use random number(s) only at the beginning.

Systematic sampling is more efficient than simple random sampling because only one or a very few random numbers need to be determined at the beginning.

Disadvantages of Systematic Sampling. Although systematic sampling is simpler, less time consuming, and less expensive to employ than simple random sampling, it is less representative in the final analysis than simple random sampling because it arbitrarily places population members into groups before the sample is selected. Nonetheless, the small loss in sample precision is more than counterbalanced by the economic savings, so systematic sampling is often chosen when simple random sampling is impractical or too expensive. The greatest danger in the use of systematic sampling lies in the listing of the population (sample frame). Sample frame error is a major concern for telephone directories because of unlisted numbers. It is also a concern for lists that are not current. In both instances, the sample frame will not include certain population members, and these members have no chance of being selected into the sample because of this fact.

> With systematic sampling the small loss in sampling precision is counterbalanced by its economic savings.

Cluster Sampling Another form of probability sampling is known as **cluster sampling**, in which the population is divided into subgroups, called "clusters," each of which represents the entire population. Note that the basic concept behind cluster sampling is very similar to the one described for systematic sampling, but the implementation differs. The procedure identifies identical clusters. Any one cluster, therefore, will be a satisfactory representation of the population. Cluster sampling is advantageous when there is no electronic database of the population. It is easy to administer, and cluster sampling goes a step further in striving to gain economic efficiency over simple random sampling by simplifying the sampling procedure used. We illustrate cluster sampling by describing a type of cluster sample known as area sampling.

> A cluster sampling method divides the population into groups, any one of which can be considered a representative sample.

Area Sampling as a Form of Cluster Sampling. In **area sampling**, the researcher subdivides the population to be surveyed into geographic areas, such as census tracts, cities, neighborhoods, or any other convenient and identifiable geographic designation. The researcher has two options at this point: a one-step approach or a two-step approach. In the **one-step area sample** approach, the researcher may believe the various geographic areas to be sufficiently identical to permit him or her to concentrate his or her attention on just one area and then generalize the results to the full population. But the researcher would need to select that one area randomly and perform a census of its members. Alternatively, he or she may employ a **two-step area sample** approach to the sampling process. That is, for the first step, the researcher could select a random sample of areas, and then for the second step, he or she could decide on a probability method to sample individuals within the chosen areas. The two-step area sample approach is preferable to the one-step approach because there is always the possibility that a single cluster may be less representative than the researcher believes. But the two-step method is more costly because more areas and time are involved. Marketing Research Insight 12.4 illustrates how to take an area sample using subdivisions as the clusters.[12]

> Area sampling employs either a one-step or two-step approach.

Area grid sampling is a variation of the area sampling method. To use it, the researcher imposes a grid over a map of the area to be surveyed. Each cell within the grid then becomes a cluster. The difference between area grid sampling and area sampling lies primarily in the use of a grid framework, which cuts across natural or artificial boundaries such as streets, rivers, city limits, or other separations normally used in area sampling. Geodemography has been used to describe the demographic profiles of the various clusters.[13] Regardless of how the population is sliced up, the researcher has the option of a one-step or a two-step approach.[14]

Disadvantage of Cluster (Area) Sampling. The greatest danger in cluster sampling is cluster specification error that occurs when the clusters are not homogeneous. For

How to Take an Area Sampling Using Subdivisions

STEP 1: Determine the geographic area to be surveyed and identify its subdivisions. Each subdivision cluster should be highly similar to all others.

> **Example:** 10 subdivisions within 5 miles of the proposed site for our new restaurant; assign each a number

STEP 2: Decide on the use of one-step or two-step cluster sampling.

> **Example:** use two-step cluster sampling

STEP 3: (assuming two-step): Using random numbers, select the subdivisions to be sampled.

> **Example:** select four subdivisions randomly, say numbers 3, 5, 2, and 9

STEP 4: Using some probability method of sample selection, select the members of each chosen subdivision to be included in the sample.

> **Example:** identify a random starting point; instruct field-workers to drop off the survey at every fifth house (systematic sampling)

example, if a subdivision association used area sampling to survey its members using its streets as cluster identifiers, and one street circumnavigated a small lake in the back of the subdivision, the "Lake Street" homes might be more expensive and luxurious than most of the other homes in the subdivision. If by chance, Lake Street was selected as a cluster in the survey, it would most likely bias the results toward the opinions of the relatively few wealthy subdivision residents. In the case of one-step area sampling, this bias could be severe.

Stratified Sampling All of the sampling methods we have described thus far implicitly assume that the population has a normal or bell-shaped distribution for its key properties. That is, there is the assumption that every potential sample unit is a fairly good representation of the population, and any who are extreme in one way are perfectly counterbalanced by opposite extreme potential sample units. Unfortunately, it is common to work with populations in marketing research that contain unique subgroupings; you might encounter a population that is not distributed symmetrically across a normal curve. With this situation, unless you make adjustments in your sample design, you will end up with a sample described as "statistically inefficient" or, in other words, inaccurate. One solution is **stratified sampling**, which separates the population into different subgroups and then samples all of these subgroups.

> With stratified sampling, the population is separated into different strata and a sample is taken from each stratum.

Working with Skewed Populations. A **skewed population** deviates quite a bit from what is assumed to be the "normal" distribution case in the use of simple random, systematic, or cluster sampling. Because of this abnormal distribution, there exists the potential for an inaccurate sample. For example, let's take the case of a college that is attempting to assess how its students perceive the quality of its educational programs.

A researcher has formulated the question, "To what extent do you value your college degree?" The response options are along a 5-point scale where 1 equals "not valued at all" and 5 equals "very highly valued." The population of students is defined by year: freshman, sophomore, junior, and senior. It is believed that the means will differ by the respondent's year status because seniors probably value a degree more than do juniors who value a degree more than do sophomores, and so on. At the same time, it is expected that seniors would be more in agreement (have less variability) than would underclass-persons. This belief is due to the fact that

> Stratified sampling is appropriate when we expect that responses will vary greatly from stratum to stratum.

freshmen are students who are trying out college, some of whom are not serious about completing it and do not value it highly, but some of whom are intending to become doctors, lawyers, or professionals whose training will include graduate degree work as well as their present college work. The serious freshmen students would value a college degree highly, whereas the less serious ones would not. So, we would expect much variability in the freshmen students, less in sophomores, still less in juniors, and the least with college seniors. The situation might be something similar to the distributions illustrated in Figure 12.1.

What would happen if we used a simple random sample of equal size for each of our college groups? Because sample accuracy is determined by the variability in the population, we would be least accurate with freshmen and most accurate with seniors. To state this situation differently, we would be statistically overefficient with seniors and statistically underefficient with freshmen because we would be oversampling the seniors and undersampling the freshmen. To gain overall statistical efficiency, we should draw a larger sample of freshmen and a smaller one of seniors. We might do this by allocating the sample proportionately based on the total number of the freshmen, sophomores, juniors, and seniors, each taken as a percentage of the whole college population. (Normally, there are fewer seniors than juniors than sophomores than freshmen in a college.) Thus, we would be drawing the smallest sample from the seniors group, who have the least variability in their assessments of the value of their college education, and the largest sample from the freshmen, who have the most variability in their assessments. We discuss this more fully in the next chapter.

Stratified sampling is used when the researcher is working with a skewed population divided into strata and wishes to achieve high statistical efficiency.

With stratified random sampling, one takes a skewed population and identifies the subgroups or **strata** contained within it. Simple random sampling, systematic sampling, or some other type of probability sampling procedure is then applied to draw a sample from each stratum. The stratum sample sizes can differ based on knowledge of the variability in each population stratum and with the aim of achieving the greatest statistical efficiency.

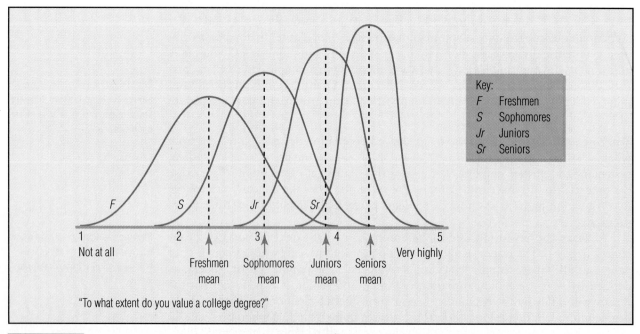

Figure 12.1 **Stratified Random Sampling: Using College Year Status as a Stratification Basis**

Area sampling uses subdivisions as its clusters.

Accuracy of Stratified Sampling. How does stratified sampling result in a more accurate overall sample? Actually, there are two ways this accuracy is achieved. First, stratified sampling allows for explicit analysis of each stratum. The college degree example illustrates why a researcher would want to know about the distinguishing differences between the strata in order to assess the true picture. Each stratum represents a different response profile, and by allocating sample size based on the variability in the strata profiles, a more efficient sample design is achieved.

Second, there is a procedure that allows the estimation of the overall sample mean by use of a **weighted mean**, whose formula takes into consideration the sizes of the strata relative to the total population size and applies those proportions to the strata's means. The population mean is calculated by multiplying each stratum by its proportion and summing the weighted stratum means. This formula results in an estimate that is consistent with the true distribution of the population when the sample sizes used in the strata are not proportionate to their shares of the population. Here is the formula that is used for two strata:

Formula for weighted mean

$$\text{Mean}_{\text{population}} = (\text{mean}_A)(\text{proportion}_A) + (\text{mean}_B)(\text{proportion}_B)$$

where A signifies stratum A, and B signifies stratum B.

Here is an example. A researcher separated a population of households that rent videos on a regular basis into two strata. Stratum A was families without young children, and stratum B was families with young children. When asked to use a scale of 1 = "poor" and 5 = "excellent" to rate their video rental store on its video selection, the means were computed to be 2.0 and 4.0, respectively, for the samples. The researcher knew from census information that families without young children accounted for 70 percent of the population, whereas families with young children accounted for the remaining 30 percent. The weighted mean rating for video selection was then computed as $(.7)(2.0) + (.3)(4.0) = 2.6$.

A stratified sample may require the calculation of a weighted mean to achieve accuracy.

How to Apply Stratified Sampling. There are a number of instances in which stratified sampling is used in marketing research because skewed populations are often encountered. Prior knowledge of populations under study, augmented by research objectives sensitive to subgroupings, sometimes reveals that the population is not normally distributed. Under these circumstances, it is advantageous to

To apply stratified sampling, researchers often use an easily identified surrogate as the stratification mechanism.

Researchers should select a basis for stratification that reveals different responses across the strata.

The weighted mean formula is not needed with a proportionate sample.

apply stratified sampling to preserve the diversity of the various subgroups. Usually, a **surrogate measure**, which is some observable or easily determined characteristic of each population member, is used to help partition or separate the population members into their various subgroupings. For example, in the instance of the college, the year classification of each student is a handy surrogate. With its internal records, the college could easily identify students in each stratum, and this determination would be the stratification method. Of course, there is the opportunity for the researcher to divide the population into as many relevant strata as necessary to capture different subpopulations. For instance, the college might want to further stratify on college of study, gender, or grade point average (GPA) ranges. Perhaps professional school students value their degrees more than do liberal arts students, women differently from men students, and high GPA students more than average GPA or failing students. The key issue is that the researcher should use some basis for dividing the population into strata that results in different responses across strata. There is no need to stratify if all strata respond alike.

If the strata sample sizes are faithful to their relative sizes in the population, you have what is called a **proportionate stratified sample** design. Here you do not use the weighted formula because each stratum's weight is automatically accounted for by its sample size. But with **disproportionate stratified sampling**, the weighted formula needs to be used because the strata sizes do not reflect their relative proportions in the population. We have provided a step-by-step description of stratified sampling in Marketing Research Insight 12.5.

Nonprobability Sampling Methods

All of the sampling methods we have described thus far embody probability sampling assumptions. In each case, the probability of any unit being selected from the population into the sample is known, even though it cannot be calculated precisely.

MARKETING RESEARCH

INSIGHT
12.5

Additional Insights ◀

How to Take a Stratified Sample

STEP 1:   Be certain that the population's distribution for some key factor is not bell-shaped and that separate subpopulations exist.

   Example: cellular telephone owners differ from nonowners in their use of long-distance calls

STEP 2:   Use this factor or some surrogate variable to divide the population into strata consistent with the separate subpopulations identified.

   Example: use a screening question on ownership/nonownership of a cellular telephone. This may require a screening survey using random digit dialing to identify respondent pools for each stratum.

STEP 3:   Select a probability sample from each stratum.

   Example: use a computer to select simple random samples for each stratum

STEP 4:   Examine each stratum for managerially relevant differences.

   Example: do owners differ from nonowners in their long-distance calls? Answer: owners average 35 minutes per month; nonowners average 20 minutes per month.

STEP 5:   If stratum sample sizes are not proportionate to the stratum sizes in the population, use the weighted mean formula to estimate the population value(s).

   Example: if owners are 20 percent and nonowners are 80 percent of the population, the estimate is $(35)(.20) + (20)(.80) = 23$ minutes per month.

The critical difference between probability and nonprobability sampling methods is the mechanics used in the sample design. With a nonprobability sampling method, selection is not based on probability. That is, you cannot calculate the probability of any one person in the population being selected into the sample. Still, each nonprobability sampling method claims to draw a representative sample. There are four nonprobability sampling methods: convenience samples, judgment samples, referral samples, and quota samples (Table 12.2). A discussion of each method follows.

> With nonprobability sampling methods, every member of the population does not have a chance of being included in the sample.

Convenience Samples **Convenience samples** are samples drawn at the convenience of the interviewer. Accordingly, the most convenient areas to a researcher in terms of time and effort turn out to be high-traffic areas such as shopping malls or busy pedestrian intersections. The selection of the place and, consequently, prospective respondents is subjective rather than objective. Certain members of the population are automatically eliminated from the sampling process.[15] For instance, there are those people who may be infrequent or even nonvisitors of the particular high-traffic area being used. On the other hand, in the absence of strict selection procedures, there are members of the population who may be omitted because of their physical appearance, general demeanor, or by the fact that they are in a group rather than alone. One author states, "Convenience samples . . . can be seriously misleading."[16]

> Convenience samples may misrepresent the population.

Mall-intercept companies often use a convenience sampling method to recruit respondents. For example, shoppers are encountered at large shopping malls and quickly qualified with screening questions. For those satisfying the desired population characteristics, a questionnaire may be administered or a taste test performed. Alternatively, the respondent may be given a test product and asked if he or she would use it at home. A follow-up telephone call some days later solicits his or her reaction to the product's performance. In this case, the convenience extends beyond easy access of respondents into considerations of setup for taste tests, storage of products to be distributed, and control of the interviewer workforce. Additionally,

> Mall intercepts are convenience samples.

Table **12.2**   **Four Different Types of Nonprobability Sampling Methods**

Convenience Sampling

The researcher or interviewer uses a high-traffic location such as a busy pedestrian area or a shopping mall to intercept potential respondents. Error occurs in the form of members of the population who are infrequent or nonusers of that location.

Judgment Sampling

The researcher uses his or her judgment or that of some other knowledgeable person to identify who will be in the sample. Subjectivity enters in here, and certain members of the population will have a smaller chance of selection than will others.

Referral Sampling

Respondents are asked for the names or identities of others like themselves who might qualify to take part in the survey. Members of the population who are less well known, disliked, or whose opinions conflict with the respondent have a low probability of being selected.

Quota Sampling

The researcher identifies quota characteristics such as demographic or product use factors and uses these to set up quotas for each class of respondent. The sizes of the quotas are determined by the researcher's belief about the relative size of each class of respondent in the population. Often quota sampling is used as a means of ensuring convenience samples will have the desired proportion of different respondent classes.

large numbers of respondents can be recruited in a matter of days. The screening questions and geographic dispersion of malls may appear to reduce the subjectivity inherent in the sample design, but in fact the vast majority of the population was not there and could not be approached to take part. Yet, there are ways of controlling convenience sample selection error using a quota system, which we discuss shortly.

Judgment Samples **Judgment samples** are somewhat different from convenience samples in concept because they require a judgment or an "educated guess" as to who should represent the population. Often the researcher or some individual helping the researcher who has considerable knowledge about the population will choose those individuals that he or she feels constitute the sample. It should be apparent that judgment samples are highly subjective and, therefore, prone to much error.

Focus group studies often use judgment sampling rather than probability sampling. In a recent focus group concerning the need for a low-calorie, low-fat microwave oven cookbook, 12 women were selected as representative of the present and prospective market. Six of these women had owned a microwave oven for ten or more years; three of the women had owned the oven for less than ten years; and three of the women were in the market for a microwave oven. In the judgment of the researcher, these 12 women represented the population adequately for the purposes of the focus group. It must be quickly pointed out, however, that the intent of this focus group was far different from the intent of a survey. Consequently, the use of a judgment sample was considered satisfactory for this particular phase in the research process for the cookbook. The focus group findings served as the foundation for a large-scale regional survey conducted two months later that relied on a probability sampling method.

Referral Samples **Referral samples,** sometimes called "snowball samples," require respondents to provide the names of additional respondents. Such lists begin when the researcher compiles a short list of sample units that is smaller than the total sample he or she desires for the study. After each respondent is interviewed, he or she is queried about the names of other possible respondents. In this manner, additional respondents are referred by previous respondents. Or, as the other name implies, the sample grows just as a snowball grows when it is rolled downhill.

Referral samples are most appropriate when there is a limited and disappointingly short sample frame and when respondents can provide the names of others who would qualify for the survey. The nonprobability aspects of referral sampling come from the selectivity used throughout. The initial list may also be special in some way, and the primary means of adding people to the sample is by tapping the memories of those on the original list. Referral samples are often useful in industrial marketing research situations.[17]

Quota Samples The **quota sample** establishes a specific quota for various types of individuals to be interviewed. It is a form of nonprobability sampling used prevalently by marketing researchers. The quotas are determined through application of the research objectives and are defined by key characteristics used to identify the population. In the application of quota sampling, a field-worker is provided with screening criteria that will classify the potential respondent into a particular quota cell. For example, if the interviewer is assigned to obtain a sample quota of 50 each for black females, black males, white females, and white males, the qualifying characteristics would be race and gender. Assuming our field-workers were working mall intercepts, each would determine through visual inspection where the prospective respondent falls and work toward filling the quota in each of the four cells. So a quota system overcomes much of the nonrepresentativeness danger inherent in convenience samples.

With a judgment sample, one "judges" the sample to be representative.

A referral sample asks respondents to provide the names of additional respondents.

Quota samples rely on key characteristics to define the composition of the sample.

Quota samples require interviewers to select respondents with specific demographic or other characteristics.

Quota samples are often used by companies that have a firm grasp on the features characterizing the individuals they wish to study in a particular marketing research project. A large bank, for instance, might stipulate that the final sample be one-half adult males and one-half adult females because in the bank's understanding of its market, the customer base is equally divided between males and females.

Sample quotas are sometimes used to facilitate field-worker control. Often there is considerable opportunity for field-workers to apply their own judgment in the selection of respondents. However, if the field-worker is given guidelines establishing quotas for various types of individuals to be included in the sample, the researcher has an assurance that the final sample composition will be faithful to his or her prior specifications. In no way does this approach eliminate the subjectivity or the nonprobability aspects of the sampling method; however, it does gain the necessary control to ensure that the final sample will include people within the marketing researcher's definition of the population. Or it may guarantee that he or she has sufficient subsample sizes for meaningful subgroup analysis.

When done conscientiously and with a firm understanding of the quota characteristics, quota sampling can rival probability sampling in the minds of researchers. One researcher has commented, "Probability sampling is the recommended method, but in the 'real world,' statistical inferences are often based on quota samples and other nonrandom sampling methods. Strangely, these heretical uses of statistical theory, in my experience, seem to work just as well as they do for 'purist' random samples."[18]

Quota samples are appropriate when you have a detailed demographic profile of the population on which to base the sample.

PICTURES SAY A THOUSAND WORDS: A GRAPHICAL PRESENTATION OF SAMPLE METHODS

Figure 12.2 contains representations of each of the eight types of sample methods. The population in every instance is comprised of 25 consumers. One-fifth (20%) of the consumers are unsatisfied, two-fifths (40%) are satisfied, and two-fifths (40%) are indifferent or neutral about our brand. With each probability sample method

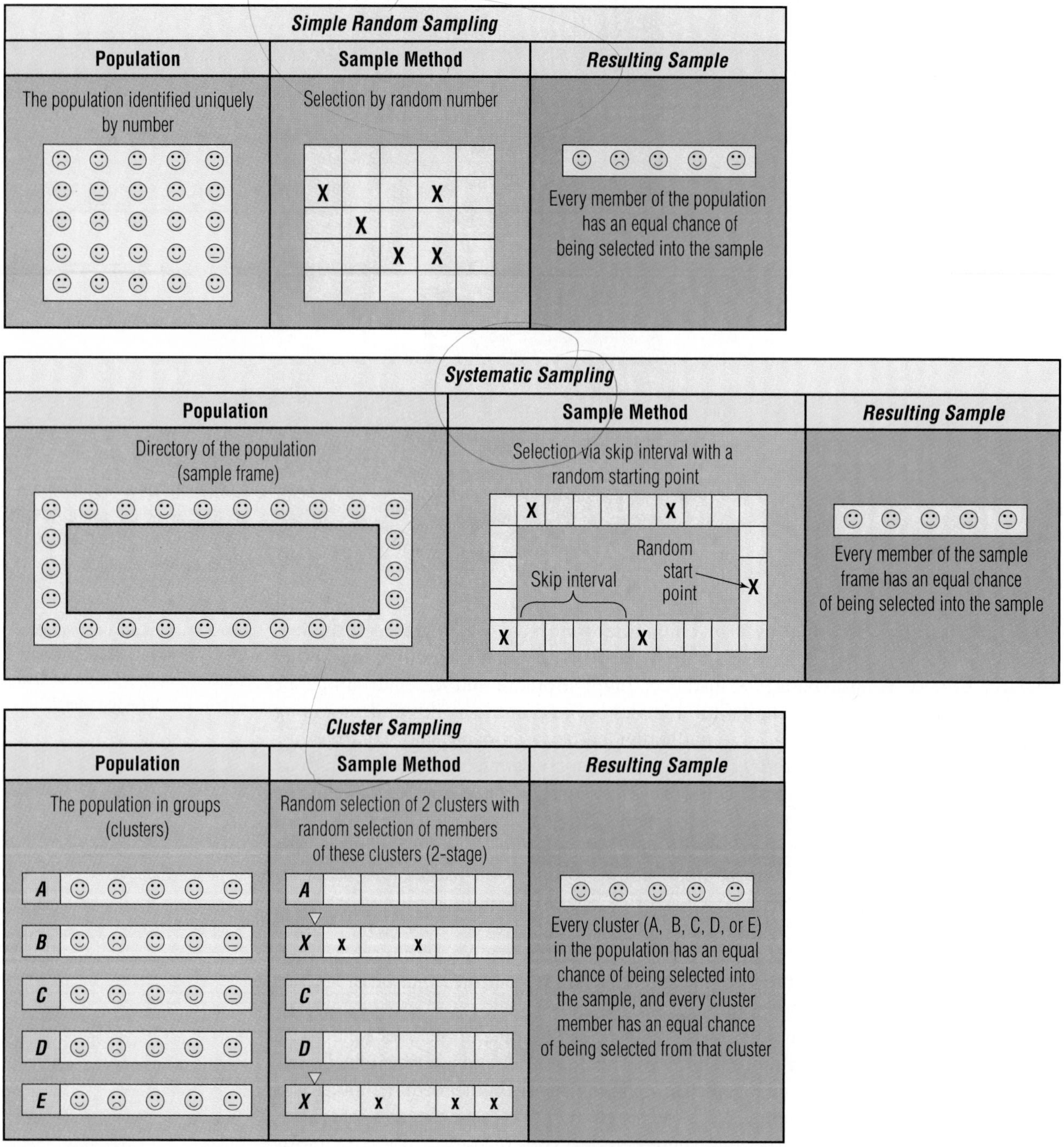

Simple Random Sampling
Population
Sample Method
Resulting Sample
The population identified uniquely by number
Selection by random number
X X
X
X X
Every member of the population has an equal chance of being selected into the sample
Systematic Sampling
Population
Sample Method
Resulting Sample
Directory of the population (sample frame)
Selection via skip interval with a random starting point
X X
Random start point
Skip interval
X
X X
Every member of the sample frame has an equal chance of being selected into the sample
Cluster Sampling
Population
Sample Method
Resulting Sample
The population in groups (clusters)
Random selection of 2 clusters with random selection of members of these clusters (2-stage)
A
B
C
D
E
A
X x x
C
D
X x x x
Every cluster (A, B, C, D, or E) in the population has an equal chance of being selected into the sample, and every cluster member has an equal chance of being selected from that cluster

Figure 12.2A **Graphical Presentations for the Various Sampling Methods**

(simple random sample, systematic sample, cluster sample, and stratified random sample), the resulting sample's satisfaction profile is consistent with the population. That is, each probability sample has five consumers, with one unsatisfied, two satisfied, and two indifferent.

However, with each of the nonprobability sample methods (convenience sample, judgment sample, referral sample, and quota sample), the resulting sample's sat-

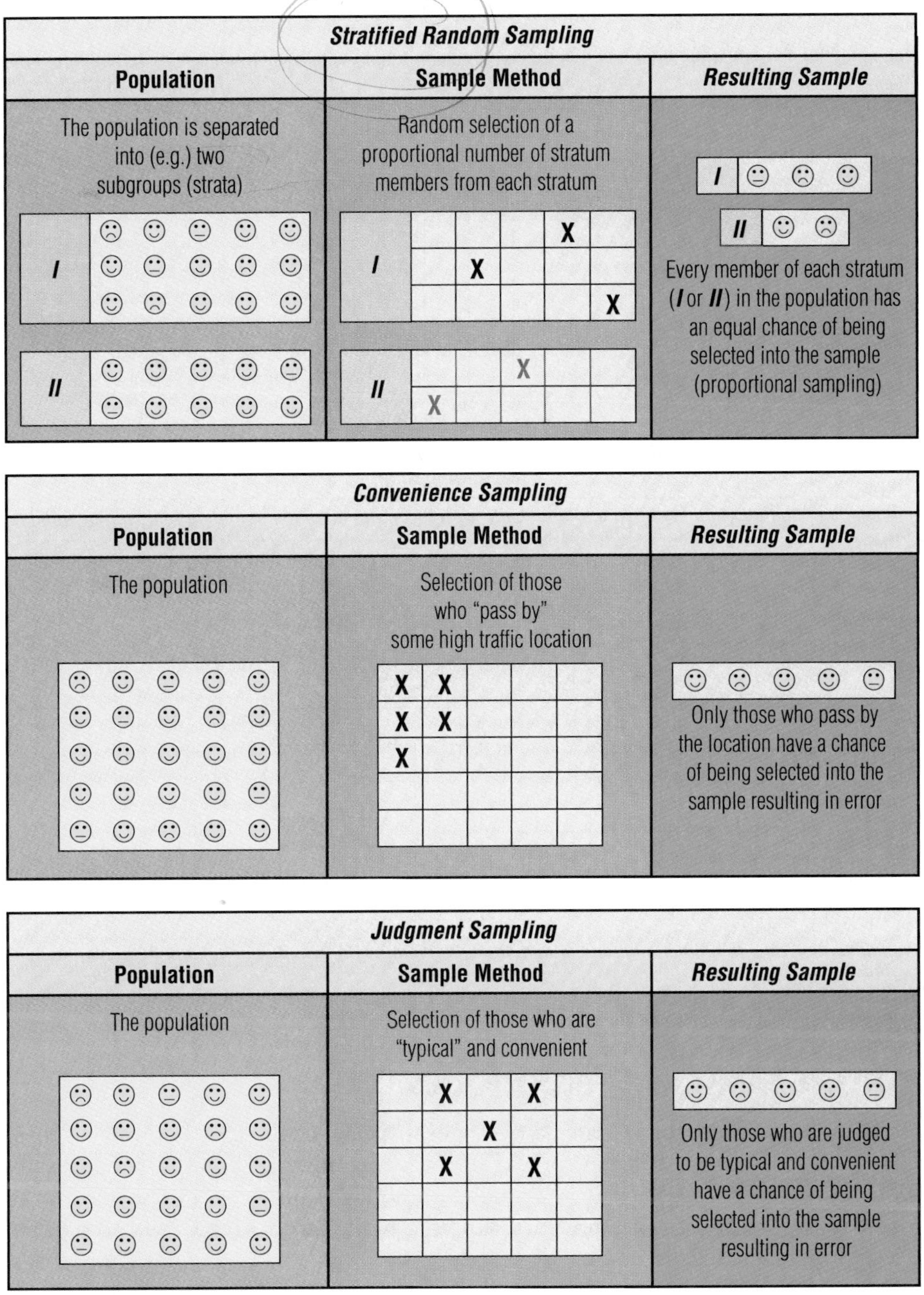

Stratified Random Sampling

Population	Sample Method	Resulting Sample
The population is separated into (e.g.) two subgroups (strata)	Random selection of a proportional number of stratum members from each stratum	Every member of each stratum (**I** or **II**) in the population has an equal chance of being selected into the sample (proportional sampling)

Convenience Sampling

Population	Sample Method	Resulting Sample
The population	Selection of those who "pass by" some high traffic location	Only those who pass by the location have a chance of being selected into the sample resulting in error

Judgment Sampling

Population	Sample Method	Resulting Sample
The population	Selection of those who are "typical" and convenient	Only those who are judged to be typical and convenient have a chance of being selected into the sample resulting in error

Figure **12.2B**

(*figure continues*)

isfaction profile is not a good representation of the population. If you look at the X's in the middle frame that depicts the sample's selection specifics, the nonprobability sample method X's are concentrated in specific areas of the population, whereas they are scattered across the entire population with probability samples. The concentration aspect of nonprobability sampling means that some members of the population have a disproportionate chance of being selected into the sample, resulting in sample selection error.

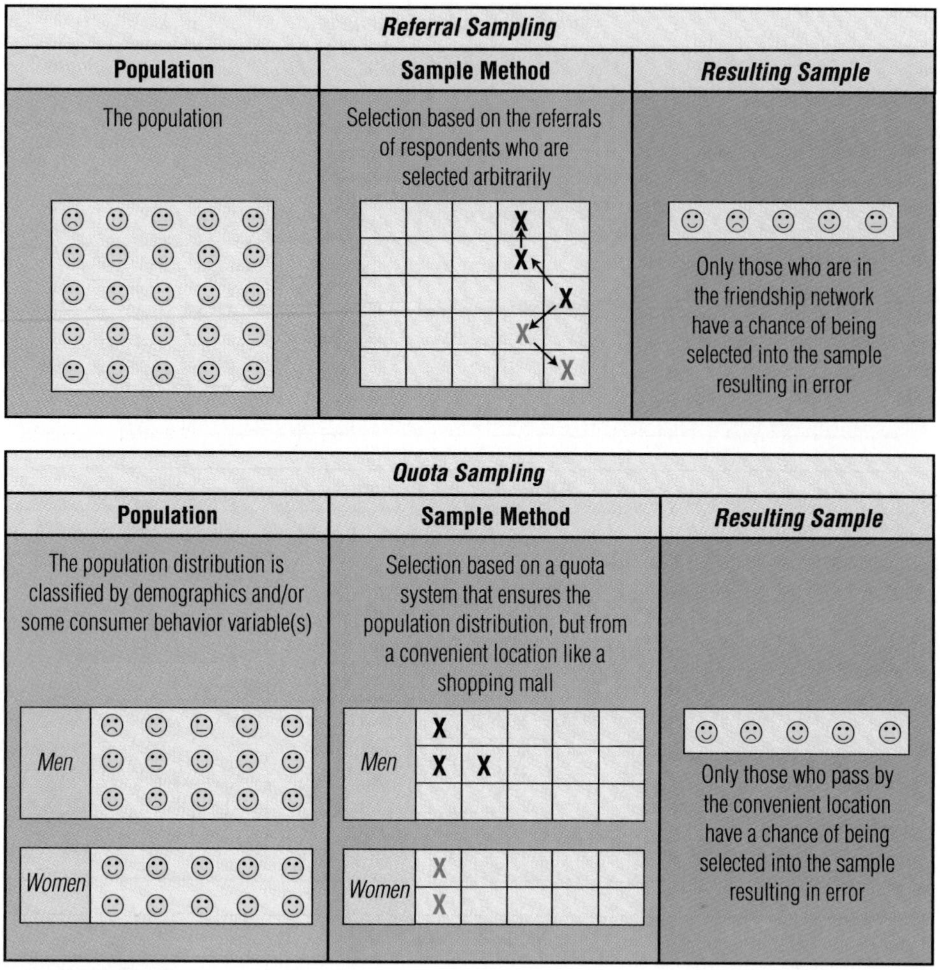

Referral Sampling		
Population	**Sample Method**	**Resulting Sample**
The population	Selection based on the referrals of respondents who are selected arbitrarily	Only those who are in the friendship network have a chance of being selected into the sample resulting in error

Quota Sampling		
Population	**Sample Method**	**Resulting Sample**
The population distribution is classified by demographics and/or some consumer behavior variable(s)	Selection based on a quota system that ensures the population distribution, but from a convenient location like a shopping mall	Only those who pass by the convenient location have a chance of being selected into the sample resulting in error

Figure 12.2C

ONLINE SAMPLING TECHNIQUES

Online sampling can be interpreted in the context of traditional sampling techniques.

To be sure, sampling for Internet surveys poses special challenges, but most of these issues can be addressed in the context of our probability and nonprobability sampling concepts.[19] The trick is to understand how the online sampling method in question works and to interpret the sampling procedure correctly with respect to basic sampling concepts.[20]

For purposes of illustration, we will describe four types of online sampling: (1) random online intercept sampling, (2) invitation online sampling, (3) online panel sampling, and (4) other online sampling types.

Random Online Intercept Sampling

Random online intercept sampling relies on a random selection of Web site visitors. There are a number of Java-based or other html-imbedded routines that will select Web site visitors on a random basis such as time of day or random selection from the stream of Web site visitors. If the population is defined as Web site visitors, then this is a simple random sample of these visitors within the time frame of the survey. If the sample selection program starts randomly and incorporates a skip interval system, it is a systematic sample,[21] and if the sample program treats the population of Web site visitors like strata, it uses stratified simple random sampling as long as random selection procedures are used faithfully. However, if the population is other than Web site visitors, and the Web site is used because there are many visitors, the sample is akin to a mall-intercept sample (convenience sample).

Invitation Online Sampling

Invitation online sampling is when potential respondents are alerted that they may fill out a questionnaire that is hosted at a specific Web site.[22] For example, a retail store chain may have a notice that is handed to customers with their receipts notifying them that they may go online to fill out the questionnaire. However, to avoid spam, online researchers must have an established relationship with potential respondents who expect to receive an e-mail survey. If the retail store uses a random sampling approach such as systematic sampling, a probability sample will result. Similarly, if the e-mail list is a truly representative group of the population, and the procedures embody random selection, it will constitute a probability sample. However, if in either case there is some aspect of the selection procedure that eliminates population members or otherwise overrepresents elements of the population, the sample will be a nonprobability one. A good example of a sampling system that overcomes this problem is Opinion Place[sm]. It uses a proprietary sampling method where visitors learn about Opinion Place[sm] through promotions placed throughout America Online (AOL) properties, the Internet, and various rewards programs. Additionally, AOL members can access the area quickly through a permanent placement in AOL Member Perks or through AOL Keyword: Opinion Place. Visitors to Opinion Place[sm] proceed through a complex, sophisticated screening process to ensure random representation across all surveys.[23]

To learn more about the unique sample method used at Opinion Place[sm] and to see a comparison to online panels, read Marketing Research Insight 12.6. When you read about Opinion Place[sm], you will find that it is operated by Digital Marketing Services, a wholly owned subsidiary of America Online. We have also provided a thumbnail sketch of Chuck Miller, executive vice president of DMS, in Marketing Research Insight 12.7.

> Four online sampling types are (1) random, (2) invitation, (3) panel, and (4) other.

▶ **An Online Application**

When Is a Panel Not a Panel?
(When It's Opinion Place[sm]!)

MARKETING RESEARCH
INSIGHT
12.6

Research panels are a common data collection tool for many researchers. These panels typically consist of prescreened respondents who have answered a series of profiling questions prior to participating in any actual studies and who have agreed to participate in future research studies conducted by the panel manager. The panel manager uses the information from the profiling questions to help balance the panel to represent a specific market (frequently the U.S. population) or target group (e.g., teens). They may also use the profiling questions to identify respondents who potentially meet the screening requirements for a specific project.

In the past, most of the interaction between the panelist and the manager was conducted via mail. This meant that panel managers sent out paper questionnaires to respondents, who wrote out their answers to those questions.

They then mailed the completed survey back to the panel manager.

More recently, the advent of the Internet produced new opportunities for the market research industry, as it did for so many others. For researchers, this meant a new way to contact and survey respondents. Panel managers reacted by quickly moving their panels online. Instead of mailing questionnaires to respondents, now panel managers e-mail invitations to respondents with information on how to complete the survey online. Respondents complete the survey and submit it—all online. Without question, this process can be much faster than mail and more convenient for respondents.

In contrast, one research company looked at the emerging Internet and saw a way to reinvent respondent interaction, while maintaining the benefits of random selection. Rather

(box continues)

than using the same group of preidentified respondents repeatedly for multiple research studies such as panels, Digital Marketing Services (DMS), a wholly owned subsidiary of America Online, envisioned an innovative method of data collection. DMS realized that the traffic on the Internet could provide a continual flow of new respondents to a specific online location (i.e., Opinion Place^sm) for the sole purpose of participating in research studies. Of course, there had to be a reason for respondents to do this and, thus, DMS also created an online incentive program that rewarded every respondent for participating in research studies.

Not surprisingly, many in the industry questioned this new development since researchers are by their nature very methodical in accepting new research methods and somewhat risk averse. Many parallel tests were conducted, in which data were collected via both a traditional methodology (i.e., phone, mall, or mail panel) and online. In general, the results of these tests showed that online data collection could provide comparable results to traditional methodologies and that these results were valid and reliable.

But many researchers still found it hard to comprehend a completely new method of data collection. They tried to classify Opinion Place^sm as just another online panel. In reality, it operates very differently, with many unique features and capabilities. One common analogy used to illustrate the difference describes Opinion Place^sm as a free-flowing river, with fresh respondents continuously flowing to surveys. In contrast, an online panel might be compared to a pond of water; occasionally new drops arrive, but the majority of the water stays the same.

Thus, although panels are very useful tools and provide many benefits when used in the online environment, it is important to remember that Opinion Place^sm incorporates capabilities and respondent opportunities distinctive from online panels. In other words, a river is not a pond.

The accompanying table details more differences between Opinion Place^sm and standard online panels.

Topic	Opinion Place (OP)	Online Panel
Population Base	More than 80% of the online population has direct access to OP.	The largest online panels may have up to 5 million records.
Respondents	First-time respondents flow to OP from the AOL Properties (AOL, CompuServe, etc.) and the Internet (AAdvantage, Netcenter, etc.), representing a significant majority of the online population.	Panel members are initially recruited from individual Web sites and may represent a small slice of the online universe. Panelists return repeatedly to participate in surveys.
Frequency of Participation	Respondent participation is limited through the use of access controls, preventing the development of "professional respondents."	Panel members may receive invitations to participate in multiple surveys within the space of a week or two.
Recruitment Process	Ongoing promotions alert respondents to OP, who then determine when it is convenient to participate.	Respondents are selected from the panel and mailed an invitation, which may state the content of the survey.
Screening Process	Demographic and other screening questions are asked each time a respondent enters OP. Qualified participants are then randomly assigned to a survey based on their answers.	Profiling data are gathered during the sign-up process. Questions are not repeated during subsequent surveys. Respondents are preidentified for participation in a specific survey or allowed to self-select which survey they complete.
Low-Incidence Targets	The flow of traffic through OP allows low-incidence groups to be identified at a rate relative to the degree of incidence.	Profiling questions enable panels to identify qualified respondents prior to mailing an e-mail invitation.
Incentive	Multiple incentive programs provide value to all segments of the population. Incentives are given to each respondent who completes a survey.	Incentives are typically in the form of sweepstakes, access to results, or charity donations and may have different levels of value to various respondent groups.
Response Rate	Respondents initiate contact with OP making response rates irrelevant. Among those who begin surveys, 85% or more complete the interview.	Current figures indicate that a significant majority of e-mail invitations to panel surveys are not accepted.

Chuck Miller heads the operations and technology group at Digital Marketing Services. One of the original founders of DMS, much of the current success of the company is largely due to the innovations, experience, and technical leadership of Miller. DMS was the first company to create a system that executed self-administered Web surveys capable of real-time data evaluation and complex quota controlling, moving the industry beyond e-mail and form-based surveys.

Prior to his tenure at AOL, Miller worked at the M/A/R/C Group for 10 years in a number of positions ranging from account management to the development of quality standards. While at M/A/R/C, Miller was widely recognized for his success in developing automated analysis and reporting systems.

Miller is highly regarded for his expertise in transforming more traditional research methodologies to online applications. Miller regularly shares his expertise when speaking at conferences and through his work with many industry organizations.

Online Panel Sampling

Online panel sampling refers to consumer or other respondent panels that are set up by marketing research companies for the explicit purpose of conducting online surveys with representative samples. There is a growing number of these companies, and online panels afford fast, convenient, and flexible access to preprofiled samples.[24] Typically, the panel company has several thousand individuals who are representative of a large geographic area, and the market researcher can specify sample parameters such as specific geographic representation, income, education, family characteristics, and so forth. The panel company then uses its database on its panel members to broadcast an e-mail notification to those panelists who qualify according to the sample parameters specified by the market researcher. Although online panel samples are not probability samples, they are used extensively by the marketing research industry.[25] A major exception is the probability sample panel of Knowledge Networks described in Marketing Research Insight 12.1. In some instances, the online panel company creates the questionnaire; at other times, the researcher composes the questionnaire on the panel company's software, or some other means of questionnaire design might be used, depending on the services of the panel company. One of the greatest pluses of online panels is the high response rate, which ensures that the final sample closely represents the population targeted by the researcher.

Other Online Sampling Approaches

Other online sampling approaches are feasible and limited only by the creativity of the sample designers. To identify the underlying sample method, you simply need to analyze the specifics of how potential respondents are selected. For instance, a respondent may be asked to forward the survey site to his or her friends (referral sampling), or there may be a survey page that pops up after every customer makes an online purchase (census). Regardless of the approach, if you analyze it carefully in the context of basic sampling techniques that are described in this chapter, you should be able to determine if it is a probability or a nonprobability sample.

DEVELOPING A SAMPLE PLAN

Up to this point, we have discussed various aspects of sampling as though they were discrete and seemingly unrelated decisions. However, they are logically joined together, and there is a definite sequence of steps, called the **sample plan**, that the researcher goes through in order to draw and ultimately arrive at the final sample. These steps are

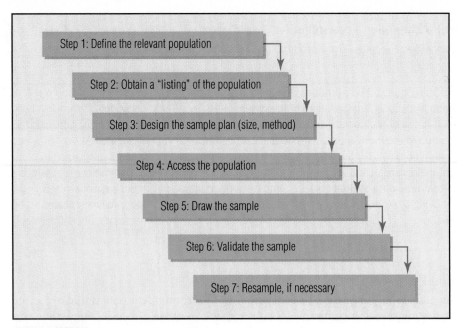

Figure **12.3**   **Steps in the Sampling Process**

illustrated in Figure 12.3. Now that you are acquainted with basic terms, definitions, and concepts involved with sampling, we can describe these steps in detail.

Step 1: Define the Relevant Population

A sample plan begins with the population definition.

As you know, the very first step to be considered in the sampling process requires a definition of the target population under study. We indicated earlier in the chapter that the target population is identified by the marketing research study objectives; however, typically at the beginning of the sampling phase of a research project, the focus on the relevant population is necessarily sharpened. This sharpening involves the translation of nebulous descriptions of the target population into fairly specific demographic or other characteristics that separate the target population from other populations. The task here is for the researcher to specify the sample unit in the form of a precise description of the type of person to be surveyed.

For example, with a fast-food restaurant survey done for Taco Bell, it might be assumed that an important descriptor helping to define the relevant population is that its members have very limited time for lunch—many of them have only 30 minutes (actually less, if one were to consider driving or walking time). A population description can result from previous studies, or it may be the collective wisdom of marketing decision makers who have catered to this particular population for a number of years and have had the opportunity to observe members' behaviors and to listen to their comments.

Step 2: Obtain a Listing of the Population

Lists to be considered as sample frames should be assessed in terms of sample frame error.

Once the relevant population has been defined, the researcher begins searching for a suitable list to serve as the sample frame. In some studies, candidate lists are readily available in the form of databases of various sorts—company files or records, either public or private, that are made available to the researcher. In other instances, the listing is available at a price from a third party. Unfortunately, it is rare that a listing is perfectly faithful to the target population. Most lists suffer from sample frame error; or, as we noted earlier, the database does not contain a complete enumeration of members of the population. Alternatively, the listing may be a distorted accounting of the population in that some of those listed may not belong to the population.

A good example of working with sample frame error is a survey that might be conducted for the American Automobile Association (AAA) that guarantees 24-hour emergency road service for its subscribers. As a means of winning new customers, AAA might consider marketing an "automobile travelers' maintenance and emergency kit." This kit comes in a tough plastic case about 10 inches long, 6 inches wide, and 4 inches deep. Inside are found various car maintenance devices such as a tire pressure gauge, a quart of oil, a bottle of windshield wiper solvent, a road flare, and a waterless cleaner for your hands. Of course, the kit has the AAA roadside emergency benefits and sign-up telephone number emblazoned prominently on the top. A marketing research company is contacted and asked to come up with a proposal for a survey to determine consumer reactions to this kit at various prices. This company claims that the most appropriate list of the population would be voter registration records. What sample frame error is evident here, and how severe is it?

The answer should be apparent once you realize a list of registered voters is incomplete in that it omits new state residents. Also, it would not be a complete listing of all drivers in your state because, prior to the Motor Voter Act of 1993, not everyone who drove bothered to register to vote. Motor vehicle registration records, on the other hand, would be a more accurate listing of this population. Furthermore, most states mandate that a new resident must acquire state license plates within 60 days of acquiring an address in that state. Obviously, the motor vehicle registration list would be more complete and more current, not to mention more relevant. So why did the research company not recommend motor vehicle registrations as its sample frame? Unfortunately, vehicle registration records typically are not available for outside inspection or sampling procedures. Voter registration records, on the other hand, are available. Consequently, the use of a less accurate list is necessary because of the impracticality involved in securing a more complete listing.

The key to assessing sample frame error lies in two factors: (1) judging how different the people listed in the sample frame are from the population and (2) estimating what kinds of people in the population are not listed in the sample frame. With the first factor, screening questions at the beginning of an interview will usually suffice as a means of disqualifying those contacted who are not consistent with the population definition. As we noted in an earlier chapter, the percentage of people on a list who qualify as members of the population is referred to as the **incidence rate**. For instance, a researcher may have a list of automobile owners in a metropolitan area, but if the survey seeks only drivers who have had an accident in the past year, the incidence rate might be 1 percent or one out of every 100 automobile owners. With the second consideration, if the researcher cannot find any reason that those population members who were left off the list would adversely affect the final sample, the degree of frame error is judged tolerable. In the emergency highway kit example using voter registration records, the incidence rate should be high, and unregistered state residents constitute only a tiny portion of drivers in most states, plus they probably do not differ from registered residents in their gasoline purchasing. So voter registration records would serve as an acceptable sample frame for this survey.

If the population is global and has a low-incidence rate, researchers typically turn to compiled lists, and sampling companies such as Survey Sampling, Inc. have developed services to accommodate this especially problematic aspect of global marketing research. We have written Marketing Research Insight 12.8 to describe how the Survey Sampling, Inc. Global SSI-LITe™ services works.

Now that you have learned about one of Survey Sampling, Inc.'s sampling products, you can meet two of the principals of this impressive company. We have asked Terrence Coen and Chris De Angelis to provide thumbnail descriptions of themselves, and you will find these in Marketing Research Insights 12.9 and 12.10.

Two forms of sample frame error occur when the names of some people on the list are not part of the population, or when members of the population are not on the list.

Lists with high-incidence rates are good candidates for use as sample frames.

MARKETING RESEARCH
INSIGHT

12.8

Survey Sampling, Inc. Provides Global E-Mail Samples

A major challenge for online sampling is to find an adequate sample frame. This challenge is multiplied many times when the population involves global marketing or, at the least, a population of consumers in a single foreign country.

Survey Sampling, Inc. (**www.ssisamples.com**) has been a leading sample provider in the United States for the past two decades, and in the late 1990s, it greatly expanded its global samples capabilities. At the same time, it launched a special online survey sampling services called Global SSI-LITe™.

Survey Sampling, Inc. compiles master lists with e-mail addresses of Internet users who have agreed to answer online surveys on specific topics such as financial matters and money management, computer game usage, children's education, health, child-rearing practices, and toys. In addition, these individuals agree to answer e-mail surveys on general topics such as pets, autos, computers, entertainment, health, music, sports, and travel.

Presently, the Global SSI-LITe™ service exists for consumers in virtually every European country, and it is rapidly growing to represent all countries where Internet usage is commonplace. This sampling system is especially valuable for researchers seeking to sample in low-incidence situations, that is, seeking to find consumers who are difficult to find in the general population, such as Siamese cat owners or vinyl record collectors.

How does it work? A researcher designs and posts an online questionnaire. Then he or she contacts Survey Sampling, Inc. to communicate what countries, what types of respondents, and how many are to be drawn into the sample. Survey Sampling, Inc. then uses its extensive databases that comprise its Global SSI-LITe™ system to send out e-mail invitations to the target populations, telling these individuals where the researcher's online questionnaire is posted.

MARKETING RESEARCH
INSIGHT

12.9

Terrence Coen of Survey Sampling, Inc.
Vice President Sales and Marketing, Survey Sampling, Inc.

Terry Coen has been vice president of sales and marketing for Survey Sampling since 1988.

From 1974 until that time he held a variety of executive positions with organizations responsible for processing large establishment–oriented databases. From the mid-1970s to the mid-1980s he was vice president, sales and marketing, for Market Data Retrieval. As a principal of the company he was instrumental in bringing a start-up company to sales of $25 million a year.

In the mid-1980s Coen served as president of National Business Lists and in the late 1980s was vice president for alternate channels of distribution for Dun & Bradstreet.

▶ **Meet a Marketing Researcher**

MARKETING RESEARCH
INSIGHT
12.10

Chris De Angelis of Survey Sampling, Inc.
Survey Sampling, Inc. (SSI)

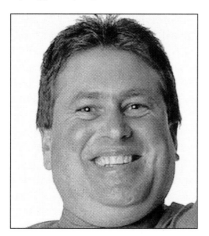

Chris De Angelis is SSI's national sales manager. He has been with SSI since 1986 serving as an account executive

for five years and senior account executive for another five years before moving to the role of national sales manager in January 1997.

De Angelis has over a decade of sampling experience working closely on a day-to-day basis with SSI customers. He has worked with clients throughout the United States on all types of sample designs. This extensive experience has proven valuable in helping customers develop creative solutions to sampling challenges. He has provided consultation, expertise, and sampling solutions for a wide variety of commercial, government, and academic research projects.

De Angelis has a B.A. in economics from Bates College, studied economics in the United Kingdom for one year, and has an M.B.A. in marketing from the University of Bridgeport. He has been an active Market Research Association member for many years and is a member of American Association for Public Opinion Research.

Step 3: Design the Sample Plan (Size and Method)

Armed with a precise definition of the population and an understanding of the availability and condition of lists of the target population, the researcher progresses directly into the design of the sample itself. At this point, the costs of various data collection method factors come into play. That is, the researcher begins to simultaneously balance sample design, data collection costs, and sample size. We discuss sample size determination in the next chapter, and you will learn that it is a trade-off between the desire for statistical precision and the requirements of efficiency and economy.

Regardless of the size of the sample, the specific sampling method or combination of sampling methods to be employed must be stipulated in detail by the researcher. There is no one "best" sampling method. The sample plan varies according to the objectives of the survey and its constraints.[26]

The sampling method description includes all of the necessary steps to draw the sample. For instance, if we decided to use systematic sampling, the sampling method would detail the sample frame, the sample size, the skip interval, how the random starting point would be determined, qualifying questions, recontacts, and replacement procedures. That is, all eventualities and contingencies should be foreseen and provisions should be made for each of them. These contingency plans are most apparent in the directions given to interviewers or provided to the data collection company. Obviously, it is vital to the success of the survey that the sampling method be adhered to throughout the entire sampling process.

Sample size and sample method are separate steps in the sample plan.

Step 4: Draw the Sample

Drawing the sample is a two-phase process. First, the sample unit must be selected. Second, information must be gained from that unit. Simply put, you need to choose a person and ask him or her some questions. However, as you realize, not everyone will agree to answer. So there comes the question of substitutions.[27] Substitutions occur whenever an individual who was qualified to be in the sample proves to be unavailable, unwilling to respond, or unsuitable. The question here is, "How is the substitution respondent determined?" If the marketing research project director wishes to ensure that a particular sampling method is used faithfully, the question of substitutions must be addressed. There are three substitution methods in practice: drop-downs, oversampling, and resampling.

Substitutions in the sample may be determined with drop-downs, oversampling, or resampling.

The **drop-down substitution** is often used with systematic sampling. Let us say that we are using a telephone directory as our sample frame, and you are the interviewer who is instructed to call every 100th name. On your first call, the person qualifies but refuses to take part in the survey. If the drop-down method of substitution is in effect, your responsibility is to call the name immediately following the one you just called. You will not skip 100 names but just drop down to the next one below the refusal. If that person refuses to take part, you will drop down another name and so on until you find a cooperative respondent. Then you will resume the 100 skip interval, using the original name as your beginning point. Obviously, interviewers must be provided the complete sample frame to use drop-down substitution.

Oversampling is an alternative substitution method, and it takes place as a result of the researcher's knowledge of incidence rates, nonresponse rates, and unusable responses. For example, if the typical response rate for a mail survey questionnaire hovers around 20 percent, in order to obtain a final sample of 200 respondents, 1,000 potential respondents must be drawn into the mailout sample. Each data collection method constitutes separate oversampling implications, and it is up to the marketing research project director to apply his or her wisdom to determine the appropriate degree of oversampling. Otherwise, resampling will be necessary at a later point in the marketing research study in order to obtain the desired sample size.

Incidence rates and response rates determine the need for sample substitutions.

Resampling constitutes a third means of respondent substitution. Resampling is a procedure in which the sample frame is tapped for additional names after the initial sample is drawn. Here the response rate may turn out to be much lower than anticipated, and more prospective respondents must be drawn. CATI random digit dialing uses resampling implicitly because the numbers are generated until the desired sample size is reached. Of course, provision must be made that prospective respondents appearing in the original sample are not included in the resample.

Step 5: Assess the Sample

The final activity in the sampling process is the assessment stage. Sample assessment can take a number of forms, one of which is to compare the sample's demographic profile with a known profile such as the census. With quota sample validation, of course, the researcher must use a demographic characteristic other than those used to set up the quota system. The essence of **sample validation** is to assure the client that the sample is, in fact, a representative sample of the population about which the decision maker wishes to make decisions. Although not all researchers perform sample validation, it is recommended when prior knowledge exists about the population's demographic profile. When no such prior information exits, validation is not possible, and the sample selection method bears the full burden of convincing clients that the sample is representative of the population.

Sample validation assures the client that the sample is representative, but sample validation is not always possible.

Step 6: Resample If Necessary

When a sample fails assessment, it means that it does not adequately represent the population. This problem may arise even when sample substitutions are incorporated.[28] Sometimes when this condition is found, the researcher can use a weighting scheme in the tabulations and analyses to compensate for the misrepresentation. On the other hand, it is sometimes possible to perform resampling by selecting more respondents and adding them to the sample until a satisfactory level of validation is reached.

Here is how our Blue Ribbon Panel members answered our question about how online research is wrestling with issues of representativeness of online samples.

Q: *One of the issues in online survey research has been the questioning of online survey respondents' representativeness. The charges have been made that Internet users cannot be representative of the entire population and that people who respond to online surveys are not even representative of all Internet users. Now, after a few years of experience with online surveys and evaluating the results of those surveys, how would you respond to the question of representativeness of online survey respondents?*

Note: To learn about the panel members, see the Preface of this book.

Bill MacElroy
President
Socratic Technologies

A: I am in total agreement with the statement regarding the problems of representativeness of online samples being used to model the entire population for many types of study. At the very least, a hybrid methodology should be used in which at least 60 percent of the population is not online and/or in which reasonable bias can be hypothesized. For online populations, however, I have no reason to find that nonresponse makes projecting to that population any more difficult than nonresponse in traditional methods makes projecting to off-line populations. I have not encountered any online research findings that are not as good, if not better, at capturing a representative demographic sample of the online population being studied.

Allen Hogg
President
Burke, Inc.

A: One of the paradoxes of online research is that it can be a poor method of capturing a representative set of opinions about topics relating to the Internet. People who are able and willing to take online surveys will tend to be heavier users of the Internet than all people with online access. They will also tend to engage in a wider variety of online activities.

Obviously, opinions of people who complete online surveys will also not be representative of those of the entire population on many topics. By the same token, those who are willing to take telephone surveys will not be representative of the entire population on some issues, nor will those who make the effort to complete mail questionnaires. Whether findings from a particular survey method and sample source will be less representative of the views of the target population depends very much on the specifics of the study.

Before an organization dives wholeheartedly into online research, it is wise to use parallel studies to see how both sample population and methodological differences will affect results.

George Harmon
Senior Vice President
Digital Marketing
Services (DMS)

A: DMS has conducted over 300 online comparability studies side by side with traditional methods that claim to have representative sampling. In each of these we found our online methods yielded similar results and, more importantly, the business decisions would be similar. These findings are not unique to DMS. In January 1999 the Advertising Research Foundation (ARF) held a conference about online validity in which a dozen online companies presented overwhelming evidence of online comparability and validity.

Although many population subsets are underrepresented online, quota sampling can be employed to build appropriate samples. It should be noted that only a small portion of market research studies is designed to represent the total United States. Typically marketing studies are designed to screen for category users with specific ages and gender quotas rather than the general population.

Keith Price
Vice President
Greenfield Online

A: The Internet population is forecasted to grow by 65 percent between 2000 and 2003 and is predicted to reach 1 billion by the year 2005 (source: PriceWaterhouse Coopers). At this point, the Web is largely comprised of users with higher annual incomes as compared with the general U.S. population, but the fastest-growing segment of the Internet user population is households with incomes of less than $25,000 a year (source: MediaMetrix, The Dollar Divide, August 2000). Although Internet usage levels do not match the U.S. census data and there is no true sampling frame, weighting techniques can be applied.

Lee Smith
CEO
Insight Express

A: The demographics of the online population continue to shift as Internet penetration grows. Currently, more than two-thirds of all U.S. households are online. The online population is rapidly converging to that of the general U.S. population—increasingly enabling researchers to use online methodologies for many applications and decreasing representativeness concerns.

Although online research may not currently be suitable for all research needs, certainly every marketer has one or more segments of its customers, markets, or target markets that are well represented online. It is simply a matter of time until Internet penetration drives convergence and representativeness for all market segments.

Doss Struse
Senior Vice President
Client Service
Knowledge Networks,
Inc.

A: There is no question that consumers volunteering or opting to complete online surveys do not accurately reflect the population of the United States (or even the online population). The biases are weakly correlated to demographics or other characteristics that might enable developing adjustment factors. The lack of a workable sampling frame requires setting up panels selected according to probability theory. Although such panels bring with them issues around conditioning of panelists and attrition, these are much more easily solved.

SPSS Student Assistant Online
Red Lobster: Recoding and
Computing Variables

SUMMARY

This chapter described various sampling methods. It began by acquainting you with various terms such as *population, census,* and *sample frame.* A sample is taken because it is too costly to perform a census, and there is sufficient information in a sample to allow it to represent the population. We described four probability sampling methods in which there is a known chance of a member of the population being selected into the sample: (1) simple random sampling, (2) systematic sampling, (3) cluster sampling using area sampling as an example, and (4) stratified sampling. We also described four nonprobability sampling methods: (1) convenience sampling, (2) judgment sampling, (3) referral sampling, and (4) quota sampling. The growing trend to draw online samples was noted, and we related (1) random online intercept sampling, (2) invitation online sampling, and (3) other online sampling types. Finally, we described seven steps needed to develop a sample plan: (1) define the relevant population; (2) obtain a listing of the population; (3) design the sample plan (size and methods); (4) access the population; (5) draw the sample; (6) validate the sample; and (7) resample if necessary.

KEY TERMS

Population (p. 334)
Sample (p. 334)
Sample unit (p. 335)
Census (p. 335)
Sampling error (p. 335)
Sample frame (p. 335)
Sample frame error (p. 336)
Probability samples (p. 338)
Nonprobability samples (p. 338)
Simple random sampling (p. 338)
Blind draw method (p. 338)
Table of random numbers (p. 339)
Random digit dialing (RDD) (p. 341)
Plus-one dialing procedure (p. 341)
Systematic sampling (p. 342)
Skip interval (p. 342)
Cluster sampling (p. 344)
Area sampling (p. 344)
One-step area sample (p. 344)
Two-step area sample (p. 344)
Stratified sampling (p. 345)

Skewed population (p. 345)
Strata (p. 346)
Weighted mean (p. 347)
Surrogate measure (p. 348)
Proportionate stratified sample (p. 348)
Disproportionate stratified sampling (p. 348)
Convenience samples (p. 349)
Judgment samples (p. 350)
Referral samples (p. 350)
Quota sample (p. 350)
Random online intercept sampling (p. 354)
Invitation online sampling (p. 355)
Online panel sampling (p. 357)
Sample plan (p. 357)
Incidence rate (p. 359)
Drop-down substitution (p. 362)
Oversampling (p. 362)
Resampling (p. 362)
Sample validation (p. 362)

REVIEW QUESTIONS/APPLICATIONS

1. Distinguish a nonprobability from a probability sampling method. Which one is the preferable method and why? Indicate the pros and cons associated with probability and nonprobability sampling methods.

2. List and describe briefly each of the probability sampling methods described in the chapter.

3. What is meant by the term "random"? Explain how each of the following embodies randomness: (a) table of random numbers, (b) blind draw, (c) use of random digit dialing, and (d) use of a computer.

4. In what ways is a systematic sample more efficient than a simple random sample? In what way is systematic sampling less representative of the population than simple random sampling?

5. Distinguish cluster sampling from simple random sampling. How are systematic sampling and cluster sampling related?

6. Differentiate one-step from two-step area sampling, and indicate when each one is preferred.

7. What is meant by a "skewed" population? Illustrate what you think is a skewed population distribution variable and what it looks like.

8. What are the popular online sampling methods? Describe each one.

9. Briefly describe each of the four nonprobability sampling methods.

10. Why is quota sampling often used with a convenience sampling method such as mall intercepts?

11. Describe each of the three methods of substitution for individuals who are selected into the sample but refuse to participate in the survey or who did not qualify.

12. Provide the marketing researcher's definitions for each of the following populations:

a. Columbia House, a mail-order house specializing in tapes and compact discs, wants to determine interest in a 10-for-1 offer on jazz CDs.

b. The manager of your student union is interested in determining if students desire a "universal" debit ID card that will be accepted anywhere on campus and in many stores off campus.

c. Joy Manufacturing Company decides to conduct a survey to determine the sales potential of a new type of air compressor used by construction companies.

13. Here are four populations and a potential sample frame for each one. With each pair, identify (1) members of the population who are not in the sample frame and (2) sample frame items that are not part of the population. Also, for each one, would you judge the amount of sample frame error to be acceptable or unacceptable?

POPULATION	SAMPLE FRAME
a. Buyers of Scope mouthwash	Mailing list of *Consumer Reports* subscribers
b. Listeners of a particular FM radio classical music station in your city	Telephone directory
c. Prospective buyers of a new day planner and prospective clients tracking kit	Members of Sales and Marketing Executives International (a national organization of sales managers)
d. Users of weatherproof decking materials (to build outdoor decks)	Individuals' names registered at a recent home and garden show

14. Taco Bell approaches an official at your university and proposes to locate one of its restaurants on the campus. Because it would be the first commercial interest of this sort on your campus, the administration requires Taco Bell to conduct a survey of full-time students to assess the desirability of this operation. Analyze the practical difficulties encountered with doing a census in this situation, and provide specific examples of each one. For instance, how long might such a census take, how much might it cost, what types of students are more accessible than others, and what capacity constraints might be operating here?

15. A state lottery (weekly lottery in which players pick numbers from 1 to 20) player is curious about the randomness of winning lottery numbers. He has kept track of the winning numbers in the past five weeks and finds that most numbers were selected 25 percent of the time, but the number 6 was one of the winning numbers 50 percent of the time. Will he be more or less likely to win if he picks a 6 in this week's lottery, or will it not make any difference in his chances? Relate your answer to simple random sampling.

16. Pet Insurers Company markets health and death benefits insurance to pet owners. It specializes in coverage for pedigreed dogs, cats, or expensive and exotic pets such as miniature Vietnamese pot-bellied pigs. The veterinary care costs of these pets can be high, and their deaths represent substantial financial loss to their owners. A researcher working for Pet Insurers finds that a listing company can provide a list of 15,000 names, which includes all current subscribers to *Cat Lovers, Pedigreed Dog,* and *Exotic Pets Monthly.* If the final sample size is to be 1,000, what should be the skip interval in a systematic sample for each of the following: (a) a telephone survey using drop-down substitution, (b) a mail survey with an anticipated 30 percent response rate, and (c) resampling to select 250 more prospective respondents? Also, assess the incidence rate for this sample frame.

17. A market researcher is proposing a survey for the Big Tree Country Club, a private country club that is contemplating several changes in its layout to make the golf course more championship caliber. The researcher is considering three different sample designs as a way to draw a representative sample of the club's golfers. The three alternative designs are:

    a. Station an interviewer at the first hole tee on one day chosen at random, with instructions to ask every 10th golfer to fill out a self-administered questionnaire.

    b. Put a stack of questionnaires on the counter where golfers check in and pay for their golf carts. There would be a sign above the questionnaires, and there would be an incentive for a "free dinner in the clubhouse" for three players who fill out the questionnaires and whose names are selected by a lottery.

    c. Using the city telephone directory, a plus-one dialing procedure would be used. With this procedure a random page in the directory would be selected, and a name on that page would be selected, both using a table of random numbers. The plus-one system would be applied to that name and every name listed after it until 1,000 golfers are identified and interviewed by telephone.

        Assess the representativeness and other issues associated with this sample problem. Be sure to identify the sample method being contemplated in each case. Which sample method do you recommend using and why?

18. A financial services company wants to take a survey of Internet users to see if they are interested in using the company's financial-planning and asset-tracking Internet services. Previous studies have shown that Internet usage differs greatly by age, education, and gender. The total sample size will be 1,000. Using actual information about Internet usage or supplying reasonable assumptions, indicate how stratified simple random sampling should be applied for each of the following stratification situations: (1) 18–25, 26–50, and 51–65 age ranges; (2) education levels of high school diploma, some college, college degree, and graduate degree; and (3) gender: males versus females.

INTERACTIVE LEARNING

Visit the Web site at www.prenhall.com/burnsbush. For this chapter, work through the Self-Study Quizzes, and get instant feedback on whether you need additional studying. On the Web site, you can review the chapter outlines and case information for Chapter 12.

CASE 12.1   BYU's Creamery on North[29]

In the fall of 2001, the Brigham Young University (BYU) Foodservice Department launched a bold extension of its traditional food services by opening the "Creamery on North." The facility is a grocery-and-drugstore located on BYU's campus and catering specifically to BYU students, faculty, and staff, but primarily to students. The university-run supermarket was described in the following manner by the director of dining services at the grand opening: "It will be a full-line grocery with fresh meats, produce, an in-house bakery, and an expanded line of canned and paper goods."

Almost 30,000 students attend BYU, and although most do not live on campus, the Creamery on North is located on the eastern edge of the BYU campus close to a large university apartment complex and a residential area where many off-campus students live. Because its closest competitor is approximately 4 miles away, it is very convenient for most BYU students.

The college crowd is one of the most difficult food preference profiles to figure out because college students are in a volatile period when they are transitioning from their parent-controlled, high school–determined, and/or juvenile peer–influenced meals and food fads to entirely self-decided meals. But they are busy with studies, social activities, or work, and most are not experienced in making home-cooked meals. The "freshman 15" myth predicts that first-year college students will gain 15 pounds due to their diets and appetites being uncontrolled. In short, college students' eating habits and the foods they like to eat are in no way mainstream.

So the BYU Foodservice Department has a formidable challenge in its need to monitor and predict BYU student food choices in order to stock the items that are going to be "hot." At the same time, it is tasked with the general well-being of BYU students who buy food or eat at any of the several Foodservices facilities on campus.

In an attempt to measure the grocery store purchasing preference of its target market, the director of the Foodservice Department contacted the chairman of the BYU Marketing Department, who agrees to have a student team perform a survey. The team meets with Creamery on North managers, brainstorms, conducts a focus group, and comes up with the following objectives.

- ▶ To determine the typical student's perception of the Creamery on North's food assortment.
- ▶ To ascertain the typical BYU student's preferences for various grocery items.
- ▶ To identify what acceptable "healthy" items should be added to the grocery store's shelves.

The student team has decided to design a self-administered questionnaire to collect its data in this survey, and it is now debating the sample plan. Somehow the plan must allow for the research team members to access all BYU students who might use the Creamery on North for grocery purchases, hand the questionnaire to each potential respondent, and retrieve the questionnaire once it is completed.

1. Specify a sample plan for each of the following types of probability sampling methods: simple random sampling, systematic sampling, cluster sampling, and stratified sampling.
2. Specify a sample plan for each of the following types of nonprobability sampling methods: convenience sampling, judgment sampling, and quota sampling.

Don't forget to include all of the necessary mechanics of each plan.

CASE 12.2 The Cobalt Group: Online Survey for MyCarTools™

The Cobalt Group (www.cobaltgroup.com) touts itself as a leading provider of e-business products and services for the automotive industry. It claims almost 9,000 Web site clients and about the same number of parts locator clients. There are several Cobalt Group products, and a number are geared toward the automobile dealer–automobile buyer/owner relationship. One of Cobalt Group's products is MyCarTools™, which provides auto dealers with the ability to give personal Web space to its auto buyers. This Web space is set up to let the car owner input his or her auto usage, to track service records, or to schedule a service appointment online. The auto dealership can use this Web space service as a direct-marketing tool of its own, for as its customers enter their information on their Web spaces, the dealership's database of owners grows. This database can be used to identify customer types and trends, to target specific customer segments with advertisements and special promotions, or even to alert customers to product recalls.

There is great potential value in MyCarTools™, for it is a means of maintaining close contact with buyers of autos from the dealership over the life of their automobiles. If satisfying to the customer, this contact may well translate into a strong propensity in that customer to return to the dealership when he or she is thinking about replacing the auto. Of course, the degree of participation in MyCarTools™ is entirely voluntary, and it depends on a number of factors. First, the auto buyer must agree to be entered into the dealer's Web space, and, second, the buyer must have computer availability and Internet connectivity. Finally, the buyer must use the service on a regular basis.

In an online chat problem-solving forum, automobile dealers who use Cobalt Group dealership software brainstormed questions about the value of MyCarTools™. The top question was, "Does the use of MyCarTools™ increase the propensity of a car buyer to return to the dealership where he or she bought the auto as compared to those who do not use MyCarTools™?"

The Cobalt Group Special Projects Team was assigned the task of researching this question. The team immediately created an online questionnaire using Websurveyor, but it is having difficulty deciding on the sample plan.

1. What should be the population definition for this marketing research situation?
2. Given this population definition, what should be the sample frame?
3. Should the Special Projects Team use an e-mail invitation or a Web site pop-up invitation sampling method? Why did you recommend this method over the other option?

CASE 12.3 *Your Integrated Case*

Hobbit's Choice Restaurant

This is your integrated case described on pages 42–43.

After some deliberation, Cory Rogers has narrowed the data collection method for The Hobbit's Choice Restaurant down to two choices: to use either a telephone sample or an online panel. In order for his forecasting model to work properly, Cory needs to use a sample design that will result in a sample that represents the entire greater metropolitan area.

1. Should Cory use a systematic sample using the metropolitan area telephone book as the sample frame? What are the advantages and disadvantages of this sample plan?
2. Should Cory use random digit dialing for the sample plan? What are the advantages and disadvantages of this sample plan?
3. Should Cory use a probability online panel such as the one maintained by Knowledge Networks, Inc? With respect to sample design, what are the advantages and disadvantages involved with using this approach? (You may want to review Knowledge Networks, Inc. services by visiting its Web site at **www.knowledgenetworks.com**.)

Determining the Size of a Sample

SCIENTIFIC TELEPHONE SAMPLES

Practitioner Viewpoint

How much sample size is enough? The common answer is "its never enough." Sample size is typically a result of budget or timing considerations, and there are more subtle and much more important factors to consider. One issue to think about is the difference between the interviews you collect and the interviews you will use to make the final decision. Good research, therefore, must anticipate possible types of outcomes and make provisions to ensure there will be more than "never enough." Over all, it is probably better to conduct fewer studies with more funding behind them, while developing more meaningful results.

Steven C. Clark
Partner
Scientific Telephone Samples (STS)

Ipsos-Reid Decides the Sample Size for a Survey Representing 3 Billion Consumers

Where We Are:
1. Establish the need for marketing research
2. Define the problem
3. Establish research objectives
4. Determine research design
5. Identify information types and sources
6. Determine methods of accessing data
7. Design data collection forms
8. **Determine sample plan and size**
9. Collect data
10. Analyze data
11. Prepare and present the final research report

Ipsos-Reid is one of the top 10 marketing research companies in the world with four offices in the United States in the cities of New York, Washington, DC, Minneapolis, and San Francisco, plus offices in six other cities around the globe. This research company has strong presence in the following industries: financial services, health care, lottery and gambling, agrifood (including biotechnology), technology of all types, travel, youth, and global marketing.

While Ipsos-Reid designs and executes custom marketing research, it has developed an omnibus global survey for clients whose research needs are more standard. The Ipsos-Reid Global Express is a survey conducted quarterly in each of 50 different countries. These countries comprise representation of practically every major industrialized country on every continent with the exception of Africa.

There are many uses of the Ipsos-Reid omnibus survey, and companies rely on it for a number of needs, including market size determination, market share and penetration, concept tests, awareness and purchase studies, demographic profiling, brand equity, brand image, benchmarking, consumer attitudes, market segmentation, and trend analyses.

The sample size for every country, except the United States, is 500, and if you do the math of 1,000 (U.S.) + 49 other countries times 500, the result is a sample size of 25,500 respondents who represent over 3 billion people in these 50 countries.

Here is a snapshot of the sample sizes that Ipsos-Reid uses in its Ipsos-Reid Global Express omnibus survey.

COUNTRY	COUNTRY POPULATION	GLOBAL EXPRESS SAMPLE SIZE
China	1.2 billion	500
India	1 billion	500
United States	283 million	1,000
Japan	127 million	500
Thailand	62 million	500
Sweden	9 million	500

Despite these huge differences in the populations of the various countries in the Ipsos-Reid omnibus survey, Ipsos-Reid claims in its promotional literature that the sample size "gives you statistically reliable results in each national market."[1]

Ipsos-Reid must be doing something right, for it claims that it has conducted over 10,000 surveys in the past decade.

The Ipsos-Reid Global Express example illustrates that there is something counterintuitive about sample size, which refers to the number of respondents in a survey rather than how these respondents are selected. If you believe that Ispos-Reid is correct in its sample sizes, it appears that the size of the sample has nothing to do with how representative that sample is of the population. Unfortunately, many managers falsely believe that sample size and sample representativeness are related, but they are not. Perhaps you were shocked to find that a sample of 500 is adequate for

Marketing managers are typically uninformed about the factors that determine proper sample size.

What size sample is large enough to represent India's one billion residents? Would you believe 500 is acceptable?

China with a population of 1.2 billion as well as for Sweden with its population of only 9 million. Do not be concerned as this only means that you are like most marketing managers.

Here is a way to convince yourself that there is no relationship between the size of a sample and its representativeness of the population from which it is drawn. Suppose we want to find out what percentage of the U.S. workforce dresses "business casual" most of the workweek. So we take a convenience sample by standing on a corner of Wall Street in New York City. We ask everyone who will talk to us about whether or not they dress business casual at work. At the end of one week, we have questioned over 5,000 respondents in our survey. Are these people representative of the U.S. workforce population? No, of course, they are not. In fact, conceivably they are not even representative of New York City workers because an uncontrolled nonprobability sampling method was used. What if we had asked 10,000 New Yorkers? No matter what its size, the sample would still be unrepresentative for the same reason.

> **The selection method—not the size of the sample—determines a sample's representativeness.**

Instead of determining representativeness, the size of the sample affects the sample accuracy of results. **Sample accuracy** refers to how close a random sample's statistic (for example, mean of the responses to a particular question) is to the true population's value it represents. Sample size will have a direct bearing on how accurate the sample's findings are relative to the true values in the population. If a random sample (any sample selected using a probability sampling method) of U.S. Social Security card holders had 5 respondents, it would be more accurate than if it had only 1; 10 respondents would be more accurate than 5, and so forth. Common sense tells us that larger random samples are more accurate than smaller random samples. But, as you will learn in this chapter, 5 is not 5 times more accurate than 1, and 10 is not twice as accurate as 5. The important points to remember at this time are that (1) sample size is not related to representativeness, but (2) sample size is related to accuracy. Precisely how accuracy is affected constitutes a major section of this chapter.

> **The accuracy of a sample is a measure of how closely it reports the true values of the population it represents.**

This chapter is concerned with sample size determination methods. To be sure, sample size determination can be a complicated process,[2,3,4] but we have tried to make it uncomplicated and intuitive. To begin, we share with you some axioms about sample size. These statements serve as the basis for the confidence interval approach, which is the best sample size determination method to use, so we describe its underlying notions of variability, allowable sample error, and level of confidence. These are combined into a simple formula to calculate sample size, and we give some examples of how the formula works. Next, we describe four other popular, but mostly incorrect, methods used to decide on a sample's size. Finally, there are practical considerations and special situations that affect the final sample size, and we briefly mention some of these.

SAMPLE SIZE AXIOMS

How to determine the number of respondents in a particular sample is actually one of the simplest decisions within the marketing research process.[5] However, because formulas are used, it often appears to be very bewildering. In reality, a sample size decision is usually a compromise between what is theoretically perfect and what is practically feasible. Although it is not the intent of this chapter to make you a sampling expert, it is important that you understand the fundamental concepts that underlie sample size decisions.[6]

There are two good reasons a marketing researcher should have a basic understanding of sample size determination. First, many practitioners have a **large sample size bias,** which is a false belief that sample size determines a sample's representativeness. These practitioners ask questions such as "How large a sample should we have to be representative?" However, as you just learned, there is no relationship between sample size and representativeness. So, you already know one of the basics of sample size determination. Second, a marketing manager should have a firm understanding of sample size determination because the size of the sample is often a major cost factor, particularly for personal interviews but even with telephone surveys. Consequently, understanding how sample size is determined will help the manager manage his or her resources better.

We wish to contradict the large sample size bias found in many marketing research clients with Table 13.1 which lists eight axioms about sample size and how this size relates to the accuracy of that sample. An axiom is a universal truth, meaning that the statement will always be correct. However, we must point out that these

> The size of a sample has nothing to do with its representativeness. Sample size affects the sample accuracy.

Table **13.1**	**The Axioms of Sample Size and Sample Accuracy**

1. The only perfectly accurate sample is a census.
2. A probability sample will always have some inaccuracy (sample error).
3. The larger a probability sample is, the more accurate it is (less sample error).
4. Probability sample accuracy (error) can be calculated with a simple formula, and expressed as a ± % number.
5. You can take any finding in the survey, replicate the survey with the same probability sample size, and you will be "very likely" to find the same finding within the ± range of the original finding.
6. In almost all cases, the accuracy (sample error) of a probability sample is independent of the size of the population.
7. A probability sample size can be a very tiny percentage of the population size and still be very accurate (have little sample error).
8. The size of a probability sample depends on the client's desired accuracy (acceptable sample error) balanced against the cost of data collection for that sample size.

Marketing managers are shocked when they learn that small samples are highly accurate.

axioms pertain only to probability samples, so they are true only as long as the sample in question is a random one. As we describe the confidence interval method of sample size determination, we will refer to each axiom in turn and help you understand it.

THE CONFIDENCE INTERVAL METHOD OF DETERMINING SAMPLE SIZE

The confidence interval approach is the correct method by which to determine sample size.

The most correct method of determining sample size is the **confidence interval approach,** which applies the concepts of accuracy (sample error), variability, and confidence interval to create a "correct" sample size. Because it is the theoretically most correct method, it is the one used by national opinion polling companies and most marketing researchers. To describe the confidence interval approach to sample size determination, we first describe its four underlying concepts.

Sample Size and Accuracy

The only perfectly accurate sample is a census.

The first axiom, "The only perfectly accurate sample is a census," is easy to understand. Accuracy is referred to as "sample error." You should be aware that a survey has two types of error: nonsampling error and sampling error. **Nonsampling error** pertains to all sources of error other than the sample selection method and sample size, so nonsampling error includes things such as problem specification mistakes, question bias, and incorrect analysis. **Sampling error** is the difference between the sample finding and the true population value due to the fact that a sample was taken. Because a census accounts for every single individual, it is completely accurate, meaning that it has no sample error whatsoever.

However, a census is almost always infeasible due to cost and for practical reasons. This fact brings us to the second axiom, "A probability sample will always have some inaccuracy (sample error)." This axiom notifies you that no random sample is a perfect representation of the population. However, it is important to remember that a random sample is nonetheless a *very good* representation of the population, even if it is not perfectly accurate.

The third axiom, "The larger a probability sample is, the more accurate it is (less sample error)," serves notice that there is a relationship between sample size and the accuracy of that sample. This relationship is presented graphically in Figure 13.1. In this figure, sample error (accuracy) is listed on the vertical axis and sample size is noted on the horizontal one. The graph shows the accuracy levels of samples ranging in size from 50 to 2,000. The shape of the graph is consistent with the third axiom, as the sample size increases as sample error decreases. However, you should immediately notice that the graph is not a straight line. In other words, doubling sample size does not result in halving the sample error. The relationship is a curved one. It looks a bit like a ski jump lying on its back.

> **The larger the size of the (probability) sample, the less is its sample error.**

There is another important property of the sample error graph. As you look at the graph, note that at a sample size of around 500, the accuracy level drops below ±5 percent (actually ±4.4%), and it decreases at a very slow rate with larger sample sizes. In other words, once a sample is greater than, say, 500, large gains in accuracy are not realized with large increases in the size of the sample. In fact, if it is already ±4.4 percent in accuracy, there is not much more accuracy possible.

With the lower end of the sample size axis, however, large gains in accuracy can be made with a relatively small sample size increase. For example, with a sample size of 50, the accuracy level is ±13.9 percent, whereas with a sample size of 250 it is ±6.2 percent, meaning the accuracy of the 250 sample is roughly double that of the 50 sample. But as was just described, such huge gains in accuracy are not the case at the other end of the sample size scale because of the nature of the curved relationship.

> **With a sample size of 1,000 or more, very little gain in accuracy occurs even with doubling or tripling the sample to 2,000 or 3,000.**

The sample error graph was produced via the fourth axiom, "Probability sample accuracy (error) can be calculated with a simple formula, and expressed as a ± percent number," and the formula follows:

Sample error formula $\pm$ Sample error % = 1.96 times $\sqrt{\dfrac{p * q}{n}}$

This formula is simple as "*n*" is the sample size, and there is a constant, 1.96. But what are *p* and *q*?

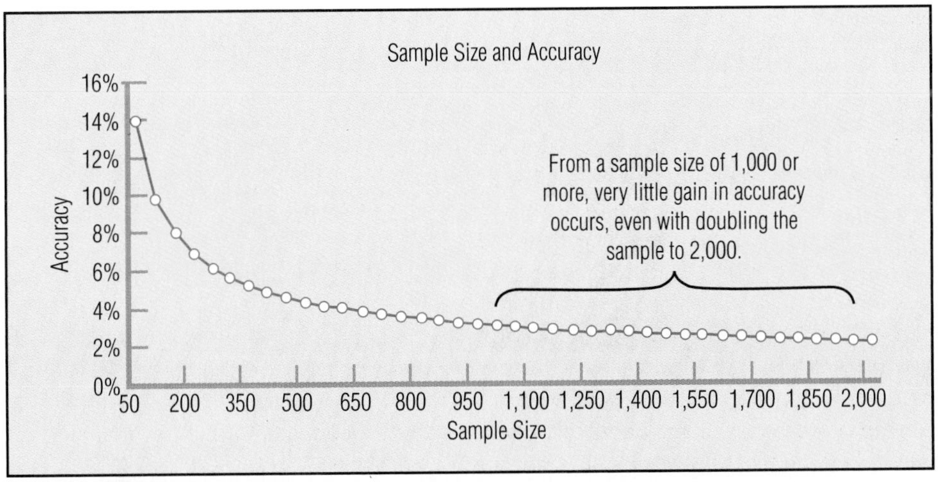

Figure 13.1   **The Relationship Between Sample Size and Sample Error**

p and *q*: The Notion of Variability

Variability refers to how similar or dissimilar responses are to a given question.

When we find a wide dispersion of responses—that is, when we do not find one response item accounting for a large number of respondents relative to the other items—we say that the results have much variability. **Variability** is defined as the amount of dissimilarity (or similarity) in respondents' answers to a particular question. If most respondents indicated the same answer on the response scale, the distribution would be indicative of little variability. On the other hand, if respondents were found to be evenly spread across the question's response options, there would be much variability.

Conceptualizing variability changes depending on the data used. With nominal data, or data in which the response items are categorical, the responses may be lopsided. The greater this lopsidedness, the less the variability in the responses. For example, we may find that the question "The next time you order a pizza, will you use Domino's?" yields a 90 to 10 percent distribution split between "yes" versus "no." In other words, most of the respondents gave the same answer, meaning that there is much similarity in the responses, and the variability would be low. In contrast, if the question had resulted in a 50 to 50 percent split, the overall response pattern would be (maximally) dissimilar, and there would be much variability. You can see the variability of responses in Figure 13.2. With the 90 to 10 percent split, the graph has one high side (90%) and one low side (10%), meaning almost everyone agreed on Domino's, or with disagreement or much variability in people's answers, it has both sides at even levels (50%–50%).

A 50–50 split in response signifies maximum variability (dissimilarity) in the population, whereas a 90–10 split signifies little variability.

The Domino's Pizza example relates to *p* and *q* in the following way:

p = percent

$q = 100\% - p$

In other words, *p* and *q* will always sum to 100 percent as in the cases of 90% + 10% and 50% + 50%.

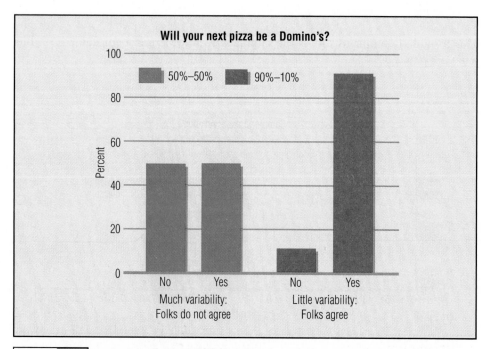

Will your next pizza be a Domino's?

50%–50%   90%–10%

No   Yes
Much variability:
Folks do not agree

No   Yes
Little variability:
Folks agree

Figure **13.2** **Graph of Variability 50/50–90/10**

The amount of variability is reflected in the spread of the distribution.

Sample size should be larger with more differences evident between population members.

In the sample error formula, *p* and *q* are multiplied together. The largest possible product of *p* times *q* is 2,500 or 50% times 50%. You can verify this fact by multiplying other combinations of *p* and *q* such as 90/10, 80/20, or 60/40. Every one will have a result smaller than 2,500, and, in fact, the most lopsided combination of 99/1 yields the smallest product. So, if we assume the worst possible case of maximum variability or 50/50 disagreement, the sample error formula becomes even simpler and can be given with two constants, 1.96 and 2,500 as follows:

Sample error formula with **p** *= 50% and* **q** *= 50%* $\pm \text{Sample error \%} = 1.96 \text{ times } \sqrt{\dfrac{2,500}{n}}$

This is the formula used to create the sample error graph in Figure 13.1. To determine how much sample error is associated with a random sample, all you need to do is to "plug in" the sample size in this fomula.

The Notion of a Confidence Interval

The fifth sample size axiom states, "You can take any finding in the survey, replicate the survey with the same probability sample size, and you will be very likely to find the same finding within the ± percent range of the original finding." This axiom is based on the idea of a "confidence interval."

A **confidence interval** is a range whose endpoints define a certain percentage of the responses to a question. Figure 13.3 reveals that the properties of the normal curve are such that 1.96 times the standard deviation theoretically defines the endpoints for 95 percent of the distribution.

A confidence interval defines endpoints based on knowledge of the area under a bell-shaped curve.

There is a theory called the **central limit theorem** that underlies many statistical concepts, and this theory is the basis of the sixth axiom. A replication is a repeat of the original, so if we repeated our Domino's survey a great many times—perhaps 1,000—with a fresh random sample of the same size, and we made a bar chart of all 1,000 percents of "yes" results, the central limit theorem holds that our bar chart would look like a normal curve. Figure 13.4 illustrates how the bar chart would look if 50 percent of our population members intended to use Domino's the next time they ordered a pizza.

Figure 13.4 reveals that 95 percent of the replications fall within ±1.96 times the sample error. In our example, 1,000 random samples, each with sample size (*n*) equal

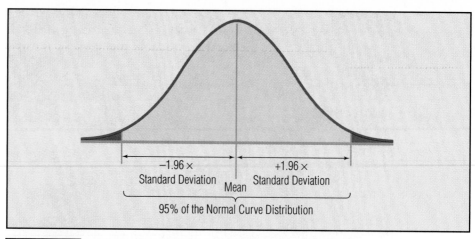

Figure **13.3** **A Normal Curve with Its 95% Properties Identified**

to 100, were taken and the percentage of "yes" answers was calculated for each sample and all of these were plotted as you see in Figure 13.4. The sample error for a sample size of 100 is calculated as follows:

$$\pm \text{Sample error \%} = 1.96 \text{ times } \sqrt{\frac{2,500}{n}}$$

Sample error formula with p = 50%, q = 50%, and n = 100

$$= 1.96 \text{ times } \sqrt{\frac{2,500}{100}}$$

$$= 1.96 \text{ times } \sqrt{25}$$

$$= 1.96 \text{ times } 5$$

$$= \pm 9.8\%$$

The confidence interval is calculated as follows:

Confidence interval formula   Confidence interval = $p \pm$ sample error

This means that the limits of the 95 percent confidence interval in our example is 50% ± 9.8%, or 40.2% to 59.8%.

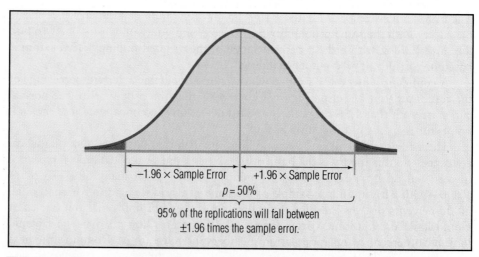

Figure **13.4** **Plotting the Findings of 1,000 Replications of the Domino's Pizza Survey: Central Limit Theorem Illustration**

How can a researcher use the confidence interval? This is a good time to leave the theoretical and move to the practical aspects of sample size. The confidence interval approach allows the researcher to predict what would be found if a survey were replicated many, many times. Of course, no client would agree to the cost of 1,000 replications, but the researcher can say, "I found that 50 percent of the sample intends to order Domino's the next time. I am very confident that the true population percentage is between 40.2 percent and 59.8 percent; in fact, I am confident that if I did this survey over 1,000 times, 95 percent of the findings will fall in this range."

What if the confidence interval was too wide? That is, what if the client felt that a range from about 40 percent to 60 percent was not precise enough? Figure 13.5 shows how the sample size affects the shape of the theoretical normal curve distribution and, more important, the confidence interval range.

> The confidence interval gives the range of findings if the survey were replicated many, many times with the identical sample size.

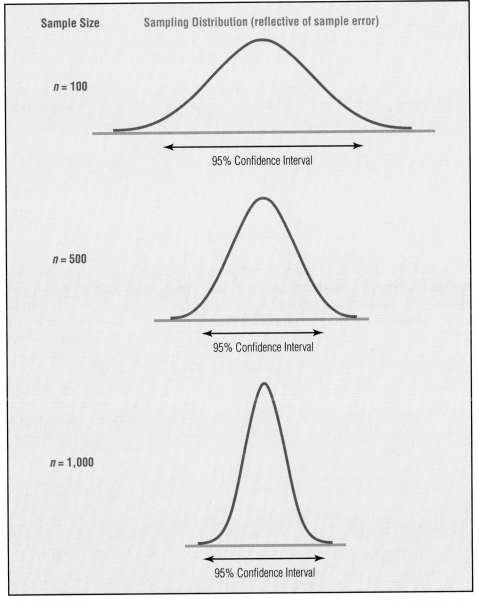

Figure **13.5** **Sampling Distributions Showing How the Sample Error Is Less with Larger Sample Sizes**

Perhaps you noticed something that is absent in all of these discussions and calculations, and that element is mentioned in the sixth sample size axiom, "In almost all cases, the accuracy (sample error) of a probability sample is independent of the size of the population." Our formulas do not include N, the size of the population! We have been calculating sample error and confidence intervals without taking the size of the population into account. Does this mean that a sample of 100 will have a sample error of ±5% (confidence interval of ±9.8%) for a population of 20 million people who watched the last Super Bowl, 2 million Kleenex tissue buyers, and 200,000 Scottish Terrier owners? Yes, it does. The only time that the population size is a consideration in sample size determination is in the case of a small population, and this possibility is discussed in the last section in this chapter.

Because the size of the sample is independent of the population size, the seventh sample size axiom, "A probability sample size can be a very tiny percentage of the population size and still be very accurate (have little sample error)," can now be understood. National opinion polls tend to use sample sizes ranging from 1,000 to 1,200 people, meaning that the sample error is around ±3 percent, or highly accurate. A sample size of 5,000 yields an error of ±1.4 percent, which is a very small error level, yet 5,000 is less than 1 percent of 1 million, and a great many consumer markets—cola drinkers, condominium owners, debit card users, allergy sufferers, home gardeners, Internet surfers, and so on—are each comprised of many millions of customers.

With few exceptions, the sample size and the size of the population are not related to each other.

THE SAMPLE SIZE FORMULA

You are now acquainted with the basic axioms essential to understanding sample size determination using the confidence interval approach. To calculate the proper sample size for a survey, only three factors need to be considered: (1) the amount of variability believed to be in the population, (2) the desired accuracy, and (3) the level of confidence required in your estimates of the population values. This section will describe the formula used to compute sample size via the **confidence interval method**. As we describe the formula, we will present some of the concepts you learned earlier a bit more formally.

To compute sample size, only three factors need to be considered: variability, accuracy, and confidence level.

A researcher can calculate sample size using either a percentage or a mean. We describe the percentage approach here, and we show you how to determine sample size using a mean in Marketing Research Insight 13.1. Although the formulas are different, the basic concepts involved are identical.

Determining Sample Size via the Confidence Interval Formula

As you would expect, there is a formula that includes our three considerations. When estimating a percentage, the formula is as follows:

Standard sample size formula for a mean
$$n = \frac{z^2(pq)}{e^2}$$

where

n = the sample size

z = standard error associated with the chosen level of confidence (1.96)

p = estimated percent in the population

$q = 100 - p$

e = acceptable sample error

► **Additional Insights**

Determining Sample Size Estimating a Mean

On occasion, a market researcher finds he or she is working with metric scale data, not nominal data. For instance, the researcher might have a 10-point importance scale or a 7-point satisfaction scale that is the critical variable with respect to determining sample size. Estimating a mean calls for changes in the sample size formula, the logic of sample size determination is the same as it is in the instance of a percentage.

First, this situation calls for the use of the standard deviation to indicate the amount of variation. In this case, the sample size formula changes slightly to be the following:

Sample size formula for a mean $n = \dfrac{s^2 z^2}{e^2}$

where

n = the sample size

z = standard error associated with the chosen level of confidence (1.96)

s = variability indicated by an estimated standard deviation

e = the amount of precision or allowable error in the sample estimate of the population

Although this formula looks different from the one for a percentage, it applies the same logic and key concepts in an identical manner. As you can see, the formula determines sample size by multiplying the squares of the variability (s) and level of confidence values (z) and dividing that product by the square of the desired precision value (e). First, let us

look at how variability of the population is a part of the formula. It appears in the form of s, or the estimated standard deviation of the population. This means that, because we are going to estimate the population mean, we need to have some knowledge of or at least a good guess at how much variability there is in the population. We must use the standard deviation because it expresses this variation. But unlike our percentage sample size case, there is no "50 percent equals the most variation" counterpart, so we have to rely on some prior knowledge about the population for our estimate of the standard deviation.

Next, we must express e, which is the acceptable error around the sample mean when we ultimately estimate the population mean from our survey. If information on the population variability is truly unknown and a pilot study is out of the question, a researcher can use a range estimate and knowledge that the range is approximated by the mean ±3 standard deviations. Suppose, for example, that a critical question on the survey involved a scale in which respondents rated their satisfaction with the client company's products on a scale of 1 to 10. If respondents use this scale, the theoretical range would be 10, and 10 divided by 6 equals a standard deviation of 1.7, which would be the variability estimate. Note that this would be a conservative estimate as respondents might not use the entire 1–10 scale, or the mean might not equal 5, the midpoint, meaning that 1.7 is the largest variability estimate possible in this case.[7]

Variability: *p* Times *q* This formula is used if we are focusing on some nominally scaled question in the survey. For instance, when conducting the Domino's Pizza survey, our major concern might be the percentage of pizza buyers who intend to buy Domino's. If no one is uncertain, there are two possible answers: those who do and those who do not. Earlier, we illustrated that if our pizza buyers population has very little variability, that is, if almost everyone, say, 90 percent, is a raving Domino's Pizza fan, this belief will be reflected in the sample size. With little variation in the population, we know that we can take smaller samples because this is accommodated by the formula by *p* times *q*. The estimated percentage in the population, *p*, is the mechanism that performs this translation along with *q*, which is always determined by *p* as $q = 100\% - p$.

Desired Accuracy: *e* The formula includes another factor—acceptable sample error. We hope you are not surprised at this factor, as we developed it in the previous section that explained many of the sample size axioms. **Acceptable error** is, in fact, the very same concept that was introduced to you earlier. That is, the term, *e*, is the amount of sample error that will be associated with the survey. It is used to indicate how close your sample percentage finding will be to the true population percentage if you were to report the study many, many times.

The standard sample size formula is applicable if you are concerned with the nominally scaled questions in the survey such as "yes or no" questions.

That is, if we performed any survey with a *p* value that was to be estimated—who intends to buy from Wal-Mart, IBM, Shell, AllState, or any other vendor versus any other vendor—the acceptable sample error notion would hold. High accuracy (small sample error) translates into a small percentage, such as ±4 percent or less, whereas low accuracy (high sample error) translates into a large percentage, such as ±10 percent or higher.

Level of Confidence: z Last, we need to decide on a level of confidence or, to relate to our previous section, the percentage of area under the normal curve described by our calculated confidence intervals. Thus far, we have used the constant, 1.96, because 1.96 is the *z* value that pertains to 95 percent confidence intervals. Researchers typically only worry about the 95 percent or 99 percent level of confidence. The 95 percent level of confidence is by far the most commonly used one, so we used 1.96 in the examples earlier and referred to it as a constant because it is the chosen *z* in most cases. Also, 1.96 rounds up to 2, which is convenient in case you do not have a calculator handy and you want to do a quick approximation of the sample size.

> In marketing research, a 95 percent or 99 percent level of confidence is standard practice.

Actually, any level of confidence ranging from 1 percent to 100 percent is possible, but you would need to consult a *z* table in order to find the corresponding value. Market researchers almost never deviate from 95 percent, but if they do, 99 percent is the likely level to be used. We have itemized the *z* values for the 99 percent and 95 percent levels of confidence in Table 13.2, so you can turn to it quickly if you need to.

We are now ready to calculate sample size. Let us assume there is great expected variability (50%) and we want ±10 percent accuracy at the 95 percent level of confidence. To determine the sample size needed, we calculate as follows:

Sample size computed with p = *50%,*
q = *50%, and* e = *10%*

$$n = \frac{1.96^2(50 \times 50)}{10^2}$$

$$= \frac{3.84(2,500)}{100}$$

$$= \frac{9,600}{100}$$

$$= 96$$

Just to convince you of the use of the confidence interval approach, recall our previous comment that most national opinion polls use sample sizes of about 1,100 and they claim ±3 percent accuracy. Using the 95 percent level of confidence, the computations would be:

Sample size computed with p = *50%,*
q = *50%, and* e = *3%*

$$n = \frac{1.96^2(50 \times 50)}{3^2}$$

$$= \frac{3.84(2,500)}{9}$$

$$= \frac{9,600}{9}$$

$$= 1,067$$

In other words, if these national polls were to be ±3 percent accurate at the 95 percent confidence level, they would need to have sample sizes of 1,067 (or about 1,100 respondents). The next time you read in the newspaper or see on television something about a national opinion poll, check the sample size and look to see if there is a footnote or reference on the "margin of error." It is a good bet that you will find the error to be somewhere close to ±3% and the sample size to be in the 1,100 range.

Table 13.2	Values of *z* for 95% and 99% Levels of Confidence

LEVEL OF CONFIDENCE	z
95%	1.96
99%	2.58

What if the researcher wanted a 99 percent level of confidence in his or her estimates? The computations would be as follows:

$$n = \frac{2.58^2(50 \times 50)}{3^2}$$

99% confidence interval
sample size computed with p = *50%,*
q = *50%, and* e = *3%*

$$= \frac{6.66(2,500)}{9}$$

$$= \frac{16,650}{9}$$

$$= 1,850$$

Thus, if a survey were to be ±3 percent accurate at the 99 percent level of confidence, it would need to have a sample size of 1,850, assuming the maximum variability (50%).

In all of our examples, we are, of course, calculating the final sample size, meaning that we must adjust for incidence rates and cooperation levels of prospective respondents. Read Marketing Research Insight 13.2 to see how Scientific Telephone Samples (STS) describes the typical way to calculate the number of telephone numbers you would need to effect a desired final sample size of completed interviews. After this, you can learn about the career of Steven Clark, Partner, STS.

▶ **An Online Application**

MARKETING RESEARCH
INSIGHT
13.2

How Many RDD Numbers Should You Buy
to Achieve Your Desired Final Sample Size?

As you have learned, random digit dialing (RDD) overcomes the unlisted number sample frame error that researchers encounter when they use standard telephone books as the sample frame. Scientific Telephone Samples (STS) is a company that specializes in supplying current telephone numbers for designated geographic areas. It provides the following advice on achieving a target sample size of 100 completions.[8]

The traditional industry approach is to multiply the expected "hit rate" (the percentage of a sample that will be working residential telephones) times the net effective incidence (NEI) times an expected cooperation rate (varies from 30% to 40% depending on the telephone bank). Then you must divide the resulting figure into 100 to arrive at an esti-

mate for how many numbers will be needed. Normally, it is assumed the hit rate from major sampling suppliers will range from 65 percent to 70 percent.

For instance, at a hit rate of 70 percent, a 60 percent incidence, and a 30 percent respondent cooperation rate, the calculations would look as follows:

▶ 70 (hit rate) × .60 (incidence) × .3 (coop rate) = 12.6
▶ 100 divided by 12.6 = 7.93 numbers needed per completion

So in this sample for a sample size of 100, you will need to order 793 numbers, 555 of which will be working numbers (hit rate).

MARKETING RESEARCH
INSIGHT
13.3

Meet Steve Clark of Scientific Telephone Samples
Steven C. Clark, Partner, Scientific Telephone Samples (STS)

Steve Clark is a partner and cofounder of Scientific Telephone Samples (STS), one of the leading providers of random digit dialing (RDD), listed, and business sampling for the marketing research industry. Steve has a B.S. from the University of Southern California with dual majors in business administration and entrepreneurship. In addition, he is an accomplished software developer, database administrator, and codeveloper of CATIHelp, a phone-bank management system. Steve has over 15 years of experience in marketing research.

PRACTICAL CONSIDERATIONS IN SAMPLE SIZE DETERMINATION

Although we have discussed how variability, desired sample error, and confidence level are used to calculate sample size, we have not discussed the criteria used by the marketing manager and researcher to determine these factors. General guidelines follow.

How to Estimate Variability in the Population

Two alternatives are: (1) expect the worst case or (2) estimate what the actual variability is. We have shown you that with percentages, the **worst case**, or most, **variability** is 50 percent/50 percent. This assumption is the most conservative one, and it will result in the calculation of the largest possible sample size.

On the other hand, a researcher may want to estimate p, or the percentage, in order to lower the sample size. Remember that any p/q combination other than 50 percent/50 percent will result in a lower calculated sample size. A lower sample size means less effort, time, and cost, so there are good reasons for a researcher to try to estimate p.

Surprisingly, information about the target population often exists in many forms. There are census tract descriptions available in the form of secondary data, and there are compilations and bits of information that may be gained from groups such as chambers of commerce, local newspapers, state agencies, groups promoting commercial development, and a host of other similar organizations. Moreover,

If p is estimated to be more or less than 50 percent, the researcher can reduce the sample size and save money.

To estimate variability, you can use prior research, experience, or a pilot study.

many populations under study by firms are known to them either formally through prior research studies or informally through prior business experiences. All of this information combines to help the research project director to grasp the variability in the population. If the project director has conflicting information or is worried about the timeliness or some other aspect of the information about the population's variability, he or she may conduct a pilot study in order to estimate p more confidently.[9,10]

How to Determine the Amount of Desired Sample Error

By now, you know that sample findings are nothing more than estimates of population values. The act of estimating incurs a certain degree of error because an estimate will not be precisely the population value; however, it will be close to the population value. From our descriptions in this chapter, you should know that the size of the sample has a direct bearing on the sample error, and this error translates into the accuracy of the sample statistic value.

The marketing manager knows that small samples are less accurate, on the average, than are large samples. But it is rare for a marketing manager to think in terms of sample error. Thus, it is almost always up to the researcher to educate the manager on what might be acceptable or "standard" sample error.

Translated in terms of precision, the more precise the marketing decision maker desires the estimate to be, the larger must be the sample size. Thus, it is the task of the marketing research director to extract from the marketing decision maker the acceptable range of allowable error sufficient for him or her to make a decision. As you have learned, the acceptable sample error is specified as a plus or minus percentage. That is, the researcher might say to the marketing decision maker, "I can deliver an estimate that is within ±10 percent of the actual figure." If the marketing manager is confused at this, the researcher can next say, "This means that if I find that 45 percent of the sample is thinking seriously about leaving your competitors and buying your brand, I will be telling you that between 35 percent and 55 percent of your competitors' buyers are thinking about jumping over to be your customers." The conversation would continue until the marketing manager, working with the researcher, sets the amount of sample error.

Marketing researchers often must help decision makers understand the sample size implications of their requests for high precision, expressed as allowable error.

How to Decide on the Level of Confidence Desired

All marketing decisions are made under a certain amount of risk, and it is mandatory to incorporate the estimate of risk, or at least some sort of a notion of uncertainty, into sample size determination. Because sample statistics are estimates of population values, the proper approach is to use the sample information to generate a range in which the population value is anticipated to fall. Because the sampling process is imperfect, it is appropriate to use an estimate of sampling error in the calculation of this range. Using proper statistical terminology, the range is what we have called the confidence interval. The researcher reports the range and the confidence he or she has that the range includes the population figure.

As we have indicated, the typical approach in marketing research is to use the standard confidence interval of 95 percent. As we have also indicated, this level translates into a z of 1.96. As you may recall from your statistics course, any level of confidence between 1 percent and 99.9 percent is possible, but marketing researchers primarily use 95 or 99 percent level of confidence. With the 99 percent level of confidence, the corresponding z value is 2.58. The 99 percent level of confidence means that if the survey were replicated many, many times with the sample size determined by using 2.58 in the sample size formula, 99 percent of the sample p's would fall in the sample error range.

Use of 95 percent or 99 percent level of confidence is standard in sample size determination.

However, because the z value is in the numerator of the sample size formula, an increase from 1.96 to 2.58 will increase the sample size. In fact, for any given sample error, the use of a 99 percent level of confidence will increase the sample size by about 73 percent. So, using the 99 percent confidence level has profound effects on the calculated sample size. Are you surprised that most marketing researchers opt for a z of 1.96?

How to Balance Sample Size with the Cost of Data Collection

Perhaps you thought we had forgotten to comment on the last sample size axiom, "The size of a probability sample depends on the client's desired accuracy (acceptable sample error) balanced against the cost of data collection for that sample size." This is a very important axiom as it describes the reality of almost all sample size determination decisions. Hopefully, you will remember that in one of the very early chapters of this textbook, we commented on the cost of the research versus the value of the research, and that there was always a need to make sure that the cost of the research did not exceed the value of the information expected from that research.

The researcher must take cost into consideration when determining sample size.

Nowhere, it seems, do the cost and value issues come into play more vividly than with sample size determination and data collection cost considerations. You just learned that using the 99 percent level confidence impacts the sample size considerably, and you also learned that for this reason market researchers almost always use the 95 percent level of confidence.

In order to help you understand how to balance sample size and cost, let's consider the typical sample size determination case. First, 95 percent level of confidence is used, so $z = 1.96$. Next, the $p = q = 50\%$ situation is customarily assumed as it is the worst possible case of variability. Then the researcher and marketing manager decide on a *preliminary* acceptable sample error level. As an example, a researcher works with a client who owns a large water park who is thinking about adding a water toboggan run. The client wants to know if her water park will become more popular as a family fun spot with the water toboggan run. The researcher and water park owner initially agree to a ±3.5 percent sample error.

Using the sample size formula, the sample size, n, is calculated as follows:

Sample size computed with $p = 50\%$, $\dot{q} = 50\%$, *and* $e = 3.5\%$

$$n = \frac{1.96^2(50 \times 50)}{3.5^2}$$
$$= \frac{3.84(2,500)}{12.25}$$
$$= \frac{9,600}{12.25}$$
$$= 784 \ (rounded \ up)$$

What must happen next involves a dialogue between the researcher and the manager. You will find this conversation in Marketing Research Insight 13.4.

OTHER METHODS OF SAMPLE SIZE DETERMINATION

In practice, a number of different methods are used to determine sample size. The more common methods are described briefly in this section. As you will soon learn, most have critical flaws that make them undesirable, even though you may find instances in which they are used and proponents who argue for their use. Plus, there are other correct methods that are beyond the scope of this textbook.[11] Since you are acquainted with the eight sample size axioms, and you know how to calculate

▶ **Additional Insights**

How the Cost of the Sample Figures into Sample Size

Larry, our researcher has worked with Dana, the water park owner, to develop the research objectives and basic research design for a survey to see if there is sufficient interest in a water toboggan run ride. Yesterday, Dana indicated that she wanted to have an accuracy level of ±3.5 percent because this was "just a little less accurate than your typical national opinion poll."

Larry has done some calculations and created a table that he faxes to Dana. The table looks like this.

**Water Toboggan Run Survey
Schedule of Sample Error and Sample Data
Collection Cost**

SAMPLE ERROR	SAMPLE SIZE	SAMPLE COST*
±3.5%	784	$15,680
±4.0%	600	$12,000
±4.5%	474	$9,480
±5.0%	384	$7,680
±5.5%	317	$6,340
±6.0%	267	$5,340

*Estimated at $20 per completed interview

The following telephone conversation then takes place.

Larry: "Did the fax come through okay?"

Dana: "Yes, but maybe I wish it didn't."

Larry: "What do you mean?"

Dana: "There is no way I am going to pay over $15,000 just for the data collection."

Larry: "Yes, I figured this when we talked yesterday, but we were thinking about the accuracy of a national opinion poll then, and we are talking about your water park survey now. So, I prepared a schedule with some alternative accuracy levels, the sample sizes, and their costs."

Dana: "Gee, can you really get an accuracy level of ±6 percent with just 267 respondents? That seems like a very small sample."

Larry: "Small in numbers, but it is still somewhat hefty in price as the data collection company will charge $20 per completed telephone interview. You can see that it will still amount to over $5,000."

Dana: "Well, that's nowhere near $15,000! What about the 384 size? It will come to $7,680 according to your table, and the accuracy is ±5 percent. How does the accuracy thing work again?"

Larry: "If I find that, say, 70 percent of the respondents in the survey want the water toboggan ride at your water park, then you can be assured that between 65 to 75 percent of all of your customers want it."

Dana: "And with $7,680 for data collection, the whole survey comes in under $15,000?"

Larry: "I am sure it will. If you want me to, I can calculate a firm total cost using the 384 sample size."

Dana: "Sounds like a winner to me. When can you get it to me?"

Larry: "I'll have the proposal completed by Friday. You can study it over the weekend."

Dana: "Great. I'll set up a tentative meeting with the investors for the middle of next week."

---

sample size using the confidence interval method formula, you should comprehend the flaws as we point each one out.

A table that relates data collection cost and sample error is a useful tool when deciding on the survey sample size.

Arbitrary "Percentage Rule of Thumb" Sample Size

The **arbitrary approach** may take on the guise of a "percentage rule of thumb" statement regarding sample size: "A sample should be at least 5 percent of the population in order to be accurate." In fact, it is not unusual for a marketing manager to respond to a marketing researcher's sample size recommendation by saying, "But that is less than 1 percent of the entire population!"

You must agree that the arbitrary percentage rule of thumb approach certainly has some intuitive appeal in that it is very easy to remember, and it is simple to apply. Surely, you will not fall into the seductive trap of the percentage rule of thumb, for you understand that sample size is not related to population size at all. Just to convince yourself, consider these sample sizes. If you take 5 percent samples

Arbitrary sample size approaches rely on erroneous rules of thumb.

of populations with sizes 10,000, 1,000,000, and 10,000,000, the *n*'s will be 500, 50,000, and 500,000, respectively. Now, think back to the sample accuracy graph in Figure 13.1. The highest sample size on that graph was 2,000, so obviously the percentage rule of thumb method can yield sample sizes that are absurd with respect to accuracy. Furthermore, you have also learned from the sample size axioms that a sample can be a very, very small percentage of the total population and have very great accuracy.

In sum, arbitrary sample sizes are simple and easy to apply, but they are neither efficient nor economical. With sampling, we wish to draw a subset of the population in an economical manner and to estimate the population values with some predetermined degree of accuracy. Percentage rule of thumb methods lose sight of the accuracy aspect of sampling; they certainly violate some of the axioms about sample size, and, as you just saw, they certainly are not economical when the population under study is large.

Arbitrary sample sizes are simple and easy to apply, but they are neither efficient nor economical.

Conventional Sample Size Specification

The **conventional approach** follows some "convention" or number believed somehow to be the right sample size. A manager may be knowledgeable about national opinion polls and notice that they are often taken with sample sizes of between 1,000 and 1,200 respondents. This may appear to the manager as a "conventional" number, and he or she may question a market researcher whose sample size recommendation varies from this convention. On the other hand, the survey may be one in a series of studies a company has undertaken on a particular market, and the same sample size may be applied each succeeding year simply because it was used last year. The convention might be an average of the sample sizes of similar studies, it might be the largest sample size of previous surveys, or it might be equal to the sample size of a competitor's survey that the company somehow discovered.

Using conventional sample size can result in a sample that may be too small or too large.

The basic difference between a percentage rule of thumb and a conventional sample size determination is that the first approach has no defensible logic, whereas the conventional approach appears logical. However, the logic is faulty. We just illustrated how a percentage rule of thumb approach such as a 5 percent rule of thumb explodes into huge sample sizes very quickly; however, the national opinion poll convention of 1,200 respondents would be constant regardless of the population size. Still, this characteristic is one of the conventional sample size determination method's weaknesses, for it assumes that the manager wants an accuracy of around ±3% and it assumes that there is maximum variability in the population.

Adopting past sample sizes or taking those used by other companies can be criticized as well, for both approaches assume that whoever determined sample size in the previous studies did so correctly (that is, not with a flawed method). If a flawed method was used, you simply perpetuate the error by copying it, and if the sample size method used was not flawed, the circumstances and assumptions surrounding the predecessor's survey may be very different from those encompassing the present one. Thus, the conventional sample size approach ignores the circumstances surrounding the study at hand and may well prove to be much more costly than would be the case if the sample size were determined correctly.

Conventional sample sizes ignore the special circumstances of the survey at hand.

Statistical Analysis Requirements of Sample Size Specification

On occasion, a sample's size will be determined using a **statistical analysis approach** because there is some overriding statistical analysis consideration. We have not discussed statistical procedures as yet in this text, but we can assure you that some advanced techniques require certain minimum sample sizes in order to be reliable or

▶ **Additional Insights**

Sample Sizes Used by the American Heart Association

MARKETING RESEARCH
INSIGHT
13.5

The following quote was provided for use in this textbook by Allison Groom, marketing research consultant at the American Heart Association in Dallas, Texas.[12]

> The AHA determines the sample size for each research study based on the business decisions to be made. For instance, if the study is to be projected to the entire U.S. population, a sample size of at least 1,000 is typically used. The sample size is also driven by the degree of analysis needed, ensuring that at least 100 respondents are included in each cell for comparison purposes. Often certain ethnic groups such as Hispanics and African Americans are oversampled in order to ensure their representativeness.

to safeguard the validity of their statistical results.[13] Sample sizes based on statistical analysis criteria can be quite large.[14]

Statistical analysis is used to analyze subgroups within a sample. Many marketing research projects are undertaken to gain a sensitivity for segments of people within a population. We have included Marketing Research Insight 13.5, which is a quote from a marketing research consultant who works with the American Heart Association to illustrate how conventional sample size and subgroup sample size requirements are central in determining the final sample sizes of its surveys.

Even the least powerful personal computer allows for extensive "subgroup analysis,"[15] which is nothing more than a reasonably thorough investigation of subsegments within the population such as the American Heart Association example. As you would expect, the desire to gain knowledge about subgroups has direct implications for sample size. It should be possible to look at each subgroup as a separate population and to determine sample size for each subgroup, along with the appropriate methodology and other specifics to gain knowledge about that subgroup. Once this is accomplished, all of the subgroups can be combined into a large group in order to obtain a complete population picture.

Sometimes the researcher's desire to use particular statistical techniques influences sample size.

A "cookie cutter" approach should not be used to determine sample size. Sample size should be calculated for each study undertaken.

Cost Basis of Sample Size Specification

Sometimes termed the **"all you can afford" approach**, this method uses cost as a basis for sample size. As you learned with our presentation of the eighth sample size axiom, managers and marketing research professionals are vitally concerned with survey costs. If there were no sampling costs of marketing research, everything could be accomplished with a census, and there would be no concern about sample accuracy. Unfortunately, costs are very relevant, and the costs of data collection, particularly for personal interviews, telephone surveys, and even for mail surveys in which incentives are included in the envelopes mailed out, can mount quickly. So it is not surprising that cost sometimes becomes the basis for sample size.

Exactly how the "all you can afford" approach is applied varies a great deal. In some instances, the marketing research project budget is determined in advance, and set amounts are specified for each phase. Here the budget may have, for instance, $10,000 for interviewing, or it might specify $5,000 for data collection. A variation is for the entire year's marketing research budget amount to be set and to have each project carve out a slice of that total. With this approach, the marketing research project director is forced to stay within the total project budget, but he or she can allocate the money across the various cost elements, and the sample size ends up being whatever is affordable within the budget.

Using cost as the sole determinant of sample size may seem wise, but it is not.

But using the "all you can afford" sample size specification is a case of the tail wagging the dog. That is, instead of the value of the information to be gained from the survey being a primary consideration in the sample size, the sample size is determined by budget factors that usually ignore the value of the survey's results to management. Alternatively, because many managers harbor a large sample size bias, it is possible that their marketing research project costs are overstated for data collection when smaller sample sizes could have sufficed quite well. As can be seen in Marketing Research Insight 13.6 unscrupulous market researchers can use this bias selfishly. However, we cannot ignore cost altogether.

Still, you know from the last sample size axiom that you cannot decide on sample size without taking cost into consideration. The key is to remember *when* to

---

consider cost. In the "all you can afford" approach examples we just described, cost drives the sample size completely. When we have $5,000 for interviewing and a data collection company tells us that it charges $25 per completed interview, our sample is set at 200 respondents. The correct approach is to consider cost relative to the value of the research to the manager. If the manager requires extremely precise information, the researcher will surely suggest a large sample and then estimate the cost of obtaining the sample. The manager, in turn, should then consider this cost in relation to how much the information is actually worth. Using the cost schedule concept, the researcher and manager can then discuss alternative sample sizes, different data collection modes, costs, and other considerations. This is a healthier situation, for now the manager is assuming some ownership of the survey and a partnership arrangement is being forged between the manager and the researcher. The net result will be a better understanding on the part of the manager as to how and why the final sample size was determined. This way cost will not be the only means of determining sample size, but it will be given the consideration it deserves.

The appropriateness of using cost as a basis for sample size depends on when cost factors are considered.

SPECIAL SAMPLE SIZE DETERMINATION SITUATIONS

The final section of this chapter takes up two special cases: sample size when sampling from small populations and sample size when using a nonprobability sampling method.

Sampling from Small Populations

Implicit to all sample size discussions thus far in this chapter is the assumption that the population is very large. This assumption is reasonable because there are multitudes of households in the United States, millions of registered drivers, hundreds of thousands of persons over the age of 65, and so forth. So it is common, especially with consumer goods marketers, to draw samples from very large populations. Occasionally, however, the population is much smaller, and this is not unusual in the case of industrial marketers. This case is addressed by the condition stipulated in our sixth sample size axiom, "In almost all cases, the accuracy (sample error) of a probability sample is independent of the size of the population."

As a general rule, a **small population** situation is one in which the sample exceeds 5 percent of the total population size. Notice that a small sample is defined by the size of the population under consideration. If the sample is less than 5 percent of the total population, you can consider the population to be of large size, and you can use the procedures described earlier in this chapter. On the other hand, if it is a small population, the sample size formula needs some adjustment with what is called a **finite multiplier**, which is an adjustment factor that is approximately equal to the square root of that proportion of the population not included in the sample. For instance, suppose our population size was considered to be 1,000 companies, and we decided to take a sample of 500. That would result in a finite multiplier of about 0.71, or the square root of 0.5, which is ((1,000 − 500)/1,000). That is, we could use a sample of only 355 (or .71 times 500) companies, and it would be just as accurate as one of size 500 if we had a large population.

With small populations, you should use the finite multiplier to determine sample size.

The formula for computation of a sample size using the finite multiplier is as follows:

Small population Small population
sample size formula sample size = sample size formula $\times \sqrt{\dfrac{N-n}{N-1}}$

Here is an example using the 1,000 company population. Let us suppose we want to know the percentage of companies that are interested in a substance abuse counseling program for their employees offered by a local hospital. We are uncertain about the variability, so we use our 50–50 "worst case" approach. We decide to use a 95 percent level of confidence, and the director of counseling services at Claremont Hospital would like the results to be accurate ±5 percent. The computations are as follows:

Sample size computed with p = 50%, q = 50%, *and* e = 5%

$$n = \frac{1.96^2(pq)}{e^2}$$

$$= \frac{1.96^2(50 \times 50)}{5^2}$$

$$= \frac{3.84(2,500)}{25}$$

$$= \frac{9,600}{25}$$

$$= 384$$

Now, applying the finite multiplier to adjust the sample size for a small population,

Small size population sample
$$= n \sqrt{\frac{N - n}{N - 1}}$$

Example:
Sample size formula to adjust for a small population size

$$= 384 \sqrt{\frac{1,000 - 384}{1,000 - 1}}$$

$$= 384 \sqrt{\frac{616}{999}}$$

$$= 384 \sqrt{.62}$$

$$= 384 \times .79$$

$$= 303$$

Appropriate use of the finite multiplier formula will reduce a calculated sample size and save money when performing research on small populations.

In other words, we need a sample size of 303, not 384, because we are working with a small population. By applying the finite multiplier, we can reduce the sample size by 81 respondents and achieve the same accuracy level. If this survey required personal interviews, we would gain a considerable cost savings.

Sample Size Using Nonprobability Sampling

All sample size formulas and other statistical considerations treated in this chapter assume that some form of probability sampling method has been used. In other words, the sample must be unbiased with regard to selection, and the only sampling error present is due to sample size. Remember, sample size determines the accuracy, not the representativeness, of the sample. The sampling method determines the representativeness. All sample size formulas assume that representativeness is guaranteed with use of a probability sampling procedure.

When using nonprobability sampling, sample size is unrelated to accuracy, so cost–benefit considerations must be used.

The only reasonable way of determining sample size with nonprobability sampling is to weigh the benefit or value of the information obtained with that sample against the cost of gathering that information. Ultimately, this is a very subjective exercise, as the manager may place significant value on the information for a number or reasons. For instance, the information may crystallize the problem, it may open the manager's eyes to vital additional considerations, or it might even make him or her aware of previously unknown market segments. But because of the unknown bias introduced by a haphazard sample selection[16] process, it is inappropriate to apply sample size formulas. For nonprobability sampling, sample size is a judgment based almost exclusively on the value of the information to the manager, rather than desired precision, relative to cost.

SUMMARY

SPSS Student Assistant Online

Noxzema Skin Cream:

Selecting Cases

We began this chapter by notifying you of the large sample size bias that many managers hold. To counter this myth, we listed 8 sample size axioms that relate the size of a random sample to its accuracy or closeness of its findings to the true population value. These axioms were used to describe the confidence interval sample size determination method, which is the most correct method because it relies on statistical concepts of variability, confidence intervals, and sample error. From the descriptions of these concepts, we moved to the standard sample size formula used by market researchers. This formula uses variability (p and q), level of confidence (z), and sample error (e) to compute the sample size, n. We indicated that for confidence level, typically 95 percent or 99 percent levels are applied. These equate to z values of 1.96 and 2.58, respectively. For variability with percentage estimates, the researcher can fall back on a 50 percent/50 percent split, which is the greatest variability possible. The standard sample size formula is best considered a starting point for deciding the final sample size, for data collection costs must be taken into consideration. Normally, the researcher and manager will discuss the alternative sample error levels and their associated data collection costs to come to agreement on an acceptable sample size.

Although most are flawed, there are other methods of determining sample size: (1) designating size arbitrarily, (2) using a conventional size, (3) basing size on the requirements of statistical procedures to be used, and (4) letting cost determine the size. Finally, the chapter discussed two special sampling situations. With a small population, the finite multiplier should be used to adjust the sample size determination formula. Last, with nonprobability sampling, a cost–benefits analysis should take place.

KEY TERMS

Sample accuracy (p. 372)
Large sample size bias (p. 373)
Confidence interval approach (p. 374)
Nonsampling error (p. 374)
Sampling error (p. 374)
Variability (p. 376)
Confidence interval (p. 377)
Central limit theorem (p. 377)
Confidence interval method (p. 380)

Acceptable error (p. 381)
Worst-case variability (p. 384)
Arbitrary approach (p. 387)
Conventional approach (p. 388)
Statistical analysis approach (p. 388)
"All you can afford" approach
  (p. 390)
Small population (p. 391)
Finite multiplier (p. 391)

REVIEW QUESTIONS/APPLICATIONS

1. Describe each of the following methods of sample size determination and indicate a critical flaw in the use of each one.
   a. Using a "rule of thumb" percentage of the population size.
   b. Using a "conventional" sample size such as the typical size pollsters use.
   c. Using the amount in the budget allocated for data collection to determine sample size.
2. Describe and provide illustrations of each of the following notions: (a) variability, (b) confidence interval, and (c) sample error.

3. What are the three fundamental considerations involved with the confidence interval approach to sample size determination?

4. When calculating sample size, how can a researcher decide on the level of accuracy to use? What about level of confidence? What about variability with a percentage?

5. Using the formula provided in your text, determine the approximate sample sizes for each of the following cases, all with precision (allowable error) of ±5 percent:
   a. Variability of 30 percent, confidence level of 95 percent.
   b. Variability of 60 percent, confidence level of 99 percent.
   c. Unknown variability, confidence level of 95 percent.

6. Indicate how a pilot study can help a researcher understand variability in the population.

7. Why is it important for the researcher and the marketing manager to discuss the accuracy level associated with the research project at hand?

8. What are the benefits to be gained by knowing that a proposed sample is more than 5 percent of the total population's size? In what marketing situation might this be a common occurrence?

9. A researcher knows from experience the average costs of various data collection alternatives:

DATA COLLECTION METHOD	COST/RESPONDENT
Personal interview	$50
Telephone interview	$25
Mail survey	$ 0.50 (per mailing)

If $2,500 is allocated in the research budget for data collection, what are the levels of accuracy for the sample sizes allowable for each data collection method? Based on your findings, comment on the inappropriateness of using cost as the only means of determining sample size.

10. Last year, Lipton Tea Company conducted a mall-intercept study at six regional malls around the country and found that 20 percent of the public preferred tea over coffee as a midafternoon hot drink. This year, Lipton wants to have a nationwide telephone survey performed with random digit dialing. What sample size should be used in this year's study in order to achieve an accuracy level of ±2.5 percent at the 99 percent level of confidence? What about at the 95 percent level of confidence?

11. Allbookstores.com has a used textbook division. It buys its books in bulk from used book buyers who set up kiosks on college campuses during final exams, and it sells the used textbooks to students who log on to the allbookstores.com Web site via a secured credit card transaction. The used texts are then sent by United Parcel Service to the student.

   The company has conducted a survey of used book buying by college students each year for the past four years. In each survey, 1,000 randomly selected college students have been asked to indicate whether or not they bought a used textbook in the previous year. The results are as follows:

	YEARS AGO			
	1	2	3	4
Percentage buying used text(s)	45%	50%	60%	70%

What are the sample size implications of these data?

12. American Ceramics, Inc. (ACI) has been developing a new form of ceramic that can stand high temperatures and sustained use. Because of its improved properties, the project development engineer in charge of this project thinks that the new ceramic will compete as a substitute for the ceramics currently used in spark plugs. She talks to ACI's market research director about conducting a survey of prospective buyers of the new ceramic material. During their phone conversation, the research director suggests a study using about 100 companies as a means of determining market demand. Later that day, the research director does some background using the *Thomas Register* as a source of names of companies manufacturing spark plugs. A total of 312 companies located in the continental United States are found in the *Register*. How should this finding impact the final sample size of the survey?

13. Here are some numbers that you can use to sharpen your computational skills for sample size determination. Crest toothpaste is reviewing plans for its annual survey of toothpaste purchasers. With each case that follows, calculate the sample size pertaining to the key variable under consideration. Where information is missing, provide reasonable assumptions.

CASE	KEY VARIABLE	VARIABILITY	ACCEPTABLE ERROR	CONFIDENCE LEVEL
1	Market share of Crest toothpaste last year	23% share	4%	95%
2	Percentage of people who brush their teeth per week	Unknown	5%	99%
3	How likely Crest buyers are to switch brands	30% switched last year	5%	95%
4	Percentage of people who want tartar-control features in their toothpaste	20% two years ago; 40% one year ago	3.5%	95%
5	Willingness of people to adopt the toothpaste brand recommended by their family dentist	Unknown	6%	99%

14. Do managers really have a large sample size bias? Because you cannot survey managers easily, this exercise will use surrogates. Ask any five seniors majoring in business administration who have not taken a marketing research class the following questions. Indicate whether each of the following statements is true or false.
    a. A random sample of 500 is large enough to represent all of the full-time college students in the United States.
    b. A random sample of 1,000 is large enough to represent all of the full-time college students in the United States.
    c. A random sample of 2,000 is large enough to represent all of the full-time college students in the United States.
    d. A random sample of 5,000 is large enough to represent all of the full-time college students in the United States.
    What have you found out about sample size bias?

15. The Andrew Jergens Company markets a "spa tablet" called ActiBath, which is a carbonated moisturizing treatment for use in a bath. From previous research, Jergens management knows that 60 percent of all women use some form of skin moisturizer and 30 percent believe their skin is their most beautiful asset.

There is some concern among management that women will associate the drying aspects of taking a bath with ActiBath and not believe that it can provide a skin moisturizing benefit. Can these facts about use of moisturizers and concern for skin beauty be used in determining the size of the sample in the ActiBath survey? If so, indicate how. If not, indicate why and how sample size can be determined.

16. Donald Heel is the microwave oven division manager of Sharp Products. Don proposes a $40 cash rebate program as a means of promoting Sharp's new crisp-broil-and-grill microwave oven. However, the Sharp president wants evidence that the program would increase sales by at least 25 percent, so Don applies some of his research budget to a survey. He uses the National Phone Systems Company to conduct a nationwide survey using random digit dialing. National Phone Systems is a fully integrated telephone polling company, and it has the capability of providing daily tabulations. Don decides to use this option, and instead of specifying a final sample size, he chooses to have National Phone Systems perform 50 completions each day. At the end of five days of fieldwork, the daily results are as follows:

	Day				
	1	2	3	4	5
Total sample size	50	100	150	200	250
Percentage of respondents who would consider buying a Sharp microwave with a $40 rebate	50%	40%	35%	30%	33%

For how much longer should Don continue the survey? Indicate your rationale.

INTERACTIVE LEARNING

Visit the Web site at www.prenhall.com/burnsbush. For this chapter, work through the Self-Study Quizzes, and get instant feedback on whether you need additional studying. On the Web site, you can review the chapter outlines and case information for Chapter 13.

CASE 13.1   Peaceful Lake Subdivision

Located on the outskirts of a large city, the subdivision of Peaceful Lake comprises approximately 600 upscale homes. The subdivision came about 10 years ago when a developer built an earthen dam on Peaceful Brook and created Peaceful Lake, a meandering five-acre body of water. The lake became the centerpiece of the subdivision, and the first 100 one-half acre lots were sold as lakefront property. Now Peaceful Lake Subdivision is fully developed, and its residents are primarily young, professional, dual-income families with one or two school-age children.

Controversy has come to Peaceful Lake. The Subdivision Steering Committee has recommended that a subdivision swimming pool, tennis court, and meeting room facility be constructed on four adjoining vacant lots in the back of the subdivision. Cost estimates range from $250,000 to $500,000, depending on how large the facility will be. Currently, every Peaceful Lake Subdivision homeowner pays a voluntary $150 annual fee for maintenance, security, and upkeep of the subdivision. To construct the proposed recreational facility, each homeowner would be expected to pay a one-time fee of $500, and annual fees would increase by $100.

Objections to the recreational facility come from various quarters. For some, the one-time fee is unacceptable; for others, the notion of a recreational facility is not appealing. Some have their own swimming pools, belong to local tennis clubs, or otherwise have little use for a meeting room facility. Other Peaceful Lake Subdivision homeowners see the recreational facility as a wonderful addition where they could have their children learn to swim, play tennis, or just hang out under supervision.

The president of the Subdivision Association has decided to conduct a survey to poll the opinions and preferences of Peaceful Lake Subdivision homeowners regarding the swimming pool, tennis court, and meeting room facility concept.

1. If the steering committee agrees to a survey that is accurate to ±5 percent and at a 95 percent level of confidence, what sample size should be used?
2. Should the survey be a sample or a census of Peaceful Lake Subdivision homeowners? Defend your choice. Be certain to discuss any practical considerations that enter into your choice.

CASE 13.2 The Cobalt Group: Online Survey for My Car Tools, Part II

The background for this case is found as Case 12.2 on page 368.

A decision is made to use a pop-up invitation that will appear randomly on every automobile dealership Web site over the course of one complete week, beginning at midnight on Sunday and ending at 11:59:59 P.M. on Saturday of that week. There are approximately 9,000 automobile dealerships with Cobalt Group Web sites, but only about 2,000 use the My Car Tools feature. A quick check of the Web site's database suggests that automobile dealerships experience about 100 "serious" hits per week. A serious hit is when the Web site visitor stays on the Web site for 2 minutes or longer. In other words, there are about 100 times 2,000 or 20,000 serious hits on these dealer Web sites in a typical week.

There is a decision to be made as to what percentage of these serious hits the pop-up invitation should appear. The decision is complicated by the unknown factor of the response rate: What percentage of the dealer Web site visitors who are invited to move to the Websurveyor online survey will actually fill out and submit it? Some online marketing research sources say that a 10 percent response rate is standard.

1. Determine the sample error (at 95 percent level of confidence) that will accompany the expected sample size for each of the following alternatives.
   a. Invite every twentieth visitor.
   b. Invite every tenth visitor.
   c. Invite every fifth visitor.
2. Using what you found in your answers to the preceding question, and taking into consideration other factors that are related to sample size, what sample size approach do you recommend in this case and why?

Chapter 14

Data Collection in the Field, Nonresponse Error, and Questionnaire Screening

Learning Objectives:

To learn about total error and how nonsampling error is related to it

To understand the sources of data collection errors and how to minimize them

To learn about the various types of nonresponse error and how to calculate response rate in order to measure nonresponse error

To read about questionnaire inspection procedures used during and after data collection

Practitioner Viewpoint

The quality of the data can and will be impacted by the human bias of the interviewer. The goal of the practitioner is to make the data collection process as homogeneous as possible by training interviewers to be neutral in tone while at the same time probing in their technique. The use of leading questions or major changes in voice inflection will impact the responses collected during the interview in a way subtle enough to impact the data, but most times not detectable with the use of online monitoring or callback validation.

To ensure quality in the collection of data, great attention must be placed on the interviewers and the training that they receive prior to the start of a study. This one area can most impact and cause the single largest source of nonsampling error.

Howard Gershowitz[1]
Executive Vice President
Mktg Inc.

When Is It the Best Time to Call Someone for a Telephone Interview?[2]

American Demographics, a company that studies and documents household and consumer trends of all types, recently commissioned E-Poll to find out how Americans spend their leisure time. E-Poll conducts online surveys of various types, and it applied its expertise to execute an online survey that was representative of the U.S. general population. Here is what E-Poll found out about the average American's typical week.

DAY OF THE WEEK	WHAT HE OR SHE IS LIKELY TO BE DOING IN THE EVENING
Monday	Working late, working out, running errands, and/or catching up on correspondence
Tuesday	Attending meetings and/or catching up on correspondence
Wednesday	Watching television; least likely "family night"
Thursday	Watching television; highest percentage of any "school night"
Friday	Going out to dinner and/or a movie, watching television, or spending time with the family
Saturday	Running errands, going out to dinner and/or a movie, watching television, or spending time with the family
Sunday	Paying bills, watching television, and/or spending time with the family

Over all, Americans are most likely to work late (11 percent) or workout (10 percent) on Monday; attend a club meeting on Tuesday (8 percent), and stay at home and watch TV or a movie on Friday night (22 percent). Saturday is the most popular night for attending a movie, concert, or theater performance (46 percent); going out for dinner or drinks (33 percent); running errands (25 percent); or enjoying "family night" (21 percent). Sundays are reserved for stay-at-home activities such as catching up on correspondence (21 percent) and paying bills (18 percent).

The pattern of typical evening leisure time usage reveals that Wednesday evening is the best time for a telephone interviewer to call as potential respondents will probably be home and watching television but least likely to consider this as "quality" family time. Thursday evening is also a good time slot. On Monday, Friday, and Saturday, the telephone interviewer should expect a lot of "not at homes." The survey found that one out of five Americans is likely to be paying bills on Sunday evening, so they will probably not be in a good mood.

Our *American Demographics*/E-Poll findings are revealing because they identify some of the underlying reasons for data collection errors. Sometimes potential respondents are just not available; sometimes they are enjoying their families; sometimes they are distracted with worries or a favorite television show; and sometimes they have other correspondence on their minds. There are two kinds of errors in survey research. The first is sampling error, which arises from the fact that we have taken a sample. You learned in Chapter 13 that you can actually control sampling error through the standard sample size formula. But what about the error that arises from a respondent who does not listen carefully to the question or an interviewer who is almost burned out from listening to answering machines or having prospective respondents hang up? This is the second type of error, which is called nonsampling error. In this chapter you will learn the sources of nonsampling error and what controls you can use to minimize it in our research.

You previously learned that you can expect to have sampling errors and that you can control for the level of sampling error. But nonsampling error cannot be measured; it can only be controlled with safeguards. Thus, you must understand the sources of these nonsampling errors and learn how they may be minimized. This chapter teaches you the sources of nonsampling errors. Along with a discussion of each source of error, we suggest how you can minimize the negative effect of each type of error. We also teach you how to calculate the response rate in order to measure the amount of nonresponse error. We relate what a researcher looks for in preliminary questionnaire screening after the survey has been completed in order to spot respondents whose answers may exhibit bias, such as always responding positively or negatively to questions.

NONSAMPLING ERROR IN MARKETING RESEARCH

In the two previous chapters, we discussed sampling. We learned that the sample plan and sample size are important in predetermining the amount of sampling error that you will experience. The significance of understanding sampling is that we may control sampling error.[3] However, as we indicated to you, sampling error is only one of the two components of total error in a survey. The counterpart to sampling error

MARKETING RESEARCH
INSIGHT
14.1

Meet a Marketing Researcher

Howard Gershowitz Knows How to Reduce Nonsampling Error
Howard Gershowitz, Executive Vice President, Mktg Inc.

Howard Gershowitz is executive vice president of Mktg Inc., one of the country's largest telephone data collection companies. He has served as the national president of the Marketing Research Association. Currently he serves on the board of the Council of Marketing and Opinion Research and is the legislative chair of that organization. He was the initial chair of the Marketing Research Association Institute, an organization that provides a distance learning program to practitioners within the marketing research industry.

is **nonsampling error**, which is defined as all errors in a survey except those due to the sample plan and the sample size. Nonsampling error includes the following: (1) all types of nonresponse error, (2) data gathering errors, (3) data handling errors, (4) data analysis errors, and (5) interpretation errors. It also includes errors in problem definition, question wording, and, in fact, anything other than sampling error. Generally, the greatest potential for large nonsampling error occurs during the data collection stage, so we discuss errors that can occur during this stage at some length. Also, because nonsampling error cannot be measured by a formula as sampling error can, we describe the various controls that can be imposed on the data collection process to minimize the effects of nonsampling error.[4]

> Nonsampling error is defined as all errors in a survey except those due to the sample plan and the sample size.

POSSIBLE ERRORS IN FIELD DATA COLLECTION

As we stated before, many nonsampling errors occur during data collection. We divide these errors into two general types and further specify errors within each general type. The first general type is **field-worker error**, defined as errors committed by the persons who administer the questionnaires. It is important to keep in mind that field-worker error can occur with the professional data collection worker as well as with the do-it-yourselfer. The other general type is **respondent error**, which refers to errors on the part of the respondent. These, of course, can occur regardless of the method of data collection. Within each general type, we identify two classes of error: intentional errors, or errors that are committed deliberately, and unintentional errors, or errors that occur without willful intent.[5] Figure 14.1 lists the various types of errors described in this section under each of the four headings.

> Nonsampling errors are committed by field-workers and respondents.

Intentional Field-Worker Errors

Intentional field-worker errors occur whenever a data collection person willfully violates the data collection requirements set forth by the researcher. There are two variations of intentional field-worker errors that we describe: interviewer cheating and leading the respondent. Both are constant concerns of all researchers.

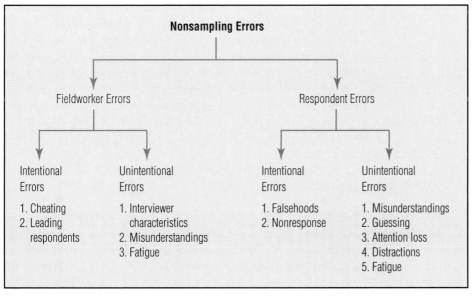

Figure **14.1** **Nonsampling Errors**

Interviewer cheating is a concern, especially when compensation is based on the number of interviews completed.

Interviewer cheating occurs when the interviewer intentionally misrepresents respondents. You might think to yourself, "What would prompt an interviewer to intentionally falsify responses?" The cause is often found in the compensation system.[6] Interviewers may work by the hour, but a common compensation system is to reward them by completed interviews. That is, a telephone interviewer or a mall-intercept interviewer may be paid at a rate of $3.50 per completed interview, so at the end of an interview day, he or she simply turns in the completed questionnaires, and the number is credited to the interviewer. Or the interviewers may cheat by interviewing someone who is convenient instead of a person designated by the sampling plan. Again, the by-completed-interview compensation may provide the incentive for this type of cheating.

There is some defensible logic for a paid-by-completion compensation system. Interviewers do not always work like production-line workers. With mall intercepts, for instance, there are periods of inactivity, depending on mall shopper flow and respondent qualification requirements. Telephone interviewers working out of their homes may take breaks, or they may be waiting for periods of time in order to satisfy the number of callbacks policy for a particular survey. However, as you may already know, the compensation levels for field-workers are low, the hours are long, and the work is frustrating at times.[7] So the temptation to turn in bogus completed questionnaires is present, and some interviewers give in to this temptation.

The second error that we are categorizing as intentional on the part of the interviewer is **leading the respondent**, and it is defined as occurring when the interviewer influences the respondent's answers through wording, voice inflection, or body language. In the worst case, the interviewer may actually reword a question so it is leading. For instance, consider the question, "Is conserving electricity a concern for you?" An interviewer can influence the respondent by changing the question to "Isn't conserving electricity a concern for you?"

There are other less obvious instances of leading the respondent. One way is to subtly signal the type of response that is expected. If, for example, a respondent says "yes" in response to our question, the interviewer might say, "I thought you would say 'yes' as over 90 percent of my respondents have agreed on this issue." A comment such as this plants a seed in the respondent's head that he or she should continue to agree with the majority.

Another area of subtle leading occurs in the interviewer's cues. In a personal interview, for instance, the interviewer might ever so slightly shake his or her head "no" to questions he or she disagrees with and "yes" to those he or she agrees with while posing the question. The respondent may perceive these cues and begin responding in the expected manner signaled by the interviewer's head movements while he or she reads the questions. Over the telephone, an interviewer might give verbal cues such as "unhuh" to responses he or she disagrees with or "okay" to responses he or she agrees with, and this continued reaction pattern may subtly influence the respondent's answers. Again, we have categorized this example as an intentional error because professional interviewers are trained to avoid them, and if they commit them, they should be aware of their violations.

Interviewers should not influence respondents' answers.

Unintentional Field-Worker Errors

Interviewer errors can occur without the interviewer being aware of them.

An **unintentional interviewer error** occurs whenever an interviewer commits an error while believing that he or she is performing correctly. There are three general sources of unintentional interviewer errors. These sources are interviewer personal characteristics, interviewer misunderstandings, and interviewer fatigue. Unintentional interviewer error is found in the interviewer's **personal characteristics** such as accent, sex, or demeanor. Under some circumstances, even the interviewer's gender can be a source of bias.[8]

Interviewer misunderstanding occurs when an interviewer believes he or she knows how to administer a survey but instead does it incorrectly. As we have described, a questionnaire may include various types of instructions for the interviewer, varying response scale types, directions on how to record responses, and other complicated guidelines that must be adhered to by the interviewer. As you can guess, there is a considerable education gap between marketing researchers who design questionnaires and interviewers who administer them. This gap may translate into a communication problem in which the instructions on the questionnaire are confusing to the interviewer. In this circumstance, the interviewer will usually struggle to comply with the researcher's wishes but may fail to do so to some degree or another.

The third type of unintentional interviewer error pertains to **fatigue-related mistakes**, which can occur when an interviewer becomes tired. Fatigue sets in because interviewing can become tedious and monotonous. It is repetitive at best. Toward the end of a long interviewing day, the interviewer may be less mentally alert than earlier in the day, and this condition can cause slipups and mistakes to occur. The interviewer may fail to obey a skip pattern, might forget to check the respondent's reply to a question, might hurry through a section of the questionnaire, or might appear or sound weary to a potential respondent who refuses to take part in the survey as a result.

Unintentional interviewer errors include misunderstandings and fatigue.

Intentional Respondent Errors

Unfortunately, **intentional respondent errors** occur when there are respondents who willfully misrepresent themselves in surveys, and this intentional respondent error must be guarded against. There are at least two major intentional respondent errors that require discussion: falsehoods and refusals. **Falsehoods** occur when respondents fail to tell the truth in surveys. They may feel embarrassed, they might want to protect their privacy, or they may even suspect that the interviewer has a hidden agenda such as suddenly turning the interview into a sales pitch. Certain topics denote greater potential for misrepresentation. For instance, the income level of the respondent is a sensitive topic for many people, marital status disclosure is a concern for women living alone, age is a delicate topic for some, and personal hygiene questions may offend some respondents. Energy conservation is a normative topic, and because respondents know what they should be doing to conserve, some of them may resort to lying so they will not be perceived as wasteful or unpatriotic.

Sometimes respondents do not tell the truth.

The second type of intentional respondent error is nonresponse. **Nonresponse** is defined as a failure on the part of a prospective respondent to take part in the survey or to answer specific questions on the questionnaire. In fact, nonresponse of various types is probably the most common intentional respondent error that researchers encounter. Some observers believe that survey research is facing tough times ahead because of a growing distaste for survey participation, increasingly busy schedules, and a desire for privacy.[9] By one estimate, the refusal rate of U.S. consumers is almost 50 percent.[10] Telephone surveyors are most concerned.[11] Although most agree that declining cooperation rates present a major threat to the industry,[12] some believe the problem is not as severe as many think.[13] Nonresponse in general, and refusals in particular, are encountered in virtually every survey conducted. We devote an entire section to this important source of error later on in this chapter.

Nonresponse is defined as failure on the part of a prospective respondent to take part in a survey or to answer a question.

Unintentional Respondent Errors

An **unintentional respondent error** occurs whenever a respondent gives a response that is not valid but that he or she believes is the truth. There are five instances of unintentional respondent errors: respondent misunderstanding, guessing, attention

Unintentional respondent errors include misunderstanding, guessing, attention loss, distractions, and fatigue.

Even when respondents think they are giving valid responses, they may commit unintentional errors.

Sometimes a respondent will answer without understanding the question.

loss, distractions, and respondent fatigue. First, **respondent misunderstanding** is defined as situations in which a respondent gives an answer without comprehending the question and/or the accompanying instructions. Potential respondent misunderstandings exist in all surveys. Such misunderstandings range from simple errors, such as checking two responses to a question when only one is called for, to complex errors, such as misunderstanding terminology. For example, a respondent may think in terms of net income for the past year rather than income before taxes as desired by the researcher. Any number of misunderstandings such as these can plague a survey.

Whenever a respondent guesses, error is likely.

A second form of unintentional respondent error is **guessing**, in which a respondent gives an answer when he or she is uncertain of its accuracy. Occasionally, respondents are asked about topics they have little knowledge of or low recall about, but they feel compelled to provide an answer to the questions being posed. Thus, the respondent might guess the answer. All guesses are likely to contain errors. Here is an example of guessing. If you were a respondent and were asked to estimate the number of gallons of gasoline you used in your automobile last month, how many would you say you used?

A third unintentional respondent error occurs when a respondent's interest in the survey wanes, known as **attention loss**. The typical respondent is not as excited about the survey as is the researcher, and some respondents will find themselves less and less motivated to take part in the survey as they work their way through the questionnaire.

Fourth, **distractions**, such as interruptions, may occur while the questionnaire administration takes place. For example, during a mall-intercept interview, a respondent may be distracted when an acquaintance walks by and says hello. A parent answering questions on the telephone might have to attend to a toddler, or a mail survey respondent might be diverted from the questionnaire by a telephone call. A distraction may cause the respondent to get "off track" or otherwise not take the survey as seriously as is desired by the researcher.

Fifth, unintentional respondent error can take the form of **respondent fatigue**, in which the respondent becomes tired of participating in the survey. Whenever a respondent tires of a survey, deliberation and reflection will abate. The respondent might even opt for the "no opinion" response category just as a means of quickly finishing the survey because he or she has grown tired of answering questions.

FIELD DATA COLLECTION QUALITY CONTROLS

Fortunately, there are precautions that can be implemented to minimize the effects of the various types of errors just described. Please note that we said "minimize" and not "eliminate," as the potential for error always exists. However, by instituting the following controls a researcher can be assured that the nonsampling error factor involved with data collection will be diminished. The field data collection quality controls we describe are listed in Table 14.1.

Control of Intentional Field-Worker Error

There are two general strategies to guard against cases in which the interviewer might intentionally commit an error. These strategies are supervision and validation.[14] **Supervision** uses administrators to oversee the work of field data collection workers. Most centralized telephone interviewing companies have a "listening in" capability that the supervisor can use to tap into and monitor any interviewer's line during an interview. The respondent and the interviewer may be unaware of the monitoring, so the "listening in" samples a representative interview performed by that interviewer. If the interviewer is leading or unduly influencing respondents, this procedure will spot the violation, and the supervisor can take corrective action such

Intentional field-worker error can be controlled with supervision and validation procedures.

Table **14.1** **How to Control Data Collection Errors**	
TYPES OF ERRORS	**CONTROL MECHANISMS**
Intentional field-worker errors	
Cheating	Supervision
Leading respondent	Validation
Unintentional field-worker errors	
Interviewer characteristics	Selection and training of interviewers
Misunderstandings	Orientation sessions and role playing
Fatigue	Require breaks and alternate surveys
Intentional respondent errors	
Falsehoods	Assuring third-person anonymity and confidentiality
	Incentives
	Validation checks
	Third-person technique
Nonresponse	Assuring third-person anonymity and confidentiality
	Incentives
	Third-person technique
Unintentional respondent errors	
Misunderstandings	Well-drafted questionnaire
	Direct questions
Guessing	Well-drafted questionnaire
	Response options (e.g., "unsure")
Attention loss	
Distractions	Reversal of scale endpoints
Fatigue	Prompters

as a reprimand of that interviewer. With personal interviews, the supervisor might accompany an interviewer to observe that interviewer while administering a questionnaire in the field. Because "listening in" without the consent of the respondent could be considered a breach of privacy, most companies inform respondents that all or part of the call may be monitored and/or recorded.

An industry standard is verification of 10 percent of the completed surveys.

Validation verifies that the interviewer did the work. This strategy is aimed at the falsification/cheating problem. There are various ways to validate the work. One type of validation is for the supervisor to recontact the respondent to find out whether he or she took part in the survey. An industry standard is to randomly select 10 percent of the completed surveys for purposes of making a callback to validate that the interview was actually conducted. A few sample questions might even be readministered for comparison purposes. In the absence of callback validation, some supervisors will inspect completed questionnaires, and, with a trained eye, they may spot patterns in an interviewer's completions that raise suspicions of falsification. Interviewers who turn in bogus completed questionnaires are not always careful about simulating actual respondents. The supervisor might find inconsistencies, such as very young respondents with large numbers of children, that raise doubts as to a questionnaire's authenticity.

Control of Unintentional Field-Worker Error

Unintentional field-worker errors can be reduced with supervised orientation sessions and role playing.

The supervisor is instrumental in minimizing unintentional interviewer error. We describe three mechanisms commonly used by professional field data collection companies in this regard: selection and training, orientation sessions, and role playing. Interviewer personal characteristics that can cause unintentional errors are best taken care of by careful selection of interviewers. Following selection, it is important to train them well so as to avoid any biases resulting from manner, appearance, and so forth. **Orientation sessions** are meetings in which the supervisor introduces the survey and questionnaire administration requirements to the field-workers.[15] The supervisor might highlight qualification or quota requirements, note skip patterns, or go over instructions to the interviewer that are embedded throughout the questionnaire. Finally, often as a means of becoming familiar with a questionnaire's administration requirements, interviewers will conduct **role-playing sessions**, which

Orientations, supervision, training, and validation help control for field-worker errors.

are dry runs or dress rehearsals of the questionnaire with the supervisor or some other interviewer playing the respondent's role. Successive role-playing sessions serve to familiarize interviewers with the questionnaire's special administration aspects. To control for interviewer fatigue, some supervisors require interviewers to take frequent breaks and/or alternate surveys, if possible.

Whenever an interviewer and a respondent interact, the respondent may ask for clarification of questions. Thus, there is the possibility of bias being introduced by the interviewer's answers to the respondent's questions. Interviews can be trained for either "standardized" or "conversational" interviewing. Read Marketing Research Insight 14.2 to find out about these two approaches and how they have been found to impact the quality of the data gathered.

Control of Intentional Respondent Error

To control intentional respondent error, it is important to minimize falsehoods and nonresponse on the parts of respondents. Tactics useful in minimizing intentional respondent error include anonymity, confidentiality, incentives, validation checks, and third-person technique.[16] **Anonymity** occurs when the respondent is assured that his or her name will not be associated with his or her answers. **Confidentiality** occurs when the respondent is given assurances that his or her answers will remain private. Both assurances are believed to be helpful in forestalling falsehoods. The belief here is that when respondents are guaranteed they will remain nameless, they will be more comfortable in self-disclosure and will refrain from lying or misrepresenting themselves.

> Tactics useful in minimizing intentional respondent error include anonymity, confidentiality, incentives, validation checks, and third-person technique.

▶ **Additional Insights**

MARKETING RESEARCH
INSIGHT
14.2

Standardized or Conversational Interviewing: A Dilemma for Telephone Survey Companies?[17]

The research industry standard for telephone interviewing is the "standardized interview" in which the interviewer reads each question directly from the questionnaire. With a standardized interview, interviewers are instructed to leave the interpretation of the question entirely to the respondent. In the extreme application of standardized interviewing, interviewers are not allowed to answer respondents' queries about the questions. The interviewer must do everything in his or her power to remain neutral and, thus, keep to a minimum any bias that might be introduced by the give-and-take of respondent inquiries and interviewer answers.

An opposite theory of the interviewing is "conversational interviewing" in which the interviewer engages in a conversation with the respondent in order to clarify any doubts, ambiguities, or misunderstandings in the respondent's mind. Of course, the interviewer is still trained to avoid biasing the answers, but he or she can use any words or phrases that serve to clarify the question for the respondent.

In a recent study, two professors compared standardized and conversational interviewing by looking at what changes in their initial answers (to a more correct answer) respondents made under each type of interviewing. It was found that whereas respondents changed their initial answers about 6 percent of the time with standardized interviewing, they did so about 21 percent of the time with conversational interviewing. Also, conversational interviewing was found to cause more accurate reporting of purchases. In other words, conversational interviewing resulted in higher-quality data being collected in a telephone survey.

However, it was also discovered that conversational interviewing takes about 80 percent more time than does standardized interviewing. So a 10-minute standardized telephone interview would take about 18 minutes when conversational interviewing is used. Thus, the dilemma is that although conversational interviewing garners higher-quality information, because respondents value their time, they may balk at the longer interview contact. (The researchers caution that their findings pertain only to factual or behavioral information, and it cannot be generalized to attitude questions or sensitive topics.)

Incentives sometimes compel respondents to be more truthful, and they also discourage nonresponse.

Another tactic for reducing falsehoods is the use of **incentives**, which are cash payments, gifts, or something of value promised to respondents in return for their participation. For participating in a survey, the respondent may be paid cash or provided with a redemption coupon. He or she might be given a gift such as a ballpoint pen or a T-shirt. Here, in a sense, the respondent is being induced to tell the truth by direct payment. The respondent may now feel morally obligated to tell the truth because he or she will receive compensation. Or he or she may feel guilty at receiving an incentive and then not answering truthfully. Unfortunately, practitioners and academic researchers are only beginning to understand how to entice prospective respondents to take part in a survey.[18] Incentives also encourage respondents to take part in surveys, which reduces nonresponse.

A different approach for reducing falsehoods is the use of **validation checks**, in which information provided by a respondent is confirmed. For instance, in an in-home survey on baldness medication, the interviewer might ask to see the respondent's medication as a verification or validation check. A more unobtrusive validation is to have the interviewer, who is trained to be alert to untrue answers, check for old-appearing respondents who say they are young, shabbily dressed respondents who say they are wealthy, and so on. A well-trained interviewer will note suspicious answers in the margin of the questionnaire.[19]

With an embarrassing question, the third-person technique may make the situation less personal.

Finally, there is a questionnaire design feature that a researcher can use to reduce intentional respondent errors. Sometimes the opportunity arises in which a **third-person technique** can be used in a question. Instead of directly quizzing the respondent, the question is couched in terms of a third person who is similar to the respondent. For instance, a question posed to a middle-aged man might be, "Do you think a person such as yourself uses Minoxidil as a baldness medication?" Here the respondent will most probably think in terms of his own circumstances, but because the subject of the question is some unnamed third party, the question is not seen as personal. In other words, he will not be divulging some personal and private information by talking about this fictitious other person. The third-person technique may be used to reduce both falsehoods and nonresponse.

Control of Unintentional Respondent Error

Ways to combat unintentional respondent error include well-drafted questionnaire instructions and examples, reversals of scale endpoints, and use of prompters.

The control of unintentional respondent error takes various forms as well, including well-drafted questionnaire instructions and examples, reversals of scale endpoints, and use of prompters. With regard to misunderstanding, well-drafted questionnaire instructions and examples are commonly used as a way of avoiding respondent confusion. We described these in Chapter 11 on questionnaire design. Also, researchers sometimes resort to direct questions to assess respondent understanding. For example, after describing a five-point agree–disagree response scale, in which 1 = strongly disagree, 2 = disagree, 3 = neither disagree nor agree, 4 = agree, and 5 = strongly agree, the interviewer might be instructed to ask, "Are these instructions clear?" If the respondent answers in the negative, the instructions are repeated until the respondent understands them. Guessing may be reduced by alerting respondents to response options such as "no opinion," "do not recall," or "unsure."

A tactic we described when we discussed the semantic differential is **reversals of scale endpoints**, in which instead of putting all of the negative adjectives on one side and all the positive ones on the other side, a researcher will switch the positions of a few items. Such reversals are intended to warn respondents that they must respond to each bipolar pair individually. With agree–disagree statements, this tactic is accomplished by negatively wording a statement every now and then to induce respondents to attend to each statement individually. Both of these tactics are intended to heighten the respondent's attention.

Finally, long questionnaires often use **prompters,** such as "We are almost finished," or "That was the most difficult section of questions to answer," or other statements strategically located to encourage the respondent to remain on track. Sometimes interviewers will sense an attention lag or fatigue on the part of the respondent and provide their own prompters or comments intended to maintain the respondent's full participation in the survey.

> Prompters are used to keep respondents on task and alert.

Final Comment on the Control of Data Collection Errors with Traditional Surveys

As you can see, a wide variety of nonsampling errors can occur on the parts of both interviewers and respondents during the data collection stage of the marketing research process. Similarly, a variety of precautions and controls are used to minimize nonsampling error. Each survey is unique, of course, so we cannot provide universally applicable guidelines. We will, however, stress the importance of good questionnaire design in reducing these errors. Also, professional field data collection companies whose existence depends on how well they can control interviewer and respondent error are commonly relied on by researchers who understand the true value of their services. Finally, technology is dramatically changing data collection and helping in the control of its errors.[20] For example, in certain research situations, there is good opportunity to use multiple data collection methods that, in combination, derive an accurate picture of the topic being researched. Read Marketing Research Insight 14.3 to learn about how Sorensen Associates does this, and you can read about Michael Zeman, Vice President of Client Services, Sorensen Associates along with his advice to you.

▶ **Additional Insights**

MARKETING RESEARCH
INSIGHT
14.3

How Sorensen Associates Uses Multiple Data Collection Methods

Often marketing research studies use more than one method of collecting data. Focus groups are often conducted before conducting large-scale surveys. Sorensen Associates is a marketing research firm that specializes in in-store research. One of their clients needed to understand how consumers shop products within its product's category to develop strategies to maintain and increase market share. Beyond strategic direction, the information will be used to develop in-store merchandising support, new shelf displays, new packaging graphics, and new package sizes as well as provide the retail account with information to use to manage the client's product category.

An in-store method provided the combination of observation and intercept interview needed to collect the breadth of information required to fully understand the shopping experience and to segment consumers along a few different dimensions. One piece of the initial research used video cameras to record shopping behaviors. Small cameras were mounted to capture shopper behaviors from different angles. The videotapes were then analyzed to record specific behaviors.

Several thousand shopping events were recorded and analyzed. The research was conducted in several cities using several different grocery chains. Ease of shopping and time spent shopping were correlated qualitatively with the store layout, typical shopper path, and key merchandising elements. This analysis determined which layouts and designs consumers preferred. Next, in-depth interviews gathered vital themes of information to include in the quantitative study. The qualitative interviews collected the range of issues in consumer language that would be used for the larger quantitative survey work. The in-depth interviews also recorded information repeated by nearly all consumers. This information led to recommendations as well. The preliminary findings fed into a large quantitative study on over 1,000 shoppers.

The large sample size provided the ability to analyze different consumer segments. The segments were developed using cluster analysis on shopper attitudes. The attitude battery covered the full spectrum of consumer attitudes toward the category. Several different cluster solutions were reviewed before finalizing a five-cluster

(box continues)

solution. The additional shopper data profiled these segments to allow for comparisons and contrasts. No single cluster or segment dominated the share of the market. Rather, all five segments comprised between 15 percent and 26 percent of the total market. The overall strategies developed for this category had to encompass at least three of the consumer segments to dominate the category.

Time spent shopping the category also proved very valuable. If shoppers are spending an above average amount of time shopping the category, they may be confused by the number of SKUs or may have difficulty just finding the product they most want to purchase. The accompanying chart illustrates time spent shopping for a variety of (disguised) food and nonfood products. Products near the high end of the time range have an opportunity to simplify the buying process and gain market share in the category.

Products at the low end of the range are considered "grab and go" purchases. These products either have very high brand loyalty or very little differentiation. Shoppers are likely to make their purchase decision before entering the store. The implication in either case is that spending on in-store materials would have little impact on shoppers. Shoppers are not standing still long enough for any point-of-purchase materials to have an impact. Other media should be used to maintain the brand's strength. Sorensen Associates used several different methods of collecting data for this in-store research that led to useful information for its client.

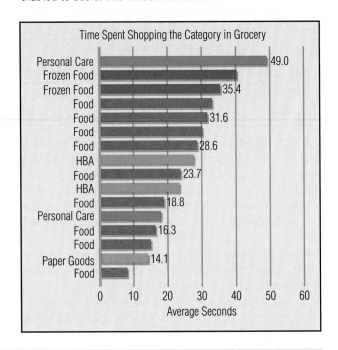

Time Spent Shopping the Category in Grocery

Category	Average Seconds
Personal Care	49.0
Frozen Food	
Frozen Food	35.4
Food	
Food	31.6
Food	
Food	28.6
HBA	
Food	23.7
HBA	
Food	18.8
Personal Care	
Food	16.3
Food	
Paper Goods	14.1
Food	

MARKETING RESEARCH
INSIGHT
14.4

Meet a Marketing Researcher ◄

Meet Michael Zeman of Sorensen Associates
Vice President of Client Services, Sorensen Associates

Michael Zeman received his B.A. in economics with honors from the University of Chicago and his M.B.A. with a marketing research concentration from the University of Minnesota. He is currently the vice president of client services, in charge of the midwestern office for Sorensen Associates, the in-store research company. He has experience on both the supplier and client sides. He previously worked with Rabin Research, NFO, Market Structure Research, and Andersen Windows. He provides marketing research consulting and project management to clients in new-product development, packaging, pricing, competitive benchmarking, and name development. Besides involvement in research, he leads the management team and leads the company in several training initiatives.

Michael Zeman's Advice

Understanding the various research techniques and methods is very important, but don't forget to look at the big picture. In other words, do not spend 80 percent of your time working on statistics—spend 80 percent of your time fitting the research with the overall strategy of the company. Your impact will be greater over the long term if you understand and align with the overall strategic direction than with the details of sample size on statistical significance. Remember that life is a marathon, not a sprint. Keep the long-term perspective. The marathon analogy works in many situations. Always treat people fairly. In the future they may be your boss or key customer. You need to keep something in reserve for the future. Occasions will exist for short sprints, but if you have no extra energy, you will not be effective during these key times.

DATA COLLECTION ERRORS WITH ONLINE SURVEYS

In many ways, an online survey is similar to a self-administered questionnaire because there is no interviewer. At the same time, unless controls are in place, there can be misrepresentations in online surveys. There are three data collection errors unique to online surveys: (1) multiple submissions by the same respondent, (2) bogus respondents and/or responses, and (3) misrepresentation of the population.

The typical online questionnaire is fast and easy to take. Unless there is a control in place, it is possible for a respondent to make **multiple submissions** of his or her completed questionnaire in a matter of minutes. If the person is free to submit multiple responses, this error will result in an overrepresentation of that individual's views and opinions. The customary control for multiple submissions is to ask the respondent for his or her e-mail address, and an electronic block is activated if the e-mail address is repeated. Of course, this control does not eliminate multiple e-mail addresses from the same respondent.

The anonymity of the Internet can inspire individuals to log into a questionnaire site as a fictitious person or to disguise himself or herself as another person. Under this disguise, the individual may feel inspired to give nonsense, polarized, or otherwise false responses. Coupled with multiple submissions, a **bogus respondent** has the potential to create havoc with an online survey. If this concern is great, researchers turn to online panels or other options in which the respondents are prequalified or preidentified in some manner to control for bogus respondents.

We alluded to the problem of **population misrepresentation** in our sample design chapter, but it must be reiterated that all consumers are not equally Internet connected or Web literate.[21] In fact, some segments of the population—such as elderly citizens, low-income families, folks in remote areas where Internet connection is sparse and/or expensive, or technophobic people—are not good prospects for an online survey. By the same token, some individuals are more connected than others in their respective market segments, so there is the very real possibility that, for instance, a Web-based survey of insurance agents would result in a responding sample overrepresenting those agents who are very comfortable with the Web and underrepresenting those agents who use the Web just for perfunctory purposes.

As you learned in Chapter 3, online surveys in no way avoid the requirements of data collection codes of good conduct, and, in fact, the online environment represents additional security and privacy of information concerns. Research associations are responding to these with these issues with new codes of conduct. Marketing Research Insight 14.5 lists the 12 requirements of online data collection that are advocated by the Market Research Society, based in England.

Online surveys can have errors of multiple submissions, bogus respondents, and population misrepresentation.

NONRESPONSE ERROR

Although nonresponse was briefly described earlier in our discussion of mail surveys, we will now describe the nonresponse issue more fully, including various types of nonresponse, how to assess the degree of **nonresponse error**, and some ways of adjusting or compensating for nonresponse in surveys. The identification, control, and adjustments necessary for nonresponse are critical to the success of a survey. Nonresponse has been labeled the marketing research industry's biggest problem,[22,23] and it is multinational in scope.[24] Compounding the problem has been the increase in the numbers of surveys, which means the likelihood of being asked to participate in a survey has increased. With several researchers chasing the same population,

MARKETING RESEARCH
INSIGHT
14.5

An Online Application ◀

Marketing Research Society Online Interview Requirements[25]

The following items are modified from *Confidential Survey Research Quantitative Data Collection Guidelines*, published by the Market Research Society located in London, England. Only items pertaining to online surveys are listed here.

1. Assure the respondent that the survey is for research purposes only and that there will be no selling involved, either during the interview or afterward.
2. Adequately describe the nature of the survey, and if the client agrees, the identity of the client.
3. Inform the respondent how much of his or her time will be incurred by agreeing to be interviewed.
4. Allow the respondent to refuse to take part or withdraw at any stage; under no circumstances must the respondent be coerced into taking part.
5. Where lists are used, it is expected that the list source will be revealed at the start or end of every interview.
6. The research agency instructions/briefing must include an explanation of the sampling method so that research agencies can honestly answer respondent queries on their selection.
7. The research agency shall normally include a cover letter, introduction, or script that specifies the following:
   ▶ Guaranteed anonymity of the respondent.

   ▶ Explanation of the reasons the respondent has been chosen to participate, and what the likely benefits are to him or her.
   ▶ Contact name and telephone number of research agency.
8. The respondent must be advised of any costs that he or she might incur (e.g., if online time) if they cooperate in the survey.
9. Researchers must reasonably ensure that any confidential information provided to them by clients or others is protected (e.g., by firewall, encryption, etc.) against unauthorized access.
10. Before data are sent over the Internet to another country, researchers must check with competent authorities that the data transfer is permissible and must provide safeguards necessary for the protection of the data.
11. It must be remembered that a respondent's e-mail address is personal data and must, therefore, be treated as such.
12. Researchers should keep unsolicited e-mail to a minimum and reduce any inconvenience or irritation such e-mail might cause to the respondent by clearly stating its purpose in the first sentence and keeping the total message as brief as possible.

---

there is always a constant battle to keep response rates from dropping. Some industry observers believe that the major problems leading to nonresponse are caused by fears of invasion of privacy, skepticism of consumers regarding the benefits of participating in research, and the use of research as a guise for telemarketing. (At this point, you may want to recall our discussion of sugging and frugging in Chapter 2).

There are three types of non-response error: refusals to participate in the survey, break-offs during the interview, and refusals to answer specific questions (item omissions).

Nonresponse is defined as a failure on the part of a prospective respondent to take part in the survey or to answer specific questions on the questionnaire. There are at least three different types of potential nonresponse error lurking in any survey: refusals to participate in the survey, break-offs during the interview, and refusals to answer specific questions, or item omission. Table 14.2 briefly describes each type of nonresponse.

Table **14.2** **The Three "Faces" of Nonresponse**

☹ A prospective respondent may refuse to participate in the survey.
☹ A respondent may break off or stop answering in the middle of the survey.
☹ A respondent may refuse to answer a particular question but continue to answer following questions.

Even online surveys encounter high refusal rates.

Refusals to Participate in the Survey

Refusal rates differ by area of the country as well as by demographic differences. The reasons for **refusals** are many and varied. The person may be busy, he or she may have no interest in the survey, something about the interviewer's voice or approach may have turned the person off, or the refusal may simply reflect how that person always responds to surveys. Part of the problem for a refusal to participate is because the respondents do not want to take the time or because they regard it as an intrusion of their privacy.

Refusals to participate in surveys are increasing worldwide.

As we previously mentioned, one way to overcome refusals is to use incentives as a token of appreciation. In a review of 15 different mail surveys, researchers found that inclusion of a small gift, such as a $1.50 rollerball pen, increased response rates by nearly 14 percent. A second feature that contributes to refusals is the length of the questionnaire.[26] The study previously cited found that for every additional minute it takes to fill out the questionnaire, the response rate drops by 0.85 percent. Response rates to mail surveys are also influenced by the type of appeal that is made in the cover letter. Results from one study indicated that a social utility appeal was more effective in increasing response rates when an educational institution was the sponsor. On the other hand, an egoistic appeal was more effective when the sponsor was a commercial organization. An egoistic appeal is a suggestion that the respondent's individual responses are highly important in completing the research task.[27]

Our knowledge of nonresponse and break-offs with online surveys is at a very early stage. However, some practitioners report that some types of online surveys have what must be considered quite low nonresponse.[28] Read Marketing Research Insight 14.6 to learn about it.

Break-Offs During the Interview

Break-off occurs when a respondent reaches a certain point and then decides not to answer any more questions for the survey. Reasons for break-offs, as you would expect, are varied. The interview may take longer than the respondent initially believed, the topic and specific questions may prove to be distasteful or too personal, the instructions may be too confusing, a sudden interruption may occur, or the respondent may choose to take an incoming call on call-waiting and stop the

If tired, confused, or uninterested, respondents may "break off" in the middle of an interview.

MARKETING RESEARCH
INSIGHT
14.6

An Online Application ◀

Online Survey Response Rates and Break-Offs[29]

Mr. Bill MacElory, president of Socratic Technologies, a company that specializes in online surveys, recently shared his company's experience with response rates to various types of online surveys. Here is a summary of his estimates.

RECRUITMENT METHOD	RESPONSE RATE ESTIMATE
Off-line recruiting by mail or newspaper ads	1–3%
Off-line recruiting by telephone	50–60% of those who agree to participate
Online banners, buttons, hypertext, etc.	1% or less
"Pop-up" windows	15–30%
E-mail invitation to a sample from a customer registration database	20–50%
Prerecruited online panel members	40–50%

Mr. MacElory notes that recruiting by telephone is expensive, so the high response rate indicated for "off-line recruiting by telephone" must be balanced against the increased cost of telephone recruiting.

A problem noted is that the partial completions or instances of respondents breaking off from the survey before they have completed all questions are high for online surveys, estimated to be from 20 to 30 percent. If the researcher has a "pickup" option programmed in the online survey so respondents can return and resume their responses from where they stopped, up to 50 percent of the break-offs can be converted to completions.

interview. Sometimes with self-administered surveys, a researcher will find a questionnaire in which the respondent has simply stopped filling it out.

Marketing Research Insight 4.6 includes one method for reducing break-offs in online research. Where interviews are used, they can play a major role in reducing break-offs. Howard Gershowitz, senior vice president of Mktg Inc., said, "I think the interviewers have to be taken out of the vacuum and be included in the process. Companies that are succeeding right now realize that the interviewers are the key to their success."[30]

Refusals to Answer Specific Questions (Item Omission)

Even if a failure to participate or break-off situation does not occur, a researcher will sometimes find that specific questions have lower response rates than others. In fact, if a marketing researcher suspects ahead of time that a particular question, such as the respondent's annual income for last year, will have some degree of refusals, it is appropriate to include the designation "refusal" on the questionnaire. Of course, it is not wise to put these designations on self-administered questionnaires, because respondents may use this option simply as a cop-out, when they might have provided accurate answers if the designation were not there. **Item omission** is the term sometimes used to identify the percentage of the sample that refused to answer a particular question.

> Occasionally, a respondent will refuse to answer a particular question that he or she considers too personal or a private matter.

Completed Interview

As we learned earlier, you will experience both break-offs and item omissions. At which point does a break-off still constitute a completed interview? At which level of item omission do we deem a survey to be incomplete? You must determine your definition for a completed interview. Almost all interviews will have some questions for which the subject does not wish to (or cannot) answer. However, simply because a few questions remain unanswered does not mean you do not have a completed interview. But how many questions must be answered before you have a completed interview? This will vary with each marketing research project. In some cases, it may be necessary that the respondent has answered all of the questions. In others, you may adopt some decision rule to allow you to define completed versus not completed interviews. For example, in most research studies there are questions directed at the primary purpose of the study. Also, there are usually questions asked for purposes of adding additional insights into how respondents answered the primary questions. Such secondary questions often include a list of demographic questions. Demographics, because they are more personal in nature, are typically placed at the end of the questionnaire. Because they are not the primary focus of the study, a **completed interview** may be defined as one in which all the primary questions have been answered. In this way, you will have data for your primary questions and most of the data for your secondary questions. Interviewers can then be given a specific statement as to what constitutes a completed survey such as, "If the respondent answers through question 18, you may count it as a completion." (The demographics begin with question 19.) Likewise, the researcher must adopt a decision rule for determining the extent of item omissions necessary to invalidate a survey or a particular question.

> You must define a "completed" interview.

Measuring Nonresponse Error in Surveys

Most marketing research studies report their response rate. The **response rate** essentially enumerates the percentage of the total sample with which interviews were completed. It is, therefore, the opposite of the nonresponse rate (a measure of nonresponse error). If you have a 75 percent response rate, then you have a nonresponse error in the amount of 25 percent.

For many years there was much confusion about the calculation of response rates. There was no one universally accepted definition, and different firms used different methods to calculate response rates. In fact, there were many terms in common usage including *completion rate, cooperation rate, interview rate, at-home rate*, and *refusal rate*, among others. In 1982, however, CASRO (Council of American Survey Research Organizations) published a special report in an attempt to provide a uniform definition and method for calculating the response rate.[31]

> The research industry has an accepted way to calculate a survey's response rate.

According to the CASRO report, response rate is defined as the ratio of the number of completed interviews to the number of eligible units in the sample. In many studies respondents may or may not be eligible as respondents. If we were conducting a survey of department store customer satisfaction with shopping in a particular department, we would determine their eligibility for the survey by asking them the screening question, "Have you shopped in the kitchenware department at any time during the last three months?" We have our sample of 1,000 shoppers, and the results of the survey are:

> Ineligible people, those who refuse the survey, and those who cannot be reached are included in the formula for response rate.

Completions = 400

Ineligible = 300

Refusals = 100

No answer, busy, not at home = 200

This information allows you to calculate the number of sample units that are (a) eligible, (b) noneligible, and (c) not ascertained. When calculating the response rate, we have the number of completions in the numerator (as usual). However, in the denominator we have the number of completions plus the percentage of those who refused and who were busy, and not-at-home who were eligible. Because we do not talk to those who refuse, don't answer, have busy signals, or who are not at home, how do we determine the percentage of these people that would have been eligible? We multiply their number by the percentage of those that we did talk with who are eligible. By doing this, we are assuming that the same percentage of eligibles exists in the population of those whom we did talk with (of the 700 we talked with, 0.57 were eligible) as exists in the population of those whom we did not get to talk with (due to refusals, no answers, busy, or not at home). The formula for calculating the response rate for this situation is:

CASRO
Response Rate   Response rate =
Formula

$$\text{Response rate} = \frac{\text{completions}}{\text{completions} + \left(\dfrac{\text{completions}}{\text{completions} + \text{ineligible}} \right) \times (\text{refusals} + \text{not reached})}$$

Here are the calculations.

$$\text{Response rate} = \frac{400}{400 + \left(\dfrac{400}{400 + 300} \right)(100 + 200)}$$

Calculation of
CASRO
Response Rate

$$= \frac{400}{400 + (0.57)(300)}$$

$$= 70.0\%$$

Whereas the CASRO formulas seems simple and straightforward, questions arise as to exactly how to interpret them when dealing with individual research projects. We provide you with a complete example of calculation of response rate for a telephone survey in Marketing Research Insight 14.7.

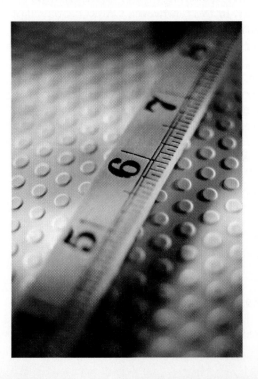

Nonresponse can be measured with the CASRO formula.

▶ **Additional Insights**

How to Calculate a Response Rate Using the CASRO Formula

We are providing you with this example because it seems that all research projects are unique when we are trying to calculate a response rate. Our attempt here is to provide you with a generic telephone survey and to give you as much detail as possible so that you will understand how to calculate a response rate.

> *Population*: Survey of car-buying attitudes and behavior in households with telephones in Anytown, USA
> *Sampling frame*: Telephone directory
> *Eligibility of respondents*: The survey seeks information about car dealers and recent car-purchasing behavior. Your client wants information collected *only from individuals who have purchased an automobile within the last year*. Consequently, a screening question was asked at the beginning of the survey to determine if the respondent, or anyone in the household, had purchased a car within the last year.

Assume you are doing this survey as a class project and you have been assigned the task of completing five interviews. You have been instructed to draw 25 telephone listings from the telephone directory. Your instructor asks you to draw 25 numbers because she has learned that it takes approximately five calls to make a completed interview. You draw your 25 numbers from the directory using a systematic sample.

As you call each number, you record one of the following codes by the number:

> *D* = Disconnected; message from phone company stating number no longer in service.
> *WT* = Wrong target (ineligible); that is, number is a business phone and you are interested only in residences.
> *IR* = Ineligible respondent; no one in household has purchased an automobile within last year.
> *R* = Refusal; subject refuses to participate.
> *T* = Terminate; subject begins survey but stops before completing all questions.
> *C* = Completed; questionnaire is completed.

For each of the following codes you will need to make at least two callback attempts.

> *BSY* = Busy signal; record the time and attempt callback at later time.
> *NA* = No answer; record time and attempt callback at a later time. This includes TADs (telephone answering devices). You may leave a message and state that you will call back later.
> *CB* = Call back; subject has instructed you to call back at more convenient time; record callback time and date and return call.

When you have reached your quota of completions, you are ready to calculate your response rate. Let us assume that your list of numbers and codes looks like the following:

TELEPHONE NUMBER	FIRST ATTEMPT	SECOND ATTEMPT	THIRD ATTEMPT
474-2892	*NA*	*NA*	Completed
474-2668	*BSY*	Ineligible Respondent	
488-3211	Disconnected		
488-2289	Completed		
672-8912	Wrong Target		
263-6855	*BSY*	*BSY*	Busy
265-9799	Terminate		
234-7160	Refusal		
619-6019	*CB*	*BSY*	Busy
619-8200	Ineligible Respondent		
474-2716	Ineligible Respondent		
774-7764	*NA*	No Answer	
474-2654	Disconnected		
488-4799	Wrong Target		
619-0015	*BSY*	Completed	
265-4356	*NA*	*NA*	Completed
265-4480	Wrong Target		
263-8898	*NA*	*NA*	No Answer
774-2213	Completed		

(box continues)

You should note that you completed your quota of five completed interviews with only 19 of your 25 names. Therefore, the response rate computation should not include anything about the six telephone numbers that you did not have to call in your part of the survey.

Look at the last code you recorded for each number and count the number of each code. Insert these numbers into the following response rate formula:

Calculation of survey Response rate

$$\text{Response rate} = \frac{C}{C + \left(\dfrac{C}{C + IR + WT}\right)(BSY + D + T + R + NA)}$$

$$= \frac{C(5)}{C(5) + \left(\dfrac{C(5)}{C(5) + IR(3) + WT(3)}\right)} \\ (BSY(2) + D(2) + T(1) + R(1) + NA(2))$$

$$= \frac{5}{5 + (.455)(8)}$$

$$= 57.9\%$$

Note how ineligibles were handled in the formula. Both IR and WT were counted as ineligibles. The logic is that the percentage of eligibles among those who were talked with is the same as among those not talked with (BSY, D, T, R, and NA).

REDUCING NONRESPONSE ERROR

We have now learned the sources of nonresponse error and how to calculate the extent of nonresponse error by calculating the response rate. Now, what can we do to ensure that we minimize nonresponse (maximize the response rate)? Each survey data collection mode represents a unique potential for nonresponse. Mail surveys historically represent the worst case, but even with these, there are many strategies employed by marketing researchers to increase response rates. Such strategies include **advance notification** via postcard or telephone, **monetary incentives**, and **follow-up contacts**. Identification of respondents prior to mailing the survey can increase response rates for a 10-minute survey from 27.5 percent to 33.7 percent. In addition to respondent identification, if respondent cooperation can be secured in advance, the response rate can be improved to 40 percent. Researchers are now experimenting with other data collection methods such as faxes, e-mail, and so on, as means of increasing response rates. However, one has to contend with other problems such as a restricted population, loss of anonymity, and inability to have longer questionnaires.[32]

> Tactics such as advance notification, monetary incentives, and follow-up mailings are used to increase response rates.

To reduce the not-at-homes, busy signals, and no answers, several **callback attempts** should be made. Interviewers should be trained to write the time and date when the respondent is not at home, the phone is busy, or there is no answer. Callback attempts, usually three or four, should be made at a later time and date. Marketing research firms have designed special forms that can keep track of the several callback attempts that may be made to obtain a completed survey from a particular respondent.

> Callback forms are essential tools for tracking attempts to reduce nonresponses.

A typical sheet allows for a total of four callback attempts. There are provisions to mark the time and date of the call as well as the result. The results are coded so that the data analyst can find out whether the nonresponse was due to a disconnected number, language problems, refusal to answer, and so on.

We discussed using replacement samples in Chapter 12. There are many methods that may be followed to replace samples. Essentially, they all strive to replace a nonrespondent (noncontact or refusal) with an equivalent respondent during the survey. For instance, if a telephone interviewer is given a telephone book and instructed to interview every twenty-fifth name, he or she may find that one of these people refuses to participate in the survey. To replace the nonrespondent, the interviewer can be directed to use a "drop-down" replacement procedure. That is, the interviewer will call the next name below that one rather than skipping to the next twenty-fifth name. He or she can continue calling names in this manner until a replacement is secured for the refusal. On finding a replacement, the original 25-name skip interval would be resumed. The basic strategy for treating nonresponse error during the conduct of the survey involves a combination of judicious use of incentives and persuasion to cooperate and repeated attempts to reach the original prospective respondent. Systematic replacement of those respondents who, for whatever reason, do not take part in the survey helps achieve desired levels of allowable error.

> If a researcher believes that nonresponse will be a problem, he or she may opt to oversample in order to compensate.

PRELIMINARY QUESTIONNAIRE SCREENING

As we have indicated, nonresponses appear in practically every survey. At the same time, there are respondents whose answers have a suspicious pattern to them. Both of these necessitate a separate phase of the data collection stage in the marketing research process that involves the inspection of questionnaires as they are being prepared for entry into a computer file for tabulation and analysis. Researchers develop a sixth sense about the quality of responses, and they can often spot errors just by inspecting raw questionnaires. Granted, some data collection companies provide for direct entry of responses to a computer file, and this is becoming standard practice in online research. Nonetheless, it is good practice to perform a screen step to catch respondent errors before tabulation of the data takes place.

Unsystematic and Systematic Checks of Completed Questionnaires

Despite the ongoing checks of questionnaires by supervisors during the data collection phase, it is worthwhile to perform a more complete inspection at this time. There are two options available: unsystematic and systematic checks. With an **unsystematic check**, the researcher flips through the stack in an arbitrary fashion. With a **systematic check**, the researcher selects questionnaires with a random or systematic sampling procedure. Alternatively, he or she may draw a sample for each interviewer or even opt for a full inspection of every completed questionnaire depending on time, resources, and judged necessity.

> Completed questionnaires should be screened for errors.

What to Look for in Questionnaire Inspection

What is the purpose of questionnaire checks? Despite all of the precautions described thus far, the danger still exists that problem questionnaires are included in the completed stack. So the purpose of completed questionnaire inspection is to determine the degree of "bad" questionnaires and, if deemed advisable, to pull the ones with severe problems. Problem questionnaires are ones that fall into the following categories: They have questionable validity; they have unacceptable patterns of incompleteness; they have unacceptable amounts of apparent respondent misunderstanding; or they have other complications such as illegible writing, damage in transit, or some other obvious problem. Five different

Table 14.3	**Types of Response Problems Found During Questionnaire Inspection**
PROBLEM TYPE	**DESCRIPTION**
Incomplete questionnaire	Questionnaire is incomplete. The respondent apparently stopped answering questions at some point.
Nonresponse to specific questions	The respondent refused to answer particular questions but answered others before and after it (item omissions).
Yea- or nay-saying patterns	Respondent exhibits a persistent tendency to respond favorably or unfavorably, respectively, regardless of the questions.
Middle-of-the-road patterns	Respondent indicates "no opinion" to most questions.
Unreliable responses	Respondent is not consistent on a reliability check.

problems that can be identified with screened completed questionnaires can be described: incomplete questionnaires, nonresponses to specific questions, yea- or nay-saying patterns, middle-of-the-road patterns, and unreliable responses. We describe each problem, and Table 14.3 summarizes each one. In industry jargon, these are "exceptions," and they signal possible field data collection errors to a researcher.

Incomplete Questionnaires Incomplete questionnaires are those in which the later questions or pages of a questionnaire are left blank. We just described this type of nonresponse error as a "break-off," which is its common label with personal or telephone interviews. That is, the researcher might find that a respondent answered the first three pages of questions, and then, for some reason, the respondent stopped. The researcher must determine if enough questions are answered to meet the definition of a completed questionnaire.

> Some questionnaires may be only partially completed.

Nonresponses to Specific Questions (Item Omissions) Also, as we just noted in our descriptions of the various types of nonresponse, for whatever reasons, respondents will sometimes leave a question blank. The researcher must judge if there are too many item omissions to render the questionnaire unusable.

> When a respondent does not answer a particular question, it is referred to as an item omission.

Yea- or Nay-Saying Patterns Even when questions are answered, there can be signs of problems. A **yea-saying** pattern may be evident on one questionnaire in the form of all "yes" or "strongly agree" answers.[33] The yea-sayer has a persistent tendency to respond in the affirmative regardless of the question, and yea-saying implies that the responses are not valid. The negative counterpart to the yea-saying is **nay-saying**, identifiable as persistent responses in the negative. Such questionnaires should not be used.

> Yea-saying and nay-saying are persistent tendencies in some respondents to agree or disagree, respectively, with most of the questions.

Middle-of-the-Road Patterns The **middle-of-the-road pattern** is seen as a preponderance of "no opinion" responses. No opinion is in essence no response, and prevalent no opinions on a questionnaire may signal low interest, lack of attention, or even objections to being involved in the survey. True, a respondent may not have an opinion on a topic, but if one gives a great many no opinion answers, questions arise as to how useful that respondent is to the survey.

> Some respondents will hide their opinions by indicating "no opinion" throughout the survey.

UNRELIABLE RESPONSES

We defined reliability in a previous chapter as the consistency in a respondent's answers. Sometimes a researcher will deliberately include a consistency check. For instance, if a respondent encountered the question "Is the amount of electricity used by your kitchen appliances a concern to you?" the person might respond with a "yes." Later in the survey this question appears: "When you use your electric coffee maker, toaster, or electric can opener, do you think about how much electricity is being used?" Now, suppose that respondent answers "no" to this question. This signals an inconsistent or **unreliable respondent** who should be eliminated from the sample.

There are other bothersome problems that can pop up during questionnaire screening. For example, you might find that a respondent has checked more than one response option when only one was supposed to be checked. Another respondent may have failed to look at the back of a questionnaire page and, thus, missed all of the questions there. A third respondent may have ignored the agree–disagree scale and written in comments about energy conservation. Usually, detecting these errors requires physically examining the questionnaires.

Here is how our Blue Ribbon Panel members answered our question about decline in respondent cooperation rates and their views about online research response rates.

> **Problems found when screening completed questionnaires include incomplete questionnaires, non-responses to specific questions, yea- or nay-saying patterns, middle-of-the-road patterns, and unreliable responses.**

Q: *Do you agree that respondent cooperation has been declining for traditional data collection methods? What has been your experience with the response rates for the studies you have conducted online?*

Note: To learn about the panel members, see the Preface of this book.

BLUE RIBBON PANEL on [Online Research]

Bill MacElroy
President
Socratic Technologies

A: When online surveying was brand new (five to six years ago), participation rates were huge (50% to 60%) compared to telephone/mail (less than 15%). Although that rate has dropped (25% to 30%), it is still several times that of traditional methodologies. Part of the high initial response rates no doubt had to do with the novelty factor that accompanies any new channel of communication. But, of course, novelty wears off (until the next new thing); so the drop-off from the initial rates is not surprising. Reasons for continuing high rates of participation versus phone:

▶ Convenience: Surveys are done on respondent's time schedule.
▶ Speed: Online surveys take 60 percent of the time needed for phone.
▶ Entertainment: Online surveys are still generally thought to be more engaging.
▶ Permission: Online surveys should only be conducted with people who have agreed to participate in advance; phone is considered to be an invasion of privacy.

Allen Hogg
President
Burke, Inc.

A: There is definitely a downward trend in cooperation rates for more traditional data collection methods. Although effective survey design and incentives can bolster response rates for particular projects, poor practices within and outside the marketing research industry have "abused" potential respondents to the point where people increasingly believe it is, in general, not worth their time to participate in survey research.

People do appreciate that with online research they can take surveys when it is convenient for them. It also can take less time to complete a survey online than through more traditional methods. In side-by-side research, people who have taken Web surveys are significantly more likely than those who have taken identical phone surveys to say they would participate in similar studies in the future.

The completion rate for online surveys nevertheless varies greatly depending on the target population, the recruiting method, the incentive offered, the survey topic, and the survey length. For research projects that attempt to recruit respondents as they are visiting Web sites, response rates have been declining as "surfers" are increasingly bombarded with online advertising and the novelty of taking online surveys wanes.

George Harmon
*Senior Vice President
Digital Marketing
Services*

A: The past 20 years of refusal rates and nonresponse rates are well documented. (See the graph.)

The "river approach" DMS created draws respondents from the largest Internet sampling frame and randomly assigns respondents to surveys. Once in a survey, completion rates are very high at 85 to 95 percent depending on questionnaire length and difficulty.

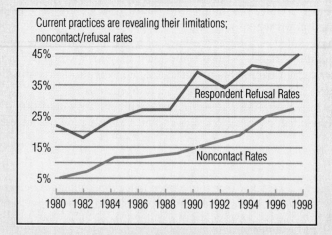

Current practices are revealing their limitations; noncontact/refusal rates

George Terhanian
*Vice President of
Internet Research
Harris Interactive,
Inc.*

A: The growth of technological barriers (e.g., cellular phones, caller ID, answering machines, and multiple lines), the negative impact of telemarketing, declining contact rates, increasing refusal rates, and the declining proportion of working residential numbers are continuing to threaten telephone data collection methods in particular. These barriers are also continuing to threaten those organizations whose revenues depend on telephone data collection methods. (Although mail, central location, and face-to-face methodologies are still in use, their use and usefulness have also continued to decline due in large part to the cost and associated burden of data collection.) Online research that depends on the participation of volunteers who receive intrinsic and extrinsic rewards as compensation does not seem similarly plagued. Response rates to Harris Interactive's online surveys, for instance, have increased steadily since we mounted our first online survey four years ago. As we continue to identify ways to further improve the friendliness of our surveys without sacrificing reliability or validity, we expect to see response rates continue to increase.

Keith Price
*Vice President
Greenfield Online*

A: Interview refusal rates are close to 60 percent for both telephone and mail studies (source: Iconcocast). More and more companies are participating in telemarketing efforts under the guise of conducting valid research, which is adding to a general lack of consumer participation in traditional forms of marketing research.

It is now necessary to gather feedback in nontraditional ways. Greenfield Online has developed an online panel of 100 percent opt-in participants, and as a result, our panel-based studies can experience completion rates of 50 percent and higher.

Lee Smith
*CEO
Insight Express*

A: It is well documented that cooperation rates for traditional research methods have been declining for many reasons. Fortunately, online cooperation rates have remained relatively constant. However, as the novelty of online surveys begins to wane, it is incumbent upon online researchers to consider the factors that may affect cooperation rates. All online surveys should include a clear invitation indicating the purpose of the research, why an individual has been selected, an accurate expression of time required to complete the survey, and a motivating statement to encourage participation. When respondent expectations are appropriately aligned with the demands of the research initiative, a positive respondent experience can be delivered and cooperation rates can easily be maintained.

Doss Struse
Senior Vice President
Client Service
Knowledge Networks,
Inc.

A: There is no question that respondent contact rates and cooperation have both been declining over the last 10 years, with a significant drop in the last five years. CMOR has documented this in detail. Knowledge Networks' studies are not at all typical because of the unique nature of our panel. However, there are indicators from our experience that are generally useful. A common theme for why Knowledge Networks maintains high survey response rates is that we make it convenient for consumers to express their opinions. Although our request for participation is intrusive, panelists can respond at their convenience within a reasonable period of time.

SUMMARY

SPSS Student Assistant Online
Getting SPSS Help

Total error in survey research is a combination of sampling error and nonsampling error. Sampling error may be controlled by the sample plan and the sample size. Researchers must know both the sources of nonsampling error and how to minimize the effect on total error. The data collection phase of marketing research holds great potential for nonsampling errors. There are intentional as well as unintentional errors on the parts of both interviewers and respondents that must be regulated. Dishonesty, misunderstanding, and fatigue affect field-workers; whereas falsehoods, refusals, misunderstanding, and fatigue affect respondents. We described the several controls and procedures used to overcome these sources of error.

At the same time, nonresponse errors of various types are encountered in the data collection phase. Nonresponse error is measured by the calculation of the response rate. There are several methods for improving the response rate and thereby lowering nonresponse error. Once the interviews are completed, the researcher must screen them for errors. Invariably, incomplete questionnaires and refusals are present, and tendencies such as yea-saying may be seen as well.

KEY TERMS

Nonsampling error (p. 401)
Field-worker error (p. 401)
Respondent error (p. 401)
Intentional field-worker errors (p. 401)
Interviewer cheating (p. 402)
Leading the respondent (p. 402)
Unintentional interviewer errors (p. 402)
Personal characteristics (p. 402)
Interviewer misunderstanding (p. 403)
Fatigue-related mistakes (p. 403)
Intentional respondent errors (p. 403)
Falsehoods (p. 403)
Nonresponse (p. 403)
Unintentional respondent error (p. 403)

Respondent misunderstanding (p. 404)
Guessing (p. 404)
Attention loss (p. 404)
Distractions (p. 404)
Respondent fatigue (p. 405)
Supervision (p. 405)
Validation (p. 406)
Orientation sessions (p. 406)
Role-playing sessions (p. 406)
Anonymity (p. 407)
Confidentiality (p. 407)
Incentives (p. 408)
Validation checks (p. 408)
Third-person technique (p. 408)

Reversals of scale endpoints (p. 408)
Prompters (p. 409)
Multiple submissions (p. 411)
Bogus respondents (p. 411)
Population misrepresentation (p. 411)
Nonresponse error (p. 411)
Refusals (p. 413)
Break-offs (p. 413)
Item omission (p. 414)
Completed interview (p. 415)
Response rate (p. 416)

Advance notification (p. 418)
Monetary incentives (p. 418)
Follow-up contacts (p. 418)
Call-back attempts (p. 418)
Unsystematic check (p. 419)
Systematic check (p. 419)
Yea-saying (p. 420)
Nay-saying (p. 420)
Middle-of-the-road pattern (p. 420)
Unreliable respondent (p. 421)

REVIEW QUESTIONS/APPLICATIONS

1. Distinguish sampling error from nonsampling error.
2. Because we cannot easily calculate nonsampling errors, how must the prudent researcher handle nonsampling error?
3. Identify different types of intentional field-worker error and the controls used to minimize them. Identify different types of unintentional field-worker error and the controls used to minimize them.
4. Identify different types of intentional respondent error and the controls used to minimize them. Identify different types of unintentional respondent error and the controls used to minimize them.
5. Define "nonresponse." List three types of nonresponse found in surveys.
6. If a survey is found to have resulted in significant nonresponse error, what should the researcher do?
7. Why is it necessary to perform preliminary screening of completed questionnaires?
8. Identify five different problems that a researcher might find while screening completed questionnaires.
9. What is an "exception," and what is typically done with each type of exception encountered?
10. Your church is experiencing low attendance with its Wednesday evening Bible classes. You volunteer to design a telephone questionnaire aimed at finding out why church members are not attending these classes. Because the church has limited funds, members will be used as telephone interviewers. List the steps necessary to ensure good data quality in using this "do-it-yourself" option of field data collection.
11. A new mall-intercept company opens its offices in a nearby discount mall, and its president calls on the insurance company where you work to solicit business. It happens that your company is about to do a study on the market reaction to a new whole life insurance policy it is considering to add to its line. Make an outline of the information you would want from the mall-intercept company president in order to assess the quality of its services.
12. Acme Refrigerant Reclamation Company performs large-scale reclamation of contaminated refrigerants as mandated by the U.S. Environmental Protection Agency. It wishes to determine what types of companies will have use of this service, so the marketing director designs a questionnaire intended for telephone administration. Respondents will be plant engineers, safety engineers, or directors of major companies throughout the United States. Should Acme use a professional field data collection company to gather the data? Why or why not?

13. You work part time in a telemarketing company. Your compensation is based on the number of credit card applicants you sign up with the telemarketing approach. The company owner has noticed that the credit card solicitation business is slowing down, and so she decides to take on some marketing research telephone interview business. When you start work on Monday, she says that you are to do telephone interviews and gives you a large stack of questionnaires to have completed. What intentional field-worker errors are possible under the circumstances described here?

14. Indicate what specific intentional and unintentional respondent errors are likely with each of the following surveys.

    a. The Centers for Disease Control sends out a mail questionnaire on attitudes and practices concerning prevention of AIDS.

    b. Eyemasters has a mall-intercept survey performed to determine opinions and uses of contact lenses.

    c. Boy Scouts of America sponsors a telephone survey on Americans views on humanitarian service agencies.

15. How do you define a "completion," and how does this definition help a researcher deal with incomplete questionnaires?

16. What is nay-saying and how does it differ from yea-saying? What should a researcher do if he or she suspects a respondent of being a nay-sayer?

17. On your first day as a student marketing intern at the O-Tay Research Company, the supervisor hands you a list of yesterday's telephone interviewer records. She tells you to analyze them and to give her a report by 5 P.M. Well, get to it!

	RONNIE	MARY	PAM	ISABELLE
Completed	20	30	15	19
Refused	10	2	8	9
Ineligible	15	4	14	15
Busy	20	10	21	23
Disconnected	0	1	3	2
Break-off	5	2	7	9
No answer	3	2	4	3

INTERACTIVE LEARNING

Visit the Web site at www.prenhall.com/burnsbush. For this chapter, work through the Self-Study Quizzes, and get instant feedback on whether you need additional studying. On the Web site, you can review the chapter outlines and case information for Chapter 14.

CASE 14.1   Associated Grocers, Inc.

Associated Grocers, Inc. (AG) is a food store wholesaler cooperative located in Whitewater, Wisconsin. AG operates a large warehouse distribution center and serves approximately 100 independent grocery stores in the state of Wisconsin. Most of these grocery stores are family-owned, medium-sized supermarkets such as Jacob's, Cravitt's, or Wimberly's, but about one-quarter are banded together in local chainlike associations such as Hi Neighbor, Blue Bonnet, or Associated Food Stores. All compete against the national food store chains such as Winn-Dixie, SuperFresh, or Kroger.

A recent statewide survey done by the University of Wisconsin–Madison has revealed that the major chains dominate the market, accounting for over 90 percent of the market. AG stores have very low awareness and represent less than 5 percent of grocery purchases. This finding prompted AG executives to begin a corporate identity program. They talked to a professor of marketing from the University of Wisconsin–Whitewater, who suggested that the first step is to ascertain the positions of the major grocery chains and the desires of grocery shoppers as a way of identifying positioning alternatives for AG. The professor advised AG to do a statewide survey on the grocery market as a first step. He also informed AG that he advises a student marketing group called Pi Sigma Epsilon that does various types of marketing projects. He suggested that AG use the Pi Sigma Epsilon members for data collection in a telephone survey as a means of holding costs down.

AG officials were skeptical of the ability of students to execute this survey, but they had very little money to devote to this project. The professor proposed to meet with AG officials and the marketing research projects director of Pi Sigma Epsilon to discuss the matter. When he returned to campus, he informed the Pi Sigma Epsilon president of the opportunity and told her to have the marketing research projects director draft a list of the quality control safeguards that would be used in a statewide telephone survey in which 20 student interviewers would be calling from their apartments or dorm rooms.

1. Take the role of the marketing research projects director and draft all of the interviewer controls you believe are necessary to effect data collection comparable in quality to that gathered by a professional telephone interviewing company.
2. The Pi Sigma Epsilon chapter president calls the marketing research projects director and says, "I'm concerned about the questionnaire's length. It will take over 20 minutes for the typical respondent to complete over the phone. Isn't the length going to cause problems?" Again, take the role of the marketing research projects director. Indicate what nonresponse problems might result from the questionnaire's length, and recommend ways to counter each of these problems.

CASE 14.2   Big West Research: CATI or Online Panel?

Big West Research, Inc. is a full-service interview company located in 10 regional malls throughout the western United States, extending as far south as San Diego. Each location is equipped with a complete focus group facility that accounts for approximately 25 percent of Big West's revenues. Another 25 percent is derived from Big West's mall-intercept interviewing, and the remaining 50 percent of the business is obtained from centralized telephone interview services. Work has been reasonably steady in all three areas over the past five years. But the company has continually wrestled with quality problems in its telephone interview area. The major difficulty is retention of interviewers. An internal study has revealed that the average location needs six telephone interviewers to work full-time and another six part-timers who are hired as the volume of work requires. When work is slack, the full-time interviewers are laid off, and when the workload increases beyond the ability of the full-time interviewers, the part-timers are used for the time when they are needed. The average length of time full-time telephone interviewers work for Big West Research is just under six months.

Quality control problems have affected business. One major account recently informed Big West that it would no longer use its services when a major error was found in how Big West's interviewers administered a critical question on its survey. Other accounts have complained that Big West is slow in turning telephone interview work around, and they have also noted errors in the work that has been done. To make matters more complicated, the marketing research trade publications are reporting a general decline in telephone research due to nonresponse problems, issues of privacy, and various "call blocking" systems that consumers can use to screen their incoming calls.

Ned Allen, the manager responsible for telephone interviewing, has met with various computer services companies about the problem. Ned is thinking of recommending that Big West move away from centralized telephone interviewing to computer-assisted telephone interviewing (CATI). Ned has done some preliminary analysis, and he figures that CATI would greatly eliminate interviewer errors. He thinks that the ease of a CATI system will probably entice interviewers to stay with Big West longer. Also, because CATI can be integrated across all 10 locations, it would serve to spread the work evenly across the full-time interviewers. Right now, each location operates like a stand-alone data collection company but work is allocated to each through Big West's main office located in San Francisco.

Ned finds that a fully integrated CATI system would require somewhere around $250,000 in installation costs, and annual maintenance/upgrading is going to be about $150,000. Also Big West would need to levy clients a setup charge of $250 per page to convert the questionnaire to a CATI format.

Ned is also contemplating an online panel that would be representative of the "Upscale West United States." This online panel would consist of 20,000 online panelists with 1,000 in each of the 20 largest cities in the "Upscale West" (California, Oregon, Washington, Arizona, and Nevada). The panel respondents would be upscale consumers who would be compensated in catalog buying points for responding to at least three online surveys per month. Ned estimates the annual panelist compensation cost alone would be $2 million. The programming of the online service will cost about $250,000, and the Internet fees to maintain the online panel are estimated to be about the same amount.

1. Using your knowledge of the data collection concepts and issues described in this chapter, make a pro and con list for Ned concerning the CATI system.
2. What is your advice concerning the online panel system that is a great deal more expensive than the CATI system? Should Ned just focus his attention on the CATI system, or should he pursue the online panel idea? Why?

Basic Data Analysis: Descriptive Statistics

Practitioner Viewpoint

Most market researchers will tell you that they are always gathering data. But the successful researcher knows how to use those data to answer difficult marketing questions. Knowing what to analyze, how to analyze, and how to interpret the results are what makes your research worthwhile. Understanding the basics of statistical analysis is a must for a successful career in the marketing research field.

In this chapter, you will learn the basics of statistical data analysis in marketing research. You will learn what data to use, how to prepare these data for analysis, how to determine what type of analysis to perform, and how to conduct descriptive analyses of your data using your statistical analysis package—SPSS®.

Jack Noonan
President, SPSS, Inc.

The Digital Divide for Hispanic U.S. Consumers[1]

Although the African American segment has been the largest minority consumer market in the United States for a great many years, the Hispanic population has been steadily gaining. It is estimated from census comparisons and other sources that the Hispanic market segment grew by more than 40 percent in the past decade. At this rate, Hispanics will overtake African American consumers in total population. There are currently about 32,500,000 Hispanic U.S. residents, accounting for approximately 11 percent of the total U.S. population.

What will be the consumer market impacts of the Hispanic minority growth? One industry that will be definitely affected is consumer electronics. A recent survey of what electronics products are owned by U.S. Hispanic households revealed that although Hispanic households are equal to other U.S. households in possession of some consumer electronics products, there are several "digital divides" when its findings were compared to the general U.S. population. Figure 15.1 is a snapshot of the divide.

Hispanics are significantly behind in personal computers, portable CD players, and car CD players, whereas they are equal in camcorder and DVD player ownership. Plus, they are actually 6 percent ahead in digital camera ownership.

Where We Are:

1. Establish the need for marketing research
2. Define the problem
3. Establish research objectives
4. Determine research design
5. Identify information types and sources
6. Determine methods of accessing data
7. Design data collection forms
8. Determine sample plan and size
9. Collect data
10. **Analyze data**
11. Prepare and present the final research report

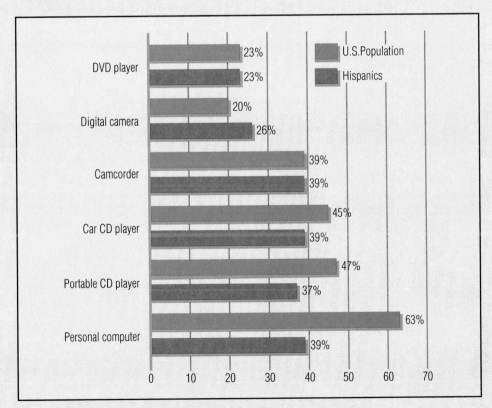

Figure **15.1** **Hispanic Electronics Ownership Compared to the U.S. Population**

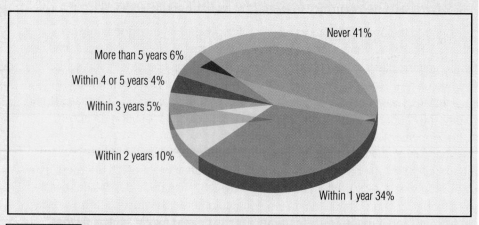

Figure **15.2**   **Hispanics' Intentions to Purchase First DVD Player**

When will the Hispanic electronics purchase wave wash ashore? No one can answer this question with certainty, but the graph in Figure 15.2 that depicts when they intend to purchase their first DVD player gives some insight.

This pie chart immediately reveals that about one-third of all Hispanics who do not have a DVD player intend to buy one in the coming year. Assuming there are 3 family members per household, the 32.5 million Hispanic U.S. residents represent about 10.8 million households. The survey reveals that 77 percent of these households do not own a DVD player, and 34 percent of them intend to purchase a DVD player in the coming year. Thirty-four percent of 77 percent of 10.8 million households translates into over 2.8 million DVD players to be purchased in the coming year.

Hispanic consumers in the United States represent a very large segment of the consumer electronics market.

This chapter begins our discussion of the various statistical techniques available to the marketing researcher. As you will soon learn, these really are devices to convert formless data into meaningful information just as was done in the "Hispanics Digital Divide" example. These techniques summarize and communicate patterns found in the data sets marketing researchers analyze. We begin the chapter by describing data coding and the code book. Then we introduce data reduction and the four functions it accomplishes. Here we preview five different types of statistical analyses commonly used by marketing researchers. Next, we define descriptive analysis and discuss measures of central tendency such as the mode, median, and mean. We also discuss measures of variability, including the frequency distribution, range, and standard deviation. It is important to understand when each measure is appropriate, so this topic is addressed. Last, we show you how to obtain the various descriptive statistics available in SPSS.

CODING DATA AND THE DATA CODE BOOK

After questionnaires are screened and exceptions are dealt with, the researcher moves to the data entry stage of the data analysis process. **Data entry** refers to the creation of a computer file that holds the raw data taken from all of the questionnaires deemed suitable for analysis. A number of data entry options exist, ranging from manual keyboard entry of each and every piece of data to computer scanning systems that scan entire sets of questionnaires and convert them to a data file in a matter of minutes. There are, in fact, integrated questionnaire design and analysis software programs, such as Websurveyor, that include computer scanning operations in their systems.

Data entry requires an operation called **data coding**, defined as the identification of codes that pertain to the possible responses for each question on the questionnaire. Typically, these codes are numerical because numbers are quick and easy to input, and computers work with numbers more efficiently than they do with alphanumeric codes. Recall that we discussed precoding the questionnaire in Chapter 11. You have also encountered data codes in your work with SPSS thus far using your SPSS Student Assistant. In large-scale projects, and especially in cases in which the data entry is performed by a subcontractor, researchers utilize a **data code book**, which identifies all of the variable names and code numbers associated with each possible response to each question that makes up the data set. With a code book that describes the data file, any researcher can work on the data set, regardless of whether or not that researcher was involved in the research project during its earlier stages.

Researchers utilize data coding when preparing and working with a computer data file.

With online surveys, such as the use of Websurveyor, the data file is built as respondents submit their completed online questionnaires. That is, with a Web-based survey, the codes are programmed into the html questionnaire document, but they do not appear as code numbers such as those customarily placed on a paper-and-pencil questionnaire. In the case of Web-based surveys, the code book is vital as it is the researcher's only map to decipher the numbers found in the data file and to correlate them to the answers to the questions on the questionnaire.

With SPSS, it is easy to obtain the coding. With the data file opened, and all of the variables and their variable labels defined, use the Utilities-File Info or Utilities-Variables commands. The first one gives a list of all variables in the SPSS output window, whereas the second one uses a window that isolates the variable information one by one. See Figure 15.3.

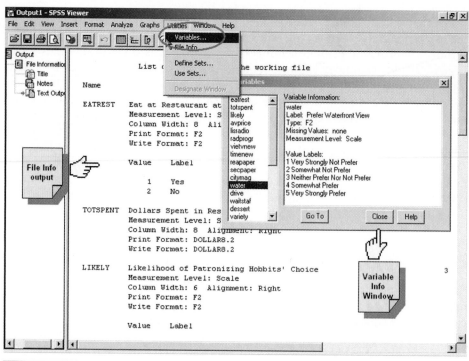

Figure 15.3 **SPSS Variables Commands Reveal the Underlying Code Book for The Hobbit's Choice Restaurant Survey Data**

TYPES OF STATISTICAL ANALYSES USED IN MARKETING RESEARCH

As you have learned through using SPSS, experimenting with the data sets we have provided, and becoming familiar with how SPSS works, marketing researchers work with data matrices. A **data matrix** is the coded raw data from a survey. These data are arranged in columns, which represent answers to the various questions on the survey questionnaire, and rows, which represent each respondent or case. The problem confronting the marketing researcher when faced with a data matrix is **data reduction**, which is defined as the process of describing a data matrix by computing a small number of measures that characterize the data set. Data reduction condenses the data matrix while retaining enough information so the client can mentally envision its salient characteristics.[2] Data reduction is actually any statistical analysis that accomplishes one or more of the following functions: (1) It summarizes the data; (2) it applies understandable conceptualizations; (3) it communicates underlying patterns; and (4) it generalizes sample findings to the population.[3] Refer to Table 15.1.

Table 15.1 **The Four Functions of Data Reduction**

FUNCTION	EXAMPLE
Summarizes the data	The *average* respondent's age is . . .
Applies understandable conceptualizations	*Few* respondents are younger than 30 . . .
Communicates underlying patterns	Most *satisfied customers recommend our brand* to their friends . . .
Generalizes sample findings to the population	This means that *from 70% to 80% of the target market* is . . .

Table **15.2** **Five Types of Statistical Analysis Used by Marketing Researchers**

TYPE	DESCRIPTION	EXAMPLE	STATISTICAL CONCEPTS
Descriptive (Chapter 15)	Data reduction	Describe the typical respondent; describe how similar respondents are to the typical respondent	Mean, median, mode frequency distribution, range, standard deviation
Inferential (Chapter 16)	Determine population parameters, test hypotheses	Estimate population values	Standard error Null hypothesis H_0
Differences (Chapter 17)	Determine if differences exist between groups	Evaluate statistical significance of difference in the means of two groups in a sample	*t* test of differences, analysis of variance
Associative (Chapter 18)	Determine associations	Determine if two variables are related in a systematic way	Correlation, cross-tabulation
Predictive (Chapter 19)	Forecast, based on a statistical model	Estimate the level of *Y*, given the amount of *X*	Regression

To reduce a data matrix [handwritten annotation]

There are five basic types of statistical analyses that can be used by marketing researchers to reduce a data matrix: descriptive analysis, inferential analysis, differences analysis, associative analysis, and predictive analysis (Table 15.2). Each one has a unique role in the data analysis process; moreover, they are usually combined into a complete analysis of the information in order to satisfy the research objectives. As you can see in Figure 15.4, these techniques are progressively more complex, but at the same time, they convert raw data into increasingly more useful information as they increase in complexity.

These introductory comments will provide a preview of the subject matter that will be covered in this and other chapters. Because this is an introduction, we use the names of statistical procedures, but we do not define or describe them here. The specific techniques are all developed later in this textbook. It is important, however, that you understand each of the various categories of analysis available to the marketing researcher and comprehend generally what each is about.

Descriptive Analysis

Certain measures such as the mean, mode, standard deviation, and range are forms of **descriptive analysis** used by marketing researchers to describe the sample data matrix in such a way as to portray the "typical" respondent and to reveal the general pattern of responses. Descriptive measures are typically used early in the analysis process and become foundations for subsequent analysis.

Descriptive analysis is used to describe the variables (question responses) in a data matrix (all respondents' answers).

Inferential Analysis

When statistical procedures are used by marketing researchers to generalize the results of the sample to the target population that it represents, the process is referred to as **inferential analysis**. In other words, such statistical procedures allow a researcher to draw conclusions about the population based on information contained in the data matrix provided by the sample. Inferential statistics include

Inferential analysis is used to generate conclusions about the population's characteristics based on the sample data.

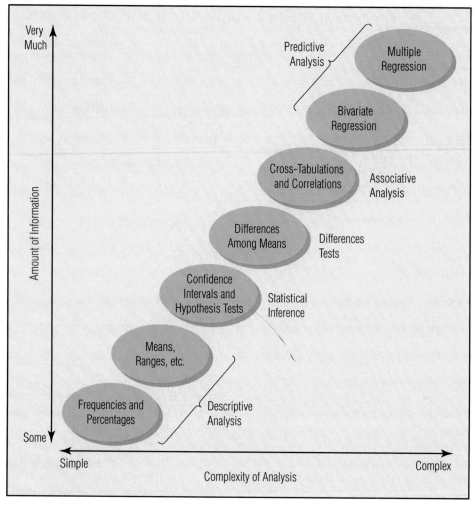

Figure 15.4 **Levels of Analysis Used in Marketing Research**

hypothesis testing and estimating true population values based on sample information. We describe basic statistical inference in Chapter 16.

Differences Analysis t test, variance

Occasionally, a marketing researcher needs to determine whether two groups are different. For example, the researcher may be investigating credit card usage and want to see if high-income earners differ from low-income earners in how often they use American Express. The researcher may statistically compare the average annual dollar expenditures charged on American Express by high- versus low-income buyers. Important market segmentation information may come from this analysis. Or he or she may run an experiment to see which of several alternative advertising themes garners the most favorable impression from a sample of target audience members. The researcher uses **differences analysis** to determine the degree to which real and generalizable differences exist in the population in order to help the manager make an enlightened decision on which advertising theme to use. Statistical differences analyses include the *t* test for significant differences between groups and analysis of variance. We define and describe them in Chapter 17.

Difference analysis is used to compare the mean of the responses of one group to that of another group, such as satisfaction ratings for "heavy" users versus "light" users of a product or service.

Associative Analysis   correlation, cross tab

Other statistical techniques are used by researchers to determine systematic relationships among variables. **Associative analysis** investigates if and how two variables are related. For instance, are advertising recall scores positively associated with intentions to buy the advertised brand? Are expenditures on sales force training positively associated with sales force performance? Depending on the statistic used, the analysis may indicate the strength of the association and/or the direction of the association between two questions on a questionnaire in a given study. Techniques are also available if the researcher is interested in determining complex patterns of associations; these procedures are beyond the scope of this textbook. We devote Chapter 18 to descriptions of cross-tabulations and correlations that are basic associative analysis methods used in marketing research.

> Associative analysis determines the strength and direction of relationships between two or more variables (questions in the survey).

Predictive Analysis   regression

Statistical procedures and models are available to the marketing researcher to help him or her make forecasts about future events, and these fall under the category of **predictive analysis**. Regression analysis or time series analysis are commonly used by the marketing researcher to enhance prediction capabilities. Because marketing managers are typically worried about what will happen in the future given certain conditions such as a price increase, prediction is very desirable. Regression analysis is described in depth in Chapter 19.

> Predictive analysis allows one to make forecasts of future events.

It is not our intention to make you an expert in statistical analysis. Rather, the primary objective of our chapters on statistical analysis is to acquaint you with the basic concepts involved in each of the selected measures. You will certainly do basic statistical analysis throughout your marketing career, and it is very likely that you will encounter information summarized in statistical terms. So it is important for you to have a conceptual understanding of the commonly used statistical procedures. Our descriptions are intended to show you when and where each measure is appropriately used and to help you interpret the meaning of the statistical result once it is reported. We also rely heavily on computer statistical program output because you will surely encounter statistical program output in

> Differences analysis will tell you if high income owners use their American Express account differently from lower income owners.

your company's marketing information system and/or summarized in a marketing research study report.

UNDERSTANDING DATA VIA DESCRIPTIVE ANALYSIS

RETURN TO   *Your Integrated Case*

The Hobbit's Choice Restaurant SPSS Data Set

We now turn to the several tools in descriptive analysis available to the researcher to describe the data obtained from a sample of respondents. In this chapter and in all other data analysis chapters, we are going to use The Hobbit's Choice Restaurant survey data set. That way, you can reconstruct the data analysis on your own with your Student Version of SPSS using the data set. To download this data set, go to the following Web site, and find the data set download area.

Web site address for textbook data set is **www.prenhall.com/burnsbush**.

For your information and as a quick review, the questionnaire was posted on Websurveyor, and qualified respondents answered the questions and submitted their questionnaires in the time period allotted for the online survey. The data were downloaded, imported into SPSS, set up with variable names and value labels, and cleaned. The final data set has a total of 400 respondents who answered all of the questions on the questionnaire. It exists as an SPSS data file called "**hobbitdata.sav.**" At your earliest convenience, you should download the "**hobbitdata.sav**" file and use SPSS to examine the questions and response formats that were used in The Hobbit's Choice Restaurant survey. We will refer to some of these as we instruct you on the use of SPSS for various types of analyses described in this chapter and other chapters that follow it.

From now on, you are going to "watch over the shoulder" of the marketing researcher confronted with analyzing this data set. As you know, an SPSS data set is made up of rows and columns (in the data view window). The columns are the variables that correspond to the questions and parts of questions on the questionnaire, and the individual rows represent each respondent. Refer to Figure 15.5 to see The Hobbit's Choice

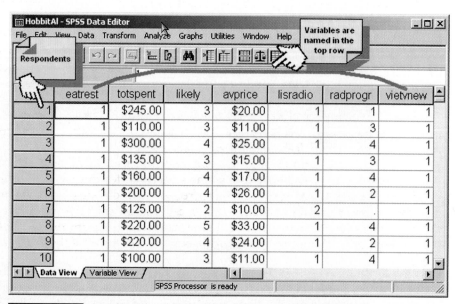

Figure **15.5**   **The SPSS Data Editor View Shows a Data Matrix**

Restaurant survey data in their row and column arrangement in SPSS. Of course, it is not possible to show all of the variables (columns) and respondents (rows), and Figure 15.5 shows only the first 10 respondents in the data set with the first seven questions (variables) visible.

Two sets of measures are used extensively to describe the information obtained in a sample. The first set involves measures of central tendency or measures that describe the "typical" respondent or response. The second set involves measures of variability or measures that describe how similar (dissimilar) respondents or responses are to (from) "typical" respondents or responses. Other types of descriptive measures are available, but they do not enjoy the popularity of central tendency and variability. In fact, they are rarely reported to clients.

Commonly used descriptive analysis measures reveal central tendency (typical response) and variability (similarity of responses).

Measures of Central Tendency: Summarizing the "Typical" Respondent

The basic data reduction goal involved in all **measures of central tendency** is to report a single piece of information that describes the most typical response to a question. The term "central tendency" applies to any statistical measure used that somehow reflects a typical or frequent response.[4] Three such measures of central tendency are commonly used as data reduction devices. They are the mode, the median, and the mean. We describe each one in turn.

Three measures of central tendency are mode, median, and mean.

Mode The **mode** is a descriptive analysis measure defined as that value in a string of numbers that occurs most often. In other words, if you scanned a list of numbers constituting a field in a data matrix, the mode would be that number that appeared more than any other. For example, in Figure 15.5, the first variable, "eatrest," pertains to the qualifying question, "Do you eat at this type of restaurant at least once every two weeks?" Respondents who said "no" were not qualified, and they do not appear in the data set. Thus, the mode for this question is "1," the code for "yes." The mode is most appropriate for categorical data such as nominal (e.g., yes/no) or ordinal (e.g., rankings) scales.

Let's look at a more interesting categorical question, "To which type of radio programming do you most often listen?" The response options and their codes are (1) country and western, (2) easy listening, (3) rock, (4) talk/news, and (5) no preference. A simple method is available to find the mode. First, the frequency or percentage distribution for each number in the string is tabulated, and then the researcher scans for the largest incidence, or he or she may use a bar chart or histogram as a visual aid. If you do a quick count using just the codes that can be seen for this variable in Figure 15.5, you will find that there is one 1, two 2's, two 3's, and four 4's. Since "4" is the most prevalent, then talk/news shows is the mode. (There is also a period (.) which you will learn about later in this chapter.)

With a string of numbers, the mode is that number appearing most often.

You should note that the mode is a relative measure of central tendency, for it does not require that a majority of responses occurred for this value. Instead, it simply specifies the value that occurs most frequently, and there is <u>no</u> requirement that this occurrence is 50 percent or more. It can take on any value as long as it is the most frequently occurring number. If a tie for the mode occurs, the distribution is considered to be "bimodal." Or it might even be "trimodal" if there is a three-way tie.

Median An alternative measure of central tendency is the **median**, which expresses that value whose occurrence lies in the middle of an ordered set of values. That is, it is the value such that one-half of all of the other values is greater than the median

The median expresses the value whose occurrence lies in the middle of a set of ordered values.

and one-half of the remaining values is less than the median. Thus, the median tells us the approximate halfway point in a set or string of numbers that are arranged in ascending or descending order while taking into account the frequency of each value. With an odd number of values, the median will always fall on one of the values, but with an even number of values, the median may fall between two adjacent values.

To determine the median, the researcher creates a frequency or percentage distribution with the numbers in the string in either ascending or descending order. In addition to the raw percentages, he or she computes cumulative percentages and, by inspecting these, finds where the 50–50 break occurs.

Let us just take the first 10 respondents that can be seen in Figure 15.5. In order to determine a median, the codes must be ordered, meaning that they cannot be categorical. We can use the likelihood of patronizing Hobbit's Choice (the variable called "likely"), which is an interval scale. There is one 2, four 3's, four 4's, and one 5. This means that the median is exactly between 4 (somewhat likely) and 3 (neither likely nor unlikely) because the 2 and 3 codes account for exactly 50 percent, and the 4 and 5 codes account for the remaining 50 percent. In our 10-respondent example, the median is 3.5.

The mean is the arithmetic average of a set of numbers.

You should notice that the median supplies more information than does the mode, for a mode may occur anywhere in the string, but the median must be at the halfway point. It should be pointed out that most frequency distributions are not symmetric, and the 50–50 point often falls on a particular value rather than between two adjacent ones.

Mean   A third measure of central tendency is the mean, sometimes referred to as the "arithmetic mean." The **mean** is the average value characterizing a set of numbers. It differs from the mode and the median in that a computation is made to determine the average. The mean is computed through the use of the following formula:

Formula for a mean

$$\text{Mean } (\bar{x}) = \frac{\sum\limits_{i-1}^{n} x_i}{n}$$

where:

n = the number of cases

x_i = each individual value

$\sum$ signifies that all the x_i values are summed

As you can see, all of the members in the set of n numbers, each designated by x_i, are summed and that total is divided by the number of members in that set. The resulting number is the mean, a measure that indicates the central tendency of those values. It approximates the typical value in the set. To compute the mean average price of a restaurant evening meal entrée, we must first sum the 10 prices visible in Figure 15.5. If you want to, you can verify that this sum is $192. Then the sum is divided by 10 respondents to yield a mean of $19.20. Because the mean is determined by taking every member of the set of numbers into account through this formula, it is more informative than the median. Means communicate a great deal of information, and they can be plotted for quick interpretations. Read Marketing Research Insight 15.1 for an illustration.

Just as a quick break in Marketing Research Insight 15.2, read about Richard Brumfield, a marketing researcher who deals with basic statistical measures a great deal of the time.

► **A Global Perspective**

Global Plot Means on a Graph to Communicate Them Effectively

In global marketing, there is a debate as to whether a local country brand (national brand), a local private brand, or a global brand name is most effective. To investigate this issue, researchers in Israel asked consumers to rate shampoo on nine different product characteristics using a 1–7 scale where 1 meant the lowest rating and 7 corresponded to the highest rating.[5] The respondents rated three types of brands: private, national, or global.

The means were calculated and plotted as shown on the accompanying line graph.

The graph clearly shows that local private brands are at a disadvantage to national and global brand names in all but one characteristic. However, global brands are seen as more expensive (low rating on price). Global brands are attractive to consumers who are least price sensitive, whereas local country private brands are attractive to those consumers who are price sensitive.

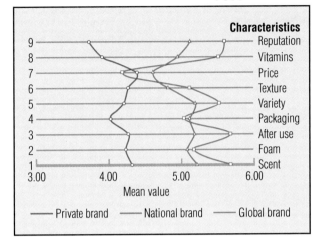

Measures of Variability: Visualizing the Diversity of Respondents

Although they are extremely useful, measures of central tendency are incomplete descriptors of the variety of values in a particular set of numbers. That is, they do not indicate the variability of responses to a particular question or, alternatively, the diversity of respondents on some characteristic measured in our survey. To gain sensitivity for the diversity or variability of values, the marketing researcher must turn to measures of variability. All **measures of variability** are concerned with depicting the "typical" difference between the values in a set of values.

It is one matter to know the mean or some other measure of central tendency, but it is quite another matter to be aware of how close to that mean or measure of central tendency the rest of the values fall. For example, we ascertained that the average expected cost for an entrée in an upscale restaurant such as The Hobbit's Choice is $19.20, but until we have a notion of the variability of the price estimates provided by our respondents, we are clueless as to the existence of individuals who

Measures of variability reveal the typical difference between the values in a set of values.

► **Meet a Marketing Researcher**

Learn About Richard Brumfield of Marketing Research Services, Inc.
Vice President, Marketing Research Services, Inc. (MRSI)

Richard has worked in consumer research since 1978. Before joining MRSI in 1988, Richard worked with Burke Marketing Research for seven years. While at Burke, Richard held several positions, including group director of analytical and consulting services. At MRSI, Richard services the needs of clients in the retail, shopping center development, and shopping center management fields. Richard holds an M.A. in sociology and an M.S. in marketing from the University of Cincinnati, with an emphasis in quantitative analysis, statistics, research design, and scientific sampling techniques.

might be expecting to pay twice or three times that much. This information is vital to Jeff Dean's understanding of the price sensitivity of various market segments that might patronize The Hobbit's Choice.

Thus, knowing the variability of the data could greatly impact a marketing decision based on the data because it expresses how similar the respondents are to one another on the topic under examination. There are three measures of variability: frequency distribution, range, and standard deviation. Each measure provides its own unique version of information that helps to describe the diversity of responses.

Frequency Distribution A **frequency distribution** is a tabulation of the number of times that each different value appears in a particular set of values. Frequencies themselves are raw counts, and normally these frequencies are converted into percentages for ease of comparison. The conversion is arrived at very simply through a quick division of the frequency for each value by the total number of observations for all of the values, resulting in a percent, called a **percentage distribution**. For instance, we stated in the example of a mode for listening to the radio that in the "lisradio" column, you will find nine 1's and one 2 (Figure 15.5). This is the frequency distribution, and to determine the percentage distribution, each frequency must be divided by the number of respondents, or 10 in this case. So the percentage distribution is this: yes (90%) and no (10%). Apparently, just about everyone in our 10-person example listens to the radio regularly.

In sum, a frequency distribution affords an accounting of the responses to values in a set. It quickly communicates all of the different values in the set, and it expresses how similar the values are. The percentage distribution is often used here. Figure 13.2 on page 376 illustrates how quickly percentage distributions communicate variability when they are converted to bar charts.[6] For instance, if our percentage distribution happened to have only a few very similar values in it, it would appear as a very steep, spike-shaped histogram to such as the one for our "little variability" bar graph; however, if the set of values happened to be made up of many dissimilar numbers, the histogram would be much more spread out, with small peaks and valleys. This is the case with the "much variability" bar graph. This pattern indicates a great deal of dispersion in the numbers, whereas the spiked distribution indicates little variability in the set of numbers.

Range The **range** identifies the distance between lowest value (minimum) and the highest value (maximum) in an ordered set of values. Stated somewhat differently, the range specifies the difference between the endpoints in a distribution of values arranged in order. The range does not provide the same amount of information supplied by a frequency distribution; however, it identifies the interval in which the distribution occurs. The range also does not tell you how often the maximum and minimum occurred, but it does provide some information on the dispersion by indicating how far apart the extremes are found. For example, if you scan the "totspent" column, representing the estimated total dollars spent in restaurants in a typical month by each of our 10 respondents in Figure 15.5, you will find the lowest number to be $100, and the highest one to be $300, so the range is 300 − 100, or $200.

Standard Deviation The **standard deviation** indicates the degree of variation or diversity in the values in such a way as to be translatable into a normal or bell-shaped curve distribution. Although marketing researchers do not always rely on the normal curve interpretation of the standard deviation, they often encounter the standard deviation on computer printouts, and they usually report it in their tables. So it is worthwhile to digress for a moment to discuss this statistical concept.

Measures of variability include frequency distribution, range, and standard deviation.

A frequency (percentage) distribution reveals the number (percent) of occurrences of each number in a set of numbers.

The range identifies the maximum and minimum values in a set of numbers.

A standard deviation indicates the degree of variation in a way that can be translated into a bell-shaped curve distribution.

Variability indicates how different respondents are on a common topic such as buying fresh vegetables.

Table 15.3 shows the properties of a bell-shaped or normal distribution of values. As we have indicated in our chapter on sample size determination, the usefulness of this model is apparent when you realize that it is a symmetric distribution: Exactly 50 percent of the distribution lies on either side of the midpoint (the apex of the curve). With a normal curve, the midpoint is also the mean. Standard deviations are standardized units of measurement that are located on the horizontal axis. They relate directly to assumptions about the normal curve. For example, the range of one standard deviation above and one standard deviation below the midpoint includes 68 percent of the total area underneath that curve. Because the bell-shaped distribution is a theoretical or ideal concept, this property never changes. Moreover, the proportion of area under the curve and within plus or minus any number of standard deviations from the mean is perfectly known. For the purposes of this presentation, normally only two or three of these values are of interest to marketing researchers. Specifically, ± 2.58 standard deviations describes the range in which 99 percent of the area underneath the curve is found, ± 1.96 standard deviations is associated with 95 percent of the area underneath the curve, and ± 1.64 standard deviations corresponds to 90 percent of the bell-shaped curve's area. Remember, we must assume that the shape of the frequency distribution of the numbers approximates a normal curve, so keep this in mind during our following examples.

Table 15.3 **Normal Curve Interpretation of Standard Deviation**

NUMBER OF STANDARD DEVIATIONS FROM THE MEAN	PERCENT OF AREA UNDER CURVE[a]	PERCENT OF AREA TO RIGHT (OR LEFT)[b]
± 1.00	68%	16.0%
± 1.64	90%	5.0%
± 1.96	95%	2.5%
± 2.58	99%	0.5%
± 3.00	99.7%	0.1%

[a]This is the area under the curve with the number of standard deviations as the lower (left-hand) and upper (right-hand) limits and the mean equidistant from the limits.

[b]This is the area left outside of the limits described by plus or minus the number of standard deviations. Because of the normal curve's symmetric properties, the area remaining below the lower limit (left-hand tail) is exactly equal to the area remaining above the upper limit (right-hand tail).

MARKETING RESEARCH

INSIGHT
15.3

Are You a Genius? (Understanding Standard Deviation)

You probably took an IQ (intelligence quotient) test sometime in the past. They are regularly administered to elementary school children as a means of placing them into appropriate learning environments or otherwise determining their learning abilities. In addition, there are a number of online IQ tests that you can take for fun or self-discovery.

The Wechsler Intelligence Scale is an IQ test used by a great many school systems, learning diagnostic centers, and educational professionals. The theoretical distribution of the Wechsler IQ scores is illustrated in the accompanying figure. It shows that the average score is 100, meaning that 50 percent of the population has an IQ of less than 100, while the other 50 percent has an IQ greater than 100. The standard deviation of this IQ scale is 15 (see shading in figure), and as you can see in the figure, individuals with an IQ between 85 and 115 fall in the "normal" range, and as you can see, this accounts for 68 percent of the population. The range of 115 to 130 is sometimes referred to as the "bright" level, and individuals with IQ's in this range account for about 14 percent of the population. With an IQ of between 130 and 145, a person is in the "gifted" range, and as you can see, these

individuals account for only about 2 percent of the population. To be considered a "genius," one's IQ must be 145 or higher. Geniuses are quite rare as they amount to less than 0.02 percent of the population.

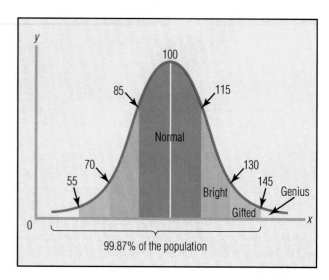

The standard deviation embodies the properties of a bell-shaped distribution of values.

Standard deviation is sometimes difficult to understand because of all the percentages. We have prepared Marketing Research Insight 15.3 to help you comprehend this statistical concept.

It is now time to review the calculation of the standard deviation. The equation typically used for the standard deviation is as follows:

Formula for a standard deviation

$$\text{Standard deviation } (s) = \sqrt{\frac{\sum_{i-1}^{n}(x_i - \bar{x})^2}{n - 1}}$$

The squaring operation in the standard deviation formula is used to avoid the cancellation effect.

In this equation, x_i stands for each individual observation and $\bar{x}$ stands for the mean, as indicated earlier. We use the average price spent for an entrée in our 10-respondent Hobbit's Choice Restaurant survey example to illustrate the calculations for a standard deviation. We already know that the mean amount spent is $19.20. Applying the standard deviation formula, the computations are as follows:

$$s = \sqrt{\frac{\sum_{i-1}^{n}(x_i - \bar{x})^2}{n - 1}}$$

Example of how to compute a standard deviation

$$= \sqrt{\frac{(20 - 19.20)^2 + (11 - 19.20)^2 + \dots + (11 - 19.20)^2}{10 - 1}}$$

$$= \$7.71$$

It may seem strange to square differences, add them up, divide them by (*n* − 1), and then take the square root. If we did not square the differences, we would have positive and negative values; and if we summed them, there would be a cancellation effect. That is, large negative differences would cancel out large positive differences, and the numerator would end up being close to zero. But this result is contrary to what we know is the case with large differences: There is variation, which is expressed by the standard deviation. The formula remedies this problem by squaring the subtracted differences before they are summed. Squaring converts all negative numbers to positives and, of course, leaves the positives positive. Next, all of the squared differences are summed and divided by 1 less than the number of total observations in the string of values; 1 is subtracted from the number of observations to achieve what is typically called an "unbiased" estimate of the standard deviation. But we now have an inflation factor to worry about because every comparison has been squared. To adjust for this, the equation specifies that the square root be taken after all other operations are performed. This final step adjusts the value back down to the original measure (e.g., dollars rather than squared dollars). By the way, if you did not take the square root at the end, the value would be referred to as the **variance.** In other words, the variance is the standard deviation squared.

Now, whenever a standard deviation is reported along with a mean, a specific picture should appear in your mind. Assuming that the distribution is bell shaped, the size of the standard deviation number helps you envision how similar or dissimilar the typical responses are to the mean. If the standard deviation is small, the distribution is greatly compressed. On the other hand, with a large standard deviation value, the distribution is consequently stretched out at both ends. With our 10-respondent Hobbit's Choice sample the standard deviation was found to be $7.71. Assuming that the responses approximate a bell-shaped distribution, the range for 95 percent of the responses would be calculated to be 19.20 ± (1.96 × 7.71), which turns out to be 19.20 ± 15.11, or $34.31 to $4.09. That is, 95 percent of the respondents spend between $4.09 and $34.31.

With a bell-shaped distribution, 95 percent of the values lie within ±1.96 times the standard deviation away from the mean.

We have prepared Marketing Research Insight 15.4 as a means of helping you remember the various descriptive statistics concepts that are commonly used by marketing researchers.

▶ **Additional Insights**

MARKETING RESEARCH
INSIGHT
15.4

Descriptive Statistics: What They Mean and How to Compute Them

Invariably, a researcher has to make "sense" out of a set of numbers that represents the ways respondents answered the questions in the survey. The answers are normally coded; that is, they are converted to numbers such as 1 for "yes," 2 for "no," and 3 for "maybe." Sometimes the numbers pertain to responses on a scale such as when a respondent indicates that his or her PCS wireless phone company rates a "4" on a 5-point scale where 1 means "poor" service and a 5 means "excellent" service, or the number might be the actual number of years he or she has used that PCS wireless phone company.

Descriptive statistics are basic to marketing research and essential to the researcher's understanding of how the respon-

dents answered each question. Here is a data set comprising the answers 10 different respondents gave when asked to rate the quality of their PCS wireless phone service.

Respondent	Rating	Respondent	Rating
1	4	6	4
2	5	7	3
3	4	8	4
4	2	9	5
5	3	10	4

To illustrate the nine descriptive statistics concepts, the ratings of our 10 respondents are analyzed in the following table.

(box continues)

Statistical Concept	What Is It?	How Do You Compute It?	Using the Ratings Example
Frequency	The number of times a number appears in the data set	Count the number of times the number appears in the set of numbers	The number 4's frequency is 5
Frequency distribution	The number of times each different number in the set appears	Count the number of times each different number appears in the set, and make a table that shows each number, its count, and the total count (all counts totaled)	Rating Count 2 1 3 2 4 5 5 <u>2</u> Total 10
Percentage distribution	The presence of each different number expressed as a percent	Divide each frequency count for each rating number by the total count, and report the result as a percent	Rating Percent 2 10% 3 20% 4 50% 5 <u>20%</u> Total 100%
Cumulative distribution (frequency or percentage)	A running total of the counts or percentages	Arrange all the different numbers in descending order and indicate the sum of the counts (percentages) of all preceding numbers plus the present one	Cum. Rating Percent Percent 2 10% 10% 3 20% 30% 4 50% 80% 5 <u>20%</u> 100% Total 100%
Median	The number in the set of numbers such that 50% of the other numbers are larger, and 50% of the other numbers are smaller	Use the cumulative percentage distribution to locate where the cumulative percent equals 50% or where it includes 50%	Cum. Rating Percent 2 10% 3 30% 4 80% ← Median 5 100%
Mode	In a frequency or a percentage distribution, the number that has the largest count or percentage (ties are acceptable)	By inspection, determine which number has the largest frequency or percentage in the distribution	The number 4 accounts for 50%, the largest of any other rating
Mean	The arithmetic average of the set of numbers	Add up all the numbers and divide this sum by the total number of numbers in the set	$(4 + 5 + 4 + 2 + 3 + 4 + 3 + 4 + 5 + 4)/10 = 3.8$
Range	An indication of the "spread" or span covered by the numbers	Find the lowest and highest numbers in the set and identify them as the minimum and maximum, respectively	The minimum is 2, and the maximum is 5; so the range is $5 - 2$, or 3.
Standard deviation	An indication of how similar or dissimilar the numbers are in the set, interpretable under the assumptions of a normal curve of that result	Sum the square of each number subtracted from the mean, divide that sum by the total number of numbers less one, and then take the square root	$\{((4 - 3.8)^2 + (5 - 3.8)^2 + \ldots + (4 - 3.8)^2)/$ $10 - 1)\}^{1/2} = .84$

WHEN TO USE A PARTICULAR DESCRIPTIVE MEASURE

In Chapter 10, you learned that the level of measurement for a scale affects how it may be statistically analyzed. Remember, for instance, that nominal question forms contain much less information than do those questions with interval scaling assumptions. Similarly, the amount of information provided by each of the various measures of central tendency and dispersion differs. As a general rule, statistical measures that communicate the most amount of information should be used with scales that contain the most amount of information, and measures that communicate the least amount of information should be used with scales that contain the least amount of information. The level of measurement determines the appropriate measure; otherwise, the measure will be uninterpretable.

At first reading, this rule may seem confusing, but on reflection it should become clear that the level of measurement of each question dictates the measure that should be used. It is precisely at this point that you must remember the arbitrary nature of coding schemes. For instance, if on a demographic question concerning religious preference, "Catholic" is assigned a "1," "Protestant" is assigned a "2," "Jewish" is assigned a "3," and so forth, a mean could be computed. But what would be the interpretation of an average religion of 2.36? It would have no practical interpretation because the mean assumes interval or ratio scaling, whereas the religion categories are nominal. The mode would be the appropriate central tendency measure for these responses.

Table 15.4 indicates how the level of measurement relates to each of the three measures of central tendency and measures of variation. The table should remind you that a clear understanding of the level of measurement for each question on the questionnaire is essential because the researcher must select the statistical procedure and direct the computer to perform the procedure. The computer cannot distinguish level of measurement because we typically convert all of our data to numbers for ease of entry.

As you might suspect, there is a much potential for misunderstanding when a researcher communicates the results of his or her descriptive analyses to the marketing manager. We have noted some of the common misconceptions held by managers in Marketing Research Insight 15.5. If a researcher knowingly allows these misunderstandings, he or she is acting unethically.

> The level of measurement underlying a question determines which statistic is appropriate.

Table **15.4** **Appropriate Scaling Situations for Various Descriptive Statistics**

	Type of Scale		
LEVEL OF MEASUREMENT	NOMINAL	ORDINAL	INTERVAL OR RATIO
Central tendency (characterizes the most typical response)	Mode	Median	Mean
Dispersion (variability) (indicates how similar the responses are)	Frequency or percentage distribution	Cumulative percentage distribution	Standard deviation Range

MARKETING RESEARCH
INSIGHT
15.5

It is sometimes said, "Statistics do not lie, but liars can use statistics." This caution is especially pertinent to communication of basic data analysis findings in which the audience is unfamiliar with statistical concepts and misperceptions can distort meanings. Here are some statements that might be made by a researcher, what each statement means in terms of descriptive analysis, and possible misperceptions that might occur in a manager who is not accustomed to working with survey findings.

WHAT IS SAID	WHAT IT MEANS	POSSIBLE MISPERCEPTIONS
"The modal answer was . . ."	The answer given by more respondents than any other answer	Most or all of the respondents gave the answer
"A majority responded . . ."	Over 50% of the respondents answered this way	Most or all of the respondents gave the answer
"A plurality responded . . ."	The answer was given by more respondents than any other answer, but less than 50% gave that answer	A majority of respondents gave the answer
"The median response was . . ."	The answer such that 50% answered above it and 50% answered below it	Most respondents gave this answer
"The mean response was . . ."	The arithmetic average of all respondents' answers or responded very close to this answer	Most respondents gave this answer
"There was some variability in the responses . . ."	Respondents gave a variety of responses with some agreement	There was no agreement among the respondents
"Missing values were omitted from the analysis."	Respondents who did not answer were not included and, thus, the sample size for that question was reduced	An adjustment was made to allow for respondents who did not answer, but the sample size was not affected
"The standard deviation was . . ."	The value was computed by applying the standard deviation formula	No comprehension

Remember, these are very basic statistical concepts, and there are a great many more sophisticated statistics that a researcher may use to completely analyze a data set. Obviously, clients will differ in their familiarity and comprehension of statistical concepts. Here are some approaches that can be used to make certain that the audience will not misunderstand the researcher's words.

1. Some companies have prepared handbooks or glossaries that define marketing research terms, including statistical concepts. They are given to clients at the onset of work.
2. Some researchers include an appendix in the final report that defines and illustrates the statistical concepts mentioned in the report.

3. Definitions of statistical concepts are included in the text of the final report where the concept is first mentioned.
4. Footnotes and annotations are included in the tables and figures that explain the statistical concepts used.

No ethical researcher would intentionally mislead a client in reporting findings, and because statistical concepts have high potential for misperceptions such as those illustrated here, ethical researchers go to considerable lengths to prevent misunderstandings.

RETURN TO   *Your Integrated Case*

The Hobbit's Choice Survey: Obtaining Descriptive Statistics with SPSS

Beginning with this chapter and all subsequent chapters dealing with statistical analyses, we provide illustrations with the use of SPSS in two ways. First, in your textbook descriptions, we indicate step-by-step the procedures used with SPSS to obtain the statistical analyses being described. Plus, we have included examples of SPSS output in these sections. The second way is with the use of your SPSS Student Assistant Online. By now, you are well acquainted with the online Student Assistant. We prompt you to look at these statistical analysis sections that illustrate how to operate SPSS, as well as how to find specific statistical results in SPSS output.

Obtaining a Frequency Distribution and the Mode with SPSS
There were many questions on The Hobbit's Choice survey that had categorical response options and, thus, embodied nominal scaling assumptions. With a nominal scale, the mode is the appropriate measure of central tendency, and variation must be assessed by looking at the distribution of responses across the various response categories.

Earlier, to illustrate how to determine the mode of our 10-person Hobbit's Choice data set, we used the radio programming listening preferences variable as it is a nominal scale. We will now use this variable with the entire 400-completions data set to illustrate how to instruct SPSS to create a frequency distribution and find the mode.

Figure 15.6 shows the clickstream sequence to find a mode for the radio station listening preferences using the entire Hobbit's Choice survey data set. As you can see, the primary menu sequence is ANALYZE-DESCRIPTIVE STATISTICS-FREQUENCIES. This sequence opens up the variable selection window where you specify the variable(s) to be analyzed, and the Statistics . . . button opens up the Statistics window that has several statistical concepts as options. Since we are working only with the mode, you would click in the check mark box beside the Mode. Continue will close this window and OK will close the variable selection and cause SPSS to create a frequency distribution and to identify the

Descriptive statistics are needed to see The Hobbit's Choice survey's basic findings.

A frequency distribution and mode are appropriate for nominal scales.

Use the ANALYZE-DESCRIPTIVE STATISTICS-FREQUENCIES procedure to produce descriptive statistics for variables with nominal or ordinal scaling.

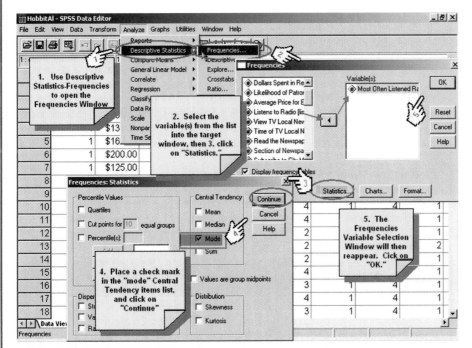

Figure **15.6**   **The SPSS Clickstream to Obtain a Frequency Distribution and the Mode**

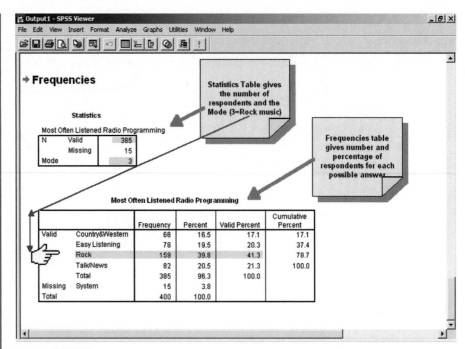

Figure **15.7** The SPSS Output for a Frequency Distribution and the Mode

mode. You can see this output in Figure 15.7 where the code number of "3" is specified as the mode response, and the frequency distribution shows that rock is the most popular station format with 159 respondents selecting it, or 39.8 percent of the total 100 percent.

As you look at the output, you should notice that the variable labels and value labels were defined, and they appear on the output. The DESCRIPTIVE STATISTICS-FREQUENCIES procedure creates a frequency distribution and associated percentage distribution of the responses for each question. Its output includes a statistics table and a table for each variable that includes the variable label, value labels, frequencies, percent, valid percent, and cumulative percent.

Our Hobbit's Choice Restaurant survey data set is typical because there are missing answers. As you learned in Chapter 14, it is not uncommon for respondents to refuse to answer a question in a survey or for them to be unable to answer a question. Alternatively, a respondent may be directed to skip a question if his or her previous answer does not qualify him or her for the subsequent question. If any of these occurs, and the respondent is still included in the data set, we have an instance of "missing data." This is absolutely no problem for SPSS and most other data analysis programs, but the output will be adjusted to compensate for the missing data. Read Marketing Research Insight 15.6 to learn about what SPSS specifies as "valid percent."

SPSS Student Assistant Online
Descriptive Statistics for Nominal
Data: Frequencies, Percents, Mode

Finding the Median with SPSS

It is also a simple matter to determine the median using the ANALYZE-DESCRIPTIVE STATISTICS-FREQUENCIES menu sequence. As we indicated, in order for the median to be a sensible measure of central tendency, the values must have some logical order to them. In our 10-respondent example, we used the likelihood of patronizing Hobbit's Choice Restaurant to obtain the median from the full data set. The procedure is very similar to the mode procedure. There are two differences. First, the "likely" variable is selected in the variable selection window and, second, the median is checked in the statistics window. Refer to Figure 15.6, and just imagine that the likelihood of patronizing is the chosen variable, and that the median is checked instead of the mode.

The resulting SPSS output will have the frequency distribution of our likelihood variable, and it will show that code number 3, pertaining to "neither likely nor unlikely" is the 50/50 location in the scale, or the median. You can confirm that 3 is the median by running the analysis yourself using our Hobbit's Choice Restaurant survey data set. Use Figure 15.6 as a guide, but select the likelihood variable for the analysis and place a check mark in the median checkbox.

With SPSS Descriptives it was found that respondents spend a little less than $19 for an evening meal entrée.

SPSS

When using SPSS DESCRIPTIVES, always bear in mind the variables being analyzed should be interval or ratio scaled.

SPSS

SPSS Student Assistant Online Descriptive Statistics for Scaled Data: Mean, Standard Deviation, Median, Range

Finding the Mean, Range, and Standard Deviation with SPSS

As we have mentioned, computer statistical programs cannot distinguish the level of measurement of various questions. Consequently, it is necessary for the analyst to discern the level of measurement and to select the correct procedure(s). One question in the survey asked, ". . . what would you expect an average evening meal entrée item alone to be priced?" Respondents answered with a specific dollar amount, so we have a ratio scale.

Here we do not want a frequency table for two reasons. First, the average price variable is ratio scaled and, second, a frequency table will have to be quite large to accommodate all of the different monthly fees. So we will use the ANALYZE-DESCRIPTIVE STATISTICS-DESCRIPTIVES commands, and click on the Options button after we have selected average price as the variable for analysis. In the Options panel, you can select the mean, standard deviation, range, and so forth. Refer to Figure 15.8 for the SPSS clickstream sequence.

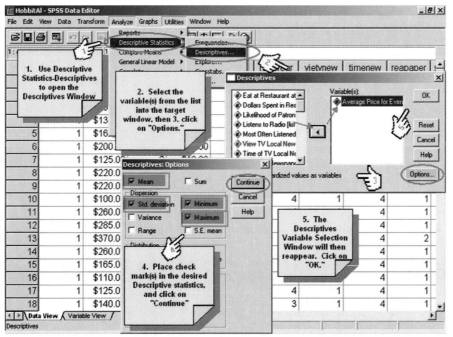

Figure **15.8** **The SPSS Clickstream to Obtain a Mean, Standard Deviation, and the Range**

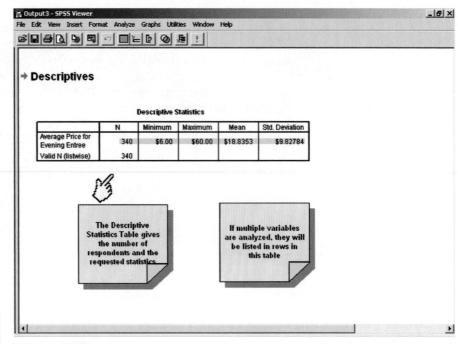

Figure **15.9** **SPSS Output for a Mean, Standard Deviation, and the Range**

Figure 15.9 presents the output generated from this option. In our Hobbit's Choice survey, the output reveals that the average expected entrée price estimate was $18.84, and the standard deviation was $9.83 (both rounded up). You can also see that the lowest estimate (minimum) was $6, and the highest (maximum) was $60, making the range equal to $54.

MARKETING RESEARCH
INSIGHT
15.6

Additional Insights ◀

Valid Percents: How SPSS Handles Missing Data

You saw in Figure 15.7 that SPSS produces a frequency table that has four columns of statistical information: (1) frequency, or raw count, (2) percent, or frequency divided by the total respondents, (3) valid percent, which we will discuss here, and (4) cumulative percent. When there are no missing values, that is, when all respondents have answered the question, the percent and the valid percent columns will be identical. "Missing cases" are those instances in which a respondent did not answer a particular question because (1) the question did not apply, (2) it was overlooked, or (3) the respondent refused to answer that question. Normally, missing cases are input as blanks or special codes in the data set that the statistical analysis software is programmed to identify as missing data and to exclude in any

analysis. With SPSS frequency distributions, this exclusion is noted under the column called "Valid Percent."

However, if there are missing data items, this will be signaled with the "Missing" row that appears when missing data are encountered. When there are missing data, the researcher should use the "Valid Percent" column. In other words, the valid percentages are determined after any missing values are removed. Note in Figure 15.7 that 15 respondents are listed as missing. The "Percent" column is as we described it. For example 159/400 is 39.8 percent, but the "Valid Percent" column adjusts by taking out the missing values. Thus, the valid percent is 159/385, or 41.3 percent, because 15 respondents did not answer this question because they indicated "no" to the previous question asking them if they listen to the radio regularly.

SPSS Student Assistant Online
Working with SPSS Output, Including
"What's This?"

SUMMARY

This chapter introduced you to the descriptive statistics researchers use to inspect basic patterns in data sets. These measures help researchers summarize, conceptualize, and generalize their findings. We also previewed the five types of statistical analysis: descriptive, inferential, differences, associative, and predictive. Descriptive analysis is performed with measures of central tendency such as the mean, mode, or median, each of which portrays the typical respondent or the typical answer to the question being analyzed. The chapter contained formulas and examples of how to determine these central tendency measures. Measures of variability, including the frequency distribution, range, and standard deviation, provide bases for envisioning the degree of similarity of all respondents to the typical respondent. The chapter also contained instructions and formulas of key variability measures. Basically, descriptive analysis yields a profile of how respondents in the sample answered the various questions in the survey. The chapter also provides information on how to instruct SPSS to compute descriptive analyses with SPSS using The Hobbit's Choice Restaurant survey data set. Both clickstream sequences for setting up the analyses and the resulting output are shown.

KEY TERMS

Data entry (p. 431)
Data coding (p. 431)
Data code book (p. 431)
Data reduction (p. 432)
Descriptive analysis (p. 433)
Inferential analysis (p. 433)
Differences analysis (p. 434)
Associative analysis (p. 435)
Predictive analysis (p. 435)
Measures of central tendency (p. 437)

Mode (p. 437)
Median (p. 437)
Mean (p. 438)
Measures of variability (p. 439)
Frequency distribution (p. 440)
Percentage distribution (p. 440)
Range (p. 440)
Standard deviation (p. 440)
Variance (p. 443)

REVIEW QUESTIONS/APPLICATIONS

1. Indicate what data reduction is and why it is useful.
2. Define and differentiate each of the following: (a) descriptive analysis, (b) inferential analysis, (c) associative analysis, (d) predictive analysis, and (e) differences analysis.
3. Indicate why a researcher might refrain from reporting the use of highly sophisticated statistical analyses and opt for simpler forms of analysis.
4. What is a data matrix and how does it appear?
5. What is a measure of central tendency and what does it describe?
6. Indicate the concept of variability and relate how it helps in the description of responses to a particular question on a questionnaire.
7. Using examples, illustrate how a frequency distribution (or a percentage distribution) reveals the variability in responses to a Likert-type question in a lifestyle study. Use two extreme examples of much variability and little variability.
8. Indicate what a range is and where it should be used as an indicator of the amount of dispersion in a sample.
9. With explicit reference to the formula for a standard deviation, show how it measures how different respondents are from one another.
10. Why is the mean an inappropriate measure of central tendency in each of the following cases: (a) gender of respondent (male or female); (b) marital status

(single, married, divorced, separated, widowed, other); (c) a taste test in which subjects indicate their first, second, and third choices of Miller Lite, Bud Light, and Coors Silver Bullet?

11. For each of the cases in question 10, what is the appropriate central tendency measure?

12. In a survey on magazine subscriptions, respondents write in the number of magazines they subscribe to regularly. What measures of central tendency can be used? Which is the most appropriate and why?

13. If you use the standard deviation as a measure of the variability in a sample, what statistical assumptions have you implicitly adopted?

14. A manager has commissioned research on a special marketing problem. He is scheduled to brief the board of directors on the problem's resolution in a meeting in New York tomorrow morning. Unfortunately, the research has fallen behind schedule, but the research director works late that night in the downtown San Francisco headquarters and completes the basic data analysis, which will be sufficient for the presentation. However, he now has stacks of computer output and less than an hour before the manager calls him for an early-morning briefing on the survey's basic findings. The researcher looks around at the equipment in his office and an idea flashes in his head. He immediately grabs a blank questionnaire. What is he about to do to facilitate the quick communication of the study's basic findings to the manager?

INTERACTIVE LEARNING

Visit the Web site at www.prenhall.com/burnsbush. For this chapter, work through the Self-Study Quizzes, and get instant feedback on whether you need additional studying. On the Web site, you can review the chapter outlines and case information for Chapter 15.

CASE 15.1   Tinseltown Theaters Improvement Survey

Mary Smith graduated from college in June 2002. On graduation, she took a job as a marketing research assistant with Tinseltown Theaters, a movieplex theater chain located in the midwestern United States, headquartered in St. Louis, Missouri. It was not the position she wanted, but she did want to work in a large company, and Tinseltown had 25 cineplex theaters in the Midwest, and she figured she would be promoted into a marketing management position in a year or two if she did well.

When Mary began working, the marketing research department was in the middle of a huge telephone survey of Tinseltown moviegoers across its five-state market area. The objectives of the survey included (1) to determine why people select a movie theater, (2) to identify how many and why people use more than one movie theater, (3) to investigate satisfaction or dissatisfaction with Tinseltown Theaters, (4) to generate suggestions for improved Tinseltown services, and (5) to compare profiles of Tinseltown "regular" customers with the profiles of customers who are "regulars" at competing movie theaters.

Mary was assigned the responsibility of data analysis because she was fresh out of college. She was informed that Tinseltown headquarters uses a statistical analysis program called WINSTATS for its data analysis. All of the 5,000 respondents' answers have been put on the computer, and all that is left is for someone to use WINSTATS to perform the necessary analyses. Of course, someone has to interpret the results, too. It is Mary's responsibility to do the analysis and to interpret it.

The questionnaire designers created a code sheet of the scales used in the survey. This code book is duplicated in the following table:

VARIABLE	RESPONSE SCALE USED
Age	Actual age in years
Income	Ranges in $10,000 increments
Gender	Male, female
Marital status	Single, married, other
Satisfaction with service	10-point scale from "poor" to "excellent"
10 possible improvements in service	A 5-point, disagree–agree scale for each improvement
Preferred movie theater	Tinseltown or "some other"
Usage of various services	Yes or no for each of 15 different services such as purchase tickets over the phone, receive mail listings of upcoming movies, use coupons, etc.
Movie theater loyalty	Total number of different services used at that preferred movie theater (0 to 15)
Exposure to mail advertising	Yes or no to recall receiving mail advertising last month from Tinseltown Theaters

1. What type of descriptive data analysis should Mary instruct WINSTATS to perform to determine basic patterns in the factors listed on the code sheet? For each variable, identify the type of descriptive analysis, describe its aspects, and indicate why it is appropriate.
2. Give an example of what each result might "look like" and how it should be interpreted.

CASE 15.2   Auto Online Web Site Usage Survey (Part I)

Auto Online is a Web site where prospective automobile buyers can find information about the various makes and models. Individuals can actually purchase a make and model with specific options and features online. Recently, Auto Online posted an online questionnaire on the Internet, and it mailed invitations to the last 5,000 automobile buyers who visited Auto Online. Some of these buyers bought their car from Auto Online, whereas the remaining individuals bought their autos from a dealership. However, they did visit Auto Online at least one time prior to that purchase.

The questionniare that was posted online is produced here, and its code numbers are included for your information.

Auto Online *Online Survey Questionnaire*

Please answer the following questions to the best of your ability. When you have answered all questions, click on the "Submit" button at the end. Please do not respond to this questionnaire more than one time.

1. Have you visited the Auto Online Web site in the past 3 months?
   ____ Yes (1)   ____ No (2)
2. How often do you make purchases through the Internet?

Very Often	Often	Occasionally	Almost Never	Never
5	4	3	2	1

3. Indicate your opinion on each of the following statements. For each one, please indicate if you strongly disagree, somewhat disagree, are neutral, somewhat agree, or strongly agree.

	STRONGLY DISAGREE		NEUTRAL		STRONGLY AGREE
I like using the Internet.	1	2	3	4	5
I use the Internet to research purchases I make.	1	2	3	4	5
I think purchasing items from the Internet is safe.	1	2	3	4	5
The Internet is a good tool to use when researching an automobile purchase.	1	2	3	4	5
The Internet should not be used to purchase vehicles.	1	2	3	4	5
Online dealerships are just another way of getting you into the traditional dealership.	1	2	3	4	5
I like the process of buying a new vehicle.	1	2	3	4	5
I don't like to hassle with car salesmen.	1	2	3	4	5

4. About how many times before you bought your automobile did you visit the Auto Online Web site?

    _____ times

5. How did you find out about Auto Online? Indicate all of the ways that you can recall.
    _____ From a friend (0,1)   _____ Web surfing (0,1)   _____ Theater (0,1)
    _____ Billboard (0,1)   _____ Search engine (0,1)   _____ Newspaper (0,1)
    _____ Internet banner ad (0,1)   _____ Television (0,1)   _____ Other (0,1)

6. What is your reaction to the following statements about the Auto Online Web site?

	STRONGLY DISAGREE		NEUTRAL		STRONGLY AGREE
The Web site was easy to use.	1	2	3	4	5
I found the Web site was very helpful in my purchase.	1	2	3	4	5
I had a positive experience using the Web site.	1	2	3	4	5
I would use this Web site only for research.	1	2	3	4	5
The Web site influenced me to buy my vehicle.	1	2	3	4	5
I would feel secure to buy from this Web site.	1	2	3	4	5

7. Did you buy your new vehicle on the Auto Online Web site?
    _____ Yes (1)   _____ No (2)

    a. If yes, was it a better experience than buying at a traditional dealership visit?
        _____ Yes (1)   _____ No (2)

    b. If yes, indicate how much better.
        _____ A great deal better   (1)   _____ Somewhat better   (3)
        _____ Much better   (2)   _____ Just a bit better   (4)

8. The next six statements are possible reasons why people may not buy a car from start to finish off the Internet. Please indicate the degree to which you agree or disagree with each statement.

	STRONGLY DISAGREE		NEUTRAL		STRONGLY AGREE
People feel that the Internet is not a safe place for personal information.	1	2	3	4	5
People want to test the performance of the vehicle before buying it.	1	2	3	4	5
People feel they can negotiate a better price by talking with a sales representative in person.	1	2	3	4	5
People usually have trade-ins that are too complicated to deal with online.	1	2	3	4	5
People like to have a "hands-on" situation when buying different options for their vehicle.	1	2	3	4	5
People want to see the vehicle before they buy it to check for imperfections.	1	2	3	4	5

The next few questions pertain to the vehicle you just purchased.

9. For how many weeks were you actively searching for your vehicle? ____ weeks
10. If you traded in a vehicle, approximately how much was it worth? $____
11. What was the approximate sticker price of your new vehicle? $____
12. What was the approximate actual price you paid for it? $____

There are only a few more questions for clarification purposes.

13. What is your age? ____ years
14. What is your marital status?

____ Single (1)   ____ Married (2)   ____ Widowed (3)   ____ Divorced (4)   ____ Separated (5)

15. How many children under the age of 18 are living with you? _____
16. What is the highest level of education you have completed?

____ Less than high school (1)   ____ High school (2)   ____ Some college (3)

____ Undergraduate degree (4)   ____ Graduate degree (5)____ Other (Specify: _____) (6)

17. What is your race?

____ Caucasian (1)____ Black (2)____ Asian (3)____ American Indian (4)

____ Hispanic (5)____ Other (6)

18. What range includes your total household income before taxes for last year?

____ Under $35,000 (1)   ____ $35,000–$50,000 (2)   ____ $50,000–$65,000 (3)

____ $65,000–$80,000 (4)   ____ $80,000–95,000 (5)   ____ $95,000–$110,000 (6)

____ Over $110,000 (7)

19. Your gender is . . .

____ Male (1)   ____ Female (2)

A total of 1,400 respondents answered the Auto Online survey, and the SPSS data set is named **AutoOnline.sav**. To download this data set, go to the following Web site, and find the dataset download area at **www.prenhall.com/burnsbush**.

Perform the proper descriptive analysis with SPSS Student Version on all of the questions on the questionnaire.

CASE 15.3   *Your Integrated Case*

This is your integrated case, described on pages 42–43. The Hobbit's Choice Restaurant Survey SPSS data set can be downloaded from the text Web site www.prenhall.com/burnsbush.

The Hobbit's Choice Restaurant Survey Descriptive Analysis

Cory Rogers was happy to call Jeff Dean to inform him that The Hobbit's Choice Restaurant survey data were collected and ready for analysis. Of course, Cory had other marketing research projects and meetings scheduled with present and prospective clients, so he called in his marketing intern, Celeste Brown. Celeste was a senior marketing major at Able State University, and she had taken marketing research in the previous semester. Celeste had "aced" this class, which she enjoyed a great deal. Her professor had invited Cory Rogers to give a talk on "a typical day in the life of a market researcher," and Celeste had approached Cory the very next day about a marketing research internship. Like every dedicated marketing major, Celeste had kept her Burns and Bush marketing research textbook for future reference.

Cory called Celeste into his office, and said, "Celeste, it is time to do some analysis on the survey we did for Jeff Dean. For now, let's just get a feel for what the data look like. I'll leave it up to your judgment as to what basic analysis to run. Let's meet tomorrow at 2:30 P.M. and see what you have found."

Your task in Case 15.3 is to take the role of Celeste Brown, marketing intern. As we indicated in this chapter, the file name is HobbitData.sav, and it is in SPSS data file format. We have used this data set in some of the examples of various types of descriptive analysis in this chapter.

1. Determine what variables are categorical (either nominal or ordinal scales), perform the appropriate descriptive analysis, and interpret it.
2. Determine what variables are metric scales (either interval or ratio scales), perform the appropriate descriptive analysis, and interpret it.

Chapter 16

Generalizing a Sample's Findings to Its Population and Testing Hypotheses About Percents and Means

Practitioner Viewpoint

Research is typically conducted to improve the chances of marketing success and reduce the risks of career-ending failure. Companies can't afford to interview everyone when they need to make a marketing decision, of course, so the gods have given us a miracle called "sampling" that allows us to talk to a few to learn what the many are thinking. Sometimes we use nonprobability samples because, in the right circumstances, it is sufficient for us to make a decision based on what x number of people have told us. However, in other cases, when we want to make estimates of the population parameters with a known level of precision, we must use probability sample plans. Thus, if you have used a probability sampling plan, you can then use SPSS to assess how precise your sample statistic is to the true population parameter you are trying to estimate. (Of course, you learned in Chapter 13 that the size of the sample determines how accurate your sample estimate will be.) In this chapter, you will learn how to estimate the accuracy of statistics based on a sample, and you will learn how to test hypotheses, using the concepts of statistical inference.

Jerry W. Thomas
President/CEO
Decision Analyst, Inc.

Kit Kat's Annual Mindshare Survey

Nestlé's Kit Kat competes with a vast variety and huge number of candy bars. To name just a few, its competitors include Almond Joy, Chunky, Heath Bars, Hershey Bars, M&M's, Milky Way, Rocky Road, Snickers, Tootsie Roll, and Zagnut. The marketing managers of Kit Kat know that although there are candy bar consumers who tend to be very brand loyal, such as Milky Way fanatics, a great many candy bar buyers constantly jump from brand to brand. Furthermore, Kit Kat has found from its research that many of these volatile candy buyers often make up their minds as to what bar to buy as soon as the craving hits them. So, although Kit Kat knows its Kit Kat fans will always buy a Kit Kat, it also knows that it must be prominent in the minds of the other candy bar buyers who are not focused on their favorite brand.

That is, a candy bar buyer prospect feels the craving for chocolate or something sweet, and he or she then quickly conjures up a small number of competing candy bar brands in his or her head. The decision as to which one is then made mentally while the person is headed to the store or the closest vending machine. Kit Kat's challenge then is to have "mindshare." Mindshare is similar to market share, except it exists in the consumer's awareness set and, hopefully, in the consideration set. The awareness set is all the brands of which the consumer is aware in a product category, and the consideration set is those brands in the awareness set that the consumer would consider buying when the purchase urge hits.

To track consumers and, further, to assess the effectiveness of its promotional campaigns aimed at increasing Kit Kat's mindshare, Kit Kat commissioned an annual survey. Here is the conversation between Stan, the Kit Kat marketing manager, and Barbara, the research project director, which took place recently.

Statistical inference can help Kit Kat study its mindshare changes.

Stan: "I see that you have the results of our annual Kit Kat Mindshare survey."

Barbara: "I certainly do. We don't have the report finished yet, but I have some notes, and I can summarize our major findings."

Stan: "Great. I certainly hope this is good news and not bad news."

Barbara: "I bring good news. Should I deliver it?"

Stan: "I can't wait to hear it."

Barbara: "All right, here goes. You probably recall that we found Kit Kat to have 50 percent mindshare last year, so we calculated confidence intervals and told you that Kit Kat had between 42 percent and 58 percent mindshare."

Stan: "Yes, I do recall, and it was the basis for our promotional campaign target this year. We are striving for 70 percent mindshare."

Barbara: "Goals are always good. The movement is in the right direction, so you are doing something right. This year we found 65 percent mindshare for Kit Kat. That computes to a 95 percent confidence interval of 62 to 68 percent."

Stan: "So we almost made our 70 percent goal. Wait a minute. Last year, we had 50 percent plus or minus 8 percent, and this year we have 65 percent plus or minus 3 percent. If we had the 8 percent from last year, we can say we reached our 70 percent goal. What gives?"

Barbara: "Two things are different. The 65 percent means more people are in agreement that Kit Kat will be considered when they get the craving, and we increased the sample by one-quarter. We have less variability and more sample accuracy, so the plus or minus number is smaller."

Stan: "Oh. Well, you're the expert."[1]

As you learned in Chapter 15, descriptive measures of central tendency and measures of variability adequately summarize the findings of a survey. However, whenever a probability sample is drawn from a population, it is not enough to simply report the sample's descriptive statistics, for these measures contain a certain degree of error due to the sampling process. Every sample provides some information about its population, but there is always some sample error that must be taken into account. That is what Barbara is communicating to Stan in our opening case. By reading and comprehending the material in this chapter, you should be able to understand Barbara's comments on variability and sample accuracy.

We begin the chapter by noting that the term "statistic" applies to a sample, whereas the term "parameter" pertains to the related population value. Next, we describe the concept of logical inference and show how it relates to statistical inference. There are two basic types of statistical inference, and we discuss both cases. First, there is parameter estimation in which a value, such as the population mean, is estimated based on a sample's mean and its size. Second, there is hypothesis testing where an assessment is made as to how much of a sample's findings support a manager's or researcher's *a priori* belief regarding the size of a population value. We provide formulas and numerical examples and also show you examples of SPSS procedures and output using The Hobbit's Choice Restaurant survey data.

STATISTICS VERSUS PARAMETERS

Statistics are sample values, whereas parameters are corresponding population values.

We begin the chapter by defining the concepts of statistics and parameters. There is a fundamental distinction you should keep in mind. Values that are computed from information provided by a sample are referred to as the sample's **statistics,** whereas

Table **16.1**	**Population Parameters and Their Companion Sample Statistics**	
STATISTICAL CONCEPT	**POPULATION PARAMETER (GREEK LETTERS)**	**SAMPLE STATISTIC (ROMAN LETTERS)**
Average	μ (mu)	$\bar{x}$
Standard deviation	σ (sigma)	s
Percentage	π (pi)	p
Slope	β (beta)	b

values that are computed from a complete census, which are considered to be precise and valid measures of the population, are referred to as **parameters**. Statisticians use Greek letters when referring to population parameters and Roman letters when referring to statistics. As you can see in Table 16.1, the notation used for a percentage is p for the statistic and π for the parameter, the notations for standard deviation are s (statistic) and σ (parameter), and the notations for the mean are $\bar{x}$ (statistic) and μ (parameter). Because a census is impractical, the sample statistic is used to estimate the population parameter. This chapter describes the procedures used when estimating various population parameters.

THE CONCEPTS OF INFERENCE AND STATISTICAL INFERENCE

We begin by defining inference because an understanding of this concept will help you understand what statistical inference is all about. **Inference** is a form of logic in which you make a generalization about an entire class based on what you have observed about a small set of members of that class. When you infer, you draw a conclusion from a small amount of evidence. For example, if two of your friends each bought a new Chevrolet and they both complained about their cars' performances, you might infer that all Chevrolets perform poorly. On the other hand, if one of your friends complained about his Chevy, whereas the other one did not, you might infer that your friend with the problem Chevy happened to buy a lemon.

Inference is drawing a conclusion based on some evidence.

Inferences are greatly influenced by the amount of evidence in support of the generalization. So, if 20 of your friends bought new Chevrolets, and they all complained about poor performance, your inference would naturally be stronger or more certain than it would be in the case of only two friends' complaining.

Statistical inference is a set of procedures in which the sample size and sample statistics are used to make estimates of population parameters. For now, let us concentrate on the percentage, p, as the sample statistic we are using to estimate the population percentage, π, and see how sample size enters into statistical inference. Suppose that Chevrolet suspected that there were some dissatisfied customers, and it commissioned two independent marketing research surveys to determine the amount of dissatisfaction that existed in its customer group. (Of course, our Chevrolet example is entirely fictitious. We don't mean to imply that Chevrolets perform in an unsatisfactory way.)

Statistical inference takes into account that large random samples are more accurate than are small ones.

In the first survey, 100 customers who had purchased a Chevy in the last six months were called on the telephone and asked, "In general, would you say that you are satisfied or dissatisfied with the performance of your Chevrolet since you bought it?" The survey found that 30 respondents (30 percent) are dissatisfied. This finding could be inferred to be the total population of Chevy owners who had bought one in the last six months, and we would say that there is 30 percent dissatisfaction. However, we know that our sample, which, by the way, was a probability sample,

Statistical inference is based on sample size and variability, which then determine the amount of sampling error.

must contain some sample error, and in order to reflect this you would have to say that there was *about* 30 percent dissatisfaction in the population. In other words, it might actually be more or less than 30 percent if we did a census because the sample provided us with only an estimate.

In the second survey, 1,000 respondents—that's 10 times more than in the first survey—were called on the telephone and asked the same question. This survey found that 35 percent of the respondents are "dissatisfied." Again, we know that the 35 percent is an estimate containing sampling error, so now we would also say that the population dissatisfaction percentage was *about* 35 percent. This means that we have two estimates of the degree of dissatisfaction with Chevrolets. One is about 30 percent, whereas the other is about 35 percent.

How do we translate our answers (remember they include the word "about") into more accurate numerical representations? Let us say you could translate them into ballpark ranges. That is, you could translate them so we could say "30 percent plus or minus *x* percent" for the sample of 100 and "35 percent plus or minus *y* percent" for the sample of 1,000. How would *x* and *y* compare? To answer this question, think back on how your logical inference was stronger with 20 friends than it was with 2 friends with Chevrolets. To state this in a different way, with a larger sample (or more evidence), we have agreed that you would be more certain that the sample statistic was accurate with respect to estimating the true population value. In other words, with a larger sample size you should expect the range used to estimate the true population value to be smaller. Intuitively, you should expect the range for *y* to be smaller than the range for *x* because you have a large sample and less sampling error.

As these examples reveal, when the statistician makes estimates of population parameters such as the percentage or mean, the sample statistic is used as the beginning point, and then a range is computed in which the population parameter is estimated to fall. The size of the sample, or *n*, plays a crucial role in this computation, as you will see in all of the statistical inference formulas we present in this chapter.

The three types of statistical inference are parameter estimation, hypothesis tests, and tests of significant differences.

Three types of statistical inferences are often used by marketing researchers. We will introduce them here and describe them more completely later in the chapter. They are: parameter estimation, hypothesis testing, and tests of significant differences. Parameter estimation is used to estimate the population value (parameter) through the use of confidence intervals. Hypothesis testing is used to compare the sample statistic with what is believed (hypothesized) to be the population value prior to undertaking the study. **Tests of significant differences** are used to compare the sample statistics of two (or more) subgroups in the sample to see whether or not there are statistically significant differences between their corresponding population values. (Although we distinguished between differences analysis and inference analysis in the previous chapter, strictly speaking, differences tests are a form of statistical inference.) We describe the first two types of statistical inference in this chapter and differences tests in Chapter 17. Also, for quick reference, we have listed and described the three types of statistical inference in Table 16.2 with examples of findings of an online survey conducted for RealPlayer™.

PARAMETER ESTIMATION

To estimate a population parameter you need a sample statistic (mean or percentage), the standard error of the statistic, and the desired level of confidence (95% or 99%).

Estimation of population parameters is a common type of statistical inference used in marketing research survey analysis. As indicated earlier, inference is largely a reflection of the amount of sampling error believed to exist in the sample statistic. When the *New York Times* conducts a survey and finds that readers spend an average of 45 minutes daily reading the *Times*, or when McDonald's determines through a nationwide sample that 78 percent of all Egg McMuffin Breakfast buyers buy a

Table **16.2**	**The Three Types of Statistical Inference: Results of Online Music Listeners Survey Conducted for RealPlayer™**	
TYPE	**DESCRIPTION**	**EXAMPLE**
Parameter estimation	Estimate the population value (parameter) through the use of confidence intervals.	The percent of PC users who listen to music online is 30% ± 10%, or from 20% to 40%.
Hypothesis testing	Compare the sample statistic with what is believed (hypothesized) to be the population value prior to undertaking the study.	Online music listeners listen an average of 45 ± 15 minutes per day, not 90 minutes as believed by RealPlayer managers.
Tests of significant differences	Compare the sample statistics of two (or more) subgroups in the sample to see whether or not there are statistically significant differences between their corresponding population values.	Online music listeners who are under 20 years old listen 60 minutes, whereas those over 20 listen 30 minutes, on average, and the difference is statistically significant.

Note: The examples are fictitious.

cup of coffee, both companies may want to determine more accurately how close these estimates are to the actual population parameters.

Parameter estimation is the process of using sample information to compute an interval that describes the range of a parameter such as the population mean (μ) or the population percentage (π). It involves the use of three values: the sample statistic (such as the mean or the percentage), the standard error of the statistic, and the desired level of confidence (usually 95% or 99%). A discussion of how each value is determined follows.

In parameter estimation, the sample statistic is usually a mean or a percentage.

Sample Statistic

You should recall from the formula provided in Chapter 15 that the mean is the average of a set of interval- or ratio-scaled numbers. For example, you might be working with a sample of golfers and researching the average number of golf balls they buy per month. Or you might be investigating how much high school students spend, on average, on fast foods between meals. For a percentage, you could be

McDonald's can use statistical inference to estimate the percentage of Egg McMuffin buyers who order a cup of coffee.

examining what percentage of golfers buy only Maxfli golf balls, or you might be looking at what percentage of high school students buy from Taco Bell between meals. In either case, the mean or percentage is derived from a sample, so it is the sample statistic.

Standard Error

The standard error is a measure of the variability in a sampling distribution.

There usually is some degree of variability in the sample. That is, our golfers do not all buy the same number of golf balls per month and they do not all buy Maxfli. Not all of our high school students eat fast food between meals and not all of the ones who do go to Taco Bell. In Chapter 15, we introduced you to variability with a mean by describing the standard deviation, and we used the percentage distribution as a way of describing variability when percentages are being used. Also, in Chapter 13, we described how, if you theoretically took many, many samples and plotted the mean or percentage as a frequency distribution, it would approximate a bell-shaped curve called the sampling distribution. The **standard error** is a measure of the variability in the sampling distribution based on what is theoretically believed to occur were we to take a multitude of independent samples from the same population. We described the standard error formulas in Chapter 13, but we repeat them here because they are vital to statistical inference in that they tie together the sample size and its variability.

The formula for mean standard error differs from a percentage standard error.

The formula for **the standard error of the mean** is as follows:

Formula for standard error of the mean
$$s_{\bar{x}} = \frac{s}{\sqrt{n}}$$

where

$s_{\bar{x}}$ = standard error of the mean

s = standard deviation

n = sample size

The formula for the **standard error of the percentage** is as follows:

Formula for standard error of the percentage
$$s_p = \sqrt{\frac{p \times q}{n}}$$

where

s_p = standard error of the percentage

p = the sample percentage

$q = (100 - p)$

n = sample size

In both equations, the sample size n is found in the denominator. This means that the standard error will be smaller with larger sample sizes and larger with smaller sample sizes. At the same time, both of these formulas for the standard error reveal the impact of the variation found in the sample. Variation is represented by the standard deviation s for a mean and by $(p \times q)$ for a percentage. In either equation, the variation is in the numerator, so the greater the variability, the greater the standard error. Thus, the standard error simultaneously takes into account both the sample size and the amount of variation found in the sample. The following examples illustrate this fact.

The standard error takes into account sample size and the variability in the sample.

Suppose that the *New York Times* survey on the amount of daily time spent reading the *Times* had determined a standard deviation of 20 minutes and had used a sample size of 100. The resulting standard error of the mean would be as follows:

$$s_{\bar{x}} = \frac{s}{\sqrt{n}}$$

Calculation of standard error of the mean with standard deviation = 20

$$s_{\bar{x}} = \frac{20}{\sqrt{100}}$$

$$= \frac{20}{10}$$

$$= 2 \text{ minutes}$$

On the other hand, if the survey had determined a standard deviation of 40 minutes, the standard error would be as follows:

Notice how sample variability affects the standard error in these two examples.

$$s_{\bar{x}} = \frac{s}{\sqrt{n}}$$

Calculation of standard error of the mean with standard deviation = 40

$$s_{\bar{x}} = \frac{40}{\sqrt{100}}$$

$$= \frac{40}{10}$$

$$= 4 \text{ minutes}$$

As you can see, the standard error of the mean from a sample with little variability (20 minutes) is smaller than the standard error of the mean from a sample with much variability (40 minutes), as long as both samples have the same size. In fact, you should have noticed that when the variability was doubled from 20 to 40 minutes, the standard error also doubled, given identical sample sizes. Refer to Figure 16.1.

The standard error of a percentage mirrors this logic, although the formula looks a bit different. In this case, as we indicated earlier, the degree of variability is inherent in the $(p \times q)$ aspect of the equation. Very little variability is indicated if p and q are very different in size. For example, if a survey of 100 McDonald's breakfast buyers determined that 90 percent of the respondents ordered coffee with their Egg McMuffin and 10 percent of the respondents did not, there would be very little variability because almost everybody orders coffee with breakfast. On the other hand, if the sample determined that there was a 50–50 split between those who had and those who had not ordered coffee, there would be a great deal more variability because any two customers would probably differ in their drink orders.

With a 90–10 percent split there is little variability.

We can apply these two results to the standard error of percentage for a comparison. Using a 90–10 percent split, the standard error of percentage is as follows:

$$s_p = \sqrt{\frac{p \times q}{n}}$$

$$= \sqrt{\frac{(90)(10)}{100}}$$

Calculation of standard error of the percent with p = 90 and q = 10

$$= \sqrt{\frac{900}{100}}$$

$$= \sqrt{9}$$

$$= 3\%$$

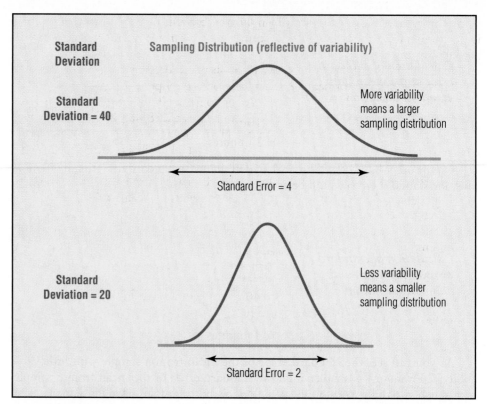

Figure 16.1 **The Variability Found in the Sample Directly Affects the Standard Error (same sample size)**

Using 50–50 percent split, the standard error of the percentage is as follows:

$$s_p = \sqrt{\frac{p \times q}{n}}$$

$$= \sqrt{\frac{(50)(50)}{100}}$$

$$= \sqrt{\frac{2{,}500}{100}}$$

$$= \sqrt{25}$$

$$= 5\%$$

Calculation of standard error of the percent with p = 50 and q = 50

A 50–50 percent split has a larger standard error than a 90–10 one when sample size is the same.

Again, these examples show that greater variability in responses results in a larger standard error of the percentage at a given sample size.

Confidence Intervals

Population parameters are estimated with the use of confidence intervals.

Confidence intervals are the degree of accuracy desired by the researcher and stipulated as a level of confidence in the form of a percentage. We also introduced confidence intervals in Chapter 13, and we briefly review them here. Because there is always some sampling error when a sample is taken, it is necessary to estimate the population parameter with a range. We did this in the Chevrolet owners' example earlier. One factor affecting the size of the range is how confident the researcher wants to be that the range includes the true population percentage. Normally, the researcher first decides on how confident he or she wants to be. The sample statistic is the beginning of the estimate, but because there is sample error present, a "plus" amount and an identical "minus" amount is added and subtracted from the sample statistic to determine the maximum and minimum, respectively, of the range.

Typically, marketing researchers rely only on the 90 percent, 95 percent, or 99 percent levels of confidence, which correspond to ±1.64, ±1.96, and ±2.58 standard errors, respectively. They are designated z_α, so $z_{0.99}$ is ±2.58 standard errors. By far, the **most commonly used level of confidence** in marketing research is the 95 percent level, corresponding to 1.96 standard errors. In fact, the 95 percent level of confidence is usually the default level found in statistical analysis programs such as SPSS. Now that the relationship between the standard error and the measure of sample variability—be it the standard deviation or the percentage—is apparent, it is a simple matter to determine the range in which the population parameter will be estimated. Simply use the appropriate **formula for population parameter estimation** for a mean on a percentage that appears below this paragraph. We use the sample statistics, $\bar{x}$ or p, compute the standard error, and then apply our desired level of confidence. In notation form these are as follows:

> The range of your estimate of the population mean or percentage depends largely on the sample size and the variability found in the sample.

Formula for population parameter Estimation (Mean) $\bar{x} \pm z_\alpha s_{\bar{x}}$

where

$\bar{x}$ = sample mean

z_α = z value for 95 percent or 99 percent level of confidence

$s_{\bar{x}}$ = standard error of the mean

> Confidence intervals are estimated using these formulas.

Formula for population parameter Estimation (Percentage) $p \pm z_\alpha s_p$

where

p = sample percentage

z_α = z value for 95 percent or 99 percent level of confidence

s_p = standard error of the percentage

If you wanted to be 99 percent confident that your range included the true population percentage, for instance, you would multiply the standard error of the percentage s_p by 2.58 and add that value to the percentage p to obtain the upper limit, and you would subtract it from the percentage to find the lower limit. Notice that you have now taken into consideration the sample statistic p, the variability that is in the formula for s_p, the sample size n, which is also in the formula for s_p, and the degree of confidence in your estimate.

How do these formulas relate to inference? Recall that we are estimating a population parameter. That is, we are indicating a range into which it is believed that the true population parameter falls. The size of the range is determined by those three bits of information we have about the population on hand as a result of our sample. The final ingredient is our level of confidence or the degree to which we want to be correct in our estimate of the population parameter. If we are conservative and wish to assume the 99 percent level of confidence, then the range would be more encompassing than if we are less conservative and assume only the 95 percent level of confidence because 99 percent is associated with ±2.58 standard errors and 95 percent is associated with ±1.96 standard errors.

> Marketing researchers typically use only a 95 or a 99 percent confidence interval.

Using these formulas for the sample of 100 *New York Times* readers with a mean reading time of 45 minutes and a standard deviation of 20 minutes, the 95 percent and the 99 percent confidence interval estimates would be calculated as follows.

$$\bar{x} \pm 1.96 \times s_x$$

$$45 \pm 1.96 \times \frac{20}{\sqrt{100}}$$

Calculation of a 95 percent confidence interval for a mean

$$45 \pm 1.96 \times 2$$

$$45 \pm 3.9$$

$$41.1\text{--}48.9 \text{ minutes}$$

Here are two examples of confidence interval computations with a mean.

$$\bar{x} \pm 2.58 \times s_{\bar{x}}$$

$$45 \pm 2.58 \times \frac{20}{\sqrt{100}}$$

Calculation of a 99 percent confidence interval for a mean

$$45 \pm 2.58 \times 2$$

$$45 \pm 5.2$$

$$39.8\text{--}50.2 \text{ minutes}$$

If 50 percent of the 100 Egg McMuffin eaters orders coffee, the 95 percent and 99 percent confidence intervals would be computed using the percentage formula.

$$p \pm 1.96 \times s_p$$

$$p \pm 1.96 \times \sqrt{\frac{p \times q}{n}}$$

Calculation of a 95 percent confidence interval for a percentage

$$50 \pm 1.96 \times \sqrt{\frac{50 \times 50}{100}}$$

$$50 \pm 1.96 \times 5$$

$$50 \pm 9.8$$

$$41.2\%\text{--}59.8\%$$

Here are two examples of confidence interval computations with a percentage.

$$p \pm 2.58 \times s_p$$

$$p \pm 2.58 \times \sqrt{\frac{p \times q}{n}}$$

Calculation of a 99 percent confidence interval for a percentage

$$50 \pm 2.58 \times \sqrt{\frac{50 \times 50}{100}}$$

$$50 \pm 2.58 \times 5$$

$$50 \pm 12.9$$

$$37.1\%\text{--}62.9\%$$

A 99 percent confidence interval is always wider than a 95 percent confidence interval if all other factors are equal.

Notice that the only thing that differs when you compare the 95 percent confidence interval computations to the 99 percent confidence interval computations in each case is z_α. It is 1.96 for 95 percent and 2.58 for 99 percent of confidence. The confidence interval is always wider for 99 percent than it is for 95 percent when the sample size is the same and variability is equal. Table 16.3 lists the steps used to compute confidence intervals.

Table **16.3**	**Steps for How to Compute Confidence Intervals for a Mean or a Percentage**

Step 1. Find the sample statistic, either the mean, $\bar{x}$, or the percentage, p.
Step 2. Determine the amount of variability found in the sample in the form of standard error of the mean, $s_{\bar{x}}$, or standard error of the percentage, s_p.
Step 3. Identify the sample size, n.
Step 4. Decide on the desired level of confidence to determine the value for z: $z_{.95}$ (1.96) or $z_{.99}$ (2.58).
Step 5. Compute your (95%) confidence interval as: $\bar{x} \pm 1.96s_{\bar{x}}$ or $p \pm 1.96s_p$.

How to Interpret an Estimated Population Mean or Percentage Range

How are these ranges interpreted? The interpretation is quite simple when you remember that the sampling distribution notion is the underlying concept. If we were using a 99 percent level of confidence, and if we repeated the sampling process and computed the sample statistic many times, 99 percent of these repeated samples results would produce a range that includes the population parameter. The bell-shaped distribution assumption assures us that the sampling distribution is symmetric.

Obviously, a marketing researcher would take only one sample for a particular marketing research project, and this restriction explains why estimates must be used. Furthermore, it is the conscientious application of probability sampling techniques that allows us to make use of the sampling distribution concept. Thus, statistical inference procedures are the direct linkages between probability sample design and data analysis. Do you remember that you had to grapple with confidence levels when we determined sample size? Now we are on the other side of the table, so to speak, and we must use the sample size for our inference procedures. Confidence intervals must be used when estimating population parameters, and the size of the random sample used is always reflected in these confidence intervals.

There are five steps to computing a confidence interval.

What does this mean? The researcher can say the following about a *New York Times* reading: "My best estimate is that readers spend 45 minutes reading the *Times*. In addition, I am 95 percent confident that the true population value falls between 41.1 and 48.9 minutes." With the tools of statistical inference, a researcher has a good idea of how closely the sample statistic represents the population parameter.

With confidence intervals, Jeff Dean will know what percentage of his target market listens to "rock" radio programs.

As a final note, we want to remind you that the logic of statistical inference is identical to the reasoning process you go through when you weigh evidence to make a generalization or conclusion of some sort. The more evidence you have, the more precise you will be in your generalization. The only difference is that with statistical inference we must follow certain rules that require the application of formulas so our inferences will be consistent with the assumptions of statistical theory. When you make a nonstatistical inference, your judgment can be swayed by subjective factors, so you may not be consistent with others who are making an inference with the same evidence. But in statistical inference, the formulas are completely objective and perfectly consistent. Plus, they are based on accepted statistical concepts.

RETURN TO   *Your Integrated Case*

The Hobbit's Choice Restaurant Survey: How to Obtain a Confidence Interval with SPSS

We will now show you how to use SPSS to obtain confidence intervals.

How to Obtain a Confidence Interval for a Percent with SPSS

Your SPSS program will not calculate the confidence intervals for a percentage. This is because with a categorical variable such as the radio programming format of The Hobbit's Choice Restaurant survey, there may be many different categories. But you know now that the computation is fairly easy, and all you need to know is the value of p and the sample size, both of which you can obtain using the "Frequencies" procedure in SPSS.

Here is an example using The Hobbit's Choice data set. We found in our descriptive analysis that "rock" was the most preferred radio show format, and 41.3 percent of the respondents listened to it. We can calculate the confidence intervals at 95 percent level of confidence easily as we know that the sample size was 400. Here are the calculations.

Calculation of a 95 percent confidence interval for the "rock" radio format percentage in The Hobbit's Choice population

$$p \pm 1.96 \times s_p$$

$$p \pm 1.96 \times \sqrt{\frac{p \times q}{n}}$$

$$41.3 \pm 1.96 \times \sqrt{\frac{41.3 \times 58.7}{400}}$$

$$41.3 \pm 1.96 \times 2.46$$

$$41.3 \pm 4.8$$

$$36.5\%\text{--}46.1\%$$

Now we can say, "Our best estimate of the percentage of the population that prefers 'rock' radio is 41.3 percent, and we are 95 percent confident that the true population value is between 36.5 percent and 46.1 percent."

How to Obtain a Confidence Interval for a Mean with SPSS

Fortunately, because the calculations are a bit more complicated and tedious, your SPSS program will calculate the confidence interval for a mean. To illustrate this feature, we will revisit some very critical comments that Cory Rogers, research project manager, made to Jeff Dean. In fact, Cory Rogers had already made some estimates of demand using the forecasting model. He told Jeff that if only 4 percent of heads of households in the 12 zip code areas claimed they were "very likely" to patronize the restaurant and if these same people spent an average of $200 per month in restaurants and were willing to pay an average of $18 for an à la carte entrée, then the model predicted a very successful restaurant operation.

You should have already found via your descriptive analysis (Case 15.3, page 455), that 18 percent of the respondents indicated "very likely." If you calculate the 95 percent confidence intervals for the population estimate, you will find the range to be 14.2 percent to 21.8 percent, so the first condition is satisfied. The next requirement is an average of $200 per month. We can test this with a 95 percent confidence interval for the mean dollars spent on restaurants for the "very likely" respondents who represent the "very likely" population.

The requirement says that the "very likely" individuals must spend an average of $200 per month, so we must select only those respondents for this analysis. You learned earlier how to select respondents, and you should recall that it is accomplished with the DATA-SELECT CASES menu sequence. Then all we need to specify is the selection condition of "is likely to patronize Hobbit's Choice Restaurant" = 5. With this operation, SPSS will analyze only these respondents.

Figure 16.2 shows the clickstream sequence to accomplish a 95 percent confidence interval estimate using SPSS. As you can see, the correct SPSS procedure is a "One Sample t-test," and you use the ANALYZE-COMPARE MEANS-ONE SAMPLE T TEST menu clickstream sequence to open up the proper window. Refer to Figure 16.2 to see that all you need to do is to select the "Dollars spent in restaurants per month" variable into the Test Variables area, and then click "OK."

Figure 16.3 shows the results of ANALYZE-COMPARE MEANS-ONE SAMPLE T TEST for dollars spent per month in a restaurant. As you can see, the average monthly restaurant expenditures for our "very likely" folks are about $282, and the 95 percent confidence interval is $266.99 to $296.92. To repeat our interpretation of this finding: If we conducted a great many replications of this survey using the same sample size, we would find that 95 percent of the sample average monthly restaurant expenditures for the "very likely" respondents would fall between about $267 and $297.

SPSS Student Assistant Online
Establishing Confidence Intervals
for Means

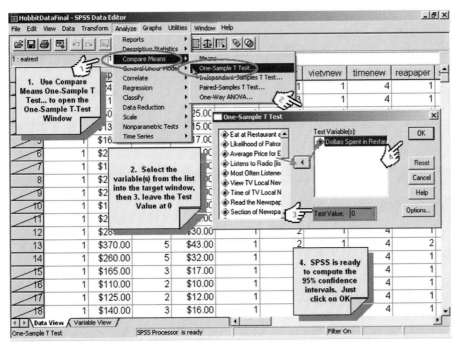

Figure **16.2** **The SPSS Clickstream to Obtain a 95% Confidence Interval for a Mean**

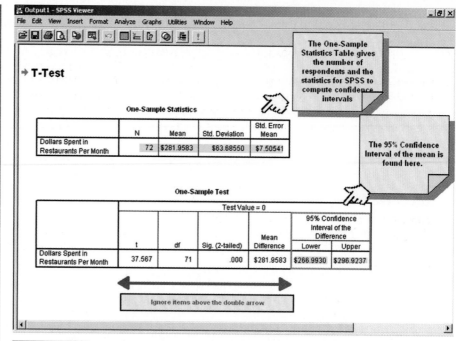

Figure **16.3** The SPSS Output for a 95% Confidence Interval for a Mean

This is very good news for our budding restaurateur, Jeff Dean, as we have satisfied two of the three conditions specified by researcher Cory Rogers: the percentage of individuals in the population who are very likely to visit the proposed restaurants exceeds 4 percent, and these people are spending more than an average of $200 per month on restaurants.

In fact, with our findings, we can estimate the total market potential for all upscale restaurants in the metropolitan area. See Marketing Research Insight 16.1.

Estimating market potential is only one of many useful applications of statistical inference using survey and other data. A company that has built a global reputation in marketing research and decision-making statistical techniques is Decision Analyst, Inc. of Arlington, Texas. You can meet Jerry Thomas, CEO of Decision Analyst, Inc. in our "Meet a Marketing Researcher" item on page 471.

HYPOTHESIS TESTING

A hypothesis is what the manager or researcher expects the population mean (or percentage) to be.

Sometimes someone, such as the marketing researcher or marketing manager, makes a statement about the population parameter based on prior knowledge, assumptions, or intuition. This statement, called a **hypothesis**, most commonly takes the form of an exact specification as to what the population parameter value is.

Hypothesis testing is a statistical procedure used to "accept" or "reject" the hypothesis based on sample information. With all hypothesis tests, you should keep in mind that the sample is the only source of current information about the population. Because our sample is a probability sample and therefore representative of the population, the sample results are used to determine whether or not the hypothesis about the population parameter has been supported.

▶ Additional Insights

How to Estimate Market Potential Using a Survey's Findings

A common way to estimate total market potential is to rely on the definition of a market. A market is people with the willingness and ability to pay for a product or a service. This definition can be expressed somewhat like a formula, in the following way.

> Market potential = Population base times percent likely to buy times amount they are willing to pay

In The Hobbits' Choice Restaurant case, we know that the metropolitan population is about 500,000, which translates to about 167,000 households. We also know that not every household dines out regularly. A recent article in the *City Magazine* reported that one out of 10 households eats evening meals at the major restaurants in the city. So there are about 16,700 households comprising the "sit down" restaurant market population base.

We found the 95 percent confidence intervals for the individuals (who represent households) who are "very likely" to patronize an upscale restaurant to be 14.2 percent to 21.8 percent, and we found that they spend about $282, on aver-

age, each month at restaurants. With these facts, findings, and confidence intervals, we can make three estimates of the market potential for an upscale restaurant.

PESSIMISTIC ESTIMATE	BEST ESTIMATE	OPTIMISTIC ESTIMATE
16,700	16,700	16,700
times 14.2%	times 18.0%	times 21.8%
times $282	times $282	times $282
= **$668,735**	= **$847,692**	= **$1,026,649**

Using the 95 percent confidence intervals and the sample percentage, the total market potential is found to be between about $0.7 million and $1.0 million dollars per month, which amounts to $8.4 million to $12.0 million per year. The best annual estimate is about $850,000. It is "best" because it is based on the sample percentage, which is the best estimate of the true population percentage of "very likely" households. The 95 percent confidence interval estimates are possible, but if many, many replications of the survey were to take place, most of the percentages would fall near 18 percent.

▶ Meet a Marketing Researcher

Meet Jerry W. Thomas, President/CEO of Decision Analyst, Inc.

Jerry W. Thomas, president and chief executive officer, is the founder of Decision Analyst, chairman of the board of directors, and a member of the executive committee. His principal responsibilities include strategic planning and general management of the firm. He is deeply involved in internal research and development activities and in the development of research techniques and study designs used throughout the company.

He is a widely published author of articles on marketing research and marketing strategy and a frequent public speaker on these topics. He currently serves as chairman of the advisory board for the Master of Science in Marketing Research (MSMR) program at the University of Texas at Arlington.

His strengths are creative study design and problem solving, business and marketing strategy, and the translation of research data into actionable marketing recommendations. His expertise spans both qualitative and quantitative techniques. His experience has been concentrated in the packaged goods, food service, and computer and related high-technology industries.

(box continues)

Before founding Decision Analyst, he was a senior vice president at M/A/R/C in Dallas, Texas. Before that, he worked in product management at Anderson Clayton Foods and in marketing planning at Hallmark Cards, Inc. in Kansas City. He holds an M.B.A. degree from the University of Texas, with additional postgraduate studies in economics at Southern Methodist University.

People test and revise intuitive hypotheses often without thinking about it.

All of this might sound frightfully technical, but it is a form of inference that you do every day. You just do not use the words "hypothesis" or "parameter" when you do it. Here is an example to show how hypothesis testing occurs naturally. Your friend, Bill, does not wear his seat belt because he thinks only a few drivers actually wear them. But Bill's car breaks down, and he has to ride with his coworkers to and from work while it is being repaired. Over the course of a week, Bill rides with five different coworkers, and he notices that four out of the five buckle up. When Bill begins driving his car the next week, he begins fastening his seat belt.

People engage in intuitive hypothesis testing constantly.

This is intuitive hypothesis testing in action; Bill's initial belief that few people wear seat belts was his hypothesis. **Intuitive hypothesis testing** (as opposed to statistical hypothesis testing) is when someone uses something he or she has observed to see if it agrees with or refutes his or her belief about that topic. Everyone uses intuitive hypothesis testing; in fact, we rely on it constantly. We just do not call it hypothesis testing, but we are constantly gathering evidence that supports or refutes our beliefs, and we reaffirm or change our beliefs based on our findings. Read Marketing Research Insight 16.3 and see that you perform intuitive hypothesis testing a great deal.

Obviously, if you had asked Bill before his car went into the repair shop, he might have said that only a small percentage, perhaps as low as 10 percent, of drivers wear seat belts. His week of car rides is analogous to a sample of five observations, and he observes that 80 percent of his coworkers buckle up. Now his initial hypothesis is not supported by the evidence. So Bill realizes that his hypothesis is in error, and it must be revised. If you asked Bill what percentage of drivers wear seat belts after his week of observations, he undoubtedly would have a much higher percentage in mind than his original estimate. The fact that Bill began to fasten his seat belt suggests he perceives his behavior to be out of the norm, so he has adjusted his belief and his behavior as well. In other words, his hypothesis was not supported, so Bill revised it to be consistent with what is actually the case.

The logic of statistical hypothesis testing is very similar to this process that Bill has just undergone.

There are five steps in hypothesis testing.

There are five basic steps involved in hypothesis testing, and we have listed them in Table 16.4. We have also described with each step how Bill's hypothesis that only 10 percent of drivers buckle their seat belt is tested via intuition.

A hypothesis test gives you the probability of support for your hypothesis based on your sample evidence and sample size.

Due to the variation that we know will be caused by sampling, it is impossible to be absolutely certain that our assessment of the acceptance or rejection of the hypothesis will be correct if we simply compare our hypothesis arithmetically to the sample finding. Therefore, you must fall back on the sample size concepts discussed in Chapter 13 and rely on the use of probabilities. The statistical concept underlying hypothesis testing permits us to say that if many, many samples were drawn, and a comparison made for each one, a true hypothesis would be accepted, for example, 99 percent of these times.

Statistical hypothesis testing involves the use of four ingredients: the sample statistic, the standard error of the statistic, the desired level of confidence, and the hypothesized population parameter value. The first three values were discussed in the section on parameter estimation. The final value is simply what the researcher believes the population parameter (π or μ) to be before the research is undertaken.

Intuitive Hypothesis Testing: We Do It All the Time!

People do intuitive hypothesis testing all the time to reaffirm their beliefs or to reform them to be consistent with reality. The following diagram illustrates how people perform intuitive hypothesis testing.

Here is an everyday example. As a student studying marketing research, you believe that you will "ace" the first exam if you study hard the night before the exam. You take the exam, and you score a 70 percent. Ouch. You now realize that your belief was wrong, and you need to study more for

the next exam. So your hypothesis was refuted, and you now have to come up with a new one.

You ask the student beside you, who did ace the exam, how much study time he put in. He says he studied for the three nights before the exam. Notice that he has found evidence (his A grade) that supports his hypothesis, so he will not change his study habits belief. You, on the other hand, must change your hypothesis or suffer the consequences.

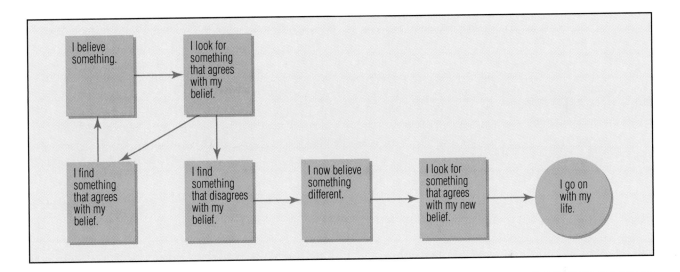

Table **16.4**   **The Five Basic Steps Involved in Hypothesis Testing (Using Bill's Seat Belt Hypothesis)**

THE STEPS	BILL'S INTUITIVE HYPOTHESIS TEST
Step 1. Begin with a statement about what you believe exists in the population, that is, the population mean or percentage.	In our example, Bill believed only 10% of drivers buckle their seat belts.
Step 2. Draw a probability sample and determine the sample statistic.	Bill found that 80% of his friends buckled up.
Step 3. Compare the statistic to the hypothesized parameter.	Bill noticed that 80% is different from 10%.
Step 4. Decide whether the sample supports the original hypothesis.	The observed 80% of drivers does not support the hypothesis that 10% buckle up.
Step 5. If the sample does not support the hypothesis, revise the hypothesis to be consistent with the sample's statistic.	The actual incidence of drivers who buckle their seat belts is about 80%. (*Bill, your hypothesis of 10% is not supported; you need to buckle up like just about everyone else.*)

MARKETING RESEARCH

INSIGHT

16.4

What Is an Alternative Hypothesis?

Whenever you test a stated hypothesis, you always automatically test its alternative. The **alternative hypothesis** takes in all possible cases that are not treated by the stated hypothesis. For example, if you hypothesize that 50 percent of all drivers fasten their seat belts, you are saying that the population percentage is equal to 50 percent (stated hypothesis), and the alternative hypothesis is that the population percentage is not equal to 50 percent. To say this differently, the alternative hypothesis is that the population percentage can be any percentage other than 50 percent, the stated hypothesis. The alternative hypothesis is always implicit, but sometimes statisticians will state it along with the stated hypothesis.

To avoid confusion, we do not formally provide the alternative hypotheses in this textbook. But here are some stated hypotheses and their alternatives. You may want to refer back to this exhibit if the alternative hypothesis is important to your understanding of the concepts being described.

The importance of knowing what the alternative hypothesis stems from the fact that it is a certainty that the sample results must support either the stated hypothesis or the alternative hypothesis. There is no other outcome possible. If the findings do not support the stated hypothesis, then they must support the alternative hypothesis because it covers all possible cases not specified in the stated hypothesis. Of course, if the stated hypothesis is supported by the findings, the alternative hypothesis is not supported.

STATED HYPOTHESIS	ALTERNATIVE HYPOTHESIS
Population Parameter Hypothesis	
The population mean is equal to $50.	The population mean is not equal to $50.
The population percentage is equal to 60 percent.	The population percentage is not equal to 60 percent.
Directional Hypothesis	
The population mean is greater than 100.	The population mean is less than or equal to 100.
The population percentage is less than 70 percent.	The population percentage is greater than or equal to 70 percent.

There is always an alternative hypothesis.

Statisticians often refer to the alternative hypothesis when performing statistical tests. This concept is important for you to know about. We have included Marketing Research Insight 16.4 as a way to introduce you to the idea of an alternative hypothesis and to understand how it is used in statistical hypothesis tests.

Test of the Hypothesized Population Parameter Value

The **hypothesized population parameter** value can be determined using either a percentage or a mean. The equation used to test the hypothesis of a population percentage is as follows:

Formula for test of a hypothesis about a percent

$$z = \frac{p - \pi_H}{s_{\bar{x}}}$$

where

p = the sample percentage

π_H = the hypothesized percentage

s_p = the standard error of the percentage

Here are formulas used to test a hypothesized population parameter.

The equation used to test the hypothesis of a mean is identical in logic, except it uses the mean and standard error of the mean.

Formula for test of a hypothesis about a mean

$$z = \frac{\bar{x} - \mu_H}{s_{\bar{x}}}$$

where

$\bar{x}$ = the sample mean

μ_H = the hypothesized mean

$s_{\bar{x}}$ = the standard error of the mean

Tracking the logic of the equation for a mean, one can see that the sample mean ($\bar{x}$), is compared to the hypothesized population mean (μ_H). Similarly, the sample percentage (p) is compared to the hypothesized percentage (π_H). In this case, "compared" means "take the difference." This difference is divided by the standard error to determine how many standard errors away from the hypothesized parameter the sample statistic falls. The standard error, you should remember, takes into account the variability found in the sample as well as the sample size. A small sample with much variability yields a large standard error, so our sample statistic could be quite far away from the mean arithmetically but still less than one standard error away in certain circumstances. All the relevant information about the population as found by our sample is included in these computations. Knowledge of areas under the normal curve then comes into play to translate this distance into a probability of support for the hypothesis.

To a statistician, "Compare means" amounts to "Take the difference."

Here is a simple illustration using Bill's seat belt hypothesis. Let us assume that instead of observing his friends buckling up, Bill reads that a Harris Poll finds that 80 percent of respondents in a national sample of 1,000 wear their seat belts. The hypothesis test would be computed as follows (notice we substituted the formula for s_p in the second step):

$$z = \frac{p - \pi_H}{s_p}$$

Calculation of a test of a Bill's hypothesis that only 10% of drivers "buckle up."

$$= \frac{p - \pi_H}{\sqrt{\dfrac{p \times q}{n}}}$$

$$= \frac{80 - 10}{\sqrt{\dfrac{80 \times 20}{1,000}}}$$

An example of no support for Bill's seat belt hypothesis.

$$= \frac{70}{\sqrt{\dfrac{1,600}{1,000}}}$$

$$= \frac{70}{\sqrt{1.6}}$$

Sorry, Bill. No support for you.

$$= 55.6$$

The crux of statistical hypothesis testing is the **sampling distribution concept.** Our actual sample is one of the many, many theoretical samples comprising the assumed bell-shaped curve of possible sample results using the hypothesized value as the center of the bell-shaped distribution. There is a greater probability of finding a sample result close to the hypothesized mean, for example, than of finding one that is far away. But there is a critical assumption working here. We have conditionally accepted from the outset that the person who stated the hypothesis is correct. So, if our sample mean turns out to be within ±2.58 standard errors of the hypothesized mean, it supports the hypothesis maker at the 99 percent level of confidence because it falls within 99 percent of the area under the curve.

The sampling distribution concept says that our sample is one of many, many theoretical samples that comprise a bell-shaped curve with the hypothesized value as the mean.

You always assume the sample information to be more accurate than any hypothesis.

But what if the sample result is found to be outside this range? Which is correct—the hypothesis or the researcher's sample results? The answer to this question is always the same: Sample information is invariably more accurate than a hypothesis. Of course, the sampling procedure must adhere strictly to probability sampling requirements and assure representativeness. As you can see, Bill was greatly mistaken because his hypothesis of 10 percent of drivers wearing seat belts was 55.3 standard errors away from the 80 percent finding of the national poll.

The following example serves to describe the hypothesis testing process with a mean. Northwestern Mutual Life Insurance Company has a college student internship program. The program allows college students to participate in an intensive training program and to become field agents in one academic term. Arrangements are made with various universities in the United States whereby students will receive college credit if they qualify for and successfully complete this program. Rex Reigen, district agent for Idaho, believed, based on his knowledge of other programs in the country, that the typical college agent will be able to earn about $2,750 in his or her first semester of participation in the program. He hypothesizes that the population parameter, that is, the mean, will be $2,750. To check Rex's hypothesis, a survey was taken of current college agents, and 100 of these individuals were contacted through telephone calls. Among the questions posed was an estimate of the amount of money made in their first semester of work in the program. The sample mean is determined to be $2,800, and the standard deviation is $350.

Does the sample support Rex's hypothesis that student interns make $2,750 in the first semester?

In essence, the amount of $2,750 is the hypothesized mean of the sampling distribution of all possible samples of the same size that can be taken of the college agents in the country. The unknown factor, of course, is the size of the standard error in dollars. Consequently, although it is assumed that the sampling distribution will be a normal curve with the mean of the entire distribution at $2,750, we need a way to determine how many dollars are within ±1 standard error of the mean, or any other number of standard errors of the mean for that matter. The only information available that would help to determine the size of the standard error is the standard deviation obtained from the sample. This standard deviation can be used to determine a standard error with the application of the standard error formula.

The amount of $2,800 found by the sample differs from the hypothesized amount of $2,750 by $50. Is this amount a sufficient enough difference to cast doubt on Rex's estimate? Or, in other words, is it far enough from the hypothesized mean to reject the hypothesis? To answer these questions, we compute as follows (note that we have substituted the formula for the standard error of the mean in the second step):

$$z = \frac{\bar{x} - \mu_H}{s_{\bar{x}}}$$

$$= \frac{\bar{x} - \mu_H}{\frac{s}{\sqrt{n}}}$$

Calculation of a test of Rex's hypothesis that Northwestern Mutual interns make an average of $2,750 in their first semester of work.

$$= \frac{2,800 - 2,750}{\frac{350}{\sqrt{100}}}$$

How many standard errors is $2,800 away from $2,750?

$$= \frac{50}{35}$$

Rex is right!

$$= 1.43$$

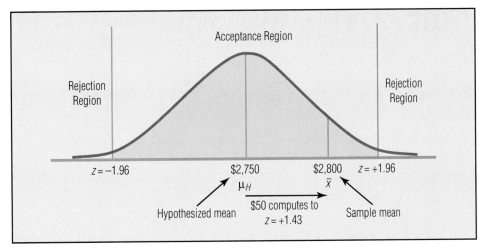

The Sample Findings Support the Hypothesis in This Example

The sample variability and the sample size have been used to determine the size of the standard error of the assumed sampling distribution. In this case, one standard error of the mean is equal to $35. When the difference of $50 is divided by $35 to determine the number of standard errors away from which the hypothesized mean the sample statistic lies, the result is 1.43 standard errors. As is illustrated in Figure 16.4, 1.43 standard errors is within ±1.96 standard errors of Rex's hypothesized mean. It also reveals that the hypothesis is supported because it falls in the acceptance region.

Although the exact probability of support for the hypothesized parameter can be determined from the use of a table, it is often handy just to recall the two numbers, 1.96 and 2.58; as we have said, these two are directly associated to the intervals of 95 percent and 99 percent, respectively. Anytime that the computed z value falls outside 2.58, the resulting probability of support for the hypothesis is 0.01 or less. Of course, computer statistical programs such as SPSS will provide the exact probability because they are programmed to look up the probability in the z table just as you would have to do if you did the test by hand calculations and you wanted the exact probability.

The z is calculated to be 1.43 standard errors. What does this mean?

A computed z of 1.43 is less than 1.96, so the hypothesis is supported.

Directional Hypotheses

It is sometimes appropriate to indicate a directional hypothesis. A **directional hypothesis** is one that indicates the direction in which you believe the population parameter falls relative to some target mean or percentage. That is, the owner of a toy store might not be able to state the exact number of dollars parents spend each time they buy a toy in that store, but the owner might say, "They spend under $100." A directional hypothesis is usually made with a "more than" or "less than" statement. For example, Rex Reigen might have hypothesized that the average college agent working for Northwestern Mutual Life earns *more than* $2,750. In both the "more than" case and the "less than" case, identical concepts are brought into play, but one must take into account that only one side (one tail) of the sampling distribution is being used.

A directional hypothesis is one in which you specify the hypothesized mean (or percentage) to be less than or greater than some amount.

Table **16.5** **With a Directional Hypothesis Test, the Critical Points for z Must Be Adjusted, and the Sign (+ or −) Is Important**

LEVEL OF CONFIDENCE	DIRECTION OF HYPOTHESIS[a]	z VALUE
95%	Greater than	+1.64
	Less than	−1.64
99%	Greater than	+2.33
	Less than	−2.33

[a]Subtract the sample statistic (mean or percentage) *from* the hypothesized parameter (μ or π).

When testing a directional hypothesis, you must look at the sign as well as the size of the computed z value.

There are only two differences to keep in mind for directional hypothesis tests. First, you must be concerned with the sign determined for the z value as well as its size. When you subtract the hypothesized mean from the sample mean, the sign will be positive with "greater than" hypotheses, whereas the sign will be negative for "less than" hypotheses if the hypothesis is true. To use Rex's example again, the hypothesized target of $2,750 would be subtracted from the sample mean of $2,800 yielding a +$50, so the positive sign does support the "greater than" hypothesis. But is the difference statistically significant?

To answer this question requires our second step: to divide the difference by the standard error of the mean to compute the z value. We did this earlier and determined the z value to be 1.43. Because we are working with only one side of the bell-shaped distribution, we need to adjust the critical z value to reflect this fact. As Table 16.5 shows, a z value of ±1.64 standard errors defines the end-points for 95 percent of the normal curve, and a z value of ±2.33 standard errors defines the endpoints for 99 percent confidence levels. Now the "greater than" directional hypothesis is supported at that level of confidence if the computed z value is larger than the critical cut point, *and*, of course, its sign is consistent with the direction of the hypothesis. Otherwise, the directional hypothesis is not supported at our chosen level of confidence. Although the computed z value is close (1.43), it is not equal to or greater than 1.64, so Rex's directional hypothesis is not supported.

How to Interpret Hypothesis Testing

How do you interpret hypothesis tests? The interpretation of a hypothesis test is again directly linked to the sampling distribution concept. If the hypothesis about the population parameter is correct or true, then a high percentage of sample means must fall close to this value. In fact, if the hypothesis is true, then 99 percent of the sample results will fall between ±2.58 standard errors of the hypothesized mean. On the other hand, if the hypothesis is incorrect, there is a strong likelihood that the computed z value will fall outside ±2.58 standard errors. In other words, you must adjust the "standard" number of standard errors (1.96 or 2.58) for directional hypothesis tests. We have done this for you in Table 16.5.

With the directional hypothesis test z values, the interpretation remains the same. The further away the hypothesized value is from the actual case, the more likely the computed z value will not fall in the critical range. Failure to support the hypothesis essentially tells the hypothesizer that his or her assumptions about the population are in error, and that they must be revised in light of the evidence from the sample. This revision is achieved through estimates of the population parameter

If a hypothesis is not supported by a random sample finding, use the sample statistic and estimate the population parameter.

Like all businesspersons, restaurant owners make marketing strategy decisions based on their hypotheses about what their target market wants.

just discussed in the previous section. These estimates can be used to provide the manager or researcher with a new mental picture of the population through confidence interval estimates of the true population value.

HOW TO USE SPSS TO TEST A HYPOTHESIS FOR A PERCENTAGE

As you found out earlier, SPSS does not perform statistical tests on percentages, so if you have a hypothesis about a percentage, you are required to do the calculations with your handy calculator. You should use the SPSS "Frequencies" procedure to have it calculate the sample p value and to determine the sample size if you do not know it precisely. Then apply the percentage hypothesis test formula to calculate the z value. If the value is inside the range of ±1.96, the hypothesized percentage is supported at the 95 percent level of confidence, and if it is inside ±2.58, it is supported at the 99 percent level. You will have an opportunity to use SPSS and do these calculations in Case 16.2 at the end of this chapter.

SPSS does not perform percentages hypothesis tests, but you can use it to obtain the necessary information to do one by hand calculation.

RETURN TO *Your Integrated Case*

The Hobbit's Choice Restaurant Survey: How to Use SPSS to Test a Hypothesis for a Mean

We can take Cory Rogers's third condition—that the "very likely" customers must be "willing to pay an average of $18 for an à la carte entrée"—as a hypothesis, and we can test it with our Hobbit's Choice Restaurant sample findings. Your SPSS software can be easily directed to make a mean estimation or to test a hypothesis for a mean.

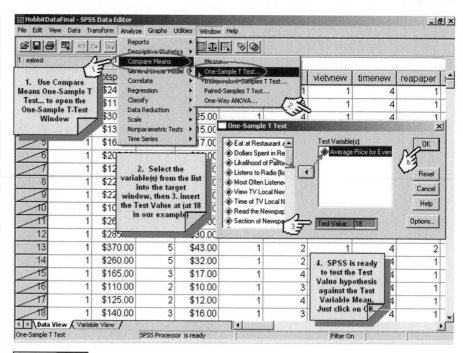

Figure **16.5** The SPSS Clickstream to Test a Hypothesis About a Mean

To test a hypothesis about a mean with SPSS, use the ANALYZE-COMPARE MEANS-ONE SAMPLE T TEST command sequence.

SPSS Student Assistant Online

Testing a Hypothesis for a Mean

To perform a mean hypothesis test, SPSS provides a Test Value box in which the hypothesized mean can be entered. As you can see in Figure 16.5, you get to this box by using the ANALYZE-COMPARE MEANS-ONE SAMPLE T TEST command sequence. You then select the variable, "average price for evening entrée." Next, enter in an "18" as Test Value and click on the OK button. (Remember that we selected only the "very likely" respondent cases earlier, and that selection will remain in place until we direct SPSS to "select all" cases or make a different case selection.)

The resulting output is contained in Figure 16.6. When you look at it, you will notice that the information layout for the output is identical to the previous output table. It indicates that 72 respondents were selected, and the mean of their answers was calculated to be $34.06 (rounded up.) The output indicates our test value equal to 18, and the bottom contains 95 percent confidence intervals for the estimated population parameter (the population parameter is the difference between the hypothesized mean and the sample mean, expected to be 0). There is a mean difference of $16.0556, which was calculated by subtracting the hypothesized mean value (18) from the sample mean (34.0556), and the standard error is provided in the upper half ($.97662). A t value of 16.440 is determined by dividing 16.0556 by .97662. It is associated with a two-tailed significance level of 0.000. (For now, assume the t value is the z value we have used in our formulas and explanations. We describe use of the t value in Chapter 17.)

In other words, our Hobbit's Choice Restaurant sample finding of a willingness to pay an average of about $34 does not support the hypothesis of $18. The true mean is, in fact, quite a bit greater than $18. (Do not use the information reported under "95% Confidence Intervals" when testing a hypothesis with SPSS.)

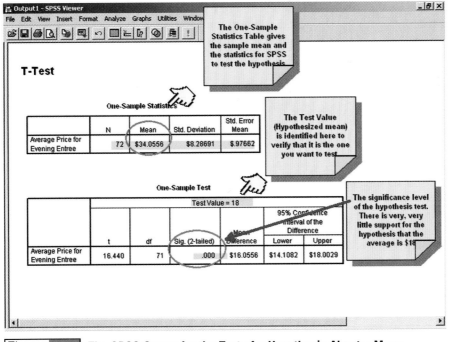

Figure **16.6** **The SPSS Output for the Test of a Hypothesis About a Mean**

If you were Jeff Dean, and you just learned that the hypothesis of $18 per entrée was not supported, and the true population mean was almost twice as large, how would you feel? Surely, you would feel great because this satisfied the third and last condition specified by his researcher's model. Jeff should think seriously about buying a bottle of champagne.

SUMMARY

This chapter began by distinguishing a sample statistic from its associated population parameter. We then introduced you to the concept of statistical inference, which is a set of procedures for generalizing the findings from a sample to the population. A key factor in inference is the sample size, n. It appears in statistical inference formulas because it expresses the amount of sampling error: Large samples have less sampling error than do small samples given the same variability. We illustrated the two inference types commonly used by marketing researchers. First, we described how a population parameter, such as a mean, can be estimated by using confidence intervals computed by application of the standard error formula. Second, we related how a researcher can use the sample findings to test a hypothesis about a mean or a percentage.

We used SPSS and The Hobbit's Choice Restaurant data to illustrate how you can direct SPSS to calculate 95 percent confidence intervals for the estimation of a mean as well as how to test a hypothesis about a mean. Both are accomplished with

SPSS Student Assistant Online
SPSS Results Coach and Case
Studies

the SPSS menu item—One-Sample T Test procedure. For parameter estimation or test of a hypothesis with a percentage, you can use SPSS to determine the percentage, but you must use the formulas in this chapter to calculate the confidence interval or perform the significance test.

KEY TERMS

Statistics (p. 458)
Parameters (p. 459)
Inference (p. 459)
Statistical inference (p. 459)
Tests of significant differences (p. 460)
Parameter estimation (p. 461)
Standard error (p. 462)
Standard error of the mean (p. 462)
Standard error of the percentage (p. 462)
Confidence intervals (p. 464)
Most commonly used level of
  confidence (p. 465)

Formula for population parameter
  estimation (p. 465)
Hypothesis (p. 470)
Hypothesis testing (p. 470)
Intuitive hypothesis testing (p. 472)
Alternative hypothesis (p. 474)
Hypothesized population parameter
  (p. 474)
Sampling distribution concept (p. 475)
Directional hypothesis (p. 477)

REVIEW QUESTIONS/APPLICATIONS

1. What essential factors are taken into consideration when statistical inference takes place?
2. What is meant by "parameter estimation," and what function does it perform for a researcher?
3. How does parameter estimation for a mean differ from that for a percentage?
4. List the steps in statistical hypothesis testing. List the steps in intuitive hypothesis testing. How are they similar? How are they different?
5. When a researcher's sample evidence disagrees with a manager's hypothesis, which is right?
6. What does it mean when a researcher says that a hypothesis has been supported at the 95 percent confidence level?
7. Distinguish a directional from a nondirectional hypothesis, and provide an example of each one.
8. Here are several computation practice exercises to help you identify which formulas pertain and learn how to perform the necessary calculations. In each case, perform the necessary calculations and write your answers in the column identified by a "question mark."
   a. Determine confidence intervals for each of the following.

Sample Statistic	Sample Size	Confidence Level	Your Confidence Intervals?
Mean: 150 Std. Dev: 30	200	95%	
Percent: 67%	300	99%	
Mean: 5.4 Std. Dev: 0.5	250	99%	
Percent: 25.8%	500	99%	

b. Test the following hypothesis and interpret your findings.

Hypothesis	Sample Findings	Confidence Level	Your Test Results
Mean = 7.5	Mean: 8.5 Std dev: 1.2 $n = 670$	95%	
Percent = 86%	$p = 95$ $n = 1000$	99%	
Mean > 125	Mean: 135 Std dev: 15 $n = 500$	95%	
Percent < 33%	$p = 31$ $n = 120$	99%	

9. The manager of the aluminum recycling division of Environmental Services wants a survey that will tell him how many households in the city of Seattle, Washington, will voluntarily wash out, store, and then transport all of their aluminum cans to a central recycling center located in the downtown area and open only on Sunday mornings. A random survey of 500 households determines that 20 percent of households would do so, and that each participating household expects to recycle about 100 cans monthly with a standard deviation of 30 cans. What is the value of parameter estimation in this instance?

10. It is reported in the newspaper that a survey sponsored by *Forbes* magazine with *Fortune* 500 company executives has found that 75 percent believe that the United States trails Japan and Germany in automobile engineering. The article notes that executives were interviewed at a recent "Bring the U.S. Back to Competitiveness" symposium held on the campus of the University of Southern California. Why would it be incorrect for the article to report confidence intervals?

11. Alamo Rent-A-Car executives believe that Alamo accounts for about 50 percent of all Cadillacs that are rented. To test this belief, a researcher randomly identifies 20 major airports with on-site rental car lots. Observers are sent to each location and instructed to record the number of rental company Cadillacs observed in a four-hour period. About 500 are observed, and 30 percent are observed being returned to Alamo Rent-A-Car. What are the implications of this finding for the Alamo executives' belief?

INTERACTIVE LEARNING

Visit the Web site at www.prenhall.com/burnsbush. For this chapter, work through the Self-Study Quizzes, and get instant feedback on whether you need additional studying. On the Web site, you can review the chapter outlines and case information for Chapter 16.

CASE 16.1   Auto Online Survey (Part II)

You will find Case 15.2 (Part I) of the Auto Online survey on pages 453–455. You will need to refer to the questionnaire on these pages in order to perform the proper analysis with SPSS. You may assume that the respondents to this survey are representative of the population of automobile buyers who visited the Auto Online Web site during their vehicle purchase process.

1. In order to describe this population, estimate the population parameters for the following.
   a. How often they make purchases online.
   b. Number of visits they made to Auto Online.
   c. The percentage who actually bought their vehicle from Auto Online.
   d. The percentage of those who felt it was a better experience than buying at a traditional dealership.
   e. How do people feel about the Auto Online Web site (question 6 on the questionnaire)?
2. Auto Online principals have the following beliefs. Test these hypotheses.
   a. People will "strongly agree" to all eight statements concerning use of the Internet and purchase (question 3 on the questionnaire).
   b. Prior to buying a vehicle, people will visit the Auto Online Web site approximately five times.
   c. Just about everyone will say that buying a vehicle online is "a great deal better" than buying it at a traditional dealership.
   d. Those who buy their vehicles from Auto Online will be adults in their mid-thirties.
   e. Those who buy from Auto Online will pay an average of $3,500 below the sticker price, whereas those who buy elsewhere will pay only an average of $2,000 less than the vehicle sticker price.

CASE 16.2   *Your Integrated Case*

This is your integrated case, described on pages 42–43.

The Hobbit's Choice Restaurant Survey Inferential Analysis

Cory Rogers was pleased with Celeste Brown's descriptive analysis. Celeste had done all of the proper descriptive analyses, and she had copied the relevant tables and findings into a Word document with notations that Cory could refer to quickly.

Cory says, "Celeste, this is great work. I am going to Jeff Dean's in an hour to show him what we have found. In the meantime, I want you to look a bit deeper into the data. I have jotted down some items that I want you to analyze. This is the next step in understanding how the sample findings generalize to the population of the greater metropolitan area."

Your task in Case 16.2 is to again take the role of Celeste Brown, marketing intern. Using The Hobbit's Choice Restaurant survey SPSS data set, perform the proper analysis, and interpret the findings for each of the following questions specified by Cory Rogers.

1. What are the population estimates for each of the following?
   a. Preference for "easy listening" radio programming
   b. Viewing of 10 P.M. local news on TV
   c. Subscribe to *City Magazine*
   d. Average age of heads of households
   e. Average price paid for an evening meal entrée

2. Because Jeff Dean's restaurant will be upscale, it will appeal to high-income consumers. Jeff hopes that at least 25 percent of the households have an income level of $100,000 or higher. Test this hypothesis.

3. With respect to those who are "very likely" to patronize The Hobbit's Choice Restaurant, Jeff believes that they will either "very strongly" or "somewhat" prefer each of the following: (a) waitstaff with tuxedos, (b) unusual desserts, (c) large variety of entrées, (d) unusual entrées, (e) elegant décor, and (f) jazz combo music. Does the survey support or refute Jeff's hypotheses? Interpret your findings.

Chapter 17

Testing for Differences Between Two Groups or Among More Than Two Groups

Practitioner Viewpoint

In many of the studies we perform, clients are interested in knowing how subgroups within the sample differ on certain important issues. For example, a client from the beverage industry may want to know if the preference for a new beverage concept differs depending on whether the respondent is or is not a current consumer of the company's brands. Another client from the retail industry may want to know if customer satisfaction scores differ between customers who shop online or shop in person at their retail outlets. In both these cases, we want to know if significant differences exist between two groups of shoppers. Sometimes there will be more than two groups. A client from the political arena may want to know if opinions about a new tax plan differ depending on whether the respondent is a Republican, Democrat, or Independent. In this chapter, you will learn how to use SPSS to test for significant statistical differences between two groups or among more than two groups.

Melinda Smith de Borrero
Vice President and Managing Director
Knowledge Networks

Differences Within "Heavy" Catalog Purchasers as Well as Within Catalog Nonbuyers[1]

People who bought seven or more catalog purchases last year constitute the more frequent catalog buyers. A recent study has revealed interesting similarities and differences between different types of heavy catalog buyers.

Here are findings for catalog buying in general:

▶ Over 80 percent said convenience was the major reason for catalog buying.

▶ "The price was right" was a reason given more often by men than by women.

▶ "Uniqueness of merchandise" was given as a reason more often by women than by men.

▶ "Uniqueness of merchandise" was more important to those with high income than to those with low income.

▶ Impulse purchase were less prevalent with frequent catalog buyers than with less frequent catalog buyers.

The study also investigated online catalog buying. Here are its findings.

▶ Convenience was the more important reason for online catalog shopping, but it was more important for women than it was for men.

▶ With online catalog buying, price was more of a factor for younger shoppers (35 years and younger) than for older shoppers.

▶ The importance of price in online catalog shopping was about the same for all household income levels.

Where We Are:

1. Establish the need for marketing research
2. Define the problem
3. Establish research objectives
4. Determine research design
5. Identify information types and sources
6. Determine methods of accessing data
7. Design data collection forms
8. Determine sample plan and size
9. Collect data
10. **Analyze data**
11. Prepare and present the final research report

Analysis reveals differences among various types of catalog merchandise buyers.

Finally, the study investigated individuals who did not make a single catalog purchase in the past year. Here are some similarities and differences that were found.

▶ Inability to see the product was the primary reason for individuals to not make a single catalog purchase.

▶ Lack of trust in ordering by mail or phone was the second most mentioned reason for not making a catalog purchase.

▶ Younger (18–25) noncatalog buyers were more distrustful of ordering by mail or phone than were older nonbuyers.

▶ Lower-income noncatalog buyers were more distrustful than higher-income noncatalog buyers.

▶ The highest-income noncatalog buyers were more likely to say that they never see what they want than were lower-income noncatalog buyers.

▶ Lower-income noncatalog buyers were more prone to say that the items cost too much than higher-income noncatalog buyers.

▶ Women noncatalog buyers found price to be more of an issue than did men noncatalog buyers.

▶ Not having Internet access was a more prevalent reason for not buying from an online catalog with older individuals than with younger ones.

▶ (A surprise) Wired catalog nonbuyers who are younger are more distrustful of online ordering than older catalog nonbuyers.

▶ (Another surprise) Wired higher-income catalog nonbuyers are more suspicious of online buying than lower-income catalog nonbuyers.

▶ Not being able to see the product was more of a problem for wired men catalog nonbuyers than for wired women catalog nonbuyers.

As you learned in Chapter 16, it is possible to make inferences about measures of central tendency such as means and percentages found in a probability sample survey. These inferences take the form of confidence intervals or tests of hypotheses. A different type of inference concerns differences. That is, are two means statistically significant in their difference? In this chapter, we describe the logic of differences tests, and we show you how to use SPSS to conduct various types of differences tests.

We begin this chapter discussing why differences are important to marketing managers, and we give some guidelines for researchers and managers when interpreting differences tests. Next, we introduce you to differences (percentages or means) between two independent groups, such as a comparison high-speed cable versus DSL telephone Internet users on how satisfied they are with their Internet connection service. We next show you that it is possible to test if a difference exists between the averages of two similarly scaled questions. For instance, do buyers rate a store higher in "merchandise selection" than they rate its "good values?" Finally, we introduce you to ANOVA, a scary name but a simple way to compare the means of several groups simultaneously and to quickly spot patterns of significant differences. We provide formulas and numerical examples, and also show you examples of SPSS procedures and output using The Hobbit's Choice Restaurant survey data.

WHY DIFFERENCES ARE IMPORTANT

Perhaps one of the most vital marketing management concepts is market segmentation. In a nutshell, market segmentation holds that different types of consumers have different requirements, and these differences can be the bases of marketing strategies. For example, the Iams Company, which markets pet foods, has approximately 12 different varieties of dry dog food geared to the dog's age (puppy versus adult), weight situation (normal versus overweight), and activity (active versus inactive). Toyota Motors has 17 models including the two-seat Spyder sports car, the four-door Avalon luxury sedan, the Highlander SUV, and the Tacoma truck. Even Boeing Airlines has seven different types of commercial jets and a separate business jets division for corporate travel.

> Market segmentation is based on differences between groups of consumers.

Let's look at differences from the consumer's side. Everyone washes his or her hands, but the kind of soap required differs for weekend gardeners with potting soil under their fingernails, factory workers whose hands are dirty with solvents, preschoolers who have sticky drink residue on their hands and faces, or aspiring beauty princesses who wish their hands to look absolutely flawless. The needs and requirements of each of these market segments differ greatly from the others, and an astute marketer will customize his or her marketing mix to each target market's unique situation.[2]

These differences, of course, are quite obvious, but as competition becomes more intense with prolific market segmentation and target marketing being the watchword of most companies in an industry, there is a need to investigate difference among consumer groups for consumer marketers and business establishments for B2B marketers. One commonly used basis for market segmentation is the discovery of stable, meaningful, statistically significant differences that are actionable. We have dissected this statement into its four components with a brief explanation of each one. Refer to Table 17.1.

We will discuss each requirement briefly. In our comments, we will assume that we are working with a pharmaceuticals company that markets cold remedies.

The differences must be significant. As you know, the notion of statistical significance underpins much of marketing research. **Statistical significance of differences** means that the differences found in the sample(s) may be assumed to exist in the population(s) from which the probability samples are drawn. Thus, the differences that are apparent between and among market segments must be subjected to tests that assess the statistical significance of these differences. This is the topic of this chapter, and we will endeavor to teach you how to perform and interpret tests of the statistical significance of differences. With our cold remedy marketer, we could ask cold sufferers, "How important is it that your cold remedy relieves your . . . ?" The respondents

> To be potentially useful to the marketing researcher or manager, differences must, at minimum, be statistically significant.

Table **17.1**   **The Four Requirements of Differences Analysis to Be Useful for Market Segmentation**

REQUIREMENT	EXPLANATION
The differences must be statistically significant.	Statistically significant differences should be demonstrated between the groups.
The differences must be meaningful.	The differences between the market segments should be of such a magnitude that the marketer can target them individually.
The differences must be stable.	The differences should not be short term or transitory.
The differences must be actionable.	The market segment groups should be identified and suitable for target marketing.

would respond using a scale of 1 = not important to 10 = very important for each cold symptom such as fever, sore throat, congestion, aching muscles, and so on, and statistical tests such as those described in this chapter would determine if the responses were significantly different.

The differences must be meaningful. A finding of statistical significance in no way guarantees "meaningful" difference. In fact, with the proliferation of data mining analysis due to scanner data with tens of thousands of records, online surveys that garner thousands of respondents, and other ways to capture very large samples, there is a very real danger of finding a great deal of statistical significance that is not meaningful. The reason for this danger is that statistical significance is determined to a very great deal by the sample size.[3] You will see in this chapter by examining the formulas we provide that the sample size n is instrumental in the calculation of z, the determinant of the significance level. Large samples, those in excess of 1,000 per sample group, often yield statistically significant results when the absolute differences between the groups are quite small. A **meaningful difference** is one that the marketing manager can potentially use as a basis for marketing decisions. We will offer some guidelines on what might be statistically significant and "meaningful" differences later in the chapter.

With our cold remedy example, we might find that relieving one's aches has an average of 8 for importance, whereas reducing congestion has an average of 7.7. If these means were found to be statistically significant in their difference, there would not be a reason for the marketer to differentiate them because both symptoms are at essentially the same level of importance.

The differences should be stable. Stability refers to the requirement that we are not working with a short-term or transitory set of differences. Thus, a **stable difference** is one that will be in place for the foreseeable future. For example, there is a very real difference between cold symptoms and flu symptoms. To be sure, colds are inconvenient and uncomfortable, but the flu is much more painful, and it can be

To be useful to the marketing researcher or manager, differences must, if statistically significant, also be meaningful.

To be useful to the marketing researcher or manager, differences must, if statistically significant and meaningful, also be stable.

Differences in cold sufferers are used as market segmentation bases by pharmaceutical companies.

very dangerous for certain people such as infants, the elderly, or those with weak-ened immune systems. For this reason, pharmaceutical companies have developed and market flu-symptoms products markedly differently from their colds-symptoms products because they know that the symptoms of the flu sufferers will be signifi-cantly more severe than the symptoms of cold sufferers. By the same token, the over-the-counter medicine needed by flu sufferers is much stronger than that required by people with colds, and this is a persistent and stable difference between the two groups. Even within the colds medicines, companies have targeted infants, children, and individuals with stable susceptibilities (such as always getting a sore throat, always being congested, etc.) with custom-designed versions of their products because they know from experience and research that certain consumers will be con-sistent (stable) in seeking certain types of relief or specific product benefits when they suffer from colds.

The differences must be actionable. Market segmentation requires that standard or innovative market segmentation bases must be used and that these bases must uniquely identify the various groups so they can be analyzed and put in the mar-keter's targeting mechanisms. An **actionable difference** means that the marketer can focus various marketing strategies and tactics, such as advertising, on the market segments to make use of the differences between the segments. There are a great many segmentation bases that are actionable such as demographics, lifestyles, and product benefits. As we pointed out earlier, there are many symptoms manifested by colds sufferers including congestion, muscle aches, and sore throat. Thus, a cold remedy product line that concentrates on each one of these separately is possible. Similarly, infants' cold remedy needs differ from those of children, which differ from adults' needs. A quick glance at the cold remedies section of your local drugstore will verify the actionability of the sufferer's age and cold symptoms.

> To be useful to the marketing researcher or manager, differ-ences must, if statistically signif-icant, meaningful, and stable, also be actionable.

You may be confused about meaningful and actionable differences. Recall the words "potentially use" in our definition of a meaningful difference. With our cold remedies example, a pharmaceutical company could potentially develop and market a cold remedy that was specific to every type of cold symptom as experienced by every demographic group and further identified by lifestyle differences. For exam-ple, there could be a cold medicine to alleviate the runny noses of teenage girls who participate in high school athletics and a different one for the sniffles in teenage boys who play high school sports. But it would be economically unjustifiable to offer so many different cold medicines, so the pharmaceutical companies and other mar-keters must assess actionable differences based on market segment size and prof-itability considerations. Nevertheless, the fundamental differences are based on sta-tistical significance, meaningfulness, and stability assessments.

To be sure, the bulk of this chapter deals strictly with statistically significant dif-ferences, because it is the beginning point for market segmentation and savvy target marketing. Meaningfulness, stability, and actionability are not statistical issues; rather, they are the marketing manager's judgment calls.

SMALL SAMPLE SIZES: THE USE OF A *t* TEST OR A *z* TEST AND HOW SPSS ELIMINATES THE WORRY

Most of the equations in this chapter will lead to the computation of a *z* value. But there are special instances in which the *z* test is not appropriate. We pointed out in the previous chapter that computation of the *z* value makes the assumption that the raw data for most statistics under scrutiny have normal or bell-shaped distributions. However, statisticians have shown that this normal curve assumption is invalid

The *t* test should be used when the sample size is 30 or less.

when the sample size is 30 observations or less. In this instance, a *t* value is computed instead of a *z* value. The *t* **test** is defined as the statistical inference test to be used with small sample sizes ($n \leq 30$). Instead of a constant normal distribution, the *t* test relies on Student's *t* distribution. The *t* distribution's shape is determined by the number of degrees of freedom defined as being equal to the sample size minus the number of population parameters estimated, which is ($n - 1$) here because the population parameter is the difference between the two population means. The smaller the number of degrees of freedom, the more spread out the curve becomes. It still retains a bell shape, but it flattens out a little bit with each successive loss of a sample unit below 30. Any instance when the sample size is 30 or greater requires the use of a *z* **test**.

Most computer statistical programs report only the *t* value because it is identical to the *z* value with large samples.

The great advantage to using statistical analysis routines on a computer is that they are programmed to compute the correct statistic. In other words, you do not need to decide whether you want the program to compute a *t* value, a *z* value, or some other value. With SPSS, the analyses of differences are referred to as "*t* tests," but now that you realize that SPSS will always determine the correct significance level whether it is a *t* or a *z*, you do not need to worry about which statistic to use. The talent you need to acquire is how to interpret the significance level that is reported by SPSS. We have provided Marketing Research Insight 17.1 to introduce you to a "flag waving" analogy that students have told us is helpful in this regard.

MARKETING RESEARCH
INSIGHT
17.1

Additional Insights ◀

Flag Waving and Significance in Statistical Analysis

The output from statistical procedures in all software programs can be envisioned as "flag-waving" devices. When the flag is waving briskly, statistical significance is present. Then, and only then, is it warranted to look at the findings more closely to determine the pattern of the findings; but if the flag is not waving, your time will be wasted by looking any further. To read statistical flags, you need to know two things. First, where is the flag located? Second, how much does it need to wave for you to pay attention to it and to delve further into the analysis in order to interpret it?

Where Is the Flag?

Virtually every statistical test or procedure involves the computation of some critical statistic, and that statistic is used to determine the statistical significance of the findings. The critical statistic's name changes depending on the procedure and its underlying assumptions, but usually the statistic is identified as a letter: *z*, *t*, *F*, or something similar. Statistical analysis computer programs will automatically identify and compute the correct statistic, so although it is helpful to know ahead of time what statistic will be computed, it is not essential to know it. Moreover, the statistic is not the flag; rather it is just a computation necessary to raise

the flag. You might think of the computed statistic as the flagpole.

The computer program will also raise the flag on the flagpole, but its name changes a bit depending on the procedure. The flags, called *p* values by statisticians, are identified by the term "significance" or "probability." Sometimes abbreviations such as "Sig" or "Prob" are used to economize on the output. To find the flag, locate the "Sig" or "Prob" designation in the analysis, and look at the number that is associated with it. The number will be a decimal perhaps as low as 0.000 but ranging to as high as 1.000. When you locate it, you have found the statistical significance flag.

How Much Is the Flag Waving?

Perhaps an analogy about hurricane-force winds will help. Gentle winds blow all the time, and we are not concerned about them; but when hurricane-force winds build, we become concerned, and we pay a great deal of attention to the weather. Because hurricanes are very rare, the probability of their coming our way is very small, perhaps as small as 0.01 or even 0.001. So very small probabilities signal that hurricane-force winds are imminent, and we had better look into it to see where they are headed whenever .05 or less occurs.

TESTING FOR SIGNIFICANT DIFFERENCES BETWEEN TWO GROUPS

Often a researcher will want to compare two groups that exist in the same sample. That is, the researcher may have two independent groups such as walk-ins versus loyal customers, and he or she may want to compare their answers to the same question. The question may require either a nominal scale or a metric (interval or ratio) scale. A categorical scale requires that the researcher compare percentages, whereas he or she will compare means when a metric scale is involved. As you know by now, the formulas differ depending on whether percentages or means are being tested.

There are statistical tests for when a researcher wants to compare the means or percentages of two different groups or samples.

Differences Between Percentages with Two Groups (Independent Samples)

When a marketing researcher is interested in making comparisons between two groups of respondents to determine whether or not there are statistically significant differences between them, in concept, he or she is considering them as two potentially different populations. The question to be answered then becomes whether or not their respective population parameters are different. But, as always, a researcher can work only with the sample results. Therefore, the researcher must fall back on statistical inference to determine whether the difference that is found between the two sample statistics is a true population difference. You will shortly discover that the logic of differences tests is very similar to the logic of hypothesis testing that you learned about in the previous chapter.

Independent samples are treated as representing two potentially different populations.

Again, we refer to the intuitive approach you use every day when comparing two things to make an inference. Let us assume you have read a *Business Week* article about college recruiters that quotes a Louis Harris poll of 100 randomly selected companies, indicating that 65 percent of them will be visiting college campuses to interview business majors. The article goes on to say that a similar poll taken last year with 300 companies found only 40 percent for the sample percentages. You

Are your job prospects better this year than last year? Yes, if significantly more companies will visit your campus.

cannot be completely confident of your conclusion about the populations they represent because of sampling error. If the difference between the percentages was very large, say, 80 percent for this year and 20 percent for last year, you would be more inclined to believe that a true change had occurred. But if you found out this large difference was based on small sample sizes, you would be less confident with your inference that last year's college recruiting and this year's college recruiting are different. Intuitively, you have taken into account two critical factors in determining whether statistically significant differences exist between a percentage or a mean compared between two samples: the magnitude of the difference between the compared statistic (65 percent versus 40 percent) and sample sizes (100 versus 300).

The null hypothesis states there is no difference between the percentages or means being compared.

To test whether a true difference exists between two group percentages, we test the **null hypothesis** or the hypothesis that the difference in their population parameters is equal to zero. The alternative hypothesis is that there is a true difference between them. To perform the test of **significance of differences between two percentages**, each representing a separate group (sample), the first step requires a "comparison" of the two percentages. By "comparison," we mean that you find the arithmetic difference between them. The second step requires that this difference be translated into a number of standard errors away from the hypothesized value of zero. Once the number of standard errors is known, knowledge of the area under the normal curve will yield an assessment of the probability of support for the null hypothesis.

With a differences test, you test the null hypothesis that no differences exist between the two group percentages or means.

We realize that it is confusing to keep in mind the null hypothesis, the alternative hypothesis, and to understand all these equations as well. Just as in Chapter 16 where we provided a Marketing Research Insight on what is an alternative hypothesis for a hypothesis test, we have provided one in this chapter that describes what is the alternative hypothesis for the differences tests that are described in this chapter.

MARKETING RESEARCH
INSIGHT
17.2

What Is the Alternative Hypothesis for a Differences Test?

In Chapter 16, Marketing Research Insight 16.4 "What Is an Alternative Hypothesis?" introduced you to the concept of an alternative hypothesis. To refresh your memory, the alternative hypothesis takes in all possible cases that are not treated by the stated hypothesis.

With differences tests, the stated hypothesis, called the "null hypothesis," is that the arithmetic difference between one parameter (e.g., mean) and another one is zero. That is, the statistical test begins with the assumption that the two means (or percentages) are exactly the same value. Thus, the alternative hypothesis of a differences test is that they are not the same value. In other words, the difference is not equal to zero.

Here are the stated and alternative hypotheses for the two types of differences tests described in this chapter.

STATED HYPOTHESIS	ALTERNATIVE HYPOTHESIS
Differences Between Two Means Hypothesis	
No difference exists between means of two groups (populations)	A difference does exist between the means of two groups (populations).
The mean of one group (population) is greater than the mean of another group (population).	The mean of one group (population) is less than or equal to the mean of another group (population).
Differences in Means Among More Than Two Groups	
No difference exists between the means of all paired groups (populations).	A difference exists between the means of at least one pair of groups (populations).

For a percentage, the equation looks like this:

Formula for significance
of the difference between $z = \dfrac{p_1 - p_2}{s_{p_1 - p_2}}$
two percentages

where

p_1 = percentage found in sample 1

p_2 = percentage found in sample 2

$s_{p_1 - p_2}$ = standard error of the difference between two percentages

The standard error of the difference between two percentages is calculated with the following formula:

Formula for the standard
error of the difference $s_{p_1 - p_2} = \sqrt{\dfrac{p_1 \times q_1}{n_1} + \dfrac{p_2 \times q_2}{n_2}}$
between two percentages

Again, if you compare these formulas to the ones we used in hypothesis testing, you will see two differences. First, in the numerator, we subtract one sample's statistic (p_2) from the other sample's statistic (p_1). You should have noticed that we use the subscripts 1 and 2 to refer to the two different sample statistics. The second difference comes in the form of the sampling distribution that is expressed in the denominator. The sampling distribution under consideration now is the assumed sampling distribution of the differences between the percentages. That is, the assumption has been made that the differences have been computed for comparisons of the two sample statistics for many repeated samplings. If the null hypothesis is true, this distribution of differences follows the normal curve with a mean equal to zero and a standard error equal to one. Stated somewhat differently, the procedure requires us, as before, to accept the (null) hypothesis as true until it lacks support from the statistical test. Consequently, the differences of a multitude of comparisons of the two sample percentages generated from many, many samplings would average zero. In other words, our sampling distribution is now the distribution of the difference between one sample and the other, taken over many, many times. The following example will walk you through the point we just made.

Here is how you would perform the calculations for the Harris poll on companies coming to campus to hire college seniors. Recall that last year's poll with 300 companies reported 40 percent were coming to campus while this year's poll with 100 companies reported that 65 percent were visiting campuses.

Computation of the significance
of the difference between
p_1 = 65% and p_2 = 40%
(n_1 = 100 and n_2 = 300)

$$z = \frac{p_1 - p_2}{s_{p_1 - p_2}}$$

$$= \frac{65 - 40}{\sqrt{\dfrac{65 \times 35}{100} + \dfrac{40 \times 60}{300}}}$$

$$= \frac{25}{\sqrt{22.75 + 12.8}}$$

$$= \frac{25}{5.55}$$

$$= 4.51$$

We compare the computed z value with our standard z of 1.96 for 95 percent level of confidence, and the computed z is larger than 1.96. A computed z value that is larger than the standard z value amounts to *no* support for the null hypothesis. Thus, there is a statistically significant difference between the two percentages and we are confident that if we repeated this comparison many, many times with a multitude of independent samples, we would conclude that there is a significant difference in at least 95 percent of these replications. Of course, we would never do many, many replications, but this is the statistician's basis for the level of significance.

Using SPSS for Differences Between Percentages of Two Groups

SPSS does not perform tests of the significance of the difference between the percentages of two groups, but you can use SPSS to generate the relevant information and perform a hand calculation.

As with most statistical analysis programs, SPSS does not perform tests of the significance of the difference between the percentages of two groups. You can, however, use SPSS to determine the sample percentage on your variable of interest along with its sample size. Repeat this descriptive analysis for the other sample, and you will have all the values required (p_1, p_2, n_1, and n_2) to perform the calculations by hand or in a spreadsheet program. (Recall that you can compute q_1 and q_2, based on the "$p + q = 100$" relationship.)

Differences Between Means with Two Groups (Independent Samples)

The procedure for testing **significance of difference between two means** from two different groups (samples) is identical to the procedure used in testing two percentages. As you can easily guess, however, the equations differ because a metric scale is involved. Here is the equation for the test of the difference between two sample means:

If the null hypothesis is true, when you subtract one group mean from the other, the result should be about zero.

Formula for significance of the difference between two means

$$z = \frac{\bar{x}_1 - \bar{x}_2}{s_{\bar{x}_1 - \bar{x}_2}}$$

where

$\bar{x}_1$ = mean found in sample 1

$\bar{x}_2$ = mean found in sample 2

$s_{\bar{x}_1 - \bar{x}_2}$ = standard error of the difference between two means

Here are formulas for the standard errors of the difference between two means.

The standard error of the difference is easy to calculate and again relies on the variability that has been found in the samples and their sizes. For example, the formula for the standard error of a difference between two means is:

Formula for the standard error of the difference between two means

$$S_{\bar{x}_1 - \bar{x}_2} = \sqrt{\frac{s_1^2}{n_1} + \frac{s_2^2}{n_2}}$$

where

s_1 = standard deviation in sample 1

s_2 = standard deviation in sample 2

n_1 = size of sample 1

n_2 = size of sample 2

Here are the calculations for a test of the difference between the means of two groups.

To illustrate how significance of difference computations are made, we use the following example that answers the question "Do male teens and female teens drink different amounts of sports drinks?" In a recent survey, teenagers were asked to indicate how many 20-ounce bottles of sports drinks they consume in a typical week. The descriptive statistics revealed that males consume 9 bottles on average and females consume 7.5 bottles of sports drinks on average. The respective standard deviations were found to be 2 and 1.2. Both samples were of size 100.

Applying this information to the formula for the test of statistically significant differences, we get the following:

$$z = \frac{\overline{x}_1 - \overline{x}_2}{\sqrt{\dfrac{s_1^2}{n_1} + \dfrac{s_2^2}{n_2}}}$$

$$= \frac{9.0 - 7.5}{\sqrt{\dfrac{2^2}{100} + \dfrac{1.2^2}{100}}}$$

Computation of the significance of the difference between $\overline{x}_1 = 9.0$ and $\overline{x}_2 = 7.5$ ($n_1 = 100$ and $n_2 = 100$)

$$= \frac{1.5}{\sqrt{.04 + .0144}}$$

$$= \frac{1.5}{0.233}$$

$$= 6.43$$

Figure 17.1 indicates how these two samples compare on the sampling distribution assumed to underlie this particular example. We have included the standard error of the difference curve. The probability of support for the null hypothesis of no difference between the two means is less than 0.01 because 6.43 is greater than 2.58.

How do you interpret this test for significance of differences? As always, the sampling distribution concept underlies our interpretation. If the hypothesis were true, were we to draw many, many samples and do this explicit comparison each time, then 99 percent of differences would fall within ±2.58 standard errors of zero. Of course, only one comparison can be made, and you have to rely on the sampling distribution concept and its attendant assumptions to determine whether this one

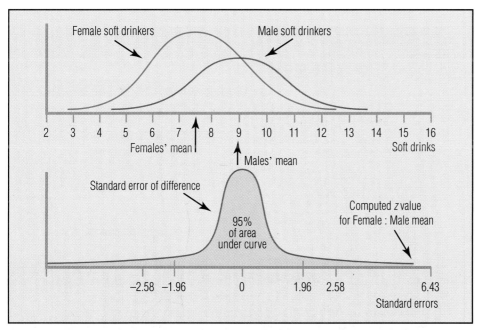

Figure 17.1 **A Significant Difference Exists Between the Two Means Because z is Calculated to Be Greater Than 2.58 (99 Percent Level of Confidence)**

particular instance of information supports or refutes the hypothesis of no significant differences found between the means (or percentages) of your two groups.

Directional hypotheses are also feasible in the case of tests of statistically significant differences. The procedure is identical to directional hypotheses that are stipulated in hypothesis tests. That is, you must first look at the sign of the computed z value to check that it is consistent with your hypothesized direction. Then you would use a cutoff z value such as 2.33 standard errors for 99 percent level of confidence because only one tail of the sampling distribution is being used.

RETURN TO　*Your Integrated Case*

The Hobbit's Choice Restaurant Survey: How to Perform an Independent Samples Significance of Differences Between Means Test with SPSS

In the previous chapter on statistical inference, we illustrated the use of SPSS to answer some critical questions on the survival potential of Jeff Dean's The Hobbit's Choice Restaurant. You should recall that we discovered that the survey held good news because all three criteria specified by Cory Rogers, research project director, were met.

To demonstrate an independent samples significance test, we will take up Jeff's questions on how to promote The Hobbit's Choice Restaurant. One question Jeff voiced during the problem definition stage was whether or not he should use the *City Magazine* as an advertising vehicle. The questionnaire asked if respondents subscribed or did not subscribe to *City Magazine*, so we have two groups: subscribers and nonsubscribers. We can test the mean of the likelihood of patronizing The Hobbit's Choice Restaurant. This construct was measured on a five-point scale where 1 = very unlikely and 5 = very likely.

The clickstream that directs SPSS to perform an independent samples *t* test of the significance of the difference between means is displayed in Figure 17.2. As you can see, you begin with the ANALYZE-COMPARE MEANS-INDEPENDENT SAMPLES *t* TEST ... menu sequence. This sequence opens up the selection menu, and the "likelihood of patronizing Hobbit's Choice (likely)" is clicked into the "Test Variable" area, while the "Subscribe to City

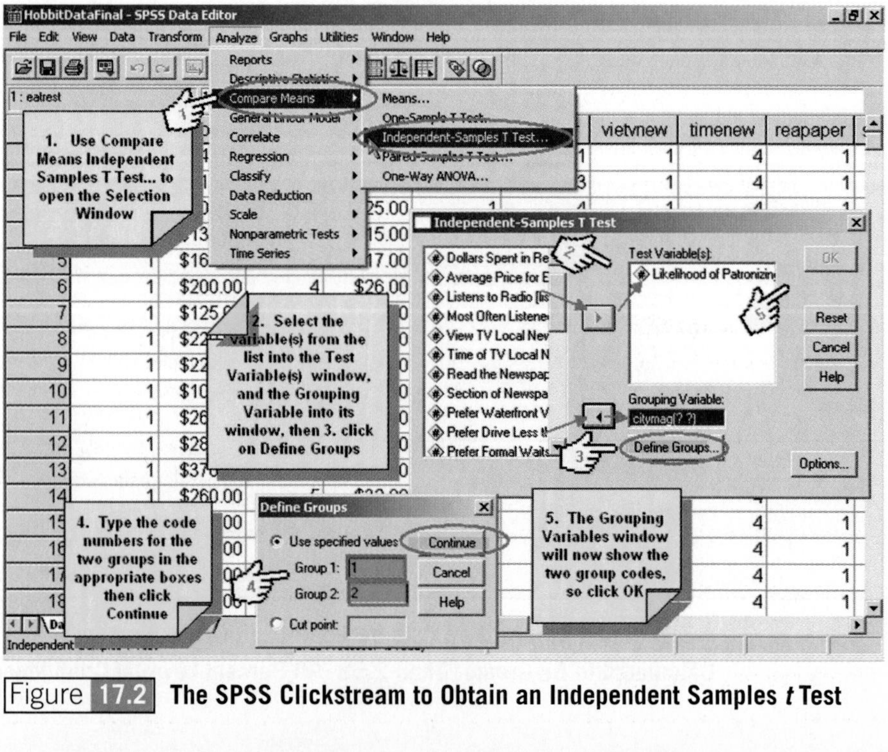

To determine the significance of the difference in the means of two groups with SPSS, use the ANALYZE-COMPARE MEANS-INDEPENDENT SAMPLES t TEST ... menu sequence.

Figure 17.2　**The SPSS Clickstream to Obtain an Independent Samples *t* Test**

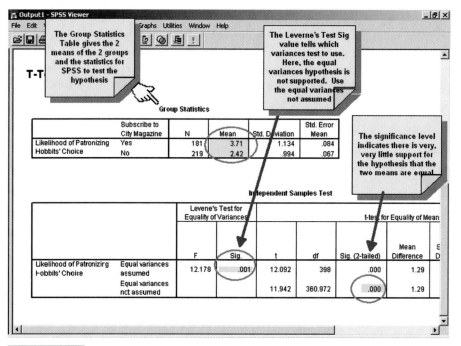

Figure **17.3** **SPSS Output for an Independent Samples *t* Test**

Magazine (citymag)" variable is clicked into the "Grouping Variable" box. Using the "Define Groups" button, a window opens to let us identify the codes of the two groups (1 = yes and 2 = no). This sets up the *t* test, and a click on OK executes it.

The annotated output is found in Figure 17.3. The first table reveals that the mean of the 181 *City Magazine* subscribers is 3.71, whereas the mean for the 219 nonsubscribers is 2.42.

The statistical test for the difference between the two means is given next. However, SPSS computes the results two different ways. One is identified as the "equal variances assumed," and the other is called the "equal variances not assumed." In our previous descriptions, we omitted a detail involved in tests for the significance of difference between two means. In some cases, the variances (standard deviations) of the two samples are about the same; that is, they are not significantly different. If so, you can use the formula pertaining to the equal variances (same variance for both samples), but if the standard deviations are statistically significant in their differences, you should use the unequal variances line on the output.

How do you know which one to use? The null hypothesis here is that there is no difference between the variances (standard deviations), and it is tested with an *F* value printed in the top row of the independent samples test table. The *F* test is just another statistical test, and it is the proper one here. (Recall that we stated earlier that SPSS will always select and compute the correct statistical test.) The *F* value is based on a procedure called "Levene's Test for Equality of Variances." In our output, the *F* value is identified as 12.178 (flagpole) with a Sig (probability) of 0.001 (flag waving). The probability reported here is the probability that the variances are equal, so anytime the probability is *greater than*, say, 0.05, then you would use the equal variance line on the output. If the probability associated with the *F* value is *small, say, 0.05 or less*, then the variances null hypothesis is not supported, and you should use the unequal variance line. If you forget this rule, then just look at the standard deviations, and try to remember that if they are about the same size, you would use the equal variances *t* value.

Using the unequal variance estimate information, you will find that the computed *t* value is –11.942, and the association probability of support for the null hypothesis of no difference between the *City Magazine* subscribers' mean and the nonsubscribers' mean is .000. In other words, they differ significantly. Subscribers are more likely to patronize The Hobbit's Choice Restaurant. So, the *City Magazine* would definitely be an advertising vehicle that targets potential customers.

SPSS Student Assistant Online
Assessing Differences Between
Means for 2 Groups (Independent)

Differences Between Two Means Within the Same Sample (Paired Sample)

Occasionally, a researcher will want to test for differences between the means of two variables within the same sample. For example, in our pharmaceuticals company cold remedy situation described earlier in this chapter, a survey can be used to determine "How important is it that your cold remedy relieves your . . ." using a scale of 1 = not important and 10 = very important for each cold symptom. The question then becomes, "Are any two average importance levels significantly different?" To determine the answer to this question, we must run a **paired samples test for the difference between two means**, which is a test to determine if two means of two different questions using the same scale format, and answered by the same respondents in the sample, are significantly different.

But the same respondents answered both questions, so you do not have two independent groups. Instead, you have two independent questions with one group. The logic and equations we have described still apply, but there must be an adjustment factor because there is only one sample involved. We do not provide the equations, but in the following SPSS section we describe how to perform and to interpret a paired samples t test.[4]

> You can test the significance of the difference between two means for two different questions answered by the same respondents using the same scale.

  RETURN TO   *Your Integrated Case*

The Hobbit's Choice Restaurant Survey: How to Perform a Paired Samples Significance of Differences Between Means Test with SPSS

Let's analyze restaurant décor. In the survey, respondents indicated their preferences on a five-point scale where 1 = very strongly not prefer and 5 = very strongly prefer for a "simple décor" to "elegant décor."

The SPSS clickstream sequence to perform a paired samples t test of the significance of the difference between means is displayed in Figure 17.4. As you can see, you begin with

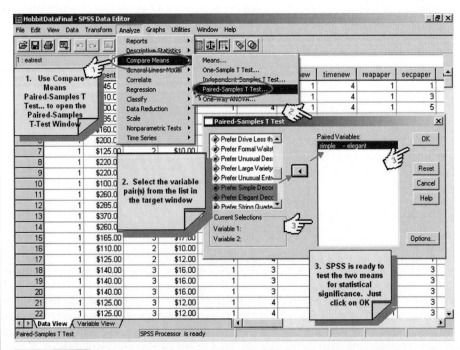

Figure **17.4** **The SPSS Clickstream to Obtain a Paired Samples *t* Test**

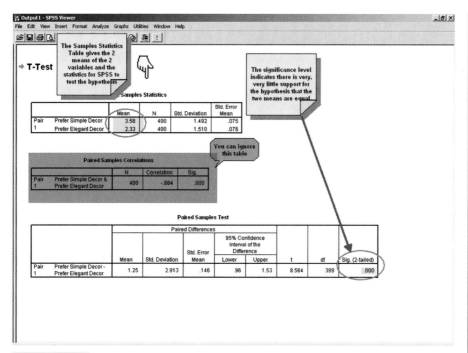

Figure **17.5** SPSS Output for a Paired Samples *t* Test

SPSS

SPSS Student Assistant Online

Assessing Differences Between

Means for 2 Questions (Paired)

the ANALYZE-COMPARE MEANS-PAIRED SAMPLES *t* TEST . . . menu sequence. This sequence opens up the selection menu, and via cursor clicks, you can select "Prefer Simple Décor" and "Prefer Elegant Décor" as the variable pair to be tested. This sets up the *t* test, and a click on OK executes it.

The resulting annotated output is found in Figure 17.5. You should notice that the table is similar, but not identical, to the independent samples output. The relevant information includes (1) 400 respondents gave answers to each statement and were analyzed; (2) the means for simple décor and elegant décor are 3.58 and 2.33, respectively; (3) the computed *t* value is 8.564; and (4) the two-tailed significance level is 0.000. In words, the test gives almost no support for the null hypothesis that the means are equal. The simple décor option is definitely preferred over the elegant décor for all restaurant patrons.

To test the significance of difference between two means for questions answered by the same respondents, use the SPSS ANALYZE-COMPARE MEANS-PAIRED SAMPLES *t* TEST . . . menu sequence.

Whew! It is time for a break from all of these statistics. What about meeting a market researcher? Read about Melinda Smith de Borrero in our item on page 502.

ONLINE SURVEYS AND DATABASES—A "SIGNIFICANCE" CHALLENGE TO MARKETING RESEARCHERS

You should be aware that sample size has a great deal to do with statistical significance. Sample size *n* appears in every statistical formula we have described in this chapter on differences and in the previous chapter that dealt with confidence intervals and hypothesis tests. As we indicated earlier in this chapter, a statistician considers any sample greater than 30 to be a "large" sample. With the fast, easy, and inexpensive data collection that accompanies online surveys, it is common for market researchers to have samples that are comprised of several thousands of respondents. Furthermore, databases such as those built by checkout scanners can easily

have hundreds of thousands of individuals. With these megasamples, statistical tests are almost always found to be significant. In other words, the significance is determined by the immense sample sizes and not by the actual differences between the groups being compared

What is a researcher to do when just about everything is statistically significant? The answer is found in our earlier comments about the importance of differences to marketing managers. Not only should the difference in question be statistically significant, but it must also be meaningful. We have prepared Marketing Research Insight 17.4 which has some rules of thumb that can be used to judge the meaningfulness of statistically significant differences.

TESTING FOR SIGNIFICANT DIFFERENCES IN MEANS AMONG MORE THAN TWO GROUPS: ANALYSIS OF VARIANCE

ANOVA is used when comparing the means of three or more groups.

Often a researcher will want to compare the means of several different groups. Analysis of variance, sometimes called ANOVA, should be used to accomplish such multiple comparisons.[5] Read our AT&T example in Marketing Research Insight 17.5 for an example. The use of the word "variance" in the name "analysis of variance" is perhaps misleading—it is not an analysis of the standard deviations of the groups. To be sure, the standard deviations are taken into consideration, and so are the sample sizes just as you saw in all of our other statistical inference formulas. Fundamentally, **ANOVA (analysis of variance)** is an investigation of the differences between the group means to ascertain whether sampling errors or true population differences explain their failure to be equal.[6] That is, the word "variance" signifies for our purposes differences between two or more groups' means—do they vary from one another significantly? Although a term like "ANOVA" sounds frightfully technical, it is nothing more than a statistical procedure that embodies inference when you are looking at the means of several groups. The following sections explain to you the basic concepts involved with analysis of variance and also how it can be applied to marketing research situations.

An Online Application

Statistical Significance and Meaningfulness: How Online Surveys Require a "Difference Percent" to Assess Managerial Meaningfulness

As you learned in Chapter 4, the researcher and the manager are from different worlds, and sometimes in the heat of statistical analysis, the researcher can lose sight of what is relevant to his client-manager.

Researchers are trained to be vigilant to statistical significance. They scour computer output screens looking for p values or "Sig." numbers that are less than .05. They become very excited when they find a value like .01, and they can become downright jubilant when a .000 pops up.

Online surveys are capable of producing thousands of respondents in a short time period. In case you did not notice this fact, the sample size n is always in the "denominator of the denominator" of statistical significance tests, such as a t test for the significance of the difference between means of two groups. We did not share the ANOVA formulas, but the sample size is, in fact, in the denominator of the computed F statistic ANOVA.

This fact means that as the sample size increases, the denominator decreases, and the t, z, or F value increases. Thus, with very large sample sizes, any difference can be statistically significant regardless of how small its arithmetic difference is.

Here is how one author characterizes this situation.

For example, suppose that we conduct a study with 1,000,000 people and find that women score an average of 86 on a math test and men score an average of 87. With such a big sample size, we would probably find the difference to be statistically

significant. However, what would we conclude about the practical significance of a one-point difference between genders on a 100-point exam? Are men "superior" to women in math? Will we have adverse impact? Should I discourage my daughter from a career in science? Probably not. The statistical significance allows me to confidently say that there is little difference between men and women on this variable.[7]

With this situation, it is vital that a researcher provide a way for the manager to assess the meaningfulness of the difference between two means or percentages. One possibility is to provide a "percent difference" that is calculated by the following formula:[8]

Formula for "percent difference"
$$\text{Percent difference} = \frac{(\text{mean}_1 - \text{mean}_2)}{\text{scale range}}$$

(Note: The sign is irrelevant.)

In our math example, this would compute to be a 1 percent difference ((absolute $(86 - 87)/100$)) and hardly worth worrying about. If it was 10 percent or more, the manager's attention would be warranted.

Here are some guidelines to help the manager assess the meaningfulness of statistically significant differences.[9]

Assessing Meaningfulness of Statistical Significance

PERCENT DIFFERENCE	INTERPRETATION
Less than 10%	Not meaningful
10% to 20%	Probably meaningful
Greater than 20%	Definitely meaningful

Additional Insights

How AT&T Uses Market Research to Determine Customer Loyalty Differences[10]

Market research is an important tool in determining the optimal marketing mix required to drive a successful marketing offer or launch. Research can also be used to determine how a successful product experience can reinforce the quality and strength of the customer relationship.

At AT&T, research was conducted following the launch of an innovative new-product* offering that was truly differentiated from its competitors. AT&T researchers wanted to determine the extent to which ownership of this particular product influenced subsequent brand purchase decisions.

Research was conducted among multiple customer groups: customers who purchased this product, customers

who were targeted for messaging about the product but who did not buy, and a control group of customers who were not marketed to for this particular product.

Results indicated that customers who had purchased this product were significantly more likely to associate positive brand attitudes with AT&T and to say that they would do additional business with AT&T in the future than either of the other two groups. This research enabled marketing managers to claim that this positive brand equity impact was related to ownership of the new product.

*The product is not identified for proprietary reasons.

Basic Logic in Analysis of Variance

The basic logic of analysis of variance is a desire on the part of a researcher to determine whether a statistically significant difference exists between the means for *any two groups* in his or her sample with a given variable regardless of the number of groups. The end result of analysis of variance is an indication to the marketing researcher as to whether a significant difference at some chosen level of statistical significance exists (*p* value) between *at least* two groups' means. Significant differences may exist between all of the groups' means, but analysis of variance results will not communicate how many pairs of means are statistically significant in their differences.

ANOVA is a **flagging procedure**, meaning that if at least one pair of means has a statistically significant difference, ANOVA will signal this by indicating significance. Then it is up to the researcher to conduct further tests to determine precisely how many statistically significant differences actually exist and which ones they are. Of course, if the flag does not pop up, the researcher knows that no significant differences exist.

Let us elaborate just a bit on how ANOVA works. ANOVA uses some complicated formulas, and we have found from experience that market researchers do not memorize them. Instead, a researcher understands the basic purpose of ANOVA, and he or she is adept in interpreting ANOVA output. Let's assume that we have three groups, A, B, and C. In concept ANOVA uses all possible independent samples *t* tests for significant differences between the means, comparing, in our A, B, C example, A:B, A:C, and B:C. ANOVA is very efficient as it makes these comparisons simultaneously, not individually as you would need to do if you were running independent samples *t* tests. ANOVA's null hypothesis is that no pair of means is significantly different. Because multiple pairs of group means are being tested, ANOVA uses the *F* test statistic, and the *p* value that appears on the output in this *F* test is the probability of support for the null hypothesis.

ANOVA will "flag" when at least one pair of means has a statistically significant difference, but it does not tell which pair.

ANOVA is a "flagging" procedure that signals when at least one pair of means is significantly different.

Table **17.2A** **Results of Five Independent Samples *t* Tests of How Likely Patrons Are to Return to the Same Department to Make Their Next Major Purchase**

GROUPS COMPARED	GROUP MEANS	*p* VALUE
Electronics: Home and Garden	5.1: 5.3	.873
Electronics: Sporting Goods	5.1: 5.6	.469
Electronics: Automotive	5.1: 2.2	.000
Home and Garden: Sporting Goods	5.3: 5.6	.656
Home and Garden: Automotive	5.3: 2.2	.000
Sporting Goods: Automotive	5.6: 2.2	.000

Here is an example that will help you to understand how ANOVA works and when to use it. A major department store conducts a survey, and one of the questions on the survey is, "At what department did you last make a purchase for over $250?" There are four departments where significant numbers of respondents made these purchases: (1) electronics, (2) home and garden, (3) sporting goods, and (4) automotive. Another question on the survey is, "How likely are you to purchase another item for over $250 from that department the next time?" The respondents indicate how likely they are to do this on a seven-point scale where 1 = very unlikely and 7 = very likely. It is easy to calculate the mean of how likely each group is to return to the department store and purchase another major item from that same department.

The researcher who is doing the analysis decides to compare these means statistically, so six different independent samples *t* tests of the significance of the differences are performed. A summary of the findings is found in Table 17.2A. It may take a few minutes, but if you examine Table 17.2A, you will see that the automotive department's mean is significantly different and lower than the likelihood means of the other three departments. Also, there is no significant difference in the other three department patrons' means.

In other words, there is a good indication that the patrons who bought an item for more than $250 from the department store's automotive department are not as likely to buy again as are patrons who bought from any other department.

Now, look at Table 17.2B. It is an abbreviated ANOVA output. Instead of looking at several *p* values as in Table 17.2A, all the researcher needs to do is to look at

The Sig. value in the ANOVA table indicates the level of significance.

Table **17.2B** **Results of ANOVA Analysis of How Likely Patrons Are to Return to the Same Department to Make Their Next Major Purchase by Department of Last Major Purchase**

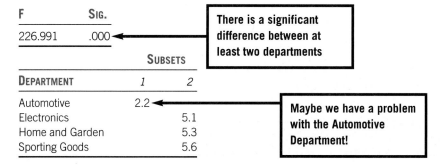

F	SIG.		
226.991	.000		

There is a significant difference between at least two departments

	SUBSETS	
DEPARTMENT	1	2
Automotive	2.2	
Electronics		5.1
Home and Garden		5.3
Sporting Goods		5.6

Maybe we have a problem with the Automotive Department!

MARKETING RESEARCH
INSIGHT
17.6

How Are American Tourists Seen by Foreign Country Tour Guides?

What type of an impression do American tourists leave on their foreign tour guides? This is an intriguing question as tour guides act according to how they perceive their tourist groups will react and behave. At the same time, tour guides may serve as opinion leaders in their communities with respect to others' attitudes toward foreigners.

In an attempt to see if American tourists are seen uniformly or differently, a researcher surveyed tour guides operating in four different countries.[11] The countries and number of tour guides who took part in the survey were Great Britain (97), Israel (97), Korea (44), and Holland (48). These respondents rated American tourists on 20 different behaviors such as interacting with other tourists, shopping constantly, being adventuresome, and preferring local food and drinks, each with a five-point scale. The means for each tour guide country group were compared for each of the 20 characteristics by the use of ANOVA.

Differences were found, but three of the four tourist guide nationality groups agreed (had no differences) that American tourists . . .

- ▶ have a slight preference for local food and drinks
- ▶ plan moderately their visit to a destination
- ▶ constantly interact with other tourists
- ▶ purchase many souvenirs
- ▶ shop extensively
- ▶ play it safe rather than be adventurous
- ▶ are mildly active
- ▶ socialize with other tourists
- ▶ are fairly trustful of tourist-trade people
- ▶ are more interested in people than in artifacts
- ▶ write many letters and postcards to friends and relatives at home

---

ANOVA is much more advantageous than running multiple *t* tests of the significance of the difference between means.

the significance level (Sig.) for the *F* test. It is .000, so now it is worth the researcher's time and effort to look at the next table to find where the significant differences are. This table is arranged so the means that are not significantly different fall in the same column, whereas those that are significantly different fall in separate columns, and each column is identified as a unique subset. The means are arranged in the second table from the lowest mean to the highest mean, and it is immediately apparent that the automotive department has a problem.

ANOVA has two distinct advantages over performing multiple *t* tests of the significance of the difference between means. First, it immediately notifies the researcher if there is any significant difference, because all he or she needs to do is to look at the "Sig." value. Second, in our example, it arranges the means so the significant differences can be located and interpreted easily.

This "Sig." or *p* value is the flag that we referred to earlier and in Marketing Research Insight 17.1. When the flag is waving, the researcher is then justified at looking at each pair of means to find which one(s) are significantly different. Once you learn how to read SPSS ANOVA output, it is quite easy to identify these cases. Of course, if the *F* statistic *p* value flag is not waving, meaning that the *p* value is *greater than .05*, it is a waste of time to look at the differences between the pairs of means, as no difference will be statistically significant at the 95 percent level of confidence. For an example of how ANOVA can be used in global marketing research, read Marketing Research Insight 17.6.

A Bit More on Determining Specific Statistically Significant Differences Between Group Means

Post hoc tests are options that are available to determine where the pair(s) of statistically significant differences between the means exist(s). As you will soon see in our SPSS example, there are over a dozen of these to choose from, including Scheffe's and

Tukey's that you may recognize from statistics courses. It is beyond the scope of this book to provide a complete delineation of the various types of tests. Consequently, only one test, Duncan's multiple range test, will be shown as an illustration of how the differences may be determined. **Duncan's multiple range test** provides output that is mostly a "picture" of what pair(s) of means are significantly different, and it is much less statistical than most of the other post hoc tests, so we have chosen to use it here for this reason. The picture provided by the Duncan's post hoc test is the arrangement of the means as you saw them in Table 17.2B.

The Duncan multiple range test is our preferred post hoc test because its output is easy to interpret.

RETURN TO *Your Integrated Case*

The Hobbit's Choice Restaurant Survey: How to Run Analysis of Variance on SPSS

In The Hobbit's Choice Restaurant survey, there are a number of categorical variables that have more than two groups. Let's take a promotional decision that concerns Jeff Dean: In what section of the newspaper should he place his ads? The questionnaire asked which newspaper section respondents read most frequently, and the options were editorial, business, local, classifieds, life (health and entertainment), or no preference.

One-way ANOVA in this case is done under the ANALYZE-COMPARE MEANS-ONE-WAY ANOVA menu command sequence illustrated in Figure 17.6. A window opens to set up the ANOVA analysis. The "Dependent list" is where you click in the variable(s) pertaining to the means, whereas the "Factor" variable is the grouping variable. In our example, the likelihood of patronizing The Hobbit's Choice is our dependent one, and the "Section of Newspaper Read Most Often" is the grouping variable. Figure 17.6 also shows how to select the Duncan's Multiple Range option under the Post Hoc . . . Tests menu. Returning to the selection window and clicking on "OK" commences the ANOVA procedure.

To run analysis of variance with SPSS, use the ANALYZE-COMPARE MEANS-ONE-WAY ANOVA menu command sequence.

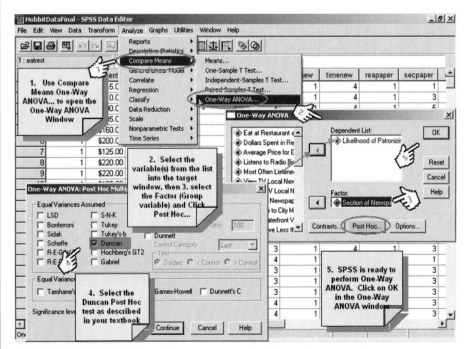

Figure **17.6** **The SPSS Clickstream to Perform Analysis of Variance (ANOVA)**

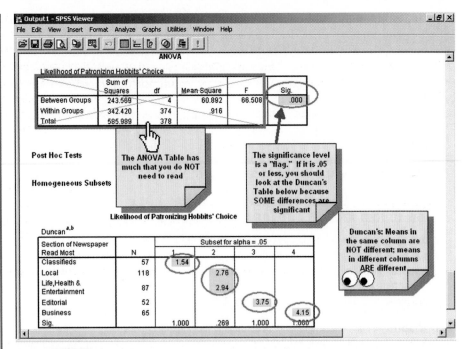

Figure **17.7**   **SPSS Output for Analysis of Variance (ANOVA)**

Figure 17.7 is an annotated ANOVA output. The first table contains a number of intermediate and additional computational results, but our attention should be focused on the "Sig." column. Here is the support for the null hypothesis that not one pair of means is significantly different. Since, the Sig. value is .000, we are assured that there is at least one significantly different pair. The next table is the Duncan's test output. Specifically, the table is arranged so the means ascend in size from top left to bottom right, and the columns represent subsets of groups that are significantly different from groups in the other columns. You can immediately see that business (4.15), editorial (3.75) life, health and entertainment and local (2.94 and 2.76, but not significantly different from each other), and classifieds (1.54) define four unique groupings of likelihood to patronize The Hobbit's Choice. People who read the business section are the most likely patrons, so it makes sense for Jeff to place his ads in this section because its readers are more prone to be looking for an upscale restaurant.

What about the editorial page? We have a statistically significant difference between the business section frequent readers (4.15) and the editorial page frequent readers (3.75), but is it a *meaningful* difference? If we apply our guideline for meaningfulness, we find that the difference is 7 percent (i.e., absolute (4.15 – 3.75)/5 = 8 percent). This is less than 10 percent, so based on our rule of thumb, it is not definitely meaningful. Instead, it is possibly meaningful, and Jeff may want to experiment by varying his ad placements in these two newspaper sections to see what type of responses are generated.

n-Way ANOVA

The Hobbit's Choice Restaurant survey newspaper section reading example illustrates what is normally termed **one-way ANOVA** because there is only one independent factor used to set up the groups. However, it is not unusual to look at two or more grouping factors simultaneously, in which case one would use ***n*-way ANOVA**. For example, a manager might decide to use age groups and occupation classifications at the same time to test for differences. Or, with a test market experiment, the researcher might want to see the effect of a high versus a low price operating with a newspaper versus billboard advertising. The overlaying of various independent factors permits the marketing researcher to investigate "interaction effects." **Interaction effects** are cases in which the independent factors are operating in concert and simultaneously affecting the means of the groups. Conceptually, *n*-way ANOVA operates identically to the one-way ANOVA regardless of the number of treatment classification schemes being used. Of course, the formulas and computations are more complicated.

n-Way ANOVA with SPSS

n-way ANOVA is found in SPSS under the ANALYZE-GENERAL LINEAR MODEL-UNIVARIATE menu command sequence, which leads to a dialogue box where you can select the Fixed Factors, or independent grouping variables, and the Dependent variables, or the one being used to calculate the group means. There are many features to *n*-way ANOVA on your SPSS program that we have not mentioned. We suggest that you refer to more advanced sources if you are interested in using *n*-way ANOVA.

SUMMARY

The chapter began with a discussion on why differences are important to marketing managers. Basically, market segmentation implications underlie most differences analyses. It is important that differences are statistically significant, but it is also vital that they are meaningful, stable, and a basis of marketing strategy.

We then described how differences between two percentages in two samples can be tested for statistical significance. Then we described the same test procedure using means. In addition, you were introduced to the *t* test procedure in SPSS that is used to test the significance of the difference between two means from two independent samples. We gave an illustration of how to use SPSS for this analysis using The Hobbit's Choice Restaurant data set. Additionally, you learned about a paired samples test and how to perform and interpret it using SPSS.

When a researcher has more than two groups and wishes to compare their various means, the correct procedure involves analysis of variance, or ANOVA. ANOVA is a flagging technique that tests all possible pairs of means for all the groups involved and indicates via the Sig. (significance) value in the ANOVA table if at least one pair is statistically significant in its difference. If the Sig. value is greater than .05, the researcher will waste his or her time inspecting the means for differences. But if the Sig. value is .05 or less, the researcher can use a post hoc procedure, such as Duncan's multiple range test, to identify the pair or pairs of groups where the means are significantly different.

KEY TERMS

Statistical significance of differences
  (p. 489)
Meaningful difference (p. 490)
Stable difference (p. 490)
Actionable difference (p. 491)
t test (p. 492)
z test (p. 492)
Null hypothesis (p. 494)
Significance of differences between
  two percentages (p. 494)
Significance of difference between
  two means (p. 496)

Paired samples test for the difference
  between two means (p. 500)
ANOVA (analysis of variance) (p. 502)
Flagging procedure (p. 504)
Post hoc tests (p. 506)
Duncan's multiple range test (p. 507)
One-way ANOVA (p. 508)
n-way ANOVA (p. 508)
Interaction effects (p. 509)

REVIEW QUESTIONS/APPLICATIONS

1. What are differences and why should marketing researchers be concerned with them? Why are marketing managers concerned with them?
2. What is considered to be a "small sample," and why is this concept a concern to statisticians? To what extent do marketing researchers concern themselves with small samples? Why?
3. When a marketing researcher compares the responses of two identifiable groups with respect to their answers to the same question, what is this called?
4. With regard to differences tests, briefly define and describe each of the following:
   a. Null hypothesis
   b. Sampling distribution
   c. Significant difference
5. Relate the formula and identify each formula's components in the test of significant differences between two groups for when the question involved is
   a. A "yes/no" type of question
   b. A metric scale type of question
6. Are the following two sample results significantly different?

SAMPLE 1	SAMPLE 2	CONFIDENCE LEVEL	YOUR FINDING?
Mean: 10.6 Std. dev: 1.5 $n = 150$	Mean: 11.7 Std. dev: 2.5 $n = 300$	95%	
Percent: 45% $n = 350$	Percent: 54% $n = 250$	99%	
Mean: 1,500 Std. dev: 550 $n = 1,200$	Mean: 1,250 Std. dev: 500 $n = 500$	95%	

7. What is a paired samples test? Specifically how are the samples "paired?"
8. When should one-way ANOVA be used and why?
9. When a researcher finds a significant F value in an analysis of variance, why can it be considered a "flagging" device?
10. The circulation manager of the *Daily Advocate* commissions a market research study to determine what factors underlie the circulation attrition. Specifically, the survey is designed to compare current *Daily Advocate* subscribers with those who have dropped their subscriptions in the past year. A telephone survey is conducted with both sets of individuals. Following is a summary of the key findings from the study.

ITEM	CURRENT SUBSCRIBERS	LOST SUBSCRIBERS	SIGNIFICANCE
Length of residence in the city	20.1 years	5.4 years	.000
Length of time as a subscriber	27.2 years	1.3 years	.000
Watch local TV news program(s)	87%	85%	.372
Watch national news program(s)	72%	79%	.540
Obtain news from the Internet	13%	23%	.025
Satisfaction[a] with . . .			
Delivery of newspaper	5.5	4.9	.459
Coverage of local news	6.1	5.8	.248
Coverage of national news	5.5	2.3	.031
Coverage of local sports	6.3	5.9	.462

Item	Current Subscribers	Lost Subscribers	Significance
Satisfaction[a] with . . .			
Coverage of national sports	5.7	3.2	.001
Coverage of local social news	5.8	5.2	.659
Editorial stance of the newspaper	6.1	4.0	.001
Value for subscription price	5.2	4.8	.468

[a]Based on a seven-point scale where 1 = very dissatisfied and 7 = very satisfied

Interpret these findings for the circulation manager.

11. A researcher is investigating different types of customers for a sporting goods store. In a survey, respondents have indicated how much they exercise in approximate minutes per week. These respondents have also rated the performance of the sporting goods store across 12 difference characteristics such as good value for the price, convenience of location, helpfulness of the sales clerks, and so on. The researcher used a 1–7 rating scale for these 12 characteristics where 1 = poor performance and 7 = excellent performance. How can the researcher investigate differences in the ratings based on the amount of exercise reported by the respondents?

12. A marketing manager of Collections, Etc., a Web-based catalog sales company, uses a segmentation scheme based on the incomes of target customers. The segmentation system has four segments: (1) low income, (2) moderate income, (3) high income, and (4) wealthy. The company database holds information on every customer's purchases over the past several years, and the total dollars spent at Collections, Etc. is one of the prominent variables. Using Microsoft Excel on this database, the marketing manager finds that the average total dollar purchases for the four groups are as follows.

Market Segment	Average Total Dollar Purchases
Low income	$101
Moderate income	$120
High income	$231
Wealthy	$595

Construct a table that is based on the Duncan's multiple range test table concept discussed in the chapter that illustrates that the low- and moderate-income groups are not different from each other, but the other groups are significantly different from one another.

13. How would a grocery store chain company go about constructing and validating a market segmentation system? Take the possible segmentation variables of family type (single, couple, or with children) and occupation (skilled labor, professional, or retired). Indicate the steps you would take and any considerations you would take into account as a researcher investigating if there was a useful segmentation system for the grocery store chain company using these two demographic variables as the basis.

INTERACTIVE LEARNING

Visit the Web site at www.prenhall.com/burnsbush. For this chapter, work through the Self-Study Quizzes, and get instant feedback on whether you need additional studying. On the Web site, you can review the chapter outlines and case information for Chapter 17.

CASE 17.1 General Hospital Cafeteria Importance-Performance Survey

General Hospital is a large regional hospital that employs over 2,000 full- and part-time workers, including custodial personnel, nurses, medical technicians, and doctors. On the ground floor of General Hospital there is a cafeteria that is operated by the hospital with Ms. Connie Wilson as its manager. Almost all employees use the cafeteria for lunch. There have been complaints about the cafeteria for many years, and Ms. Wilson has decided to look into these problems with a survey. She recruits the hospital's marketing research director to design a questionnaire that asks cafeteria patrons to rate the cafeteria on a seven-point satisfaction scale with 1 meaning "very dissatisfied" and 7 meaning "very satisfied." Based on a focus group, 17 different cafeteria attributes are rated. In addition, the importance of each attribute is also rated on an importance scale where 1 means "unimportant" and 7 means "very important" to a respondent's decision to eat at a particular location.

Using systematic sampling over a period of one week, cafeteria users who are General Hospital employees are identified during lunch and asked to fill out a questionnaire. A total of 340 usable questionnaires are gathered by the end of the data collection phase. The marketing research director prepares the following two tables. In each table, the researcher separated the 240 weekday from the 100 weekend cafeteria users with the rationale that weekend workers are generally part-time employees. They are also younger than full-time employees. Their mean responses follow.

TABLE A
Importance of Selected Cafeteria Attributes by Type of Patron

Cafeteria Attribute	Weekday	Weekend	Sig.
Courteous employees	5.28	5.18	0.978
Helpful employees	5.20	5.15	0.876
Quality of service	5.07	4.98	0.540
Freshness of lunch items	5.07	4.50	0.034
High nutritional value of lunch items	5.03	4.44	0.045
Overall quality of lunch items	4.97	4.53	0.035
Comfortable seating	4.96	4.95	0.986
Discounts for employees	4.89	4.75	0.752
Appetizing look of lunch items	4.88	4.02	0.052
Speed of lunch service	4.83	4.97	0.650
Relaxed atmosphere	4.83	5.23	0.001
Good-tasting lunch items	4.80	4.02	0.012
Adequate lighting	4.71	4.80	0.659
Good variety of lunch menu	4.60	3.53	0.002
Low price of lunch items	4.52	4.20	0.102
Large portions	4.34	3.87	0.034
Clean surroundings	4.25	4.50	0.286

TABLE B
Evaluation of Cafeteria Performance on Selected Attributes by Type of Patron

Cafeteria Attribute	Weekday	Weekend	Sig.
Courteous employees	5.79	5.46	0.182
Helpful employees	5.83	5.51	0.044
Quality of service	5.54	5.60	0.276
Freshness of lunch items	5.80	4.46	0.001

Cafeteria Attribute	Weekday	Weekend	Sig.
High nutritional value of lunch items	5.29	5.23	0.197
Overall quality of lunch items	4.48	4.46	0.568
Comfortable seating	4.63	4.53	0.389
Discounts for employees	5.45	4.56	0.009
Appetizing look of lunch items	5.65	4.64	0.045
Speed of lunch service	5.52	4.22	0.010
Relaxed atmosphere	4.96	5.63	0.061
Good-tasting lunch items	5.31	4.37	0.048
Adequate lighting	4.52	4.62	0.369
Good variety of lunch menu	4.98	3.75	0.019
Low price of lunch items	5.35	6.86	0.045
Large portions	4.43	5.43	0.038
Clean surroundings	5.56	5.24	0.286

1. Interpret these findings for Ms. Wilson. What do they say about the two subpopulations of weekday and weekend workers?
2. What managerial implications are apparent from these findings?

CASE 17.2   *Your Integrated Case*

This is your integrated case, described on pages 42–43.

The Hobbit's Choice Restaurant Survey Differences Analysis

Cory Rogers called a meeting with Jeff Dean and with Celeste Brown attending. At the beginning of the meeting, Cory's wife called with news that their 5-year-old daughter was having a stomachache at school, and Cory had to pick her up and take her to the doctor. Cory excused himself, saying, "I am sorry about this, but these things happen when you are a dual-career household. Celeste, sit with Jeff for a bit and find out what questions he has about the survey findings. Then take a shot at the analysis, and we'll meet about it tomorrow afternoon. I am sure that my daughter will be over her stomach ailment by then."

After meeting for about 20 minutes, Celeste had a list of six questions that Jeff Dean was especially interested in. Celeste's notes follow.

Your task in this case is to take Celeste's role, using The Hobbit's Choice Restaurant survey SPSS data set, perform the proper analysis, and interpret the findings for each of the following questions.

1. Jeff wonders if The Hobbit's Choice Restaurant is more appealing to women than it is to men or vice versa. Perform the proper analysis, interpret it, and answer Jeff's question.
2. With respect to the location of The Hobbit's Choice Restaurant, is a waterfront view preferred more than a drive of less than 30 minutes?
3. With respect to the restaurant's atmosphere, is a string quartet preferred over a jazz combo?
4. What about unusual entrées versus unusual desserts?
5. In general, upscale establishments are appealing to higher-income households, whereas they are less appealing to lower-income households. Is this pattern the case for The Hobbit's Choice Restaurant?
6. Jeff and Cory speculated that the different geographic areas that they identified by zip codes would have different reactions to the prospect of patronizing a new upscale restaurant. Are these anticipated differences substantiated by the survey? Perform the proper analysis and interpret your findings.

Chapter 18

Determining and Interpreting Associations Among Variables

Practitioner Viewpoint

Market researchers are most often interested in what people want and in how they utilize products or services. This causes them to ask: How important is price in determining purchase intent? What product features are most desirable to potential customers? Are brands perceived differently by product users compared to non-users?

After specifying the variables we wish to study and collecting the data, we organize the data in terms of frequencies, crosstabs, and correlations. These descriptive summaries help to identify the relationships among the variables. Then we employ tests of statistical significance (such as chi-square tests or t tests) to help us determine the likelihood that the observed relationships are valid.

Randall K. Thomas
Research Scientist
Harris Interactive

Using Associations to Assess Customer Satisfaction

Customer satisfaction is the ultimate goal of marketing orientation. It is firmly believed that satisfied customers lead to profit and longevity for a company that is competing with other companies in any market. However, sensing what customers want and bringing these wants to the attention of the company are formidable challenges.

In a recent study, a researcher[1] sought to identify the "best practices" that distinguish companies that have a good system for understanding their customers' problems, monitoring customer satisfaction, and delivering goods and services that lead to satisfied and loyal customers. He found that the premier companies use multiple methods of customer value and satisfaction research. Although each method is unique, the underlying purpose of each one is to discover if a pattern exists, or is developing, in the company's customers. One of the simplest patterns to detect is a direct relationship between some facet of customer satisfaction and some customer characteristic. For example, are single customers less satisfied with some aspect of the company's products than are married customers? Are more complaints coming from customers with higher incomes than from those with lower incomes? Are longtime customers more satisfied than those who have used the products for short time periods? That is, as customer satisfaction increases or decreases, is there some customer characteristic that simultaneously increases or decreases?

Each method found by the researcher to be among the best practices is described in the following table with questions to guide a market researcher when looking into the data derived from these methods to understand associations with customer satisfaction.

Association analysis helps marketers to identify customer types who are more or less likely to be satisfied.

Where We Are:

1. Establish the need for marketing research
2. Define the problem
3. Establish research objectives
4. Determine research design
5. Identify information types and sources
6. Determine methods of accessing data
7. Design data collection forms
8. Determine sample plan and size
9. Collect data
10. **Analyze data**
11. Prepare and present the final research report

CUSTOMER SATISFACTION RESEARCH METHOD	DESCRIPTION OF THE METHOD	EXAMPLE ASSOCIATION TO EXAMINE
Critical Incident Survey	Ask customers what specific incident with the company caused them to be loyal (or to be disloyal)	Are some types of incidents more likely to occur with certain types of customers? For example, are men more likely to have tried our brand because of friends' recommendations?
Relationship Survey	Determine customers' perceptions of the company's performance and service quality	Are performance evaluations related to some customer characteristic? For example, are older customers more (or less) satisfied than younger ones?
Customer Complaints	Have a formal system to monitor complaints and look for trends	Do types of complaints come from specific classes of customers? For example, are complaints about slow delivery more prevalent in one region of the country than in other regions?
Life Cycle	Segment customers by stage in the life cycle and analyze satisfaction changes from one stage to the next	Is satisfaction related to stage in the life cycle? For example, are empty nesters less satisfied than full nesters with our brand?
Benchmark	Determine customers' perceptions of competitors' performance, particularly market leaders	Is a competitor's image related to some customer characteristic? For example, is competitor A seen as performing better in the eyes of our higher-income customers?
Won-Lost Why?	Survey customers immediately once they have been lost to a competitor or have come to your company from a competitor	Are lost customers of a certain type? For example, are we losing most of our medium income customers to a particular competitor?
Problem Resolution	For customers who have experienced problems, determine what they were and how they were resolved	Is satisfaction related to the type of resolution? For example, when we replace a defective product, does how long the customer has been loyal to our brand correlate with how satisfied he or she is with the resolution?

This chapter illustrates the usefulness of statistical analyses beyond simple descriptive measures and statistical inference. Often marketers are interested in relationships among variables. For example, Frito-Lay wants to know what kinds of people and under what circumstances these people choose to buy Doritos, Fritos, and any of the other items in the Frito-Lay line. The Pontiac Division of General Motors wants to know what types of individuals would respond favorably to the various style changes proposed for the Firebird. A newspaper wants to understand the lifestyle characteristics of its prospective readers so that it is able to modify or change sections in the newspaper to better suit its audience. Furthermore, the newspaper desires information about various types of subscribers so as to communicate this information to its advertisers, helping them in copy design and advertisement placement within the various newspaper sections. In our introductory case, there are a great many of these types of questions beyond the example we noted for each customer satisfaction research method. For all of these cases, there are statistical procedures available, termed *associative analyses*, which determine answers to these questions. **Associative analyses** determine whether stable relationships exist between two variables; they are the central topic of this chapter.

We begin the chapter by describing the four different types of relationships possible between two variables. Then we describe cross-tabulations and indicate how a cross-tabulation can be used to compute a chi-square value that, in turn, can be assessed to determine whether or not a statistically significant association exists between the two variables. From cross-tabulations, we move to a general discussion of correlation coefficients, and we illustrate the use of Pearson product moment correlations. As in our previous analysis chapters, we show you SPSS steps to perform these analyses and the resulting output.

Associative analyses determine whether stable relationships exist between two variables.

TYPES OF RELATIONSHIPS BETWEEN TWO VARIABLES

In order to describe a relationship between two variables, we must first remind you of the scale characteristic called "description" that we introduced to you in Chapter 10. Every scale has unique descriptors, sometimes called levels, that identify the different labels of that scale. The term "levels" implies that the scale is metric, namely, interval or ratio, whereas the term "labels" implies that the scale is not metric, namely, ordinal or interval. A simple label is a "yes" or "no" one, for instance, if a respondent is a buyer (yes) or nonbuyer (no) of a particular product or service. Of course, if the researcher measured how many times a respondent bought a product, the level would be the number of times, and the scale would be metric because this scale would satisfy the assumptions of a ratio scale.

A **relationship** is a consistent and systematic linkage between the levels or labels for two variables. This linkage is statistical, not necessarily causal. A causal linkage is one in which you are certain one variable affected the other one, but with a statistical linkage you cannot be certain because some other variable might have had some influence. Associative analysis procedures are useful because they determine if there is a consistent and systematic relationship between the presence (label) or amount (level) of one variable and the presence (label) or amount (level) of another variable. There are four basic types of relationships between two variables: nonmonotonic, monotonic, linear, and curvilinear. A discussion of each follows.

A relationship is a consistent and systematic linkage between the levels or labels for two variables.

Nonmonotonic Relationships

A **nonmonotonic relationship** is one in which the presence (or absence) of one variable is systematically associated with the presence (or absence) of another variable. The term "nonmonotonic" means essentially that there is no discernible direction to the relationship, but a relationship exists. For example, McDonald's knows from experience that morning customers typically purchase coffee whereas afternoon customers typically purchase soft drinks. The relationship is in no way exclusive—there is no guarantee that a morning customer will always order coffee or that an afternoon customer will always order a soft drink. In general, though, this relationship exists, as can be seen in Figure 18.1. The nonmonotonic relationship is simply that morning customers tend to purchase breakfast foods, such as eggs, biscuits, and coffee, and the afternoon customers tend to purchase lunch items, such as burgers, fries, and soft drinks.

Here are some other examples of nonmonotonic relationships: (1) People who live in apartments do not buy lawn mowers but homeowners do; (2) tourists in Daytona Beach, Florida, during "bike week" are likely to be motorcycle owners, not

A nonmonotonic relationship means two variables are associated, but only in a very general sense.

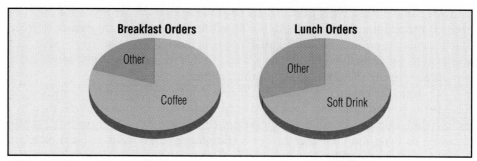

Figure 18.1 **McDonald's Example of a Nonmonotonic Relationship for the Type of Drink Ordered for Breakfast and for Lunch**

college students; and (3) Play Station game players are typically children, not adults. Again each example reports that the presence (absence) of one aspect of some object tends to be joined to the presence (absence) of an aspect of some other object. But the association is very general, and we must state each one by spelling it out verbally. In other words, we know only the general pattern of presence or nonpresence with a nonmonotonic relationship.

Monotonic Relationships

A monotonic relationship means you know the general direction of the relationship between two variables.

Monotonic relationships are ones in which the researcher can assign only a general direction to the association between the two variables. There are two types of monotonic relationships: increasing and decreasing. Monotonic increasing relationships are those in which one variable increases as the other variable increases. As you would guess, monotonic decreasing relationships are those in which one variable increases as the other variable decreases. You should note that in neither case is there any indication of the exact amount of change in one variable as the other changes. "Monotonic" means that the relationship can be described only in a general directional sense. Beyond this, precision in the description is lacking. The following example should help to explain this concept.

Monotonic relationships can be increasing or decreasing.

The owner of a shoe store knows that older children tend to require larger shoe sizes than do younger children, but there is no way to equate a child's age with the right shoe size. No universal rule exists as to the rate of growth of a child's foot nor to the final shoe size he or she will attain. There is, however, a monotonic increasing relationship between a child's age and shoe size. At the same time, a monotonic decreasing relationship exists between a child's age and the amount of involvement of the parents in the purchase of their child's shoes. As Figure18.2 illustrates, very young children often have virtually no input into the purchase decision, whereas older children tend to gain more and more control over the purchase decision process until they ultimately become adults and have complete control over the decision. Once again, no universal rule operates as to the amount of parental influence or the point in time at which the child becomes independent and gains complete control over the decision-making process. It is simply known that younger children have less influence in the decision-making process and older children have more influence in the shoe purchase decision. The relationship is, therefore, monotonic.

Linear Relationships

A linear relationship means the two variables have a "straight-line" relationship.

Now we will turn to a more precise relationship. Perhaps the most intuitive association between two variables is a linear relationship. A **linear relationship** is a "straight-line association" between two variables. Here knowledge of the amount of one variable will automatically yield knowledge of the amount of the other variable

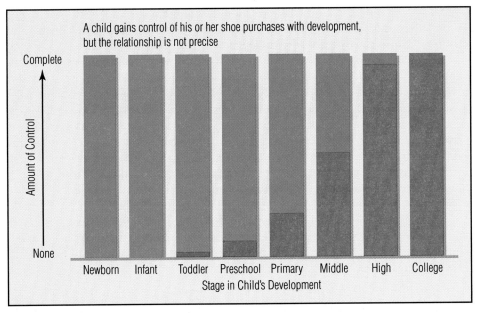

A child gains control of his or her shoe purchases with development, but the relationship is not precise

Amount of Control

Complete

None

Newborn | Infant | Toddler | Preschool | Primary | Middle | High | College

Stage in Child's Development

Figure **18.2** **A Child's Control of His or Her Shoe Purchases: Monotonic Increasing Relationship**

as a consequence of applying the linear or straight-line formula that is known to exist between them. In its general form, a **straight-line formula** is as follows:

Formula for a straight line $y = a + bx$

where

y = the dependent variable being estimated or predicted

a = the intercept

b = the slope

x = the independent variable used to predict the dependent variable

Generally, as a child grows, he or she has more influence in his or her shoe purchases. It is a monotonic relationship.

The terms "intercept" and "slope" should be familiar to you, but if they are not, do not be concerned as we describe the straight-line formula in detail in the next chapter. We also clarify the terms "independent" and "dependent" in Chapter 19.

It should be apparent to you that a linear relationship is much more precise and contains a great deal more information than does a monotonic relationship. By simply substituting the values of *a* and *b*, an exact amount can be determined for *y* given any value of *x*. For example, South-Western Book Company hires college student representatives to work in the summer. These student representatives are put through an intensified sales training program and then they are divided into teams. Each team is given a specific territory, and each individual is assigned a particular district within that territory. The student representative then goes from house to house in the district making cold calls, attempting to sell children's books. Let us assume that the amount of sales is linearly related to the number of cold calls made. In this special case, no sales calls determines zero sales, or *a* = 0. If, on average, every tenth sales call resulted in a sale and the typical sale is $62, then the average per call would be $6.20. The linear relationship between total sales (*y*) and number of sales calls (*x*) is as follows:

Straight-line formula example $y = \$0 + \$6.20x$

Thus, if the college salesperson makes 100 cold calls in any given day, the expected total revenues would be $620 ($6.20 times 100 calls). Certainly, our student sales rep would not derive exactly $620 for every 100 calls, but the linear relationship shows what is expected to happen on average.

Linear relationships are quite precise.

Curvilinear Relationships

A curvilinear relationship means that some smooth curve pattern describes the association.

Now we turn to the last type of relationship. **Curvilinear relationships** are those in which one variable is associated with another variable, but the relationship is described by a curve rather than a straight line. In other words, the formula for a curved relationship is used rather than the formula for a straight line. Many curvilinear patterns are possible. For example, the relationship may be an S-shape, a J-shape, or some other curved-shape pattern. An example of a curvilinear relationship with which you should be familiar is the product life-cycle curve that describes the sales pattern of a new product over time that grows slowly during its introduction, then spurts upward rapidly during its growth stage, and finally plateaus or slows down considerably as the market becomes saturated. Curvilinear relationships are beyond the scope of this text; nonetheless, it is important to list them as a type of relationship that can be investigated through the use of special-purpose statistical procedures.

CHARACTERIZING RELATIONSHIPS BETWEEN VARIABLES

Depending on the type, a relationship can be characterized in three ways: by its presence, direction, and strength of association. We need to describe these before taking up specific statistical analyses of associations between two variables.

Presence

The presence of a relationship between two variables is determined by a statistical test.

Presence refers to whether any systematic relationship exists between the two variables of interest. Presence is a statistical issue. By this statement, we mean that the marketing researcher relies on statistical significance tests to determine whether a particular association is present in the data. The previous chapter on statistical inference introduced the concept of a null hypothesis. With associative analysis, the null hypothesis states there is no association present and the appropriate statistical test is applied to test this hypothesis. If the test results reject the null hypothesis, then an association is present. We describe the statistical tests used in associative analysis later in this chapter.

Direction

In the case of monotonic and linear relationships, associations may also be described with regard to direction. As we described earlier, a monotonic relationship may be increasing or decreasing. In the case of the slope b of a linear relationship, if b is positive, then the linear relationship is increasing; and if b is negative, then the linear relationship is decreasing. But positive or negative direction is inappropriate for nonmonotonic relationships, because we can only describe the pattern verbally. It will soon become clear to you that the level of measurement of variables having a nonmonotonic association negate the directional aspects of the relationship. Nevertheless, we can verbally describe the association as we have in our examples, and that statement substitutes for direction.

Direction means that you know if the relationship is positive or negative.

Strength of Association

Again, depending on the type of relationship being investigated, the strength of association between two variables can be envisioned as strong, moderate, weak, or nonexistent. The nonexistent case occurs when the marketing researcher finds no presence of a consistent and systematic linkage between two variables. When a consistent and systematic association is found to be present between two variables, it is then up to the marketing researcher to ascertain the strength of association. Strong associations are those in which there is a high probability of the two variables exhibiting a dependable relationship, regardless of the type of relationship being analyzed. A low degree of association, on the other hand, is one in which there is a low probability of the two variables exhibiting a dependable relationship. The relationship exists between the variables, but it is less evident.

Strength means you know how consistent the relationship is.

There is an orderly procedure for determining presence, direction, and strength of a relationship. First, you must decide what type of relationship can exist between the two variables of interest. The answer to this question depends on the level of measurement of the variables; as we illustrated earlier, low-level (nominal) scales can embody only imprecise relationships, but high-level (interval or ratio) scales can incorporate very precise relationships. Once you identify the appropriate relationship type as either monotonic, nonmonotonic, or linear, the next step is to determine whether that relationship actually exists in the population you are analyzing. This step requires a statistical test and, again, we describe the proper test for each of these three relationship types beginning with the next section of this chapter.

Based on scaling assumptions, first determine the type of relationship and then perform the appropriate statistical test.

Once you determine that a true relationship does exist in the population by means of the correct statistical test, you then establish its direction. Again, the type of relationship dictates how you describe its direction. You might have to inspect the relationship in a table or graph, or you might need only to look for a positive or negative sign before the computed statistic. Finally, the strength of the relationship remains to be judged. Some associative analysis statistics indicate the strength in a very straightforward manner—that is, just by their absolute size. With nominal-scaled variables, however, you must inspect the pattern to judge the strength. We describe this procedure next.

It is critical in today's marketing environment to have a customer-driven marketing orientation, and an excellent example of a customer-driven company is AT&T. Just think about it: how many times have you been asked to switch your telephone company? Despite this constant attack that has gone on for a great number of years, AT&T remains the largest telephone services provider in the United States with the most loyal customers. One reason for this intense loyalty is that AT&T

MARKETING RESEARCH
INSIGHT
18.1

Randy Zeese is responsible for championing the AT&T brand through research and marketing initiatives that grow brand equity. In this role, Randy conducts market research to determine the impact of corporate communications on market perceptions and customer behavior. This includes the analysis and tracking of AT&T customer perceptions, determination of the linkages between key drivers of customer behavior, and the effectiveness of advertising in the marketing mix. Randy is also responsible for ensuring that the "voice of the customer" is at the forefront of business decision making.

In prior roles at AT&T, Randy has held additional customer-related positions in both the residential and business markets. Most recently, he was involved in customer loyalty programs. He has also held various marketing and sales positions at AT&T. Randy was a member of AT&T's Consumer Communications Services application team for the Malcolm Baldrige National Quality Award and was a subject matter expert in the area of customer satisfaction for that effort. He has received several awards at AT&T for his customer-focused initiatives.

Randy has more than 25 years of market research and brand management experience in the telecommunications industry, with undergraduate and graduate studies in journalism and business administration. In addition, Randy has completed several AT&T executive training programs.

constantly researches its customer base and finds relationships between telephone services use and key customer characteristics that it then uses in effective marketing strategies geared to heighten customer satisfaction and capitalize on AT&T's brand equity. We asked Randall Zeese, Brand Research Director, AT&T to provide a brief description of his background for you to read in our "Meet a Marketing Researcher" item in this chapter.

CROSS-TABULATIONS

Cross-tabulation and the associated chi-square value are used to assess whether a nonmonotonic relationship exists between two nominal-scaled variables. Remember that nonmonotonic relationships are those in which the presence of one variable coincides with the presence (or absence) of another variable.

Inspecting the Relationship with a Bar Chart

Bar charts can be used to "see" a nonmonotonic relationship.

A handy graphical tool that illustrates a nonmonotonic relationship is a stacked bar chart. With a stacked bar chart, two variables are shown simultaneously in the same bar graph. Each bar in the stacked bar chart stands for 100 percent, and it is divided proportionately by the amount of relationship that one variable shares with the other variables. For instance, you can see in Figure 18.3 that there are two variables: buyer type and occupational category. The two bars are made up of two types of individuals: buyers of Michelob Beer and nonbuyers of Michelob. There are two types of occupations: professional workers who might be called "white-collar" employees, and manual workers who are sometimes referred to as "blue-collar" workers. With the buyers stacked bar, you can see that a large percentage of the white-collar stacked bar is accounted for by the Michelob buyers, while a smaller percentage of Michelob buyers is apparent on the blue-collar workers bar graph.

You should remember that we described a nonmonotonic relationship as an identifiable association in which the presence of one variable is paired with the presence (or absence) of another. This pattern is apparent in the stacked bar chart in Figure 18.3: Buyers tend to be professional workers, whereas nonbuyers tend to be manual workers.

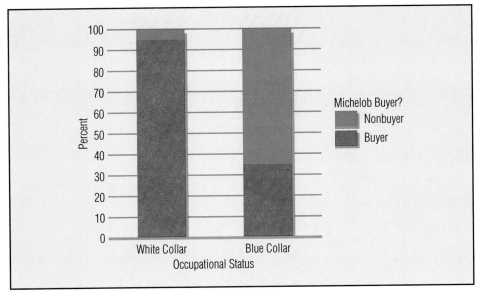

Figure **18.3** **Michelob Light Purchases and Occupational Status**

Cross-Tabulation Table

Whereas a stacked bar chart provides a way of visualizing nonmonotonic relationships, the most common method of presentation for these situations is through the use of a **cross-tabulation table**, defined as a table in which data are compared using a row and column format. A cross-tabulation table is sometimes referred to as an "$r \times c$" (r-by-c) table because it comprises rows and columns. The intersection of a row and a column is called a **cross-tabulation cell**. A cross-tabulation table for the stacked bar chart that we have been working with is presented in Table 18.1. Notice that we have identified the four cells with lines for the rows and columns. The columns are in vertical alignment and are indicated in this table as either "Buyer" or "Nonbuyer" of Michelob Light, whereas the rows are indicated as "White Collar" or "Blue Collar" for occupation.

A cross-tabulation consists of rows and columns defined by the categories classifying each variable.

Types of Frequencies and Percentages in a Cross-Tabulation Table

Look at the Frequencies Table section in Table 18.1. The upper left-hand cell number identifies people in the sample who are both white-collar workers and buyers of Michelob Light (152), and the cell to its right identifies the number of individuals who are white-collar workers who do not buy Michelob Light (8). These cell numbers represent frequencies, that is, the number of respondents who possess the quality indicated by the row label as well as the quality indicated by the column label.

Table 18.1 illustrates how at least four different sets of numbers can be computed for cells in the table. These four sets are the frequencies table, the raw percentages table, the column percentages table, and the row percentages table. The **frequencies table** contains the raw numbers determined from the preliminary tabulation. The lower right-hand number of 200 refers to the total sample size, sometimes called the "grand total." Just above it are the totals for the number of white-collar (160) and blue-collar (40) occupation respondents in the sample. Going to the left of the grand total are the totals for Michelob Light nonbuyers (34) and buyers (166) in the sample. The four cells are the totals for the intersection points: 152 white-collar Michelob Light buyers, 8 white-collar nonbuyers, 14 blue-collar Michelob Light buyers, and 26 blue-collar nonbuyers.

A cross-tabulation table can have four types of numbers in each cell: frequency, raw percentage, column percentage, and row percentage.

Table 18.1 Cross-Tabulation Tables for a Michelob Light Survey

Frequencies Table

		Buyer	**Nonbuyer**	**Totals**
	White Collar	152	8	160
Occupational Status	Blue Collar	14	26	40
	Totals	166	34	200

152 + 14 = 166
8 + 26 = 34

152 + 8 = 160
14 + 26 = 40

Raw Percentages Table

		Buyer	**Nonbuyer**	**Totals**
	White Collar	76% (152)	4% (8)	80% (160)
Occupational Status	Blue Collar	7% (14)	13% (26)	20% (40)
	Totals	83% (166)	17% (34)	100% (200)

152/200 = 76%

Column Percentages Table

		Buyer	**Nonbuyer**	**Totals**
	White Collar	92% (152)	24% (8)	80% (160)
Occupational Status	Blue Collar	8% (14)	76% (26)	20% (40)
	Totals	100% (166)	100% (34)	100% (200)

152/166 = 92%

Row Percentages Table

		Buyer	**Nonbuyer**	**Totals**
	White Collar	95% (152)	5% (8)	100% (160)
Occupational Status	Blue Collar	35% (14)	65% (26)	100% (40)
	Totals	83% (166)	17% (34)	100% (200)

152/160 = 95%

Raw percentages are cell frequencies divided by the grand total.

These raw frequencies can be converted to raw percentages by dividing each by the grand total. The second cross-tabulation table, the **raw percentages table**, contains the percentages of the raw frequency numbers just discussed. The grand total location now has 100 percent (or 200/200) of the grand total. Above it are 80 percent and 20 percent for the raw percentages of white-collar occupational respondents and blue-collar occupational respondents, respectively, in the sample. Divide a couple of the cells just to verify that you understand how they are derived. For instance 152 ÷ 200 = 76 percent.

Two additional cross-tabulation tables can be presented, and these are more valuable in revealing underlying relationships. The **column percentages table** divides the raw frequencies by its column total raw frequency. That is, the formula is as follows:

Formula for a column cell percentage

$$\text{Column cell percentage} = \frac{\text{Cell frequency}}{\text{Cell column total}}$$

For instance, it is apparent that of the nonbuyers, 24 percent were white-collar and 76 percent were blue-collar respondents. Note the reverse pattern for the buyers group: 92 percent of white-collar respondents were Michelob Light buyers and 8 percent were blue-collar buyers. You are beginning to see the non-monotonic relationship.

The **row percentages table** presents the data with the row totals as the 100 percent base for each. That is, a row cell percentage is computed as follows:

Formula for a row cell percentage

$$\text{Row cell percentage} = \frac{\text{Cell frequency}}{\text{Cell row total}}$$

Row (column) percentages are row (column) cell frequencies divided by the row (column) total.

Now it is possible to see that, of the white-collar respondents, 95 percent were buyers and 5 percent were nonbuyers. As you compare the row percentages table to the column percentages table, you should detect the relationship between occcupational status and Michelob Light beer preference. Can you state it at this time?

An unequal percentage concentration of individuals in a few cells, as we have in this example, illustrates the possible presence of a nonmonotonic association. If we had found that approximately 25 percent of the sample had fallen in each of the four cells, no relationship would be found to exist—it would be equally probable for any person to be a Michelob Light buyer or nonbuyer and a white- or a blue-collar worker. However, the large concentrations of individuals in two particular cells here suggests that there is a high probability that a buyer of Michelob Light beer is also a white-collar worker, and there is also a tendency for nonbuyers to work in blue-collar occupations. In other words, there is probably an association between occupational status and the beer-buying behavior of individuals in this particular sample.

CHI-SQUARE ANALYSIS

Chi-square (χ^2) analysis is the examination of frequencies for two nominal-scaled variables in a cross-tabulation table to determine whether the variables have a non-monotonic relationship.[2] The formal procedure for chi-square analysis begins when the researcher formulates a statistical null hypothesis that the two variables under investigation are not associated. Actually, it is not necessary for the researcher to state this hypothesis in a formal sense, for chi-square analysis always implicitly takes this hypothesis into account. Stated somewhat differently, chi-square analysis always begins with the assumption that no association exists between the two nominal-scaled variables under analysis.

Chi-square analysis assesses non-monotonic associations in cross-tabulation tables.

Observed and Expected Frequencies

The statistical procedure is as follows. The first cross-tabulation table in Table 18.1 contains **observed frequencies**, which are the actual cell counts in the cross-tabulation table. These observed frequencies are compared to **expected frequencies**, which are defined as the theoretical frequencies that are derived from this hypothesis of no association between the two variables. The degree to which the observed frequencies depart from the expected frequencies is expressed in a single number called the chi-square statistic. The computed chi-square statistic is then compared to a table chi-square value (at a chosen level of significance) to determine whether the computed value is significantly different from zero.

Here's a simple example to help you understand what we just stated. Suppose you perform a blind taste test with 10 of your friends. You let each one try Diet Pepsi served in a paper cup with no identification and ask them to guess whether it is Diet Pepsi or Diet Coke. If your friends had no idea of which brand was involved, they would guess randomly, so you would expect five to guess Diet Pepsi and five to guess Diet Coke. This is your null hypothesis: There is no relationship between the diet cola brand being

Observed frequencies are the counts for each cell found in the sample.

Expected frequencies are calculated based on the null hypothesis of no association between the two variables under investigation.

Associations between brand preferences and demographic characteristics help marketers identify their target markets.

tested and the guess. But you find that eight of your friends correctly guess Diet Pepsi, and two incorrectly guess Diet Coke. In other words, you have found a departure in your observed frequencies from the expected frequencies. It looks like your friends can correctly identify Diet Pepsi about 80 percent of the time. There seems to be a relationship, but we are not certain of its statistical significance, because we have not done any significance tests. The chi-square statistic is used to perform such a test.

The expected frequencies are those that would be found if there were no association between the two variables. Remember that this is the null hypothesis. About the only "difficult" part of chi-square analysis is in the computation of the expected frequencies. The computation is accomplished using the following equation:

Formula for an expected cell frequency

$$\text{Expected cell frequency} = \frac{\text{Cell column total} \times \text{Cell row total}}{\text{Grand total}}$$

The application of this equation generates a number for each cell that would have occurred if the study had taken place and no associations existed. Returning to our Michelob Light beer example, you were told that 160 white-collar and 40 blue-collar consumers had been sampled, and it was found that there were 166 buyers and 34 nonbuyers of Michelob Light. The expected frequency for each cell, assuming no association, calculated with the expected cell frequency is as follows:

Calculations of expected cell frequencies using the Michelob beer example

$$\text{White-collar buyer} = \frac{160 \times 166}{200} = 132.8$$

$$\text{White-collar nonbuyer} = \frac{160 \times 34}{200} = 27.2$$

$$\text{Blue-collar buyer} = \frac{40 \times 166}{200} = 33.2$$

$$\text{Blue-collar nonbuyer} = \frac{40 \times 34}{200} = 6.8$$

The Computed χ^2 Value

Next compare the observed frequencies to these expected frequencies. The formula for this computation is as follows:

Chi-square formula
$$\chi^2 = \sum_{i-1}^{n} \frac{(\text{Observed}_i - \text{Expected}_i)^2}{\text{Expected}_i}$$

where

Observed$_i$ = observed frequency in cell i

Expected$_i$ = expected frequency in cell i

n = number of cells

The computed chi-square value compares observed to expected frequencies.

Applied to our Michelob beer example,

Calculation of chi-square value (Michelob example)
$$\chi^2 = \frac{(152 - 132.8)^2}{132.8} + \frac{(8 - 27.2)^2}{27.2}$$
$$+ \frac{(14 - 33.2)^2}{33.2} + \frac{(26 - 6.8)^2}{6.8} = 81.64$$

You can see from the equation that each expected frequency is compared to the observed frequency and squared to adjust for any negative values and to avoid the cancellation effect. This value is divided by the expected frequency to adjust for cell size differences, and these amounts are summed across all of the cells. If there are many large deviations of observed frequencies from the expected frequencies, the computed chi-square value will increase; but if there are only a few slight deviations from the expected frequencies, the computed chi-square number will be small. In other words, the computed chi-square value is really a summary indication of how far away from the expected frequencies the observed frequencies are found to be. As such, it expresses the departure of the sample findings from the null hypothesis of no association.

The chi-square statistic summarizes how far away from the expected frequencies the observed cell frequencies are found to be.

Some researchers think of an expected-to-observed comparison analysis as a "goodness of fit" test. It assesses how closely the actual frequencies fit the pattern of expected frequencies. We have provided Marketing Research Insight 18.2 as an illustration of the goodness-of-fit notion.[3]

Chi-square analysis is sometimes referred to as a "goodness-of-fit" test.

Let us apply this equation to the example of your 10 friends guessing about Diet Pepsi or Diet Coke. We already agreed that if they guessed randomly, you would find five guessing for each brand, on a 50–50 split. But if we found an 80–20 vote for Diet Pepsi, you would conclude that they could recognize Diet Pepsi. How did you decide that your friends could identify Diet Pepsi? You probably compared the observed 80 percent to the expected 50 percent and found a difference of 30 percent. If your friends were random guessers, the difference would be 0, so you decided that 30 percent was sufficiently far from 0 to justify your conclusion that your null hypothesis was not supported.

To determine the chi-square value, we calculate as follows:

Calculation of chi-square value using diet cola taste test
$$\chi^2 = \sum_{i-1}^{n} \frac{(\text{Observed}_i - \text{Expected}_i)^2}{\text{Expected}_i}$$
$$= \frac{(8 - 5)^2}{5} + \frac{(2 - 5)^2}{5}$$
$$= 3.6$$

Remember that you need to use the frequencies, not the percentages.

MARKETING RESEARCH

INSIGHT
18.2

"Zeroing In" on Goodness of Fit

Can you guess the next number based on the apparent pattern of 1, 3, 5? Okay, what about this series: 1, 6, 11, 16?

In the first series, you realize that 2 was added to determine the next number (1, 3, 5, 7, 9, and so on). You looked at the series and noticed the equal intervals of 2. You then created a mental expectation of the series based on your suspected pattern.

Let us take the second series because it is a bit more difficult. Suppose your first intuition was to add a 3 to the previous number. Here is your expected series and the actual one compared:

Expected	1	4	7	10
Actual	1	6	11	16
Difference	0	2	4	6

Oops, not much of a match here. So let's try a 4.

Expected	1	5	9	13
Actual	1	6	11	16
Difference	0	1	2	3

Getting closer, but still not there. Now try a 5.

Expected	1	6	11	16
Actual	1	6	11	16
Difference	0	0	0	0

You have been performing goodness-of-fit tests. Notice that the differences became smaller as you zeroed in on the true pattern. (Catch the pun?) In other words, when the actual numbers are equal to the expected numbers, there is no difference, and the fit is perfect. This is the concept used in chi-square analysis. When the differences are small, you have a good fit to the expected values. When the differences are larger, you have a poor fit, and your hypothesis (the expected number sequence) is incorrect.

The Chi-Square Distribution

Now that you've learned how to calculate a chi-square value, you need to know if it is statistically significant. In a previous chapter, we described how the normal curve or z distribution, the F distribution, and Student's t distribution, all of which exist in tables, are used by a computer statistical program to determine level of significance. Chi-square analysis requires the use of a different distribution. The **chi-square distribution** is skewed to the right and the rejection region is always at the right-hand tail of the distribution. It differs from the normal and t distributions in that it changes its shape depending on the situation at hand, but it does not have negative values. Figure 18.4 shows examples of two chi-square distributions.

The chi-square distribution's shape changes depending on the number of degrees of freedom.

The chi-square distribution's shape is determined by the number of degrees of freedom. The figure shows that the more the degrees of freedom, the more the curve's tail is pulled to the right. Or, in other words, the more the degrees of freedom, the larger the chi-square value must be to fall in the rejection region for the null hypothesis.

It is a simple matter to determine the number of degrees of freedom. In a cross-tabulation table, the degrees of freedom are found through the following formula:

Formula for chi-square degrees of freedom   Degrees of freedom $= (r - 1)(c - 1)$

where

r = number of rows

c = number of columns

The computed chi-square value is compared to a table value to determine statistical significance.

A table of chi-square values contains critical points that determine the break between acceptance and rejection regions at various levels of significance. It also

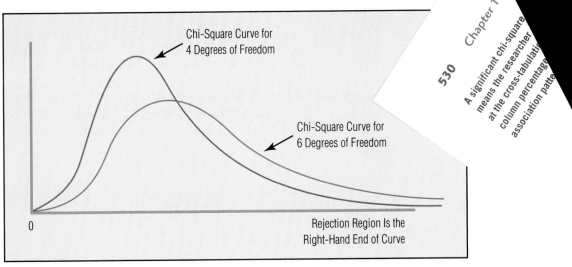

530   Chapter 18

A significant chi-square
means the researcher
at the cross-tabulati
column percentag
association patte

Figure **18.4**   **The Chi-Square Curve's Shape Depends on Its Degrees of Freedom**

takes into account the numbers of degrees of freedom associated with each curve. That is, a computed chi-square value says nothing by itself—you must consider the number of degrees of freedom in the cross-tabulation table because more degrees of freedom are indicative of higher critical chi-square table values for the same level of significance. The logic of this situation stems from the number of cells. With more cells, there is more opportunity for departure from the expected values. The higher table values adjust for potential inflation due to chance alone. After all, we want to detect real nonmonotonic relationships, not phantom ones.

SPSS and virtually all computer statistical analysis programs have chi-square tables in memory and print out the probability of the null hypothesis. Let us repeat this point: The program itself will take into account the number of degrees of freedom and determine the probability of support for the null hypothesis. This probability is the percentage of the area under the chi-square curve that lies to the right of the computed chi-square value. When this probability is .05 or less (at the 95 percent level of confidence), we have found a statistically significant nonmonotonic association existing between the two variables.

Computer statistical programs look up table chi-square values and print out the probability of support for the null hypothesis.

How to Interpret a Chi-Square Result

How does one interpret a chi-square result? The chi-square analysis yields the probability that the researcher would find evidence in support of the null hypothesis if he or she repeated the study many, many times with independent samples. By now, you should be well acquainted with the concept of many, many independent samples. For example, if the chi-square analysis yielded a 0.02 probability for the null hypothesis, the researcher would conclude that only 2 percent of the time he or she would find evidence to support the null hypothesis. This means there is a significant association.

It must be pointed out that chi-square analysis is simply a method to determine whether a nonmonotonic association exists between two variables. A chi-square result does not indicate the nature of the association, and it indicates only roughly the strength of association by its size. It is best interpreted as a prerequisite to looking more closely at the two variables to discern the nature of the association that exists between them. That is, the chi-square test is another of our "flags" that tell us whether or not it is worthwhile to inspect all those rows and columns percentages.

When the computed chi-square value is small, then the null hypothesis or the hypothesis of independence between the two variables is generally assumed to be true. It is not worth the marketing researcher's time to focus on associations, because they are more a function of sampling error than they are of meaningful relationships between the two variables. However, when chi-square analysis identifies a relationship with a significance level of .05 or less (the flag is waving), the researcher can be assured that he or she is not wasting time and is actually pursuing a real association, a relationship that truly exists between the two variables in the population.

RETURN TO *Your Integrated Case*

The Hobbit's Choice Restaurant Survey:
Analyzing Cross-Tabulations for Significant Associations
by Performing Chi-Square Analysis with SPSS

We are going to use our The Hobbit's Choice Restaurant survey data to demonstrate how to perform and interpret cross-tabulation analysis with SPSS. You may recall that we used the subscription to *City Magazine* as a grouping variable and performed an independent samples *t* test in Chapter 16. We found that *City Magazine* subscribers were more likely to intend to patronize The Hobbit's Choice Restaurant. We can use cross-tabulation analysis to get a better picture of the effectiveness of *City Magazine* as an advertising medium. Subscription to *City Magazine* is a nominal variable because respondents indicated "yes" or "no." We can categorize the respondents based on how likely they are to patronize The Hobbit's Choice. By taking those who are "very likely" or are "somewhat likely," we can create a "probable patron of The Hobbit's Choice Restaurant" variable where respondents are classified as either "probable patron" or "not probable patron."

> **With SPSS, chi-square is an option under the "Crosstabs" analysis routine.**

The clickstream command sequence to perform a chi-square test with SPSS is ANALYZE-DESCRIPTIVE STATISTICS-CROSSTABS, which leads to a dialogue box in which you can select the variables for chi-square analysis. In our example in Figure 18.5, we have selected Subscribe to *City Magazine* as the row variable and Probable Patron of Hobbit's Choice Restaurant as the column variable. There are three options buttons at the bottom of the box. The Cells . . . option leads to the specification of observed frequencies, expected frequencies, row percentages, column percentages, and so forth. We have opted for just the observed frequencies (raw counts) and the column percents. The Statistics . . . button opens up a menu of statistics that can be computed from cross-tabulation tables. Of course, the only one we want is the Chi-square option.

The resulting output is found in Figure 18.6. In the Case Processing Summary table, it is apparent that 400 cases were processed, and there were no missing cases. In the middle table, you can see that we have variable and value labels, and the table contains the raw frequency as the first entry in each cell. Also, the row percentages are reported along with each row and column total. In the final table, there is information on the chi-square analysis result. For our purposes, the only relevant statistic is the "Pearson Chi-Square," which you can see has been computed to be 112.878. The df column pertains to the number of degrees of freedom, which is 1; and the Asymp. Sig. corresponds to the probability of support for the null hypothesis. Significance in this example is .000, which means that there is practically no support for the hypothesis that subscription to *City Magazine* and Probable Patron of Hobbit's Choice Restaurant are not associated. In other words, they are related. (Actually, the probability is not exactly equal to zero because SPSS reports only three decimal places. If it reported, say, 10 places, you would see a number somewhere past the third decimal place.)

SPSS Student Assistant Online
Setting Up and Analyzing
Cross-Tabulations

> **With chi-square analysis, interpret the SPSS significance level as the amount of support for *no* association between the two variables being analyzed.**

Thus, SPSS has effected the first step in determining a nonmonotonic association. Through chi-square analysis it has signaled that a statistically significant association actually exists. The next step is to fathom the nature of the association. Remember that with a nonmonotonic relationship, you must inspect the pattern and describe it verbally. When we looked for the pattern in our example, we converted the frequencies into row and column

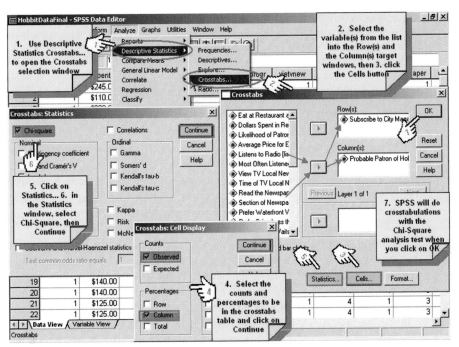

Figure **18.5** **The SPSS Clickstream to Create Cross-Tabulation with Chi-Square Analysis**

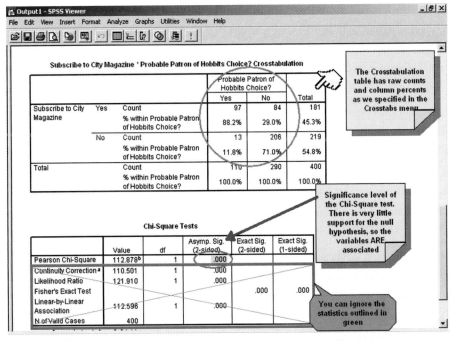

Figure **18.6** **SPSS Output for Cross-Tabulations with Chi-Square Analysis**

percentages. Now you have a cross-tabulation table with row percentages in their respective cells. The row percentages show that about 88 percent of Probable patrons are *City Magazine* subscribers. At the same time, 71 percent of the Non Probable patrons are non-subscribers to *City Magazine*. You can interpret this finding in the following way. If Jeff places an ad in *City Magazine* for The Hobbit's Choice Restaurant, there is a chance of reaching almost 90 percent of his target market with this medium.

In other words, because the significance was less than .05, it was worthwhile to inspect and interpret the percentages in the cross-tabulation table. By doing this, we can discern the pattern or nature of the association, and the percentages indicate its relative strength. More importantly, because the relationship was determined to be statistically significant, you can be assured that this association and the relationship you have observed will hold for the population that this sample represents.

You have no doubt observed that SPSS output tables are filled with information, and they are often confusing to a nonresearcher for this reason. Surely, you have experienced a good deal of frustration when trying to find and make sense of the numbers, percentages, and statistics we have referred to in describing the cross-tabulation output in Figure 18.6. SPSS has long realized that the detail in its output is essential for researchers, but these same details are not appreciated by managers who are looking for the critical difference or association that will provide insight into their marketing problems. Recently, SPSS has developed a feature that addresses the manager's need to "see" the results. Read Marketing Research Insight 18.3 to find out about how SPSS OLAP tables accomplish this end.

CORRELATION COEFFICIENTS AND COVARIATION

A correlation coefficient standardizes the covariation between two variables into a number ranging from −1.0 to +1.0.

The **correlation coefficient** is an index number, constrained to fall between the range of −1.0 and +1.0, that communicates both the strength and the direction of association between two variables. The amount of association between two variables is communicated by the absolute size of the correlation coefficient, whereas its sign communicates the direction of the association. Stated in a slightly different manner, a correlation coefficient indicates the degree of "covariation" between two variables. **Covariation** is defined as the amount of change in one variable systematically associated with a change in another variable. The greater the absolute size of the correlation coefficient, the greater is the covariation between the two variables, or the stronger is their association.

To use a correlation, you must first establish that it is statistically significant from zero.

Let us take up the statistical significance of a correlation coefficient first. Regardless of its absolute value, a correlation that is not statistically significant has no meaning at all. This is because of the null hypothesis, which states that the population correlation coefficient is equal to zero. If this null hypothesis is rejected (statistically significant correlation), then you can be assured that a correlation other than zero will be found in the population. But if the sample correlation is found to not be significant, the population correlation will be zero. Here is a question. If you can answer it correctly, you understand the statistical significance of a correlation. If you repeated a correlational survey many, many times and computed the average for a correlation that was not significant across all of these surveys, what would be the result? (The answer is zero because if the correlation is not significant, the null hypothesis is true, and the population correlation is zero.)

How do you determine the statistical significance of a correlation coefficient? Tables exist that give the lowest value of the significant correlation coefficients for given sample sizes. However, most computer statistical programs will indicate the statistical significance level of the computed correlation coefficient. Your SPSS pro-

▶ **SPSS**

Using SPSS OLAP Cubes to "See" Patterns in Data

An innovation developed by SPSS affords a unique way to "look" at data and to see the patterns that are signified by statistical analysis finding. OLAP (for "Online Analytical Processing") Cubes is a graphical command method of instantaneously changing the arrangement of rows and columns in a Pivot table. (This is the tables format for all SPSS output.) At the same time, this feature lets you select which of several descriptive statistics are to be reported in the table. For instance, in our Michelob Light example, when you were confronted with a cross-tabulation table such as Table 18.1, it probably was very difficult to identify the patterns we have described for you when looking at Figure 18.3. Actually, it is easy for a trained researcher to see the patterns, but it is much more of a challenge for a manager or untrained individual to identify the patterns.

OLAP Cubes is designed to help researchers eliminate the superfluous aspects of SPSS output and to isolate the critical parts of the output, and the output can even be for-matted into a presentation-quality table "on the fly." For example, using our Michelob Light example data, with a few mouse clicks, the OLAP Cubes feature of SPSS can be applied to create the following two tables.

These tables vividly illustrate the pattern of white-collar versus blue-collar occupation drinking preferences for Michelob beer. In Table 18.2, the 95/5 percent preference pattern of the white-collar respondents is clearly evident, and it is easy to see that the blue-collar respondents' preferences are 35/65 percent.

Granted, this table is still in the unsophisticated SPSS output format; however, by using the TableLooks feature of SPSS, it is quick and easy to direct SPSS to format the table into any one of several alternative table styles. See Table 18.3 for one that was created with two or three mouse clicks.

OLAP Cubes is a great innovation on the part of SPSS, and this feature is consistent with its mission of achieving "Real Stats. Real Easy."

Table 18.2   SPSS Crosstabulation Output Table Modified by OLAP Cubes

Occupation Classification* Buyer or Nonbuyer of MICH Crosstabulation

			BUYER OR NONBUYER OF MICH		
			Buyer	Nonbuyer	TOTAL
OCCUPATION CLASSIFICATION	WHITE COLLAR	% within OCCUPATION CLASSIFICATION	95.0%	5.0%	100.0%
	BLUE COLLAR	% within OCCUPATION CLASSIFICATION	35.0%	65.0%	100.0%

Table 18.3   SPSS Table "Dressed Up" with SPSS TableLooks Feature

Who Buys Michelob Beer?

		BUYER OR NONBUYER OF MICHELOB		
		Buyer	Nonbuyer	TOTAL
OCCUPATION CLASSIFICATION	WHITE COLLAR	95.0%	5.0%	100.0%
	BLUE COLLAR	35.0%	65.0%	100.0%

gram provides the significance in the form of the probability that the null hypothesis is supported. In SPSS, this is a "Sig." value that we will identify for you when we show you SPSS correlation output. In addition, it will also allow you to indicate a directional hypothesis about the size of the expected correlation just as with a directional means hypothesis test.

Rules of Thumb for Correlation Strength

Rules of thumb exist concerning the strength of a correlation based on its absolute size.

After we have established that a correlation coefficient is statistically significant, we can talk about some general rules of thumb concerning the *strength of association*. Correlation coefficients that fall between +1.00 and +.81 or between −1.00 and −.81 are generally considered to be "high." That is, the association between the two variables is strong. Those correlations that fall between +.80 and +.61 or −.80 and −.61 generally indicate a "moderate" association. Those that fall between +.60 and +.41 or −.60 and −.41 are typically considered to be "low," and they denote a weak association. Finally, any correlation that falls between the range of ±.21 and ±.40 is usually considered indicative of a very weak association between the variables. Next, any correlation that is equal to or less than ±.20 is typically uninteresting to marketing researchers because it rarely identifies a meaningful association between two variables. We have provided Table 18.4 as a reference on these rules of thumb. As you use these guidelines, remember two things: First, we are assuming that the statistical significance of the correlation has been established. Second, researchers make up their own rules of thumb, so you may encounter someone whose guidelines differ slightly from those in the table.

In any case, it is helpful to think in terms of the closeness of the correlation coefficient to zero or to ±1.00. Correlation coefficients that are close to zero show that there is no systematic association between the two variables, whereas those that are closer to +1.00 or −1.00 express that there is some systematic association between the variables.

The Correlation's Sign

A correlation indicates the strength of association between two variables by its size. The sign indicates the direction of the association.

But what about the sign of the correlation coefficient? The sign indicates the *direction of the association*. A positive sign indicates a positive direction; a negative sign indicates a negative direction. For instance, if you found a significant correlation of 0.83 between years of education and hours spent reading *National Geographic*, it would mean that people with more education spend more hours reading this magazine. But if you found a significant negative correlation between education and cigarette smoking, it would mean that more educated people smoke less.

Graphing Covariation Using Scatter Diagrams

We addressed the concept of covariation between two variables in our introductory comments on correlations. It is now time to present covariation in a slightly different manner. Here is an example: A marketing researcher is investigating the possible relationship between total company sales for Novartis, a leading pharmaceuticals sales company, in a particular territory and the number of salespeople assigned to that territory. At the researcher's fingertips are the sales figures and number of salespeople assigned for each of 20 different Novartis territories in the United States.

Table 18.4 **Rules of Thumb About Correlation Coefficient Size***

COEFFICIENT RANGE	STRENGTH OF ASSOCIATION*
±.81 to ±1.00	Strong
±.61 to ±.80	Moderate
±.41 to ±.60	Weak
±.21 to ±.40	Very weak
±.00 to ±.20	None

*Assuming the correlation coefficient is statistically significant.

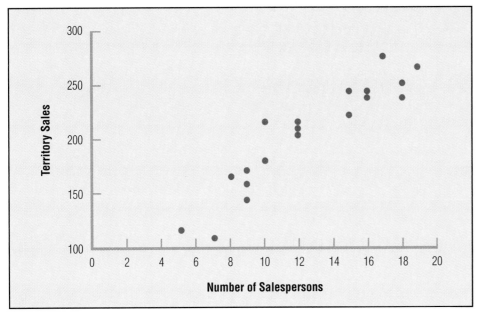

It is possible to depict the raw data for these two variables on a scatter diagram such as the one in Figure 18.7. A **scatter diagram** plots the points corresponding to each matched pair of x and y variables. In this figure, the vertical axis (y) is Novartis sales for the territory and the horizontal axis (x) contains the number of salespeople in that territory. The arrangement or scatter of points appears to fall in a long ellipse. Any two variables that exhibit systematic covariation will form an ellipse-like pattern on a scatter diagram. Of course, this particular scatter diagram portrays the information gathered by the marketing researcher on sales and the number of salespeople in each territory and only that information. In actuality, the scatter diagram could have taken any shape, depending on the relationship between the points plotted for the two variables concerned.[4]

A number of different types of scatter diagram results are portrayed in Figure 18.8. Each of these scatter diagram results is indicative of a different degree of covariation. For instance, you can see that the scatter diagram depicted in Figure 18.8(a) is one in which there is no apparent association or relationship between the two variables; the points fail to create any identifiable pattern. Instead, they are clumped into a large, formless shape. Those points in Figure 18.8(b) indicate a negative relationship between variable x and variable y; higher values of x tend to be associated with lower values of y. Those points in Figure 18.8(c) are fairly similar to those in Figure 18.8(b), but the angle or the slope of the ellipse is different. This slope indicates a positive relationship between x and y, because larger values of x tend to be associated with larger values of y.

What is the connection between scatter diagrams and correlation coefficients? The answer to these questions lies in the linear relationship described earlier in this chapter. Look at Figures 18.7 and 18.8(b) and 18.8(c). All form ellipses. Imagine taking an ellipse and pulling on both ends. It would stretch out and become thinner until all of its points fall on a straight line. If you happened to find some data that formed an ellipse with all of its points falling on the axis

Covariation can be examined with use of a scatter diagram.

Two highly correlated variables will yield a scatter diagram pattern of a tight ellipse.

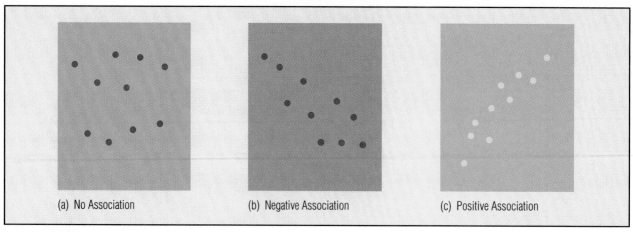

(a) No Association   (b) Negative Association   (c) Positive Association

Figure **18.8** **Scatter Diagrams Illustrating Various Relationships**

line and you computed a correlation, you would find it to be exactly 1.0 (plus 1.0 if the ellipse went up to the right and minus 1.0 if it went down to the right). Now imagine pushing the ends of the ellipse until it became the pattern in Figure 18.8(a). There would be no identifiable straight line. Similarly, there would be no systematic covariation. The correlation for a ball-shaped scatter diagram is zero because there is no discernable linear relationship. In other words, a correlation coefficient indicates the degree of covariation between two variables, and you can envision this relationship as a scatter diagram. The form and angle of the scatter pattern are revealed by the size and sign, respectively, of the correlation coefficient.

Your Student Assistant movie shows graphical representations of covariation.

THE PEARSON PRODUCT MOMENT CORRELATION COEFFICIENT

The Pearson product moment correlation coefficient measures the degree of linear association between two variables.

The **Pearson product moment correlation** measures the linear relationship between two interval- and/or ratio-scaled variables such as those depicted conceptually by scatter diagrams. The correlation coefficient that can be computed between the two variables is a measure of the "tightness" of the scatter points to the straight line. You already know that in a case in which all of the points fall exactly on the straight line, the correlation coefficient indicates this as a plus or minus 1. In the case in which it was impossible to discern an ellipse, such as in scatter diagram Figure 18.8(a), the correlation coefficient approximates zero. Of course, it is extremely unlikely that you will find perfect 1.0 or 0.0 correlations. Usually, you will find some value in between that could be interpreted as "high," "moderate," or "low" correlation using the rules of thumb given earlier.

The formula for calculating a Pearson product moment correlation is complicated, and researchers never compute it by hand as they invariably find these on computer output. However, some instructors believe that students should understand the workings of the correlation coefficient formula. We have described this formula and provided an example in Marketing Research Insight 18.4.

▶ **Additional Insights**

How to Compute a Pearson Product Moment Correlation Coefficient

Marketing researchers almost never compute statistics such as chi-square or correlation, but it is insightful to learn about this computation.

The computational formula for Pearson product moment correlations is as follows:

Formula for Pearson product moment correlation

$$r_{xy} = \frac{\sum_{i=1}^{n}(x_i - \bar{x})(y_i - \bar{y})}{ns_x s_y}$$

where

x_i = each x value
$\bar{x}$ = mean of the x values
y_i = each y value
$\bar{y}$ = mean of the y values
n = number of paired cases
s_x, s_y = standard deviations of x and y, respectively

We briefly describe the components of this formula to help you see how the concepts we just discussed fit in. In the statistician's terminology, the numerator represents the cross-products sum and indicates the covariation or "covariance" between x and y. The cross-products sum is divided by n to scale it down to an average per pair of x and y values. This average covariation is then divided by both standard deviations to adjust for differences in units. The result constrains r_{xy} to fall between −1.0 and +1.0.

Here is a simple computational example. You have some data on population and retail sales by county for 10 counties in your state. Is there a relationship between population and retail sales? You do a quick calculation and find the average number of people per county is 690,000, and the average retail sales is $9.54 million. The standard deviations are 384.3 and 7.8, respectively, and the cross-products sum is 25,154. The computations to find the correlation are:

Calculation of a correlation coefficient

$$r_{xy} = \frac{\sum_{i=1}^{n}(x_i - \bar{x})(y_i - \bar{y})}{ns_x s_y}$$

$$= \frac{25,154}{10 \times 7.8 \times 384.4}$$

$$= \frac{25,154}{29,975.4}$$

$$= .84$$

A correlation of 0.84 is a high positive correlation coefficient for the relationship. This value reveals that the greater the number of citizens living in a county, the greater the county's retail sales.

Pearson product moment correlation and other linear association correlation coefficients indicate not only the degree of association but the direction as well. As we described in our introductory comments on correlations, the sign of the correlation coefficient indicates the direction of the relationship. Negative correlation coefficients reveal that the relationship is opposite: As one variable increases, the other variable decreases. Positive correlation coefficients reveal that the relationship is increasing: Larger quantities of one variable are associated with larger quantities of another variable. It is important to note that the angle or the slope of the ellipse has nothing to do with the size of the correlation coefficient. Everything hinges on the width of the ellipse. (The slope will be considered in Chapter 19 under regression analysis.)

Whenever you work with correlation, there is danger of misinterpreting a strong correlation to consider that the two variables are the same level. For example, you might find a strong correlation between sales and advertising, but it does not make sense to interpret this finding to mean that your advertising level must equal your sales level. In other words, do not make the error that was committed by Mark Reese of SmartCon described in Marketing Research Insight 18.5.

A positive correlation signals an increasing linear relationship, whereas a negative correlation signals a decreasing one.

MARKETING RESEARCH
INSIGHT
18.5

Don't Confuse Correlation with Equality![5]

The Bedford Group had conducted a survey for its client, SmartCon of Indiana, to determine demand for video accelerator boards. SmartCon had developed a board to be used with Microsoft Windows that greatly increased the speed of the video display. Windows requires continual updating of the video display, and owners of personal computers with the "old" processors (processors that are 9 months old or older) would benefit greatly from inserting the SmartCon "Extreme Accelerator" board in their machines.

Mark Reese, SmartCon marketing manager, was briefed by the Bedford Group project manager on the findings of the survey. Mark then presented the findings to SmartCon's top management team. Mark felt he had good news for his management and he began with an eye opener.

"Ladies and gentlemen," Mark began, "I have what I believe is an important finding to report to you. As you know, in our survey, we asked respondents how many hours, on the average, they used their personal computers. We also asked them on a scale of 1 to 10, where 1 indicated 'not likely at all' and 10 indicated 'very likely,' their intentions to buy a SmartCon 'Extreme Accelerator' video board in the next six months. There is a strong positive correlation between how many hours PC owners use their computers and their inten-

tions to buy a SmartCon video board. I predict that heavy PC users will be buying a SmartCon video board soon."

Pamela Del Santiago, SmartCon's comptroller, then interrupted with, "Mark, in the preliminary results you showed us last month, the intentions-to-buy average was 2.5 and the standard deviation was 1.0. That's pretty low on a 10-point intentions-to-purchase scale, and there is not much variability. So, I'm confused as to how all these sales are going to materialize."

Pamela was right to ask this question, and here is the reason: Mark has mistaken a correlation for an equality. Correlation measures only the covariation or relative distance from the average for PC use and intentions. It does not compare the averages themselves. For illustration, take the standard deviation of 1 for intentions. A "heavy" PC user would be 2 or more standard deviations from the average, and so would his or her intentions score. Adding two standard deviations (2×1) to the average of 2.5 yields 4.5. With a 10-point intentions-to-purchase scale, our heavy PC user is still near the neutral intentions position. The correlation coefficient simply tells us the degree to which respondents' answers to the two questions tend to occupy the same relative positions on their respective scales.

RETURN TO   *Your Integrated Case*

The Hobbit's Choice Restaurant Survey: How to Obtain Pearson Product Moment Correlation(s) with SPSS

With SPSS, it takes only a few clicks to compute correlation coefficients. Once again, we will use The Hobbit's Choice Restaurant survey case study as you are familiar with it. If you recall, we have determined from previous analysis, that a waterfront view is generally preferred among all 400 respondents. Remembering this, you would probably feel very confident about recommending this location to Jeff. But let's take a closer look using correlation analysis. Correlation analysis can be used to find out what people want with the waterfront view. That is, high positive correlations would indicate that they wanted the waterfront location and the items that are highly correlated with this location preference. Conversely, high negative correlations would signal that they did not want those items with the waterfront location. Recall that there were several menu, décor, and atmosphere questions being mulled over by Jeff Dean. Correlation analysis is very powerful as it can reveal to what extent people prefer (or not prefer) these items as they prefer the waterfront view. We'll only do a few of the items here, and you can do the rest in your SPSS integrated case analysis work specified at the end of the chapter.

Thus, we need to perform correlation analysis with the waterfront location preference variable and the other factors that will determine The Hobbit's Choice Restaurant's "per-

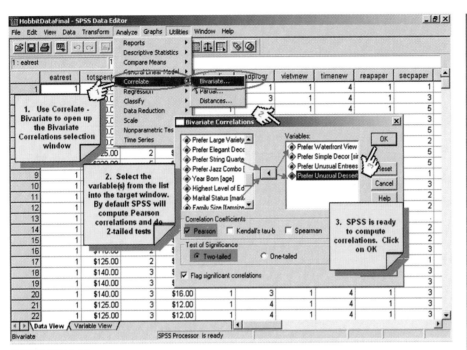

Figure **18.9** **The SPSS Clickstream to Obtain Correlations**

sonality." The clickstream sequence is ANALYZE-CORRELATE-BIVARIATE that leads, as can be seen in Figure 18.9, to a selection box to specify which variables are to be correlated. Note that we have selected the waterfront location and several other items related to décor, atmosphere, and menu. Different types of correlations are optional, so we have selected Pearson's, and the two-tailed test of significance is the default.

The output generated by this command is provided in Figure 18.10. Whenever you instruct SPSS to compute correlations, its output is a symmetric correlation matrix composed of rows and columns that pertain to each of the variables. Each cell in the matrix contains three items: (1) the correlation coefficient, (2) the significance level, and (3) the sample size. As you can see in Figure 18.10, the computed correlations between "prefer waterfront location" and three of Jeff's questions—Simple décor? Prefer unusual entrées? Prefer unusual desserts?—are +.780, −.782, and −.810, respectively. They all have a "Sig." value of .000 that translates into a .001 or less probability that the null hypothesis of zero correlation is supported. If you look at our correlation printout, you will also notice that a correlation of 1.000 is reported where a variable is correlated with itself. This reporting may seem strange, but it serves the purpose of reminding you that the correlation matrix that is generated with this procedure is symmetric. In other words, the correlations in the matrix above the diagonal 1s are identical to those correlations below the diagonal. With only a few variables, this fact is obvious; however, sometimes several variables are compared in a single analysis, and the 1s on the diagonal are handy reference points.

Since we now know that the correlations are statistically significant, or significantly different from zero, we can assess their strengths. They hover around .80, which, according to our rule of thumb on correlation size, indicates a moderately strong association. In other words, we have some relationships that are stable and fairly strong. Last, we can use the signs to interpret the associations. What is your interpretation?

Here is what we have found. People who prefer to eat at a restaurant with a waterfront view also prefer a simple décor. At the same time, they do *not* want unusual entrées or unusual desserts. Apparently, when folks go to a waterfront restaurant they want to kick

With SPSS, correlations are computed with the CORRELATE-BIVARIATE feature.

With correlation analysis, each correlation will have a unique significance level.

A correlation matrix is symmetric with 1s on the diagonal.

SPSS Student Assistant Online

Working with Correlations

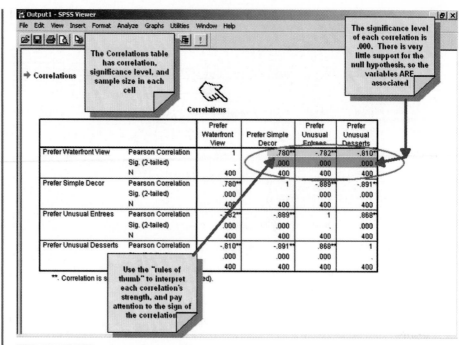

Figure 18.10 **SPSS Output for Correlations**

back, be comfortable, and not be bothered with choosing from a variety of curious dishes or an array or exotic desserts. They probably want seafood. An upscale Hobbit's Choice Restaurant with unusual entrées and desserts would definitely not fit the preferences of these people. So, now how do you feel about your previous recommendation to locate The Hobbit's Choice Restaurant on some expensive waterfront property?

Special Considerations in Linear Correlation Procedures

To begin, the scaling assumptions underlying linear correlation should be apparent to you, but it does not hurt to reiterate that the correlation coefficient discussed in this section assumes that both variables share interval-scaling assumptions at minimum. If the two variables have nominal-scaling assumptions, the researcher would use cross-tabulation analysis, and if the two variables have ordinal-scaling assumptions, the researcher would opt to use a rank order correlation procedure. (We do not discuss rank order correlation in this chapter as its use is relatively rare.)

Interpretation of the Pearson product moment correlation is not difficult, but there are three restrictions or assumptions within the interpretation you should understand. First, the correlation coefficient takes into consideration only the relationship between two variables. It does not take into consideration interactions with any other variables. In fact, it explicitly assumes that they do not have any bearing on the relationship with the two variables of interest. All other factors are considered to be constant or "frozen" in their bearing on the two variables under analysis.

Correlation does not demonstrate cause and effect.

Second, the correlation coefficient explicitly does not assume a **cause and effect relationship,** which is a condition of one variable bringing about the other variable. Although you might be tempted to believe that more company salespeople cause more company sales or that an increase in the competitor's sales force in a territory takes away sales, correlation should not be interpreted to demonstrate such cause-and-effect relationships. Just think of all of the other factors that affect sales: price,

When dining on seafood, restaurant patrons like to keep it simple.

product quality, service policies, population, advertising, and more. It would be a mistake to assume that just one factor causes sales. Instead, a correlation coefficient merely investigates the presence, strength, and direction of a linear relationship between two variables.

Third, the Pearson product moment correlation expresses only linear relationships. Consequently, a correlation coefficient result of approximately zero does not necessarily mean that the scatter diagram that could be drawn from the two variables defines a formless ball of points. Instead, it means that the points do not fall in a well-defined elliptical pattern. Any number of alternative curvilinear patterns such as an S-shape or a J-shape pattern are possible, and the linear correlation coefficient would not be able to communicate the existence of these patterns to the marketing researcher. Any one of several other systematic but nonlinear patterns is entirely possible and would not be indicated by a linear correlation statistic. Only those cases of linear or straight-line relationships between two variables are identified by the Pearson product moment correlation. In fact, when a researcher does not find a significant or strong correlation but still believes some relationship exists between two variables, he or she may resort to running a scatter plot. This procedure allows the researcher to visually inspect the plotted points and possibly to spot a systematic nonlinear relationship. You already know that your SPSS program has a scatter plot option that will provide a scatter diagram that you can use to obtain a sense of the relationship, if any, between two variables.

Correlation will not detect nonlinear relationships between variables.

CONCLUDING COMMENTS ON ASSOCIATIVE ANALYSES

The scaling assumptions of the data being analyzed are the key to understanding associative analysis.[6] Sometimes a marketing researcher must use categorical measurements (nominal scale). As you know, nominal measurement provides the least amount of information about an object, whereas ratio measures provide the greatest amount of information. The amount of information in scales directly impacts the amount of information yielded by their appropriate associative test. So the chi-square statistic that uses two nominal-scaled variables cannot have as much information as the Pearson product moment correlation that may be used for two interval- or

Researchers always test the null hypothesis of no association or no correlation, even though they hope to find a significant association or correlation to yield useful managerial implications.

ratio-scaled variables. Similarly, the underlying relationships reflect the differences in information. Chi-square describes a nonmonotonic relationship, a Pearson product moment correlation describes a linear relationship, and a rank order correlation's relationship falls between these two with a monotonic relationship.

Finally, throughout our descriptions of various statistical tests, we have referred to the "null hypothesis." For example, with chi-square analysis, there is the null hypothesis of no association between the two nominal-scaled variables, and with correlation analysis there is the null hypothesis of no correlation. But marketing managers really want to find strong evidence of an association that exists and can be used to their advantage. That is, they really want to find support for the "alternative hypothesis" that an association does exist. So why do we always test the null hypothesis? Here is an example that answers this question.

The Tree-Free Company of Medford, Massachusetts, makes paper products from 100 percent recycled paper. As a strategy to entice Kleenex to buy its tissue boxes, Tree-Free might conduct a survey asking, "If you learned that a company used recycled paper boxes, would that fact influence your decision to purchase a particular brand of tissue?" and "Do you typically buy Kleenex, or do you buy some other brand of facial tissue?" Of course, what Tree-Free management would love to discover is that buyers of some brand other than Kleenex are sensitive to the recycled paper issue. Then they could make a persuasive argument that Kleenex should use Tree-Free tissue boxes, advertise how it is helping the environment, and increase its market share over tissue brands that do not use recycled paper boxes. The "hypothesis of interest" is a strong association between a "yes" answer to the first question and a "some other brand" answer to the second question.

In truth, marketing managers and researchers typically have hypotheses of interest in mind. But statistical tests do not exist that can assess these hypotheses conveniently. Instead, the researcher must use the two-step process we have described. First, the existence of an association must be demonstrated. If there is no association, there is no sense in looking for evidence of the hypothesis of interest. However, when the null hypothesis is rejected, an association does exist in the population, and the researcher is then justified to look at the direction of the association. When the second step takes place, the researcher is in pursuit of the hypothesis of interest. Now the strength and direction aspects of the relationship are assessed to see if they correspond with the suspicions held by the marketing manager who wants to turn this association into managerial action.

> When the null hypothesis is rejected, then the researcher may have a managerially important relationship to share with the manager.

Just think of the millions of boxes used by the facial tissue industry for packaging. Now do you see why Tree-Free has such a strong interest in a hypothesis other than the null? To do competent work, a researcher must ferret out all of the hypotheses of interest during the problem definition stage.

SPSS

SPSS Student Assistant Online
Genie in the Bottle: SPSS Statistics
Coach

SUMMARY

This chapter dealt with instances in which a marketing researcher wants to see if there is a relationship between the responses to one question and the responses to another question in the same survey. Four different types of relationships are possible. First, there is a nonmonotonic relationship where the presence (or absence) of one variable is systematically associated with the presence (or absence) of another. Second, a monotonic relationship indicates the direction of one variable relative to the direction of the other variable. Third, a linear relationship is characterized by a straight-line appearance if the variables are plotted against another on a graph. Fourth, curvilinear relationship means the pattern has a definite curved shape. Associative analyses are used to assess these relationships statistically.

Associations can be characterized by presence, direction, and strength, depending on the scaling assumptions of the questions being compared. With chi-square analysis, a cross-tabulation table is prepared for two nominal-scaled questions, and the chi-square statistic is computed to determine whether the observed frequencies (those found in the survey) differ significantly from what would be expected if there were no nonmonotonic relationship between the two. If the null hypothesis of no relationship is rejected, the researcher then looks at the cell percentages to identify the underlying pattern of association.

A correlation coefficient is an index number, constrained to fall between the range of +1.0 to −1.0, that communicates both the strength and the direction of association between two variables. The sign indicates the direction of the relationship and the absolute size indicates the strength of the association. Normally, correlations in excess of ±.81 are considered strong. With two questions that are interval and/or ratio in their scaling assumptions, the Pearson product moment correlation coefficient is appropriate as the means of determining the underlying linear relationship. A scatter diagram can be used to inspect the pattern.

KEY TERMS

Associative analyses (p. 517)
Relationship (p. 517)
Nonmonotonic relationship (p. 517)
Monotonic relationships (p. 518)
Linear relationship (p. 518)
Straight-line formula (p. 519)
Curvilinear relationship (p. 520)
Cross-tabulation table (p. 523)
Cross-tabulation cell (p. 523)
Frequencies table (p. 523)
Raw percentages table (p. 524)
Column percentages table (p. 524)

Row percentages table (p. 525)
Chi-square (χ^2) analysis (p. 525)
Observed frequencies (p. 525)
Expected frequencies (p. 525)
Chi-square formula (p. 527)
Chi-square distribution (p. 528)
Correlation coefficient (p. 532)
Covariation (p. 532)
Scatter diagram (p. 535)
Pearson product moment correlation (p. 536)
Cause-and-effect relationship (p. 540)

REVIEW QUESTIONS/APPLICATIONS

1. Explain the distinction between a statistical relationship and a causal relationship.
2. Define and provide an example for each of the following types of relationship: (a) nonmonotonic, (b) monotonic, (c) linear, and (d) curvilinear.
3. Relate the three different aspects of a relationship between two variables.
4. What is a cross-tabulation? Give an example.
5. With respect to chi-square analysis, describe or identify each of the following: (a) r-by-c table, (b) frequencies table, (c) observed frequencies, (d) expected frequencies, (e) chi-square distribution, (f) significant association, (g) scaling assumptions, (h) row percentages versus column percentages, and (i) degrees of freedom.
6. What is meant by the term "significant correlation"?
7. Briefly describe the connections among the following: covariation, scatter diagram, correlation, and linear relationship.
8. Indicate, with the use of a scatter diagram, the general shape of the scatter of data points in each of the following cases: (a) a strong positive correlation, (b) a weak negative correlation, (c) no correlation, (d) a correlation of −.98.
9. What are the scaling assumptions assumed by Pearson product moment correlation?

10. Following are various factors that may have relationships that are interesting to marketing managers. With each one identify the type of relationship, indicate its nature or direction, and specify how knowledge of the relationship could help a marketing manager in designing marketing strategy.

    a. Readership of certain sections of the Sunday newspaper and age of the reader for a sporting goods retail store.

    b. Ownership of a telephone answering machine and household income for a telemarketing service being used by a public television broadcasting station soliciting funds.

    c. Number of miles driven in company cars and need for services such as oil changes, tune-ups, or filter changes for a quick auto service chain attempting to market fleet discounts to companies.

    d. Plans to take a five-day vacation to Jamaica and the exchange rate of the Jamaican dollar to that of other countries for Sandals, an all-inclusive resort located in Montego Bay.

    e. Amount of do-it-yourself home repairs and declining state of the economy (e.g., a recession) for Ace Hardware stores.

11. Indicate the presence, nature, and strength of the relationship involving purchases of intermediate size automobiles and each of the following factors: (a) price, (b) fabric versus leather interior, (c) exterior color, and (d) size of rebate.

12. With each of the following examples, compose a reasonable statement of an association you would expect to find existing between the factors involved, and construct a stacked bar chart expressing that association.

    a. Wearing braces to straighten teeth by children attending expensive private schools versus those attending public schools.

    b. Having a Doberman pinscher as a guard dog, using a home security alarm system, and owning of rare pieces of art.

    c. Adhering to the "diet pyramid" recommended by the Surgeon General of the United States for healthful living and family history of heart disease.

    d. Purchasing toys as gifts during the Christmas buying season versus other seasons of the year by parents of preschool-aged children.

13. Following is some information about 10 respondents to a mail survey concerning candy purchasing. Use SPSS to construct the four different types of cross-tabulation tables that are possible. Label each table, and indicate what you perceive to be the general relationship apparent in the data.

RESPONDENT	BUY PLAIN M&Ms	BUY PEANUT M&Ms
1	Yes	No
2	Yes	No
3	No	Yes
4	Yes	No
5	No	No
6	No	Yes
7	No	No
8	Yes	No
9	Yes	No
10	No	Yes

14. Morton O'Dell is the owner of Mort's Diner, which is located in downtown Atlanta, Georgia. Mort's opened up about 12 months ago, and it has experienced success, but Mort is always worried about what food items to order as inventory on a weekly basis. Mort's daughter, Mary, is an engineering student at Georgia Tech, and she offers to help her father. She asks him to provide

sales data for the past 10 weeks in terms of pounds of food bought. With some difficulty, Mort comes up with the following list.

WEEK	MEAT	FISH	FOWL	VEGETABLES	DESSERTS
1	100	50	150	195	50
2	91	55	182	200	64
3	82	60	194	209	70
4	75	68	211	215	82
5	66	53	235	225	73
6	53	61	253	234	53
7	64	57	237	230	68
8	76	64	208	221	58
9	94	68	193	229	62
10	105	58	181	214	62

Mary uses these sales figures to construct scatter diagrams that illustrate the basic relationships among the various types of food items purchased at Mort's Diner over the past 10 weeks. She tells her father that the diagrams provide some help in his weekly inventory ordering problem. Construct Mary's scatter diagrams with your SPSS to indicate what assistance they are to Mort. Perform the appropriate associative analysis with SPSS and interpret your findings.

INTERACTIVE LEARNING

Visit the Web site at www.prenhall.com/burnsbush. For this chapter, work through the Self-Study Quizzes, and get instant feedback on whether you need additional studying. On the Web site, you can review the chapter outlines and case information for Chapter 18.

CASE 18.1   Friendly Market Versus Circle K

Friendly Market is a convenience store located directly across the street from a Circle K convenience store. Circle K is a national chain, and its stores enjoy the benefits of national advertising campaigns, particularly the high visibility these campaigns bring. All Circle K stores have large red-and-white store signs, identical merchandise assortments, standardized floor plans, and they are open around the clock. Friendly Market, in contrast, is a one-of-a-kind "mom-and-pop" variety convenience store owned and managed by Bobby James. Bobby's parents came to the United States from Palestine when Bobby was 15 years old. The family members became American citizens and adopted the last name of James. Bobby had difficulty making the transition to U.S. schools, and he dropped out without finishing high school. For the next 10 years of his life, Bobby worked in a variety of jobs, both full- and part-time, and for most of the past 10 years, Bobby has been a Circle K store employee.

In 1999, Bobby made a bold move to open his own convenience store. Don's Market, a mom-and-pop convenience store across the street from the Circle K where Bobby was working at the time, had closed six months before, and Bobby watched it month after month as it remained boarded up with a for sale sign on the front door with no apparent interested parties. Bobby gathered up his life savings and borrowed as much money as he could from friends, relatives, and his bank. He bought the old Don's Market building and equipment, renamed it Friendly Market, and opened its doors for business in November 1999. Bobby's core business philosophy was to greet everyone who came in and to get to know all his customers on a first-name basis. He also watched Circle K's prices closely and sought to have lower prices on at least 50 percent of the merchandise sold by both stores.

To the surprise of the manager of the Circle K across the street, Friendly Market prospered. In 2001, Bobby's younger sister, who had gone on to college and earned an M.B.A. degree at Indiana University, conducted a survey of Bobby's target market to gain a better understanding of why Friendly Market was successful. She drafted a simple questionnaire and did the telephone interviewing herself. She used the local telephone book and called a random sample of over 150 respondents whose residences were listed within three miles of Friendly Market. She then created an SPSS data set with the following variable names and values.

Variable Name	Value Labels
FRIENDLY	0 = Do not use Friendly Market regularly; 1 = Use Friendly Market regularly
CIRCLE K	0 = Do not use Circle K regularly; 1 = Use Circle K regularly
DWELL	1 = Own home; 2 = Rent
SEX	1 = Male; 2 = Female
WORK	1 = Work full-time; 2 = Work part-time; 3 = Retired or Do not work
COMMUTE	0 = Do not pass by Friendly Market/Circle K corner on way to work; 1 = Do pass by Friendly Market/Circle K corner on way to work

In addition to these demographic questions, respondents were asked if they agreed (coded 3), disagreed (coded 1), or neither agreed nor disagreed (coded 2) with each of five different lifestyle statements. The variable names and questions follow.

Variable Name	Lifestyle Statement
BARGAIN	I often shop for bargains.
CASH	I always pay cash.
QUICK	I like quick, easy shopping.
KNOW ME	I shop where they know my name.
HURRY	I am always in a hurry.

The data set is available to you to be downloaded from the data files area of the textbook Web site (**www.prenhall.com/burnsbush**). It is named "friendly.sav." Use SPSS to perform the associative analyses necessary to answer the following questions.

1. Do Friendly Market and Circle K have the same customers?
2. What is the demographic profile associated with Friendly Market's customers?
3. What is the demographic profile associated with Circle K's customers?
4. What is the lifestyle profile associated with Friendly Market's customers?

CASE 18.2 *Your Integrated Case*

This is your integrated case, described on pages 42–43.

The Hobbit's Choice Restaurant Survey Associative Analysis

Cory's little daughter's stomach ailment turned out to be much worse than Cory Rogers expected, and he called in to inform Celeste that it would probably be several days before he would be able to get back in to the office. Cory said to Celeste, "I know you are a bit lost with The Hobbit's Choice Restaurant project, but why don't you take a look at the proposal, and see if there is any further analysis that you can do while I am out? Have Tonya pull the proposal from the file."

Celeste looked at the research proposal, and she jotted down some notes with respect to research questions that need to be addressed. Her notes follow.

Your task in Case 18.2 is to use The Hobbit's Choice Restaurant SPSS data set and perform the proper analysis. You will also need to interpret the findings.

1. Perform the correct analysis and interpret your findings with regard to The Hobbit's Choice Restaurant menu, décor, and atmosphere for those people who prefer to drive less than 30 minutes to get to the restaurant.

2. Do older or younger people want unusual desserts and/or unusual entrées?

3. Create a variable that distinguishes the "Probable patrons" (likely to patronize Hobbit's Choice =1 or =2) from the "Not probable patrons" (likely to patronize Hobbit's Choice =3, =4, or =5). If the probable patrons constitute The Hobbit's Choice Restaurant's target market, what is the demographic makeup of this target market? Use the demographics of household income, education level, gender, and zip code.

4. Celeste knows (from the analysis described in this chapter) that the *City Magazine* is a viable advertising medium for Jeff Dean to use. Are there other viable promotion vehicles that Jeff should know about?

Chapter 19

Predictive Analysis in Marketing Research

Practitioner Viewpoint

We often use regression analysis both to examine simple relationships and as the starting point in investigating more complex relationships. For example, we might look at the relationship between a B2B customer's ratings of your company's sales support and the customer's overall satisfaction with your company. We seldom expect a high correlation between one measured item and overall satisfaction.

Why don't we expect a high correlation between any one item and overall satisfaction? If you look at the cross-tabulation that follows you will see a typical data set.

Satisfaction Rating

		1	2	3	4	5
Sales	*1*	3	4	2	1	0
Support	*2*	3	6	5	4	3
Rating	*3*	1	4	5	5	5
	4		2	4	14	8
	5		1	2	8	11

The correlation between satisfaction and sales support is .55. By looking at those ratings on the highlighted diagonal, you can observe that, although there is a relationship, it is not strong. Every person whose ratings were "off the diagonal" reduced the correlation. This leads us to using multiple regression to better explain factors (such as price, product quality, customer service, and so forth) that are related to customer satisfaction. In this chapter, you will learn more about simple and multiple regression analysis using SPSS.

Ronald L. Tatham
Chief Executive Officer
Burke, Inc.

Gambler Target Market Similarities and Differences Between Atlantic City and Las Vegas

Although a number of casinos and other gambling venues have opened up across the United States in the past several years, the "granddaddy" locations remain Las Vegas and Atlantic City. Las Vegas has been the gambling capital for most of the last century, beginning with the legalization of gambling in the 1930s. In the 1950s Las Vegas exploded into the single most notorious gambling mecca in the United States with the development and aggressive marketing of "The Strip" with the famous Sands Hotel and a number of other well-known casinos such as the Mirage, Rivera, and Frontier.

Perhaps jealous of Las Vegas's ability to attract tourists, New Jersey legalized gambling in Atlantic City in the 1970s. What immediately followed was a flurry of casino building projects that transformed the famous Atlantic City boardwalk into a city with several casinos such as Bally's, Caesar's, and the Trump Taj Mahal.

Do Las Vegas and Atlantic City compete for U.S. gamblers? This is an important marketing question, for if they do compete, the strategies of their promoters should be very different than if they do not compete. If they are not competing and drawing local, regional, or otherwise unique gamblers, the marketing strategies should be designed around these considerations. On the other hand, if Las Vegas and Atlantic City are competing for the same market of gamblers across the United States, then the two gambling capitals should be aggressively battling each other for market share.

A researcher investigated the characteristics of Las Vegas gamblers and Atlantic City gamblers.[1] The researcher used the American Travel Survey data made available by the U.S. Department of Transportation's Bureau of Transportation Statistics. This survey identifies destinations of U.S. travelers, and it includes a number of demographic and lifestyle questions. Using a sophisticated form of multiple regression

Predictive analysis reveals that Las Vegas and Atlantic City do not compete for the same U.S. gamblers.

Table 19.1	Characteristics of Las Vegas and Atlantic City Gamblers	
CHARACTERISTIC	**LAS VEGAS GAMBLERS**	**ATLANTIC CITY GAMBLERS**
Income	More trips with higher income	More trips with higher income
Education	More trips with more education	More trips with more education
Distance to Las Vegas	More trips the closer he or she lives to Las Vegas	Less trips the closer he or she lives to Las Vegas
Distance to Atlantic City	Less trips the closer he or she lives to Atlantic City	More trips the closer he or she lives to Atlantic City
Own home	More trips with ownership	Not related
Home in Midwest	More trips by Midwesterners	Less trips by Midwesterners
Home in Northeast	Not related	More trips by Northeasterners
Home in South	Not related	Less trips by Southerners
Retired	More trips if retired	Not related
Student	More trips if a student	Not related
Asian	More trips if Asian	Not related
Black	Not related	More trips if Black

analysis, the researcher answered the question, "Do Las Vegas and Atlantic City compete for U.S. gamblers?" Table 19.1 lists his findings.

The highlighted cells are the ones that distinguish the market segment profiles that differentiate Las Vegas from Atlantic City gamblers. Specifically, both Las Vegas and Atlantic City are drawing gamblers who live closer to their respective locations, and they both are attracting higher income and higher education groups. In addition, Las Vegas gamblers are more likely to be (1) homeowners, (2) Midwesterners, (3) retired, or (4) students, and (5) Asian, and not Northeasterners, Southerners, or Blacks. Atlantic City, in contrast, is attractive to gamblers who are Northeasterners and Blacks, but it is definitely not attracting gamblers who are Midwesterners or Southerners. Compared to Las Vegas, Atlantic City is not attracting homeowners, retirees, students, or Asians. From this set of findings, the two great American gambling destinations do not compete for the same gamblers.

This chapter is the last one in which we discuss statistical procedures frequently used by marketing researchers. A researcher sometimes wishes to predict what might result if the manager were to implement a certain alternative. Alternatively, the researcher may be seeking a parsimonious way to describe market segments or the differences between various types of consumers such as was the case in our introductory case about Las Vegas versus Atlantic City gamblers. In this chapter, we will describe regression analysis. Although it may seem like an intimidating procedure, we will show you how regression relates directly to the scatter diagrams and linear relationship you learned about in the previous chapter. Three types of regression analysis are described in this chapter. The first, bivariate regression, simply takes correlation analysis between two variables into the realm of prediction. Next, multiple regression analysis introduces the concept of simultaneously using two or more variables to make the prediction of a target variable such as sales. Finally, we will briefly introduce you to stepwise regression. This is a technique used by a researcher when faced with a large number of candidate predictors, and he or she is looking for the subset of these that best predicts or describes the phenomenon under study.

UNDERSTANDING PREDICTION

A **prediction** is a statement of what is believed will happen in the future made on the basis of past experience or prior observation. We are confronted with the need to make predictions on a daily basis. For example, you must predict whether it will rain to decide whether to carry an umbrella. You must predict how difficult an examination will be in order to properly study. You must predict how heavy the traffic will be in order to decide what time to start driving to make your dentist appointment on time.

Marketing managers are also constantly faced with the need to make predictions, and the stakes are much higher than in the three examples just cited. That is, instead of getting wet, receiving a grade of C rather than a B, or being late for a dentist appointment, the marketing manager has to worry about competitors' reactions, changes in sales, wasted resources, and whether profitability objectives will be achieved. Making accurate predictions is a vital part of the marketing manager's workaday world.

Prediction is a statement of what is believed will happen in the future made on the basis of past experience or prior observation.

Two Approaches to Prediction

There are two ways of making a prediction: extrapolation and predictive modeling. In **extrapolation**, you can use past experience as a means of predicting the future. This process identifies a pattern over time and projects that pattern into the future. For example, if the weather forecaster has predicted an 80 percent chance of rain every day for the past week and it had rained every day, you would expect it to rain if he or she predicted an 80 percent chance of rain today. Similarly, if the last two exams you took under a professor were quite easy, you would predict the next one would be easy as well. Of course, it might not rain or the professor might administer a hard exam, but the observed patterns argue for rain today and an easy next exam. In both cases, you have detected a consistent pattern over time and based your predictions on this pattern.

The two approaches to prediction are extrapolation and predictive modeling.

In the other case, prediction relies on an observed relationship perceived to exist between the factor you are predicting and some condition you believe influences the factor. For example, how does the weather forecaster make his or her predictions? He or she inspects several pieces of evidence such as wind direction and velocity, barometric pressure changes, humidity, jet stream configuration, and temperature. That is, he or she goes far beyond taking what happened yesterday and forecasting that it will happen today. He or she builds a predictive model, using the relationships believed to exist among variables to make a prediction. A **predictive model** relates the conditions expected to be in place and influencing the factor you are predicting. It is not an extrapolation of a consistent pattern over time; rather, it is an observed relationship that exists across time.

Extrapolation detects a pattern in the past and projects it into the future. Predictive modeling uses relationships found among variables to make a prediction.

How to Determine the "Goodness" of Your Predictions

Regardless of the method of prediction, you will always want to judge the "goodness" of your predictions, which is how good your method is at making those predictions. But because predictions are for the future and we can never know the future until it occurs, how can you judge the accuracy of your predictions? Here is a simple example that will explain the basic approach. Imagine that you are away at college. Your little brother, who is a high school sophomore, works part-time at the movie theater in your hometown. He is rather cocky about himself. When you come home for the weekend, he claims that he can predict the theater's popcorn sales for each day in the week. It turns out that you also worked at the theater while in high school, and you know the theater manager very well. She agrees to keep a record of popcorn sales and to provide the daily amount to you for the next week. So you challenge your little brother to write down the sales for the next seven days. After the week passes, how would you determine the accuracy of your brother's prediction?

All predictions should be judged as to their "goodness" (accuracy).

By comparing your brother's predictions of popcorn sales to actual sales, you can assess the "goodness" of his predictions.

The goodness of a prediction is based on examination of the residuals.

Residuals are the errors: comparisons of predictions to actual values.

The easiest way would be to compare the predictions for each day's popcorn sales to the actual amount sold. We have done this in Table 19.2. When you look at the table, you will see that we have calculated the difference between your brother's prediction and the actual sales for each day. Notice that for some days, the predictions were high, whereas for others, the predictions were low. When you compare how far the predicted values are from the actual or observed values, you are performing **analysis of residuals**. Stated differently, assessment of the goodness of a prediction requires you to compare the pattern of errors in the predictions to the actual data. Analysis of residuals underlies all assessments of the accuracy of a forecasting method, and because researchers cannot wait a month, a quarter, or a year to compare a prediction with what actually happens, they fall back on past data. In other words, they select a predictive model and apply it to the past data. Then they examine the residuals to assess the model's predictive accuracy.

There are many ways to examine residuals. For example, in the case of your little brother's forecast, you could judge it either on a total basis or an individual basis. On a total basis, you might compute the average as we have done in the table, or you could sum all of the daily residuals. Of course, you would need to square the daily residuals or use the absolute values to avoid cancellation of the positive differ-

Table 19.2 **Weekly Popcorn Sales: Using Residuals to Assess the Goodness of a Forecast**

DAY OF WEEK	YOUR BROTHER'S FORECAST	ACTUAL SALES	RESIDUAL (DIFFERENCE)	TYPE OF ERROR
Monday	$100	$125	−25	Very low
Tuesday	$110	$130	−20	Low
Wednesday	$120	$135	−15	Low
Thursday	$125	$125	0	Exact
Friday	$260	$225	+35	Very high
Saturday	$300	$250	+50	Very high
Sunday	$275	$235	+40	Very high
Averages	**$185**	**$175**	**+10**	**High**

ences by the negative differences. (You have seen the necessary squaring operation before, for instance, in the formula for a standard deviation or the sums of squares formulas we described in Chapter 15.) For the individual error, you might look for some pattern.[2] On an individual basis, you might notice a pattern: Your little brother tends to underestimate how much popcorn will be bought on weekdays, which are low-sales days, whereas he overestimates it for Friday through Sunday, which are high-sales days. As you can see, the goodness of a prediction approach depends on how closely it predicts a set of representative values judged by examining the residuals (or errors).

Now that you have a basic understanding of prediction and how you determine the goodness of your predictions, we turn our attention to regression analysis.

BIVARIATE REGRESSION ANALYSIS

We first define **bivariate regression analysis** as a predictive analysis technique in which one variable is used to predict the level of another by use of the straight-line formula. We review the equation for a straight line and introduce basic terms used in regression. We also describe basic computations and significance with bivariate regression. We show how a regression prediction is made and we illustrate how to perform this analysis on SPSS.

With bivariate regression, one variable is used to predict another variable.

A straight-line relationship underlies regression, and it is a powerful predictive model. Figure 19.1 illustrates a straight-line relationship, and you should refer to it as we describe the elements in a general straight-line formula. The formula for a straight line is:

The straight-line equation is the basis of regression analysis.

Formula for a straight-line $y = a + bx$
relationship

where

y = the predicted variable

x = the variable used to predict y

a = the **intercept,** or point where the line cuts the y-axis when $x = 0$

b = the **slope** or the change in y for any 1-unit change in x

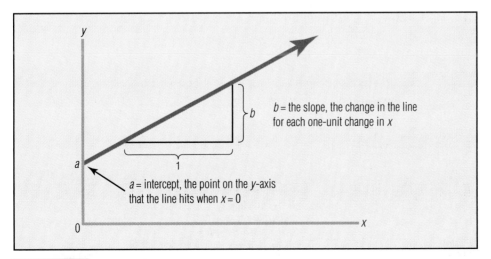

y

b = the slope, the change in the line for each one-unit change in x

a = intercept, the point on the y-axis that the line hits when $x = 0$

a

1

0

x

Figure **19.1** **The General Equation for a Straight Line in Graph Form**

Regression is directly related to correlation by the underlying straight-line relationship.

You should recall the straight-line relationship we described underlying the correlation coefficient: When the scatter diagram for two variables appears as a thin ellipse, there is a high correlation between them. Regression is directly related to correlation. In fact, we use one of our correlation examples to illustrate the application of bivariate regression shortly.

Basic Procedure in Bivariate Regression Analysis

We now describe independent and dependent variables and show how the intercept and slope are computed. Then we use SPSS output to show how tests of significance are interpreted.

In regression, the independent variable is used to predict the dependent variable.

Independent and Dependent Variables   As we indicated, bivariate regression analysis is a case in which only two variables are involved in the predictive model. When we use only two variables, one is termed *dependent* and the other is termed *independent*. The **dependent variable** is that which is predicted, and it is customarily termed y in the regression straight-line equation. The **independent variable** is that which is used to predict the dependent variable, and it is the x in the regression formula. We must quickly point out that the terms "dependent" and "independent" are arbitrary designations and are customary to regression analysis. There is no cause-and-effect relationship or true dependence between the dependent and the independent variable. It is strictly a statistical relationship, not causal, that may be found between these two variables.

Computing Slope and Intercept   To compute a and b, a statistical analysis program needs a number of observations of the various levels of the dependent variable paired with different levels of the independent variable, identical to the ones we illustrated previously when we were demonstrating how to perform correlation analysis.

The formulas for calculating the slope (b) and the intercept (a) are rather complicated, but some instructors are in favor of their students learning these formulas, so we have included them in Marketing Research Insight 19.1.

MARKETING RESEARCH
INSIGHT
19.1

Additional Insights ◄

How to Calculate the Intercept and Slope of a Bivariate Regression

In the following example we are using the Novartis pharmaceuticals company sales territory and number of salespersons data found in Table 19.3. Intermediate regression calculations are included in Table 19.3.

The formula for computing the regression parameter b is:

Formula for b, the slope, in bivariate regression

$$b = \frac{n\sum_{i=1}^{n} x_i y_i - \left(\sum_{i=1}^{n} x_i\right)\left(\sum_{i=1}^{n} y_i\right)}{n\sum_{i=1}^{n} x_i^2 - \left(\sum_{i=1}^{n} x_i\right)^2}$$

where

x_i = an x variable value
y_i = a y value paired with each x_i value
n = the number of pairs

The calculations for b, the slope, are as follows:

$$b = \frac{n\sum_{i=1}^{n} x_i y_i - \left(\sum_{i=1}^{n} x_i\right)\left(\sum_{i=1}^{n} y_i\right)}{n\sum_{i=1}^{n} x_i^2 - \left(\sum_{i=1}^{n} x_i\right)^2}$$

Calculation of b, the slope, in bivariate regression using Novartis sales territory data

$$= \frac{20 \times 58{,}603 - 251 \times 4{,}325}{20 \times 3{,}469 - 251^2}$$

$$= \frac{1{,}172{,}060 - 1{,}085{,}575}{69{,}380 - 63{,}001}$$

$$= \frac{86{,}485}{6{,}379}$$

$$= 13.56$$

Table **19.3** **Bivariate Regression Analysis Data and Intermediate Calculations**

TERRITORY (i)	SALES ($ MILLIONS) (y)	NUMBER OF SALESPERSONS (x)	xy	x^2
1	102	7	714	49
2	125	5	625	25
3	150	9	1,350	81
4	155	9	1,395	81
5	160	9	1,440	81
6	168	8	1,344	64
7	180	10	1,800	100
8	220	10	2,200	100
9	210	12	2,520	144
10	205	12	2,460	144
11	230	12	2,760	144
12	255	15	3,825	225
13	250	14	3,500	196
14	260	15	3,900	225
15	250	16	4,320	256
16	275	16	4,400	256
17	280	17	4,760	289
18	240	18	4,320	324
19	300	18	5,400	324
20	310	19	5,890	361
Sums	**4,325** (Average = 216.25)	**251** (Average = 12.55)	**58,603**	**3,469**

The formula for computing the intercept is:

Formula for a, the intercept, in bivariate regression $a = \bar{y} - b\bar{x}$

The computations for a, the intercept, are as follows:

Calculation of a, the intercept, in bivariate regression using Novartis sales territory data

$$a = \bar{y} - b\bar{x}$$
$$= 216.25 - 13.56 \times 12.55$$
$$= 216.25 - 170.15$$
$$= 46.10$$

In other words, the bivariate regression equation has been found to be:

Novartis sales regression equation $y = 46.10 + 13.56\,x$

The interpretation of this equation is as follows. Annual sales in the average Novartis sales territory are $46.10 million, and they increase $13.56 million annually with each additional salesperson.

When SPSS or any other statistical analysis program computes the intercept and the slope in a regression analysis, it does so on the basis of the "least squares criterion." The **least squares criterion** is a way of guaranteeing that the straight line that runs through the points on the scatter diagram is positioned so as to minimize the vertical distances away from the line of the various points. In other words, if you draw a line where the regression line is calculated and measure the vertical distances of all the points away from that line, it would be impossible to draw any other line that would result in a lower total of all of those vertical distances. Or, to state the least squares criterion using residuals analysis, the line is the one with the lowest total squared residuals.

The least squares criterion used in regression analysis guarantees that the "best" straight-line slope and intercept will be calculated.

RETURN TO *Your Integrated Case*

The Hobbit's Choice Restaurant Survey: How to Run and Interpret Bivariate Regression Analysis on SPSS

Now let us illustrate bivariate regression with SPSS using The Hobbit's Choice Restaurant survey data with which you are well acquainted. Our purpose is to help you learn the basic SPSS commands for bivariate regression and to familiarize you with SPSS output and various regression statistics found on it.

The first step in bivariate regression analysis is to identify the dependent and independent variables. For our example, we will use the amount spent in restaurants per month as our dependent variable. Logically, we would expect expenditures to be related to income, so the before-tax household income level is a logical independent variable. However, we have used a code system for income level: The code numbers are not in dollars or dollar units (such as thousands). In any regression, it is best to use realistic values because realistic values are easiest to interpret. Consequently, we will recode the income values to represent the midpoints of the income ranges on the questionnaire. For example, we will recode the "less than $15,000" to 7.5 meaning $7,500, so our recoded units are in thousands of dollars. The recoded income values are $7.5, $20.0, $37.5, $62.5, $87.5, $125, and $175. Notice that the highest income level of "$150,000 or higher" did not have an upper limit, so we arbitrarily use the range of the income level just below it.

As you can see in Figure 19.2, the SPSS menu commands clickstream to run bivariate regression is ANALYZE-REGRESSION-LINEAR. This opens up the linear regression selection window where you would indicate which variable is the dependent variable and the independent variable. In our example, we are investigating what you would expect to be a linear relationship between the amount spent per month in restaurants (dependent vari-

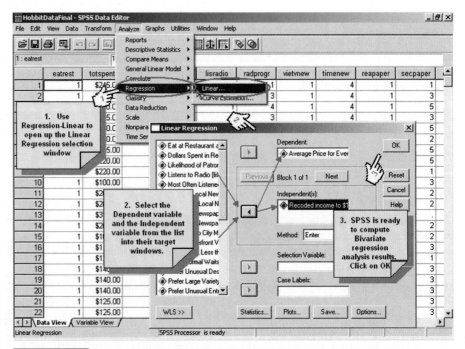

Figure 19.2 **The SPSS Clickstream for Bivariate Regression Analysis**

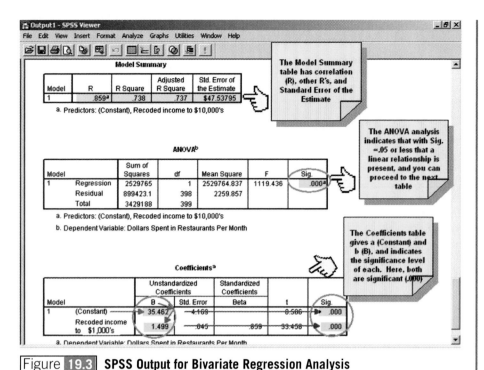

Figure **19.3** **SPSS Output for Bivariate Regression Analysis**

able) and household income (independent variable). When these variables are clicked into their respective locations on the SPSS Linear Regression setup window, clicking on OK will generate the SPSS output we are about to describe.

There are several pieces of information provided with a regression analysis such as this. First, there is information on "Variables Entered/Removed," which indicates that the regression analysis used a method designated as "Enter." This designation refers to the regression method we are using. (There are several methods, but most are beyond the scope of our textbook.)

The annotated SPSS linear regression output is shown in Figure 19.3. In the Model Summary table, three types of "Rs" are indicated. For bivariate regression, R Square (.738 on the output) is the square of the correlation coefficient of 0.859. The Adjusted R Square (.737) reduces the R^2 by taking into account the sample size and number of parameters estimated. This R Square value is very important, because it reveals how well the straight-line model fits the scatter of points. Because a correlation coefficient ranges from −1.0 to +1.0, its square will range from 0 to +1.0. The higher the R Square value, the better is the straight line's fit to the elliptical scatter of points. A standard error value is reported, and we explain its use later.

Next, an Analysis of Variance (ANOVA) section is provided. As you can see, regression is related to analysis of variance.[3] We must determine whether the straight-line model we are attempting to apply to describe these two variables is appropriate. The F value is significant (.000) so we reject the null hypothesis that a straight-line model does not fit the data we are analyzing. Just as in ANOVA, this test is a flag, and the flag has now been raised, making it justifiable to continue inspecting the output for more significant results. If the ANOVA F test is not significant, we would have to abandon our regression analysis attempts with these two variables. Finally, you can see in the Coefficients Table that the values of b and a are listed under "Unstandardized Coefficients." The

SPSS Student Assistant Online
Running and Interpreting Bivariate
Regression

constant (*a*) is 35.462 whereas *b*, identified as "B," is 1.499. In other words, rounding to hundredths, the regression equation has been found to be the following.

Bivariate regression equation determined by SPSS using The Hobbit's Choice data

Dollars spent in restaurants per month
= \$35.46 + \$1.50 × Income in \$1,000's

To relate this finding to our regression line in Figure 19.1, it says that the regression line will intercept the dollars spent in restaurants per month (the *y*-axis) at \$35.46, and the line will increase \$1.50 per month for each \$1,000 unit increase in the income level (the *x*-axis).

You must always test the regression model, intercept, and slope for statistical significance.

Testing for Statistical Significance of the Intercept and the Slope Simply computing the values for *a* and *b* is not sufficient for regression analysis, because the two values must be tested for statistical significance. The intercept and slope that are computed are sample estimates of population parameters of the true intercept, α (alpha), and the true slope, β (beta). The tests for statistical significance are tests as to whether the computed intercept and computed slope are significantly different from zero (the null hypothesis). To determine statistical significance, regression analysis requires that a *t* test be undertaken for each parameter estimate. The interpretation of these *t* tests is identical to other significance tests you have seen. We describe what these *t* tests mean next.

In our example, you would look at the "Sig." column in the Coefficients table. This is where the slope and intercept *t* test results are reported. Both of our tests have significance levels of .000, which are below our standard significance level cutoff of .05, so our computed intercept and slope are valid estimates of the population intercept and slope. If *x* and *y* do not share a linear relationship, the population regression slope will equal zero and the *t* test result will support the null hypothesis. However, if a systematic linear relationship exists, the *t* test result will force rejection of the null hypothesis, and the researcher can be confident that the calculated slope estimates the true one that exists in the population. Remember that we are dealing with a statistical concept, and you must be assured that the straight-line parameters α and β really exist in the population before you can use your regression analysis findings as a prediction device.

Regression analysis predictions are estimates that have some amount of error in them.

Making a Prediction and Accounting for Error Now, there is one more step to relate, and it is the most important one. How do you make a prediction? The fact that the line is a best-approximation representation of all the points means we must account for a certain amount of error when we use the line for our predictions. The true advantage of a significant bivariate regression analysis result lies in the ability of the marketing researcher to use that information gained about the regression line through the points on the scatter diagram and to estimate the value or amount of the dependent variable based on some level of the independent variable. For example, with our regression result calculated for the relationship between total monthly restaurant purchases and income level, it is now possible to estimate the dollar amount of restaurant purchases predicted to be associated with a specific income level. However, we know that the scatter of points does not describe a perfectly straight line because the correlation is .859, not 1.0. So our regression prediction can only be an estimate.

The standard error of the estimate is used to calculate a range of the prediction made with a regression equation.

Generating a regression prediction is conceptually identical to estimating a population mean. That is, it is necessary to express the amount of error by estimating a range rather than stipulating an exact estimate for your prediction. Regression analysis provides for a **standard error of the estimate**, which is a measure of the

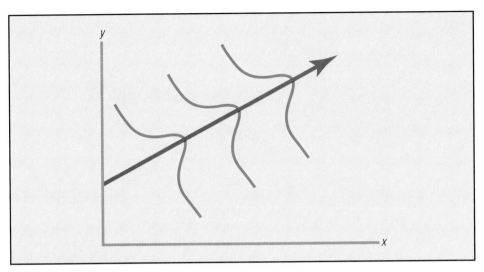

Figure **19.4** **Regression Assumes That Data Points Form a Bell-Shaped Curve Around the Regression Line**

accuracy of the predictions of the regression equation. This standard error value is listed in the top half of the SPSS output and just beside the Adjusted R Square in Figure 19.3. It is analogous to the standard error of the mean you used in estimating a population mean from a sample, but it is based on the residuals, or how far away each predicted value is from the actual value. Do you recall the popcorn sales example of residuals we described earlier in this chapter? SPSS does the same comparison by using the regression equation it computed to predict the monthly restaurant purchases dollar amount for each respondent, and this predicted value is compared to the actual amount given by the respondent. The differences, or residuals, are translated into a standard error of estimate value. In our Hobbit's Choice Restaurant survey example, the standard error of the estimate was found to be $47.54 (rounded to the nearest cent).

One of the assumptions of regression analysis is that the plots on the scatter diagram will be spread uniformly and in accord with the normal curve assumptions over the regression line. Figure 19.4 illustrates how this assumption might be depicted graphically. The points are congregated close to the line and then become more diffuse as they move away from the line. In other words, a greater percentage of the points is found on or close to the line than is found further away. The great advantage of this assumption is that it allows the marketing researcher to use his or her knowledge of the normal curve to specify the range in which the dependent variable is predicted to fall. For example, if the researcher used the predicted dependent value result ±1.96 times the standard error of the estimate, he or she would be stipulating a range with a 95 percent level of confidence; whereas if the researcher uses ±2.58 times the standard error of the estimate, he or she would be stipulating a range with a 99 percent level of confidence. The interpretation of these confidence intervals is identical to interpretations for previous confidence intervals: Were the prediction made many times and an actual result determined each time, the actual results would fall within the range of the predicted value 95 percent or 99 percent of these times.

Figure 19.5 illustrates how you can envision a regression prediction. Let us use the regression equation to make a prediction about the dollar amount of monthly

The use of 95 percent or 99 percent confidence interval is standard.

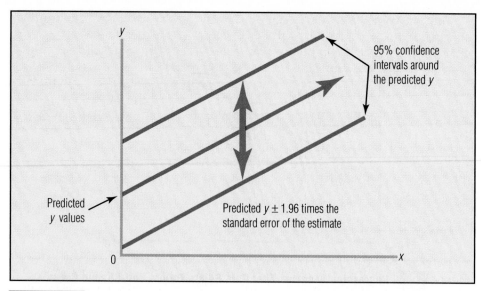

Figure **19.5** **To Predict with Regression, Apply Levels of Confidence Around the Regression Line**

restaurant purchases that would be associated with an income level of $75,000. Applying the regression formula, we have the following:

$$y = a + b_x$$

Calculation of monthly restaurant purchases predicted with an income level of $75,000

Dollars spent in restaurants per month = $35.46 + $1.50 × Income in $1,000's
= $35.46 + $1.50 × 75
= $35.46 + $112.5
= $147.96

Regression predictions are made with confidence intervals.

Next, to reflect the imperfect aspects of the predictive tool being used, we must apply confidence intervals. If the 95 percent level of confidence were applied, the computations would be:

Predicted $y \pm z_\alpha$ Standard error of the estimate

Calculation of 95% confidence intervals for the predicted monthly restaurant purchases

$147.96 ± 1.96 × $47.54
$147.96 ± 93.18
$54.78 to $241.14

As you can see, the predicted y is the monthly dollar amount of restaurant purchases we just computed for an income level of $75,000, the 1.96 pertains to 95 percent level of confidence, and the standard error of the estimate is the value indicated in the regression analysis output. The interpretation of these three numbers is as follows. For a typical individual in The Hobbit's Choice Restaurant survey population, if that person's household income before taxes was $75,000, the monthly restaurant purchases amount that would be expected would be about $148, but because there are differences between income ranges and monthly restaurant purchases, the restaurant purchases would not be exactly that amount. Consequently, the 95 percent confidence interval reveals that the sales figure should fall between $55 and $241. Finally, the prediction is valid only if conditions remain the same as they were for the time period from which the original data were collected.[4]

You may be troubled at the large range of our confidence intervals, and you are right to be concerned. If you recall our popcorn sales estimation example in the beginning of the chapter, you should remember that it is important to assess the precision of the predictions generated by a predictive model. How precisely a regression analysis finding predicts is determined by the size of the standard error of the estimate, a measure of the variability of the predicted dependent variable. In our Hobbit's Choice survey case, the average dollars spent on restaurants per month may be predicted by our bivariate regression findings; however, if we repeated the survey many, many times, and made our $75,000 income prediction of the average dollars spent every time, 95 percent of these predictions would fall between $55 and $241. There is no way to make this prediction more exact because its precision is dictated by the variability in the data.

The precision of a prediction based on a regression analysis finding depends on the size of the standard error of the estimate.

MULTIPLE REGRESSION ANALYSIS

Now that you are familiar with bivariate regression analysis, you are ready to step up to a higher level. In this section, we will introduce you to multiple regression analysis. You will find that all of the concepts in bivariate regression apply to multiple regression, except you will be working with more than one independent variable.

An Underlying Conceptual Model

In Chapter 4 in which you learned about marketing research problem definition, we referred to a model as a structure that ties together various constructs and their relationships. In that chapter, we indicated that it is beneficial for the marketing manager and the market researcher to have some sort of model in mind when designing the research plan. The bivariate regression equation that you just learned about is a model that ties together an independent variable and its dependent variable. The dependent variables that market researchers are interested in are typically sales, potential sales, or some attitude held by those who make up the market. For example, in the Novartis

Because consumers are influenced by many factors, it is best to use a general conceptual model as the basis for multiple regression analysis.

example, the dependent variable was territory sales. If Dell computers commissioned a survey, it might want information on those who intend to purchase a Dell computer, or it might want information on those who intend to buy a competing brand as a means of understanding these consumers and perhaps dissuading them. The dependent variable would be purchase intentions for Dell computers. If Maxwell House Coffee was considering a line of gourmet iced coffee, it would want to know how coffee drinkers feel about gourmet iced coffee, that is, their attitudes toward buying, preparing, and drinking it would be the dependent variable.

Figure 19.6 provides a general conceptual model that fits many marketing research situations, particularly those that are investigating consumer behavior. A **general conceptual model** identifies independent and dependent variables and shows their basic relationships to one another. In Figure 19.6, you can see that purchases, intentions to purchase, and preferences are in the center, meaning they are dependent. The surrounding concepts are possible independent variables. That is, any one could be used to predict any dependent variable. For example, one's intentions to purchase an expensive automobile like a Lexus could depend on one's income. It could also depend on friends' recommendations (word of mouth), one's opinions about how a Lexus would enhance one's self-image, or experiences riding in or driving a Lexus.

In truth, consumers' preferences, intentions, and actions are potentially influenced by a great number of factors as would be very evident if you listed all of the subconcepts that make up each concept in Figure 19.6. For example, there are probably a dozen different demographic variables; there could be dozens of lifestyle dimensions, and a person is exposed to a great many types of advertising media every day. Of course, in the problem definition stage, the researcher and manager slice the myriad of independent variables down to a manageable number to be included on the questionnaire. That is, they have the general model structure in Figure 19.6 in mind, but they identify and measure specific variables that pertain to the problem at hand.

Our underlying conceptual model example is one of many different conceptual models that researchers have available to them. In truth, every research project has a unique conceptual model that depends entirely on the research objectives. As an example of how regression analysis can be applied to how consumers from two different countries view certain questionable sales tactics, read Marketing Research Insight 19.2. We have also provided Marketing Research Insight 19.3 on page 563

There is an underlying general conceptual model in multiple regression analysis.

The researcher and the manager identify, measure, and analyze specific variables that pertain to the general conceptual model in mind.

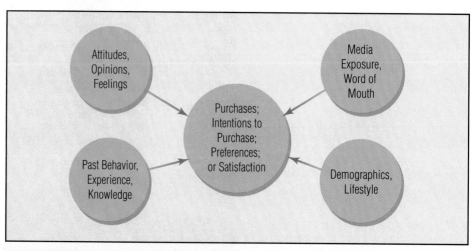

Figure 19.6 **A Conceptual Model for Multiple Regression Analysis**

► **A Global Perspective**

Regression Analysis Shows Ethical Reactions to Questionable Business Practices Differ Between Two Countries[5]

Situation 1: How would you feel if you found that you were overcharged $80 on a purchase of a new suit? What about a $5 overcharge?

Situation 2: What would be your reaction if you just bought a $25 membership in a health club and you found out it might go out of business the very next day? What if you paid $700?

Variations of these situations were presented to samples of American and Greek college students. Among these variations, the dollar value of the situation was systematically varied. For the suit, the overcharged amounts used were $5, $40, and $80, whereas for the health club membership the amounts were $25, $200, and $700. The gender and organizational status of the culprit (salesperson, general manager, and owner) were also varied. The students gave their

reactions to each situation by responding to scales, one of which pertained to how ethical or unethical they considered the act to be.

Using a form of regression called conjoint analysis, the researchers found that Greek and American college students are similar in many ways. For example, both groups felt that the suit purchase situation was more ethically offensive than the health club one. However, the Greek students saw the situations as more unethical than did the American students.

With respect to what factors influenced the students' reactions, American and Greek students were in agreement that the least important factor was the actor's gender, and the most important factor was the dollar size of the transgression. However, Greek students were more affected by the dollar size than were American students.

► **A Global Perspective**

Does "Buy American" in the United States Work as Well as "Buy Japanese" in Japan?

The global economy works in both directions. Products from the home country compete with products produced in foreign countries, and the home country's products are exported to foreign countries where they are the foreign country products. For instance, a consumer in Chicago may be comparing U.S.-made televisions to those produced in Korea, Japan, or Germany. Similarly, a German consumer in Berlin may be comparing the very same brands, but now the German brand is the home country brand.

Suppose you are Japanese and you are in the market for a mountain bike. If you are Japanese, you are a member of a collectivist culture that values cooperation, collectivism, and teamwork. You can find Japanese mountain bikes and American import mountain bikes. After you do some research, you find that some Japanese bikes are better than some of the American bikes, and that some of the American bikes are better than some of the Japanese bikes. What bike will you buy: a superior Japanese one, a superior American one, a lesser Japanese bike, or a lesser U.S. bike?

Now, let's assume that you are an American looking for that mountain bike. Americans are nurtured in an individualistic culture, so you value competition, self-reliance, and being distinctive. You will find the same marketscape: supe-

rior Japanese bikes, lesser Japanese bikes, superior American bikes, and lesser American bikes. Which mountain bike will you buy?

These questions are vital ones for global marketers because the ways consumers make decisions about products with foreign country origins have important implications about the marketing strategies a global marketer should use to gain competitive advantage in each of the countries where its products are sold.

Two researchers[6] investigated the exact situations we have just posed for you: Japanese consumers considering superior and lesser Japanese and American mountain bike brands and American consumers considering superior and lesser American and Japanese mountain bike brands. Using various techniques including regression analysis, they found that Japanese consumers favored Japanese-made products regardless of superiority. In other words, they always chose their own country's brand. American consumers, on the other hand, chose the superior brand, regardless of the country of origin. The researchers concluded that any global marketer must be aware of the strong home country product favoritism they will face in countries where the culture is collectivist. In these markets, the global marketer may want to

(box continues)

downplay its foreign country status. Similarly, a global marketer competing in a country where the culture is individualistic must demonstrate superior product performance even if it is the marketer's home country. The researchers caution

that "Buy American" slogans issued by U.S. marketers at U.S. consumers probably have not worked for lesser-quality products. But "Buy Japanese" seems to work quite well in Japan regardless of the quality of the Japanese products.

that illustrates how regression analysis was used to assess the success of the slogan "Buy American."

Bivariate regression analysis treats only dependent–independent pairs, and it would take a great many bivariate regression analyses to account for possible relevant dependent–independent pairs of variables in a survey. Fortunately, there is no need to perform a great many bivariate regressions, as there is a much better tool called multiple regression analysis, the last analysis technique described in this textbook. While hearing that you have only one more statistical technique to learn in this textbook, you should be aware that there are a number of statistical techniques that are beyond the scope of this textbook. A market researcher and author of a book on these techniques is Dr. Ronald Tatham, who is also the CEO of Burke Marketing Research, Inc., a world leader in marketing research. You can meet Dr. Tatham in Marketing Research Insight 19.4.

Multiple Regression Analysis Described

Multiple regression means that you have more than one independent variable to predict a single dependent variable.

Multiple regression analysis is an expansion of bivariate regression analysis in that more than one independent variable is used in the regression equation. The addition of independent variables complicates the conceptualization by adding more dimensions or axes to the regression situation. But it makes the regression model more realistic because predictions normally depend on multiple factors, not just one.

Basic Assumptions in Multiple Regression Consider our example with the number of salespeople as the independent variable and territory sales as the dependent variable. A second independent variable such as advertising levels can be added to the equation (Figure 19.7). You will note that the advertising dimension (x_2) is included

MARKETING RESEARCH
INSIGHT
19.4

Meet a Marketing Researcher ◄

Meet Ronald L. Tatham, Ph.D, Chief Executive Officer, Burke, Inc.

Dr. Ronald Tatham began his career at Burke in 1976. He has been chairman/CEO since 1989. Before joining Burke, Ron was a professor on the Graduate Business Faculty of Arizona State University and has taught at the University of Cincinnati and Kent State University. He also consulted with several organizations, including advertising agencies, retailers, as well as consumer and industrial good manufacturers and service providers. Ron holds a B.B.A. degree from the University of Texas at Austin, an M.B.A. from Texas Tech University, and a Ph.D. from the University of Alabama. He is coauthor of *Multivariate Data Analysis* (MacMillan, 4th edition, 1994). His research papers have appeared in several publications,

including the *Journal of Marketing Research*, the *Journal of Market Research Society*, *Business Horizons*, and *Management Science*. His most recent article is "Product Design and the Pricing Decision: A Sequential Approach," *Journal of the Market Research Society*, January 1995 (with Jeff Miller and Vidyut Vashi). He is a member of the Marketing Research Advisory Board at the University of Georgia and the MSMR Advisory Board at the University of Texas at Arlington. He is also active in several professional organizations and has presented over 200 seminars and papers before professional groups. His most recent teaching assignment was a class on international research at the University of Thailand.

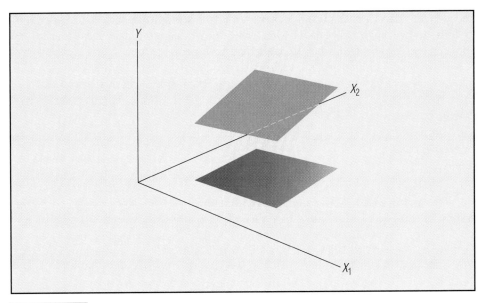

Figure **19.7** **With Multiple Regression, the Line Becomes a Plane**

at a right angle to the axis representing the number of salespeople (x_1), which creates a three-dimensional display. At the same time, the addition of a second variable turns the regression line into a regression plane. A **regression plane** is the shape of the dependent variable in multiple regression analysis. If other independent variables are added to the regression analysis, it would be necessary to envision each one as a new and separate axis existing at right angles to all other axes. Obviously, it is impossible to draw more than three dimensions at right angles. In fact, it is difficult to even conceive of a multiple-dimension diagram, but the assumptions of multiple regression analysis require this conceptualization.

With multiple regression, you work with a regression plane rather than a line.

Everything about multiple regression is essentially equivalent to bivariate regression except you are working with more than one independent variable. The terminology is slightly different in places, and some statistics are modified to take into account the multiple aspect, but for the most part, concepts in multiple regression are analogous to those in the simple bivariate case. We note these similarities in our description of multiple regression.

A multiple regression equation has two or more independent variables (x's).

The regression equation in multiple regression has the following form:

Multiple regression equation $\quad y = a + b_1x_1 + b_2x_2 + b_3x_3 + \ldots + b_mx_m$

where

y = the dependent, or predicted, variable

x_i = independent variable i

a = the intercept

b_i = the slope for independent variable i

m = the number of independent variables in the equation

As you can see, the addition of other independent variables has done nothing more than to add b_ix_i's to the equation. We still have retained the basic $y = a + bx$ straight-line formula, except now we have multiple x variables, and each one is added to the equation, changing y by its individual slope. The inclusion of each independent variable in this manner preserves the straight-line assumptions of multiple regression analysis. This is sometimes known as **additivity** because each new independent variable is added on to the regression equation.

Let's look at a multiple regression analysis result so you can better understand the multiple regression equation. Here is a possible result using our Lexus example.

Lexus purchase intention multiple regression equation example

$$
\text{Intention to purchase a Lexus} = 2 \\
+ 1.0 \times \text{attitude toward Lexus (1–5 scale)} \\
- .5 \times \text{negative word of mouth (1–5 scale)} \\
+ 1.0 \times \text{income level (1–10 scale)}
$$

This multiple regression equation says that you can predict a consumer's intention to buy a Lexus level if you know three variables: (1) attitude toward Lexus, (2) friends' negative recommendations or other negative comments about Lexus, and (3) income level using a scale with 10 income grades. Furthermore, we can see the impact of each of these variables on Lexus purchase intentions. Here is how to interpret the equation. First, the average person has a "2" intention level, or some small propensity to want to buy a Lexus. Attitude toward Lexus is measured on a 1–5 scale, and with each attitude scale point, intention goes up 1 point. That is, an individual with a strong positive attitude of "5" will have a greater intention than one with a strong negative attitude of "1." With friends' objections to the Lexus (negative word of mouth) such as "A Lexus is overpriced," the intention decreases by .5 for each level on the 5-point scale. Finally, the intention increases by 1 with each increasing income grade.

Here is a numerical example for a potential Lexus buyer whose attitude is 4, negative word of mouth is 3, and income is 5.

Calculation of Lexus purchase intention using the multiple regression equation

$$
\text{Intention to purchase a Lexus} = 2 \\
+ 1.0 \times 4 \\
- .5 \times 3 \\
+ 1.0 \times 5 \\
= 9.5
$$

Multiple *R* indicates how well the independent variables can predict the dependent variable in multiple regression.

Multiple regression is a very powerful tool, because it tells us which factors affect the dependent variable, which way (the sign) each factor influences the dependent variable, and how much (the size of b_i) each factor influences it.

Just as was the case in bivariate regression analysis in which we used the correlation between *y* and *x*, it is possible to inspect the strength of the linear relationship between the independent variables and the dependent variable with multiple regression. Multiple *R*, also called the **coefficient of determination**, is a handy measure of the strength of the overall linear relationship. Just as was the case in bivariate regression analysis, the multiple regression analysis model assumes that a straight-line (plane) relationship exists among the variables. Multiple *R* ranges from 0 to +1.0 and represents the amount of the dependent variable "explained," or accounted for, by the combined independent variables. High multiple *R* values indicate that the regression plane applies well to the scatter of points, whereas low values signal that the straight-line model does not apply well. At the same time, a multiple regression result is an estimate of the population multiple regression equation, and, just as was the case with other estimated population parameters, it is necessary to test for statistical significance.

Multiple *R* is like a lead indicator of the multiple regression analysis findings. As you will see soon, it is one of the first pieces of information provided in a multiple regression output. Many researchers mentally convert the multiple *R* into a per-

centage. For example, a multiple R of .75 means that the regression findings will explain 75 percent of the dependent variable. The greater the explanatory power of the multiple regression finding, the better and more useful it is for the researcher.

Let us issue a caution before we show you how to run a multiple regression analysis using SPSS. The **independence assumption** stipulates that the independent variables must be statistically independent and uncorrelated with one another. The independence assumption is portrayed by the right-angle alignment of each additional independent variable in Figure 19.7. The presence of moderate or stronger correlations among the independent variables is termed **multicollinearity** and will violate the independence assumption of multiple regression analysis results when it occurs.[7] It is up to the researcher to test for and remove multicollinearity if it is present.

> With multiple regression, the independent variables should have low correlations with one another.

There are statistics issued to identify this problem. One commonly used statistic is the **variance inflation factor** (**VIF**). The VIF is a single number, and a rule of thumb is that as long as VIF is less than 10, multicollinearity is not a concern. With a VIF of 10 or more associated with any independent variable in the multiple regression equation, it is prudent to remove that variable from consideration or to otherwise reconstitute the set of independent variables. In other words, when examining the output of any multiple regression, the researcher should inspect the VIF number associated with each independent variable that is retained in the final multiple regression equation by the procedure. If the VIF is greater than 10, the researcher should remove that variable from the independent variable set and rerun the multiple regression. This iterative process is used until only independent variables that are statistically significant and that have acceptable VIFs are in the final multiple regression equation. SPSS calculates all VIFs.

> Multicollinearity can be assessed and eliminated in multiple regression with the VIF statistic.

RETURN TO   *Your Integrated Case*

The Hobbit's Choice Restaurant Survey: How to Run and Interpret Multiple Regression Analysis on SPSS

Running multiple regression is almost identical to performing simple bivariate regression with SPSS. The only difference is that you will select more than one independent variable for the analysis. Let's think about a general conceptual model that might predict how much people spend on restaurants per month. We already know from our bivariate regression analysis work with The Hobbit's Choice Restaurant data set that income predicts this dependent variable. Another predictor could be family size as larger families will order more entrées because there are more family members. So, we will add this independent variable. A third independent variable could be preferences. People who prefer an elegant décor surely will pay for this atmosphere as elegant décors are typically found in the most expensive restaurants. To summarize, we have determined our conceptual model: The average amount paid at restaurants per month may be predicted by (1) household income level, (2) family size, and (3) preference for restaurants with elegant décors.

Just as with bivariate regression, the ANALYZE-REGRESSION-LINEAR command sequence is used to run a multiple regression analysis, and the variable, dollars spent in restaurants per month, is selected as the dependent variable, while the other three are specified as the independent variables. You will find this annotated SPSS clickstream in Figure 19.8.

As the computer output in Figure 19.9 shows, the Adjusted R Square value (Model Summary table) indicating the strength of relationship between the independent variables and the dependent variable is .749, signifying that there is some linear relationship present. Next, the printout reveals that the ANOVA F is significant, signaling that the null hypothesis of no linear relationship is rejected, and it is justifiable to use a straight-line relationship to model the variables in this case.

Just as we did with bivariate regression, it is necessary in multiple regression analysis to test for statistical significance of the b_i's (betas) determined for the independent variables. Once again, you must determine whether sampling error is influencing the results and giving a false reading. You should recall that this test is a test for significance from zero (the null hypothesis) and is achieved through the use of separate t tests for each b_i. The SPSS output in Figure 19.9 indicates the levels of statistical significance. In this particular example, it is apparent the recoded income level and the preference for an elegant dining décor are significant as both have significance levels of .000. The constant (a) also is significant as it, too, has a significance level of .000. However, the size of family independent variable

The SPSS ANALYZE-REGRESSION-LINEAR command is used to run multiple regression.

With multiple regression, look at the significance level of each calculated beta.

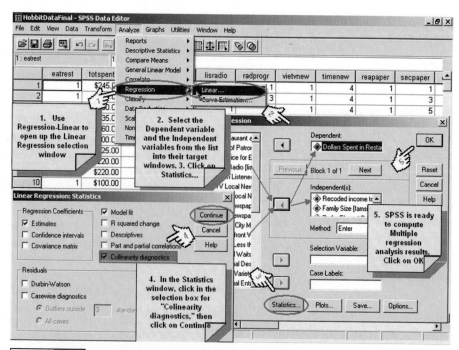

Figure **19.8**   **The SPSS Clickstream for Multiple Regression Analysis**

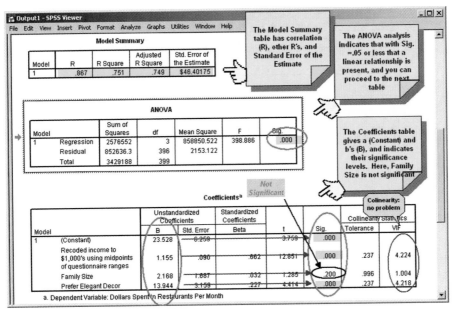

Figure **19.9** **SPSS Output for Multiple Regression Analysis**

is not significant because its significance level is .200 and, therefore, above our standard cutoff value of .05.

What do you do with the mixed significance results we have just found in our dollars spent on restaurants per month multiple regression example? Before we answer this question, you should be aware that this mixed result is very likely, so how to handle it is vital to your understanding of how to perform multiple regression analysis successfully. Here is the answer: It is standard practice in multiple regression analysis to systematically eliminate those independent variables that are shown to be insignificant through a process called "trimming." You then rerun the trimmed model and inspect the significance levels again. This series of eliminations or iterations helps to achieve the simplest model by eliminating the nonsignificant independent variables. The trimmed multiple regression model with all significant independent variables is found in Figure 19.10. Notice that the VIF diagnostics were not examined because they were examined on the untrimmed SPSS output and found to be acceptable.

This additional run enables the marketing researcher to think in terms of fewer dimensions within which the dependent variable relationship operates. Generally, successive iterations sometimes cause the Adjusted R to decrease somewhat, and it is advisable to scrutinize this value after each run. You can see that the new Adjusted R is still .749, so in our example, there has been no decrease. Iterations will also cause the beta values and the intercept value to shift slightly; consequently, it is necessary to inspect all significance levels of the betas once again. Through a series of iterations, the marketing researcher finally arrives at the final regression equation expressing the salient independent variables and their linear relationships with the dependent variable. A concise predictive model has been found.

Using Results to Make a Prediction

The use of a multiple regression result is identical in concept to the application of a bivariate regression result—that is, it relies on an analysis of residuals. Remember, we began this chapter with a description of residuals and indicated that residuals analysis is a way to determine the goodness of a prediction. Ultimately, the marketing researcher wishes to

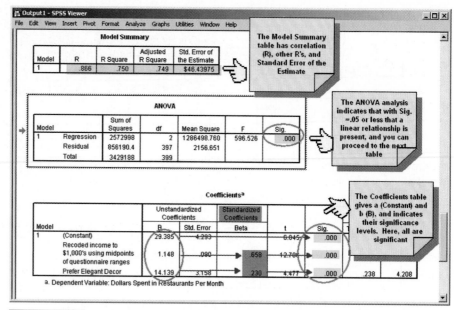

predict the dependent variable based on assumed or known values of the independent variables that are found to have significant relationships within the multiple regression equation. The standard error of the estimate is provided on all regression analysis programs, and it is possible to apply this value to forecast the ranges in which the dependent variable will fall, given levels of the independent variables.

Making a prediction with multiple regression is identical to making one with bivariate regression except you use the multiple regression equation. For a numerical example, let us assume that we are interested in upscale restaurant patrons so we can give Jeff Dean an estimate of how much they spend monthly on restaurants. We'll specify an upscale restaurant patron as someone with household income of $100K and who very strongly prefers an elegant décor. To "very strongly prefer" means a "5" on the 5-point scale of preferences for various restaurant features.

Using our SPSS trimmed multiple regression findings, we can predict the amount of dollars spent on restaurants each month by upscale consumers. The calculations follow. Remember the constant and betas are from the trimmed multiple regression output in Figure 19.10.

Here is an example of a prediction using multiple regression.

Calculation of monthly restaurant purchases predicted with an income level of $100,000 and preference for elegant décor of "5"	$$\begin{aligned} y &= a + b_1x_1 + b_2x_2 \\ &= \$29.39 + \$1.15 \times 100 + \$14.14 \times 5 \\ &= \$29.39 + \$115{,}000 \times \$70.70 \\ &= \$215.09 \end{aligned}$$

The calculated prediction is about $232; however, we must take into consideration the sample error and variability of the data with a confidence interval, that is, the predicted dollars spent on restaurants per month ±1.96 times the standard error of the estimate.

Calculation of 95% confidence interval for a prediction based on multiple regression findings with The Hobbit's Choice Restaurant survey	Predicted y ± 1.96 × standard error of the estimate $215.09 ± 1.96 × $46.45 $215.09 ± 91.04 $124.05 to $306.13

The interpretation would be that those individuals with a household income before taxes of $100,000 and who very strongly prefer an elegant décor when they dine can be expected to spend between about $124 and $306 monthly on restaurants, averaging about $215. Again, the confidence interval range is quite large, but it is perfectly reflective of the variability in the data and in no way a flaw in the multiple regression analysis.

Special Uses of Multiple Regression Analysis

There are a number of special uses and considerations to keep in mind when running multiple regression analysis. These include using a "dummy" independent variable, using standardized betas to compare the importance of independent variables, and using multiple regression as a screening device.

Using a "Dummy" Independent Variable A **dummy independent variable** is defined as one that is scaled with a nominal 0-versus-1 coding scheme. The 0-versus-1 code is traditional, but any two adjacent numbers could be used, such as 1-versus-2. The scaling assumptions that underlie multiple regression analysis require that the independent and dependent variables both be at least interval scaled. However, there are instances in which a marketing researcher may want to use an independent variable that does not embody interval-scaling assumptions. It is not unusual, for instance, for the marketing researcher to wish to use a dichotomous or two-level variable, such as gender, as an independent variable, in a multiple regression problem. For instance, a researcher may want to use gender coded as 0 for male and 1 for female as an independent variable. Or you might have a buyer–nonbuyer dummy variable that you want to use as an independent variable. In these instances, it is usually permissible to go ahead and slightly violate the assumption of metric scaling for the independent variable to come up with a result that is in some degree interpretable.

> The interval-at-minimum scaling assumption requirement of multiple regression may be relaxed by use of a dummy variable.

Using Standardized Betas to Compare the Importance of Independent Variables
Regardless of the application intentions of the marketing researcher, it is usually of interest to the marketing researcher to determine the relative importance of the independent variables in the multiple regression result. Because independent variables are often measured with different units, it is wrong to make direct comparisons between the calculated betas. For example, it is improper to directly compare the b coefficient for family size to another for money spent per month on personal grooming because the units of measurement are so different (people versus dollars). The most common approach is to standardize the independent variables through a quick operation that involves dividing the difference between each independent variable value and its mean by the standard deviation of that independent variable. This results in what is called the **standardized beta coefficient**. In other words, standardization translates each independent value into the number of standard deviations away from its own mean. Essentially, this procedure transforms these variables into a set of values with a mean of zero and a standard deviation equal to 1.0.

When they are standardized, direct comparisons may be made between the resulting betas. The larger the absolute value of a standardized beta coefficient, the more relative importance it assumes in predicting the dependent variable. SPSS and most other statistical programs provide the standardized betas automatically. If you review the SPSS output in Figure 19.10, you will find the standardized values under the column designated as "Standardized Coefficients." It is important to note that this operation has no effect on the final multiple regression result. Its only function is to allow direct comparisons of the relative impact of the significant independent variables on the dependent variable. As an example, if you look at the "Standardized

> The researcher can compare standardized beta coefficients' sizes directly, but comparing unstandardized betas is like comparing apples and oranges.

> Standardized betas indicate the relative importance of alternative independent variables.

Coefficients" reported in our Hobbit's Choice Restaurant regression printout (Figure 19.10), you will see that the income level is the more important variable (.658), whereas preference for an elegant restaurant décor is much less important (.230). We have highlighted these numbers with magenta color so you can identify them easily.

Using Multiple Regression as a Screening Device Another application of multiple regression analysis is as a screening or identifying device. That is, the marketing researcher may be faced with a large number and variety of prospective independent variables, and he or she may use multiple regression as a **screening device** or a way of spotting the salient (statistically significant) independent variables for the dependent variable at hand. In this instance, the intent is not to determine some sort of a prediction of the dependent variable; rather, it may be to search for clues as to what factors help the researcher understand the behavior of this particular variable. For instance, the researcher might be seeking market segmentation bases and could use regression to spot which demographic variables are related to the consumer behavior variable under study. We have prepared Marketing Research Insight 19.5 that will show you how multiple regression can be used as a screening device in developing countries for global marketers to refine their market segmentation approaches.

> Multiple regression is sometimes used to help a marketer apply market segmentation.

STEPWISE MULTIPLE REGRESSION

When the researcher is using multiple regression as a screening tool or he or she is otherwise faced with a large number of independent variables in the conceptual model that are to be tested by multiple regression, it can become tedious to narrow down the independent variables by trimming. Fortunately, there is a type of multiple regression that does the trimming operation automatically, and this is called stepwise multiple regression.

> Stepwise regression is useful if a researcher has many independent variables and wants to narrow the set down to a smaller number of statistically significant variables.

With **stepwise multiple regression**, the one independent variable that is statistically significant and explains the most variance in the dependent variable is determined, and it is entered into the multiple regression equation. Then the statistically significant independent variable that contributes most to explaining the remaining unexplained variance in the dependent variable is determined and entered. This process is continued until all statistically significant independent variables have been entered into the multiple regression equation.[8] In other words, all of the insignificant independent variables are eliminated from the final multiple regression equation based on the level of significance stipulated by the researcher in the multiple regression options. The final output contains only statistically significant independent variables. Stepwise regression is used by researchers when they are confronted with a large number of competing independent variables and they do want to narrow down the analysis to a set of statistically significant independent variables in a single regression analysis. With stepwise multiple regression, there is no need to trim and rerun the regression analysis because SPSS does the trimming automatically.

SPSS

How to Do Stepwise Multiple Regression with SPSS

A researcher executes stepwise multiple regression by using the ANALYZE-REGRESSION-LINEAR command sequence precisely as was described for multiple regression. The dependent variable and many independent variables are clicked into their respective windows as before. To direct SPSS to perform stepwise multiple regression, one uses the "Method" selection menu to select "Stepwise." The findings will be the same as those arrived at by a researcher who uses iterative trimmed multiple regressions. Of course, with stepwise multiple regression output, there will be

▶ **A Global Perspective**

MARKETING RESEARCH
INSIGHT
19.5

Multiple Regression Screening Analysis Leads to an Understanding of Women Consumers in Developing Markets

Global marketers of household and other family-oriented products are keenly interested in shifts in the workforce in developing countries. As the workforce of a country moves into higher-paying jobs, discretionary income of families increases. Similarly, with these shifts, consumers often find they have less time and they become more open to time-saving goods and services being marketed by foreign corporations in their countries. One of the most significant shifts that can happen in a developing country workforce is the large-scale movement of women into the job market. When a wife takes on employment, household income can increase substantially, and it has profound implications for the products and services that household will purchase with this new income level.

Asia is a region undergoing many economic transitions, and researchers[9] chose to study five Asian countries—Korea, Thailand, Sri Lanka, Indonesia, and the Philippines—in an attempt to understand what factors are key to women from these Asian countries entering into the labor market. A great many factors may combine to foster the movement of Asian women into the workforce, and regression analysis can be used as a screening device to narrow down the many possible factors to a set of those that are significantly related to these shifts.

The researchers speculated in their general conceptual model that a number of possible independent variables may determine whether a woman is employed outside the home or whether she remains at home. These variables included wife's age, husband's age, total number of births, number of young children, total number of children living at home, rural or urban residence, wife's illiteracy, husband's illiteracy, and level of education of the wife and of the husband (separate dummy variables of primary, middle, high school, or college education levels). A multiple regression screening analysis was conducted separately for each of the five Asian countries. Table 19.4 lists the independent variables that were found to be statistically significant for at least three of the five Asian countries. A plus sign means the beta coefficient was positive, whereas a minus sign means that the beta coefficient was found to be negative.

Global marketers targeting Asian countries should interpret these findings in the following way. Their target markets should be older women who are past the child-bearing stage and who definitely do not have young children. Rural or urban location depends on the country. When the wife graduates from college or a university, she definitely will enter the workforce. Also, since these working wives have college degrees, global marketers can expect them to be sophisticated consumers. The researchers speculate that if the husband has a high school education, he earns a higher income, and the wife does not need to work, so this group is a completely different kind of target market.

Table **19.4** **Results of a Multiple Regression Screening Analysis on Determinants of Women Entering the Workforce in Asian Countries**

FACTOR	KOREA	THAILAND	SRI LANKA	INDONESIA	PHILIPPINES
Wife's age	+	+	+	+	+
Births	+		+		+
Children at home	−		−	−	−
Young children	−	−	−	−	−
Rural location	−	−	+	−	+
Wife's college education	+	+	+	+	+
Husband's high school education	−		−		−

+ = positive relationship, − = negative relationship, blank = not significant

information on those independent variables that are taken out of the multiple regression equation based on nonsignificance, and, if the researcher wishes, SPSS stepwise multiple regression will also take into account the VIF statistic to assure that multicollinearity is not an issue.

We do not have screenshots of stepwise multiple regression as this technique is quite advanced. Please read our "Final Comments on Multiple Regression Analysis" at the end of this chapter for an explanation.

TWO WARNINGS REGARDING REGRESSION ANALYSIS

Regression is a statistical tool, not a cause-and-effect statement.

Before leaving our description of multiple regression analysis, we must issue a warning about your interpretation of regression. We all have a natural tendency to think in terms of causes and effects, and regression analysis invites us to think in terms of a dependent variable's resulting or being caused by an independent variable's actions. This line of thinking is absolutely incorrect: Regression analysis is nothing more than a statistical tool that assumes a linear relationship between two variables. It springs from correlation analysis, which is, as you will recall, a measure of the linear association and not the causal relationship between two variables. Consequently, even though two variables, such as sales and advertising, are logically connected, a regression analysis does not permit the marketing researcher to formulate cause-and-effect statements.

The second warning we have is that you should not apply regression analysis to predict outside of the boundaries of the data used to develop your regression model. That is, you may use the regression model to interpolate within the boundaries set by the range (lowest value to highest value) of your independent variable, but if you use it to predict for independent values outside those limits, you have moved into an area that is not accounted for by the raw data used to compute your regression line. For this reason, you are not assured that the regression equation findings are valid. For example, it would not be correct to use our income-dollars spent on restaurants regression equation findings on individuals who are wealthy and have annual incomes in the millions of dollars because these individuals were not represented in The Hobbit's Choice Restaurant survey.

FINAL COMMENTS ON MULTIPLE REGRESSION ANALYSIS

There is a great deal more to multiple regression analysis but it is beyond the scope of this textbook to delve deeper into this topic. The coverage in this chapter introduces you to regression analysis, and it provides you with enough information about it to run uncomplicated regression analyses on SPSS, identify the relevant aspects of the SPSS output, and to interpret the findings. As you will see when you work with the SPSS regression analysis procedures, we have only scratched the surface of this topic. There are many more options, statistics, and considerations involved. In fact, there is so much material that whole textbooks on regression exist. Our purpose has been to teach you the basic concepts and to help you interpret the statistics associated with these concepts as you encounter them in statistical analysis program output. Our descriptions are merely an introduction to multiple regression analysis to help you comprehend the basic notions, common uses, and interpretations involved with this predictive technique.[10]

Despite our simple treatment of it, we fully realize that even simplified regression analysis is very complicated and difficult to learn and that we have showered you with a great many regression statistical terms and concepts in this chapter.

Table 19.5 Regression Analysis Concepts

CONCEPT	EXPLANATION
Regression analysis	A predictive model using the straight-line relationship of $y = a + bx$
Intercept	The constant, or a, in the straight-line relationship that is the value of y when $x = 0$
Slope	The b, or the amount of change in y for a 1-unit change in x
Dependent variable	The y variable that is being predicted by the x or independent variable
Independent variable(s)	The x variable or variables that are used in the straight-line equation to predict y
Least squares criterion	A statistical procedure that assures that the computed regression equation is the best one possible
R Square	A number ranging from 0 to 1.0 that reveals how well the straight-line model fits the scatter of points; the higher, the better
Standard error of the estimate	A value that is used to make a prediction at the (e.g.) 95% level of confidence with the formula $y \pm z$ times s_e
Multiple regression analysis	A powerful form of regression where more than one x variable is in the regression equation
Additivity	A statistical assumption that allows the use of more than one x variable in a multiple regression equation: $y = a + b_1 x_1 + b_2 x_2 \ldots + b_m x_m$
Independence assumption	A statistical requirement that when more than one x variable is used, no pair of x variables has a high correlation
Multiple R	Also called the coefficient of determination, a number that ranges from 0 to 1.0 that indicates the strength of the overall linear relationship in a multiple regression; the higher, the better
Multicollinearity	The term used to denote a violation of the independence assumption that causes regression results to be in error
Variance inflation factor (VIF)	A statistical value that identifies what x variable(s) contribute to multicollinearity and should be removed from the analysis to eliminate multicollinearity. Any variable with a VIF of 10 or greater should be removed
Trimming	Removing an x variable in multiple regression because it is not statistically significant, rerunning the regression, and repeating until all remaining x variables are significant
Standardized beta coefficients	Slopes (b values) that are normalized so they can be compared directly to determine their relative importance in y's prediction
Dummy independent variable	Use of an x variable that has a 0, 1, or similar coding, used sparingly when nominal variables must be in the independent variables set
Stepwise multiple regression	A specialized multiple regression that is appropriate when there is a large number of x variables that need to be trimmed down to a small, significant set and the researcher wishes the statistical program to do this automatically

Seasoned researchers are intimately knowledgeable with them and very comfortable in using them. However, as a student encountering them for the first time, you undoubtedly feel very intimidated. Although we may not be able to reduce your anxiety, we have created Table 19.5 that lists all of the regression analysis concepts we have described in this chapter, and it provides an explanation of each one. At least, you will not need to search through the chapter to find these concepts when you are trying to learn or use them.

SUMMARY

Predictive analyses are methods used to forecast the level of a variable such as sales. Model building and extrapolation are two general options available to market researchers. In either case, it is important to assess the goodness of the prediction. This assessment is typically performed by comparing the predictions against the actual data with procedures called residuals analyses.

Market researchers use regression analysis to make predictions. The basis of this technique is an assumed straight-line relationship existing between the variables. With bivariate regression, one independent variable, x, is used to predict the dependent variable, y, using the straight-line formula of $y = a + bx$. A high R^2 and a statistically significant slope indicate that the linear model is a good fit. With multiple regression, the underlying conceptual model specifies that several independent variables are to be used, and it is necessary to determine which ones are significant. By systematically eliminating the nonsignificant independent variables in an iterative manner, a process called "trimming," a researcher will ultimately derive a set of significant independent variables that yields a significant predictive model. The standard error of the estimate is used to compute a confidence interval range for a regression prediction.

Seasoned researchers may opt to use stepwise multiple regression if faced with a large number of candidate independent variables such as several demographic, lifestyle, and buyer behavior characteristics. With stepwise multiple regression, independent variables are entered into the multiple regression equation containing only statistically significant independent variables.

KEY TERMS

Prediction (p. 551)
Extrapolation (p. 551)
Predictive model (p. 551)
Analysis of residuals (p. 552)
Bivariate regression analysis (p. 553)
Intercept (p. 553)
Slope (p. 553)
Dependent variable (p. 554)
Independent variable (p. 554)
Least squares criterion (p. 555)
Standard error of the estimate (p. 558)
General conceptual model (p. 562)

Multiple regression analysis (p. 564)
Regression plane (p. 565)
Additivity (p. 566)
Coefficient of determination (p. 566)
Independence assumption (p. 567)
Multicollinearity (p. 567)
Variance inflation factor (VIF) (p. 567)
Dummy independent variable (p. 571)
Standardized beta coefficient (p. 571)
Screening device (p. 572)
Stepwise multiple regression (p. 572)

REVIEW QUESTIONS/APPLICATIONS

1. Construct and explain a reasonably simple predictive model for each of the following cases:
   a. What is the relationship between gasoline prices and distance traveled for family automobile touring vacations?
   b. How do hurricane-force warnings relate to purchases of flashlight batteries in the expected landfall area?
   c. What do florists do with regard to inventory of flowers for the week prior to and the week following Mother's Day?
2. Indicate what the scatter diagram and probable regression line would look like for two variables that are correlated in each of the following ways (in each instance, assume a negative intercept): (a) −0.89 (b) +0.48 and (c) −0.10.
3. Circle K runs a contest, inviting customers to fill out a registration card. In exchange, they are eligible for a grand prize drawing of a trip to Alaska. The card asks for the customer's age, education, gender, estimated weekly purchases (in dollars) at the Circle K, and approximate distance the Circle K is from his or her home. Identify each of the following if a multiple regression analysis were to be performed: (a) independent variable, (b) dependent variable, (c) dummy variable.
4. Explain what is meant by the independence assumption in multiple regression. How can you examine your data for independence, and what statistic is issued by most statistical analysis programs? How is this statistic interpreted? That is,

what would indicate the presence of multicollinearity, and what would you do to eliminate it?

5. What is multiple regression? Specifically, what is "multiple" about it, and how does the formula for multiple regression appear? In your indication of the formula, identify the various terms and also indicate the signs (positive or negative) that they may take on.

6. If one uses the "Enter" method for multiple regression analysis, what statistics on an SPSS output should be examined to assess the result? Indicate how you would determine each of the following:
   a. Variance explained in the dependent variable by the independent variables.
   b. Statistical significance of each of the independent variables.
   c. Relative importance of the independent variables in predicting the dependent variable.

7. Explain what is meant by the notion of "trimming" a multiple regression result. Use the following example to illustrate your understanding of this concept.

   A bicycle manufacturer maintains records over 20 years of the following: retail price in dollars, cooperative advertising amount in dollars, competitors' average retail price in dollars, number of retail locations selling the bicycle manufacturer's brand, and whether or not the winner of the Tour de France was riding the manufacturer's brand (coded as a dummy variable where 0 = no, and 1 = yes).

   The initial multiple regression result determines the following:

Variable	Significance Level
Average retail price in dollars	.001
Cooperative advertising amount in dollars	.202
Competitors' average retail price in dollars	.028
Number of retail locations	.591
Tour de France	.032

   Using the "Enter" method, what would be the trimming steps you would expect to undertake to identify the significant multiple regression result? Explain your reasoning.

8. Using the bicycle example in question 7, what do you expect would be the elimination of variables sequence using stepwise multiple regression? Explain your reasoning with respect to the operation of this technique.

9. Using SPSS graphical capabilities, diagram the regression plane for the following variables.

Number of Gallons of Gasoline Used per Week	Miles Computed for Work per Week	Number of Riders in Carpool
5	50	4
10	125	3
15	175	2
20	250	0
25	300	0

10. The Maximum Amount is a company that specializes in making fashionable clothes in large sizes for large people. Among its customers are Sinbad and Shaquille O'Neal. A survey was performed for the Maximum Amount, and a regression analysis was run on some of the data. Of interest in this analysis was the possible relationship between self-esteem (dependent variable) and

number of Maximum Amount articles purchased last year (independent variables). Self-esteem was measured on a 7-point scale in which 1 signifies very low and 7 indicates very high self-esteem. Following are some items that have been taken from the output.

Pearson product moment correlation = +0.63
Intercept = 3.5
Slope = +0.2
Standard error = 1.5

All statistical tests are significant at the 0.01 level or less. What is the correct interpretation of these findings?

11. Wayne LaTorte is a safety engineer who works for the U.S. Postal Service. For most of his life, Wayne has been fascinated by UFOs. He has kept records of UFO sightings in the desert areas of Arizona, California, and New Mexico over the past 15 years and he has correlated them with earthquake tremors. A fellow engineer suggests that Wayne use regression analysis as a means of determining the relationship. Wayne does this and finds a "constant" of 30 separate earth tremor events and a slope of 5 events per UFO sighting. Wayne then writes an article for the *UFO Observer*, claiming that earthquakes are largely caused by the subsonic vibrations emitted by UFOs as they enter Earth's atmosphere. What is your reaction to Wayne's article?

INTERACTIVE LEARNING

Visit the Web site at www.prenhall.com/burnsbush. For this chapter, work through the Self-Study Quizzes, and get instant feedback on whether you need additional studying. On the Web site, you can review the chapter outlines and case information for Chapter 19.

CASE 19.1 Segmentation Associates, Inc.

Segmentation Associates, Inc. is a marketing research company that specializes in market segmentation studies. It has access to large and detailed databases on demographics, lifestyles, asset ownership, consumer values, and a number of other consumer descriptors. It has developed a reputation for reducing these large databases into findings that are managerially relevant to its clients. That is, Segmentation Associates is known for its ability to translate its findings into market segmentation variables for its clients to use in their marketing strategies.

In the past year, Segmentation Associates has conducted a great many market segmentation studies for diverse clients such as Ford Motor Company, Microsoft, Allstate Insurance, Delta Airlines, American Express, Snackwells, and Disney World. The company has agreed to provide disguised findings of some of its work. In the following table segmentation variables are identified, and each of three different types of automobile buyer types is identified. For each segmentation variable, Segmentation Associates has provided the results of its stepwise multiple regression findings. The values are the standardized beta coefficients of those segmentation variables found to be statistically significant. Where no value appears, that regression coefficient was not statically significant.

Segmentation Variable	Compact Automobile Buyer	Sports Car Buyer	Luxury Automobile Buyer
Demographics			
Age	−.28	−.15	+.59
Education	−.12	+.38	
Family Size	+.39	−.35	
Income	−.15	+.25	+.68

Segmentation Variable	Compact Automobile Buyer	Sports Car Buyer	Luxury Automobile Buyer
Lifestyle/Values			
Active		+.59	−.39
American Pride	+.30		+.24
Bargain Hunter	+.45	−.33	
Conservative		−.38	+.54
Cosmopolitan	−.40	+.68	
Embraces Change	−.30	+.65	
Family Values	+.69		+.21
Financially Secure	−.28	+.21	+.52
Optimistic		+.71	+.37

1. What is the underlying conceptual model used by Segmentation Associates that is apparent in these three sets of findings?
2. What are the segmentation variables that distinguish compact automobile buyers and in what ways?
3. What are the segmentation variables that distinguish sports car buyers and in what ways?
4. What are the segmentation variables that distinguish luxury automobile buyers and in what ways?
5. Contrast the segmentation variable classification differences among the three types of automobile buyers.

CASE 19.2   *Your Integrated Case*

This is your integrated case, described on pages 42–43.

The Hobbit's Choice Restaurant Survey Predictive Analysis

Jeff Dean was a very happy camper. He had learned that his dream of The Hobbit's Choice Restaurant could be a reality. Through the research conducted under Cory Rogers's expert supervision and Celeste Brown's SPSS analysis, Jeff knew the approximate size of the upscale restaurant market, and he had a good idea of what features were desired, where it should be located, and even what advertising media to use to promote it. He had all the information he needed to return to his friend, Walker Stripling, the banker, to obtain the financing necessary to design and build The Hobbit's Choice Restaurant.

Jeff called Cory on Friday morning and said, "Cory, I am very excited about everything that your work has found about the good prospects of The Hobbit's Choice. I want to set up a meeting with Walker Stripling next week to pitch it to him for the funding. Can you get me the final report by then?"

Cory was silent for a moment and then he said, "Celeste is doing the final figures and dressing up the tables so we can paste them into the report document. But I think you have forgotten about the last research objective. We still need to address the target market definition with a final set of analyses. I know that Celeste just finished some exams at school, and she has been asking if there is any work she can do over the weekend. I'll give her this task. Why don't you plan on coming over at 11:00 A.M. on Monday? Celeste and I will show you what we have found, and then we can take Celeste to lunch for giving up her weekend."

Your task in Case 19.2 is to take Celeste's role, use The Hobbit's Choice Restaurant SPSS data set, and perform the proper analysis. You will also need to interpret the findings.

1. What is the demographic target market definition for The Hobbit's Choice Restaurant?
2. What is the restaurant spending behavior target market definition for The Hobbit's Choice Restaurant?
3. Develop a general conceptual model of market segmentation for The Hobbit's Choice Restaurant. Test it using multiple regression analysis and interpret your findings for Jeff Dean.

Chapter 20

Preparing and Presenting the Research Results

Practitioner Viewpoint

In school, I didn't understand why I had to study composition and public speaking. I was going to be a scientist, not a novelist or politician. However, even the best research will not drive the appropriate action unless the audience understands the outcomes and implications. Researchers must create a clear, concise presentation of the results. Projects are often complicated, and it is easy to bury the audience in technical discussion. Understand the information your target audience wants and the appropriate depth. Distill your insights into two or three key points—that's all your busy audience will retain. Edit your work for time-pressed managers—understand how to effectively (and objectively) use sound bytes.

Michael A. Lotti
Eastman Kodak Company

Producing the Final Product

The market research for Jeff Dean is finished. Cory Rogers and his team have worked diligently to investigate the market potential for The Hobbit's Choice, and they are ready to prepare their findings and recommendations for presentation to Jeff Dean and Walker Stripling. You might think the bulk of their work is finished, but that is not the case. Now begins the task of sifting through the hundreds of pages of print-outs and other information to determine what to present and then how to present it clearly and effectively. When the members of the team have prepared the written report, they will also need to decide which elements are critical to include in the oral presentation to the client.

Compiling a market research report is a challenging (and sometimes daunting) task. Cory and his team meet to discuss what parts need to be in the report, what content needs to be in each part, what kinds of visuals to include, and what format to follow for headings and subheadings. Then they assign responsibilities to the members of the team and agree on a timetable. When they have a common understanding of what their objectives are and what each team member will do, they are ready to strike out on their individual tasks, meeting frequently to ensure that all tasks will be completed on time and to maintain consistency in their ideas and understandings.

Where We Are:

1. Establish the need for marketing research
2. Define the problem
3. Establish research objectives
4. Determine research design
5. Identify information types and sources
6. Determine methods of accessing data
7. Design data collection forms
8. Determine sample plan and size
9. Collect data
10. Analyze data
11. **Prepare and present the final research report**

The fact that this chapter is the final chapter in the textbook does not indicate that it is less important.[1] On the contrary, it means that communicating the results of your research is the culmination of the entire process. Being able to do so effectively and efficiently is critical to your success. In fact, all of your outstanding data and significant findings and recommendations are meaningless if you cannot communicate them in such a way that the client knows what you have said, understands your meaning, and responds appropriately. You, then, must be able to transfer exactly what is in your mind to the mind of the receiver of your message. The ultimate result of your hard labor is communication with your client. Mr. Lotti's advice in our Practitioner Viewpoint is right on target!

Communicating the results of your research is the culmination of the entire process.

581

The marketing research report is a factual message that transmits research results, vital recommendations, conclusions, and other important information to the client, who in turn bases his or her decision making on the contents of the report.

The **marketing research report** is a factual message that transmits research results, vital recommendations, conclusions, and other important information to the client, who in turn bases his or her decision making on the contents of the report. This chapter deals with the essentials of writing and presenting the marketing research report.

RECOGNIZING THE IMPORTANCE OF THE MARKETING RESEARCH REPORT

Researchers must provide client value in the research report. The marketing research report is the product that represents the efforts of the marketing research team, and it may be the only part of the project that the client will see. If the report is poorly written, riddled with grammatical errors, sloppy or inferior in any way, the quality of the research (including its analysis and information) becomes suspect and its credibility is reduced. If organization and presentation are faulty, the reader may never reach the intended conclusions. The time and effort expended in the research process are wasted if the report does not communicate effectively.

The time and effort expended in the research process are wasted if the report does not communicate effectively.

If, on the other hand, all aspects of the report are done well, the report will not only communicate properly, but it will also serve to build credibility. Marketing research users,[2] as well as marketing research suppliers,[3] agree that reporting the research results is one of the most important aspects of the marketing research process. Many managers will not be involved in any aspect of the research process but will use the report to make business decisions. Effective reporting is essential, and all of the principles of organization, formatting, good writing, and good grammar must be employed.

MARKETING RESEARCH

INSIGHT
20.1

Meet A Marketing Researcher ◀

Michael Lotti Knows the Importance of the Written Report

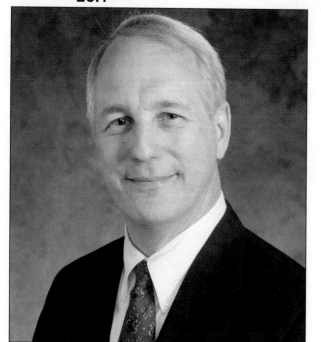

Michael A. Lotti is director, business research, and vice president, corporate marketing, for Eastman Kodak Company. The Business Research unit provides critical insight to management regarding customer needs, behavioral trends, competitive situation, and technology adoption.

Mr. Lotti's involvement with global market research and marketing began in 1980 when he joined Kodak's Asia, Africa, and Australia Region as a market research coordinator. He has had assignments in marketing management, advertising management, market research, advertising research, and manufacturing for both the worldwide and U.S. markets. He led the integrated Marketing Communications program for the Colorwatch brand in which Bill Cosby was the celebrity spokesperson. Mr. Lotti's experience also includes a three-year assignment in Kodak's Tokyo office as the director of business research for the Asia Pacific Region.

Mr. Lotti has degrees in statistics from Western Michigan University and the University of Iowa. He has an M.B.A. in marketing and finance from the University of Rochester. He is active in the American Marketing Association where he has served as vice president of AMA's Marketing Research Division and in executive positions on AMA's board of directors. He is a trustee of the Marketing Science Institute.

ORGANIZING THE WRITTEN REPORT

Marketing research reports are tailored to specific audiences and purposes, and you must consider both in all phases of the research process, including planning the report. Before you begin writing, then, you must answer some questions:

- What message do you want to communicate?
- What is your purpose?
- Who is the audience?
- If there are multiple audiences, who is your primary audience? Your secondary audience?
- What does your audience know?
- What does your audience need to know?
- Are there cultural differences you need to consider?
- What biases or preconceived notions of the audience might serve as barriers to your message?
- What strategies can you employ to overcome these negatives?
- Do demographic and lifestyle variables of your audience affect their perspective of your research?
- What are your audience's interests, values, concerns?

These and other questions must be addressed before you know how to structure your report.

When you are performing this analysis, it is often helpful "to get on the other side of the desk." Assume you are the reader instead of the sender. Doing so will help you see things through the eyes of your audience and increase the success of your communication. This is your opportunity to ask that basic (and very critical) question from the reader's point of view: "What's in it for me?"

> When you are performing this analysis, it is often helpful "to get on the other side of the desk."

Once you have performed these analyses, you need to determine the format of your document. If the organization for which you are conducting the research has specific guidelines for preparing the document, you should follow them. However, if no specific guidelines are provided, there are certain elements that must be considered when you are preparing the report. These elements can be grouped in three sections: front matter, body, and end matter. See Table 20.1 for details.

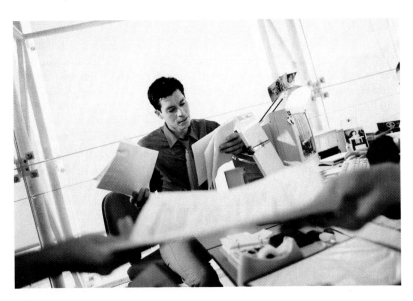

Table 20.1	The Elements of a Marketing Research Report

A. Front Matter

    1. Title Page
    2. Letter of Authorization
    3. Letter/Memo of Transmittal
    4. Table of Contents
    5. List of Illustrations
    6. Abstract/Executive Summary

B. Body

    1. Introduction
    2. Research Objectives
    3. Methodology
    4. Results
    5. Limitations
    6. Conclusions or Conclusions and Recommendations

C. End Matter

    1. Appendices
    2. Endnotes

Front Matter

Front matter consists of all pages that precede the first page of the report.

The **front matter** consists of all pages that precede the first page of the report—the title page, letter of authorization (optional), letter/memo of transmittal, table of contents, list of illustrations, and abstract/executive summary.

Title Page

The **title page** (Figure 20.1) contains four major items of information: (1) the title of the document, (2) the organization/person(s) for whom the report was prepared, (3) the organization/person(s) who prepared the report, and (4) the date of submission. If names of individuals appear on the title page, they may be in either alphabetical order or some other agreed-upon order; each individual should also be given a designation or descriptive title.

The document title should be as informative as possible. It should include the purpose and content of the report, such as "An Analysis of the Demand for a Branch Office of the CPA Firm of Saltmarsh, Cleaveland & Gund" or "Alternative Advertising Copy to Introduce the New M&M/Mars Low-Fat Candy Bar." The title should be centered and printed in all uppercase (capital) letters. Other items of information on the title page should be centered and printed in upper- and lowercase letters. The title page is counted as page i of the front matter; however, no page number is printed on it. See Figure 20.1. On the next page, the printed page number will be ii.

Letter of Authorization

The **letter of authorization** is the marketing research firm's certification to do the project and is optional. It includes the name and title of the persons authorizing the research to be performed, and it may also include a general description of the nature of the research project, completion date, terms of payment, and any special conditions of the research project requested by the client or research user. If you allude to the conditions of your authorization in the letter/memo of transmittal, the letter of authorization is not necessary in the report. However, if your reader may not know the conditions of authorization, inclusion of this document is helpful.

THE HOBBIT'S CHOICE:
A MARKETING RESEARCH STUDY
TO DETERMINE INTENTION TO PATRONIZE,
PREFERENCES FOR OPERATING/DESIGN
CHARACTERISTICS, LOCATION,
AND MEDIA HABITS

Prepared for

Mr. Jeff Dean

Prepared by

CMG Research, Inc.

May, 2003

Figure **20.1**   **A Title Page**

Letter/Memo of Transmittal

Use a **letter of transmittal** to release or deliver the document to an organization for which you are not a regular employee. Use a **memo of transmittal** to deliver the document within your own organization. The letter/memo of transmittal describes the general nature of the research in a sentence or two and identifies the individual who is releasing the report. The primary purpose of the letter/memo of transmittal is to orient the reader to the report and to build a positive image of the report. It should establish rapport between the writer and receiver. It gives the receiver a person to contact if questions arise.

Use a letter for transmittal outside your organization and a memo within your own organization.

Writing style in the letter/memo of transmittal should be personal and slightly informal. Some general elements that may appear in the letter/memo of transmittal are a brief identification of the nature of the research, a review of the conditions of the authorization to do the research (if no letter or authorization is included), comments on findings, suggestions for further research, and an expression of interest in the project and further research. It should end with an expression of appreciation for the assignment, acknowledgment of assistance from others, and suggestions for following up. Personal observations, unsupported by the data, are appropriate. Figure 20.2 presents an example of a letter of transmittal.

CMG Research, Inc.
1100 St. Louis Place
St. Louis, MO

May 21, 2003

Mr. Jeff Dean
2010 Main St.
Anytown, USA 00000

Dear Mr. Dean:

As you requested in your letter of authorization dated February 25, 2003, I have completed the marketing research analysis for The Hobbit's Choice. The results are contained in the report entitled "The Hobbit's Choice: A Marketing Research Study to Determine Intention to Patronize, Preferences for Operating/Design Characteristics, Location, and Media Habits." The report is based on interviews with 400 households in Anytown.

The complete methodology is described in the report. Standard marketing research practices were used throughout the research project. You will find that the results of the report provide the information necessary to achieve the research objectives we set out for this project. These results represent "the voice of your future consumers" and we trust you will be able to use these results to make the best decisions for The Hobbit's Choice.

Should you need further assistance please do not hesitate to call me at (877) 492-2891. I enjoyed working with you on this project and I look forward to working with you again in the future.

Sincerely,

Cory Rogers

Cory Rogers

ii

Figure **20.2**   **A Letter of Transmittal**

Contents

Section Title	Page
List of Illustrations	vi
Executive Summary	vii
Introduction	1
Background	1
Research Objectives	2
Limitations of the Study	3
Method	5
Definition of the Population	5
Sample Plan	6
Sample Size	6
Development of the Questionnaire	6
Data Collection Method	7
Nonsampling Error Reduction	9

iii

Figure 20.3 **A Table of Contents**

Table of Contents

The **table of contents** helps the reader locate information in the research report. The table of contents (Figure 20.3) should list all sections of the report that follow; each heading should read exactly as it appears in the text and should identify the number of the page on which it appears. If a section is longer than one page, list the page on which it begins. Indent subheadings under headings. All items except the title page and the table of contents are listed with page numbers in the table of contents. Front matter pages are numbered with lowercase Roman numerals: i, ii, iii, iv, and so on. Arabic numerals (1, 2, 3) begin with the introduction section of the body of the report.

List of Illustrations

Figure — Page

1. Likelihood of Patronizing The Hobbit's Choice..3

2. Radio Programming Listenership...6

Table

1. Interest in a New Upscale Restaurant...11

vi

Figure 20.4 A List of Illustrations

List of Illustrations

If the report contains tables and/or figures, include in the table of contents a **list of illustrations** with page numbers on which they appear (see Figure 20.4). All tables and figures should be included in this list, which helps the reader find specific illustrations that graphically portray the information. **Tables** are words or numbers that are arranged in rows and columns; **figures** are graphs, charts, maps, pictures, and so on. Because tables and figures are numbered independently, you may have both a Figure 1 and a Table 1 in your list of illustrations. Give each a name, and list each in the order in which it appears in the report.

Abstract/Executive Summary

Your report may have many readers. Some of them will need to know the details of your report, such as the supporting data on which you base your conclusions and recommendations. Others will not need as many details but will want to read the conclusions and recommendations. Still others with a general need to know may read only the executive summary. Therefore, the **abstract or executive summary** is a "skeleton" of your report. It serves as a summary for the busy executive or a preview for the in-depth reader. It provides an overview of the most useful information, including the conclusions and recommendations. The abstract or executive summary should be very carefully written, conveying the information as concisely as possible. It should be single spaced and should briefly cover the general subject of the research, the scope of the research (what the research covers/does not cover), identification of the type of methodology used (i.e., a mail survey of 1,000 homeowners), conclusions, and recommendations.

Abstracts are "skeletons" of reports.

Body

The **body** is the bulk of the report. It contains an introduction to the report, an explanation of your methodology, a discussion of your results, a statement of limitations, and a list of conclusions and recommendations. Do not be alarmed by the repetition that may appear in your report. Only a few people will read it in its entirety. Most will read the executive summary, conclusions, and recommendations. Therefore, formal reports are repetitious. For example, you may specify the research objectives in the executive summary and refer to them again in the findings section as well as in the conclusions section. Also, do not be concerned that you use the same terminology to introduce the tables and/or figures. In many lengthy reports, repetition actually enhances reader comprehension.

The first page of the body contains the title centered two inches from the top of the page; this page is counted as page 1, but no page number is printed on it. All other pages throughout the document are numbered consecutively.

Introduction

The **introduction** to the marketing research report orients the reader to the contents of the report. It may contain a statement of the background situation leading to the problem, the statement of the problem, and a summary description of how the research process was initiated. It should contain a statement of the general purpose of the report and also the specific objectives for the research.

Research objectives may be listed either as a separate section (see Table 20.1) or within the introduction section. The listing of research objectives should follow the statement of the problem since the two concepts are closely related. The list of specific research objectives often serves as a good framework for organizing the results section of the report.

Listing of research objectives should follow the statement of the problem.

Methodology

The **methodology** describes, in as much detail as necessary, how you conducted the research, who (or what) your subjects were, and what methods were used to achieve your objectives. Supplementary information should be placed in the appendix. If you used secondary information, you will need to document your sources (provide enough information so that your sources can be located).[4] You do not need to document facts that are common knowledge or can be easily verified. But if you are in doubt, document! Plagiarism is a serious offense; it can cost you your job.

The methodology describes in detail how the research was conducted, who (or what) the subjects were, and what methods were used to achieve the objectives.

MARKETING RESEARCH
INSIGHT

20.2

Do You Feel Like This About Documentation?

"It's just a few words."

"It's just a document for my office."

"I'm not making money off it."

"The information is from the Web; everyone can find it and use it."

"I could never say it better."

"The words are perfect; who cares who wrote it?"

"A bunch of citations just makes the report more difficult to read."

"Nobody expects me to reinvent the wheel."

Plagiarism is derived from a Latin word for kidnapping a Roman citizen's slave.[5] Words can be thought of as property. Avoiding plagiarism involves respect for the original author's work and respect for your audience's needs or desire to trace data and learn more from the source.

Just as all printed sources must be documented, so must information found online. In a letter to the *New York Times*, Marilyn Bergman, the president of the American Society of Composers, Authors, and Publishers, expressed a disturbing trend of online theft of words when she said that Americans are prompted by a "free for the taking" feeling of information on the Web.[6] The Internet is not public domain. Proper documentation of all sources helps a writer avoid public humiliation and maintain professional integrity.

Documentation of Online Sources: Why and How?

Copyright laws provide four general types of rights for an author:

1. Right to produce copies of the document
2. Right to sell or distribute document
3. Right to create new works based on the copyrighted work
4. Right to perform work in public

APA and MLA are two styles that offer formats for citation. Generally APA is used in business fields, and MLA is used in the humanities. Style books and university Web sites offer examples on documentation for a range of sources, including electronic formats.

For example, the preceding information was found on the library services Web site of the University of Maryland University College (UMUC). The source citation and format follow.

> *University of Maryland University College (1998). "Citing Internet Resources: APA Style," [On-line]. Available: http://www.umuc.edu/library/apa.html [2/4/99].*

Format:

Author, I., Author, I., & Author, I. (Year, month date). Title, [Type of medium]. Available: Site/Path/File [Access date].

UMUC library services explains each field below.

Author—The creator or compiler of the information on the Web page. This can be the Web master or the name of the organization that is responsible for the page.

Year, month date—The date that the Web page was put online; it should be the same as the "last updated" date if available.

Title—The title of the document. Often, this can be found at the top of the Web page.

Type of medium—The way the document was accessed. If the document was found on the Web or through another Internet service, this field should read "Online."

Site/Path/File—The address or URL of the Web site.

Access date—The date that you viewed the Web page or accessed the information.

In most cases, the methodology section (sometimes called the "methods" section) does not need to be long. It should, however, provide the essential information your reader needs to understand how the data were collected and how the results were achieved. It should be detailed enough that the data collection could be replicated by others for purposes of reliability. In other words, the methodology section should be clear enough that other researchers could conduct a similar study.

In some cases, the needs of the research user may dictate a very extensive methodology section. A client may, for example, want the researcher to not only thoroughly describe the methodology that was used but also discuss why other methodologies were not selected. (In situations in which research information will be provided in litigation, where there is certain to be an adversary, a researcher may be asked to provide an exhaustive description of the methods used in conducting the study and the methods that were not chosen.)

Results

The **results** section is the most important portion of your report. This section should logically present the findings of your research and be organized around your objectives for the study. The results should be presented in narrative form and accompanied by tables, charts, figures, and other appropriate visuals that support and enhance the explanation of results. Tables and figures are supportive material; they should not be overused or used as filler. Each should contain a number and title and should be referred to in the narrative.

The results section is the major portion of your report and should logically present the findings of the research.

Outline your results section before you write the report. The survey questionnaire itself can serve as a useful aid in organizing your results because the questions are often grouped in a logical order or in purposeful sections. Another useful method for organizing your results is to individually print all tables and figures and arrange them in a logical sequence. Once you have the results outlined properly, you are ready to write the introductory sentences, definitions (if necessary), review of the findings (often referring to tables and figures), and transition sentences to lead into the next topic.

Limitations

Do not attempt to hide or disguise problems in your research; no research is faultless. Always be above board and open regarding all aspects of your research. To avoid discussion of limitations often is to render suspect your integrity and your research. Suggest what the limitations are or may be and how they impact the results. You might also suggest opportunities for further study based on the limitations. Typical **limitations** in research reports often focus on but are not limited to factors such as time, money, size of sample, and personnel. Consider the following example: "... the reader should note that this study was based on a survey of graduating students at a midsized public university in the Southeast United States. Budget constraints limited the sample to this university and this region of the country. Care should be exercised in generalizing these findings to other populations."

Do not attempt to hide or disguise problems in your research. Suggest the possible limitations and how they impact the results.

Conclusions and Recommendations

Conclusions and recommendations may be listed together or in separate sections, depending on the amount of material you have to report. In any case, you should note that conclusions are not the same as recommendations. **Conclusions** are the outcomes and decisions you have reached based on your research results. **Recommendations** are suggestions for how to proceed based on the conclusions. Unlike conclusions, recommendations may require knowledge beyond the scope of the research findings themselves, that is, information on conditions within the company, the industry, and so on. Therefore, researchers should exercise caution in making recommendations. The researcher and the client should determine prior to the study whether the report is to contain recommendations. A clear understanding of the researcher's role will result in a smoother process and will help avoid conflict. Although a research user may desire the researcher to provide specific recommendations, both parties must realize that the researcher's recommendations are based solely on the knowledge gained from the research report, not familiarity with the client. Other information, if made known to the researcher, could totally change the researcher's recommendations.

Conclusions are outcomes or decisions based on results. Recommendations are suggestions for how to proceed based on conclusions.

If recommendations are required and if a report is intended to initiate further action, however, recommendations are the important map to the next step. Writing recommendations in a bulleted list and beginning each with an action verb help to direct the reader to the logical next step.

MARKETING RESEARCH

INSIGHT

20.3

An Online Application ◀

Online Reporting Software

Online reporting software is available to help researchers disseminate their research reports. These programs also allow readers to interact with the reports. Readers may use "what if" queries or build their own tables from data they select.

One such package is Beyond 20/20. This software allows researchers to disseminate a research report in a format that allows "technically nonadept" users to do their own manipulations. The program allows for a report to be disseminated over the Web or through intranets, allowing readers to interact with the data using their standard Web browser. The program supports 12 different languages.[7] Providing readers with the ability to analyze data in a way that is meaningful to them increases the usefulness of marketing research information. This means fewer marketing research reports will be used by only one entity in the client's firm and then be filed away on the company library shelf to collect dust.

Another online solution for reporting comes from Burke Interactive. Its Digital Dashboard allows users to collect survey responses and disseminate survey findings. Among the features are custom-prepared project background and executive summary sections, links from the executive summary to key findings, capability for users to manipulate data, searchable survey responses to open-ended questions, and easy monitoring of data while they are being collected.

In a study of the marketing research industry, the Advertising Research Foundation found that in 1999 almost one-half of the research firms in the study reported providing research report data in an online format. Moreover, 92 percent of the companies surveyed said that they expected this practice would increase in the next five years.[8]

End Matter

End matter contains additional information to which the reader may refer for further reading but that is not essential to reporting the data.

The **end matter** comprises the **appendices,** which contain additional information to which the reader may refer for further reading but that is not essential to reporting the data. Appendices contain the "nice to know" information, not the "need to know." Therefore, that information should not clutter the body of the report but should instead be inserted at the end for the reader who desires or requires additional information. Tables, figures, additional reading, technical descriptions, data collection forms, and appropriate computer printouts are some elements that may appear in the appendix. (If they are critical to the reader, however, they may be included in the report itself.) Each appendix should be labeled with both a letter and a title, and each should appear in the table of contents. A reference page or endnotes (if appropriate) should precede the appendix.

FOLLOWING GUIDELINES AND PRINCIPLES FOR THE WRITTEN REPORT

The parts of the research report have been described. However, you should also consider their form and format and their style.

Form and Format

Form and format concerns include headings and subheadings and visuals.

Headings and Subheadings In a long report, your reader needs signals and signposts that serve as a road map. Headings and subheadings perform this function. **Headings** indicate the topic of each section. All information under a specific heading should relate to that heading, and **subheadings** should divide that information into segments. A new heading should introduce a change of topic. Choose the kind of heading that fits your purpose—single word, phrase, sentence, question—and consistently use that form throughout the report. If you use subheadings within the divi-

Headings and subheadings act as signals and signposts to serve as a road map for a long report.

sions, the subheadings must be parallel to one another but not to the main headings. See Figure 20.5 for levels of headings.

Visuals

Visuals are tables, figures, charts, diagrams, graphs, and other graphic aids. Used properly, they can dramatically and concisely present information that might otherwise be difficult to comprehend. Tables systematically present numerical data or words in columns and rows. Figures translate numbers into visual displays so that relationships and trends become comprehensible. Examples of figures are graphs, pie charts, and bar charts.

Visuals can dramatically and concisely present information that might otherwise be difficult to comprehend.

Report Title

First-Level Subheading

Second-Level Subheading

Third-Level Subheading.

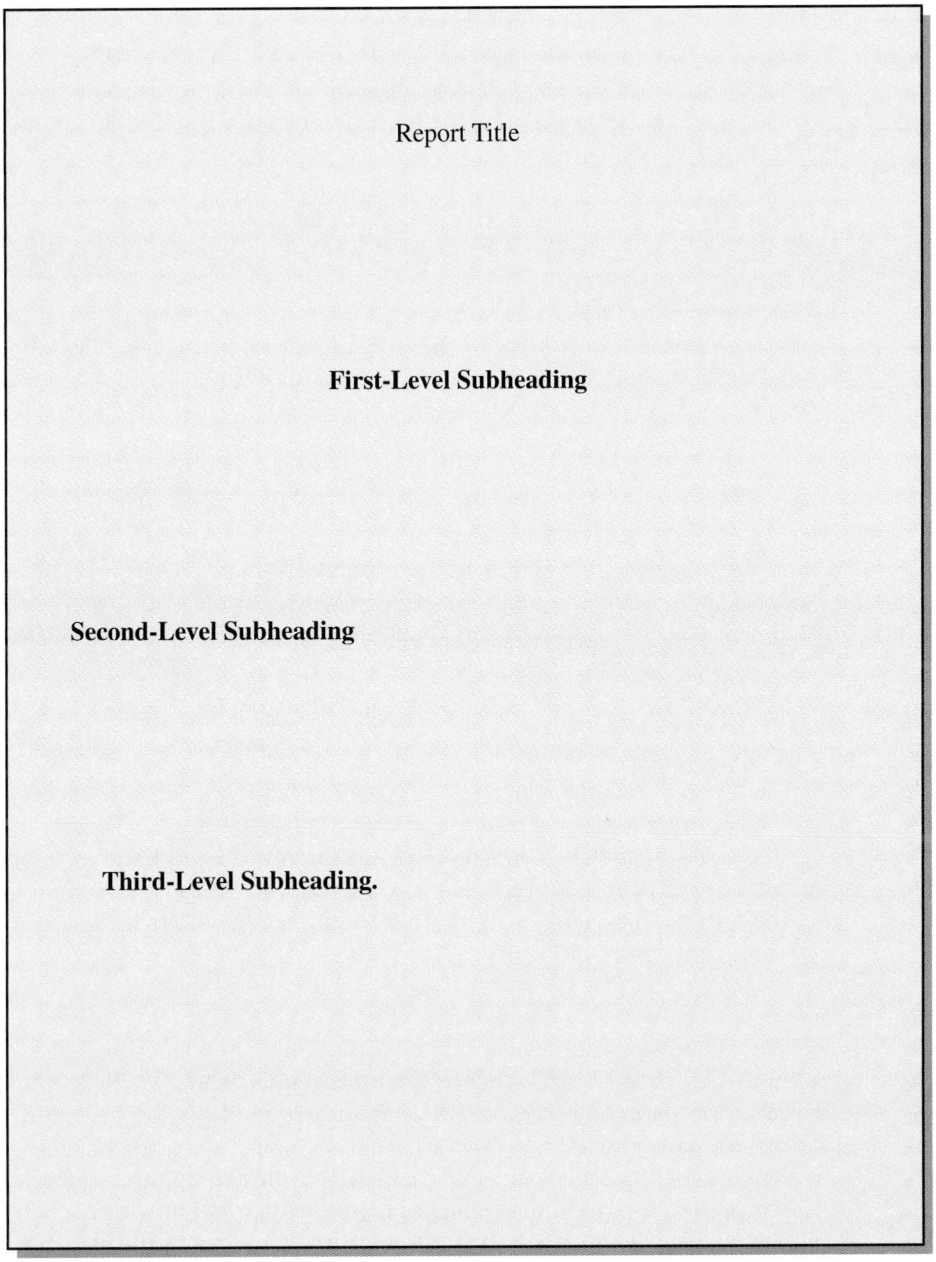

Figure 20.5 **Levels of Headings**

Visuals should tell a story; they should be uncluttered and self-explanatory. Even though they are self-explanatory, the key points of all visuals should be explained in the text. Refer to visuals by number: ". . . as shown in Figure 1." Each visual should be titled and numbered. If possible, place the visual immediately below the paragraph in which its first reference appears. Or, if sufficient space is not available, continue the text and place the visual on the next page. Visuals can also be placed in an appendix. Additional information on preparing visuals is presented later in this chapter.

Style

Stylistic devices can make the difference in whether or not your reader gets the message as you intended it.

Consider stylistic devices when you are actually writing the sentences and paragraphs in your report. These can make the difference in whether or not your reader gets the message as you intended it. Therefore, consider the following "tips" for the writer.

1. A good paragraph has one main idea, and a topic sentence should state that main idea. As a general rule, begin paragraphs with topic sentences. However, topic sentences can appear in the middle or at the end of a paragraph. Examples of good topic sentences are as follows: "The Northern Michigan market is not receptive to the New Chef's anise-flavored gumdrops" and "This research indicates that the intersection at Davis Highway and Creighton Avenue is a good location for a new Subway, Inc. franchise."

2. Avoid long paragraphs (usually those with more than nine printed lines). Long paragraphs are a strategy for burying a message because most readers do not read the middle contents of long paragraphs.

3. Capitalize on white space. Immediately before and immediately after white space (the beginning and the end of a paragraph) are points of emphasis. So are the beginning and the end of a page. Therefore, place more important information at these strategic points.

4. Use jargon sparingly. Some of your audience may understand technical terms; others may not. When in doubt, properly define the terms for your readers. If many technical terms are required in the report, consider including a glossary of terms in an appendix to assist the less-informed members of your audience.

5. Use strong verbs to carry the meaning of your sentences. Instead of "making a recommendation," "recommend." Instead of "performing an investigation," "investigate."

6. As a general rule, use the active voice. Voice indicates whether the subject of the verb is doing the action (active voice) or receiving the action (passive voice). For example, "The marketing research was conducted by Judith" uses the passive voice. "Judith conducted the marketing research" uses the active voice. Active voice is direct and forceful, and the active voice uses fewer words.

7. Eliminate extra words. Write your message clearly and concisely. Combine and reword sentences to eliminate unnecessary words. Remove opening fillers and eliminate unnecessary redundancies. For example, instead of writing, "There are 22 marketing research firms in Newark," write, "Twenty-two marketing research firms are located in Newark." Instead of saying, "the end results," say, "the results."

8. Avoid unnecessary changes in tense. Tense tells if the action of the verb occurred in the past (past tense—*were*), is happening right now (present tense—*are*), or will happen in the future (future tense—*will be*). Changing tenses within a document is an error writers frequently make.

9. In sentences, keep the subject and verb close together. The farther apart they become, the more difficulty the reader has understanding the message and the greater the chance for errors in subject/verb agreement.

10. Vary the length and structure of sentences and paragraphs.

11. Use faultless grammar. If your grammar is in any way below par, you need to take responsibility for finding ways to improve. Poor grammar can result in costly errors and loss of your job. It can jeopardize your credibility and the credibility of your research. There is no acceptable excuse for poor grammar.

12. Maintain 1-inch side margins. If your report will be bound, use a $1\frac{1}{2}$-inch left margin.

13. Use the organization's preference for double or single spacing.

14. Edit carefully. Your first draft is not a finished product; neither is your second. Edit your work carefully, rearranging and rewriting until you communicate the intent of your research as efficiently and effectively as possible. Some authors suggest that as much as 50 percent of your production time should be devoted to improving, editing, correcting, and evaluating an already written document.[9]

15. Proofread! Proofread! Proofread! After you have finished a product, check it carefully to make sure everything is correct. Double check names and numbers, grammar, spelling, and punctuation. Although spell checks and grammar checks are useful, you cannot rely on them to catch all errors. One of the best ways to proofread is to read a document aloud, preferably with a reader following along on the original. An alternative is to read the document twice—once for content and meaning and once for mechanical errors. The more important the document is, the more time and readers you need to employ for proofreading.

USING VISUALS: TABLES AND FIGURES

Visuals assist in the effective presentation of numerical data. The key to a successful visual is a clear and concise presentation that conveys the message of the report. The selection of the visual should match the presentation purpose for the data. Common visuals include the following.[10]

Tables, which identify exact values (see Marketing Research Insight 20.4).

Graphs and *charts*, which illustrate relationships among items.
   Pie charts, which compare a specific part of the whole to the whole (see Marketing Research Insight 20.5).
   Bar charts (see Marketing Research Insight 20.6) and *line graphs*, which compare items over time or show correlations among items.

Flow diagrams, which introduce a set of topics and illustrate their relationships (Figure 20.6).

Maps, which define locations.

Photographs, which present an aura of legitimacy because they are not "created" in the sense that other visuals are created. Photos depict factual content.

Drawings, which focus on visual details.

A discussion of some of these visuals follows.

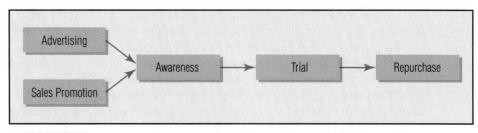

Figure **20.6**   **A Flow Diagram Introduces Topics and Shows How They Are Related**

Tables

Tables allow the reader to compare numerical data.

Tables allow the reader to compare numerical data. Effective table guidelines are as follows:

1. Do not allow computer analysis to imply a level of accuracy that is not achieved. Limit your use of decimal places (12% or 12.2% instead of 12.223%).
2. Place items you want the reader to compare in the same column, not the same row.
3. If you have many rows, darken alternate entries or double space after every five entries to assist the reader to accurately line up items.
4. Total columns and rows when relevant.

Marketing Research Insight 20.4 gives you the necessary keystroke instructions to create tables using SPSS.

MARKETING RESEARCH
INSIGHT SPSS
20.4

How to Create a Table Using SPSS

We will use The Hobbit's Choice data set (HobbitData.sav) that you are familiar with as we have been using it for all of the statistical analysis examples in previous chapters. Let's say we wish to find out the likelihood that our respondents will patronize The Hobbit's Choice. To do this, we create a simple frequency table for responses to the question on the questionnaire: "How likely would it be for you to patronize this restaurant?"

1. The first step is to create a frequency table for responses to question 1 on the questionnaire: "How likely would it be for you to patronize this restaurant?" After opening the data file, use the ANALYZE-DESCRIP-TIVE STATISTICS-FREQUENCIES and select the variable corresponding to likelihood of patronizing The Hobbit's Choice. The resulting frequency table is displayed in the SPSS output Viewer.

2. To edit the table, put the cursor anywhere on the table and double-click. This activates the table editor, which

is indicated by a shaded highlight box appearing around the table, and a red arrow pointing to the selected table. You may also see a toolbar appearing on your screen.

3. Figure 20.7 illustrates how to change the format of the table (after you have double-clicked on the table). Select FORMAT-TABLELOOKS.

4. To select a particular table format, browse through the directory and select one that suits your need. In this case, we used Boxed (VGA) format. However, because we wanted to change the fonts, we had to edit the format we had selected.

5. To edit an already available format, click EDIT LOOK while in TABLELOOKS. To change the fonts, alignment, margins, and so on, click on CELL FORMATS. Change the fonts, size, style, and so on to suit your needs. To change borders, click on BORDERS and select appropriate borders. An example of a finished table is in Figure 20.7.

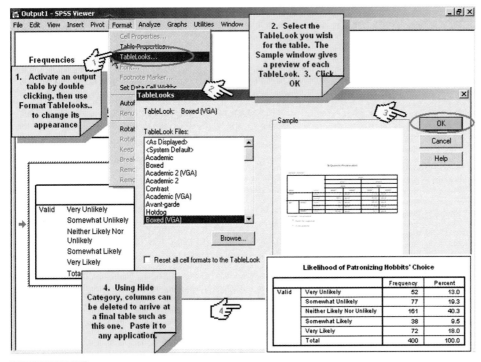

Figure 20.7

6. After adjusting the table properties for the attributes you want, save your customized table format by clicking on SAVE AS within the TABLELOOKS dialog box and saving the table under a new file name. Keep reading. We show you how to recall this new table format for all the tables you make without having to reedit each new table. You can use this customized table look for any future tables you create. After you click SAVE AS and name the table format to be saved, click SAVE-OK.

7. You are now back in the table edit mode. The next step is to change the text in specific cells. To do this, double-click on the cell in which you want to change the text. The selected text will be highlighted. Simply type over and press Enter when you are done.

Pie Charts

Pie charts are particularly useful for illustrating relative size or static comparisons. The **pie chart** is a circle divided into sections. Each section represents a percentage of the total area of the circle associated with one component. Today's data analysis programs easily and quickly make pie charts. Your SPSS Interactive Graphics program, for example, allows you to build customized pie charts.

The pie chart should have a limited number of segments (four to six). If your data have many small segments, consider combining the smallest or the least important into an "other" or "miscellaneous" category. Because internal labels are difficult to read for small sections, labels for the sections should be placed outside the circle.

Marketing Research Insight 20.5 gives you the keystroke instructions for creating pie charts using SPSS.

Pie charts are particularly useful for illustrating relative size or static comparisons.

MARKETING RESEARCH
INSIGHT SPSS

SPSS ◀

20.5

How to Create a Pie Chart Using SPSS

We again use data from The Hobbit's Choice survey (HobbitData.sav) to demonstrate the creation of a simple pie graph using SPSS. Let us say we want to show responses to the question, "To which type of radio programming do you most often listen?" in the form of a pie chart.

1. Create a pie chart for responses to the question on the questionnaire: "To which type of radio programming do you most often listen?"

   Figure 20.8 shows that you use the Command sequence of GRAPHS and PIE. Click Summaries for Groups of Cases and then Define.

   The next screen allows you to choose the variable that you want to graph. Select the variable corresponding to the question on the questionnaire, click the button for Define Slices By, and the variable will be entered.

   You can choose what you want your slices to represent. In this case, we selected the pies to represent % of cases.

2. At this stage, you can also enter the titles and footnotes for the chart by clicking on all caps and entering the appropriate labels.

   Using the command OPTIONS, you can decide how you want missing values to be treated. Here we have not included missing values in the chart by clicking off the check mark (3) on the Display Groups Defined by Missing Values.

   Click OK and the resulting pie chart will appear in the SPSS Viewer. You are now ready to edit the chart.

   If you have an existing template of a pie graph, you can request the output to be formatted according to template specifications by clicking on Use Chart Specifications From and selecting the saved file name.

3. Scroll down to the pie chart. To edit the chart, double-click the chart. This takes you to the SPSS Chart Editor screen. You will do all your editing in this screen.

4. Figure 20.9 shows how the Chart Editor works with our pie chart. To edit the filled patterns and colors of the slices of the pie chart, first click once on the pie slice you wish to edit. Use command FORMAT-FILL PATTERN (or COLOR). You can see the pie chart presented in Figure 20.9.

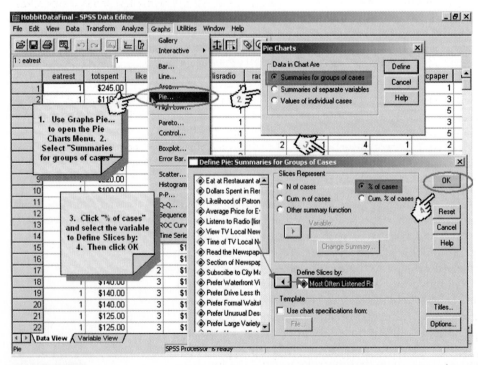

Figure **20.8**

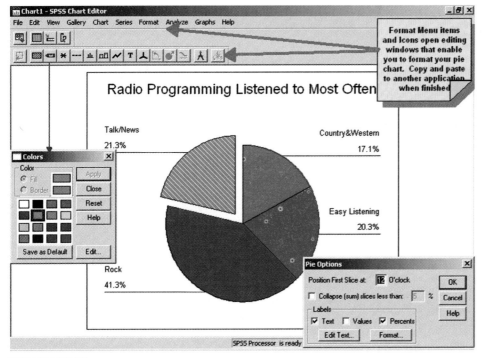

Figure 20.9

5. To edit the textual content and justification, select the text you want to edit by clicking once with the mouse. When your text is selected, a box or a set of markers will appear around the text. Now, double-click and you will get a Pie Options box that allows you to edit text and format.

To change the font and size of the text, select the text by clicking once on the text with the mouse. Now, use command FORMAT-TEXT and select the fonts and sizes you want. To edit and position the labels, use command CHART-OPTIONS. This takes you to a box titled Pie Options. Here you also have the option of collapsing slices that are less than 5 percent by summing them.

You can choose to have your labels presented with values and percentages. In the pie chart presented in Figure 20.9, we have opted to present the text and the percentages by clicking on the Text and Percents boxes in the Pie Options box.

6. To fit the entire chart with a frame, use command options CHART-OUTER FRAME.

7. After making all the changes, you can save your customized chart by using command options FILE-SAVE CHART TEMPLATE. For future charts, you can call up the customized template, saving you the need to edit every pie chart you create.

8. The chart is now ready to be transferred to a word processing document. The chart that we have created is shown in Figure 20.9.

Bar Charts

Several types of **bar charts** can be used. Figure 20.10 shows a simple bar chart created by SPSS 11.0. Marketing Research Insight 20.6 gives you the keystroke instructions for creating bar charts of various types using SPSS. Study the types of bar charts available to you in SPSS. Your selection of the type of bar chart will depend on what you are trying to communicate to your reader.

MARKETING RESEARCH

INSIGHT

20.6

SPSS ◄

How to Create a Bar Chart Using SPSS

We use data from The Hobbit's Choice (HobbitData.sav) to demonstrate the creation of a simple bar graph using SPSS. Let us say we want to show graphically the frequency distribution of the likelihood of respondents patronizing The Hobbit's Choice.

1. Create a bar chart for responses to question 4 on the questionnaire: "How likely would it be for you to patronize this restaurant?"

   As you can see in Figure 20.10, after opening the data file, use the Command GRAPHS and BAR. You have the option of choosing from three different styles of bar charts. In this case, we used the simple chart. Click Summaries for Groups of Cases and then Define.

   The next screen allows you to choose the variable that you want to graph. Select the variable corresponding to question 4 on the questionnaire, highlight the variable, and click on the Category Axis button.

   You can choose what you want your bars to represent. In this case, we selected the bars to represent % of cases because we want to know the percentages of respondents citing likelihood to patronize The Hobbit's Choice.

2. At this stage, you can also enter the titles and footnotes for the chart by clicking on all caps and entering the appropriate labels. Also, by selecting OPTIONS, you can decide how you want missing values to be treated. Here, we have not included missing values in the chart by clicking off the check mark (✓) on the Display Groups Defined by Missing Values.

   Click OK and the resulting bar chart will appear in the SPSS Viewer. You are now ready to edit the chart.

   If you have an existing template of a bar graph while in the Define Simple Bar Summaries for Groups of Cases box, you can request the output to be formatted according to template specifications by clicking on Use Chart Specifications From, and selecting the saved file name.

3. To edit the chart, double-click the chart. This takes you to the SPSS Chart Editor screen. You will do all your editing in this screen. Figure 20.11 shows the operation of the SPSS chart editor with our bar chart.

4. To edit the bars, use command FORMAT-BAR STYLE and BAR LABEL STYLE. As you can see from the final bar chart presented in Figure 20.11, we have used the three-dimensional style for the bars.

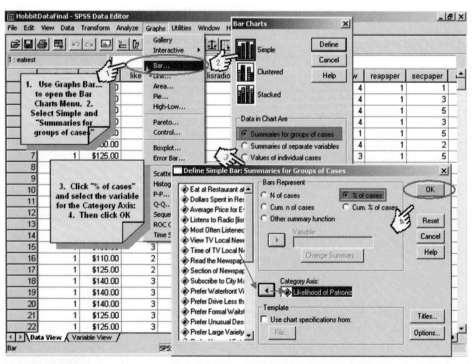

Figure 20.10

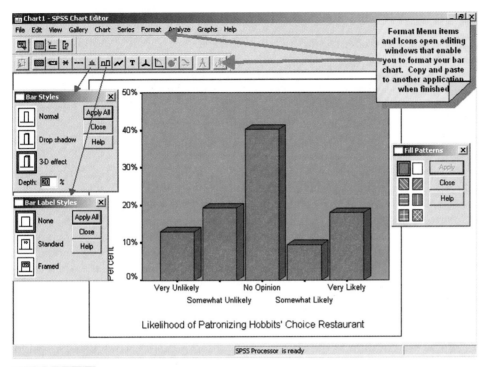

Figure **20.11**

To suppress display of any particular category such as Less than 5, and so forth, use commands SERIES-DISPLAYED, and select the category you want to hide or show.

5. To edit the textual content of the chart, select the text you want to edit by clicking once with the mouse. When your text is selected, a box or a set of markers will appear around the text. Now, use commands FORMAT-TEXT and change the fonts and sizes accordingly.

To change the contents and alignment of the text, double-click on the text to be edited. You can now make the appropriate changes in the Category Axis box.

To change the orientation of the axis labels, double-click on labels. This takes you to another box titled Category Axis: Labels. In this box, make your Orientation selection.

6. To fit the entire chart with a frame, use command CHART-OUTER FRAME. You can also edit the axis, legends, annotations, and so forth under CHART.

7. After making all the changes, you can save your customized chart by using command FILE-SAVE CHART TEMPLATE. For future charts, you can call up the customized template, saving you the need to edit every bar chart you create.

8. The chart is now ready to be transferred to a word processing document. The chart that we have created is shown in Figure 20.11.

Line Graphs

Line graphs are easy to interpret if they are designed properly. Line graphs may be drawn in SPSS using the GRAPHS option. You will notice there are several options in types of line graphs.

Flow diagrams introduce a set of topics and illustrate their relationships. Flow diagrams are particularly useful to illustrate topics that are sequential, for example, step 1, step 2, and so on. (See Figure 20.6.)

Flow diagrams introduce a set of topics and illustrate their relationships.

PRODUCING AN ACCURATE AND ETHICAL VISUAL

An ethical visual is one that is totally objective in terms of how information is presented in the research report.

A marketing researcher should always follow the doctrine of full disclosure. An **ethical visual** is one that is totally objective in terms of how information is presented in the research report. Sometimes misrepresenting information is intentional (as when a client asks a researcher to misrepresent the data in order to promote his or her "pet project") or it may be unintentional. In the latter case, those preparing a visual are sometimes so familiar with the material being presented that they falsely assume that the graphic message is apparent to all who view it.

To illustrate how one can be unethical in preparing a visual, let us assume that the entrepreneur in The Hobbit's Choice Restaurant Case, Jeff Dean, is seeking financial backing for his restaurant. He must convince potential investors that there are enough potential patrons in the local area to support an upscale restaurant. Our entrepreneur receives the results of the survey and prepares the visuals that he feels are necessary to make his presentation. Using SPSS he generates the bar chart shown in Figure 20.12 that is labeled "An Ethical Visual." SPSS automatically assigns the range of values located on the y-axis. Although it is expected that the majority of people in the local area would not patronize an upscale restaurant, the results look extremely skewed to the negative with the "neutral" respondents making the situation look even more dire. However, this is an ethical presentation of the research data. If our manager is unethical, he could use SPSS to eliminate the "no opinion" respondents to just show the opinionated respondents. Furthermore, he could eliminate the percentages identified on the vertical axis. These alterations, which result in the bar chart labeled "An Unethical Visual" shown in Figure 20.12b, gives the impression that the results are more positive than they actually are. This bar chart is unethical because it is misleading; it makes the possibility of patronizing the restaurant appear propor-

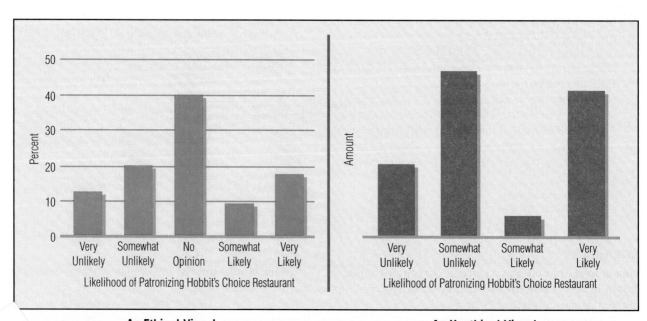

An Ethical Visual   **An Unethical Visual**

Figure **20.12**   Comparison of an Ethical Visual with an Unethical Visual

▶ **Meet a Marketing Researcher**

Jim Kershaw Knows the Importance of Report Writing

Jim Kershaw is a manager in the Consulting and Analytical Services Department of Burke, Inc., a leading provider of decision support services. In his tenure at Burke, he has analyzed marketing research data for clients in a wide range of industries, including financial services, telecommunications, hospitality, and consumer packaged goods. His research experience includes brand image/positioning, product line optimization, market segmentation, concept testing, pricing analysis, and customer satisfaction mea-

surement. Jim's prior professional experience includes analysis of survey data related to social and economic policy issues, as well as management consulting to enable business process reengineering efforts for several large organizations. He holds a B.A. in economics and sociology from Duke University and an M.B.A. in marketing and finance, with an emphasis in services marketing, from Vanderbilt University.

tionally greater than it is. As a result, potential investors may be duped into believing that the possibility of restaurant patronization is greater than what is ethically supported by the data.

To ensure that you have objectively and ethically prepared your visuals you should do the following:

1. Double and triple check all labels, numbers, and visual shapes. A faulty or misleading visual discredits your report and work.
2. Exercise caution if you use three-dimensional figures. They may distort the data by multiplying the value by the width and the height.
3. Make sure all parts of the scales are presented. Truncated graphs (having breaks in the scaled values on either axis) are acceptable only if the audience is familiar with the data.

▶ **Advice from a Marketing Researcher**

Some Advice on Report Writing

Jim Kershaw says the most successful analytical reports exhibit several attributes:

1. A focus on highlights. Rather than serving as a "data dump," the analytical report distills the information into the key findings that directly reflect research objectives.
2. Logical flow. The report must tell a story that follows from the research objectives. Think of a journalist who has many facts to report but must organize these facts in a way that readers can follow.
3. Strong writing and thorough proofing. Professional writing supports credibility.
4. Compelling graphics and exhibits. Pictures (in our case, charts and graphs) often convey findings more succinctly than text, but they must be set up to allow the reader to identify key findings quickly.

5. Action-oriented conclusions. Conclusions should address specific research objectives as closely as possible. Developing such conclusions often requires interaction with internal contacts or client contacts who can help provide the business/industry context for research findings.
6. A concise executive summary. The executive summary should convey key findings and conclusions without extraneous detail. It should act as a stand-alone document, even if it is one section of the larger report.

The presence of these elements maximizes the likelihood that the report will get read in the first place and, more importantly, be referenced frequently as a vital input to strategic planning.

PRESENTING YOUR RESEARCH ORALLY

The purpose of the oral presentation is to succinctly present the research information and to provide an opportunity for questions and discussion.

You may be asked to present an oral summary of the recommendations and conclusions of your research. The purpose of the **oral presentation** is to succinctly present the information and to provide an opportunity for questions and discussion. The presentation may be accomplished through a simple conference with the client, or it may be a formal presentation to a room full of people. In any case, says Jerry W. Thomas, CEO of Decision Analyst, research reports should "be presented orally to all key people in the same room at the same time." He believes this is important because many people don't read the research report and others may not understand all the details of the report. "An oral presentation ensures that everyone can ask questions to allow the researchers to clear up any confusion."[11] It also ensures that everyone hears the same thing.

To be adequately prepared when you present your research orally, follow these steps:

1. Identify and analyze your audience. Consider the same questions you addressed at the beginning of the research process and at the beginning of this chapter.
2. Find out the expectations your audience has for your presentation. Is the presentation formal or informal? Does your audience expect an electronic slide show?
3. Determine the key points your audience needs to hear.
4. Outline the key points, preferably on 3 × 5 cards to which you can easily refer.
5. Present your points succinctly and clearly. The written report will serve as a reference for further reading.
6. Make sure your visuals graphically and ethically portray your key points.
7. Practice your presentation. Be comfortable with what you are going to say and how you look. The more prepared you are and the better you feel about yourself, the less you will need to worry about jitters.
8. Check out the room and media equipment prior to the presentation.
9. Arrive early.
10. Be positive and confident. You are the authority; you know more about your subject than anyone else does.
11. Speak loudly enough for all in the room to hear. Enunciate clearly. Maintain eye contact and good posture. Dress professionally.

SUMMARY

The final stage of the marketing research process is the preparation and presentation of the marketing research report. This stage is as important as, if not more important than, any other stage in the research process. This importance is attributed to the fact that, regardless of the care in the design and execution of the research project itself, if the report does not adequately communicate the project to the client, all is lost. Properly "packaging" the final report can be just as important as the content itself.

Marketing research reports should be tailored to their audiences. They are typically organized into the categories of front matter, body, and end matter. Each of these categories has subparts, with each subpart having a different purpose. Conclusions are based on the results of the research, and recommendations are suggestions based on conclusions. Online reporting software is an efficient tool that assists marketing researchers in monitoring data collection and disseminating research results. It also allows data users to interact with the reports and massage data.

Guidelines for writing the marketing research report include proper use of headings and subheadings, which serve as signposts and signals to the reader, and proper use of visuals such as tables and figures. Style considerations include beginning paragraphs with topic sentences, spare use of jargon, strong verbs, active voice, consistent tense, conciseness, and varied sentence structure and length. Editing and proofreading, preferably by reading the report aloud, are important steps in writing the research report. Care should be taken to ensure that all presentations are clear and objective to the reader. Many visual aids may be distorted so that they have a different meaning to the reader. This means that ethical considerations must be made in the preparation of the research report. Reports rely on tables, figures, and graphical displays of various types. SPSS includes routines for creating report tables and graphs. We describe step-by-step commands on how to use SPSS to make professional-appearing tables and graphs.

In some cases, marketing researchers are required to orally present the findings of their research project to the client. Guidelines for making an oral presentation include knowing the audience, its expectations, and the key points you wish to make; correctly preparing visuals; practicing; checking out presentation facilities and equipment prior to the presentation; and being positive.

KEY TERMS

REVIEW QUESTIONS/APPLICATIONS

1. Discuss the relative importance of the marketing research report to the other stages in the marketing research process.
2. What are the components of the marketing research report?
3. When should you include or omit a letter of authorization?
4. Distinguish among results, conclusions, and recommendations.
5. When should you use a subheading?
6. What is the most important consideration in determining the style in which you will report your findings?
7. When should you use a letter and when should you use a memo?
8. How does online reporting software assist market researchers and report users?
9. What visual would be the best at displaying the relative changes in spending between four promotion mix variables over time?
10. What kind of visual would you use if you wanted to use images of people to illustrate the differences in employment levels among three industries?
11. Why do you think we included a discussion of ethics in preparing visuals? Can you illustrate how a visual could present data in an unethical fashion?
12. Visit your library and ask your reference librarian if he or she is aware of any marketing research reports that have been placed in the library. Chances are good that you will be able to find several reports of various kinds. Examine the reports. What commonalities do they have in terms of the sections that the authors have created? Look at the sections carefully. What types of issues were addressed in the introduction section? The methodology section? How did the authors organize all of the information reported in the results section? Are recommendations different from conclusions?

INTERACTIVE LEARNING

Visit the Web site at www.prenhall.com/burnsbush. For this chapter, work through the Self-Study Quizzes, and get instant feedback on whether you need additional studying. On the Web site, you can review the chapter outlines and case information for Chapter 20.

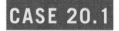 **CASE 20.1** **Branding the Beaches: South Walton County, Florida**[12]

Thirteen beach communities and destination resorts comprise the Beaches of South Walton area (www.beachesofsouthwalton.com) in the South Walton County area of Northwest Florida. The South Walton area, with its white sand beaches, excellent deep sea fishing, many golf courses, and eclectic shopping opportunities has long been a popular vacation spot for tourists. However, because the Northwest Florida tourism industry is growing at a healthy rate and regional competition for tourism dollars is intensifying, the local Tourism Development Council (TDC) believes that it has become very important to build a distinctive brand identity for the Beaches of South Walton area.

When marketing professionals seek to build strong brand identity, they are striving to create, in the minds of the market, a well-defined set of features, meanings, and outcomes that are associated with the tourism product itself as well as its representations (brand marks, names, logos, etc.). Inherent in this strategy is the implied promise that if tourists choose to visit and experience the destination product, their marketing-created expectations will be met, if not exceeded. Thus, just as the Rolls-Royce® brand means and promises an exceptional automobile to its buyers, destination brands mean and promise certain outcomes or benefits to their visitors.

According to Kriss Titus, Executive Director of the Beaches of South Walton TDC, "Customer perceptions and satisfaction are really important to us at the Beaches of South Walton because that's how we measure whether we are meeting our brand promise." As observed by Ms. Titus, continuous measurement and evaluation of customer perceptions is a mission-critical component of any brand development strategy. This information allows marketers to gauge the overall success of their strategy and make adjustments when needed.

In the summer of 2001, the Beaches of South Walton TDC and the Haas Center for Business Research and Economic Development (**www.haas.uwf.edu**) at the University of West Florida entered into a three-year partnership to measure and evaluate various outcomes of the Beaches of South Walton's marketing and branding strategies. Haas Center research staff and TDC staff collaborated to develop several research objectives for the project. A survey questionnaire was designed by Haas Center researchers to collect the data needed to meet these objectives. Several major property management firms in the area furnish quarterly guest lists, giving a sampling frame of visitors to the Beaches of South Walton area who stayed one or more nights during the quarter in a property managed by one of the participating property firms. Data are collected by an external supplier of research, The Listener Group (**www.listenergroup.com**), on a quarterly schedule using post-visit telephone surveys. A simple random sampling method is used to generate the quarterly call list. Haas Center analysts process the data and report results to the South Walton TDC.

One of the research objectives is to evaluate visitor awareness of and participation in key characteristics of the Beaches of South Walton tourism product. Nine primary activities and attractions in the area are marketed by the TDC as being key facets of the visit experience. For each of these, respondent awareness of the activity/attraction is measured. Those aware of the activity/attraction are asked if they participated in it and, if so, how satisfied they were with the activity/attraction. These data allow the computation of a *conversion rate*—in other words, the rate at which those visitors who know about the activity/attraction choose to participate in it. Conversion rates are important indicators of the extent to which visitors value the activity/attraction as a feature of their Beaches of South Walton experience. For example, 93 percent of respondents were aware of the area's unique and distinctive shops, and 88 percent of those aware actually visited those shops (Table 1). This high conversion rate indicates that unique and distinctive shopping is perceived as an integral part of the Beaches of South Walton experience. A common practice in customer satisfaction analysis is to focus on the proportion of customers who report being very satisfied, as these are the customers who are most likely to become repeat buyers and most likely to act as informal "promoters" of the product to others. Table 2 shows that 46 percent of those who shopped reported that they were very satisfied.

Haas Center researchers prepared Tables 1 and 2 to report these findings for the first quarterly survey. The lead analyst will present these data to the client at a meeting of the TDC Board of Directors. She knows that her audience will have a keen interest in the relationships among awareness, participation, and satisfaction and will expect her to visually illustrate these relationships and offer her interpretation of the data.

1. What are the key data contained in Tables 1 and 2?
2. Create a single chart or graphic that integrates these key data from Tables 1 and 2 and illustrates their interrelationships.
3. Examine the data in Table 1 for "Golf" and "Unique/Distinctive Shops," both of which have very high rates of awareness. How would you interpret the large disparity in conversion rates for these activities/attractions?
4. What other interesting relationships among the data series can you find? What are the possible strategic implications of these relationships?

Table 1
Awareness and Participation in Key Attractions and Activities

	Awareness		"Awares" who Participate	Conversion Rate
Attraction/Activity	Count	Percent	Count	Percent
Golf	154	98.1	38	24.7
Fishing	151	96.2	38	25.2
Unique/Distinctive Shops	146	93.0	128	87.7
Children's Activities	126	80.3	57	45.2
Biking	124	79.0	28	22.6
State Parks/Forests	118	75.2	28	23.7
Cultural Sites	63	40.1	16	25.4
Historical Sites	61	38.9	8	13.1
Hiking	47	29.9	8	17.0

Table 2
Participant Satisfaction with Key Attractions and Activities

Attraction/Activity	Mean	Very Satisfied	Satisfied	Neutral	Dissatisfied	Very Dissatisfied
Golf	4.5	55.3%	39.5%	2.6%	2.6%	0.0%
Fishing	3.8	31.6	34.2	18.4	13.2	2.6
Unique/Distinctive Shops	4.3	45.7	38.6	14.2	1.6	0.0
Children's Activities	4.4	50.9	36.8	10.5	1.8	0.0
Biking	4.4	50.0	35.7	14.3	0.0	0.0
State Parks/Forests	4.3	46.4	35.7	14.3	3.6	0.0
Cultural Sites	4.2	37.5	43.8	18.8	0.0	0.0
Historical Sites	4.1	44.4	22.2	33.3	0.0	0.0
Hiking	4.4	62.5	12.5	25.0	0.0	0.0

CASE 20.2 *Your Integrated Case*

The Hobbit's Choice: Making a PowerPoint Presentation

Cory Rogers completed the report for The Hobbit's Choice Restaurant. He decided he wanted to make some PowerPoint slides to use in his presentation of the findings. Working in Word, he wrote a title to his presentation: The Hobbit's Choice Restaurant: Research Findings. Then he wrote out several other comments that he wanted to include in the beginning of his presentation including the following: Survey of 400 randomly selected residents; Sample screened to include only those who eat at restaurants at least every two weeks; Findings of those Very Likely to patronize The Hobbit's Choice, and so on. When Cory wrote out a number of the statements that he thought would help him communicate the purpose and method of the study, he turned his attention to presenting the findings.

Cory thought he would begin his presentation of the findings with a frequency distribution of the question that asked for the likelihood of patronizing an "upscale" restaurant. He prepared a frequency distribution of the responses to this question using SPSS. He continued by making several key analyses of the data using SPSS.

1. Using Word (or WordPerfect), write out several of the statements that you think would be appropriate to present to the client, Jeff Dean, for an oral presentation.
2. Import the statements you prepared in question 1 into PowerPoint using copy and paste. Experiment with different color text and font sizes and styles.
3. Using SPSS, run several frequency distributions. Using TableLooks, select an output format you like and import that output into PowerPoint.
4. Using SPSS, make a bar chart of the answers to the question regarding the likelihood of patronizing an "upscale" restaurant. Experiment with the different options of bar charts available to you in SPSS. Select a bar chart and import that chart into PowerPoint using copy and paste. Experiment with making edits on your slide.

Endnotes

CHAPTER 1

1. Fine, Brian (2000). Internet research: The brave new world. In C. Chakrapani ed. *Marketing Research: State of the Art Perspectives* Chicago: American Marketing Association, p. 143.
2. Kotler, Philip (1997). *Marketing Management: Analysis, Planning Implementation, 21 and Control*, 9th ed. Upper Saddle River, NJ: Prentice Hall, p. 19.
3. Drucker, Peter (1973). *Management: Tasks, Responsibilities, Practices*. New York: Harper & Row, pp. 64–65.
4. Kotler, Philip (2000). *Marketing Management: The Mellenium Edition*. Upper Saddle River, NJ: Prentice Hall, p. 19.
5. Bennett, P. (1995). *Glossary of Marketing Terms* 2nd ed. Chicago: American Marketing Association, p. 169.
6. Clancy, K. & Krieg, P. C. (2000). *Counterintuitive Marketing: Achieve Great Results Using Uncommon Sense*. New York: The Free Press.
7. Merritt, N. J. & Redmond, W. H. (1990). Defining marketing research: Perceptions vs. practice. *Proceedings: American Marketing Association*, 146–150.
8. Tracy, K. (1998). *Jerry Seinfeld: The Entire Domain*. Secaucus, NJ: Carol Publishing Group, pp. 64–65.
9. Marconi, J. (1998, June 8). What marketing aces do when marketing research tells them, 'don't do it!' *Marketing News*; Zangwill, W. (1993, March 8). When customer research is a lousy idea. *Wall Street Journal*, p. A12.
10. Heilbrunn, J. (August, 1989). Legal lessons from the delicare affair—1. United States, *Marketing and Research Today*, vol. 17, no. 3, 156–160. Also see Frederickson, P. & Totten, J. W. (1990). Marketing research projects in the academic setting: Legal liability after Beecham vs. Yankelovich, in Capello, L. M. et al., eds., *Progress in Marketing Thought, Proceedings of the Southern Marketing Association*, pp. 250–253.
11. See www.Mintel.com.
12. Lipson, S. (2001). Giving the customer the driver's seat—the power of research manager. A presentation made at the American Marketing Association's 22nd Annual Marketing Research Conference, Atlanta, GA.
13. Bruzzone, D. & Rosen, D. (2001, March). All the right moves. *Quirk's Marketing Research Review*. 15(3), 18; 56–76.
14. Grossnickle, J. & Raskin, O. (2001). *Online Marketing Research; Knowing Your Customer Using the Net*. New York: McGraw Hill, Inc., p. xix.
15. Diet aids/ Slimming drinks/ Dieting starts early: almost 1 in 20 of America's 12-year-olds on a diet.

(2001, October). Retrieved January 25, 2002 from www.ci.mintel.com.
16. These study topics were taken from the Marketing Science Institute's research priorities list and former award-winning research papers. See www.MSI.org for additional studies designed to improve marketing as a process.
17. Hogg, A. (2002, January). Personal correspondence with the authors.
18. Hogg, A. (2002), Online research overview. Retrieved January 3, 2002 from www.marketpower.com.
19. The description of the MIS is adapted from Kotler, P. (2000). *Marketing Management: The Millennium Edition*. Upper Saddle River, NJ: Prentice Hall, 100.
20. The authors are grateful for the advice of Gregory Yost, professor of accounting, for providing input on this section.
21. Whelan, D. (2001). Ink me, stud: Tattoos and piercings decorate 15% of American bodies, but even more still disapprove of them. *American Demographics*, 23, 12, 9–11.
22. Yin, S. (2001). Grandpa gets fit: Older Americans are going to the gym—for emotional as well as health reasons. *American Demographics*, 23, 11, 13–14.

CHAPTER 2

1. Lewis, P. (2001, December 24). Peter Lewis on technology. *Fortune*, p. 176.
2. See Schlossberg, H. (1990, January 8). Cost allocation can show true value of research. *Marketing News*, 24, 2; also see Martin, J. & Chadwick, J. (1988). Factors associated with executive decisions to conduct marketing research: An exploratory study. In Moore, D. L. (ed.), Marketing forward motion. *Proceedings of the Atlantic Marketing Association*, pp. 698–709.
3. Wade, R. K. (1993, Summer). The when/what research decision guide. *Marketing Research*, 5(3), 24–27.
4. Perreault, W. D., Jr. (1992, Fall). The shifting paradigm in marketing research. *Journal of the Academy of Marketing Science*, 20(4), 369.
5. Tomasino, R. F. (1985, January 4). Integrate market research with strategic plan to get budget okay. *Marketing News*, p. 8.
6. Clancy, K. J. & Shulman, R. S. (1994). *Marketing Myths That Are Killing Business*. New York: McGraw Hill, Inc., pp. 56, 258.
7. Andreasen, A. R. (1988). *Cheap but Good Marketing Research*. Homewood, IL: Dow Jones-Irwin.
8. Wellner, A. S. (2001, April). Research on a shoestring. *American Demographics*, pp. 38–39.

9. Thomas, J. (2001, November). Marketing research. *Executive Excellence*, pp. 11–12.

10. Wellner, A. S. (2001, April). Research on a shoestring. *American Demographics*, pp. 38–39.

11. Lohse, G. L. & Rosen, D. L. (2001, Summer). Signaling quality and credibility in Yellow Pages advertising: The influence of color and graphics on choice. *Journal of Advertising*, pp. 73–85.

12. Clancy, K. J. & Shulman, R. S. (1994). *Marketing Myths That Are Killing Business*. New York: McGraw Hill, Inc., p. 63.

Chapter 3

1. Note that we are only referring to customer research. Small business owners today may need research to address opportunities and impending problems of which their customers have no knowledge.

2. Bartels, R. (1988). *The History of Marketing Thought*. Columbus, OH: Publishing Horizons, Inc., p. 125. Much of the historical information in this entire section comes from Professor Bartels's book.

3. Hardy, H. (1990). *The Politz Papers: Science and Truth in Marketing Research*. Chicago: American Marketing Association.

4. Bartels, *The History of Marketing Thought*, p. 125.

5. Honomichl, J. (2000). Practitioner viewpoint. In Burns, A. C. & Bush, R. F. (2000). *Marketing Research*. Upper Saddle River, NJ: Prentice Hall, p. 24.

6. Honomichl, J. (2000, June 4). Growth stunt: Research revenues see smaller increase in '00. *Marketing News*, p. H3.

7. Malhotra, N. K. (1999). *Marketing Research*, 3rd ed. Upper Saddle River, NJ: Prentice Hall, pp. 16–19.

8. Kinnear, T. C. & Root, A. R. (1994). *Survey of Marketing Research: Organization Function, Budget, and Compensation*. Chicago: American Marketing Association, p. 38.

9. Kinnear, T. C. & Root, A. R., *Survey of Marketing Research*, p. 12.

10. Honomichl, J. (2002, June 10). Honomichl 50. *Marketing News*. Also see: Honomichl, J. (2001, June 4). Growth stunt: Research revenues see smaller increase in '00. *Marketing News*, p. H3.

11. Honomichl, J. (2002, June 10). Honomichl 50, *Marketing News*.

12. Internet marketing research grows despite industry slump. (2002, January). *Inside Research*, 13, 1. Also see Gofton, K. (2001, July). Research agencies pool their strength. *Marketing*, p. 33.

13. Opinion Research Corporation. (2001, August 27). *Marketing News*, p. 5.

14. DMS press room. (2002, February 9). Retrieved from www.dmsdallas.com/press_releases.html.

15. SPSS Inc. and AOL announce alliance to lead market for online research. (2002, February 9). Retrieved from www.spss.com/spssmr/news/press.

16. These examples and the following paragraphs are based on Mahajan, V. & Wind, J. (1999, Fall). Rx for marketing research: A diagnosis of and prescriptions for recovery of an ailing discipline in the business world. *Marketing Research*, pp. 7–13.

17. Clancy, K. & Krieg, P. C. (2000). *Counterintuitive Marketing: Achieve Great Results Using Uncommon Sense*. New York: The Free Press.

18. Quoted in Chakrapani, C. (2001, Winter). From the editor. *Marketing Research*, 13, 4, 2.

19. What's wrong with marketing research? (2001, Winter). *Marketing Research*, 13, 4.

20. Krum, J. R. (1978, October). B for marketing research departments. *Journal of Marketing*, 42, 8–12; Krum, J. R., Rau, P. A., & Keiser, S. K. (1987–1988, December–January). The marketing research process: role perceptions of researchers and users. *Journal of Advertising Research*, 27, 9–21; Dawson, S., Bush, R. F., & Stern, B. (1994, October). An evaluation of services provided by the marketing research industry. *Service Industries Journal*, 14 (4), 515–526; also see Austin, J. R. (1991). An exploratory examination of the development of marketing research service relationships: An assessment of exchange evaluation dimensions. In M. C. Gilly, et al. (eds.), *Enhancing Knowledge Development in Marketing* (pp. 133–141). 1991 AMA Educators' Conference Proceedings; also see Swan, J. E., Trawick, I. F., & Carroll, M. G. (1981, August). Effect of participation in marketing research on consumer attitudes toward research and satisfaction with a service. *Journal of Marketing Research*, pp. 356–363; also see Malholtra, N. K., Peterson, M., & Kleiser, S. B. (1999, Spring). Marketing research: A state-of-the-art review and directions for the 21st century. *Journal of the Academy of Marketing Science*, 27 (2), 160–183.

21. Dawson, S., Bush, R. F., & Stern, B. (1994, October). An evaluation of services provided by the market research industry. *Service Industries Journal*, 144, 515–526.

22. Consensus eludes certification issue. (1989, September 11). *Marketing News*, pp. 125, 127; Stern, B. & Crawford, T. (1986, September 12). It's time to consider certification of researchers. *Marketing News*, pp. 20–21; Stern, B. L. & Grubb, E. L. (1991). Alternative solutions to the marketing research industry's "quality control" problem. In R. L. King (ed.), *Marketing: Toward the twenty-first century* (pp. 225–229). Proceedings of the Southern Marketing Association; Jones, M. A. & McKinney, R. (1993). The need for certification in marketing research. In D. Thompson (ed.), *Marketing and education: Partners in progress* (pp. 224–229). Proceedings of the Atlantic Marketing Association. Also, for an excellent review of the pros and cons of certification, see Rittenburg, T. L. & Murdock, G. W. (1994, Spring). Highly sensitive issue still sparks controversy within the industry. *Marketing Research*, 6 (2), 5–10. Also see Giacobbe, R. W. &

Segel, M. N. (1994). Credentialing of marketing research professionals: An industry perspective. In R. Archoll and A. Mitchell (eds.), *Enhancing knowledge development in marketing* (pp. 229–301). A.M.A Educators' Conference Proceedings.

23. Achenbaum, A. A. (1985, June–July). Can we tolerate a double standard in marketing research? *Journal of Advertising Research*, 25, RC3–7.

24. Murphy, P. E. & Laczniack, G. R. (1992, June). Emerging ethical issues facing marketing researchers. *Marketing Research*, 4 (2), 6–11.

25. See Steinberg, M. S. (1992, June). The "professionalization" of marketing. *Marketing Research*, 4 (2), 56. Also McDaniel, S. W. & Solano-Mendez, R. (1993). Should marketing researchers be certified? *Journal of Advertising Research*, 33 (4), 20–31.

26. Neal, W. D. (1998). Extracted from presentation at the annual conference of the Advertising Research Foundation.

27. Bernstein, S. (1990, September). A call to audit market research providers. *Marketing Research*, 2 (3), 11–16.

28. First pcms announced. (2001, September 10). *Marketing News*, 35, 19, 22.

29. Reidman, P. (2001, January 29). ABCi alliance begins. *Advertising Age*, 72, 5, 38.

30. McDaniel, S., Verille, P., & Madden, C. S. (1985, February). The threats to marketing research: An empirical reappraisal. *Journal of Marketing Research*, pp. 74–80; Akaah, I. P. & Riordan, E. A. (1989, February). Judgements of marketing professionals about ethical issues in marketing research. *Journal of Marketing Research*, pp. 112–120; Laczniak, G. R. & Murphy, P. E. *Marketing Ethics*. Lexington, MA: Lexington Books; Ferrell, O. C. & Gresham, L. G. (1985, Summer). A contingency framework for understanding ethical decision making in marketing. *Journal of Marketing Research*, pp. 87–96; Reidenbach, R. E. & Robin, D. P. (1990). A partial testing of the contingency framework for ethical decision making: A path analytical approach. In L. M. Capella, H. W. Nash, J. M. Starling, & R. D. Taylor (eds.), *Progress in marketing thought* (pp. 121–128). Proceedings of the Southern Marketing Association; LaFleur, E. K. & Reidenbach, R. E. (1993). A taxonomic construction of ethics decision rules: An agenda for research. In T. K. Massey, Jr. (ed.), *Marketing: Satisfying a diverse customerplace* (pp. 158–161). Proceedings of the Southern Marketing Association; Reidenbach, R. E., LaFleur, E. K., Robin, D. P., & Forest, P. J. (1993). Exploring the dimensionality of ethical judgements made by advertising professionals concerning selected child-oriented television advertising practices. In T. K. Massey, Jr. (ed.), *Marketing: Satisfying a diverse customerplace* (pp. 166–170). Proceedings of the Southern Marketing Association; Klein, J. G. & Smith, N. C. (1994). Teaching marketing research ethics in business school classrooms. In R. Achrol & A. Mitchell (eds.),

Enhancing knowledge development in marketing (pp. 92–99). A.M.A Educators' Conference Proceedings.

31. Dolliver, M. (2000, July 10). Keeping honest company. *Adweek*, 41, 28, 29.

32. See Kelley, S., Ferrell, O. C., & Skinner, S. J. (1990). Ethical behavior among marketing researchers: An assessment. *Journal of Business Ethics*, 9, 8, 681ff.

33. See Whetstone, J. T. (2001, September). How virtue fits within business ethics. *Journal of Business Ethics*. 33, 2, 101–114 and Pallister, J., Nancarrow, C., & Brace, I. (1999, July). Navigating the righteous course: A quality issue. *Journal of the Market Research Society*, 41, 3, 327–342.

34. Hunt, S. D., Chonko, L. B., & Wilcox, J. B. (1984, August). Ethical problems of marketing researchers. *Journal of Marketing Research*, 21, 309–324.

35. For an excellent article on ethics, see Hunt, S. D. & Vitell, S. (1986). A general theory of marketing ethics. *Journal of Macromarketing*, pp. 5–16.

36. Hunt, S. D., Chonko, L. B., & Wilcox, J. B., Ethical problems of marketing researchers.

37. For an excellent discussion of these two philosophies relative to marketing research, see Kimmel, A. J. & Smith, N. C. (2001, July). Deception in marketing research: Ethical, methodological, and disciplinary implications. *Psychology & Marketing*, 18, 7, 672–680.

38. Full code of ethics in the area of marketing research. Retrieved from www.MarketingPower.com on February 16, 2002.

39. Bowers, D. K. (1995, Summer). Confidentiality challenges. *Marketing Research*, 7(3), 34–35.

40. Hunt, S. D., Chonko, L. B., & Wilcox, J. B., Ethical problems of marketing researchers.

41. Leaders: The lessons from Enron—Enron and auditing. (2002, February 9). *The Economist*; London, 362, 8259, 10; Grace, H. S., Illiano, G., Sack, R. J. & Turner, L. (2002, January). Enron and Andersen: Auditors under the microscope. *The CPA Journal*; New York, 72, 1, 8.

42. Kiecker, P. L. & Nelson, J. E. (1989). Cheating behavior by telephone interviewers: A view from the trenches. In P. Bloom et al. (eds.), *Enhancing knowledge development in marketing* (pp. 182–188). A.M.A. Educators' Conference Proceedings.

43. Hunt, S. D., Chonko, L. B., & Wilcox, J. B., Ethical problems of marketing researchers.

44. Ibid.

45. Jarvis, S. (2002, February 4). CMOR finds survey refusal rate still rising. *Marketing News*, 36, 3, 4. Also see Bowers, D. K. (1997). CMOR's first four years. *Marketing Research*, 9, 44–45; Shea, C. Z. & LeBourveau, C. (2000, Fall). Jumping the "hurdles" of marketing research. *Marketing Research*, 12, 3, 22–30.

46. Jarvis, S. (2002, February 4). CMOR finds survey refusal rate still rising.

47. Kimmel, A. J. & Smith, N. C. (2001, July). Deception in marketing research, pp. 663–689.

48. Toy, D., Wright, L., & Olson, J. (2001, July). A conceptual framework for analyzing deception and debriefing effects in marketing research. *Psychology & Marketing*, 18, 7, 691–719.

49. Ibid., p. 693.

50. Mail abuse prevention system definition of spam. Retrieved March 1, 2002, from www.mail-abuse.org/standard.html.

51. Gillin, D. (2001, Summer). Opt in or opt out? *Marketing Research*, pp. 6–7.

52. See www.bls.gov/oco/home.htm. Retrieved on March 3, 2002.

53. Dun, T. (1999). How research providers see it: An ARF study of practices, challenges and future opportunities. New York: Advertising Research Foundation, p. 10.

54. See www.bls.gov/oco/home.htm. Retrieved on March 3, 2002.

55. Jarvis, S. (2001, August 14). Compensation prize. *Marketing News*. Retrieved from www.marketingpower.com on December 19, 2001.

56. *Marketing and Sales Career Directory*, 4th ed. (1993). Detroit, MI: Gale Research Inc., pp. 81–95.

CHAPTER 4

1. Generational differences, Research Archives, Barna Research Group of Ventura, CA, 2002. www.barna.org/.

2. Anonymous (2001, August 27). Church looks to bust image with beer. *Marketing News*, 35, 18, 12.

3. Tomas, S. (1999, May). Creative problem-solving: An approach to generating ideas. *Hospital Material Management Quarterly*, 20, 4, 33–45.

4. Moorman, C., Zaltman, G., & Despande, R. (1992, August). Relationships between providers and users of marketing research: The dynamics of trust within and between organizations. *Journal of Marketing Research*, 24, 3, 314–328.

5. Adapted from Adler, L. (1979, September 17). Secrets of when, and when not to embark on a marketing research project, *Sales & Marketing Management Magazine*, 123, 108; (1980, March 17) 124, 108, and 124, 77.

6. Ibid.

7. Chapman, R. G. (1988, Spring). False economies in survey research. *Applied Marketing Research*, 28, 1, 16–20.

8. Thomas, J. (2001, November). Marketing research. *Executive Excellence*, 18, 11, 11–12.

9. Modified from Rieck, D. (2001, October). Being smarter than the average bear. *Direct Marketing*, 64, 6, 27.

10. Semon, T. (1999, June 7). Make sure the research will answer the right question. *Marketing News*, 33, 12, H30.

11. Based on Frevert, B. (2000, Spring). Is global research different? *Marketing Research*, 12, 1, 49–51.

12. For more information on proposals and reports see Carroll, N., Mohn, M., & Land, T. H. (1989, January/February/March). A guide to quality marketing research proposals and reports. *Business*, 39, 1, 38–40.

CHAPTER 5

1. Stewart, D. W. (1984). *Secondary research: Information sources and methods*. Newbury Park, CA: Sage Publications; Davidson, J. P. (1985, April). Low cost research sources. *Journal of Small Business Management*, 23, 73–77.

2. Bonoma, T. V. Case research in marketing: Opportunities, problems, and a process. *Journal of Marketing Research*, 22, 199–208.

3. Myers, J. Wireless for the 21st century. *Telephony*, 231(6), 24–26.

4. Greenbaum, T. L. (1988). *The Practical Handbook and Guide in Focus Group Research*. Lexington, MA: D.C. Health.

5. Stoltman, J. J. & Gentry, J. W. (1992). Using focus groups to study household decision processes and choices. In R. P. Leone & V. Kumar (eds.), *AMA Educator's Conference Proceedings*: Vol. 3. Enhancing knowledge development in marketing (pp. 257–263). Chicago: American Marketing Association.

6. Rydholm, J. (1999, July). Are we getting ahead of ourselves?, *Quirk's Marketing Research Review*, pp. 19, 95–97.

7. Kinnear, T. C. & Taylor, J. R. (1991). *Marketing research: An applied approach*. New York: McGraw-Hill, p. 142.

8. Sudman, S. & Wansink, B. (2002). *Consumer Panels*. 2nd edition. Chicago, IL. This book is recognized as an authoritative source on panels.

9. Personal communication with the authors from Allison Groom, American Heart Association, March 12, 2002.

10. Lohse, G. L. & Rosen, D. L. (2002, Summer). Signaling quality and credibility in Yellow Pages advertising: The influence of color and graphics on choice. *Journal of Advertising*, 30, 2, 73–85.

11. Wyner, G. (2000, Fall). Learn and earn through testing on the Internet: The Web provides new opportunities for experimentation. *Marketing Research*, 12, 3, 37–38.

12. Kerlinger, F. N. (1986). *Foundation of Behavioral Research*, 3rd ed. New York: Holt, Rinehart, and Winston.

13. Campbell, D. T. & Stanley, J. C. (1963). *Experimental and quasi-experimental designs for research*. Chicago: Rand McNally.

14. Calder, B. J., Phillips, L. W., & Tybour, A. M. (1992, December). The concept of external validity. *Journal of Consumer Research*, 9, 240–244.

15. Gray, L. R. & Diehl, P. L. (1992). *Research Methods for Business and Management*. New York: Macmillan Publishing Company, pp. 387–390.

16. Doyle, J. (1994, October). In with the new, out with the old. *Beverage World*, 113 (1576), 204–205.

17. Brennan, L. (1988, March). Test marketing. *Sales & Marketing Management Magazine*, 140, 50–62.

18. Miles, S. (2001). MyTurn is cutting back in unusual way. *Wall Street Journal*, Eastern Edition.

19. Churchill, G. A., Jr. (2001). *Basic Marketing Research*, 4th ed. Fort Worth, TX: The Dryden Press, pp. 144–145.

20. Spethmann, B. (1985, May 8). Test market USA. *Brandweek*, 36, 40–43.

21. Zuber, A. (2002, February 11). Pizza Hut launches cal-zone-like P'Zone item. *Nation's Restaurant News*, 36, 6 pp. 4, 50.

22. Kleinman, M. (2002, January 31). Carphone trials accessories standalone. *Marketing*, p. 2.

23. Matumoto, J., Perlik, A., Sheridan, M., Silver, D., & Yee, L. (2002, January 15). Fast, faster, fastest: McDonald's tests McQuick. *Restaurants & Institutions*, 112, 2, 18.

24. Van der Pool, L. (2001, December 17). Boston Beer unveils TV blast in test markets. *Adweek*, 42, 51, 5.

25. Beirne, M. (2001, November 5). Tobacco companies roll out smoke options. *Brandweek*, 42, 41, 9.

26. Clancy, K. J. & Shulman, R. S. (1995, October). Test for success. *Sales & Marketing Management Magazine*, 147 (10), 111–115.

27. Melvin, P. (1992, September). Choosing simulated test marketing systems. *Marketing Research*, 4 (3), 14–16.

28. Ibid. Also see Turner, J. & Brandt, J. (1978, Winter). Development and validation of a simulated market to test children for selected consumer skills. *Journal of Consumer Affairs*, 266–276.

29. Blount, S. (1992, March). It's just a matter of time. *Sales & Marketing Management*, 144 (3), 32–43.

30. Power, C. (1992, August 10). Will it sell in Podunk? Hard to say. *Business Week*, pp. 46–47.

31. Nelson, E. (2001, February 2). Colgate's net rose 10 percent in period, new products helped boost sales. *Wall Street Journal*, Eastern edition, p. B6.

32. Ihlwan, M. (2002, February 4). A nation of digital guinea pigs: Korea is a hotbed of such experiments as a cash-free city. *Business Week*, p. 50.

33. Greene, S. (1996, May 4). Chattanooga chosen as test market for smokeless cigarette. *Knight-Ridder/Tribune Business News*, 5040084.

34. Hayes, J. (1995, January 3). McD extends breakfast buffet test in south-east markets. *National Restaurant News*, 29 (4), 3.

35. Kotler, P. (1991). *Marketing management: Analysis, planning, implementation, & control*. Upper Saddle River, NJ: Prentice Hall, p. 335.

36. Power, C. (1992, August 10). Will it sell in Podunk? Hard to say. *Business Week*, pp. 46–47.

37. This case was prepared by Michelle D. Steward, Ph.D. Candidate and Instructor, Arizona State University.

CHAPTER 6

1. U.S. Census Bureau. (2000). All across the USA: Population distribution and composition 2000. In *Population Profile of the United States: 2000* (Internet Release), Chapter 2. Retrieved March 23, 2002, from www.census.gov/population/www/pop-profile/profile2000.html.

2. For an example of using secondary data for a marketing research project, see Castleberry, S. B. (2001, December). Using secondary data in marketing research: A project that melds Web and off-Web sources. *Journal of Marketing Education*, 23, 3, 195–203.

3. Wagner, C. G. (2001, July–August). Technology: The promise of Internet2. *The Futurist*, 35, 4, 12–13.

4. Senn, J. A. (1988). *Information Technology in Business: Principles, Practice, and Opportunities*. Upper Saddle River, NJ: Prentice Hall, 66.

5. Grisaffe, D. (2002, January 21). See about linking CRM and MR systems. *Marketing News*, 36, 2, 13.

6. Drozdenko, R. G. & Drake, P. D. (2002). *Optimal Database Marketing*. Thousand Oaks, CA: Sage Publications.

7. McKim, R. (2001, September). Privacy notices: What they mean and how marketers can prepare for them. *Journal of Database Marketing*, 9, 1, 79–84.

8. See, for example, *U.S. Industrial Outlook 1999*. (1999). Washington, DC: International Trade Administration, U.S. Department of Commerce.

9. Gordon, L. P. (1995). *Using Secondary Data in Marketing Research: United States and Worldwide*. Westport, CT: Quorum Books, 24.

10. *Market Statistics* is a division of Bill Communications, Corporate Headquarters: 355 Park Avenue South, New York, NY 10010.

11. These questions and much of the following discussion is taken from Stewart, D. W. (1984). *Secondary Research: Information Sources and Methods*. Newbury Park, CA: Sage Publications.

12. Murray, D., Swartz, J., & Lichter, S. R. (2001). *It Ain't Necessarily So: How Media Make and Unmake the Scientific Picture of Reality*. Lanham, MD: Rowman & Littlefield Publishers, Inc.

13. Ibid., pp. 71–76.

14. Ibid., pp. vii–ix.

15. See Goldberg, B. (2002). *Bias*. Washington, DC: Regnery Publishing, Inc., and Best, J. (2001). *Damned Lies and Statistics*. Berkeley, CA: University of California Press.

16. Crossen, C. (1994). *Tainted Truth: The Manipulation of Fact in America*. New York: Simon & Schuster, 140.

17. Chapman, J. (1987, February). Cast a critical eye: Small area estimates and projections sometimes can be dramatically different. *American Demographics*, 9, 30.

18. These steps are updated and adapted from Stewart, D. W. (1984). *Secondary Research: Information Sources and Methods*. Newbury Park, CA: Sage Publications, 20–22, by Ms. Peggy Toifel, MSLS, MBA, University Librarian, University of West Florida, 2002.

19. Rogers, C. O. (1999, Spring). Census 2000 update. *Indiana Business Review*, 74, 1, 11–12.

20. America's experience with Census 2000. (2000, August). *Direct Marketing*, 63, 4, 46–51.

21. Researchers wishing to use SIC codes should refer to the *Standard Industrial Classification Manual 1987*, rev. ed. (1987). Executive office of the President, U.S. office of Management and Budget, Washington, DC: U.S. Government Printing Office.

22. Winchester, J. (1998, February). Marketers prepare for switch from SIC codes. *Business Marketing*, 1, 34.

23. Boettcher, J. (1996, April–May). NAFTA prompts a new code system for industry—The death of SIC and birth of NAICS. *Database*, 42–45.

24. Information found in this section may be referenced in *Demographics USA* (2002). Chicago: Bill Communications.

25. The authors wish to thank Gregory Yost, professor of accounting, for writing this exercise.

26. This case was prepared by David R. Eppright, Ph.D., University of West Florida. Dr. Eppright is a specialist in Internet marketing.

Chapter 7

1. Actually, virtually all these firms offer some customization of data analysis and many offer varying methods of collecting data. Still, while customization is possible, these same companies provide standardized processes and data.

2. See *Rocking the Ages: The Yankelovich Perspective on Generational Marketing.* (1997). New York: Harper Business.

3. Solutions & Services/consumer trends research/monitor annually. Retrieved from Yankelovich.com on September 6, 2002.

4. You can read more about this service at www. Yankelovich.com.

5. Harris poll. Retrieved from www.HarrisInteractive.com on September 6, 2002.

6. What does America think about? (undated publication). Wilmington, Delaware: Scholarly Resources, Inc.

7. Fish, D. (2000, November). Untangling psychographics and lifestyle. *Quirk's Marketing Research Review*, 138ff.

8. SRI Consulting Business Intelligence. Retrieved from www.sric-bi.com/VALS/ on May 10, 2002.

9. Stolzenberg, M. (2000, February). 10 tips on tracking research. *Quirk's Marketing Research Review*, 20–24.

10. For an example of analysis of supermarket data using Scantrack, see Heller, W. (2000, July). Surfing retail channels. *Progressive Grocer*, 79, 7, 48–58.

11. Retail Measurement. (2002). Retrieved from www. acnielsen.com on September 6, 2002.

12. Combined outlet consumer panel. (2002). Retrieved from www.infores.com/public/us/prodserv/factsheet/us_fact_chpcombinedoutlet.htm on May 16, 2002.

13. Marketing minds specializing in research. (2002). Retrieved from www.nfow.com/NFOPanel.asp on May 16, 2002.

14. NPD group, food and beverages worldwide. (2002). Retrieved from www.npd.com on May 16, 2002.

15. Ehrenberg, A. S. C. & Wakshlag, J. (1987, February). Repeat-viewing with people meters. *Journal of Advertising Research*, pp. 9–13; Stoddard, L. R., Jr. (1987, October). The history of people meters. *Journal of Advertising Research*, pp. 10–12.

16. By permission, Arbitron.

17. By permission, RoperASW.

18. Adnorms. (2002). RoperASW, p. iv.

19. Patchen, R. H. & Kolessar, R. S. (1999, August). Out of the lab and into the field: A pilot test of the Personal Portable Meter. *Journal of Advertising Research*, 39, 4, 55–68. Also see Moss, L. (2002, February 11). A constant companion. *Broadcasting & Cable*, 132, 6, 17.

20. Hughes, L. Q. (2001, June 18). Buyers demand more data. *Advertising Age*, 72, 25, T2.

21. Reid, A. (2000, January 28). Is ITV's tvSPAN the holy grail adland has been waiting for? *Campaign*, p. 20.

22. For a review of these discussions, see Peters, B. (1990, December). The brave new world of single-source information. *Marketing Research*, 2, 4, 16; Churchill, V. B. (1990, December). The role of ad hoc survey research in a single source world. *Marketing Research*, 2, 4, 22–26 and Metzger, G. D. (1990, December). Single source: Yes and no (the backward view). *Marketing Research*, 2, 4, 29.

23. The authors wish to thank ESRI Business Information Solutions for contributing this case.

Chapter 8

1. Raymond, J. (2002, March). All smiles. *American Demographics*, 23, 3, S18.

2. Ezzy, D. (2001, August). Are qualitative methods misunderstood? *Australian and New Zealand Journal of Public Health*, 25, 4, 294–297.

3. Clark, A. (2001, September 13). Research takes an inventive approach, *Marketing*, 25–26.

4. DeNicola, N. (2002, March 4). Casting finer net not necessary. *Marketing News*, 36, 5, 46.

5. Griffen, D. S. & Duley, R. (2000, July/August). Read all about it. *Quirks Marketing Research Review*, XIV, 7, 20–21, 104–106.

6. Smith, S. M. & Whitlark, D. B. (2001, Summer). Men and women online: What makes them click? *Marketing Research*, 13, 2, 20–25.

7. For some guidelines to direct observation, see Becker, B. (1999, September 27). Take direct route when data-gathering. *Marketing News*, 33, 20, 29, 31.

8. Piirto, R. (1991, September). Socks, ties and videotape. *American Demographics*, 6.

9. Fellman, M. W. (1999, Fall). Breaking tradition. *Marketing Research*, 11, 3, 20–34.

10. Modified from Tull, D. S., & Hawkins, D. I. (4th Ed.). (1987). *Marketing Research*. New York: Macmillan, 331.

11. Rust, L. (1993, November/December). How to reach children in stores: Marketing tactics grounded in observational research. *Journal of Advertising Research*, 33, 6, 67–72, and Rust, L. (1993, July/August). Parents and children shopping together: A new approach to the qualitative analysis of observational data. *Journal of Advertising Research*, 33, 4, 65–70.

12. Thomas, J. (1999, February). Motivational research. *Quirks Marketing Research Review*, XII, 2, 40–43.

13. Viles, P. (1992, August 24). Company measures listenership in cars. *Broadcasting*, 122, 35, 28.

14. Kephart, P. (1996, May). The spy in aisle 3. *American Demographics Marketing Tools*, www.marketingtools.com/Publications/MT/96_mt/9605MD04.htm.

15. Del Vecchio, E. (1988, Spring). Generating marketing ideas when formal research is not available. *Journal of Services Marketing*, 2, 2, 71–74.

16. Mariampolski, H. (1988, January 4). Ethnography makes comeback as research tool. *Marketing News*, 22, 1, 32, 44.

17. Hellebursch, S. J. (2000, September 11). Don't read research by the numbers. *Marketing News*, 34, 19, 25.

18. Kahn, A. (1996, September 6). Focus groups alter decisions made in business, politics. *Knight-Ridder/Tribune Business News*, 916.

19. Quinlan, P. (2000, December). Insights on a new site. *Quirk's Marketing Research Review*, XIV, 11, 36–39.

20. Hines, T. (2000). An evaluation of two qualitative methods (focus group interviews and cognitive maps) for conducting research into entrepreneurial decision making. *Qualitative Market Research*, 3, 1, 7–16.

21. Berlamino, C. (1989, December/January). Designing the qualitative research project: Addressing the process issues. *Journal of Advertising Research*, 29, 6, S7–S9.

22. Greenbaum, T. L. (1993, March 1). Focus group research is not a commodity business. *Marketing News*, 27, 5, 4.

23. Greenbaum, T. L. (1991, May 27). Answer to moderator problems starts with asking right questions. *Marketing News*, 25, 11, 8–9; Fern, E. F. (1982, February). The use of focus groups for idea generation: The effects of group size, acquaintanceship, and moderator on response quantity and quality. *Journal of Marketing Research*, 1–13.

24. Greenbaum, T. L. (1991). Do you have the right moderator for your focus groups? Here are 10 questions to ask yourself. *Bank Marketing*, 23, 1, 43.

25. PRA, Inc., 500–363 Broadway, Winnipeg, Manitoba, R3C 3N9, www.pra.ca/main.html.

26. Based on Henderson, N. R. (2000, December). Secrets of our success: Insights from a panel of moderators. *Quirk's Marketing Research Review*, XIV, 11, 62–65.

27. For guidelines for "backroom observers," see Langer, J. (2001, September 24). Get more out of focus group research. *Marketing News*, 35, 20, 19–20.

28. Grinchunas, R., & Siciliano, T. (1993, January 4). Focus groups produce verbatims, not facts. *Marketing News*, 27, 1, FG-19.

29. Zinchiak, M. (2001, July/August). Online focus groups FAQs, *Quirk's Marketing Research Review*, XV, 7, 38–46.

30. Lonnie, K. (2001, November 19). Combine phone, Web for focus groups. *Marketing News*, 35, 24, 15–16.

31. For interesting comments, see DeNicola, N. & Kennedy, S. (2001, November 19). Quality Inter(net)action. *Marketing News*, 35, 24, 14.

32. Adapted from Zinchiak, M. (2001, July/August). Online focus group FAQs.

33. Jarvis, S. & Szynal, D. (2001, November 19). Show and tell. *Marketing News*, 35, 24, 1, 13.

34. Greenbaum, T. L. (1993, September 13). Focus groups can play a part in evaluating ad copy. *Marketing News*, 27, 19, 24–25.

35. Czinkota, M. R. & Ronkainen, L. A. (1995, January). Conducting primary market research: Market research for your export operations, part 2. *International Trade Forum*, 1, 16.

36. Shermach, K. (1996, April 8). Research firms take unusual approach to kids. *Marketing News*, 30, 8, 26.

37. Greenbaum, T. (2000, December). Conducting focus groups with disabled respondents. *Quirk's Marketing Research Review*, XIV, 11, 28–31.

38. Rowan, M. M. (1991, July/August). Bankers beware! Focus groups can steer you wrong. *Bottom Line*, 8, 4, 37–41.

39. Potts, D. (1990, September 3). Bias lurks in all phases of qualitative research. *Marketing News*, 24, 18, 12–13.

40. Rodgers, A. (1993, January 4). Better, faster, cheaper doesn't always mean 'best.' *Marketing News*, 27, 1, FG-19.

41. Flores Letelier, M., Spinosa, C., & Calder, B. (2000, Winter). Taking and expanded view of customers' needs: Qualitative research for aiding innovation. *Marketing Research*, 12, 4, 4–11.

42. Kahan, H. (1990, September 3). One-on-ones should sparkle like the gems they are. *Marketing News*, 24, 18, 8–9.

43. Roller, M. R. (1987, August 28). A real in-depth interview wades into the stream of consciousness. *Marketing News*, 21, 18, 14.

44. Kahan, One-on-ones should sparkle like the gems they are.

45. An interesting article on recent developments in depth interviewing is Wansink, B. (2000, Summer). New techniques to generate key marketing insights. *Marketing Research*, 12, 2, 28–36.

46. Kates, B. (2000, April). Go in-depth with depth interviews. *Quirk's Marketing Research Review*, XIV, 4, 36–40.

47. Mitchell, V. (1993, First Quarter). Getting the most from in-depth interviews. *Business Marketing Digest*, 18, 1, 63–70.

48. Berstell, G. & Nitterhouse, D. (2001, Fall). Asking all the right questions. *Marketing Research*, 13, 3, 14–20.

49. Ibid.

50. An example is Piirto, R. (1990, December). Measuring minds in the 1990s. *American Demographics*, 12, 12, 30–35.

51. Green, P., Wind, Y., Krieger, A., & Saatsoglou, P. (2000, Spring). Applying qualitative data. *Marketing Research*, 12, 1, 17–25.

52. Clarke, A. (2001, September 13). Research takes an inventive approach. *Marketing*, 2–26.

53. Wellner, A. S. (2001, April). Research on a shoestring. *American Demographics*, 23, 4, 38–39.

54. Marshall, S., Drapeau, T., & DiSciullo, M. (2001, July/August). An eye on usability. *Quirk's Marketing Research Review*, XV, 7, 20–21, 90–92.

55. Allmon, D. E. (1988). Voice stress and likert scales: A paired comparison. In David L. Moore, ed., "Marketing: Forward Motion," *Proceedings of the Atlantic Marketing Association* (1988), 710–714.

CHAPTER 9

1. Brody, J. (2001, Spring). Defining the benefits of online medical market research. *Marketing Health Services*. 21, 1, 32–34; Anonymous (2000, Winter). Internet tool enables rapid primary market research. *Medical Industry Information Report*, 5, 1.

2. Carlson, A. G. (2001, September). Using surveys to prove or disprove claims. *The Practical Litigator*, 12, 5, 29–36.

3. Cleland, K. (1996, May). Online research costs about one-half that of traditional methods. *Business Marketing*, 81, 4, B8–B9.

4. Jang, H., Lee, B., Park, M., & Stokowski, P. A. (2000, February). Measuring underlying meanings of gambling from the perspective of enduring involvement. *Journal of Travel Research*, 38, 3, 230–238.

5. Ericson, P. I. & Kaplan, C. P. (2000, November). Maximizing qualitative responses about smoking in structured interviews. *Qualitative Health Research*, 10, 6, 829–840.

6. See Jacobs, H. (1989, Second Quarter). Entering the 1990s—The state of data collection—From a mall perspective. *Applied Marketing Research*, 30, 2, 24–26; Lysaker, R. L. (1989, October). Data collection methods in the U.S. *Journal of the Market Research Society*, 31, 4, 477–488; Gates, R., & Solomon, P. J. (1982, August/September). Research using the mall intercept: State of the art. *Journal of Advertising Research*, 43–50; Bush, A. J., Bush, R. F., & Chen, H. C. (1991). Method of administration effects in mall intercept interviews. *Journal of the Market Research Society*, 33, 4, 309–319.

7. Hornik, J., & Eilis, S. (1989, Winter). Strategies to secure compliance for a mall intercept interview. *Public Opinion Quarterly*, 52, 4, 539–551.

8. At least one study refutes the concern about shopping frequency. See DuPont, T. D. (1987, August/September). Do frequent mall shoppers distort mall-intercept results? *Journal of Advertising Research*, 27, 4, 45–51.

9. Bush, A. J., & Grant, E. S. (1995, Fall). The potential impact of recreational shoppers on mall intercept interviewing: An exploratory study. *The Journal of Marketing Theory and Practice*, 3, 4, 73–83.

10. Bush, A. J., & Hair, J. F. (1983, May). An assessment of the mall intercept as a data collection method. *Journal of Marketing Research*, 22, 158–167.

11. Sheppard. J. (2000, April). Half-empty or half-full? *Quirk's Marketing Research Review*, XIV, 4, 42–45.

12. See, for example, Xu, M., Bates, B. J., & Schweitzer, J. C. (1993). The impact of messages on survey participation in answering machine households. *Public Opinion Quarterly*, 57, 232–237; Meinert, D. B., Festervand, T. A., & Lumpkin, J. R. (1992). Computerized questionnaires: Pros and cons, in Robert L. King, ed., "Marketing: Perspectives for the 1990s." *Proceedings of the Southern Marketing Association*, 201–206.

13. Remington, T. D. (1993). Telemarketing and declining survey response rates. *Journal of Advertising Research*, 32, 3, RC-6, RC-7.

14. Bos, R. (1999, November). A new era in data collection, *Quirk's Marketing Research Review*, XII, 10, 32–40.

15. Fletcher, K. (1995, June 15). Jump on the omnibus. *Marketing*, 25–28.

16. Gates, R. H., & Jarboe, G. R. (Spring). Changing trends in data acquisition for marketing research. *Journal of Data Collection*, 27, 1, 25–29; also see Synodinos, N. E., & Brennan, J. M. (1998, Summer). Computer interactive interviewing in survey research. *Psychology and Marketing*, 117–138.

17. By permission, Opinion One.

18. DePaulo, P. J., & Weitzer, R. (1994, January 3). Interactive phone technology delivers survey data quickly. *Marketing News*, 28, 1, 15.

19. Adapted from Pettit, R. & Monster, R. (2001, November). Expanding horizons: Web-enabled technologies helping globalize marketing research. *International Research*, XV, 10, 42–48.

20. Jones, P., & Palk, J. (1993). Computer-based personal interviewing: State-of-the-art and future prospects. *Journal of the Market Research Society*, 35, 3, 221–233.

21. Heun, C. T. (2001, October 15). Procter & Gamble readies online market-research push. *Informationweek*, 859, 26.

22. For a "speed" comparison, see Cobanouglu, C., Warde, B., & Moeo, P. J. (2001, Fourth Quarter). A comparison of mail, fax and Web-based survey methods. *International Journal of Market Research*, 43, 3, 441–452.

23. Bruzzone, D. & Shellenberg, P. (2000, July/August). Track the effect of advertising better, faster, and cheaper online. *Quirk's Marketing Research Review*, XIV, 7, 22–35.

24. Sudman, S. & Blair, E. (1999, Spring). Sampling in the twenty-first century. *Academy of Marketing Science Journal*, 27, 2, 269–277.

25. Grecco, C. (2000, July/August). Research non-stop. *Quirk's Marketing Research Review*, XIV, 7, 70–73.

26. Greenberg, D. (2000, July/August). Internet economy gives rise to real-time research. *Quirk's Marketing Research Review*, XIV, 7, 88–90.

27. *The World Wide Web and the Four Ps of Marketing*, William H. MacElroy, Terra Schehr, Steven Kaiser, German Online Research Society—DGOF e.V., Georg-Elias-Mueller Institute for Psychology, University of Goettingen, May 2001.

28. Ibid.

29. Taylor, H., Bremer, J., Overmeyer, C., Siegel, J. W., & Terhanian, G. (2001, Second Quarter). The record of Internet-based opinion polls in predicting the results of 72 races in the November 2000 U.S. elections. *International Journal of Market Research*, 43, 2, 127–135.

30. Rosenblum, J. (2001, July/August). Give and take. *Quirk's Marketing Research Review*, XV, 7, 74–77.

31. Source: Nielsen//NetRatings Global Internet Trends, Q2 2000.

32. Brown, S. (1987). Drop and collect surveys: A neglected research technique? *Journal of the Market Research Society*, 5, 1, 19–23.

33. American Statistical Association (1997). More about mail surveys, ASA Series: What is a survey?

34. Nonresponse is a concern with any survey, and our understanding of refusals is minimal. See, for example, Groves, R. M., Cialdini, R. B., & Couper, M. P. (1992). Understanding the decision to participate in a survey. *Public Opinion Quarterly*, 56, 475–495.

35. See, for example, McDaniel, S. W., & Verille, P. (1987, January). Do topic differences affect survey non-response? *Journal of the Market Research Society*, 29, 1, 55–66, or Whitehead, J. C. (1991, Winter). Environmental interest group behavior and self-selection bias in contingent valuation mail surveys. *Growth & Change*, 22, 1, 10–21.

36. A large number of studies have sought to determine response rates for a wide variety of inducement strategies. See, for example, Fox, R. J., Crask, M., & Kim, J. (Winter). Mail questionnaires in survey research: A review of response inducement techniques. *Public Opinion Quarterly*, 52, 4, 467–491.

37. Yammarino, F., Skinner, S., & Childers, T. (1991). Understanding mail survey response behavior. *Public Opinion Quarterly*, 55, 613–639.

38. Conant, J., Smart, D., & Walker, B. (1990). Mail survey facilitation techniques: An assessment and proposal regarding reporting practices. *Journal of the Market Research Society*, 32, 4, 369–380.

39. Fish, D. (2000, May). Is that your final answer? *Quirk's Marketing Research Review*, XIV, 5, 22–24.

40. Jassaume Jr., R. A., & Yamada, Y. (1990, Summer). A comparison of the viability of mail surveys in Japan and the United States. *Public Opinion Quarterly*, 54, 2, 219–228.

41. Arnett, R. (1990, Second Quarter). Mail panel research in the 1990s. *Applied Marketing Research*, 30, 2, 8–10.

CHAPTER 10

1. Sometimes open-ended questions are used to develop closed-ended questions that are used later. See, for example, Erffmeyer, R. C. & Johnson, D. A. (2001, Spring). An exploratory study of sales force automation practices: Expectations and realities. *The Journal of Personal Selling & Sales Management*, 21, 2, 167–175.

2. Fox, S. (2001, May). Market research 101. *Pharmaceutical Executive*, Supplement: *Successful Product Management: A Primer*, 34.

3. Honomichl, J. (1994). Satisfaction measurement jump-starts survey research. *Marketing News*, 25, 14, 15.

4. Some researchers claim the use of a 0–10 scale over the telephone is actually better than a 3-, 4-, or 5-point scale. See Loken, B. et al. (1987, July). The use of 0–10 scales in telephone surveys. *Journal of the Marketing Research Society*, 29, 3, 353–362.

5. See, for example, Leigh, J. H. & Martin Jr., C. R. (1987). Don't know item nonresponse in a telephone survey: Effects of question form and respondent characteristics. *Journal of Marketing Research*, 29, 3, 317–339.

6. Source: Anonymous (2001, August 23). A third of young people say they chew gum daily, *Marketing*.

7. Ideally, respondents should respond to the scale as having equal intervals. See, for example, Crask, M. R. & Fox, R. J. (1987). An exploration of the interval properties of three commonly used marketing research studies: A magnitude estimation approach. *Journal of the Market Research Society*, 29, 3, 317–339.

8. See, for example, Yoon, S. & Kim, J. (2001, November/December). Is the Internet more effective than traditional media? Factors affecting the choice of media. *Journal of Advertising Research*, 41, 6, 53–60; Donthu, N. (2001, November/December). Does your Web site measure up? *Marketing Management*, 10, 4, 29–32; Finn, A., McFadyen, S., Hoskins, C. & Hupfer, M. (2001, Fall). Quantifying the sources of value of a public service. *Journal of Public Policy & Marketing*, 20, 2, 225–239.

9. See, for example, Wellner, A. S. (2002, February). The female persuasion. *American Demographics*, 24, 2, 24–29; Wasserman, T. (2002, January 7). Color me bad. *Brandweek*, 43, 1, 2; Wilke, M. & Applebaum, M. (2001, November 5). Peering out of the closet. *Brandweek*, 42, 41, 26–32.

10. Statements are taken from Wells, W. D. & Tigert, D. J. (1971). Activities, interests, and opinions. *Journal of Advertising Research*, reported in Kassarjain, H. H. & Robertson, T. S. (1973). *Perspectives in Consumer Behavior* (Glenview, IL.: Scott Foresman), 175–176.

11. Based on Vriens, M., Wedel, M. & Sandor, Z. (2001, Summer). Split-questionnaire designs: A new tool in survey design and panel management. *Marketing Research*, 13, 2, 14–19.

12. Another way to avoid the halo effect is to have subjects rate each stimulus on the same attribute and then move to the next attribute. See Wu, B. T. W. & Petroshius, S. (1987). The halo effect in store image management. *Journal of the Academy of Marketing Science*, 15, 1, 44–51.

13. The halo effect is real and used by companies to good advantage. See, for example, Moukheiber, Z. & Langreth, R. (2001, December 10). The halo effect. *Forbes*, 168, 15, 66; Anonymous (2002, March 11). Sites seeking advertising (the paid kind). *Advertising Age*, 73, 10, 38.

14. Garg, R. K. (1996, July). The influence of positive and negative wording and issue involvement on responses to Likert scales in marketing research. *Journal of the Marketing Research Society*, 38, 3, 235–246.

15. Scale development requires rigorous research. See, for example, Churchill, G. A. (1979, February). A paradigm for developing better measures of marketing constructs. *Journal of Marketing Research*, 16, 64–73 for method; Ram, S. & Jung, H. S. (1990). The conceptualization and measurement of product usage. *Journal of the Academy of Marketing Science*, 18, 1, 67–76 for an example.

16. See, for example, Bishop, G. F. (1985, Summer). Experiments with the middle response alternative in survey questions. *Public Opinion Quarterly*, 51, 220–232; Schertizer, C. B. & Kernan, J. B. (1985, October). More on the robustness of response scales. *Journal of the Marketing Research Society*, 27, 262–282.

17. See also Duncan, O. D. & Stenbeck, M. (1988, Winter). No opinion or not sure? *Public Opinion Quarterly*, 52, 513–525; Durand, R. M. & Lambert, Z. V. (1988, March). Don't know responses in survey: Analyses and interpretational consequences. *Journal of Business Research*, 16, 533–543.

18. Semon, T. T. (2001, October 8). Symmetry shouldn't be goal for scales. *Marketing News*, 35, 21, 9.

19. Elms. P. (2000, April). Using decision criteria anchors to measure importance among Hispanics. *Quirk's Marketing Research Review*, XV, 4, 44–51.

20. Siciliano, T. (1999, November). Magnitude estimations: A realistic scaling technique for international research. *Quirk's Marketing Research Review*, XIII, 10, 18–19, 82.

21. Kumar, V. & Nagpal, A. (2001, Spring). Segmenting global markets: Look before you leap. *Marketing Research*, 13, 1, 8–13.

22. Developed from Hiscock, J. (2002, February 14). Most Trusted Brands 2002, *Marketing*, 20–21.

23. Personal communication with Gavin Murry, *Reader's Digest*.

24. For example, bogus recall was found negatively related to education, income, and age but positively related to "yea-saying" and attitude toward the slogan. See Glassman, M., & Ford, J. B. (Fall 1988). An empirical investigation of bogus recall. *Journal of the Academy of Marketing Science*, 16, 3, 4, 38–41; Singh, R. (1991). "Reliability and Validity of Survey Research in Marketing: The State of the Art," in Robert L. King, ed., "Marketing: Toward the Twenty-First Century," *Proceedings of the Southern Marketing Association*, 210–213; Pressley, M. M., Strutton, H. D., & Dunn, M. G. (1991). "Demographic Sample Reliability among Selected Telephone Sampling Replacement Techniques," in Robert L. King, ed., "Marketing: Toward the Twenty-First Century," *Proceedings of the Southern Marketing Association*, 214–219; Babin, B. J., Darden, W. R., & Griffin, M. (1992). "A Note on Demand Artifacts in Marketing Research," in Robert L. King, ed., "Marketing: Perspectives for the 1990s," *Proceedings of the Southern Marketing Association*, 227–230; Dunipace, R. A., Mix, R. A., &. Poole, R. R. (1993). "Overcoming the Failure to Replicate Research in Marketing: A Chaotic Explanation," in Tom K. Massey Jr., ed., "Marketing: Satisfying a Diverse Customerplace," *Proceedings of the Southern Marketing Association*, 194–197; Malawian, K. P. & Butler, D. D. (1994). "The Semantic Differential: Is It Being Misused in Marketing Research?" in Ravi Achrol and Andrew Mitchell, eds., "Enhancing Knowledge Development in Marketing," *A.M.A. Educators' Conference Proceedings*, 19.

25. Statistical analysis can sometimes be used to assist in establishing face validity. See, for example, Wolburg, J. M. and Pokrywczynski, J. (2002, September/October). A psychographic analysis of Generation Y college students. *Journal of Advertising Research*, 41, 5, 33–52.

CHAPTER 11

1. Susan, C. (1994). Questionnaire design affects response rate. *Marketing News*, 28, H25, and Sancher, M. E. (1992). Effects of questionnaire design on the quality of survey data. *Public Opinion Quarterly*, 56, 206–217.

2. Babbie, E. (1990). *Survey research methods*, 2nd ed. Belmont, CA: Wadsworth Publishing Co., pp. 131–132.

3. This example was reported in Crossen, C. (1994). *Tainted truth: The manipulation of fact in America*. New York: Simon & Schuster.

4. Hunt, S. D., Sparkman, R. D., & Wilcox, J. (1982, May). The pretest in survey research: Issues and preliminary findings. *Journal of Marketing Research*, 26 (4), 269–273.

5. Peterson, R. A. (2000). *Constructing effective questionnaires*. Thousand Oaks, CA: Sage Publications, Inc., pp. 1–2.

6. Dillman, D. A. (1978). *Mail telephone surveys: The total design method*. New York: John Wiley & Sons, Inc.

7. Loftus, E. & Zanni, G. (1975). Eyewitness testimony: The influence of the wording of a question. *Bulletin of the Psychonomic Society*, 5, 86–88.

8. Even simple words may be interpreted differently by respondents from what researcher intends. See Barnes, J. H. & Dotson, M. J. (1989, November). The effect of mixed grammar chains on response to survey questions. *Journal of Marketing Research*, 26 (4), 468–472.

9. Most agree that the classic work in question wording is: Payne, S. L. (1951). *The art of asking questions*. Princeton, NJ: Princeton University Press.

10. These guidelines are adapted from Alreck, P. L. & Settle, R. B. (1995). *The survey research handbook*. Homewood, IL.: Richard D. Irwin, pp. 88–99. Also see Barnes, J. H. & Dotson, M. J. (1989, November). The effect of mixed grammar chains on response to survey questions. *Journal of Marketing Research*, 468–472.

11. See Valdes, M. I. (2000). *Marketing to American Latinos*. Ithaca, NY: Paramount Market Publishing Inc.

12. Humberto, V. (1990). Hispanic values and subcultural research. *Journal of Academy of Marketing Science*, 17 (1), 23–28.

13. Contributed by Mr. Joel Axelrod of BRX/Global, Inc. personal communications with authors.

14. For memory questions, it is advisable to have respondents recontruct specific events. See, for example, Cook, W. A. (1987, February–March). Telescoping and memory's other tricks. *Journal of Advertising Research*, 27 (1), RC5–RC8.

15. Patten, M. (2001). *Questionnaire research*. Los Angeles, CA: Pyrczak Publishing, p. 9.

16. Ibid., p. 12.

17. Alreck, P. L. & Settle, R. B. (1995). *The survey research handbook*, pp. 88–99.

18. Peterson, R. A. (2000). *Constructing effective questionnaires*, p. 58.

19. Ibid., p. 58.

20. We asked Allen Hogg of Burke Interactive to share his experiences on questionnaire design with you. Mr. Hogg wishes to give credit to much of the information he used in preparing this piece for you to Dillman, D. A., Tortora, R. D., & Bowker, D. (1998). *Principles for constructing Web surveys*. SESRC Technical Report 98-50, Pullman, WA, 1998. Retrieved on April 13, 2002 from survey.sesrc.wsu.edu/dillman/papers/websurveyppr.pdf and MacElroy, B. (2000, July). Variables influencing dropout rates in Web-based surveys. *Quirk's Marketing Research Review*. Retrieved on April 13, 2002 from www.quirks.com/articles/article.asp?arg_ArticleId=605.

21. In interviews with marketing research professionals, the increased use and amount of incentives seems to be universal. As consumers have become more resistant, researchers must offer them more. Even still, cooperation rates are troublesome. This is one reason why so many firms are moving toward the use of panels for data collection purposes.

22. Glassman, N. A. & Glassman, M. (1998, Fall). Screening questions: How screening questions can cause self-selection bias. *Marketing Research,* 10, 3, 27–31.

23. Screens can be used to quickly identify respondents who will not answer honestly. See Waters, K. M. (1991, Spring–Summer). Designing screening questionnaires to minimize dishonest answers. *Applied Marketing Research*, 31 (1), 51–53.

24. Based on Sudman, S. & Bradhurn, N. (1982). *Asking questions*. San Francisco: Jossey-Bass, pp. 219–221.

25. Patten, M. (2001). *Questionnaire research*, p. 19.

26. Blunch, N. J. (1984, November). Position bias in multiple choice questions. *Journal of Marketing Research*, 21, 216–220; Welch, J. L. & Swift, C. O. (1992, Summer). Question order effects in taste testing of beverages. *Journal of Academy of Marketing Science*, 265–268; Bickatt, B. A. (1993, February). Carryover and backfire effects in marketing research. *Journal of Marketing Research*, 52–62.

27. Dillman, D. A., Sinclair, M. D., & Clark, J. R. (1993). Effects of questionnaire length, respondent-friendly design, and a difficult question on response rates for occupant-addressed census mail surveys. *Public Opinion Quarterly*, 57, 289–304.

28. Question order may also affect responses. See, for example, Ayidiya, S. A. & McClendon, M. J. (1990, Summer). Response effects in mail surveys. *Public Opinion Quarterly*, 54 (2), 229–247.

29. Carroll, S. (1994). Questionnaire design affects response rate. *Marketing News*, 25 (14), 23.

30. Normally pretests are done individually, but a focus group could be used. See Long, S. A. (1991, May 27). Pretesting questionnaires minimizes measurement error. *Marketing News*, 25 (11), 12.

31. Response latency or subtle hesitations in respondents can be used as a pretest aid. See, for instance, Bassili, J. N. & Fletcher, J. F. (1991). Response-time measurement in survey research. *Public Opinion Quarterly*, 55, 331–346.

32. In fact there are concerns among social scientists about the validity of information based on what respondents say as opposed to what they do. These concerns are summarized in Foddy, W. (1994). *Constructing questions for interviews and questionnaires: Theory and practice in social research*. Cambridge, UK: Press Syndicate of the University of Cambridge. As a rule marketing researchers are aware of these issues. However, the validity of survey research has been "proven" in the marketplace. If surveys did not provide valid and reliable information, their use would have ceased long ago.

Chapter 12

1. Wyner, G. A. (2001, Fall). Representation, randomization, and realism. *Marketing Research*, 13, 3, 4–5.

2. Garland, S. (1990, September 19). Money, power and numbers: A firestorm over the census. *Business Week*, 45.

3. Sample frame error is especially a concern in business samples. See, for example, Macfarlene, P. (2002, First

Quarter). Structuring and measuring the size of business markets. *International Journal of Market Research*, 44, 1, 7–30.

4. See, for example, Stephen, E. H. & Soldo, B. J. (1990, April). How to judge the quality of a survey. *American Demographics*, 12, 4, 42–43.

5. Source: Dennis, J. M. (2001, Summer). Are Internet panels creating professional respondents? *Marketing Research*, 12, 2, 34–38.

6. Source: Knowledge Networks' Web site (www.intersurvey.com/about/about.html).

7. Bradley, N. (1999, October). Sampling for Internet surveys. An examination of respondent selection for internet research. *Market Research Society. Journal of the Market Research Society*, 41, 4, 387.

8. The Excel cell entry is ROUND(RAND()*30,1) meaning a random number from 0 to .9999 times 30, rounded to no decimal, generating random numbers from 0–30.

9. Foreman, J., & Collins, M. (1991, July). The viability of random digit dialing in the UK. *Journal of the Market Research Society*, 33, 3, 219–227; Hekmat, F. & Segal, M. (1984). "Random Digit Dialing: Some Additional Empirical Observations," in David M. Klein and Allen E. Smith, eds., "Marketing Comes of Age," *Proceedings of the Southern Marketing Association*, 176–180.

10. Random digit dialing is used by the major Web traffic monitoring companies. See Fatth, H. (2000, November 13). The metrics system, *Adweek*, 41, 46, 98–102.

11. The option of random telephone number dialing may become expensive in the future. At least one state is considering a mandatory payment to consumers who are contracted by telemarketers. See Schlossberg, H. (1993, August 16). Marketing researchers face "increasingly hostile" legislation. *Marketing News*, 27, 17, 1, 8.

12. See also Sudman, S. (1985, February). Efficient screening methods for the sampling of geographically clustered special populations. *Journal of Marketing Research*, 22, 20–29.

13. Cronish, P. (1989, January). Geodemographic sampling in readership surveys. *Journal of the Market Research Society*, 31, 1, 45–51.

14. For a somewhat more technical description of cluster sampling, see Carlin, J. B. & Hocking, J. (1999, October). Design of cross-sectional surveys using cluster sampling: An overview with Australian case studies. *Australian and New Zealand Journal of Public Health*, 23, 5, 546–551.

15. Academic marketing researchers often use convenience samples of college students. See Peterson, R. A. (2001, December). On the use of college students in social science research: Insights from a second-order meta-analysis. *Journal of Consumer Research*, 28, 3, 450–461.

16. Wyner, G. A. (2001, Fall). Representation, randomization, and realism. *Marketing Research*, 13, 3, 4–5.

17. For an application of referral sampling, see Moriarity, R. T., Jr., & Spekman, R. E. (1984, May). An empirical investigation of the information sources used during the industrial buying process. *Journal of Marketing Research*, 21, 137–147.

18. Jerry W. Thomas, President/CEO, Decision Analyst, Inc., personal communication.

19. For an historical perspective and prediction about online sampling, see Sudman, S. & Blair, E. (1999, Spring). Sampling in the twenty-first century. *Academy of Marketing Science*, 27, 2, 269–277.

20. Internet surveys can access hard-to-reach groups. See Anonymous (1999, Summer). Pro and con: Internet interviewing. *Marketing Research*, 11, 2, 33–36.

21. See as an example, Dahlen, M. (2001, July/August). Banner advertisements through a new lens. *Journal of Advertising Research*, 41, 4, 23–30.

22. For a comparison of online sampling to telephone sampling, see Couper, M. P. (2000, Winter). Web surveys: A review of issues and approaches. *Public Opinion Quarterly*, 64, 4, 464–494.

23. Provided by DMS, by permission.

24. Grossnickle, J. & Raskin, O. (2001, Summer). What's ahead on the Internet. *Marketing Research*, 13, 2, 8–13.

25. Miller, T. W. (2001, Summer). Can we trust the data of online research? *Marketing Research*, 13, 2, 26–32.

26. Rothman, J. & Mitchell, D. (1989, October). Statisticians can be creative too. *Journal of the Market Research Society*, 31, 4, 456–466.

27. The need for substitutions can be affected by the respondent selection procedure. See, for example, Hagen, D. E., & Collier, C. M. (1982, Winter). Must respondent selection procedures for telephone surveys be so invasive? *Public Opinion Quarterly*, 47, 547–556.

28. Cooperation is known to vary across demographic groups. See Guggenheim, B. (1989, February/March). All Research Is Not Created Equal! *Journal of Advertising Research*, 29, 1, RC7–RC11.

29. Based on Matsumoto, J. (2000, September 1), The educated consumer, *Restaurants & Institutions*, Vol. 110, No. 23, 93–94.

CHAPTER 13

1. www.ipsos-reid.com//pdf/products/glob_exp.pdf.

2. Lenth, R. (2001, August). Some practical guidelines for effective sample size determination. *The American Statistician*, vol. 55, no. 3, 187–193.

3. Williams, G. (1999, April). What size sample do I need? *Australian and New Zealand Journal of Public Health*, vol. 23, no. 2, 215–217.

4. Cesana, B. M, Reina, G., and Marubini, E. (2001, November). Sample size for testing a proportion in clinical trials: A "two-step" procedure combining power and confidence interval expected width. *The American Statistician*, vol. 55, no. 4, 288–292.

5. Our chapter simplifies a complex area. See, for example, Williams, G. (1999, April). What size sample do I need?

6. This chapter pertains to quantitative marketing research samples. For qualitative research situations, see, for example, Christy, R. and Wood, M. (1999). Researching possibilities in marketing. *Qualitative Market Research*, vol. 2, no. 3, 189–196.

7. For a caution on this approach, see Browne, R. H. (2001, November). Using the sample range as a basis for calculating sample size in power calculations. *The American Statistician*, vol. 55, no. 4, 293–298.

8. www.stssamples.com/RDD_Samples/RDD_Sampling_Tips/Determining_How_Many_Numbers_T/determining_how_many_numbers_t.html.

9. See Shiffler, R. E., and Adams, A. J. (1987, August). A correction for biasing effects of pilot sample size on sample size determination. *Journal of Marketing Research*, 24, 3, 319–321.

10. For more information see, Lenth, R. V. (2001, August). Some practical guidelines for effective sample size determination.

11. See, for example Cesana, B. M., Reina, G., and Marubini, E. (2001, November). Sample size for testing a proportion in clinical trials.

12. Groom, A. (personal communication, February 9, 2002).

13. Barlet, J., Kotrlik, J., and Higgins, C. (2001, Spring). Organizational research: Determining appropriate sample size in survey research. *Information Technology, Learning, and Performance Journal*, vol. 19, no. 1, 43–50.

14. Hunter, J. E. (2001, June). The desperate need for replications. *Journal of Consumer Research*, vol. 28, no. 1, 149–158.

15. A different statistical analysis determination of sample size is through use of estimated effect sizes. See, for example, Semon, T. T. (1994). Save a few bucks on sample size, risk millions in opportunity cost. *Marketing News*, 28, 1, 19.

16. For a caution on this approach, see Browne, R. H. (2001, November). Using the sample range as a basis for calculating sample size in power calculations. *The American Statistician*, vol. 55, no. 4, 293–298.

CHAPTER 14

1. Howard Gershowitz is executive vice president of Mktg Inc., one of the countries largest telephone data collection companies. He has served as the national president of the Marketing Research Association. Currently he serves on the board of the Council of Marketing and Opinion Research and is the legislative chair of that organization. He was the initial chair of the Marketing Research Association Institute, an organization which provides a distance learning program to practitioners within the marketing research industry.

2. Fetto, J. (2001, October). Pencil me in. *American Demographics*, vol. 23, no. 10, 14.

3. In Chapter 13 you learned to control sampling error by using a sample size formula that allowed you to deter-

mine the sample size required in order to control for the amount of sample error (*e*) you are willing to accept.

4. For a breakdown of the types of nonsampling errors encountered in business-to-business marketing research studies, see Lilien, G., Brown, R., & Searls, K. (1991, January 7). Cut errors, improve estimates to bridge biz-to-biz info gap. *Marketing News*, 25, 1, 20–22.

5. Intentional errors are especially likely when data are supplied by competitors. See Croft, R. (1992, Third Quarter). How to minimize the problem of untruthful response. *Business Marketing Digest*, 17, 3, 17–23.

6. To better understand this area, see Barker, R. A. (1987, July). A demographic profile of marketing research interviewers. *Journal of the Market Research Society*, 29, 279–292.

7. These problems are international in scope. See Kreitzman, L. (1990, February 22). Market research: Virgins and groupies. *Marketing*, 35–38, for the United Kingdom.

8. Pol, L. G., & Ponzurick, T. G. (1989, Spring). Gender of interviewer/gender of respondent bias in telephone surveys. *Applied Marketing Research*, 29, 2, 9–13.

9. Honomichl, J. (1991, June 24). Legislation threatens research by phone. *Marketing News*, 25, 13, 4; Cynthia Webster, "Consumers' Attitudes toward Data Collection Methods," in Robert L. King, ed., "Marketing: Toward the Twenty-First Century," Proceedings of the Southern Marketing Association (1991), 220–224.

10. Jarvis, S. (2002, February 4). CMOR finds survey refusal rate still rising. *Marketing News*, 36, 3, 4.

11. See, for example, Honomichl, J. (1991, May 27). Making a point—again—for an "industry identifier." *Marketing News*, 25, 11, H35; or Spethmann, B. (1991, June 10). Cautious consumers have surveyors wary. *Advertising Age*, 62, 24, 34.

12. Arnett, R. (1990, Second Quarter). Mail panel research in the 1990s. *Applied Marketing Research*, 30, 2, 8–10.

13. Not all observers share this view. See Schlossberg, H. (1991, January 7). Research's image better than many think. *Marketing News*, 25, 1, 24–25.

14. Of course, eliminating the interviewer entirely may be an option. See Horton, K. (1990, February). Disk-based surveys: new way to pick your brain. *Software Magazine*, 10, 2, 76–77.

15. There is a move in the United Kingdom for interviewer certification. See Hemsley, S. (2000, August 17). Acting the part. *Marketing Week*, vol. 23, no. 28, 37–40.

16. See Childers, T., & Skinner, S. (1985, January). Theoretical and empirical issues in the identification of survey respondents. *Journal of the Market Research Society*, 27, 39–53; Finlay, J. L., & Seyyet, F. J. (1988). The impact of sponsorship and respondent attitudes on response rate to telephone surveys: An exploratory investigation, in David L. Moore, ed., "Marketing: Forward Motion," Proceedings of the Atlantic Marketing Association (1988), 715–721; Goldsmith, R. E. "Spurious Response Error in a New Product

Survey," in J. Joseph Cronin Jr. & Melvin T. Stith, eds., "Marketing: Meeting the Challenges of the 1990s," Proceedings of the Southern Marketing Association (1987), 172–175; Philip E. Downs & John R. Kerr, "Recent Evidence on the Relationship between Anonymity and Response Variables," in John H. Summey, Blaise J. Bergiel, and Carol H. Anderson, eds., "A Spectrum of Contemporary Marketing Ideas," Proceedings of the Southern Marketing Association (1982), 258–264; Glisan, G. & Grimm, J. L. "Improving Response Rates in an Industrial Setting: Will Traditional Variables Work?" in John H. Summey, Blaise J. Bergiel, and Carol H. Anderson, eds., "A Spectrum of Contemporary Marketing Ideas," Proceedings of the Southern Marketing Association (1982), 265–268; Taylor, R. D., Beisel, J. & Blakney, V. "The Effect of Advanced Notification by Mail of a Forthcoming Mail Survey on the Response Rates, Item Omission Rates, and Response Speed," in David M. Klein and Allen E. Smith, eds., "Marketing Comes of Age," Proceedings of the Southern Marketing Association (1984), 184–187; Friedman, H. H. (1979, Spring). The effects of a monetary incentive and the ethnicity of the sponsor's signature on the rate and quality of response to a mall survey. *Journal of the Academy of Marketing Science*, 95–100; Goldstein, L., & Friedman, H. H. (1975, April). A case for double postcards in surveys. *Journal of Advertising Research*, 43–49; Hubbard, R., & Little, E. L. (1988, Fall). Cash prizes and mail response rates: A threshold analysis. *Journal of the Academy of Marketing Science*, 42–44; Childers, T. L., & Ferrell, O. C. (1979, August). Response rates and perceived questionnaire length in mail surveys. *Journal of Marketing Research*, 429–431; Childers, T. L., Pride, W. M., & Ferrell, O. C. (1980, August). A reassessment of the effects of appeals on response to mail surveys. *Journal of Marketing Research*, 365–370; Steele, T., Schwendig, W., & Kilpatrick, J. (1992, March/April). Duplicate responses to multiple survey mailings: A problem? *Journal of Advertising Research*, 26–33; Wilcox, J. B. (1977, November). The interaction of refusal and not-at-home sources of nonresponse bias. *Journal of Marketing Research*, 592–597.

17. Based on Conrad, F. & Schober, M. (2000, Spring). Clarifying question meaning in a household survey, *Public Opinion Quarterly*, vol. 64, no. 1, 1–28.

18. A comparison on nonresponse errors under different incentives is Barsky, J. K., & Huxley, S. J. (1992, December). A customer-survey tool: using the "quality sample." *The Cornell Hotel and Restaurant Administration Quarterly*, 33, 6, 18–25.

19. Screening questionnaires can also be used. See Waters, K. M. (1991, Spring/Summer). Designing screening questionnaires to minimize dishonest answers. *Applied Marketing Research*, 31, 1, 51–53.

20. For examples, see Prete, D. D. (1991, September 2). Clients want more specific research—and faster.

Marketing News, 25, 18, 18; Hawk, K. (1992, November 12). More marketers going online for decision support. *Marketing News*, 24, 23, 14; Riche, M. F. (1990). Look before leaping. *American Demographics*, 12, 2, 18–20; or Wolfe, M. J. (1989, September 11). New way to use scanner data and demographics aids local marketers. *Marketing News*, 23, 19, 8–9.

21. Miller, T. W. (2001, September 24). Make the call: Online results are mixed bag. *Marketing News*, 35, 20, 30–35.

22. Coleman, L. G. (1991, January 7). Researchers say nonresponse is single biggest problem. *Marketing News*, 25, 1, 32–33.

23. Landler, M. (1991, February 11). The "bloodbath" in market research. *Business Week*, 72, 74.

24. Baim, J. (1991, June). Response rates: A multinational perspective. *Marketing & Research Today*, 19, 2, 114–119.

25. Source: www.mrs.org.uk/fr-code.htm.

26. Farrell, B., & Elken, T. (1994, August 29). Adjust five variables for better mail surveys. *Marketing News*, 20.

27. Tyagi, P. K. (1989, Summer). The effects of appeals, anonymity, and feedback on mail survey response patterns from salespeople. *Journal of the Academy of Marketing Science*, 17, 3, 235–241.

28. An alternative view is that nonresponse to online surveys is unknowable. See, Couper, M. P. (2000, Winter). Web surveys: A review of issues and approaches. *Public Opinion Quarterly*, 64, 4, 464–494.

29. MacElroy, B. (2000, April). Measuring response rates in on-line surveys, *Quirk's Marketing Research Review*, vol. XIV, no. 4, 50–52.

30. Anonymous (1993, August 16). The researchers' response: Four industry leaders tell how to improve cooperation. *Marketing News*, A12.

31. Frankel, L. R. "On the Definition of Response Rates," A Special Task Force Report Published by the Council of American Survey Research Organizations, 3 Upper Devon, Belle Terre, Port Jefferson, NY 11777.

32. For a comparison of response rates by mail versus fax, see Dickson, J. P., & MacLachlan, D. L. (1996, February). Fax surveys: Return patterns and comparison with mail surveys. *Journal of Marketing Research*, 33, 1, 108–113.

33. For yea-saying and nay-saying, see Bachman, J. G., & O'Malley, P. M. (1985, Summer). Yea-saying, nay-saying, and going to extremes: Black–white differences in response styles. *Public Opinion Quarterly*, 48, 491–509.

CHAPTER 15

1. Adapted from Anonymous, (2001, October). Ka-ching! *Dealerscope*, vol. 43, no. 10, 50.

2. It is important for the researcher and client to have a partnership during data analysis. See, for example, Fitxpatrick, M. (2001, August). Statistical analysis for

direct marketers—in plain English. *Direct Marketing*, vol. 64, no. 4, 54–56.

3. For an alternative presentation, see Ehrnberg, A. (2001, Winter). Data, but no information. *Marketing Research*, vol. 13, no. 4, 36–39.

4. Some authors argue that central tendency measures are too sterile. See, for example, Pruden, D. R. & Vavra, T. G. (2000, Summer). Customer research, not marketing research. *Marketing Research*, vol. 12, no. 2, 14–19.

5. Ghose, S. & Lowengart, O. (2001, September). Perceptual positioning of international, national and private brands in a growing international market: An empirical study. *Journal of Brand Management*, vol. 9, no. 1, 45–62.

6. Gutsche, A. (2001, September 24). Visuals make the case. *Marketing News*, vol. 35, no. 20, 21–23.

CHAPTER 16

1. This introductory case is for pedagogical purposes only.

CHAPTER 17

1. Adapted from Chiger, S. (2000, November). Consumer shopping survey. *Catalog Age*, vol. 18, no. 12, 80–81.

2. For a contrary view, see Mazur, L. (2000, June 8). The only truism in marketing is they don't exist. *Marketing*, 20.

3. Meaningful difference is sometimes called "practical significance." See Thompson, B. (2002, Winter). "Statistical," "practical," and "clinical": How many kinds of significance do counselors need to consider? *Journal of Counseling and Development*, vol. 30, no. 1, 64–71.

4. For an example of the use of paired samples *t* tests, see Ryan, C. & Mo, X. (2001, December). Chinese visitors to New Zealand—demographics and perceptions. *Journal of Vacation Marketing*, vol. 8, no. 1, 13–27.

5. Hellebusch, S. J. (2001, June 4). One chi square beats two *z* tests. *Marketing News*, vol. 35, no. 11, 12, 13.

6. For illumination, see Burdick, R. K. (1983, August). Statement of hypotheses in the analysis of variance. *Journal of Marketing Research*, 20, 320–324.

7. Aamodt, M. (1999, Spring). Why are there five million types of statistics? *Public Personnel Management*, vol. 28, no. 1, 157–160.

8. A more complicated approach is Bobko, P., Roth, P. L., & Bobko, C. (2001, January). Correcting the effect size of *d* for range restriction and unreliability. *Organizational Research Methods*, vol. 4, no. 1, 46–61.

9. For a criticism of the use of difference scores in consumer research, see Paul, J. P., Churchill, Jr. G. A., & Brown, T. J. (1993, March). Caution in the use of difference scores in consumer research. *Journal of Consumer Research*, vol. 19, no. 4, 655–662.

10. Personal communication from Dr. Sarah Lipson and Mr. Randall L. Zeese, AT&T.

11. Pizam, A. (1999, November). The American group tourist as viewed by British, Israeli, Korean, and Dutch tour guides. *Journal of Travel Research*, vol. 38, no. 2, 119–126.

CHAPTER 18

1. Garver, M. S. (2001, Fall). Listening to customers. *Mid-American Journal of Business*, vol. 16, no. 2, 41–54.

2. For advice on when to use chi-square analysis, see Hellebush, S. J. (2001, June 4). One chi square beats two *z* tests. *Marketing News*, vol. 35, no. 11, 12, 13.

3. Here are some articles that use cross-tabulation analysis: Burton, S., & Zinkhan, G. M. (1987, Fall). Changes in consumer choice: Further investigation of similarity and attraction effects. *Psychology in Marketing*, 4, 255–266; Bush, A. J., & Leigh, J. H. (1984, April/May). Advertising on cable versus traditional television networks. *Journal of Advertising Research*, 24, 33–38; and Langrehr, F. W. (1985, Summer). Consumer images of two types of competing financial institutions. *Journal of the Academy of Marketing Science*, 13, 248–264.

4. For a more advanced treatment of scatter diagrams, see Goddard, B. L. (2000, April). The power of computer graphics for comparative analysis, *The Appraisal Journal*, vol. 68, no. 2, 134–41.

5. Refer, also, to Babakus, E., & Ferguson, C. E., Jr. (1988, Spring). On choosing the appropriate measure of association when analyzing rating scale data. *Journal of the Academy of Marketing Science*, 16, 95–102.

6. Source: Adapted from Branch, W. (1990, February). On interpreting correlation coefficients. *American Psychologist*, vol. 45, no. 2, 296.

CHAPTER 19

1. Reece, W. S. (2001, February). Travelers to Las Vegas and to Atlantic City. *Journal of Travel Research*, vol. 39, no. 3, 275–284.

2. Residual analysis can take many forms. See, for example, Dempster, A. P., & Gasko-Green, M. (1981). New tools for residual analysis. *Annals of Statistics*, 9, 945–959.

3. See Melnick, E. L., & Shoaf, F. R. (1977, June). Regression equals analysis of variance. *Journal of Advertising Research*, 17, 27–31.

4. We admit that our description of regression is introductory. Two books that expand our description are Michael S. Lewis-Beck, *Applied Regression: An Introduction* (1980); Larry D. Schroeder, David L. Sjoffquist, and Paula E. Stephan, *Understanding Regression Analysis: An Introductory Guide* (1986), both published by Sage Publications, Inc., Newbury Park, CA.

5. Based on Tsalikis, J, Seaton, B., & Tomaras, P. (2002, February). A new perspective on cross-cultural ethical evaluations: The use of conjoint analysis, *Journal of Business Ethics*, vol. 35, no. 4, part 2, 281–292.

6. Gurhan-Canli, Z., & Maheswarn, D. (2000, August). Cultural variations in country of origin effects, *Journal of Marketing Research*, vol. 37, no. 3, 309–317.

7. For more information, see, for example, Mason, R. L., Gunst, R. F., & Webster, J. T. (1986). Regression analysis and problems of multicollinearity in marketing models: Diagnostics and remedial measures. *International Journal of Research in Marketing*, 3, 3, 181–205.

8. Our description pertains to "forward" stepwise regression. We admit that this is a simplification of stepwise multiple regression.

9. Cameron, L. A., Dowling, M., & Worswick, C. (2001, April). Education and labor market participation of women in Asia: Evidence from five countries. *Economic Development and Cultural Change*, vol. 49, no. 3, 439–477.

10. Regression analysis is commonly used in academic marketing research. Here are some examples: Callahan, F. X. (1982, April/May). Advertising and profits 1969–1978. *Journal of Advertising Research*, 22, 17–22; Dubinsky, A. J., & Levy, M. (1989, Summer). Influence of organizational fairness on work outcomes of retail salespeople. *Journal of Retailing*, 65, 221–252; Frieden, J. B., & Downs, P. E. (1986, Fall). Testing the social involvement model in an energy conservation context. *Journal of the Academy of Marketing Science*, 14, 13–20; and Tellis, G. J., & Fornell, C. (1988, February). The relationship between advertising and product quality over the product life cycle: A contingency theory. *Journal of Marketing Research*, 25, 64–71. For an alternative to regression analysis, see Quaintance, B. S., & Franke, G. R. (1991). Neural networks for marketing research. In Robert L. King, ed., "Marketing: Toward the Twenty-First Century," Proceedings of the Southern Marketing Association (1991), 230–235.

CHAPTER 20

1. The authors wish to acknowledge that this chapter was prepared by M. R. Howard, Ed.D., and H. H. Donofrio, Ph.D. Dr. Howard has been involved in editing the chapter since the first edition of the book. For this edition, the authors asked her and Dr. Donofrio for a complete updating of the chapter.

2. Deshpande, R. & Zaltman, G. (February 1982). Factors affecting the use of market research information: A path analysis. *Journal of Marketing Research*, 19, 14–31.

3. Deshpande, R. & Zaltman, G. (February 1984). A comparison of factors affecting researcher and manager perceptions of market research use. *Journal of Marketing Research*, 21, 32–38.

4. To properly cite your sources see *MLA Handbook for Writers of Research Papers*, 5th ed. New York: The Modern Language Association of America or *Publication Manual of the American Psychological Association*, 5th ed. (2001). Washington, DC: The American Psychological Association.

5. Jameson, D. A. (June 1993). The ethics of plagiarism: How genre affects writers' use of source materials. *The Bulletin*, 18–27, 2.

6. Imperiled copywrights, *New York Times* (April 15, 1998), A24.

7. Mathews, D. (Winter 2001). Web-based online reporting. *Marketing Research*, 13, 4, 46–47.

8. Dunn, T. (1999). *How research providers see it: An ARF study of practices, challenges and future opportunities.* New York: Advertising Research Foundation, 8.

9. Guffey, M. E. (2000). *Business communication: Process and product*, 3rd ed. Cincinnati: South-Western College Publishing, 103.

10. Tufte, E. R. (1983). *The visual display of quantitative information*. Cheshire, CT: Graphics Press.

11. Thomas, J. (November 2001). Executive excellence. *Marketing Research*, 11–12.

12. This case was prepared by Gregory S. Martin, Ph.D. Dr. Martin is experienced in marketing research and has worked on several research projects including this case.

Credits

CHAPTER 1

Page 4 (Photo): NewProductWorks/photo by Robert McMath, by permission. Page 5 (Product photos): NewProductWorks/photos by Robert McMath, by permission. Page 9 (Photo): Courtesy of MRSI/Marketing Research Services, Inc. Page 10 (Photo): By permission, MSRI/Marketing Research Services, Inc. Pages 15–16 (Blue Ribbon Panel photos): By permission, Burke Interactive; by permission, Digital Marketing Services/DMS; courtesy of Harris Interactive; by permission, Greenfield Online, Inc.; by permission, Insight Express; by permission, Knowledge Networks. Page 23 (Photo): Courtesy of Socratic Technologies, Inc.

CHAPTER 2

Page 26 (Ad): Courtesy of Eastman Kodak Company. Page 31 (Photo): By permission, InfoWorld Media Group. Page 33 (Illustration): Courtesy of Sorensen Associates Path Tracker™. Page 34 (Photo): By permission, Sorensen Associates. Page 36 (Photo): Courtesy of Jeremy Walker/Getty Images, Inc. Page 43 (Photo): Courtesy of James Marshall/CORBIS.

CHAPTER 3

Page 45 (Photo): Council of American Survey Research Organization, by permission, CASRO. Page 66 (Photo): Council of American Survey Research Organization, by permission, CASRO. Pages 74–75 (Blue Ribbon Panel photos): Courtesy of Socratic Technologies, Inc.; by permission, Digital Marketing Services/DMI; courtesy of Harris Interactive; by permission, Greenfield Online, Inc.; by permission Knowledge Networks, Inc.

CHAPTER 4

Page 85 (Ad): Courtesy of Barna Research Group, Ltd., of Ventura, CA. www.bar.va.org. Page 85 (Photo): Courtesy of Getty Images, Inc. Page 90 (Photo): Courtesy of Rob Lewine/Corbis/Stock Market. Page 93 (Photo): Courtesy of Eric Marder Associates, by permission, Lawrence D. Gibson. Page 95 (Photo): Courtesy of Michael Newman/PhotoEdit. Page 104 (Photo): Courtesy of James Lafayette/Index Stock Imagery, Inc. Pages 109–111 (Blue Ribbon Panel photos): Courtesy of Socratic Technologies, Inc.; by permission, Burke, Inc.; courtesy of Harris Interactive; by permission, Greenfield Online, Inc.; by permission, Insight Express; by permission, Knowledge Networks, Inc. Page 114 (Photo): By permission, Segway Company.

CHAPTER 5

Page 118 (Ad): Property of AT&T Archives, reprinted with permission of AT&T. Page 119 (Photo): AT&T Archives, reprinted with permission AT&T. Page 121 (Photo): Eric Marder Associates, by permission, Lawrence C. Gibson. Page 126 (Ad): Property of AT&T Archives, reprinted with permission AT&T. Page 127 (Ad): By permission, Ping, Inc. Page 128 (Ads): By permission, AFFINNOVA. Pages 129–130 (Blue Ribbon Panel photos): Courtesy of Socratic Technologies, Inc.; by permission, Burke, Inc.; by permission, Greenfield Online, Inc.; by permission, Insight Express.

CHAPTER 6

Page 153 (Photo): By permission, ESRI Business Information Solutions. Page 155 (Photo): Courtesy of Strategy Research Corporation. Page 164 (Screen capture): Reprinted with permission from Microsoft Corporation. Page 164 (Screen captures): By permission, ProQuest Information & Learning.

CHAPTER 7

Page 183 (Photo): Courtesy of ESRI Business Information Solutions. Pages 188–190 (Screen captures): Courtesy of ESRI Business Information Solutions. Page 193 (Screen capture): By permission, ACNielsen. Page 197 (Photo): Courtesy of Arbitron Inc.

CHAPTER 8

Page 202 (Ad): By permission, Active Group. Page 203 (Photo): Courtesy of Anton Vengo/SuperStock, Inc. Page 205 (Photo): Courtesy of Arlene Sandler/SuperStock, Inc. Page 206 (Photo): Courtesy of Bill Bachmann/Index Stock Imagery, Inc. Page 208 (Photo): Courtesy of Rhoda Sidney/PhotoEdit. Page 221 (Screen capture): By permission, Active Group. Pages 230–231 (Blue Ribbon Panel photos): Courtesy of Socratic Technologies, Inc.; by permission, Burke, Inc.; by permission, Digital Marketing Services/DMI; courtesy of Harris Interactive; by permission, Greenfield Online, Inc.; by permission, Insight Express; by permission, Knowledge Networks, Inc.

CHAPTER 9

Page 239 (Photo): Courtesy of Barbara Peacock/Getty Images, Inc.–Taxi. Page 240 (Photo): Courtesy of SuperStock, Inc. Page 242 (Photo): Courtesy of Spencer Grant/PhotoEdit. Page 247 (Photo): By permission, Opinion One. Page 248 (Photo): Courtesy of Spencer Grant/PhotoEdit. Pages 261–262 (Blue Ribbon Panel photos): Courtesy of Socratic Technologies, Inc.; by permission, Burke, Inc.; by permission, Digital Marketing Services/DMI; courtesy of Harris Interactive; by permission, Greenfield Online, Inc.; by permission, Insight Express; by permission, Knowledge Networks, Inc.

CHAPTER 10

Page 268 (Ad): By permission, SDR Consulting. Page 269 (Photo): Courtesy of Michael Newman/PhotoEdit. Page 273 (Photo): By permission, SDR Consulting. Page 274 (Photo): Courtesy of Michael Newman/PhotoEdit. Page 275 (Photo): Courtesy of Richard Hamilton Smith/CORBIS. Pages 292–293 (Blue Ribbon Panel photos): Courtesy of Socratic Technologies, Inc.; by permission, Burke, Inc.; by permission, Digital Marketing Services/DMI; courtesy of Harris Interactive; by permission, Insight Express; by permission, Knowledge Networks, Inc.

CHAPTER 11

Page 301 (Screen capture): Courtesy of WebSurveyor. Page 309 (Photo): By permission, Cultural Access Group. Pages 314–315 (Blue Ribbon Panel photos): Courtesy of Socratic Technologies, Inc.; by permission, Burke, Inc., by permission, Digital Marketing Services/DMI; courtesy of Harris Interactive; by permission,

Credits

Index

SUBJECT INDEX